ECONOMICS OF ENVIRONMENT, CLIMATE CHANGE, AND WINE

Selected Papers of Robert N Stavins
Volume 3 (2011–2023)

ECONOMICS OF ENVIRONMENT, CLIMATE CHANGE, AND WINE

Selected Papers of Robert N Stavins
Volume 3 (2011–2023)

Robert N Stavins
Harvard University, USA

World Scientific

NEW JERSEY • LONDON • SINGAPORE • BEIJING • SHANGHAI • TAIPEI • CHENNAI

Published by

World Scientific Publishing Co. Pte. Ltd.
5 Toh Tuck Link, Singapore 596224
USA office: 27 Warren Street, Suite 401-402, Hackensack, NJ 07601
UK office: 57 Shelton Street, Covent Garden, London WC2H 9HE

Library of Congress Cataloging-in-Publication Data
Names: Stavins, R. N. (Robert N.), 1948– author
Title: Economics of environment, climate change, and wine : selected papers of Robert N. Stavins, volume 3 (2011-2023) / Robert N. Stavins. Harvard University, USA
Description: New Jersey : World Scientific, 2025. | Includes bibliographical references and index.
Identifiers: LCCN 2024050266 | ISBN 9789811292408 hardcover |
ISBN 9789811292415 ebook | ISBN 9789811292422 ebook other
Subjects: LCSH: Environmental economics | Climatic changes--Economic aspects
Classification: LCC HC79.E5 S7158 2025 | DDC 363.7--dc23/eng/20250318
LC record available at https://lccn.loc.gov/2024050266

British Library Cataloguing-in-Publication Data
A catalogue record for this book is available from the British Library.

For any available supplementary material, please visit
https://www.worldscientific.com/worldscibooks/10.1142/13820#t=suppl

Desk Editors: Soundararajan Raghuraman/Geysilla Jean

Typeset by Stallion Press
Email: enquiries@stallionpress.com

To Joanna, Daniel & Jess, Julia & Aaron, and, of course, Rudy,
with thanks for having made these efforts worthwhile!

https://doi.org/10.1142/9789811292415_fmatter

About the Editor

Robert N. Stavins is the A. J. Meyer Professor of Energy & Economic Development at Harvard Kennedy School, Director of the Harvard Environmental Economics Program, Director of Graduate Studies for the Doctoral Program in Public Policy, Co-Chair of the Harvard Business School-Kennedy School Joint Degree Programs, and Director of the Harvard Project on Climate Agreements. He is a University Fellow of Resources for the Future, a Research Associate of the National Bureau of Economic Research, an elected Fellow of the Association of Environmental and Resource Economists, Vice-Chair of the Board of Directors of Resources for the Future, and Co-Editor of the *Journal of Wine Economics*. He was Founding Editor of the *Review of Environmental Economics and Policy*, Chairman of the U.S. Environmental Protection Agency's Environmental Economics Advisory Committee, and Lead Author or Coordinating Lead Author of the Second, Third, and Fifth Assessment Reports of the Intergovernmental Panel on Climate Change. His research has focused on diverse areas of environmental economics and policy, and appeared in hundreds of articles in scholarly journals plus more than a dozen books. He has been a consultant to U.S. Administrations, Members of Congress, environmental organizations, the World Bank, the United Nations, state and national governments, and private foundations and firms. He holds a B.A. in philosophy from Northwestern University, an M.S. in agricultural economics from Cornell, and a Ph.D. in economics from Harvard.

https://doi.org/10.1142/9789811292415_fmatter

Contents

About the Editor vii

Part I Background and Overview 1

Chapter 1 Introduction: The Path to the Present 3
Robert N. Stavins

Chapter 2 Martin Weitzman: A Gift That Keeps on Giving 19
Robert N. Stavins and Gernot Wagner

Chapter 3 Rolling the Dice in the Corridors of Power: William Nordhaus's Impacts on Climate Change Policy 31
Joseph E. Aldy and Robert N. Stavins

Chapter 4 Assessing the Energy-Efficiency Gap 53
Todd D. Gerarden, Richard G. Newell, and Robert N. Stavins

Chapter 5 Climate Negotiators Create an Opportunity for Scholars 119
Joseph E. Aldy and Robert N. Stavins

Part II Policy Instruments 127

Chapter 6 The Promise and Problems of Pricing Carbon: Theory and Experience 129
Joseph E. Aldy and Robert N. Stavins

Chapter 7	The SO_2 Allowance-Trading System and the Clean Air Act Amendments of 1990: Reflections on 20 Years of Policy Innovation *Gabriel Chan, Robert N. Stavins, Robert Stowe, and Richard Sweeney*	165
Chapter 8	The SO_2 Allowance Trading System: The Ironic History of a Grand Policy Experiment *Richard Schmalensee and Robert N. Stavins*	209
Chapter 9	Lessons Learned from Three Decades of Experience with Cap and Trade *Richard Schmalensee and Robert N. Stavins*	235
Part III	**Domestic Policy**	**265**
Chapter 10	Policy Evolution under the Clean Air Act *Richard Schmalensee and Robert N. Stavins*	267
Chapter 11	The Future of US Carbon-Pricing Policy *Robert N. Stavins*	299
Chapter 12	The Relative Merits of Carbon Pricing Instruments: Taxes versus Trading *Robert N. Stavins*	367
Chapter 13	Keep Climate Policy Focused on the Social Cost of Carbon: A Proposed Shift away from the SCC is Ill Advised *Joseph E. Aldy, Matthew J. Kotchen, Robert N. Stavins, and James H. Stock*	397
Chapter 14	An Economic Perspective on the EPA's Clean Power Plan — Cross-State Coordination Key to Cost-Effective CO_2 Reductions *Meredith Fowlie, Lawrence Goulder, Matthew J. Kotchen, Severin Borenstein, James Bushnell, Lucas Davis, Michael Greenstone, Charles Kolstad, Christopher Knittel, Robert N. Stavins, Michael Wara, Frank Wolak, and Catherine Wolfram*	407

Part IV International Policy 415

Chapter 15 The IPCC at a Crossroads: Opportunities for Reform — Increase Focus on Policy-Relevant Research 417
Carlo Carraro, Ottmar Edenhofer, Christian Flachsland, Charles Kolstad, Robert N. Stavins, and Robert Stowe

Chapter 16 Reforming the IPCC's Assessment of Climate Change Economics 423
Gabriel Chan, Carlo Carraro, Ottmar Edenhofer, Charles Kolstad, and Robert N. Stavins

Chapter 17 International Climate Change Policy 443
Gabriel Chan, Robert N. Stavins, and Zou Ji

Chapter 18 Three Key Elements of Post-2012 International Climate Policy Architecture 483
Sheila M. Olmstead and Robert N. Stavins

Chapter 19 An Unambiguous Consequence of the Durban Climate Talks 509
Robert N. Stavins

Chapter 20 Post-Durban Climate Policy Architecture Based on Linkage of Cap-and-Trade Systems 515
Matthew Ranson and Robert N. Stavins

Part V The Paris Agreement 555

Chapter 21 Linkage of Greenhouse Gas Emissions Trading Systems: Learning from Experience 557
Matthew Ranson and Robert N. Stavins

Chapter 22 Facilitating Linkage of Climate Policies through the Paris Outcome 581
Daniel M. Bodansky, Seth A. Hoedl, Gilbert E. Metcalf, and Robert N. Stavins

Chapter 23	Linking Climate Policies to Advance Global Mitigation: Joining Jurisdictions Can Increase Efficiency of Mitigation *Michael A. Mehling, Gilbert E. Metcalf, and Robert N. Stavins*	605
Chapter 24	Linking Heterogeneous Climate Policies (Consistent with the Paris Agreement) *Michael A. Mehling, Gilbert E. Metcalf, and Robert N. Stavins*	613
Chapter 25	Double Counting and the Paris Agreement Rulebook: Poor Emissions Accounting Could Undermine Carbon Markets *Lambert Schneider, Maosheng Duan, Robert N. Stavins, Kelley Kizzier, Derik Broekhoff, Frank Jotzo, Harald Winkler, Michael Lazarus, Andrew Howard, and Christina Hood*	677
Part VI	**Wine Production and Consumption**	**687**
Chapter 26	The Value of Terroir: Hedonic Estimation of Vineyard Sale Prices *Robin Cross, Andrew J. Plantinga, and Robert N. Stavins*	689
Chapter 27	Terroir in the New World: Hedonic Estimation of Vineyard Sale Prices in California *Robin Cross, Andrew J. Plantinga, and Robert N. Stavins*	705
Chapter 28	Film Review: Jason Wise, Somm *Robert N. Stavins*	731
Chapter 29	Film Review: David Roach and Warwick Ross, Red Obsession *Robert N. Stavins*	737

Chapter 30 Film Review: David Kennard, A Year in Burgundy 741
Robert N. Stavins

Chapter 31 Film Review: Rudi Goldman: Burgundy: People with a Passion for Wine 747
Robert N. Stavins

Chapter 32 Book Review: Gert Crum and Jan Bartelsman: Le Domaine de la Romanée-Conti 753
Robert N. Stavins

Chapter 33 Film Review: Jason Wise, *Somm 3* 757
Robert N. Stavins

Chapter 34 Book Review: James M. Gabler: Passions: The Wines and Travels of Thomas Jefferson 763
Robert N. Stavins

Index 767

Part I

Background and Overview

https://doi.org/10.1142/9789811292415_0001

Chapter 1

Introduction: The Path to the Present

Robert N. Stavins

John F. Kennedy School of Government, Harvard University, Cambridge, MA, USA

Resources for the Future, Washington, DC, USA

National Bureau of Economic Research, Cambridge, MA, USA

robert_stavins@harvard.edu

Over the past three decades, environmental and resource economics has evolved from what was once a relatively obscure application of welfare economics to being a prominent field of economics in its own right. The number of articles on the natural environment, in particular on climate change, in mainstream economics periodicals has increased greatly, as has the number of economics journals dedicated exclusively to environmental and resource topics. Likewise, the influence of economics on public policy in this sphere has increased significantly.

This introductory essay begins with some personal reflections on the professional path that has led to my research and writing, and concludes with a brief overview of the book.

A Professional Path

In retrospect, my professional path may appear direct, if not altogether linear, but it hardly seemed so at the time as I travelled along a rather circuitous route. The path I describe took me back and forth across the

United States and to several continents, and it took me from physics to philosophy, to agricultural extension, to international development studies, to agricultural economics, and eventually to environmental economics, climate change policy, and the economics of wine. It culminated in my receipt in 1988 of a Ph.D. degree in economics at Harvard University, where I have since been a faculty member at the John F. Kennedy School of Government. During this time, much has changed in the profession.

The early ascendency of the field of environmental economics, during the period from 1970 to 1990, was centered at departments of agricultural and resource economics, mainly at U.S. universities, and at Resources for the Future (RFF), the Washington research institution (where I serve as Co-Vice Chair of the Board of Directors). Within most economics departments, environmental studies remained a relatively minor area of applied welfare economics. So, when I enrolled in the Ph.D. program in Harvard's Department of Economics in 1983, and when I received my degree five years later, no field of study was offered in the field of environmental or resource economics.

Fortunately, Harvard permitted its graduate students to develop an optional, self-designed field as one of two fields on which they were to be examined orally before proceeding to dissertation research. Without a resident environmental economist in the Department of Economics (Martin Weitzman had yet to move to Harvard from the Massachusetts Institute of Technology), I developed an outline and reading list of the field through correspondence with leading scholars from other institutions, most prominently Kerry Smith, then at North Carolina State University. My proposal to prepare for and be examined in the special field of environmental and resource economics (along with econometrics) was approved by the Department's director of graduate studies, Dale Jorgenson. So began my entry into the scholarly literature of the field.

But my interest in environmental economics pre-dated by a considerable number of years my matriculation at Harvard. Like many others before and since, I came to the field because of a personal interest in the natural environment (the origin of which I describe below). This personal interest evolved into a professional one while I was studying for an M.S. degree in agricultural economics at Cornell University in the late 1970's, where my thesis advisor and mentor was Kenneth Robinson. I had originally gone to Cornell to study for a professional degree in international development, but found agricultural economics more appealing, largely because of the opportunity to examine social questions with quantitative methods within a disciplinary framework.

The faculty at Cornell and the care given to graduate students (including masters students like myself) were outstanding. Ken Robinson, my first mentor within the economics profession, became my ongoing role model for intellectual integrity. It was a sad day in 2010 when Professor Robinson passed away.

A course in linear algebra, brilliantly taught by S. R. Searle, inspired me to pursue quantitative methods of analysis, and I was fortunate to have the opportunity to study econometrics with Tim Mount. One summer I had the great privilege of learning comparative economic systems in a small workshop setting from George Staller of the Cornell Department of Economics. Working with Bud Stanton, I had my first experience teaching at the university level, and with Olan Forker, I had my first try at serious writing. All of this led to research and writing of an M.S. thesis, "Forecasting the Size Distribution of Farms: A Methodological Analysis of the Dairy Industry in New York State." The methodology in question was a variable Markov transition probability matrix, the cells of which were estimated econometrically in a multinomial logit framework. Much to my surprise, this work subsequently received the Outstanding Master's Thesis Award in the national competition of the American Agricultural Economics Association.

Armed with my M.S. degree, I moved from Cornell to Berkeley, California, where I eventually met up with Phillip LeVeen, who had until shortly before that time been a faculty member in the Department of Agricultural and Resource Economics at the University of California, Berkeley. Phil was another superb mentor, and from him I learned the power of using simple models — by which I mean a set of supply and demand curves hastily drawn on a piece of scrap paper — to develop insights into real-world policy problems. He introduced me to a topic that was to occupy me for the next few years — California's perpetual concerns with water allocation. I remember many afternoons spent working with Phil at his dining room table on questions of water supply and demand.

This work with Phil LeVeen led to a consultancy and then a staff position with the Environmental Defense Fund (EDF), the national advocacy group consisting of lawyers, natural scientists, and — then almost unique among environmental advocacy organizations — economists. At EDF, I was able to experience for the first time the use of economic analysis in pursuit of better environmental policy. With W. R. Zach Willey, EDF's senior economist in California, as a role model, and Thomas Graff, EDF's senior attorney, as my mentor, I thrived in EDF's collegial atmosphere, while thoroughly enjoying life in Berkeley's "gourmet ghetto," as my neighborhood was known. Sadly, Tom Graff — without whose mentorship I would not be where I am today — passed away in 2009 after a heroic battle with cancer.

Although I found the work at EDF exceptionally rewarding, I worried that I would eventually be constrained — either within the organization or outside it — by my limited education. So, like many others in similar situations, I considered a law degree as the next logical step. In fact, I came very close to enrolling at Stanford Law School, but instead, in 1983, I accepted an offer of admission to the Department of Economics at Harvard, moved back east to Cambridge, Massachusetts, and began what has turned out to be a long-term relationship with the University.

But where did my interest in the natural environment begin? Not at Cornell; it was present long before those days. But it had not yet arisen when I was studying earlier at Northwestern University, from which I received a B.A. degree in philosophy, having departed from my first scholarly interest, astronomy and astrophysics.

Rather, the origins of my affinity for the natural environment and my interest in resource issues are to be found in the four years I spent in a small, remote village in Sierra Leone, West Africa, as a Peace Corps Volunteer, working in agricultural extension (in particular, paddy rice development). It was there that I was first exposed both to the qualities of a pristine natural environment and the trade-offs associated with economic development.

So, I had begun in astrophysics, moved to philosophy (both at Northwestern), then to agricultural extension in a developing country (Sierra Leone), then to international development studies and subsequently to agricultural economics (both at Cornell), then to environmental economics and policy (EDF), and eventually to graduate study in economics at Harvard.

My dissertation research at Harvard was directed by a committee of three faculty members: Joseph Kalt, Zvi Griliches, and Adam Jaffe. Joseph Kalt was the first faculty member at the Department of Economics to validate my interest in environmental and resource issues, and he was unfailingly generous to me and many other graduate students in making his office (and computer, then a rather scarce resource) available at all hours. Later a colleague at the Kennedy School, Joe provided examples never to be forgotten — that economics could be a meaningful and enjoyable pursuit, and that excellence in teaching was a laudable goal.

Zvi Griliches was not only my advisor and mentor, but my spiritual father as well. Generations of Harvard graduate students would offer similar testimony. My own father had died only a year before I entered Harvard, and Zvi soon filled for me many paternal needs. It is now more than two decades since Zvi himself passed away. I felt as if I had lost my father a second time.

If Zvi Griliches provided caring and inspiration, Adam Jaffe provided invaluable day-to-day guidance. It was Adam who convinced me not to go on the job market in my fourth year with what would have been a mediocre dissertation, but to put in another year and do it right. That turned out to be some of the best professional advice I have ever received. Our intensive faculty-student relationship from dissertation days subsequently evolved into a very productive professional (and personal) one. The name of Adam Jaffe appears frequently in my curriculum vitae as a co-author; he was much more than that.

Although they were not members of my thesis committee, I should acknowledge two other faculty members at the Harvard Department of Economics who played important roles in my education. I was fortunate to take two courses in economic history (then a department requirement) from Jeffrey Williamson, who had recently arrived from the University of Wisconsin. Williamson's class sessions were as close as anything I have seen to being economic research and teaching laboratories. In class after class, we would carefully dissect one or more articles — examining hypothesis, theoretical model, data, estimation method, results, and conclusions. If there was any time and place where I actually learned how to carry out economic research, it was in those classes.

The other name that is important to highlight is that of Lawrence Goulder, then a faculty member at Harvard, and now a professor emeritus at Stanford. I say this not simply because he was willing to be my examiner in my chosen field of environmental and resource economics, nor because he subsequently became such a close friend. Rather, what is striking about my professional relationship with Larry is the degree to which he has been an unnamed collaborator on so many projects of mine. Although he and I have co-authored no more than a few articles, his name probably appears more frequently than anyone else's in the acknowledgments of papers I have written. There is no one whose overall judgement in matters of economics I trust more, and no one who has been more helpful.

When I began graduate school at Harvard in 1983, it was my intention to return to EDF as soon as I received my degree. But by my third year in the program, I had decided to pursue an academic career, although one that was heavily flavored by involvement in the real world of public policy. Within the context of this professional objective, it was not a difficult decision to accept the offer I received in February, 1988, to become an Assistant Professor at the Kennedy School. Although some of the other offers I received at that time were also very attractive, the choice for me was obvious, and I have never regretted it — not for a moment.

I remain at the Harvard Kennedy School today, where I was promoted to Associate Professor in 1992 (an untenured rank at Harvard), and to a tenured position as Professor of Public Policy in 1997. In 1998, I accepted an appointment as the Albert Pratt Professor of Business and Government, and in 2017 as the university-funded A.J. Meyer Professor of Energy and Economic Development.

In the year 2000, I launched the Harvard Environmental Economics Program, which today brings together — from across the University — forty Faculty Fellows and twenty-five Pre-Doctoral Fellows, who are graduate students studying for the Ph.D. degree in economics, political economy and government, public policy, or health policy. The Program, which I continue to direct, forms links among faculty and graduate students engaged in research, teaching, and outreach in environmental, natural resource, and energy economics and related public policy, by sponsoring research projects, convening workshops, and supporting graduate (and undergraduate) education.

A key reason why the Program — and its various projects, including the Harvard Project on Climate Agreements — have been so successful is the marvelous administrative leadership and staff support it enjoys. Everyone who has been involved in virtually any way has come away impressed by our Executive Director, Robert Stowe, Associate Director, Jason Chapman, and Program Assistant, Meredith Landry.

At the Kennedy School, I have had an excellent mentor, William Hogan, and a superb advisor and friend, Richard Zeckhauser. Over the years, seven successive deans have provided leadership, guidance, and support (including abundant time for my research and writing) — Graham Allison, Robert Putnam, Albert Carnesale, Joseph Nye, David Ellwood. Douglas Elmendorf, and Jeremy Weinstein. At Harvard more broadly, I have benefitted from regular interactions with Daniel Schrag, director of the Harvard University Center for the Environment, and the late Martin Weitzman of the Department of Economics. For two decades, Marty and I co-hosted a bi-weekly Seminar in Environmental Economics and Policy, which provided me with frequent opportunities to learn both from seminar speakers and from Marty's questions and comments. Sadly, Marty passed away in 2019. Fortunately, James Stock of Harvard's Department of Economic stepped in, and has been co-hosting the Seminar with me for the past four years. This is particularly appreciated, because Jim is now Harvard's inaugural Vice Provost for Climate and Sustainability, and directs the new Salata Institute.

I will refrain from naming the many others at Harvard and elsewhere from whom I continue to learn — including my many co-authors — only because the list of such valued colleagues and friends is so long. Included have been a most remarkable set of Ph.D. students, many of whom have gone on to productive — indeed illustrious — careers.

Along the way, I have had my share of administrative responsibilities at Harvard, including serving as Director of Graduate Studies for the Doctoral Program in Public Policy and the Doctoral Program in Political Economy and Government, and Co-Chair of the Harvard Business School-Harvard Kennedy School Joint Degree Programs. Outside of Harvard, I have had the privilege of being a University Fellow of Resources for the Future, a Research Associate of the National Bureau of Economic Research, and the founding Editor and now Co-Editor of the *Review of Environmental Economics and Policy*, as well as a member and co-vice chair of the Board of Directors of Resources for the Future, the Scientific Advisory Board of the Fondazione Eni Enrico Mattei, and numerous editorial boards. I must also note that I serve as an editor of the *Journal of Wine Economics*. In 2009, I was elected a Fellow of the Association of Environmental and Resource Economists, and I recently accepted a six-year term as an Andrew Dickson White Professor-at-Large (visiting) at Cornell University.

What originally attracted me to the Kennedy School was the possibility of combining an academic career with extensive involvement in the development of public policy. I have not been disappointed. Indeed, a theme that emerges from this book is the interplay between scholarly economic research and implementation in real-world political contexts. This is a two-way street. In some cases, my policy involvement has come from expertise I developed through research, following a path well worn by academics. But, in many other cases, my participation in policy matters has stimulated for me entirely new lines of research.

What I have characterized as involvement in policy matters is described at the Harvard Kennedy School as faculty outreach, recognized to be of great institutional and social value, along with the two other components of our three-legged professional stool — research and teaching. Because my outreach efforts relate to a number of the papers collected in this volume, I should note that they have fallen into five broad categories: advisory work with members of Congress and the White House (for example, Project 88, a bipartisan effort co-chaired by former Senator Timothy Wirth and the late Senator John Heinz, to develop innovative approaches to environmental and resource problems); service on federal government panels (for example, my role as Chairman of the Environmental Economics Advisory Committee of the U.S. Environmental Protection Agency Science Advisory Board); on-going consulting — often on an informal basis — with environmental NGOs and private firms; advisory work with state governments; and professional interventions in the international sphere, such as service as Lead Author for the Second and the Third Assessment Reports, Coordinating Lead Author for the Fifth Assessment Report, and Science Advisor to the Chair of the Sixth Assessment Report of the Intergovernmental Panel on Climate Change, professional roles with the World Bank and other international organizations, and advisory work with foreign governments.

Finally, because this book focuses on my articles, not my books, I should note that over the years I have been co-editor with Joseph Aldy of *Post-Kyoto International Climate Policy: Implementing Architectures for Agreement* (Cambridge University Press, 2010), *Post-Kyoto International Climate Policy: Summary for Policymakers* (Cambridge University Press, 2009), and *Architectures for Agreement: Addressing Global Climate Change in the Post-Kyoto World* (Cambridge University Press, 2007); editor of four editions of *Economics of the Environment* (W. W. Norton, 2000, 2005a, 2012; Edward Elgar, 2019); co-editor with Bruce Hay and Richard Vietor of *Environmental Protection and the Social Responsibility of Firms: Perspectives from Law, Economics, and Business* (Resources for the Future, 2005); editor of *The Political Economy of Environmental Regulation* (Edward Elgar, 2004), co-editor with Paul Portney of *Public Policies for Environmental Protection* (Resources for the Future, 2000); and author of *Environmental Economics and Public Policy: Selected Papers of Robert N. Stavins, 1988–1999* (Edward Elgar, 2001), *Economics of Climate Change and Environmental Policy: Selected Papers of Robert N. Stavins, 2000–2011* (Edward Elgar, 2013).

The Current Volume

That last book is the predecessor of the current volume. Whereas the first volume (Stavins, 2001) included selected papers from the period 1988 through 1999, and the second volume (Stavins, 2013) covered the period from 2000 through 2011, this current, third volume begins with some late 2011 paper and concludes with papers published in 2023. To prepare this book, I have selected 33 articles from the many more (published and unpublished) papers I wrote — frequently with co-authors — over this most recent period. Making this selection was not an easy task, but it was a rewarding one, because choosing the papers and organizing them has forced me to step back and reflect on the set of research initiatives in which I have been engaged.

The book is divided into six parts. The chapters in Part I provides some background and an overview of environmental and resource economic by treating broadly several topics, including: the contributions of Martin Weitzman (Stavins and Wagner, *Journal of the Association of Environmental and Resource Economists*, 2022), and William Nordhaus (Aldy and Stavins, *Climate Change Economics*, 2020); the causes of the energy paradox and energy-efficiency gap (Gerarden, Newell, and Stavins, *Journal of Economic Literature*, 2017); and key developments with international climate negotiations (Aldy and Stavins, *Science*, 2012).

The chapters in Part II focus on economic, political, and legal analysis of market-based environmental policy instruments, including: a broad assessment of carbon-pricing instruments (Aldy and Stavins, *Journal of Environment and Development*, 2012); reflections on the use of market-based instruments under the U.S. Clean Air Act Amendments of 1990 (Chan, Stavins, Stowe, and Sweeney, *National Tax Journal*, 2012); four ironies about the SO_2 allowance trading system (Schmalensee and Stavins, *Journal of Economic Perspectives*, 2013); and lessons learned from thirty years of experience with cap-and-trade systems (Schmalensee and Stavins, *Review of Environmental Economics and Policy*, 2017).

Part III consists of five chapters on domestic (national) policy, beginning with a historical treatment of policy evolution under the Clean Air Act (Schmalensee and Stavins, *Journal of Economic Perspectives*, 2019); followed by examinations of: the future of U.S. carbon-pricing policy (Stavins, *Environmental and Energy Policy and the Economy*, 2020); the relative merits of carbon taxes versus carbon cap-and-trade (Stavins, *Review of Environmental Economics and Policy*, 2022); the important role of the concept and empirical estimates of the social cost of carbon (Aldy, Kotchen, Stavins, and Stock, *Science*, 2021); and an economic analysis of the U.S. Clean Power Plan (Fowlie, *et al.*, *Science*, 2014).

Part IV examines the international dimensions of climate change policy, with six chapters: challenges facing the Intergovernmental Panel on Climate Change in general (Carraro, *et al.*, *Science*, 2015), and with regard to its use of economics (Chan, *et al.*, *Climate Change Economics*, 2016); a broad view of potential international climate policy architectures (Chan, Stavins, and Zou, *Annual Review of Resource Economics*, 2018); a proposal for a specific architecture (Olmstead and Stavins, *Review of Environmental Economics and Policy*, 2012); a close-up examination of the annual Conference of the Parties of the United Nations Framework Climate Change (Stavins, *Review of Environment, Energy, and Economics*, 2012); and the potential role of linkage in international climate policy architecture (Ranson and Stavins, *Chicago Journal of International Law*, 2013).

Part V of this volume focuses on the design and implementation of the Paris Agreement, including a set of five chapters that examine: the potential role of linkage of cap-and-trade systems (Ranson and Stavins, *Climate Policy*, 2015); how linkage can be facilitated under the Paris Agreement (Bodansky, Hoedl, Metcalf, and Stavins, *Climate Policy*, 2015); the role of linkage in fostering more ambitious commitments (Mehling, Metcalf, and Stavins, *Science*, 2018); how heterogeneous national policy instruments can be linked (Mehling, Metcalf, and Stavins, *Environmental Law*, 2019); and how proper interpretation of the Paris Agreement's Article 6.2 can be used to prevent double counting of emissions reductions when national policies are linked (Schneider, *et al.*, *Science*, 2019).

Finally, Part VI turns to a different but not unrelated topic — premium wine production and consumption. Nine chapters are included, some very brief, beginning with two chapters which document hedonic analyses of vineyard sales as an approach to examining empirically the concept of terroir in the New World, first in Oregon and subsequently in California (Cross, Plantinga, and Stavins, *Journal of Wine Economics*, 2011 and 2017). Following this are a series of seven book and film reviews (Stavins, *Journal of Wine Economics*, 2013a, 2013b, 2014, 2018, 2019, 2020, and 2021).

Final Words

The process I undertook to decide what to include in this third volume of my selected papers enabled me to take note of some common themes that have emerged from this decade of research and writing. First, there is the value — or at least, the potential value — of economic analysis of environmental and climate change policy. The cause of virtually all environmental problems in a market economy is economic behavior (that is, imperfect markets affected by externalities), and so economics offers a powerful lens through which to view environmental problems, and therefore a potentially effective set of analytical tools for designing and assessing environmental policies.

Second, economists can influence environmental policy in very diverse ways, as demonstrated by Weitzman's theoretical contributions (Stavins and Wagner, 2022) and Nordhaus's empirical contributions (Aldy and Stavins, 2020). That said, it is very much a two-way street that runs between academic research and policy applications (Aldy and Stavins, 2012).

Third, the means governments use to achieve environmental objectives matter greatly, because different policy instruments have very different implications along a number of dimensions, including abatement costs in both the short and the long term. However, carbon taxes and carbon cap-and-trade systems are essentially symmetric instruments, and there is a continuous spectrum of design possibilities between the purest forms of these two approaches (Stavins, 2022).

Fourth, there is a range of potential architectures of forms of international cooperation to address climate change, and the best approaches may well involve or at least facilitate the linkage of national policy instruments, which might well be heterogeneous along a number of dimensions (Mehling, Metcalf, and Stavins, 2019).

Fifth, an economic perspective is also of considerable value (and enjoyment) when examining analytically the world of premium wine, both production and consumption. Sixth and finally, policies for addressing global climate change can benefit greatly from the application of economic thinking. Despite the many challenges, an economic perspective on this grandest of environmental threats is important for the design of public policies that are scientifically effective, economically sensible, and politically pragmatic.

On a personal level, the professional path I have taken offers some confirmation that research can influence public policy, and it also illustrates that involvement in public policy can stimulate new research. The quest — both professional and personal — that took me from Evanston, Illinois, to Sierra Leone, West Africa, to Ithaca, New York, to Berkeley, California, and finally to Cambridge, Massachusetts suggests some consistency of purpose and even function. I continue to find myself doing similar things, but in different contexts. It is fair to say that my professional life has taken me along a path that has brought me home (a home

I am fortunate to share with my wife, Joanna, as our children, Daniel and Julia, have moved with their respective spouses to their own homes in the Boston area). The words of T. S. Eliot (1943) continue to ring true:

We shall not cease from exploration
And the end of all our exploring
Will be to arrive where we started
And know the place for the first time.

Selecting the papers for this volume has forced me to reflect on the past and to think more clearly about the future. The thirty-three articles that comprise this book, the twenty-six articles that comprised the predecessor volume, and the twenty-two essays that comprised the volume before that are the product of thirty-six wonderful years on the faculty of the Harvard Kennedy School. During this time, I have learned much from colleagues, collaborators, students, friends, and inhabitants of the "real world" of public policy — individuals from government, private industry, advocacy groups, and the press. I hope that I will continue to learn as long as I can.

References

Aldy, Joseph E., and Robert N. Stavins, Eds. (2007). *Architectures for Agreement: Addressing Global Climate Change in the Post-Kyoto World.* New York: Cambridge University Press.

Aldy, Joseph E., and Robert N. Stavins (2009). *Post-Kyoto International Climate Policy: Summary for Policymakers*. New York: Cambridge University Press.

Aldy, Joseph E., and Robert N. Stavins, Eds. (2010). *Post-Kyoto International Climate Policy: Implementing Architectures for Agreement*. New York: Cambridge University Press.

Aldy, Joseph E., and Robert N. Stavins. (2012a). "Climate negotiators create an opportunity for scholars." *Science*, August 31, **337**(6098): 1043–1044.

Aldy, Joseph E., and Robert N. Stavins. (2012b). "The promise and problems of pricing carbon: Theory and experience." *Journal of Environment and Development*, **21**(2): 152–180.

Aldy, Joseph E., and Robert N. Stavins. (2020). "Rolling the dice in the corridors of power: William Nordhaus's impacts on climate change policy." *Climate Change Economics*, **11**(4): 1–18.

Aldy, Joseph E., Mathew Kotchen, Robert N. Stavins, and James Stock. (2021). "Keep climate policy focused on the social cost of carbon." *Science*, Policy Forum Insights, August 20, **373**(6557): 850–852.

Bodansky, Daniel, Seth Hoedl, Gilbert Metcalf, and Robert Stavins. (2015). "Facilitating linkage of climate policies through the paris outcome." *Climate Policy*, August 5, 1–17.

Carraro, Carlo, Ottmar Edenhofer, Christian Flaschland, Charles Kolstad, Robert Stavins, and Robert Stowe. (2015). "The IPCC at a crossroads: Opportunities for reform." *Science*, **350**(6256): 34–35.

Chan, Gabriel, Robert Stavins, and Zou Ji. (2018). "International climate change policy." *Annual Review of Resource Economics*, 10:335–360.

Chan, Gabriel, Robert Stavins, Robert Stowe, and Richard Sweeney. (2012). "The SO_2 allowance trading system and the clean air act amendments of 1990: Reflections on 20 years of policy innovation." *National Tax Journal*, June, **65**(2): 419–452.

Chan, Gabriel, Carlo Carraro, Ottmar Edenhofer, Charles Kolstad, and Robert Stavins. (2016). "Reforming the IPCC's assessment of climate change economics." *Climate Change Economics*, **7**(1): 1–16.

Cross, Robin, Andrew J. Plantinga, and Robert N. Stavins. (2011). "The value of terroir: Hedonic estimation of vineyard sale prices." *Journal of Wine Economics*, **6**(1): 1–14.

Cross, Robin, Andrew J. Plantinga, and Robert N. Stavins. (2017). "Terroir in the new world: Hedonic estimation of vineyard sale prices in California." *Journal of Wine Economics*, **12**(3): 282–301.

Eliot, T. S. (1943). "Four quartets: Little gidding." *Collected Poems, 1909–1962*. New York: Hartcourt Brace, 1963.

Fowlie, Meredith, Lawrence Goulder, Matthew Kotchen, Severin Borestein, James Bushnell, Lucas Davis, Michael Greenstone, Charles Kolstad, Christopher Knittel, Robert Stavins, Michael Wara, Frank Wolak, and Catherine Wolfram. (2014). "An economic perspective on the EPA's clean power plan." *Science*, **336**(6211): 815–816.

Gerarden, Todd D., Richard G. Newell, and Robert N. Stavins. (2017). "Assessing the energy-efficiency gap." *Journal of Economic Literature*, 2017, **55**(4): 1486–1525.

Hay, Bruce L., Robert N. Stavins, and Richard H. K. Vietor, Eds. (2005). *Environmental Protection and the Social Responsibility of Firms: Perspectives from Law, Economics, and Business*. Washington, DC: Resources for the Future Press.

Mehling, Michael A., Gilbert E. Metcalf, and Robert N. Stavins. (2018). "Linking climate policies to advance global mitigation." *Science*, March 2, **359**(6379): 997–998.

Mehling, Michael A., Gilbert E. Metcalf, and Robert N. Stavins. (2019). "Linking heterogeneous climate policies (consistent with the paris agreement)." *Environmental Law*, **8**(4): 647–698.

Olmstead, Sheila M., and Robert N. Stavins. (2012). "Three key elements of post2012 international climate policy architecture." *Review of Environmental Economics and Policy*, **6**(2): 1–22.

Portney, Paul R., and Robert N. Stavins, Eds. (2000). *Public Policies for Environmental Protection*. Second Edition. Washington, DC: Resources for the Future.

Ranson, Matthew, and Robert N. Stavins. (2013). "Post-durban climate policy architecture based on linkage of cap-and-trade systems." *The Chicago Journal of International Law*, **13**(2): 403–438.

Ranson, Matthew, and Robert N. Stavins. (2015). "Linkage of greenhouse gas emissions trading systems: Learning from experience." *Climate Policy*, February 4, 284–300.

Schmalensee, Richard, and Robert N. Stavins. (2013). "The SO_2 allowance trading system: The ironic history of a grand policy experiment." *Journal of Economic Perspectives*, Winter, **27**(1): 103–122.

Schmalensee, Richard, and Robert N. Stavins. (2017). "Lessons learned from three decades of experience with cap and trade." *Review of Environmental Economics and Policy*, Summer, **11**(1): 59–79.

Schmalensee, Richard, and Robert N. Stavins. (2019). "Policy evolution under the clean air act." *Journal of Economic Perspectives*, **33**(4): 27–50.

Schneider, L., M. Duan, R. Stavins, K. Kizzier, D. Broekhoff, F. Jotzo, H. Winkler, M. Lazarus, A. Howard, and C. Hood. (2019). "Double counting and the paris agreement rulebook." Policy Forum Insights, *Science*, **366**(6462): 180–183.

Stavins, Robert N., ed. (2000). *Economics of the Environment: Selected Readings*. Fourth Edition. New York: W. W. Norton & Company.

Stavins, Robert N. (2001). *Environmental Economics and Public Policy: Selected Papers of Robert N. Stavins, 1988–1999*. Northampton, Massachusetts: Edward Elgar Publishing, Inc.

Stavins, Robert N., ed. (2004). *The Political Economy of Environmental Regulation*. Northampton, Massachusetts: Edward Elgar Publishing, Inc.

Stavins, Robert N., ed. (2005). *Economics of the Environment: Selected Readings*. Fifth Edition. New York: W. W. Norton & Company.

Stavins, Robert N., ed. (2012a). *Economics of the Environment: Selected Readings*. Sixth Edition. New York: W. W. Norton & Company.

Stavins, Robert N. (2012b). "An Unambiguous Consequence of the Durban Climate Talks." *Review of Environment, Energy, and Economics*, March 9, 1–4.

Stavins, Robert N. (2013a). *Economics of Climate Change and Environmental Policy: Selected Papers of Robert N. Stavins, 2000–2011*. Northampton, Massachusetts: Edward Elgar Publishing, Inc.

Stavins, Robert N. (2013b). "Film review: Jason Wise, Somm." *Journal of Wine Economics*, **8**:238–241.

Stavins, Robert N. (2013c). "Film review: David Roach and Warwick Ross, red obsession." *Journal of Wine Economics*, **8**:355–360.

Stavins, Robert N. (2014). "Film review: David Leonard, a year in burgundy." *Journal of Wine Economics*, **9**:100–103.

Stavins, Robert N. (2018). "Film review: Rudi Goldman: Burgundy: People with a passion for wine." *Journal of Wine Economics*, **13**:105–108.

Stavins, Robert N., ed. (2019a). *Economics of the Environment: Selected Readings*. Seventh Edition. Northampton, Massachusetts: Edward Elgar Publishing.

Stavins, Robert N. (2019). "Book review: Gert Crum and Jan Bartelsman: Le Domaine de la Romanée-Conti." *Journal of Wine Economics*, **14**:224–227.

Stavins, Robert N. (2020a). "The future of U.S. carbon-pricing policy." *Environmental and Energy Policy and the Economy*, **1**:8–64. University of Chicago Press.

Stavins, Robert N. (2020b). "Film review: Jason Wise (Director), *Somm* 3." *Journal of Wine Economics*, **15**:423–426.

Stavins, Robert N. (2021). "Book Review: James M. Gabler: Passions: The Wines and Travels of Thomas Jefferson." *Journal of Wine Economics* **16**:102–104.

Stavins, Robert N. (2022). "The relative merits of carbon pricing instruments: Taxes versus trading." *Review of Environmental Economics and Policy*, **16**(1): 1–21.

Stavins, Robert N., and Gernot Wagner. (2022). "Martin Weitzman: A Gift That Keeps on Giving." *Journal of the Association of Environmental and Resource Economists*, **9**(5): 843–850.

https://doi.org/10.1142/9789811292415_0002

Chapter 2

Martin Weitzman: A Gift That Keeps on Giving*

Robert N. Stavins[†,‡,§,¶] **and Gernot Wagner**[‖,**]

[†]*John F. Kennedy School of Government, Harvard University, Cambridge, MA, USA*

[‡]*Resources for the Future, Washington, DC, USA*

[§]*National Bureau of Economic Research, Cambridge, USA*

[‖]*Columbia Business School, New York, USA*

[¶]*robert_stavins@harvard.edu*

[**]*gwagner@columbia.edu*

This special issue is a reminder that the world lost a truly remarkable scholar when Martin Weitzman sadly passed away in 2019. Across five decades, he explored policy options for the most challenging issues — from unemployment and inflation in the 1970s to climate change in the twenty-first century. In this chapter, we provide a brief biography and personal remembrance of Weitzman and describe how his contributions

*This chapter was originally published in *Journal of the Association of Environmental and Resource Economists*, **9**(5), 2022. https://doi.org/10.1086/721093.

advanced the thinking of environmental economists,[1] and the thoughts and actions of policy makers on many fundamental issues. We conclude with a brief description of the articles that follow in this issue.

Weitzman was a treasure — a gift that kept on giving to the research and policy worlds — for Harvard University, for economists around the world, and for the global intellectual community. His work as an economic theorist who addressed a broad set of problems, and as an environmental economist who for over a decade focused on climate change, was unparalleled and formed the basis for theoretical and empirical work carried out by legions of economists and other scholars around the world. Weitzman's contributions to environmental economics in particular were unprecedented, helped to shape the field for nearly five decades, and as the papers in this volume show undoubtedly set the direction for many more years to come.

If economic theory is about stripping a problem down to its absolute essentials and deriving meaningful insights from those essentials, then Weitzman was a master. Over and over again, he demonstrated how careful and rigorous analysis of artfully constructed theoretical models can provide valuable and often surprising insights into difficult economic problems with real implications for the design of public policies. At a symposium held at Harvard University in October 2018, to mark Weitzman's retirement and celebrate his contributions, "Frontiers in Environmental Economics and Policy: A Symposium in Honor of Martin L. Weitzman," he explained, "I'm drawn to things that are conceptually unclear, where it's not clear how to make your way through this maze." His writings were works of art as well as science, weaving Greek mythology and everyday anecdotes into his expositions like few others.

As a teacher and colleague, he left a memorable impression on many, both with his ideas and his approach to tackling some of the most important economic problems of his lifetime. He was fond of saying that the best tools of his trade were a No. 2 pencil, a yellow legal pad, and a hard, wooden chair. Across the board, the example of his rigorous and often ingenious work set high standards for theorizing in environmental economics and thereby served to elevate the entire field.

---

[1]We focus exclusively on Weitzman's contributions to environmental and resource economics, which define the scope of this journal. We thereby omit his significant contributions to several other areas, including economic planning, optimal search and technological growth, and the share economy. We treat those areas in Stavins and Wagner (2022).

Biography

Meyer Levinger was born in New York City on April 1, 1942, to Joseph and Helen Levinger.[2] His mother died of tuberculosis in the boy's infancy, and his father was apparently unable to care for him after returning from military service in the Second World War. Meyer was placed in foster care and was eventually adopted by Samuel and Fannie Weitzman, elementary school teachers on the Lower East Side of Manhattan, who raised him in the planned community of Levittown, New York, renaming him Martin Lawrence Weitzman.

Despite this rather challenging start, Weitzman emerged early as a brilliant student and was valedictorian at his high school. He received his BA in Mathematics and Physics from Swarthmore College in 1963, where the Phoenix, the student newspaper, characterized him as discussing mathematics and politics "with the intonations of a Brooklyn garage mechanic."

Just one year after graduating from Swarthmore, Weitzman received an MS degree in Statistics and Operations Research from Stanford University and three years later earned a PhD in Economics from the Massachusetts Institute of Technology (MIT), where his dissertation committee chair was Robert Solow. From 1967 to 1972, he taught in the Department of Economics at Yale University, then moved back to MIT, where he taught in the Department of Economics until 1989, when he moved to Harvard University. He was a professor of economics at Harvard until 2018, when he became an emeritus and research professor of economics.

He taught courses at all levels at Harvard, ranging from introductory courses for first-year students in Harvard College to seminars for PhD students. He cohosted (with Stavins) the Harvard Seminar in Environmental Economics and Policy for 26 years, across 52 semesters involving more than 400 seminars, each with a distinct paper and presentation by a leading scholar from across the United States and around the world. Stavins found that "Weitzman's questions and comments were often as insightful as the speaker's presentation" (Stavins, 2019b).

His research contributions were well recognized. He was elected a fellow of the Econometric Society in 1976; named a fellow of the American Academy of Arts and Sciences in 1986; three times won the annual award for "Publication of Enduring Quality" from the Association

[2]This biographical sketch draws, in part, on Hagerty (2019), Roberts (2019), Smith (2019), and Hart *et al.* (2021).

of Environmental and Resource Economists; and received the Twentieth Anniversary Prize from Fondazione Eni Enrico Mattei, the Leontief Prize, and the Eric Kempe Award in 2011.

Weitzman was a stimulating teacher and colleague with a refreshingly contrarian attitude. He was always willing to talk at length with colleagues and particularly students. The range of his attainments took one by surprise. He was knowledgeable about many areas, including history, literature, and politics, and did not advertise, for example, that he was fluent, mostly self-taught, in Russian. But in the last few months of his life, Marty began to feel that his mental acuity was deserting him. It seems likely that this situation, which he could not bear easily, caused him to take his own life on August 27, 2019.

Contributions to Environmental and Resource Economics

Martin Weitzman began his research career in a field that has since all but disappeared — comparative economic systems — studying centrally planned economies. In the 1990s, however, he turned with passion and energy almost exclusively to environmental and natural resource problems.

Green National Accounting

A topic that has pervaded decades of analysis and commentary in the environmental sphere is the reality that conventional measures of economic growth, such as gross domestic product, are not measures of welfare, since they do not account for externalities (among other nonmarket economic phenomena). Weitzman's first foray into the topic was one of the most significant contributions to this literature. In Weitzman (1976), he developed an idealized measure of economic output net of all depreciation, including natural resources, and of environmental costs. Twenty years later, this work was validated by a major report from the National Research Council (Nordhaus and Kokkelenberg, 1999). Two decades after that, at the 2018 Harvard symposium, Nordhaus emphasized Weitzman's contributions in this realm and launched his keynote by stating that Weitzman "has changed the way we think about economics and the environment." Nordhaus concluded that "if we use green national output as our standard, then environmental and safety regulations have increased true economic growth substantially in recent years. . . . For this important insight we applaud Martin Weitzman, a radically innovative spirit in economics" (Nordhaus, 2018).

Policy Instrument Choice — Prices vs. Quantities

It may be difficult to identify Weitzman's single greatest contribution to environmental economics, but his classic 1974 article, "Prices vs. Quantities," would be at or near the top of any such list. In it, Weitzman developed the simple yet powerful insight that under conditions of uncertainty, the expected relative efficiency of policy instruments based on prices (such as a pollution tax) versus those based on quantities (such as a cap-and-trade system) depends on the relative slopes of the expected marginal benefit and marginal cost functions.

That work remains one of the most frequently cited articles in all of environmental economics. It stimulated a massive literature, a fact that prompted Richard Newell to characterize it as a "gift that keeps on giving" at the Harvard symposium. Even now, the paper is at the core of analysis of carbon taxes versus carbon cap-and-trade systems to address climate change (Karp and Traeger, 2018; Mideksa and Weitzman, 2019; Stavins, 2019a).

Biodiversity

In the early 1990s, Weitzman responded to what he sensed might be the unwillingness — or the inability — of ecologists to rank ecologies in terms of their relative biodiversity, by showing how these comparisons can be made theoretically and quantitatively (Weitzman, 1992, 1993, 1998a; Metrick and Weitzman, 1996). In doing so, Weitzman taught himself and then applied set theory in ways so novel that he essentially invented the economics of species conservation.

Discounting

It was also in the 1990s that Weitzman became interested in a central issue of the economic analysis of climate change policies, namely, long-term discounting. Given the long time horizons of the climate change problem, analysis of the expected net present value of alternative policies can be dominated by the choice of discount rate, which, with conventional constant exponential discounting, will greatly diminish the relative quantitative importance of phenomena that are decades or longer in the future.

Through careful theoretical analysis, he concluded that rather than a constant discount rate being employed, a rate that itself is diminishing over time is appropriate. This important and influential work appeared in a series of articles (Weitzman, 1994, 1998b, 2001). The last of these presented the results of a survey he sent to all members of the American Economic Association, leading to his analysis demonstrating how disagreement around the "correct" discount rate in itself points to a declining discount rate over time.

Fisheries

Some will be surprised to learn that a theorist such as Weitzman was as immersed as he was in concerns about the real world of natural resource management and environmental protection. One example comes from his research and outreach in the realm of fisheries management. In part an outgrowth of his theoretical instrument choice work, Weitzman's modeling of Icelandic commercial fisheries affected thinking and discussion around the world regarding the use of taxes and quotas to regulate open-access fisheries (Weitzman, 2002). As Maureen Cropper (University of Maryland) said at the Harvard symposium, "this is another example of the use of a simple model and treatment of uncertainty that really did start a conversation among fisheries economists."

Fat Tails

In recent years, Weitzman made prominent and important contributions to thinking about long-term climate change policy with his development of what he memorably termed the "dismal theorem." In typical Weitzman fashion, he taught himself Bayesian statistics, "unlearning" frequentist statistics, as he described it; he also approached the topic from the ground up, reading assessment reports from the Intergovernmental Panel on Climate Change (IPCC) cover to cover to understand climate science as thoroughly as possible.

He quickly focused on the all-important climate sensitivity parameter, which links concentrations of carbon dioxide in the atmosphere to global average temperatures. The climate sensitivity distribution has been deeply uncertain for decades. Weitzman argued that the IPCC cut off its right tail too quickly (Wagner, 2019) and concluded that even without relying on "fat tails" per se and instead looking at "heavy-tailed" distributions, relatively low-probability, high-consequence outcomes may dwarf everything else. He described this as the "dismal theorem," because it emphasizes how much potential climate catastrophes do — or, at least, should — matter. A small subset of the papers include Weitzman (2009, 2011, 2014b). It was this work that piqued his interest in domestic and international climate change policy debates.

Domestic and International Climate Change Policy

Weitzman's recent work exploring alternative policy instruments to address climate change and his critical examinations of the form of international climate agreements provide examples of continuous search for topics that were not only interesting but also relevant and important for real-world applications. Just two of the many papers that could be cited in this context include Weitzman (2014a, 2017). During this time, Weitzman approached Wagner, his former student, to coauthor what would become a series of popular writings in major periodicals, as well as a complete book (Wagner and Weitzman, 2015). The book combined ideas around "fat tails," climate risks, uncertainties, and solar geoengineering and recognized that reducing consumption of fossil fuels would be one of the most difficult challenges modern civilization has ever faced but, at the same time, warned against complacency. Weitzman also ventured into solar geoengineering, inventing the term "free driver," in contrast to the well-known economic concept of the "free rider," in Wagner and Weitzman (2012) and formalizing the argument in Weitzman (2015).

Preview of the Special Issue

The set of articles that follow in this issue are not simply related — closely or remotely — to Weitzman's work but, rather, in nearly all cases stem quite directly from it. For example, the article by Dallas Burtraw, Charles Holt, Karen Palmer, and William Shobe starts from the important refinement by Roberts and Spence (1976) of Weitzman's (1974) relative-slopes rule to recognize that the most efficient policy might be neither a pure (and simple) price instrument nor quantity instrument but, rather, a hybrid of the two. The authors develop an implementable instrument wherein an auction for allowances in a cap-and-trade system yields not only a price but also a quantity. Picking up on a key focus of Weitzman's work on discounting — uncertainty regarding future economic growth — Richard G. Newell, William A. Pizer, and Brian Charles Prest develop a rule for identifying an appropriate discount rate to use in estimating a key climate policy metric, namely, the social cost of carbon.

David Anthoff and Richard S. J. Tol carry out an empirical test of Weitzman's dismal theorem, using three prominent integrated assessment models (IAMs) that have been used to estimate the social cost of carbon. In doing so, they find that only one of the three IAMs affirms the dismal theorem, but their meta-analysis provides "qualified support." And Christopher Costello and Matthew Kotchen directly apply Weitzman's (1974) rule to assessing the relative efficiency of price and quantity instruments in a very different context — private provision of public goods. They find that prices are more efficient than quantities and not only with cost uncertainty (as in Weitzman's analysis of government policies) but with benefit uncertainty as well.

Joseph E. Aldy and Sarah Armitage use Weitzman's (1974) relative slopes rule to compare price and quantity instruments, but in addition to abatement cost uncertainty, they add firm-specific uncertainty regarding future allowance prices under a quantity instrument. The result strongly favors the price instrument option. Frances C. Moore, Arianna Stokes, Marc Conte, and Xiaoli Dong build upon Metrick and Weitzman (1996) by examining how climate change is likely to lead to greater threats to biodiversity and thereby to increases in species listing (and consequent spending) under the US Endangered Species Act. Like the 1996 work, a very significant bias emerges for vertebrate species.

Conclusion

As this special issue illustrates, Martin Weitzman's theoretical work was important not only for other theorists but also for empirical economists. In many of the realms we describe above, his insights were fundamental as the foundation for sound empirical analysis. Michael Greenstone noted at the Harvard symposium that Weitzman's work "takes something you are kind of confused about, and then after you read it, you can't understand how in the world you were confused beforehand. It just clarifies things in a way that is really beautiful."

Weitzman was thus a real treasure — a "gift that keeps on giving" — for both the research and policy worlds. His work as a theorist on environment broadly and on climate change in particular was unparalleled, and it formed the basis of much theoretical and empirical research carried out by others over several decades. His work — from examining price versus quantity instruments in the early 1970s through his examinations in the last few years of the implications of fat tails in the probability distribution of possible climate damages — has changed the way economists and others think about the environment and policies to protect it. Shortly after Marty's death, Bill Nordhaus said, "Marty Weitzman was the pre-eminent environmental economist of the modern era, which is to say of all time" (Roberts, 2019).

References

Hagerty, James R. (2019). Martin Weitzman examined climate change from an economic viewpoint. *Wall Street Journal*, September 6.

Hart, Oliver, Eric Maskin, Robert Stavins, and James Stock. (2021). Martin L. Weitzman, 77: Memorial minute, Faculty of Arts and Sciences. *Harvard Gazette*, February 3.

Karp, Larry S., and Christian P. Traeger. (2018). "Prices versus quantities reassessed." *CESifo Working Paper*, 7331.

Metrick, Andrew, and Martin L. Weitzman. (1996). "Patterns of behavior in endangered species preservation." *Land Economics*, **72**(1): 1–16.

Mideksa, Torben K., and Martin L. Weitzman. (2019). "Prices versus quantities across jurisdictions." *Journal of the Association of Environmental and Resource Economists*, **6**(5): 883–891.

Nordhaus, William D. (2018). The intellectual footprint of Martin Weitzman in environmental economics. *Presentation at "Frontiers in Environmental Economics and Policy: A Symposium in Honor of Martin L. Weitzman,"* Harvard Kennedy School, October 11.

Nordhaus, William D., and Edward C. Kokkelenberg, Eds. (1999). *Nature's Numbers: Expanding the National Economic Accounts to include the Environment*. Washington, DC: National Academies Press.

Roberts, Marc J., and Michael Spence. (1976). Effluent charges and licenses under uncertainty. *Journal of Public Economics*, **5**(3–4): 193–208.

Roberts, Sam. (2019). Martin Weitzman, 77, top climate change economist. *New York Times*, September 5, Section B:12.

Smith, Harrison. (2019). Martin Weitzman, environmental economist who emphasized uncertainty, dies at 77. *Washington Post*, September 4.

Stavins, Robert N. (2019a). The future of US carbon-pricing policy. *NBER Working Paper* 25912, National Bureau of Economic Research, Cambridge, MA.

Stavins, Robert N. (2019b). A gift that keeps on giving: The contributions of Martin Weitzman to environmental economics. *Vox*, September 9.

Stavins, Robert N., and Gernot Wagner. (2022). Martin L. Weitzman (1942–2019). Prepared for *The Palgrave Companion to Harvard Economics*, ed. Robert Cord. Cham: Springer Nature Switzerland.

Wagner, Gernot. (2019). A tribute to Marty Weitzman, with Gernot Wagner. *Resources Radio*, September 10.

Wagner, Gernot, and Martin L. Weitzman. (2012). Playing God. *Foreign Policy*, October 24.

Wagner, Gernot, and Martin L. Weitzman. (2015). *Climate Shock: The Economic Consequences of a Hotter Planet.* Princeton, NJ: Princeton University Press.

Weitzman, Martin L. (1974). Prices vs. quantities. *Review of Economic Studies*, **41**(4): 477–491.

Weitzman, Martin L. (1976). On the welfare significance of national product in a dynamic economy. *Quarterly Journal of Economics*, **90**(1): 156–162.

Weitzman, Martin L. (1992). On diversity. *Quarterly Journal of Economics*, **107**(2): 363–405.

Weitzman, Martin L. (1993). What to preserve: An application of diversity theory to crane conservation. *Quarterly Journal of Economics*, **108**(1): 157–183.

Weitzman, Martin L. (1994). On the environmental discount rate. *Journal of Environmental Economics and Management*, **26**(2): 200–209.

Weitzman, Martin L. (1998a). The Noah's Ark problem. *Econometrica*, **66**(6): 1279–1298.

Weitzman, Martin L. (1998b). Why the far-distant future should be discounted at its lowest possible rate. *Journal of Environmental Economics and Management*, **36**(3): 201–208.

Weitzman, Martin L. (2001). Gamma discounting. *American Economic Review*, **91**(1): 260–271.

Weitzman, Martin L. (2002). Landing fees vs. harvest quotas with uncertain fish stocks. *Journal of Environmental Economics and Management*, **43**(2): 325–338.

Weitzman, Martin L. (2009). On modeling and interpreting the economics of catastrophic climate change. *Review of Economics and Statistics*, **91**(1): 1–19.

Weitzman, Martin L. (2011). Fat-tailed uncertainty in the economics of catastrophic climate change. *Review of Environmental Economics and Policy*, **5**(2): 275–292.

Weitzman, Martin L. (2014a). Can negotiating a uniform carbon price help to internalize the global warming externality? *Journal of the Association of Environmental and Resource Economists*, **1**(1/2): 29–49.

Weitzman, Martin L. (2014b). Fat tails and the social cost of carbon. *American Economic Review, Papers and Proceedings*, **104**(5): 544–46.

Weitzman, Martin L. (2015). A voting architecture for the governance of free-driver externalities, with application to geoengineering. *Scandinavian Journal of Economics*, **117**(4): 1049–1068.

Weitzman, Martin L. (2017). On a world climate assembly and the social cost of carbon. *Economica*, **84**(336): 559–586.

https://doi.org/10.1142/9789811292415_0003

Chapter 3

Rolling the Dice in the Corridors of Power: William Nordhaus's Impacts on Climate Change Policy[*]

Joseph E. Aldy[†,‡,§,||,¶] and Robert N. Stavins[†,‡,§,]**

[†]*John F. Kennedy School of Government, Harvard University, Cambridge, MA, USA*

[‡]*Resources for the Future, Washington, DC, USA*

[§]*National Bureau of Economic Research, Cambridge, USA*

[||]*Center for Strategic and International Studies, Washington, DC, USA*

[¶]*joseph_aldy@hks.harvard.edu*

[**]*robert_stavins@harvard.edu*

Introduction

The core contributions of William Nordhaus to academic economics were summarized by the citation of his 2018 Nobel Prize for "for integrating climate change into long-run macroeconomic analysis" (Nobel Foundation, 2018). But beyond those academic macroeconomic insights, Nordhaus has had significant influence on U.S. and international public policies to address climate change. Identifying those contributions is more

[*]This chapter was originally published in *Journal of Economic Perspectives*, **27**(1), 103–122, Winter 2013. http://dx.doi.org/10.1257/jep.27.1.103.

challenging, partly because such influences are more subtle. That is our purpose in this essay — to identify how Professor Nordhaus and his research have affected the path of climate change policy in the United States and around the world.

The Use of Analysis in Policy Formulation

Because academic influences on policy can be subtle, they are easily missed. For many years, economists and others have taken note of the influence — or lack thereof — of economic analysis on real world policy making. The upshot of much of that work was summarized by Thomas Schelling when he surveyed potential influences across a range of policy areas — including abortion, crime, environment, health care, illegal drugs, national defense, and race relations — and observed "how little difference economic analysis appears to make in most important policies" (Schelling, 1997). However, economics and economists can be influential without leaving a trail of evidence. Sometimes, economists' greatest influence in government is by stopping bad ideas, as opposed to successfully promoting good ones (Schultze, 1996). But, within the environmental policy realm, a case can be made that the influence of economics, even if relatively modest, has at least increased — with fits and starts — over the past four decades (Hahn, 2000; Schmalensee and Stavins, 2019).

A useful metaphor about the use of analysis in the process of policy formulation, which we learned from our colleague, Dutch Leonard, is of a "light bulb versus a rock."[1] Does the analysis provide illumination about a proposed policy, and thereby persuade policy makers to pursue said policy on its merits? Or does the analysis function as ammunition in a policy battle, used by those who already support a given policy (on its merits or for other reasons)? Evidence from the Council of Economic Advisers suggests that the use of macroeconomic analysis frequently fits the "light bulb" function (Schultze, 1996; Stein, 1996), whereas microeconomic analysis is more likely to function as a "rock" (Schelling, 1997; Schultze, 1996).

Over time, Congressional testimony by academic economists has increasingly come to fit within the category of ammunition, whether for members of a Congressional committee who are already supporters or are

[1]For an examination of how an economic analysis, even if imperfect, can shine a light on climate change policy, see: Aldy (2004).

already opponents of specific legislation (Devins, 2005). Likewise, administrations frequently contact academic economists when a new legislative proposal or administrative action is about to be rolled out, in order to develop a list of "objective academics" who can serve as validators when contacted by the press. Similarly, many academic economists have received press inquiries, wherein it becomes clear that the reporter wants a statement of validation for a particular point of view, not an objective assessment.

Three Pathways of Impacts on Climate Change Policy

In reflecting on how economists have had impacts on the formulation of public policies, we identify three distinct pathways. First, there is direct participation in the policy world, such as via full-time government service or part-time service on a government committee. In the case of Bill Nordhaus, we review, in Part II of this book, three engagements that fall into this first pathway: (1) Member, Council of Economic Advisers, 1977–1979; (2) Chairman, National Academy of Sciences (NAS) Panel on Integrated Environmental and Economic Accounting, 1996–1999; and (3) Chairman, NAS Committee on the Effects of Provisions in the Internal Revenue Code on Greenhouse Gas Emissions, 2011–2013.

The second of the three pathways is that of *directly influencing the formulation of public policies*, a pathway we believe to be considerably less frequent than commonly assumed. We find one significant example of this in the case of Nordhaus, and examine it in Part III of the article: the explicit use of the Dynamic Integrated Climate-Economy (DICE) model by an interagency working group in the Obama administration which developed quantitative estimates of the "social cost of carbon" (Interagency Working Group on Social Cost of Carbon, United States Government, 2010, 2013, 2015, 2016).

The third and final pathway is by far the most common, and we characterize this pathway as *indirectly informing public policy*. This category turns out to be in some ways the most challenging to assess, because here the picture is clouded by the first half of the well-known proverb that "success has many fathers, but failure is an orphan." Subject to that caveat, in Part IV of the article, we examine six distinct ways in which William Nordhaus's economic research has indirectly informed climate change policy.

In the fifth and final part of the article, we identify themes that emerge from this investigation — both generally and specific to climate change policy. This leads us to conclude with an appeal for modesty in thinking about the influence of economists on climate change policy.

Participation in the Policy World

An economist can share his or her views on policy without filter or interpretation by personally participating in policy debates. "Being in the room where it happened." "Holding the pen." "Clearing on the memo." These phrases represent ways that direct participation in the policy process can enable an economist's voice to be heard and influence an outcome. Our first example of Nordhaus's participation in the policy world — as a Member of the Council of Economic Advisers — is being part of the process, while the second example — chairing National Academy of Sciences panels — is providing advice to the process.

Council of Economic Advisers

On March 18, 1977, the U.S. Senate confirmed William Nordhaus as a Member of the Council of Economic Advisers (CEA), which is comprised of a Chair and two Members, and advises the President on domestic and international economic policy. In contrast with other agencies and departments of the Federal government, which may have their own interests and agendas, the CEA has "the luxury of trying to discern what is in the best interest of the country and of providing that analysis and advice directly to the President" (Feldstein, 1992, p. 1224).

As a Member of the three-person council, Nordhaus's portfolio was necessarily broad, as noted in the 1979 Economic Report of the President: "Mr. Nordhaus has supervised international economic analysis and microeconomic analysis, including analysis of policies in such areas as energy, agriculture, social welfare, and oversight of regulatory reform activities" (United States, 1979, p. 173). This service predated meaningful U.S. or international concern about climate change, but years later, Nordhaus's efforts on regulatory reform and oversight were of significance in the climate policy realm.

In 1977, while Nordhaus was a Member of CEA, President Carter created the Regulatory Analysis Review Group (RARG) and charged

CEA with its leadership (Litan and Nordhaus, 1983). The RARG could review analyses of regulations and make recommendations to regulatory agencies. Agency rules — as opposed to analyses — were not subject to RARG review, however, and recommendations were not binding on regulators. Not surprisingly, CEA advocated for more rigorous analyses of the benefits and costs of regulations (Sabin, 2016).

The next year, President Carter issued Executive Order 12044 "Improving Government Regulations," which established the objective that regulations "shall achieve legislative goals effectively and efficiently."[2] The executive order required regulatory agencies to explain the need for their regulations; consider the direct and indirect effects; evaluate potential alternatives; solicit and respond to public comments; communicate rules in plain language; estimate reporting and record-keeping burdens; and develop a plan for retrospective evaluations. However, the executive order did not formally require benefit-cost analysis, and it failed to institutionalize a centralized authority responsible for implementing it. Nevertheless, in advocating for analyses of the benefits and costs of regulations, Carter's executive order and his CEA set the stage for subsequent administrations to require such assessments from their regulatory agencies, beginning with President Reagan's Executive Order 12291 and President Clinton's Executive Order 112866 (Litan and Nordhaus, 1983; Smith, 1984; Arrow *et al.*, 1996).[3]

In Carter's CEA, Nordhaus expressed concern about the potential inflationary impacts of regulations and advocated for a regulatory budget (Sabin, 2016). This has long been a controversial proposal to impose a social cost budget on regulations akin to a spending budget on government appropriations. Of course, limiting the aggregate costs of regulations, without consideration of their societal benefits, undermines the role of benefit-cost analysis in identifying policy options that increase social welfare. A memorandum from CEA Chair Charles Schultze to President Carter in advance of the 1979 State of the Union address followed up on a meeting of the President, Vice President, Schultze, and Nordhaus on

[2] Refer to Section 1 of Executive Order 12044.

[3] The emerging role of the social cost of carbon (SCC) in monetizing the benefits of reducing carbon dioxide (CO_2) emissions in recent regulations — addressed in section "Direct Influence on Public Policy", below — reflects this legacy of promoting the explicit consideration of the benefits and costs of proposed regulatory actions.

establishing rational regulatory priorities (Schultze, 1979). The CEA Chair acknowledged disagreement among White House staff regarding the idea of a regulatory budget. In his State of the Union address, Carter avoided the issue altogether.[4]

All in all, Carter's CEA and Nordhaus's service as a Member thereof had profound long-term effects on public policy — in the climate domain and many others — by initiating thinking that led directly to the use of Regulatory Impact Analyses (RIAs) of all major Federal regulatory proposals. By the year 2000, 20 of 28 countries in the Organization for Economic Development and Cooperation had implemented requirements for such RIAs (OECD, 2002).

National Academy of Sciences

In 1979, Nordhaus departed CEA after two years of service, the norm for CEA members. But he continued to inform the policy process through another vehicle for academic experts: committees convened by the National Academies. Soon after leaving government, Nordhaus served on an early *ad hoc* committee of the National Academies focused on the economic and social aspects of climate change (National Research Council, 1980), more than a decade before the Rio de Janeiro conference that produced the United Nations Framework Convention on Climate Change.

For the next two decades, Nordhaus focused mainly on his academic work, with direct and indirect climate policy implications, as we discuss in sections "Direct Influence on Public Policy" and "Indirectly Informing Public Policy." But in 1998, Nordhaus returned to direct engagement with the policy world, co-chairing an NAS committee convened to study ways of accounting for natural resources and the environment in the National Income and Product Accounts (Nordhaus and Kokkelenberg, 1999). The National Academies published the committee's report as *Nature's Numbers*. The report examined the history of national accounting and augmented accounting, suggesting that it is important to retain conventional, core accounts, but to develop additional, supplemental accounts that capture the output and value of non-market natural services, even if

[4]Executive Order 12291 issued by President Reagan in 1981 included a reference to a regulatory budget, but the Reagan Administration did not pursue it. In 2017, President Trump issued Executive Order 13771, "Reducing Regulation and Controlling Regulatory Costs," which called for regulatory cost budgets, and effectively slowed the development and promulgation of new regulations, including those that may address climate change.

defining the scope and measurement of those augmented accounts presents challenges.

In their assessment of the valuation literature, the committee noted the opportunities and methods for accounting for climate change benefits in valuing carbon sequestration through forestry activities — an issue relevant to a variety of land use policies targeting climate change, such as multilateral programs that promote reduced deforestation and increased afforestation in developing countries and tree-planting efforts in domestic policy. They also noted how Clean Air Act benefit-cost analyses had failed to monetize the benefits of reducing carbon dioxide emissions, an issue addressed subsequently through the application of the social cost of carbon (which we address in the next section). The report included guidelines for accounting for non-renewable and renewable natural resources and environmental pollution.

In 2013, the National Academies published the report of another Nordhaus-chaired committee, *Effects of US Tax Policy on Greenhouse Gas Emissions*, convened at the request of the Department of the Treasury (Nordhaus *et al.*, 2013). This study identified the tax provisions with the greatest effect on emissions that contribute to global climate change. It focused on energy-related tax expenditures and excise taxes, biofuels provisions, and broad-based tax expenditures. The committee recognized the limitations of existing models and scholarship, and made recommendations for future research to fill these gaps. In addition, the report highlighted the inefficiencies in the existing tax code in terms of its impacts on carbon dioxide emissions, both through fossil fuel provisions that may increase emissions as well as the high costs per ton of emissions reduced through some renewable energy and energy efficiency tax provisions.

In both cases, the Nordhaus-led committees made recommendations to improve public policy to better account for the adverse impacts of pollution. Indeed, each reflected well-understood insights from economics about how appropriately pricing pollution could alter behavior and investment and thereby increase social welfare. For a variety of political reasons, the committees' recommendations to account for the natural environment in Federal statistics, as well to reform the tax code, were not adopted.[5]

[5]Muller *et al.* (2011) illustrate an application of environmental accounting within a national income accounting framework, consistent with the *Nature's Numbers* recommendations. Their application focuses on local air pollution and carbon dioxide damages, but they acknowledge that no government statistical agency had explicitly linked such damages to specific industries.

Direct Influence on Public Policy

In addition to service in government positions at CEA and on NAS committees, Nordhaus carried out some of his most influential work while back at Yale. Economists' voices can carry through to public policy when their research directly informs key elements of its design, evaluation, or implementation. This has been true in one important case with Nordhaus's research, the use of his path-breaking integrated assessment model of climate change by government analysts for the purpose of developing empirical estimates of the marginal damages of a unit of CO_2 emissions, the so-called social cost of carbon (SCC).

The DICE Model and the Social Cost of Carbon

Integrated Assessment Models (IAMs) combine scientific relationships about emission flows, atmospheric pollutant stocks, temperature impacts, with key economic relationships to summarize the effects of climate change on human welfare. The first to incorporate economics in a systematic way was Nordhaus's DICE model, which has played a critical role in both scholarly and policy endeavors by characterizing the implications of a changing climate.

Consideration of the SCC, the estimated economic damage due to the emission of one ton of CO_2 into the atmosphere in a specific year, originated in Nordhaus's scholarship in 1982 (National Academy of Sciences, 2017). While this work — and many subsequent papers — came well before meaningful policy debates about mitigating carbon dioxide (CO_2) and other greenhouse gases, these early models provided a foundation for quantitative assessment when those debates turned to real policy options.

The social cost of carbon can be used as an element in the design of climate change policy, such as in setting the tax rate for a carbon tax or informing the development of a cap-and-trade program. Also, government analysts can employ the social cost of carbon in their benefit-cost analyses of regulatory proposals that are expected to reduce CO_2 emissions (Nordhaus, 2013). This latter application of the SCC has been the norm in U.S. energy and climate policy for more than a decade.

The Social Cost of Carbon Arrives in Government

In 2008, a Federal court required the Department of Transportation to revise a fuel economy regulation because it was "arbitrary and capricious" by failing to monetize the benefits of reducing CO_2 emissions.[6] This created demand for SCC estimates. It is common for regulatory agencies to include non-monetized benefit categories in their RIAs (Aldy *et al.*, 2020), but the existence of numerical estimates (using DICE model calculations) precluded efforts to avoid monetizing CO_2 emission reduction benefits for major energy and climate regulations. Some of the initial efforts by the Department of Transportation to include SCCs relied on syntheses of the literature by Richard Tol (2005, 2008), which were influenced by Nordhaus SCC estimates from several years.

In 2009, the Obama Administration formed an Interagency Working Group on the Social Cost of Carbon (IWGSCC) to review the scientific literature on climate change damages and provide guidance for monetizing such damages in RIAs (IWGSCC, 2010). Federal agencies began to use a preliminary set of SCC estimates based on an interim review of the literature, with explicit discussion of Nordhaus's DICE model as a key input to this work, along with two other IAMs — the FUND model (Tol, 1997) and the PAGE model (Hope *et al.*, 1993).[7]

The IWGSCC (2010) issued guidance to agencies on the social cost of carbon, based on modeling runs conducted by government staff with the three IAMs. In this initial report and in subsequent technical updates (2013, 2015, 2016), the working group generated hundreds of thousands of SCC estimates, using a range of discount rates, estimates of future economic growth, population growth estimates, and climate sensitivity assumptions. The primary SCC for Regulatory Impact Analyses reflected the mean SCC across these models and modeling assumptions (with a 3 percent discount rate).

In 2010, the IWGSCC's primary SCC estimate for 2015 was \$28 per ton of CO_2.[8] As the modelers updated their models, the government updated its SCC estimates. In 2013, the working group adjusted the SCC to \$45 per ton CO_2, with a modest revision down to \$43 per ton in 2015

---

[6]Center for Biological Diversity vs. National Highway Traffic Safety Administration, U.S. Court of Appeals, Ninth Circuit, 538 F.3d 1172 (9th Cir. 2008).

[7]See, for example, the Department of Energy final rulemaking "Energy Conservation Program: Energy Conservation Standards for Refrigerated Bottled or Canned Beverage Vending Machines" (74 Federal Register 44914, August 31, 2009), which references both Nordhaus's work and the interim guidance from the interagency working group.

[8]All SCC estimates in this section are for a unit of CO_2 emissions in 2015, converted to 2018 dollars.

and 2016. Nordhaus's own updated estimates of the SCC increased in similar fashion.[9]

The SCC has been used to monetize damages across three presidential administrations, but has it had a significant impact? Hahn and Ritz (2015) reviewed more than 50 regulations over 2008–2013 with monetized benefits associated with reducing CO_2 emissions, based on the SCC. Although monetized emission reduction benefits comprised a significant fraction of total monetized benefits for some rules, overall there was little evidence that inclusion of such monetized benefits changed the sign of net social benefits, and, in only a few cases did including the SCC affect the choice among regulatory alternatives. On the other hand, Pizer *et al.* (2014) demonstrated that the choice of SCC can influence whether the monetized benefits of reducing CO_2 emissions under the (then-proposed) Clean Power Plan would exceed the estimated costs of regulation. If assessments of future CO_2 regulations are based solely on the targeted pollutant benefits, that is, not including any co-benefits of reducing local air pollution, then the rule would deliver positive net social benefits only if the carbon reduction benefits estimated with the SCC exceed the monetized costs (Aldy *et al.*, 2020).[10]

Although the Federal government has turned away from considering a global SCC, various state governments have drawn on the work of the IWGSCC to inform the design and evaluation of various state-level energy and climate change policies (Paul *et al.*, 2017). In addition, the SCC has played a meaningful role in the International Monetary Fund's (IMF) recent efforts to highlight and discourage fossil fuel subsidies around the world (Coady *et al.*, 2015, 2019). In its 2019 analysis, the IMF employed an SCC estimate of $40/t$CO_2$, citing Nordhaus (2017) and the IWGSCC (2016), to monetize climate change externalities from fossil fuel use. Thus, the SCC — used under various Federal regulatory

---

[9]Nordhaus (2008) reported a SCC estimate of $14 per ton of CO_2 for the year 2015, with Nordhaus (2014) increasing it to $23, followed by Nordhaus's (2017, 2019a) estimate of about $35 per ton of CO_2.

[10]In 2017, President Trump disbanded the Interagency Working Group with Executive Order 13868, "Promoting Energy Independence and Economic Growth" (82 Federal Register 16093, March 31, 2017). Since then, relevant regulatory agencies have continued to employ SCC estimates, but based on 3 percent and 7 percent discount rates, and focused exclusively on domestic benefits of reducing carbon dioxide emissions, resulting in empirical estimates in the range of $1 to $3 per ton of CO_2 emissions (Schmalensee and Stavins, 2019).

authorities, state planning and regulatory actions, and IMF policy guidance and evaluation — emerged as a focal point in a decentralized, patchwork approach to climate policy.

Indirectly Informing Public Policy

The third pathway is indirect and often subtle, but is, in general, the most common way academic research influences public policy. We examine six ways in which Nordhaus's economic research has indirectly informed climate change policy[11]: (1) investigations of the balance between economic growth and climate protection; (2) applications and extensions of the DICE model, both by Nordhaus and others; (3) identification of the dynamically efficient time path for global greenhouse gas (GHG) emissions; (4) promotion of cost-effective GHG emissions mitigation, particularly through carbon taxes; (5) recommendation of alternative approaches to international cooperation on climate change, in particular the use of international clubs of countries; and (6) participation in policy-relevant intellectual debates.

Balance of Economic Growth and Climate Protection

Two scientific realities of global climate change lead to important economic implications. First, greenhouse gases mix in the atmosphere, and so the location of emissions has no effect on impacts, rendering climate change a global commons problem. Hence, any jurisdiction taking action incurs the costs of its actions, but the climate benefits are distributed globally. Therefore, for virtually any jurisdiction, the climate benefits it reaps from its actions will be less than the costs it incurs (despite the fact that the global benefits may be greater — possibly much greater — than the global costs).

Second, greenhouse gases accumulate in the atmosphere (for more than 100 years in the case of carbon dioxide), and the climate impacts are a function of the stock (atmospheric concentration), not the flow

[11]Our focus here is on how specific elements of Nordhaus's research have indirectly informed climate change policy. Some of these were likely linked with Nordhaus's decades of teaching Yale undergraduate and graduate students, as well as his authoring several books for general educated audiences (1994, 2008, 2013).

(emissions). As a result, the most severe consequences of climate change will be in the long term. However, climate change policies and their attendant costs of mitigation will be up front. This combination of up-front costs and long-delayed benefits presents great political challenges.

Together, the global commons nature of the problem plus its long time horizon make climate change a difficult political challenge, and explain why there are concerns in many countries that ambitious short-term climate policy actions could undermine economic growth. Indeed, Nordhaus was the first to suggest that instead of investing in early abatement strategies, it would be more efficient to invest in conventional capital, and then use the additional resources in the future to invest heavily in climate capital (Nordhaus, 1977), presumably both for mitigation and adaptation. The same analytical framework, but with updated estimates of relevant parameters, has gradually led Nordhaus to endorse much more ambitious time paths of emissions reductions (Nordhaus, 2019a).

Applications and Extensions of the DICE Model

The DICE model, first described by Nordhaus in a *Science* article in 1992, appears to have been the first integrated assessment model (IAM) to combine basic climate science, biophysical impacts, and economics so that the benefits and costs of alternative time paths of climate change could be compared.[12] In the subsequent Regional Integrated Climate-Economy (RICE) model, Nordhaus and co-authors incorporated geographically specific information on emissions, damages, production, and consumption to compare alternative approaches to climate change policy, including market-based, cooperative, and noncooperative approaches (Nordhaus and Yang, 1996).

Importantly, because Nordhaus made the DICE/RICE models publicly available (in GAMS code), other researchers were able to use and/or extend the models for their own analyses. As described in detail in Part III of this book, the DICE model — together with the FUND and PAGE models — have been used to estimate the social cost of carbon

[12]At about the same time, William Cline (1992) published his work with his independent global macroeconomic model, from which he recommended much more aggressive policy action. The early work of both Nordhaus and Cline demonstrate that "ideas matter" in focusing attention by scholars and the public, and that diffusion from ideas to policy actions can take decades or longer (Hahn and Stavins, 1992).

(Interagency Working Group on Social Cost of Carbon, 2010, 2013, 2015, and 2016).

The Dynamically Efficient Time Path of Global GHG Emissions

Economists have long used the Kaldor-Hicks criterion (Hicks, 1939; Kaldor, 1939) to identify the most efficient policy to achieve some public purpose, by estimating the expected net present value (NPV) of alternative policies, with different time paths of actions and consequences. From early on, Nordhaus applied this thinking to identify preferred time paths of emissions (and emissions abatement), thereby distinguishing between an economically optimal path and one centered on possibly *ad hoc* quantity targets specified in terms of emissions, GHG concentrations, or temperatures (1977).

Nordhaus then used this standard to maximize the discounted net present value of utility, subject to a resource constraint, adding equations to represent activities that generate emissions into the atmosphere. He found that it was only in later time periods that it would be optimal to modify the energy system. In the short term, the optimal carbon price is low, but increases to a very high level by the end of the 21st century. He concluded, at the time, that the efficient program "requires little change in the energy allocation for 20 to 40 years" (1977). More recently, Nordhaus's analyses have led to much more ambitious time paths of recommended emissions reductions (2015, 2019a).

Cost-Effective GHG Emissions Mitigation

For 100 years, since Pigou (1920), economists have endorsed the use of pollution taxes to address environmental problems. Earlier than others, Nordhaus advocated for pricing instruments to address climate change in the form of carbon taxes (Nordhaus, 1977). In order to correct for climate externalities of GHG emissions, he emphasized the need for control strategies which were both feasible scientifically and possible to decentralize, leading to the notion of a tax on the carbon content of fossil fuels. The importance of carbon taxes remained central to Nordhaus's work on climate change for over four decades (Nordhaus, 2007b, 2013, 2019a).

Countries around the world — including nearly all of the industrialized countries and large emerging economies — have launched or are in the process of launching national policies aimed at reducing their emissions of GHGs. Of the 169 Parties to the Paris climate agreement that have submitted specific pledges (known as Nationally Determined Contributions or NDCs), more than half refer to the use of carbon pricing in their NDCs. To date, some 51 carbon-pricing policies have been implemented or are scheduled for implementation worldwide, including 26 carbon taxes and 25 emissions trading systems (Stavins, 2020). Together, these carbon-pricing initiatives will cover about 20 percent of global GHG emissions (World Bank Group, 2019).

Alternative Approaches to International Cooperation

In the nearly three decades since the United Nations Framework Convention on Climate Change (UNFCCC) was signed in 1992 in Rio de Janeiro, Brazil (United Nations, 1992), Nordhaus has consistently been critical of the approaches taken to international cooperation under the United Nations, including both the top-down approach of the Kyoto Protocol (United Nations, 1997; Nordhaus and Boyer, 1999), and the more recent bottom-up or hybrid approach of the Paris Agreement (United Nations, 2015; Nordhaus, 2020). Following work by Barrett (2003), Victor (2006), and others, Nordhaus used the DICE model to examine an alternative, largely voluntary international regime — a climate club (Nordhaus, 2015).

Nordhaus has become the most prominent analyst and spokesman on behalf of the club approach, in which the club's members (countries) agree to harmonize emissions reductions using a carbon price, keep the revenue raised for themselves, and penalize non-participants by imposing a uniform tariff on all imports from non-participants. Carbon tariffs would be incentive compatible, rewarding the punisher, and incentivizing participation. Although potentially promising as a next step if the United Nations negotiations fail to produce meaningful progress, the analysis indicates that a tariff sufficient to stabilize the climate would lead to the collapse of the club (Barrett, 2018). This approach has not received serious attention in international climate negotiations, but it remains among the most prominent alternative approaches to the United Nations scheme. Whether the climate club idea, in general, and Nordhaus's analysis and advocacy, in particular, will eventually be influential and affect the direction of international policy is anyone's guess.

Policy-Relevant Intellectual Debates

Two major debates among economists in which William Nordhaus had prominent roles stand out in terms of their policy relevance. One was about the role catastrophic risk plays in assessments of climate change policies. The other concerns the low discount rates used by Nicholas Stern in his analysis of optimal policy.

Beginning ten years ago, Martin Weitzman carried out theoretical analysis of how positive biophysical feedback loops could lead to uncertainty about the future damages of climate change that would be best characterized by a probability distribution of damages with fat tails, such as a Pareto distribution, rather than a conventional Gaussian (normal) distribution (Weitzman, 2009, 2011). The result is greater weight being given to catastrophic (but relatively small probability) outcomes, such as in net present value analyses of alternative climate change policies. In the extreme, Weitzman's "Dismal Theorem" indicates that under specific structures of uncertainty and preferences, the expected value of losses would be infinite, and so standard economic (NPV) analysis simply would not apply.

Nordhaus (2011) and Pindyck (2011) pushed back against these findings, in part by indicating that the conditions of uncertainty and risk-aversion under which Dismal Theorem is derived are very limited, as well as by noting the absence of any policy interventions in Weitzman's analysis. Nordhaus suggested that policy interventions, such as geoengineering, that can truncate a fat tail merit serious consideration. In a recent paper, Nordhaus applies his thinking to account for a catastrophic event by incorporating the melting of the Greenland ice sheet in the calculation of the social cost of carbon (Nordhaus, 2019b). He finds that the risk of disintegration of the ice sheet adds less than 5 percent to the estimated social cost of carbon, because the damages would occur much later than many other damages already incorporated in the estimated social cost.

The other climate-related intellectual debate in which Nordhaus has been a major participant involves the discount rate employed in the Stern Review (Stern, 2007; Nordhaus, 2007a), the prominent analysis of climate change and related public policy carried out for the government of the United Kingdom. Nordhaus's critique of that report centers on its use of a near-zero social rate of time preference, which Nordhaus maintains would mean that the savings rate would have been much greater than it has been historically. Capital markets, he argues, reflect how societies have chosen to distribute consumption across time, and on that and other bases, claims that Stern has underestimated the appropriate social discount rate. He notes that if transfers were allowed, using Stern's policy prescriptions would actually make the world worse off, yielding in net present value terms, negative net benefits. He also points out that with such a high value of future consumption, we would need to be willing to trade off a large fraction of today's consumption for only a small fraction of potential consumption in the distant future.

Conclusions

The seminal contributions of William Nordhaus to fundamental scholarship on the long-run macroeconomics of global climate change are abundantly clear. More challenging to identify are the impacts of Nordhaus and his research on public policy in this domain. In the short term, at least, more easily digestible symbols — for example, targets of 2°C maximum temperature change by 2100 or net zero emissions in 2050 — sometimes matter more for public policy than even the best, most rigorous scholarly research. This is hardly unique to this case, however. Many of the themes that emerge in our analysis are common to the roles played by other leading economists in this policy domain, and perhaps in some other policy domains as well.

The limited influence of economic analysis on real world policy making has long been noted, although within the realm of environmental policy, such influence has increased over recent decades. Whether as a light bulb or a rock, the work of economists such as Bill Nordhaus can affect policy making via three distinct pathways: personal participation in the policy world; directly influencing the formulation of public policies; and indirectly informing public policy.

In general, personal involvement in the policy world — in Nordhaus's case decades ago at the Council of Economic Advisers and the National Academy of Sciences — typically provides the most transparent evidentiary trail. Although even here, it is clouded by the passage of time. Some of Nordhaus's most important contributions to climate change policy from this period — such as his support at President Carter's CEA of the use of benefit-cost analysis to assess proposed government regulations — came to fruition only years later, beginning in the Reagan administration, with the first formal requirements for Regulatory Impact Analysis.

A second pathway, which many economists seem to think is important and even quite common, is that of directly influencing the formulation of public policies. When and if this occurs, the evidence ought to be abundant and compelling. So it is with the use of Nordhaus's DICE model as one of three IAMs employed by the Obama administration to estimate empirically the Social Cost of Carbon. That the SCC has itself been used repeatedly for benefit calculations in RIAs demonstrates this direct connection of Nordhaus's research and the formulation of public policies. However, it should not be surprising that we find only one example of this second pathway, because this pathway — we believe — is a rare one in the work of any environmental economist.

We find that the third pathway — indirectly informing public policy — is the most important one through which Nordhaus's work has had impacts on public policy. Reflecting on the work of other scholars suggests that this is broadly the case for academic economic research influencing public policy, at least in the environmental realm. But here the evidence can be difficult to discern, partly because "success has many fathers."

Reflecting on these three pathways reminds us of Josef Schumpeter's trichotomy of the process of technological change (Schumpeter, 1942). Schumpeter distinguished three steps in the process by which a new, superior technology permeates the marketplace. *Invention* constitutes the first development of a new product or process. In the policy context, think of a new economic theory or method, such as Nordhaus's DICE model. Most inventions never develop into an *innovation* (accomplished only when the new product/process is commercialized, that is, moves from the laboratory to the showroom floor). And most academic research, no matter how pathbreaking it may be as pure scholarship, never makes its way into influence in the real world of public policy. Last in Schumpeter's three stages of technological change is diffusion, the process of gradual adoption of a product or process. Here the analogy to the policy world is clearest, where some academic economists may work full or part time within government, directly pressing for the adoption of some specific policy, whether the policy idea is attributed to them or others.

William Nordhaus is perhaps the most important economist to have ever worked on climate change and climate change policy. If we are correct that his influence in the policy world has been as subtle and often as indirect as we have indicated, then perhaps we all should be left with a sense of greatly enhanced modesty regarding our own contributions to public policy. Our assessment in this chapter of the policy impacts of one of the most important economists to have ever worked in the environmental domain prompts us to issue an appeal to our colleagues in the profession for greater moderation overall when making claims about academic research influencing policy developments, whether specifically for climate change or more broadly in the realm of environmental, energy, and natural resource policy.

Acknowledgements

They acknowledge the excellent research assistance of Kristen McCormack and valuable comments on a previous version of the manuscript by Jason Bordoff, Robert Hahn, Arik Levinson, and Richard Schmalensee, but the authors are responsible for all remaining errors.

References

Aldy, Joseph E. (2004). "Saving the planet cost-effectively: The role of economic analysis in climate change mitigation policy." In Randall Lutter and Jason F. Shogren Eds., *Painting the White House Green: Rationalizing Environmental Policy Inside the Executive Office of the President*, Washington, DC: Resources for the Future Press, 89–118.

Aldy, Joseph E., Matthew Kotchen, Mary Evans, Meredith Fowlie, Arik Levinson, and Karen Palmer. (2020). "*Co-Benefits and Regulatory Impact Analysis: Theory and Evidence from Federal Air Quality Regulations.*" Prepared for the NBER Environmental and Energy Policy and the Economy Conference, May 21.

Arrow, Kenneth J., Maureen L. Cropper, George C. Eads, Robert W. Hahn, Lester B. Lave, Roger G. Noll, Paul R. Portney, Milton Russell, Richard Schmalensee, V. Kerry Smith, and Robert N. Stavins. (1996). "Is there a role for benefit-cost analysis in environmental, health, and safety regulation?" *Science*, **272**(5259): 221–222.

Barrett, Scott. (2003). *Environment and Statecraft: The Strategy of Environmental Treaty-Making*. London: Oxford University Press.

Barrett, Scott. (2018). "Choices in the climate commons." *Science*, **362**: 1217.

Cline, William R. (1992). *The Economics of Global Warming*. Washington, DC: Institute for International Economics.

Coady, David, Ian Parry, Nghia-Piotr Le, and Baoping Shang. (2019). "*Global Fossil Fuel Subsidies Remain Large: An Update Based on Country-Level Estimates.*" IMF Working Paper WP/19/89.

Coady, David, Ian Parry, Louis Sears, and Baoping Shang. (2015). "*How Large Are Global Energy Subsidies?*" IMF Working Paper WP/15/105.

Council of Economic Advisers. (1979). *Economic Report of the President.* Transmitted to the Congress January 1979. Washington, DC: Government Printing Office.

Devins, Neal. (2005). "The academic expert before Congress." *Duke Law Journal*, **54**(6): 1525–1554.

Feldstein, Martin. (1992). "The Council of Economic Advisers and economic advising in the United States." *The Economic Journal*, **102**: 1223–1234.

Hahn, Robert W. (2000). "The impact of economics on environmental policy." *Journal of Environmental Economics and Management*, **39**: 375–399.

Hahn, Robert W., and Robert A. Ritz. (2015). "Does the social cost of carbon matter? Evidence from US policy?" *Journal of Legal Studies*, **44**: 229–242.

Hahn, Robert W., and Robert N. Stavins. (1992). "Economic incentives for environmental protection: integrating theory and practice." *American Economic Review Papers and Proceedings*, **82**: 464–468.

Hicks, John. (1939). "The foundations of welfare economics." *The Economic Journal*, **49**: 696–712.

Hope, Christopher, John Anderson, and Paul Wenman. (1993). "Policy analysis of the greenhouse effect: An application of the PAGE model." *Energy Policy*, **21**(3): 327–338.

Interagency Working Group on Social Cost of Carbon, United States Government. (2010). "Technical support document: Social cost of carbon for regulatory impact analysis under Executive Order 12866." Washington, DC (plus Technical Updates in 2013, 2015, and 2016).

Kaldor, Nicholas. (1939). "Welfare propositions in economics and interpersonal comparisons of utility." *The Economic Journal*, **49**: 549–552.

Litan, Robert E., and William D. Nordhaus. (1983). *Reforming Federal Regulation.* New Haven: Yale University Press.

Muller, Nicholas Z., Robert Mendelsohn, and William Nordhaus. (2011). "Environmental accounting for pollution in the United States economy." *American Economic Review*, **101**(5): 1649–1675.

National Academy of Sciences. (2017). *Valuing Climate Damages: Updating Estimation of the Social Cost of Carbon Dioxide*. Washington, DC: National Academies Press.

National Research Council. (1980). Letter from the Ad Hoc Study Panel on Economic and Social Aspects of Carbon Dioxide Increase. April 18, 1980. National Academy of Sciences, Climate Research Board.

Nobel Foundation. (2018). "*Sveriges Riksbank Prize in Economic Sciences in Memory of Alfred Nobel 2018.*"

Nordhaus, William D. (1977). "Economic growth and climate: the carbon dioxide problem." *American Economic Review*, **67**: 341–346.

Nordhaus, William D. (1982). "How fast should we graze the global commons?" *American Economic Review*, **72**(2): 242–246.

Nordhaus, William D. (1992). "An optimal transition path for controlling greenhouse gases." *Science*, **258**(5086): 1315–1319.

Nordhaus, William D. (1994). *Managing the Global Commons: The Economics of Climate Change*, Cambridge, Massachusetts: MIT Press.

Nordhaus, William D. (2007a). "A review of the Stern Review on the economics of climate change." *Journal of Economic Literature*, **45**: 686–702.

Nordhaus, William D. (2007b). "To tax or not to tax: Alternative approaches to slowing global warming." *Review of Environmental Economics and Policy*, **1**: 26–44.

Nordhaus, William D. (2008). *A Question of Balance: Weighing the Options on Global Warming Policies*. New Haven, Connecticut: Yale University Press.

Nordhaus, William D. (2011). "The economics of tail events with an application to climate change." *Review of Environmental Economics and Policy*, **5**(2): 240–257.

Nordhaus, William D. (2013). *The Climate Casino: Risk, Uncertainty, and Economics for a Warming World*. New Haven: Yale University Press.

Nordhaus, William D. (2014). "Estimates of the social cost of carbon: Concepts and results from the DICE-2013R model and alternative approaches." *Journal of the Association of Environmental and Resource Economists*, **1**(1/2): 273–312.

Nordhaus, William D. (2015). "Climate clubs: Overcoming free-riding in international climate policy." *American Economic Review*, **105**: 1339–1370.

Nordhaus, William D. (2017). "Revisiting the social cost of carbon." *Proceedings of the US National Academy of Sciences*, **114**: 1518–1523.

Nordhaus, William D. (2019a). "Climate change: The ultimate challenge for economics." *American Economic Review*, **109**: 1991–2014.

Nordhaus, William D. (2019b). "Economics of the disintegration of the Greenland ice sheet." *Proceedings of the National Academy of Sciences*, **116**(25): 12261–12269.

Nordhaus, William D. (2020). "The climate club: How to fix a failing global effort." *Foreign Affairs*. May/June.

Nordhaus, William D., and Joseph G. Boyer. (1999). "Requiem for Kyoto: An economic analysis of the Kyoto Protocol." *The Energy Journal*, **20**: 93–130.

Nordhaus, William D., and Edward C. Kokkelenberg, Eds. (1999). *Nature's Numbers: Expanding the National Economic Accounts to Include the Environment*. Panel on Integrated Environmental and Economic Accounting, National Research Council. Washington, DC: The National Academies Press.

Nordhaus, William D., and Zili Yang. (1996). "A regional dynamic general-equilibrium model of alternative climate-change strategies." *American Economic Review*, **86**: 741–765.

Nordhaus, William D., Stephen A. Merrill, and Paul T. Beaton, Eds. (2013). *Effects of U.S. Tax Policy on Greenhouse Gas Emissions*. Committee on the Effects of Provisions in the Internal Revenue Code on Greenhouse Gas Emissions, National Research Council. Washington, DC: The National Academies Press.

Organization for Economic Development and Cooperation. (2002). *Regulatory Policies in OECD Countries: From Interventionism to Regulatory Governance*. OECD Reviews of Regulatory Reform. Paris, France: OECD Publishing.

Paul, Iliana, Peter Howard, and Jason A. Schwartz. (2017). "The social cost of greenhouse gases and state policy." Institute for Policy Integrity, New York University School of Law.

Pindyck, Robert S. (2011). "Fat tails, thin tails, and climate change policy." *Review of Environmental Economics and Policy*, **5**(2): 258–274.

Pizer, William, Matthew Adler, Joseph Aldy, David Anthoff, Maureen Cropper, Kenneth Gillingham, Michael Greenstone, Brian Murray, Richard Newell, Richard Richels, Arden Rowell, Stephanie Waldhoff, and Jonathan Wiener. (2014). "Using and improving the social cost of carbon." *Science*, **346**: 1181–1182.

Sabin, P. (2016). "Everything has a price: Jimmy Carter and the struggle for balance in federal regulatory policy." *Journal of Policy History*, **28**(1): 1–47.

Schelling, Thomas. (1997). "Why does economics only help with easy problems?" In P. A. G. van Bergeijk, A. L. Bovernberg, E. E. C. van Damme, and J. van Sinderen Eds., *Economic Science and Practice: The Roles of Academic Economists and Policy Makers*, 134–148. Cheltenham, United Kingdom: Edward Elgar.

Schmalensee, Richard, and Robert N. Stavins. (2019). "Policy evolution under the Clean Air Act." *Journal of Economic Perspectives*, **33**(4): 27–50.

Schultze, Charles L. (1979). "State of the Union — Language on Setting Regulatory Priorities." *Memorandum for the President of the United States*. January 20, 1979. Jimmy Carter Library.

Schultze, Charles L. (1996). "The CEA: An inside voice for mainstream economics." *Journal of Economic Perspectives*, **10**(3): 23–39.

Schumpeter, Josef. (1942). *Capitalism, Socialism and Democracy*. New York: Harper.

Smith, V. Kerry, Ed. (1984). *Environmental Policy under Reagan's Executive Order: The Role of Benefit-Cost Analysis*. Chapel Hill and London: The University of North Carolina Press.

Stavins, Robert N. (2020). "The future of U.S. carbon-pricing policy." *Environmental and Energy Policy and the Economy*, **1**: 8–64. Chicago: University of Chicago Press.

Stein, Herbert. (1996). "A successful accident: Recollections and speculations about the CEA." *Journal of Economic Perspectives*, **10**(3): 3–21.

Stern, Nicholas. (2007). *The Economics of Climate Change: The Stern Review*, Cambridge University Press.

Tol, Richard S. (1997). "On the optimal control of carbon dioxide emissions: An application of FUND." *Environmental Modeling & Assessment*, **2**(3): 151–163.

Tol, Richard S. (2005). "The marginal damage costs of carbon dioxide emissions: An assessment of the uncertainties." *Energy Policy*, **33**(16): 2064–2074.

Tol, Richard S. (2008). "The social cost of carbon: Trends, outliers and catastrophes." *Economics: The Open-Access, Open-Assessment E-Journal*, **2**.

United Nations. (1992). "United Nations Framework Convention on Climate Change." Rio de Janeiro, signed in New York, New York.

United Nations. (1997). "Kyoto Protocol to the United Nations Framework Convention on Climate Change." Kyoto, Japan.

United Nations. (2015). "Paris Agreement." Adopted December 12; entered into force November 4, 2016. New York.

United States. (1979). *Economic Report of the President, Transmitted to the Congress, January*. Washington: Government Printing Office.

Victor, David G. (2006). "Toward effective international cooperation on climate change: numbers, interests and institutions." *Global Environmental Politics*, **6**: 90–103.

Weitzman, Martin L. (2009). "On modeling and interpreting the economics of catastrophic climate change." *Review of Economics and Statistics*, **91**(1): 1–19.

Weitzman, Martin L. (2011). "Fat-tailed uncertainty in the economics of catastrophic climate change." *Review of Environmental Economics and Policy*, **5**(2): 275–292.

World Bank Group. (2019). *State and Trends of Carbon Pricing*. Washington, DC.

https://doi.org/10.1142/9789811292415_0004

Chapter 4

Assessing the Energy-Efficiency Gap*

Todd D. Gerarden[†], Richard G. Newell[‡,§,‖], and Robert N. Stavins[†,‡,‖,¶]

[†]*John F. Kennedy School of Government, Harvard University, Cambridge, MA, USA*

[‡]*Resources for the Future, Washington, DC, USA*

[§]*Duke University, Durham, USA*

[‖]*National Bureau of Economic Research, Cambridge, USA*

[¶]*robert_stavins@harvard.edu*

Introduction

Global energy consumption is on a path to grow 30–50 percent over the next twenty-five years, bringing with it, in many countries, increased local air pollution and greenhouse gas emissions. Adoption of energy-efficient technologies could potentially reap both private and social returns, in the form of economic, environmental, and other social benefits from reduced energy consumption. In response, governments and firms around the world have adopted policies and programs to increase energy efficiency

*This chapter was originally published in *Journal of Economic Literature*, **55**(4), 1486–1525, 2017. https://doi.org/10.1257/jel.20161360.

Table 1. Private and social conceptions of the energy-efficiency gap.

Potential explanations	Private gap	Public gap	Social gap
Innovation/adoption spillovers, market power, imperfect information		X	X
Too-low energy prices due to unpriced externalities		X	X
Biased beliefs about energy prices and energy usage	X		X
Inattention to operating costs, myopia, and cognitive limitations	X		X

and capture these benefits. Still, there is a broadly held view that various barriers to the adoption of energy-efficient technologies have prevented the realization of a substantial portion of these benefits. Our purpose is to survey, synthesize, and advance understanding of economics research on this "energy-efficiency gap."

We distinguish between two closely related notions of the energy-efficiency gap based on whether they are defined relative to private or social optima. We designate the "private energy-efficiency gap" as the apparent reality that some energy-efficiency technologies that would pay off for adopters are, nevertheless, not adopted. This basic definition highlights potential deviations from private optimality, and has often been referred to as the "energy paradox" in prior work. More broadly, we use the term "social energy-efficiency gap" to encompass energy-efficiency decisions where technologies that would be socially efficient are not adopted.

The private energy-efficiency gap is nested within the scope of the social energy-efficiency gap (Table 1). We view the broader social energy-efficiency gap as the appropriate lens through which to evaluate the potential net benefits of government policy, and therefore use the broader definition to define the scope of this review. Hence, we follow the convention from previous literature of using the phrase "energy-efficiency gap" to refer to deviations from either private or social optimality.

Over the last several decades, a number of scholars have observed that cost-effective energy-conservation technologies appear to diffuse at suboptimal rates. Shama (1983) and the US Department of Energy (1991/1992) noted the paradoxically slow rate of penetration of various energy-conservation technologies, and Jaffe and Stavins (1994a) provided a conceptual framework for thinking about possible explanations. Noting this phenomenon, some analysts and advocates have argued that government intervention to promote energy efficiency could produce environmental benefits at little or even negative economic cost. At the same time, the US federal government, states, and other countries have implemented policies to promote energy efficiency. But the veracity of this argument and economically efficient public-policy responses depend crucially on the underlying causes of the energy-efficiency gap.

Why do decision makers underinvest — or at least appear to underinvest — in energy-efficient technologies, relative to the predictions of some engineering and economic models? Explanations fall into three broad categories: (1) market failures, (2) behavioral explanations, and (3) modeling flaws.

Potential market-failure explanations include: information problems (such as principal–agent issues affecting decisions about the adoption of energy-efficiency technologies in renter-occupied commercial and residential properties, and asymmetric information); energy market failures (including environmental and national-security externalities, and average-cost electricity pricing); capital-market failures (such as liquidity constraints); and innovation market failures (such as information spillovers from research and development).

Potential behavioral explanations include: inattentiveness and salience issues; myopia or short sightedness; bounded rationality and heuristic decision making; prospect theory and reference-point phenomena; and systematically biased beliefs.

Finally, modeling-flaw explanations refer to reasons why the observed rate of diffusion of energy-saving technology may not be as paradoxical as it may at first appear. Evidence for the gap typically involves assumptions about the economic costs and energy use of alternative product choices, the usage profile and characteristics of consumers, and interactions among these factors. Predictions founded on incorrect assumptions could misstate the size of the energy-efficiency gap. These are model and measurement explanations and include: unobserved or understated costs of adoption; ignored product attributes; heterogeneity in benefits and costs of adoption across potential adopters; use of incorrect discount rates; and uncertainty, irreversibility, and option value.[1] In the context of Joseph Schumpeter's classic trio of invention, innovation, and diffusion,

[1]For additional discussion of the energy-efficiency gap using this taxonomy of market failures, behavioral effects, and measurement flaws, see Gillingham *et al.* (2009) and Gillingham and Palmer (2014). Allcott and Greenstone (2012) suggest the

our investigation focuses primarily — but not exclusively — on diffusion (adoption).[2]

To provide structure to the many economic elements that enter into adoption decisions related to energy efficiency, we find it useful to think in terms of the fundamental elements of cost-minimizing energy-efficiency decisions. This decomposition is deliberately simple in order to highlight the main features of the issue, and does not explicitly account for all of the factors we consider in our analysis, such as uncertainty, the dynamic nature of decisions (and resulting option value), and heterogeneity:

$$\underbrace{\min \text{Total Cost}}_{\text{objective}} = \underbrace{K(E)}_{\text{equipment purchase cost}} + \underbrace{O(E, P_E) \times D(r, T)}_{\text{discounted operating costs}} + \text{other costs}$$

where $K(E)$ = equipment purchase cost; E = annual energy use; $O(E, P_E)$ = annual operating cost; P_E = price of energy; $D(r, T)$ = present-value factor; r = discount rate; and T = time horizon.

Based on this decomposition of cost-minimizing energy-efficiency adoption decisions, we organize our synthesis of existing literature around four fundamental questions and a total of twenty-three sub-questions. Referring to the first term of the above equation, we ask whether product offerings and pricing are economically efficient. This question is examined in section "Do Spillovers, Market Power, or Informational Market Failures Prevent the Energy Efficiency and Associated Pricing of Products on the Market from Being Economically Efficient?" of the chapter.

Then, in section "Are Energy Operating Costs Inefficiently Priced, Understood, and/or Analyzed?" of the chapter, we ask whether energy operating costs are inefficiently priced and/or understood. In section "Are

energy-efficiency gap is substantially smaller than it appears to be, emphasizing the role of model and measurement errors.

[2]On innovation, see Newell *et al.* (1999) and Hall and Rosenberg (2010). For a review of technological change and the environment more generally, of which energy-efficiency technological change is one component, see Jaffe *et al.* (2002), Jaffe *et al.* (2005), and Popp *et al.* (2010).

Product Choices Cost Minimizing in Present-Value Terms?", referring to the entire equation, we ask whether product choices are cost minimizing in present-value terms. Finally, in section "Do Other Unobserved Costs Inhibit Energy-Efficient Decisions?", we focus on the final term in the above equation and ask whether other costs inhibit more energy-efficient decisions. Alternative explanations of the energy-efficiency gap become parts of sub-questions in these four sections of the chapter. In section "Conclusion", we offer some conclusions and suggestions for future research priorities.[3]

Do Spillovers, Market Power, or Informational Market Failures Prevent the Energy Efficiency and Associated Pricing of Products on the Market from Being Economically Efficient?

One set of possible explanations for the energy-efficiency gap is related to the potential economic inefficiencies associated with the first element of the cost-minimization framework — namely, the variety of energy-efficient products on the market, their energy-efficiency levels, and their pricing. Although the theory is clear, empirical evidence is limited. Going forward, more data are becoming available that can facilitate empirical research, although firm-level data are less available than data on consumer decision making.

Given the range of existing public policies in this realm (such as energy-efficiency standards, labeling, utility demand-side management programs, and public funding of research), it is unclear whether there are specific issues related to the variety, availability, and pricing of energy-efficient products, as distinct from other products. Partly because of this, we do not see this area as meriting a high priority for future research specifically in the domain of energy efficiency. Two exceptions are empirical work on whether consumers have adequate information regarding energy-efficient products, and research evaluating and improving the efficacy and efficiency of current information policies.

---

[3]The vast majority of the literature is focused on consumer decision making, although where applicable and available we also discuss energy efficiency decision making by firms.

Do Product Developers Invest too Little in Energy Efficiency Due to Technology Spillovers via Research and Development and Learning-by-Doing?

Spillovers in the energy-efficiency invention and innovation processes can contribute to the energy-efficiency gap if they lead to underinvestment in the development of new energy-efficient innovations. These spillovers are possible both in basic research and development (R&D) and in subsequent commercialization.

R&D Spillovers

In theory, firms will invest too little effort in research when the resulting knowledge benefits not only them, but other firms as well. A firm does not reap the full rewards of its investment when knowledge is non-appropriable. This effect is probably most pronounced for early stages of research, because firms cannot capture the knowledge generated in the process perfectly, whereas firms can reduce spillovers in later stages of research through intellectual-property protections (Nordhaus, 2011).

While there is little direct empirical evidence of R&D spillovers associated with energy efficiency (Popp *et al.*, 2010; Howell, 2017), there is substantial evidence of these spillovers in other industries, with empirical estimates of such spillovers ranging from close to zero to 100 percent, with most estimates between 20 and 50 percent (Griliches, 1992; Hall *et al.*, 2010).

Many countries have policies to address generic R&D spillovers. Research grants are widely used to encourage basic research, and tax incentives are used to encourage applied R&D. In addition, intellectual-property protections ameliorate the problem of non-appropriability for innovations at the stage of commercialization.

Learning-by-Doing Spillovers

Learning-by-doing (LBD) refers to productivity improvements that come with experience. The learning effect can be so strong that firms may be willing to operate at a loss when manufacturing a new product to improve productivity and become more competitive (Benkard, 2004). But knowledge from such learning can spill over to other firms, creating a free-rider problem. Firms may then under-invest or delay investment to capture knowledge from other firms, rather than incur the cost of generating the knowledge themselves (Arrow, 1962; Spence, 1981).

Empirical evidence suggests LBD spill-overs are present in many industries, with learning spilling over even to firms that are separated by national borders (Lieberman, 1984; Irwin and Klenow, 1994), although other research suggests that while learning spillovers within a firm can be significant, learning spillovers across firms can be small (Thornton and Thompson, 2001).

We are not aware of any direct empirical evidence of LBD in energy efficiency, and none about the extent of any learning *spillovers*. One possible route for research would be to study the engineering pathways by which LBD spillovers occur, building on recent efforts to understand LBD mechanisms (Levitt *et al.*, 2013) and utilizing plant-level production data and dynamic structural models of firm production functions.

Does Market Power Generate Distortions in the Number of Product Alternatives, Their Level of Energy Efficiency, or Their Prices?

It is conceivable that the socially optimal diversity of products may not be offered on the market. This could occur, for example, under monopolistic competition. Two forces contribute to this outcome. First, not all welfare-improving products are offered if firms are unable to capture the consumer surplus associated with a given product, due to the difficulty of perfect price discrimination. Second, firms introducing a new product may not internalize the impact of their product's entry on other firms' profits, which can lead to too many products on the market.[4] Despite the soundness of this theory, there is no empirical evidence on the effect of these factors in the energy-efficiency domain.

Economists generally consider energy-efficient products to be of higher quality than less efficient, but otherwise comparable, products. The theory of vertical differentiation suggests that for a single product

---

[4] In the case of complementary products, these two forces push in the same direction, leading firms to introduce too few products with too little differentiation. With substitutes, the two forces push in opposite directions, in which case, the net effect on product variety (relative to the social optimum) is ambiguous (Spence, 1976).

offering, firms will under supply product quality (including energy efficiency) relative to the social optimum if the marginal consumer values efficiency less than the average consumer. Firms respond to marginal quality valuation, while the social optimum is achieved by setting quality according to average quality valuation (Spence, 1975).[5] However, in the case of multiproduct firms, theory does not provide clear guidance on quality distortion. Indeed, for any given product, the anticipated effect is ambiguous: a firm could supply too much or too little energy efficiency relative to the social optimum, due to demand interactions with the firm's other products.

Calibrations of a theoretical model of the automobile market suggest that multiproduct manufacturers would consider these interactions when choosing fuel efficiency for each vehicle, but manufacturers may over or under supply energy efficiency in different products in response to heterogeneity in consumer valuation of fuel efficiency (Fischer, 2010). This is reminiscent of quality distortion arising in models of price discrimination: manufacturers provide too much fuel efficiency in vehicle classes demanded by consumers who value fuel efficiency highly, and too little fuel efficiency in vehicle classes demanded by consumers who value fuel efficiency less. This allows manufacturers to extract surplus from consumers according to consumers' tastes, while reducing the likelihood that consumers defect to other vehicle classes. But theory does not offer clear predictions about welfare impacts, and empirical analysis is lacking in the energy-efficiency context.

Other research on automobiles has explored the responsiveness of suppliers to changes in energy costs. Increases in fuel prices should (weakly) increase demand for more efficient vehicles relative to demand for inefficient vehicles by creating differential variation in operating costs for vehicles with different fuel efficiencies. As a result, equilibrium prices and product characteristics could change. Indeed, automobile manufacturers appear to respond to short-run fluctuations in fuel prices by offering cash incentives (Langer and Miller, 2013). The responsiveness of product offerings to long-run trends in energy prices is less clear because it is confounded by simultaneous fuel-economy mandates. Fuel economy increased significantly following increases in oil prices and coincident

[5]This is not limited to firms with market power. It holds for any profit-maximizing firm that is unable to perfectly price discriminate (Spence, 1975).

with the introduction of Corporate Average Fuel Economy (CAFE) standards in the 1970s (Pakes *et al.*, 1993; Berry *et al.*, 1996).

Changes in market structure can also affect producer incentives, but anticipated effects on product variety are ambiguous. In the case of firm mergers, the ambiguity is due to countervailing forces of cost reduction, leading to lower prices; and reduced competition, leading to higher prices (Berry and Waldfogel, 2001). Changes in the demand side of the market can also affect product quality and variety. In particular, variation in market size can alter incentives for suppliers, leading to changes in the variety and quality of products available.[6]

Public policies may also interact with and influence energy-efficient product market offerings, possibly in unanticipated ways. Recent empirical evidence from the appliance industry suggests that firms employ the Energy Star logo as a price discrimination tool, as some consumers have a high willingness to pay for this certification. This allows firms to extract surplus from consumers, and may have distributional impacts that were not widely anticipated (Houde, 2014a). Engineering–economic analysis of CAFE standards highlights the quantitative importance of considering firm compliance decisions to change product characteristics — not just prices — when estimating the net benefits of regulations (Whitefoot *et al.*, 2017). Another example of unanticipated consequences is found in the response of automobile manufacturers to the "notched" Gas Guzzler Tax, which distorts manufacturer incentives and is less efficient than a smooth linear tax (Sallee and Slemrod, 2012).[7] Attribute-based regulations — regulations designed conditional on product attributes other than the target of regulations — generate similar supply distortions (Ito and Sallee, 2014).

---

[6]In the presence of horizontal differentiation but no vertical differentiation, market concentration will decrease with market size and a greater variety of products will be offered. In a market with both horizontal and vertical differentiation, this result no longer holds. If increases in product quality require an increase in fixed costs, the highest quality offered will increase with market size, while the market will remain concentrated (Shaked and Sutton, 1987).

[7]This comparison of notched and smooth taxes hinges on the assumption of consumer rationality. Under alternative assumptions (see below), the choice between notched and smooth policies becomes considerably less clear. For example, the benefits of certifications may outweigh these supply distortions if consumers are inattentive to energy efficiency (Sallee, 2014).

A tension can exist between optimal innovation and product offerings, on the one hand, and optimal adoption of energy-efficient products, on the other hand. Firms incur fixed costs to generate energy-efficiency improvements in their products, and firms may not invest if they do not expect to recover these costs. However, innovators pricing above marginal cost, which is necessary to recoup fixed costs, could hamper rapid adoption of new products offering significant reductions in energy consumption. Optimal policy would seek to balance these two forces to encourage both innovation and adoption of energy-efficient products (Kamien and Schwartz, 1982).

This tension, as with much of the preceding discussion, is generic; that is, the issues are not specific to energy efficiency. In other domains, R&D support and intellectual property protections are the primary tools used to encourage innovation, while antitrust regulation is intended to ameliorate problems associated with market concentration. There is no existing evidence to suggest that energy-efficiency markets exhibit unique market failures that call for tools beyond these traditional policies.

The limitations of theoretical results and the small quantity of empirical evidence in this realm are striking. While empirical evidence from some sectors generally supports theoretical findings,[8] relevance for energy efficiency is unclear. Hence, empirical analysis is needed to assess the role of these factors for energy-efficient product markets. In particular, empirical research with structural models is needed to understand and predict impacts of energy-efficiency policy, particularly in industries that are highly concentrated and highly regulated.

Are There too few New Energy-Efficient Product Offerings Due to Demand Spillovers?

Product offerings may be suboptimal in number due to demand spillovers. Product innovations may exhibit information asymmetries between consumers and producers, with consumers needing to be convinced to try a new product. Firms try to generate demand with advertising and/or

[8]For example, in the restaurant industry, increasing market size is associated with lower concentration, greater variety, and more quality differentiation. In the newspaper industry, where improving quality requires higher fixed costs, larger markets remain concentrated and average quality improves (Berry and Waldfogel, 2010).

promotional pricing, the cost of which must be recouped through sales. The consequent learning by consumers can spill over to other consumers, benefiting the innovating firm. Importantly, however, the firm's competitors can also capture these demand spillovers — without paying the costs to educate consumers. The net effect of these two forces is ambiguous. If the latter effect dominates, firms will introduce too few new products.

Existing research provides little insight into the contributions of such demand spill-overs to the energy-efficiency gap, possibly due to the empirical challenge of identifying demand spillovers.[9] Hybrid vehicles are a rare example of an energy-efficient technology that has been well studied and that may be associated with learning spillovers among consumers. Empirical evidence that market penetration rates of hybrid vehicles affect future purchases is consistent with this hypothesis. Furthermore, these learning spillovers may not be fully appropriated by the original producer; higher penetration rates for the Toyota Prius have led to greater purchases of hybrids of all makes (Heutel and Muehlegger, 2015).[10]

The impact of demand spillovers on product offerings is inherently difficult to study, because researchers do not observe potentially innovative energy-efficient products that firms decide not to introduce. In the absence of such data, researchers can study the impact of learning spillovers across products that *are* introduced, which can serve as a guide for whether these spillovers appear to be significant enough to prevent the introduction of candidate products. Such research could follow the approach of research on the pharmaceutical industry (Crawford and Shum, 2005; Coscelli and Shum, 2004; Berndt *et al.*, 2003).[11] The existence and magnitude of spillovers across products appear to be correlated with the degree of substitutability of the products (Janakiraman *et al.*, 2009). This finding accords with theory and provides a useful guide for evaluating the importance of learning spillovers among energy-efficient products.

[9] See the section on learning-by-using spillovers for discussion of the difficulty of identifying demand spillovers.

[10] Of course, just as learning spillovers can increase demand for similar products, such spillovers can also dampen demand. Heutel and Muehlegger (2015) found that higher market penetration by the Honda Insight led to fewer purchases of all hybrid models, consistent with anecdotal evidence that the Insight was of lower quality.

[11] Research in pharmaceuticals examines both competition between branded and generic drugs following patent expiration and competition among branded drugs. The latter is more relevant to energy-efficient technologies.

Implementing government or utility programs that educate consumers about innovative energy-saving technologies is one possible response to significant demand spillovers.

Does Adverse Selection Due to Asymmetric Information Inhibit Energy-Efficient Product Offerings?

In theory, asymmetric information could lead to adverse selection in the marketplace, which in turn might lead to underinvestment in energy efficiency. Such underinvestment would occur if buyers cannot observe perfectly the energy efficiency of products, and as a result are unwilling to pay for its true expected value. If sellers have private information they cannot credibly communicate, some energy-efficient products may not be offered in the market (Akerlof, 1970). This problem of asymmetric information tends to be more pronounced in the secondary market, as consumers who invest in energy-efficient capital, such as home weatherization, may have difficulty capitalizing on these investments when reselling. But adverse selection in secondary markets can affect incentives for adoption of efficient technologies in primary markets. Asymmetric information is sometimes cited as a justification for disclosure policies and standards — such as energy-efficiency testing and labels.[12]

Despite widespread acceptance of the theoretical argument for adverse selection due to information asymmetries, there is little empirical evidence of this phenomenon in the context of energy efficiency, particularly in the period since energy-efficiency product testing and labeling became the norm for many energy-using appliances. By its very nature, adverse selection is difficult to study. Like an uninformed buyer, researchers are often unable to observe perfectly the energy-efficiency characteristics of a product. Unobserved heterogeneity among buyers and sellers, particularly in buyers' demand functions, complicates analysis. It is also challenging to separate, in practice, adverse selection from moral hazard.

---

[12]For example, the US government cited asymmetric information as a justification for its recent medium- and heavy-duty vehicle fuel economy standards, projecting that these standards will save industry money after accounting for both up-front costs and fuel savings (US Environmental Protection Agency and US Department of Transportation National Highway Traffic Safety Administration, 2011).

One model research design is the use of randomized experiments to isolate adverse selection from moral hazard in energy consumption (for example, Munley *et al.*, 1990). In the absence of relevant experiments, theory does provide some qualitative guidance for policy and research efforts: outcomes depend on disclosure technology; in markets where disclosure is low-cost and effective, there may be less rationale for policy intervention.[13]

Do Consumers Have Inadequate Information Regarding Energy-Efficient Products?

Lack of information could lead to private decisions to invest less in energy-efficient technologies than would otherwise be the case. Such a lack of information is one of the most commonly cited justifications for policy intervention in this realm (Palmer *et al.*, 2013; Sanstad *et al.*, 2006). Two alternative interpretations fit the available evidence: consumers may be inattentive to, or have difficulty using, readily available information; or they may have imperfect information on product availability or product characteristics. We focus here on the classic market failure of imperfect information. We turn to inattention, bounded rationality, and heuristic decision making in later sections.

Information provision has been documented to affect consumer decisions. In a recent artefactual field experiment, provision of information about the energy use of alternative light bulbs increases consumer willingness-to-pay for efficient bulbs (Allcott and Taubinsky, 2015). However, these effects were attenuated in the context of a parallel natural field experiment, possibly due to information already available in the marketplace.

Furthermore, few studies disentangle the effects of imperfect information from competing explanations of consumer behavior (e.g., inattention). One recent study attempts to do this using a stated-choice experiment to understand the relative importance of various elements of information

---

[13]See Jovanovic (1982) for an analysis of how disclosure costs affect welfare. Recent empirical evidence on the impact of disclosure costs on equilibrium prices comes from online automobile sales (Lewis, 2011). Several companies have recently faced sanctions by the US Department of Energy (DOE) for overstating the efficiency of their products, failing to meet minimum efficiency standards, or both.

labels — including the EnergyGuide, Energy Star, and European Union (EU)-style labels — while controlling for other relevant factors, such as discounting behavior (Newell and Siikamäki, 2014). This research finds that a lack of relevant information can lead to significant undervaluation of energy efficiency, and that providing simple information on the economic value of saving energy was the most important element guiding more cost-effective energy-efficiency decisions.

Past evidence in the United States and recent evidence from India suggests that imperfect information also exists among firms (as consumers of energy-efficiency technology), and that firms may fail to under-take profitable investments because they are simply unaware of them (Anderson and Newell, 2004; Bloom *et al.*, 2013). Anderson and Newell (2004) examine industrial energy audits and find that while plants accept only half of recommended projects, most plants respond to the costs and benefits presented in energy audits and, with the additional information, adopt investments that meet hurdle rates consistent with standard investment criteria.

In theory and in practice, an informed third party can fill the information gap, as many government and private labeling programs seek to do. Examples include EnergyGuide labels, Energy Star logos, automobile fuel economy labels, and Leadership in Energy and Environmental Design (LEED) certification.[14] A number of studies have analyzed the effect of such information policies. For example, Davis and Metcalf (2014) use a stated-choice experiment to quantify the welfare gains of using tailored, state-specific EnergyGuide labels rather than one label based on nationwide averages. Sallee (2014) highlights the possible supply distortions caused by coarse energy-efficiency certifications, such as the binary certification employed in the Energy Star program. But the benefits of coarse certifications may out-weigh supply distortions, given limits on consumer attention to detail about performance. Houde (2014b) evaluated the welfare effects of the Energy Star certification program and found that consumers rely heavily on the certification, indicating that the program does provide new information to the market. However, he also found that some consumers *over-rely* on the binary label, as opposed to considering actual energy savings. This induces suppliers to bunch at the certification point and could crowd out some efficiency investments (Houde, 2014a).

[14]LEED is a building rating system designed by the US Green Building Council, a non-governmental organization. See: www.usgbc.org/leed.

Hedonic analyses of two building certifications, LEED and Energy Star, suggest that certifications provide information to the market, as certification status explains some of the residual variation in rental and sales prices after conditioning on prominent property characteristics (Eichholtz *et al.*, 2010, 2013). Residential certifications are associated with higher sales prices in both the Netherlands and the United States (Brounen and Kok, 2011; Kahn and Kok, 2014; Walls *et al.*, 2013).

Experimental research on point-of-sale interventions for energy-consuming products has found heterogeneity in consumer beliefs about possible energy-cost savings. Providing information to consumers could, in theory, lead some consumers to increase energy use — or invest in inefficient technology — in response to information, in a mean-reverting pattern. Carefully designed information provision may eliminate this effect (Schultz *et al.*, 2007). In practice, some information provision interventions may generate negligible demand effects (Allcott and Sweeney, 2014).

Further research is needed to distinguish the effects of incomplete information from competing explanations of the energy-efficiency gap, such as inattention and heuristic decision making. Randomized control trials, including both revealed- and stated-choice experiments, may be the most promising method to isolate and test these mechanisms. Likewise, targeted, randomized research designs could provide practical guidance for existing and potential new policy interventions. In particular, research on the effects of online information provision is merited, because consumers increasingly obtain information about and purchase energy-consuming (and other) products online.

Are Energy Operating Costs Inefficiently Priced, Understood, and/or Analyzed?

Even if energy-consuming durable goods are available on the market and appropriately priced, energy operating costs could be inefficiently priced, understood, or analyzed. In fact, even if consumers make privately optimal decisions, energy-saving technology could — in the absence of corrective policy — diffuse more slowly than the socially optimal rate, due to negative externalities from energy production and use. In other words, even if the private energy-efficiency gap is not present, a social energy-efficiency gap might exist.

For example, the combustion of fossil fuels is associated with numerous environmental pollutants, including greenhouse gases, sulfur dioxide, oxides of nitrogen, and particulate matter, and the environmental and human health effects of these pollutants are not fully incorporated into the price of fossil fuels (and electricity generation). Such unpriced externalities and/or utility regulation can, in principle, lead to a divergence between the energy prices consumers face and the prices that would guide efficient decisions.

In addition, regardless of whether energy prices are set at efficient levels, consumers who hold biased beliefs about energy prices or their expected energy use will make decisions that do not appear optimal, given observed prices. On the other hand, analysts who overestimate the savings associated with efficiency investments or ignore consumer heterogeneity will identify an energy-efficiency gap even where none exists.

As in the previously examined realm, the theoretical arguments in this area are robust. However, unlike in the previous case, here the empirical evidence is considerable, and in some cases quite compelling. In most cases, data are likely to be available for additional research, with the exception of those sub-questions below (3.4 and 3.5) that refer to beliefs, which are challenging to recover with a sufficient degree of reliability. Furthermore, in several cases, existing policies (for example, gasoline taxes, carbon pricing, and electricity price structures) appear not to provide sufficient incentives for energy efficiency from an economic perspective, suggesting that further research is warranted. We view further research in this realm as a relatively high priority; specifically, empirical estimates of the incremental monetized social damages from energy production and use, and the degree to which such damages are already accounted for in energy prices. Where appropriate, it is useful for such estimates to be location and time-specific.

Are Retail Electricity or Natural Gas Prices Too Low (or High) Due to Regulation?

Evidence is mixed regarding whether the regulation of electricity and natural gas prices helps to explain the energy-efficiency gap, due to a divergence of prices from marginal cost. On the one hand, a lack of time-varying electricity pricing suggests that prices are sometimes too low and sometimes too high. On the other hand, average-cost pricing and other features of electricity and gas price regulation could lead to prices that exceed marginal cost systematically. The net effect of these different factors is unclear.

The dynamics of electricity markets can cause prices to be below marginal cost, particularly during peak periods. The marginal cost of electricity generation varies over time, and many pricing schemes do not reflect this variation, leading to inefficient utilization decisions (Joskow and Wolfram, 2012). Real-time electricity pricing could correct this, particularly if consumers have access to real-time feedback on consumption (Jessoe and Rapson, 2014), which could yield large efficiency gains (Borenstein, 2005), but the impact of time-of-use pricing and associated load shifting on energy-efficiency investment is ambiguous (Gillingham *et al.*, 2009). Many utilities use multipart tariffs to recover fixed costs while preserving marginal incentives (Coase, 1946). But marginal (or usage) prices are typically set above marginal costs. Natural gas customers in the United States face prices inclusive of fixed distribution costs that are well above marginal cost, with one study estimating that these additional costs are comparable to a tax of over $50 per ton of carbon dioxide (Davis and Muehlegger, 2010). Pricing above short-run marginal cost is also present in the electricity sector (Naughton, 1986; Borenstein, 2012). Equity considerations are one explanation for these markups in regulated industries (Borenstein and Davis, 2012), but this issue is not restricted to regulated firms; utilities in restructured markets facing imperfect retail competition also diverge from optimal two-part tariffs (Puller and West, 2013).

A second possible reason for inefficiently *high* prices of energy for regulated utilities comes from a principal–agent problem — regulated utilities may not minimize capital costs on behalf of consumers, and these costs cannot be perfectly observed by regulators. Under rate-of-return regulation, utilities may overcapitalize in order to increase profits (Averch and Johnson, 1962), a phenomenon that has been confirmed empirically (Spann, 1974). Comparisons of electricity generators subject to different regulatory regimes following deregulation have validated this phenomenon (Fowlie, 2010; Cicala, 2015). Other research, however, has not supported the theory that utilities overinvest to increase profits (Boyes, 1976), and recasting this problem in a dynamic framework high-lights the possibility of "regulatory hold-up" (Gilbert and Newbery, 1994), where firms may strategically limit investment if they expect regulators to refuse to allow a fair rate of return after the investment is sunk. There is empirical evidence that, due to such regulatory hold-up, utilities underinvest in infrastructure that improves reliability (Lim and Yurukoglu, 2015); this could lead to inefficiently low prices.

Inattention, rational or otherwise, may also influence consumer decisions. Recent empirical research provides evidence that retail electricity customers respond to average prices rather than marginal prices (Ito, 2014), and that feedback about electricity consumption influences the price elasticity of demand (Jessoe and Rapson, 2014). Further empirical research directed at understanding how alternative pricing schemes affect investment in energy efficiency would be valuable.

Are Electricity Prices too Low Due to Unpriced Externalities?

Electric power production is also associated with environmental externalities. Quantitative estimates of the magnitude of these externalities are limited, and only a subset of these account for marginal emissions and damages being both location and time specific (Muller and Mendelsohn, 2009; Graff Zivin *et al.*, 2014).

Coal and natural gas combustion for electric power production have received the most attention, with estimates suggesting the (non-carbon) damages from coal-powered electricity cost society about three to four cents per kilowatt-hour (kWh), and those from natural gas-powered electricity cost society much less than 1 cent per kWh on average (National Research Council, 2010). Carbon dioxide emissions from these sources approximately double these cost estimates, depending on choices of the social cost of carbon and the discount rate.[15]

In general, the full incorporation of environmental externalities into the price of electricity would likely raise electricity prices in most US regions. However, many of these externalities are already regulated and thereby indirectly — and sometimes directly — priced. But other market distortions — such as electricity price regulation — make it difficult to judge overall whether electricity prices are too low, and the answer seems

[15]Other fuel sources (for example, nuclear and renewable energy) and stages of production (for example, fuel extraction) produce externalities that are more difficult to quantify, but also potentially important. Qualitative discussions of these impacts abound, but there is little knowledge of the economic magnitudes of the externalities. See, for example, National Research Council (2010).

certain to vary by region (and time of day). More research is needed to quantify and monetize electricity generation externalities, including comprehensive assessments of which externalities are currently unpriced or underpriced and which are effectively addressed by existing policy.

Are Gasoline Prices too Low Due to Unpriced Externalities?

Some unpriced transportation-related externalities are a direct function of gasoline consumption. These include the effects of greenhouse gas emissions and oil dependency (National Research Council, 2010). Available estimates place these external costs at about thirty to forty cents per gallon (Parry *et al.*, 2007). Local pollution, congestion, and accident externalities can be approximated as mileage-related costs, and converted to per gallon costs; estimates for these are as great as $2.40 per gallon (Parry *et al.*, 2007; Anderson and Auffhammer, 2014). These externality estimates are more than five times larger than current gasoline taxes in the United States.[16] Furthermore, complementarities between gasoline consumption and leisure justify a gasoline tax significantly larger than marginal damages from externalities, due to interactions with labor taxes (West and Williams III, 2007). These inefficiencies are exacerbated by fuel subsidies in some countries (Clements *et al.*, 2013), while in others, prices may actually be inefficiently high due to existing taxes (Parry and Small, 2005).

Raising gasoline prices (whether through taxation or reduction of subsidies) is not necessarily the optimal policy response to all of these externalities. For example, the damages created by congestion are both location and time dependent and would optimally be priced accordingly. Accident externalities may be best regulated by weight-specific mileage taxes, although this could be approximated by a simpler gasoline tax (Anderson and Auffhammer, 2014).

Competing goals present another complication. Due to the rebound effect,[17] improvements in energy efficiency could lead to more vehicle miles

[16]As of July 1, 2015, the federal excise tax on gasoline was 18.4 cents per gallon and the average state excise tax was 26.49 cents per gallon (www.eia.gov/tools/faqs/faq. cfm?id=10&t=5).

[17]The rebound (or take-back) effect refers to the reduction in energy savings from the adoption of an energy-efficiency technology that is due to behavioral response, such as raising the temperature setting on a home thermostat after installing better thermal insulation in the home.

traveled, resulting in larger external costs due to congestion and accidents. Addressing congestion and accidents through gasoline taxes would provide an incentive for energy-efficiency improvements to vehicles, but would fail to satisfy economic efficiency due to interactions with other externalities.

On net, economists agree that the price of gasoline in the United States is inefficiently low, and that this contributes to the divergence between observed and socially optimal adoption of energy-efficient technology.

Are Beliefs about Current and Future Fuel Prices and/or Usage Systematically Uninformed or Biased Downward?

Imperfect understanding of energy operating costs on the part of consumers is another possible contributor to the energy-efficiency gap, but biased beliefs about fuel prices do not seem to be a major factor.

Consumer Beliefs about Fuel Prices

Downward-biased beliefs about fuel prices would tend to lead to underinvestment in energy-efficient technology. Qualitative interviews suggest that people may know current gasoline prices, but lack other essential inputs to valuing vehicle fuel economy (Turrentine and Kurani, 2007). Quantitative survey evidence suggests that, on average, consumers forecast future gasoline prices using current prices (Allcott, 2011a; Anderson *et al.*, 2013).[18]

Is the current price an unbiased predictor of future prices? It is crucial to compare *ex ante* consumer beliefs with other possible *ex ante* beliefs, rather than using outcomes to judge the beliefs of consumers *ex post*, because beliefs can turn out to be mistaken after the fact, even when they are unbiased in expectation. Some empirical evidence suggests that this no-change forecast is a better predictor of future prices than predictions derived from econometric models, professional survey forecasts, and oil futures (Alquist and Kilian, 2010). Together, these two findings — that consumers forecast using current prices, and that current prices are more accurate than other conventional forecasting techniques — do not support

[18]Allcott (2011a) compares survey respondents' fuel-price forecasts to futures prices, not current prices. However, futures prices at the time of the survey were almost identical to a scenario of constant real prices.

the argument that downwardly biased beliefs about fuel prices contribute to the energy-efficiency gap.[19]

Consumer Beliefs about Fuel Usage

There is little evidence on gasoline usage forecasts or the contribution of inaccurate usage forecasts to the energy-efficiency gap. There is evidence from other settings, however. For example, consumer decisions about mobile phone and health club contracts suggest biased beliefs about product usage (DellaVigna and Malmendier, 2006; Grubb, 2009). But in the context of automobile purchases, consumers may be less likely to misestimate future fuel usage, due to the salience of gasoline expenditures and relative stability of driving patterns for a given individual.

Future research to understand the impact of fuel-price beliefs on investments in energy-efficient technology outside the transportation sector could be valuable. Likewise, studies of the beliefs of firms, or of key decision makers within firms, could aid understanding of the energy-efficiency gap. Little research has been carried out on consumers' predictions of future usage. Without eliciting or recovering these beliefs, assessing the optimality of consumer purchases requires strong assumptions. A research design that combines elicited price and usage forecasts with choice data could possibly recover preferences without bias from heterogeneity in beliefs among consumers.

Are Beliefs about Current and Future Electricity Prices and/or Usage Systematically Uninformed or Biased Downward?

Consumer Beliefs about Electricity Prices

Limited evidence suggests that consumers may be misinformed about current electricity prices, but there is no evidence of systematic bias.

---

[19]Although average beliefs about prices may not be biased, consumer forecasts of future gasoline prices dis-play substantial heterogeneity (Allcott, 2011a; Anderson *et al.*, 2013). One survey elicited upper and lower bounds on future fuel prices, with responses exhibiting significant uncertainty. The spread between the mean response for each bound was almost two dollars, or 45 percent of the midpoint between these means (Greene *et al.*, 2013). These findings could explain underinvestment by some consumers.

Consumers respond to average, rather than marginal price (Ito, 2014), but in one study appear to *reduce* consumption in response to a reduction in price, in contrast to theoretical predictions (Jessoe *et al.*, 2014). This could be a product of consumer inattentiveness, but research is needed to distinguish this from competing explanations (Faruqui and Sergici, 2011; Ito *et al.*, 2015). In contrast, other research has provided evidence that consumers value changes in physical energy use (for example, kWh of electricity and therms of natural gas) at close to their price (Newell and Siikamäki, 2014).

Consumer Beliefs about Electricity Usage

Experimental-choice data suggest that consumers are also misinformed about electricity usage or how daily activities translate into usage; consumers provided with real-time usage feedback become significantly more price responsive than consumers without such feedback (Jessoe and Rapson, 2014).[20] In consumer surveys, respondents systematically overestimate the energy costs of low-usage goods (for example, computers) and underestimate the energy costs of high-usage goods (for example, water heaters) (Attari *et al.*, 2010).

Separately identifying beliefs and preferences is certainly challenging. Economic research in this area typically makes assumptions — sometimes quite strong assumptions — about beliefs in order to recover preferences. Future research could begin by eliciting beliefs from economic agents, and then using these beliefs to recover preferences (Manski, 2004). In some contexts, this approach could enable the researcher to isolate multiple effects of information policies (for example, isolate the effect of salience from the effect of information that alters beliefs).

Do Analysts Systematically Overestimate Energy Savings from Efficiency Investments?

Incomplete understanding of energy operating costs on the part of analysts — rather than consumers — can also help reconcile conflicting

[20] In this experiment, the treatment and control groups received the same day-ahead notifications of price changes. This research design isolates the effect of usage feedback and eliminates the potentially confounding effect of salience.

estimates of the magnitude of the energy-efficiency gap. In the past, analysts' predictions of energy savings from efficiency investments have tended to overstate the magnitude of the energy-efficiency gap. We distinguish between *ex ante* engineering–economic analyses,[21] which rely primarily on physical models to predict energy savings, and *ex post* impact evaluations, which typically rely on observed energy consumption to estimate net savings associated with energy-efficiency investments. Hybrid models combine the technological detail of engineering models with economic evaluations (Murphy and Jaccard, 2011).

Ex post economic evaluations, using actual energy usage, are generally thought to be more credible than *ex ante* engineering–economic analyses,[22] and comparisons provide evidence of a seemingly systematic bias in *ex ante* predictions (Nadel and Keating, 1991). Several explanations for the divergence between engineering models and impact evaluations have been offered: erroneous assumptions about usage; complex interactions omitted from engineering estimates (for example, the rebound effect in some cases); quality control problems (for example, problems with equipment installation); and adoption of energy-saving measures by nonparticipants (which lowers net savings attributable to utility programs).

A meta-analysis of forty-two utility conservation programs in the residential, commercial, and industrial sectors found that actual energy-savings estimates for residential retrofit programs ranged from 15 to 117 percent of *ex ante* engineering–economic estimates (Nadel and Keating,

---

[21] These are also called "bottom-up" or "technology-based" approaches. They typically utilize detailed information about the relative efficiency of various types of energy-using equipment, existing deployment, and assumptions about usage patterns, in order to estimate how energy usage, expenditures, and pollutant emissions would change in response to changes in the mix of capital goods. By making assumptions about opportunities for substitution, switching costs, and infra-marginal behavioral responses, these studies have been used to predict the effects of policies. For an early critique of these studies, see Joskow and Marron (1993). In a particularly influential engineering–economic study, McKinsey & Company estimated a supply curve of carbon-emission reductions in the United States (Granade *et al.*, 2009) and concluded that a substantial amount of reductions could be achieved at negative cost by investing in greater energy efficiency. This result generated considerable interest, and also substantial criticism, partly on the grounds that some costs of adoption were not included in the analysis.

[22] However, *ex ante* studies offer something *ex post* approaches do not, namely predictions, which are critical for evaluating proposed energy-efficiency investments on cost-effectiveness grounds, as well as for projecting energy savings associated with a given policy.

1991). Commercial retrofit programs exhibited energy savings ranging from 36 to 248 percent of engineering predictions, while a majority of programs failed to meet savings benchmarks from *ex ante* analysis (Nadel and Keating, 1991). These direct comparisons suggest that caution is warranted when interpreting *ex ante* engineering–economic evidence of the energy-efficiency gap, although this research has documented some cases in which *ex ante* analyses underestimated energy savings.

Home energy auditors use engineering-based tools to predict energy savings. These tools are one potential source of systematically biased energy-savings estimates, for reasons that include user error (for example, incorrect inputs or inaccurate assumptions about post-audit thermostat settings) and improper accounting for residents' behavioral responses, even when the underlying engineering models are correct.

In empirical research, two groups of participants in a utility-weatherization program in the 1980s achieved 47 and 78 percent of predicted savings on average (Hirst, 1986),[23] while realized savings from another utility program ranged from 50 to 81 percent of predicted electricity savings, and 14 to 42 percent of predicted natural gas savings (Sebold and Fox, 1985). In another study, a tool used for weatherization home audits overpredicted savings by 186 percent, despite accurate engineering calculations (Ternes and Gettings, 2008). Likewise, weatherization projects in New York State achieved only 57 to 69 percent of the savings predicted by the National Energy Audit Tool, and studies from other states have reached qualitatively similar conclusions (Berry and Gettings, 1998). In a randomized-utility experiment providing insulation and HVAC appliances to certain households, *ex ante* engineering estimates overstated actual conservation by 13 percent (Dubin *et al.*, 1986).

Analyses that significantly overestimate energy savings persist, despite substantial improvements in *ex ante* engineering–economic methods over time. For example, *ex post* analysis of the "Cash for Coolers" program in Mexico, which provided subsidies for the replacement of inefficient house-hold appliances, indicates that refrigerator replacement achieved only one-quarter of the annual savings predicted by the World

[23] Hirst (1986) reviews possible causes of differences between predicted and actual energy savings, including errors in audit methodology, data collection and interpretation, installation of inappropriate retrofit measures, use of poor materials, low-quality installation work, changes in occupant behavior, errors in electricity usage data, and errors in analysis of electricity-billing data.

Bank. Replacement of air conditioners led to increased electricity consumption, in stark contrast to engineering predictions of energy savings (Davis *et al.*, 2014). A randomized evaluation of the Weatherization Assistance Program in the United States found model projections exceeded realized savings by a factor of 2.5 (Fowlie *et al.*, 2015b). Nonetheless, care must be taken in generalizing these findings, as weatherization may not be representative of other energy-efficiency programs, which have been found to vary significantly in cost effectiveness (Hoffman *et al.*, 2015).

Scrutiny of the rates of return predicted by *ex ante* engineering–economic analyses also provides evidence of bias in energy-savings estimates. Econometric analysis of home energy-efficiency investments by Metcalf and Hassett (1999) suggests the median rate of return for insulation improvements was 9.7 percent, consistent with reasonable discount rates, but far below the *ex ante* estimates of Blasnik (1990). A combined engineering/econometric approach to estimating these rates of return finds broadly similar results: Dubin and Henson (1988) estimate average rates of return of 4.9 percent for ceiling insulation and 8.3 percent for wall insulation.[24]

There are significant opportunities for research in this area. First, more attention is needed to *ex post* analysis in the transportation, commercial, and industrial sectors. The preponderance of evidence brought to bear on this question of accuracy in *ex ante* energy-savings predictions has come from the residential sector, presumably because of the large number of government and utility programs that provide existing engineering analysis and rich data for *ex post* assessment. More *ex post* analyses of model predictions are needed to better judge whether *ex ante* engineering–economic analyses continue to systematically overstate the savings associated with energy-efficiency investments, or whether these

[24]Simulation-based studies, which use energy-market models to trace out energy-efficiency supply curves, improve on simpler *ex ante* analyses. These models explicitly model complex adoption decisions, consumer heterogeneity, uncertainty, and feedback effects. As a result, even if these models begin with the same technology assumptions as simpler engineering–economic models, the general equilibrium effects of these interrelationships lead to different, typically lower, predicted levels of end-use energy efficiency. One study (Huntington, 2011) found that incorporating these factors reduces by three-quarters the size of the energy-efficiency gap identified in the McKinsey & Company study (Granade *et al.*, 2009).

approaches have truly improved over time.[25] It is at least conceivable that selection bias has come about through researchers having chosen to evaluate engineering–economic analyses that have most exaggerated the savings potential of efficiency investments.

Do Analysts Insufficiently Account for Consumer Heterogeneity?

For any energy-efficiency technology, the benefits and costs of adoption can vary substantially across potential adopters (Jaffe and Stavins, 1994a, 1994b, 1995; Metcalf and Hassett, 1999; Alberini *et al.*, 2013). Even when engineering predictions correctly find that, on average, the benefits of adoption exceed the costs of adoption, this will not be true for some potential adopters. Differences in benefits and costs across agents generate variation in adoption pat-terns. These differences can explain low adoption rates for technologies that appear cost effective (Griliches, 1957), especially if benefits and costs are correlated (Suri, 2011). Similarly, heterogeneity across consumers may explain variation in the adoption of energy-efficient technology. For example, Hausman and Joskow (1982) pointed out that heterogeneity in usage profiles, capital stock, or consumer preferences could result in realized savings below average predicted savings. Failure to model heterogeneity correctly can introduce bias in estimates of the size of the energy-efficiency gap.

If the bias due to heterogeneity is systematic, analyses ignoring heterogeneity could overstate the magnitude of the energy-efficiency gap. The sign of the bias is ambiguous, but can be identified. Neglecting consumer heterogeneity appears to have produced empirical estimates that overstate the extent to which vehicle purchasers undervalue fuel economy (Bento *et al.*, 2012). Ignoring heterogeneity can bias energy-savings estimates upward: systematic differences between past and future adopters can drive a wedge between observed and potential returns for a given investment. This wedge is likely positive in a context where consumers and firms have selected the most profitable projects first, as prospective returns will likely

[25]Some assessments have been improved by accounting for "free riders" (i.e., inframarginal consumers) that would have adopted technologies even in the absence of certain programs, and by incorporating a utilization elasticity termed the "rebound effect" (Davis *et al.*, 2014; Dubin and Henson, 1988; Gillingham and Palmer, 2014; Greening *et al.*, 2000; Houde and Aldy, 2014; Sorrell *et al.*, 2009).

be below historical average returns. Heterogeneity in individual time preferences will also alter the estimated attractiveness of energy-efficiency investments, which will tend to be more problematic for analyses where a larger share of benefits are estimated to come from households with relatively high discount rates (Newell and Siikamäki, 2015).

One potential area for future research involves using randomized experiments to better understand the distribution of energy savings associated with given investments by comparing the distribution of energy outcomes for treated and control groups. This could help improve *ex ante* predictions for future decision making. Wider use of techniques from industrial organization (for example, random coefficient logit models) could improve predictions by modeling heterogeneity explicitly.

Are Product Choices Cost Minimizing in Present-Value Terms?

The framework we posited in Part 1 is one of cost-minimizing energy-efficiency decisions, and so it is natural to ask whether market failures and/or behavioral phenomena inhibit cost minimization in present-value terms.

Here the empirical evidence ranges from strong (split incentives/agency issues and inattention/salience phenomena) to moderate (heuristic decision making/bounded rationality, systematic risk, myopia/short-sightedness, and option value) to weak (learning-by-using, loss aversion, and capital-market failures). And here, as elsewhere in our review, we find that most previous work has focused on the residential sector, with much less attention given to the commercial and industrial sectors — presumably because of lack of available data. That said, the availability of data for further research varies by subtopic, with split incentives/agency issues and effects of myopia offering the most promising opportunities for further investigation.

Given the wide use of building codes and energy-efficiency standards, split incentives/agency problems in the residential, commercial, and industrial sectors may not be as severe as one would expect in the absence of interventions. Some areas merit priority for future research, such as empirical analysis of split incentives/agency issues in markets for technologies that are not subject to efficiency standards. Much more work can be done in the behavioral realm on issues such as inattention/salience, loss aversion/reference points, heuristic decision making, and myopia.

Do Split Incentives/Agency Issues Due to Asymmetric Information Inhibit Energy-Efficient Decisions?

Differences in interests between economic agents frequently arise, causing problems of agency or split incentives. In the energy-efficiency realm, prominent examples include landlord–tenant and builder–buyer problems, in which capital investors may make decisions that are not optimal from the perspective of the end user. Similarly, agency conflicts are possible within firms when investment and operating decisions are divided among individuals or business units (Tietenberg, 2009). Research has long cited these conflicts as potential explanations for the energy-efficiency gap (Blumstein *et al.*, 1980; Fisher and Rothkopf, 1989; DeCanio, 1993; Jaffe and Stavins, 1994a; Jaffe and Stavins, 1994b; Gillingham *et al.*, 2009; Tietenberg, 2009; Gillingham and Palmer, 2014).

Empirical evidence has confirmed the existence of the principal–agent problem, and comprehensive accounting exercises have sought to estimate the potential importance of this market failure by quantifying the amount of energy consumption subject to incentive conflicts (IEA, 2007). As much as 35 percent of U.S. residential energy use may be affected (Murtishaw and Sathaye, 2006). Some research has compared owner-occupied and rental properties to estimate directly the impacts of split incentives. Results are compelling: even after controlling for household income and other household characteristics, renters are significantly less likely to have energy-efficient refrigerators, clothes washers, and dish-washers, based on data from the Residential Energy Consumption Survey (Davis, 2012). Owner-occupied dwellings in California are 13–20 percent more likely to have exterior wall and ceiling insulation (Gillingham *et al.*, 2012).[26]

Other evidence supports the hypothesis that information asymmetries exist in housing markets. Data from the United States show that landlords frequently include utility costs in rental prices even when units are individually metered. This may be because landlords with energy-efficient units cannot credibly communicate this information and instead include utilities as a signal of the units' efficiency (Levinson and Niemann, 2004). Landlords may even use utility-included rental contracts to attract renters or as a signal of other unobservable forms of quality unrelated to energy efficiency. The empirical correlation between how well-maintained a unit

---

[26]In contrast, a hedonic regression analysis of survey data in Australia failed to find evidence of split incentives in rental housing (Wood *et al.*, 2012).

is and the inclusion of utilities in rent provides some support for this hypothesis (Choi and Kim, 2012).

Further insight can be gleaned by assessing the link between information asymmetries and new investment in energy efficiency. Recent work on residential housing markets finds that patterns of investment in conversion from inefficient oil heating to more efficient natural gas heating are consistent with the hypothesis of asymmetric information between landlords and tenants. The potential gains from these missed investments are not trivial: back-of-the-envelope calculations suggest the annualized cost savings from converting from oil to gas heating are 12–24 percent of annual heating expenditure on average (Myers, 2015).

More support for the hypothesis of asymmetric information comes from stated preferences. Responding to a survey, New Zealand tenants stated that they would be willing to pay higher rents in exchange for improved energy efficiency and, in many cases, respondents' willingness to pay appears to justify landlord investments in energy-efficiency improvements. Asymmetric information could explain why landlords do not make such seemingly profitable efficiency investments (Phillips, 2012). In contrast, recent research on commercial buildings finds little evidence of asymmetric information between building owners and prospective buyers or tenants (Papineau, 2015).

Although such studies provide evidence regarding the hypothesis of asymmetric information, they do not provide direct estimates of the impact of information asymmetries on investments in energy efficiency. While a market failure exists, the magnitude may be small, because the energy impacts of inefficient appliances and less insulation only amount to a few percent of total energy consumption in rental units (Davis, 2012; Gillingham *et al.*, 2012).

Alternative contract structures can con-tribute to another, less cited outcome: moral hazard. Tenants who sign energy-inclusive rental agreements face zero marginal cost from energy consumption, and therefore may use too much energy, relative to the social optimum. Indeed, tenants appear to keep indoor temperatures higher during winter months and when their homes are unoccupied when utilities are included in their leases (Maruejols and Young, 2011; Levinson and Niemann, 2004). Likewise, tenants who pay for utilities are more likely to adjust heating temperatures at night than tenants who face zero marginal cost (Gillingham *et al.*, 2012). Such findings do not relate directly to investment in energy efficiency, except to the degree that land-lords respond strategically to such behavior. However, even if landlords do respond strategically, they are more likely to invest in high-efficiency appliances or decouple rental agreements and energy use than they are to underinvest in energy efficiency. Thus, moral hazard is unlikely to contribute to the energy-efficiency gap.

The best available evidence is from the residential sector, but agency problems due to information asymmetries could also play a role in commercial and industrial-sector energy-efficiency decisions. Indeed, research confirms that firms are susceptible to internal principal–agent problems. Green Lights, a program that provides technical assistance to (voluntarily) participating firms, enabled cost-saving lighting upgrades that these firms had not installed independently. Program experience suggests that firms failed to install these cost-effective measures before the program due to internal principal–agent conflicts: capital rationing by managers and split incentives across divisions (Howarth *et al.*, 2000). Likewise, case studies of the electric-motor market in Europe identified split incentives as a barrier to investments in energy efficiency (de Almeida, 1998; Ostertag, 2003).

Despite the frequency with which the principal–agent problem is named as a contributor to the energy-efficiency gap, there are few formal agency models adapted to this setting. Experimental work is difficult in many settings, since researchers cannot randomly assign landlords and tenants to properties. Therefore, creative empirical strategies (e.g., Myers, 2015) and new data sources may be needed.

The structure of the principal–agent problem may also create opportunities for creative policy responses. Eliminating information asymmetries or innovation in the form of contracts could allow private markets to overcome misaligned incentives. For example, Japan requires vending-machine operators — rather than owners of properties where machines are installed — to pay for the machines' energy use (IEA, 2007). Despite this, vending machines are also subject to minimum efficiency standards in Japan.

Do Learning-by-Using Spillovers Inhibit More Energy-Efficient Decisions?

In many cases, consumers learn about the benefits of a given technology by adopting and experiencing it. In some cases, other consumers benefit from this information without having to adopt the technology. A positive information spillover could slow the rate of technology adoption relative to the social optimum, as each consumer has an incentive to delay adoption in order to learn from others. Put another way, the opportunity for individuals to substitute their peers' experiences for their own creates an incentive to free ride (Foster and Rosenzweig, 2010). At least in theory, this phenomenon could contribute to the energy-efficiency gap.[27]

Empirical research in other domains emphasizes the prevalence of social learning and peer effects (Case and Katz, 1991; Ammermueller and Pischke, 2009; Duflo and Saez, 2002; Foster and Rosenzweig, 1995; Emerick, 2014; Conley and Udry, 2010), but there is limited evidence regarding how information spillovers affect energy-efficient technology, and — if positive spillovers exist — whether consumers respond by free riding. The bulk of the evidence on information spillovers comes from the introduction of hybrid vehicles, drawing on both stated-preference (Mau *et al.*, 2008) and revealed-preference studies (Axsen *et al.*, 2009; Narayanan and Nair, 2013).[28] In the residential sector, a study of thermal insulation choices by homebuilders found no evidence of large knowledge externalities among builders, suggesting builders do not learn from the adoption of these technologies by competitors (Jaffe and Stavins, 1995).[29]

Theoretical research from other fields highlights the potential importance of social learning and peer effects (Manski, 1993a), and underscores the potential for social learning to lead to inefficient technology-adoption decisions, even irrespective of free rider-ship. Information spillovers in the context of irreversible technology choice with network externalities can result in proven technologies being chosen over alternatives with higher expected value (Choi, 1997). Similarly, a model in which it is rational to adopt technology based on the adoption decisions of others (for example, because the decisions of others may reflect information the agent lacks) predicts herd behavior in which agents make decisions that depart from the decision they would make using only private information.

---

[27]These spillovers are related to the effects of demand spillovers on innovation by firms, discussed above, in that they also affect product offerings.

[28]Learning spillovers from hybrid technology are not always positive. Analysis of both the Toyota Prius and the Honda Insight suggests that while higher market penetration by the Prius has led to increased adoption of all hybrids, higher market penetration by the Insight has led to *reduced* adoption (Heutel and Muehlegger, 2015).

[29]An alternative explanation acknowledged by Jaffe and Stavins (1995) is that builders have complete (or close to complete) information, so there is little or no scope for learning from the adoption decisions of others.

This can lead to inefficient outcomes, as agents collectively undermine the benefits of learning by taking cues from others, rather than relying on private information (Banerjee, 1992).

Previous research illustrates the challenge of credibly identifying spillovers using observational data (Narayanan and Nair, 2013; Manski, 1993b). The challenge is to disentangle spillover effects from unobservables (Foster and Rosenzweig, 2010). Even then, empirically testing for the presence of learning spillovers does not indicate whether the spillovers contribute to the energy-efficiency gap, such as through individuals free riding and thus slowing the overall rate of technology adoption. Further research will be needed to determine the effect of learning spillovers on the adoption of energy-efficient technology, potentially through the use of experimental techniques (Baird *et al.*, 2014).

Does Inattention to and/or a Lack of Salience of Energy Operating Costs Inhibit Energy-Efficient Decisions?

Broadly speaking, there is consider-able evidence that consumer inattention to non-salient costs affects decisions. Experiments and observational data reveal that consumers are inattentive to sales taxes (Chetty *et al.*, 2009), shipping charges (Hossain and Morgan, 2006), and out-of-pocket costs for health care (Abaluck and Gruber, 2011). Conceptually, inattention may contribute to the energy-efficiency gap to the degree that energy costs are not salient for the investment decision. In some markets, this contribution could be substantial. Almost half of surveyed vehicle buyers report making their decisions without considering fuel costs (Allcott, 2011a), which is consistent with research that found that consumers largely ignored replacement ink prices when making printer purchase decisions (Hall, 1997).

There are two fundamental ways to frame research on inattention. One is a reduced-form approach, empirically estimating an attentiveness parameter without taking a stance on the underlying structural model of inattention (DellaVigna, 2009). This approach can produce credible estimates of the relative importance of inattention in a given context, but it falls short of identifying the mechanisms that underlie inattention. The other approach is to develop a model of the decision process itself, making explicit the underlying factors at play.[30]

[30]Research following this approach from other domains could provide guidance for future work on energy efficiency. For example, one common approach is to model inattention as

Intuition suggests that consumers will only allocate attention to an attribute if the cognitive costs of doing so are less than the expected utility gains. Thus, the level of inattentiveness should vary across individuals and decision environments. Modeling inattention to energy efficiency as a result of costly information acquisition offers one way to explain decisions that are *apparently* privately suboptimal (Howarth and Andersson, 1993; Sallee, 2014).

There are two leading methods for testing for inattention to energy efficiency in empirical research. First, the reduced form of attentiveness suggests comparing demand elasticities with respect to prices and energy costs from market data, the empirical approach taken in many studies of discrete choice, which assess the trade-off consumers make between purchase price and future energy operating costs (Hausman, 1979; Dubin and McFadden, 1984; Jaffe and Stavins, 1995; Goldberg, 1998; Anderson and Newell, 2004; Sallee *et al.*, 2015; Busse *et al.*, 2013; Allcott and Wozny, 2014).[31] The primary shortcoming of this method — which these researchers acknowledge — is that price and energy-cost elasticities can diverge for multiple reasons, including discounting behavior.

Experimental manipulations of salience provide an alternative means of studying inattention to energy efficiency. Field experiments designed to study lightbulb choice provide mixed evidence on the impact of an intervention that targets both salience and information: an online intervention increased average willingness to pay for compact fluorescent lightbulbs (CFLs) by over two dollars, while an in-store intervention had no statistically significant effect on CFL demand (Allcott and Taubinsky, 2015).[32] Stated-choice experiments that vary the type of information available to consumers, be it economic, physical energy, or environmental, can also help assess which of these is most salient to consumers. However, experimental studies are limited by concerns about distinguishing inattention from incomplete information, demand effects, and external validity.

a result of costly information acquisition and processing (see Conlisk, 1996 for background and Gabaix *et al.*, 2006 for experimental evidence), while other strands of research describe how salience affects consumer decisions (e.g., Bordalo *et al.*, 2013), and formulate alternative frameworks for consumer optimization (e.g., Gabaix, 2014).

[31] We discuss these and other studies in more detail later, in the context of consumer discount rates.

[32] Recent field experiments demonstrate the potential for experimental research to advance knowledge of the energy-efficiency gap in additional markets. See Price (2015) for a summary of this literature.

Complementary use of experimental and nonexperimental techniques can ameliorate the shortcomings of each approach (Chetty *et al.*, 2009).

Economic theory and empirical research provide some guidance for policies to address inattention to energy efficiency. Targeting inattentive consumers could enhance policy cost effectiveness. Information disclosure could target consumers with biased beliefs and those inattentive to future energy costs. The success of information disclosure policies depends crucially on salience, as well as on other context-specific factors. In contrast to information disclosure, subsidies may be poorly targeted for combating inattention if the consumers who know about them also tend to be attentive to future energy costs (Allcott *et al.*, 2015).[33] That said, there is an alternative argument for poorly targeted taxes and subsidies if these interventions do raise salience or otherwise reduce inattention; such interventions can generate first-order welfare gains for inattentive consumers and only second-order distortions for attentive consumers (O'Donoghue and Rabin, 2006).

Public policies can also lower the cost of attention, and even fairly blunt policies could be justified if they lower the cost of attention sufficiently (Sallee, 2014). Several recent studies investigate firm responses to coarse policy designs, and attempt to quantify the welfare impacts of these policies (Sallee and Slemrod, 2012; Houde, 2014a, 2014b).

Debates over price and information interventions to address inattention highlight a broader question of instrument choice. A number of recent studies provide evidence on the effects of different policy instruments on welfare and energy-efficiency outcomes. Pigouvian taxes on fuels are a natural economic response to the externalities associated with energy use. There may also be a case for product-market price interventions if consumers are inattentive to energy costs (Allcott *et al.*, 2014). Minimum efficiency standards are another alternative used by regulators; in some cases, such standards can lead to an effective ban on certain classes of products (Allcott and Taubinsky, 2015). In addition to regulatory mandates for disclosure and product certification, information interventions by utilities and, in particular, peer comparisons, have been successful in

---

[33] The literature on retirement savings also speaks to this problem of targeting: for example, Chetty *et al.* (2014) conclude that automatic retirement account contributions are more effective than subsidies in promoting retirement savings, because subsidies only affect the savings of attentive workers.

reducing residential energy use and may be applicable elsewhere (Allcott, 2011b; Ayres *et al.*, 2013; Allcott and Rogers, 2014).[34]

Experimental techniques, including belief elicitation, offer promising opportunities for future research. Researchers can also directly test models of inattention, where they offer testable predictions that are unlikely to be confounded by alternative explanations (Sallee, 2014).

Does Myopia/Short-Sightedness Inhibit More Energy-Efficient Decisions?

A key issue surrounding the question of whether myopia contributes to the energy-efficiency gap involves identifying the discount rates used by consumers and analyzing whether these discount rates are consistent with maximizing present-value net benefits. There is a long history of observing consumers' choices of energy-consuming durable goods to examine the trade-off between upfront capital costs and operating costs. If consumers are seeking to minimize discounted lifecycle costs, it becomes possible to estimate implicit discount rates.[35]

The seminal study of this kind was by Hausman (1979), which found average implicit discount rates in excess of 20 percent. Many other researchers subsequently found implicit discount rates much higher than market interest rates (Dubin and McFadden, 1984; Gately, 1980).[36] Such findings have been interpreted as evidence of myopia, the existence of other behavioral issues or market failures, or alternatively as evidence of rational discounting subject to liquidity constraints. Studies that identify a discount rate while assuming cost-minimizing behavior cannot, however, distinguish myopia as an underlying cause of the energy-efficiency gap from other possible causes. For example, high implicit discount rates for home energy investments could also be rationalized by moral hazard: contractors may provide low-quality services, and consumers may use

---

[34]These interventions may operate through multiple channels other than raising salience (e.g., providing new information, changing reference points, etc.). Allcott and Rogers (2014) estimate how the effects of these treatments change over time and discuss multiple mechanisms consistent with the estimates.

[35]Of course, it is also possible that consumers are not minimizing aggregate costs because of errors regarding time horizons, their beliefs, or due to inattention, in which case such studies would not reveal true consumer discount rates (Allcott and Wozny, 2014).

[36]Train (1985) and Sanstad, Hanemann, and Auffhammer (2006) review other examples.

high hurdle rates to insulate themselves from this risk (Giraudet and Houde, 2014).[37]

Automobile purchases provide a good setting to study these questions because such purchases are major decisions, about which consumers presumably think carefully, and because the cost of gasoline has varied substantially over time. Yet the evidence on consumer valuation of fuel economy is mixed (Greene, 2010; Helfand and Wolverton, 2011). One study has found that consumers are indifferent between \$0.76 now and \$1.00 of discounted future gasoline expenditures, suggesting mild undervaluation of fuel economy that could be due to myopia (Allcott and Wozny, 2014). On the other hand, other studies have found that market outcomes are consistent with dynamically cost-minimizing behavior (Busse *et al.*, 2013; Sallee *et al.*, 2015). Evidence from gasoline and diesel car purchases in Europe in the early 1990s suggests an implicit discount rate of about 11.5 percent, only slightly above automobile loan rates at the time (Verboven, 2002). However, research has not always taken into account the fact that automobile markets have been subject to fuel economy regulation for many years, which tends to reduce the possibility for high implicit discount rates by constraining consumers' choice sets.

To assess the implications of these studies for the energy-efficiency gap, it is necessary to identify a benchmark discount rate, which depends on the cost of capital. One structured-choice experiment found that — conditional on information labeling — elicited discount rates rationalized participant decision making on average, but the use of a common discount rate of five percent for all subjects tended to lead to a conclusion that consumers significantly undervalued energy efficiency (Newell and Siikamäki, 2014). In related work, Newell and Siikamäki (2015) found considerable heterogeneity in individual discount rates and also found that individual time preferences systematically influence willingness to invest in energy efficiency, as measured through product choices, required payback periods, and energy efficiency tax credit claims.

[37]An alternative way to frame the consideration of myopia is with experimental research and alternative theories at the intersection of psychology and economics. Research on intertemporal decision making from other contexts provides robust evidence that individuals are dynamically inconsistent (Loewenstein and Thaler, 1989), and delay costly upfront action even when they acknowledge that it is in their long-run interest (Akerlof, 1991). Quasi-hyperbolic discounting provides a theoretical alternative to exponential discounting to explain these empirical anomalies (Laibson, 1997).

Direct research on intertemporal trade-offs in energy-efficiency investment decisions might clarify the contribution of myopia to the energy-efficiency gap. For example, researchers could manipulate intertemporal trade-offs through information provision and pricing interventions, and examine decision making. Another approach may be to combine elicitation of time preferences with choice data and compare choices observed across multiple domains (Bradford *et al.*, 2014).

Strategic responses by firms to consumer myopia present another area for potential research. If firms believe consumers are myopic and therefore undervalue energy efficiency, product offerings will not be optimal from a social perspective, even if firms hold incorrect beliefs about consumer preferences. Studies of the automotive industry posit several explanations for the apparently suboptimal level of fuel economy that manufacturers provide (Helfand and Wolverton, 2011).

Do Other Cognitive Limitations Inhibit More Energy-Efficient Decisions?

Cognitive limitations other than inattention and myopia could conceivably contribute to the energy-efficiency gap by preventing individuals (or possibly firms) from properly balancing present-value benefits and costs when investing in energy-using capital goods (Gillingham *et al.*, 2009). This could manifest itself in the use of heuristics or simple optimization errors. Many empirical studies are consistent with these explanations (Sanstad and Howarth, 1994). However, it is difficult to disentangle the role of heuristics and bounded rationality from competing explanations, because consumers' decision processes cannot be observed directly and because there is no unified theory of decision making subject to cognitive limitations from which to draw testable hypotheses (Conlisk, 1996).

That said, studies of vehicle fuel economy provide some support for the hypothesis of bounded rationality. First, experimental evidence has revealed that consumers systematically misperceive the information contained in fuel economy ratings, due to the inverse relationship between gasoline consumption and miles per gallon ("the MPG illusion") (Larrick and Soll, 2008; Allcott, 2013). Other research has shown that stated preferences for cars of various efficiencies depend on the metric and scale of information provided on energy labels (Camilleri and Larrick, 2014). Translations of fuel economy into multiple perfectly correlated metrics (that is, gallons per mile, estimated annual fuel cost, and greenhouse gas rating) alter stated preferences (Ungemach *et al.*, forthcoming).

This research may provide guidance for regulatory changes that would encourage greater energy efficiency. The findings suggest that tailoring the scale of energy labels based on the expected lifetime of a given product or providing multiple translations of energy-efficiency metrics could help guide decisions (Camilleri and Larrick, 2014; Ungemach *et al.*, forthcoming). To some extent, this is already happening: the US Environmental Protection Agency recently redesigned new vehicle labels to include gallons per miles, multiple cost estimates, comparisons with other vehicles in the same class, and environmental ratings (US Environmental Protection Agency, 2015).

There are numerous opportunities to study the effects of cognitive limitations on energy-efficiency decisions. Most direct evidence is from laboratory studies of stated preferences. More research on revealed preferences in real decision environments could complement these studies, but — as noted above — the key research-design challenge, particularly in revealed-preference studies, is credibly distinguishing the effects of heuristic decision making and bounded rationality from other explanations of behavior.

Do Loss Aversion or Reference Points Inhibit More Energy-Efficient Decisions?

Research in psychology has highlighted the importance of reference points and loss aversion (i.e., people's tendency to strongly prefer avoiding losses to acquiring gains) in economic decision making. Empirical insights have been formalized in prospect theory and other alternatives to expected-utility theory (Kahneman and Tversky, 1979; Thaler, 1985; Tversky and Kahneman, 1991; Kőszegi and Rabin, 2006).[38] Yet despite

[38] See also Tversky and Kahneman (1981, 1992). More recent theoretical and experimental work in psychology also highlights the importance of reference dependence. Query theory hypothesizes that consumers consider discrete arguments for or against a given alternative, and that the number of considerations and the order in which they come to mind affects decision making (Weber and Johnson, 2009; Weber *et al.*, 2007). This theory underscores the importance of defaults. As another example, Hardisty *et al.* (2013) study the combination of loss aversion and intertemporal decision making. In general, this work highlights the need to strive for a comprehensive understanding of decision making to explain the energy-efficiency gap.

strong evidence in other decision environments and general theoretical frameworks for analysis, very little is known about the impacts of loss aversion and reference points on energy-efficiency investments.

The most relevant evidence comes from an electric utility that offered residential consumers the opportunity to enroll in a nonbinding goalsetting program to reduce energy consumption (Harding and Hsiaw, 2014). Two findings from this study are consistent with reference-dependent preferences: consumers voluntarily enrolled in the program, setting personal conservation goals, and many of these consumers reduced energy use to meet their own goals.

If the importance of goal-based reference points holds in practice, governments and businesses could stimulate investments in energy efficiency by encouraging personal goal-setting or otherwise influencing reference points (Heath *et al*., 1999). Two experiments have attempted to affect reference points by providing tailored information, goals, and personalized feedback about energy consumption (Abrahamse *et al*., 2007; Carrico and Riemer, 2011). These studies suggest that providing goals can lead to reductions in energy use, but further research is needed to determine whether goals or tailored information drove observed energy use reductions and to extend this approach to interventions that encourage investment in energy-efficiency technology.

Consumers and firms considering energy-efficiency improvements are almost certainly susceptible to reference points and loss aversion, but empirical research would be needed to better quantify the importance of these phenomena. Research focused on assessing the importance of loss aversion in the context of energy-efficiency decisions has received virtually no attention, so some initial research would be of value. Such research could help determine, for example, whether evidence that consumers value energy savings less than the investment costs of energy efficiency is due to inattention, myopia, or loss aversion. Future work could synthesize previous experimental techniques to study how different types of information displayed on energy labels influence reference points. Challenges to implementing policy based on existing research include heterogeneity — that no one level of energy efficiency is right for every consumer — and concerns over paternalism, which is a valid concern if reference points can be manipulated. Research on policy interventions (such as energy labels) could inform the design of uniform interventions that minimize the welfare cost of providing blunt guidance. Carefully targeted interventions could shift reference points for some consumers without creating incentives for other consumers to alter their behavior.

Do Capital-Market Failures Influence Consumer Discount Rates for Energy-Efficiency Investments?

Capital-market failures could in principle help explain a divergence between estimated implicit discount rates and typical market interest rates. Prospective investors facing capital constraints may be unable to finance energy-efficiency investments, even if future returns would justify the upfront cost. This could result in an estimated implicit discount rate that is above normal market rates. Information asymmetries could prevent efficient lending even for collateralized investments; firms that possess private information about future cost savings from a particular investment may be unable to convince lenders of its financial potential if such savings are costly for the lender to evaluate.

In the future, theoretical and empirical findings from consumer-finance research may shed light on specific capital-market failures that are most important for energy efficiency. The actual distribution of market interest rates faced by consumers and firms through various lending mechanisms is critical to identifying the appropriate benchmark market interest rate (or range of rates) in order to quantify its impact on energy-efficiency investments. However, it may be difficult to distinguish empirically between capital-market failures leading to high discount rates and lack of underlying demand for energy-saving technology (Palmer *et al.*, 2012). While we encourage research on capital markets generally, we do not assign a high priority to future research on the impact of capital-market failures on energy-efficiency investments. Where capital-market failures do exist, it seems unlikely that policies specific to energy efficiency would be the best response, given the broad set of financial decisions that would be affected.

Does Systematic Risk Affect the Appropriate Discount Rate for Energy-Efficiency Analysis?

The capital asset pricing model (CAPM) presents one way to frame debate about the "correct" discount rate to use for energy-efficiency analysis (Fama and French, 2004). The CAPM provides a static optimization framework for determining the appropriate hurdle rate for an investment, based on the risk-free rate of interest, expected returns from a diversified portfolio of assets, and the normalized covariance (β) between the investment's returns and that of the diversified portfolio. Optimal investment depends on the *opportunity cost* of capital, not simply the nominal cost of capital.

Under the CAPM, a positive (negative) correlation between energy prices and the rest of the economy would suggest hurdle rates for energy-efficiency investments that are higher (lower) than the returns on a diversified portfolio. A negative relationship between energy prices and the greater economy ($\beta < 0$) supports the use of low hurdle rates, because energy-efficient investments can serve as a hedge. One study found such a negative correlation between the consumer price index for fuels and the S&P 500 index (Metcalf, 1994). Likewise, more recent research argues that applying the CAPM to an analysis of vehicle purchases would lower the discount rate due to the low correlation between annual changes in gasoline prices and market returns (Allcott and Wozny, 2014). For some end uses, the correlation between fuel prices and market returns is artificially low due to regulation. This could also lead to a lower discount rate under the CAPM.

However, the CAPM may fail as an appropriate benchmark for discount rates for energy-efficiency investment for two reasons. First, the model is not ideal for many energy-efficiency investments because of the CAPM's static nature, meaning that the investment choice set, expected investment returns, and covariances among investments are treated as fixed over time. In contrast, energy-efficiency investment opportunities, expected returns, and risk relationships likely vary substantially with technological change and other exogenous factors. Second, the CAPM assumes that transaction costs are zero, that the investment can be resold on a secondary market, and that investors already hold diversified portfolios when considering a new investment (Sutherland, 1991). These assumptions may be tenable in certain contexts (for example, for sizable businesses), but not in others (for example, for low-income households). Third, the model has failed numerous empirical tests (Fama and French, 2004).

On the other hand, the CAPM's simplicity generates useful intuition and sharp, testable predictions that enable researchers to assess its utility for energy-efficiency investments. One possible approach would be to use observational data on similar investments utilizing different fuels. Prices for various fuels covary heterogeneously with the greater economy. As a result, investment hurdle rates should vary across fuel types. Estimating and comparing these hurdle rates could directly test the CAPM in this realm. However, it may be difficult to eliminate correlated unobservables.

Can Option Value Help Explain the Energy-Efficiency Gap?

Option value — the net benefit of delaying an investment even when the investment's net present value is positive — is a general feature of dynamic-optimization problems with uncertainty, irreversible investment, and timing flexibility (Dixit and Pindyck, 1994; Kellogg, 2014). Consumers and firms commonly face decision problems of this type when investing in energy-consuming durable goods with little or no resale value.

This presents an alternative explanation of the energy-efficiency gap: the difference between *apparently* optimal investment and observed investment may be due to the option value of waiting. Failure to account for this option value could bias estimates of the energy-efficiency gap. In an analysis of irreversible investment in residential energy-efficiency measures under conditions of energy-price uncertainty, Hassett and Metcalf (1993) explained observed technology adoption rates without any reference to market failures.[39] Potential technological innovation, which would reduce future adoption costs, can also yield option value for delaying energy-efficiency investments (Jaffe and Stavins, 1995; Ansar and Sparks, 2009).

Energy-price uncertainty is important in some industries. Direct computation, reduced form estimation, and simulations have found large hurdle rates due to energy-price volatility based on observed investment decisions (Metcalf and Rosenthal, 1995; Diederen *et al*., 2003; Löfgren *et al*., 2008).[40] Technological change is the other prominent explanation for investment delay. Evidence from air conditioner purchases indicates that purchase timing depends on expectations about future developments

[39] Sanstad *et al*. (1995) maintained that the option value analysis of Hassett and Metcalf (1993) suggested an implicit discount rate much lower than actually observed, even when taking irreversibility into account.

[40] In this context, the hurdle rate is the multiplier on the cost of capital that corresponds to the minimum acceptable rate of return for a project to be undertaken. Diederen, van Tongeren, and van der Veen (2003) find hurdle rates of 1.76 for Dutch greenhouses based on simulation, and Löfgren *et al*. (2008) econometrically estimate hurdle rates of 3.4 to 3.6 for the Swedish energy and heating sector.

in product efficiency (Rapson, 2014). Other relevant sources of uncertainty include future product use, product efficiency, and product life.

The option value of waiting due to uncertainty regarding future energy prices or technological change may explain part of the apparently suboptimal investment in energy-efficient technologies, but probably not a large part, in most cases (Baker, 2012). The option-value explanation hinges on four assumptions: irreversibility, uncertainty, flexible timing, and lumpiness of investment (McDonald and Siegel, 1986). In practice, one or more of these conditions can fail. Not all energy-efficient investments are irreversible. There are active resale markets for many types of consumer goods and producer capital. Uncertainty may be irrelevant, as in the case of firms that have long-term energy-procurement contracts in place, which provide price certainty. In other cases, energy-price uncertainty may be relatively unimportant, as in the case of energy-consuming goods with relatively short lifetimes or in the face of other, dominant sources of uncertainty (Abadie *et al.*, 2013). Finally, the timing of investments in energy-consuming durables is not always flexible (for example, replacement of a broken water heater).

One possible way to assess the relative importance of the option value of waiting due to energy-price uncertainty would be to survey consumers and firms directly. The evidence here is mixed. Energy-price uncertainty ranked fourth out of fifteen reported reasons firms did not undertake energy-efficiency investments recommended by auditors in a survey of small-and medium-sized businesses (Fleiter *et al.*, 2012). On the other hand, a stated-choice experiment in the residential sector revealed a correlation between energy-price uncertainty and a preference for the status quo over energy-efficiency improvements (Alberini *et al.*, 2013). This result is consistent with the basic prediction of the option-value model, but does not quantify its relative importance.

Do Other Unobserved Costs Inhibit Energy-Efficient Decisions?

We turn to the final term in the cost-minimization equation described above in section "Introduction", and ask whether other costs inhibit more energy-efficient decisions. We find that the empirical evidence in this realm is generally sound, and that data for additional research are available. We assign a relatively high priority to research in this area, particularly research aimed at better understanding of consumer demand (willingness to pay) for product attributes, which can be useful for improving regulatory design.

Do Analysts Take Sufficient Account of Product Attributes?

Products of varying efficiencies differ from each other in ways that are often omitted from engineering and econometric analysis, potentially contributing to the misidentification of an energy-efficiency gap. Producers may generate efficiency improvements by trading off other product attributes for enhanced energy efficiency. For example, the color, sound, and start-up time of fluorescent lights differ from those of incandescent lights. In such a case, consumers may face opportunity costs of decreased product quality, in addition to any price change, when considering energy-efficient products. Ignoring these opportunity costs would bias estimates of consumer choice and welfare, and also bias estimates of the magnitude of the energy-efficiency gap.

The fundamental challenge to inference is omitted-variable bias. Analyses can be classified in terms of information sets: (1) attributes observed by both the analyst and the consumer; (2) attributes observed by the consumer, but not by the analyst; (3) attributes observed by the analyst, but not the consumer; and (4) attributes observed by neither the analyst nor the consumer. Engineering techniques can recover unbiased estimates unless the consumer observes attributes that the engineer does not. In contrast, appropriate econometric techniques can succeed in all four cases. Thus, the second and arguably most important case necessitates the use of econometric techniques.

Early engineering–economic studies compared capital investment and lifetime operating costs to identify cost-effective investments or infer consumer discount rates, disregarding or only partially correcting for non-energy attributes. The prominent McKinsey & Company study treated compact fluorescent lightbulbs as interchangeable with other forms of lighting (Granade *et al.*, 2009), thus ignoring a potentially important source of (unobserved) opportunity costs.

In principle, econometric methods can improve on such engineering methods by including product attributes in analyses of choice data. In practice, however, econometric analysis has been limited by the impracticality of observing and accurately measuring all product characteristics.

These characteristics are typically subsumed into error terms. Instrumental variables provide researchers an opportunity to weaken identifying assumptions needed for work with cross-sectional data by isolating variation in energy-efficiency characteristics that are uncorrelated with the error term.[41]

Modern econometric techniques improve on previous work by explicitly accounting for product attributes unobserved by the econometrician in discrete-choice models. These models can be estimated using either cross-sectional or panel data. Studies employing the random-coefficients model provide examples of this type of cross-sectional estimation. An early application found significant heterogeneity in demand for automobile fuel economy, suggesting small negative willing-ness to pay for fuel economy improvements in relatively inefficient vehicles (Berry *et al.*, 1995), reflecting heterogeneity in the distribution of consumer preferences.

Subsequent research incorporating micro data in the random-coefficients estimation strategy confirmed the importance of heterogeneity, but also found that consumers have a negative willingness to pay for fuel economy, on average (Petrin, 2002). However, the primary focus of these early studies using random coefficients was on modeling unobserved consumer heterogeneity, rather than quantifying fuel economy valuation. These studies did not instrument for fuel economy, so these coefficients are likely biased. More recent estimation strategies that focused on identifying average demand for fuel economy have used alternative instruments and have not found a negative willingness to pay for fuel economy (Verboven, 2002; Klier and Linn, 2012; Whitefoot *et al.*, 2017). One study of appliance purchases using transactions data and geographic variation in operating costs (that is, electricity prices) found that consumers undervalue operating costs, on average (Houde, 2014b).

Panel data provide another credible way to account for unobserved product attributes. Researchers using panel data can effectively condition

---

[41] Instruments have been employed in models of energy-efficiency technology adoption for decades to address concerns about price endogeneity and selection on expected usage that could generate a correlation between product efficiency and the error term in a discrete-choice model (for example, Hausman, 1979; Dubin and McFadden, 1984). However, these early studies did not directly address the possibility of additional product characteristics that are observed by the consumer, but not the econometrician, and could therefore generate omitted variable bias.

on all unobserved product attributes that are time-invariant using differencing or fixed-effects models. Recent studies of this type provide limited evidence for an energy-efficiency gap (Allcott and Wozny, 2014; Busse *et al.*, 2013; Sallee *et al.*, 2015).[42]

Choice experiments offer another possible way to control for unobserved product characteristics. One approach in a stated-preference context would be to ask subjects to treat all products they consider as identical in nonenergy attributes. This holds promise for stated-preference studies but is infeasible for revealed-preference analysis. Analyses that assess the correlation between energy and nonenergy attributes for different products could help identify where the bias from ignoring nonenergy attributes is most likely to be present.

Do Analysts Take Sufficient Account of the Costs of Implementing Energy-Efficient Options?

Omitting any (opportunity) cost of adoption from a comparison of the benefits and costs associated with a given energy-efficiency technology will contribute to the impression of an energy-efficiency gap. Such omitted costs can take many forms, including time spent researching investment alter-natives, unobserved implementation costs, and reallocation of resources within a firm. In particular, costs that are less easily quantified are more likely to be omitted by analysts (Granade *et al.*, 2009; Huntington, 2011). But these costs may serve as real barriers to investment — not optimization errors or market failures — and should be included in an unbiased analysis of the energy-efficiency gap. This has been a key criticism of the McKinsey study (Granade *et al.*, 2009).

Consumers face a set of adoption costs beyond the most obvious costs of a technology's purchase price and direct installation charges. For example, homeowners have attributed the decision not to install or upgrade attic insulation to the hassle of clearing stored items from the attic space (Caird *et al.*, 2008). A policy experiment in the United Kingdom found that lowering such costs by offering attic cleaning would increase

[42] The earlier section on myopia contains a more detailed discussion of the findings of these three papers. Also, see Bento *et al.* (2009), Greene (2010), and Helfand and Wolverton (2011) for more detailed discussions of automobile choice models and consumer valuation of fuel economy.

insulation investments (UK Department of Energy and Climate Change, 2013). Another study estimated opportunity costs for adopting thermal insulation to be more than twice the costs of materials and labor (Sharma, 2011). One possible interpretation of low participation rates in subsidized weatherization programs is that there are high nonmonetary costs associated with these improvements (Fowlie *et al.*, 2015a).

In the commercial and industrial sectors, case studies and survey evidence provide the bulk of the empirical evidence (Fleiter *et al.*, 2012), with firms indicating that production disruptions and inconvenience can preclude investment in energy efficiency (Rohdin and Thollander, 2006, Thollander and Ottosson, 2008). Survey respondents also cite lack of time as a barrier, highlighting the role of opportunity cost in simply considering investments (Sorrell *et al.*, 2004; Thollander *et al.*, 2007; Schleich, 2009; Trianni and Cagno, 2012). Furthermore, recipients of industrial energy audits who failed to undertake recommended investments attributed their decisions to unmeasured costs and risks not considered in the audit analysis (Anderson and Newell, 2004).

In principle, there is no reason analysts cannot incorporate these additional costs, but in practice, data and measurement challenges often inhibit their ability to do so. One route forward may be to treat such costs as unobservables to be recovered using structural, experimental, and quasi-experimental research designs.

Conclusion

Energy-efficient technologies offer promise for reducing the costs and environmental damages associated with energy use, but these technologies appear not to be used by consumers and businesses to the degree that would be justified, even on the basis of their private financial net benefits. With this in mind, we have examined the private energy-efficiency gap, the apparent reality that some energy-efficiency technologies that would pay off for adopters are nevertheless not adopted, as well as the broader phenomenon we characterize as the social energy-efficiency gap, the apparent reality that some energy-efficiency technologies that would be socially efficient are not adopted.

The economic literature on explanations of the energy-efficiency gap continues to evolve from its origins in Hausman's 1979 article in the *Bell Journal of Economics*. Concerns about energy conservation and independence in the 1980s brought more attention to the existence of the apparent gap, with the mid-1990s seeing greatly renewed interest, due in part to economists' attention to the issue of global climate change. In this century, concerns about energy security and climate change have combined with developments in behavioral economics, as well as increasing numbers of environmental economists, to produce a massive increase in research on the energy-efficiency gap.

We began our review and assessment of this literature by decomposing cost-minimizing energy-efficiency decisions into their fundamental elements, which allowed us to identify four major questions, the answers to which are germane to sorting out the causes (and reality or lack thereof) of the energy-efficiency gap. First, we asked whether the energy efficiency and associated pricing of products on the market are economically efficient. To answer this question, we examined the variety of energy-efficient products on the market, their energy-efficiency levels, and their pricing. Although the theory is clear, empirical evidence is quite limited. More data that could facilitate potential future empirical research are becoming available, although firm-level data are much less plentiful than data on consumers. We do not see this area as meriting high priority for future research, with the exception of research that evaluates the effectiveness and efficiency of existing energy-efficiency information policies and examines options for improving these policies.

Second, we asked whether energy operating costs are inefficiently priced and/or understood. Even if consumers make privately optimal decisions, energy-saving technology may diffuse more slowly than the socially optimal rate, because of negative externalities. So, even if the private energy-efficiency gap is not present, the social energy-efficiency gap may be. As in the first realm, the theoretical arguments are strong. Empirical evidence is considerable, and in many cases data are likely to be avail-able for additional research. Existing policies appear not to be sufficient from an economic perspective, suggesting that further research is warranted. Indeed, we assign high priority to the pursuit of research in this realm.

Third, we asked whether product choices are cost-minimizing in present-value terms, or whether various market failures and/or behavioral phenomena inhibit such cost-minimization. We found that the empirical evidence ranges from strong (split incentives/agency issues and inattention/salience phenomena) to moderate (heuristic decision making/bounded rationality, systematic risk, myopia/shortsightedness, and option value) to weak (learning-by-using, loss aversion, and capital-market failures). Importantly, here, as elsewhere in our review, the bulk of previous work has focused on the residential sector and much less attention has been given to the commercial and industrial sectors. Much more work can be done in the behavioral realm, and we view this as a priority for future research.

Fourth, we asked whether other unobserved costs may inhibit energy-efficient decisions. We found that the empirical evidence is generally sound, and that data needed for more research are available. We assign a relatively high priority to future research, particularly to aid understanding of consumer demand for product attributes that are correlated with energy efficiency, thereby informing policy and product-development decisions.

Finally, we can ask what these findings suggest about our three categories of explanations for the apparent underinvestment in energy-efficient technologies, relative to the predictions of some engineering and economic models: (1) market failures, (2) behavioral explanations, and (3) modeling flaws. It turns out that all three categories of explanations are theoretically sound and that limited empirical evidence exists for each category as well, although the empirical research is by no means consistently strong across all of the specific explanations, as we highlight above.

The validity of each of these explanations — and the degree to which each contributes to the energy-efficiency gap — are relevant for crafting sensible policies, so we hope this review can help inform both future research and future policy. Given the many energy-efficiency policies and programs that are already in place, we also place a high priority on research that evaluates the effectiveness, cost effectiveness, and overall economic efficiency of existing energy-efficiency policies, as well as options for their improvement.

Acknowledgements

This chapter draws, in part, on a workshop held at Harvard, October 24–25, 2013, "Evaluating the Energy-Efficiency Gap," cosponsored by the Duke University Energy Initiative and the Harvard Environmental Economics Program. We are grateful to all of the participants for the insights they provided on the questions addressed at the workshop. In addition, we gratefully acknowledge valuable comments on a previous version of the manuscript by Robert Stowe, anonymous referees, and the editor, editorial contributions by Marika Tatsutani, and generous financial support from the Alfred P. Sloan Foundation. The authors, however, are fully responsible for any errors and all opinions expressed in this chapter.

References

Abadie, Luis M., José M. Chamorro, and Mikel González-Eguino. (2013). "Valuing uncertain cash flows from investments that enhance energy efficiency." *Journal of Environmental Management*, **116**: 113–124.

Abaluck, Jason, and Jonathan Gruber. (2011). "Heterogeneity in choice inconsistencies among the elderly: Evidence from prescription drug plan choice." *American Economic Review*, **101**(3): 377–381.

Abrahamse, Wokje, Linda Steg, Charles Vlek, and Talib Rothengatter. (2007). "The effect of tailored information, goal setting, and tailored feedback on household energy use, energy-related behaviors, and behavioral antecedents." *Journal of Environmental Psychology*, **27**(4): 265–276.

Akerlof, George A. (1970). "The market for 'lemons': Quality uncertainty and the market mechanism." *Quarterly Journal of Economics*, **84**(3): 488–500.

Akerlof, George A. (1991). "Procrastination and obedience." *American Economic Review*. **81**(2): 1–19.

Alberini, Anna, Silvia Banfi, and Celine Ramseier. (2013). "Energy efficiency investments in the home: Swiss homeowners and expectations about future energy prices." *Energy Journal*. **34**(1): 49–86.

Alberini, Anna, Will Gans, and Charles Towe. (2013). "Free riding, upsizing, and energy efficiency incentives in Maryland homes." Fondazione Eni Enrico Mattei Nota di Lavoro 82.2013.

Allcott, Hunt. (2011a). "Consumers' perceptions and misperceptions of energy costs." *American Economic Review*, **101**(3): 98–104.

Allcott, Hunt. (2011b). "Social norms and energy conservation." *Journal of Public Economics*, **95**(9–10): 1082–1095.

Allcott, Hunt. (2013). "The welfare effects of misperceived product costs: Data and calibrations from the automobile market." *American Economic Journal: Economic Policy*, **5**(3): 30–66.

Allcott, Hunt, and Dmitry Taubinsky. (2015). "Evaluating behaviorally motivated policy: Experimental evidence from the lightbulb market." *American Economic Review*, **105**(8): 2501–2538.

Allcott, Hunt, and Michael Greenstone. (2012). "Is there an energy efficiency gap?" *Journal of Economic Perspectives*, **26**(1): 3–28.

Allcott, Hunt, and Nathan Wozny. (2014). "Gasoline prices, fuel economy, and the energy paradox." *Review of Economics and Statistics*, **96**(5): 779–795.

Allcott, Hunt, and Richard Sweeney. (2014). "The role of sales agents in information disclosure: Evidence from a field experiment." National Bureau of Economic Research Working Paper 20048.

Allcott, Hunt, and Todd Rogers. (2014). "The short-run and long-run effects of behavioral interventions: Experimental evidence from energy conservation." *American Economic Review*, **104**(10): 3003–3037.

Allcott, Hunt, Christopher Knittel, and Dmitry Taubinsky. (2015). "Tagging and targeting of energy efficiency subsidies." *American Economic Review*, **105**(5): 187–191.

Allcott, Hunt, Sendhil Mullainathan, and Dmitry Taubinsky. (2014). "Energy policy with externalities and internalities." *Journal of Public Economics*, **112**: 72–88.

Alquist, Ron, and Lutz Kilian. (2010). "What do we learn from the price of crude oil futures?" *Journal of Applied Econometrics*. **25**(4): 539–573.

Ammermueller, Andreas, and Jorn-Steffen Pischke. (2009). "Peer effects in European primary schools: Evidence from the Progress in International Reading Literacy Study." *Journal of Labor Economics*, **27**(3): 315–348.

Anderson, Michael L., and Maximilian Auffhammer. (2014). "Pounds that kill: The external costs of vehicle weight." *Review of Economic Studies*, **81**(2): 535–571.

Anderson, Soren T., and Richard G. Newell. (2004). "Information programs for technology adoption: The case of energy-efficiency audits." *Resource and Energy Economics*, **26**(1): 27–50.

Anderson, Soren T., Ryan Kellogg, and James M. Sallee. (2013). "What do consumers believe about future gasoline prices?" *Journal of Environmental Economics and Management*, **66**(3): 383–403.

Ansar, Jasmin, and Roger Sparks. (2009). "The experience curve, option value, and the energy paradox." *Energy Policy*, **37**(3): 1012–1020.

Arrow, Kenneth J. (1962). "The economic implications of learning by doing." *Review of Economic Studies*, **29**(3): 155–173.

Attari, Shahzeen Z., Michael L. DeKay, Cliff I. Davidson, and Wändi Bruine de Bruin. (2010). "Public perceptions of energy consumption and savings." *Proceedings of the National Academy of Sciences*, **107**(37): 16054–16059.

Averch, Harvey, and Leland L. Johnson. (1962). "Behavior of the firm under regulatory constraint." *American Economic Review*, **52**(5): 1052–1069.

Axsen, Jonn, Dean C. Mountain, and Mark Jaccard. (2009). "Combining stated and revealed choice research to simulate the neighbor effect: The case of hybrid-electric vehicles." *Resource and Energy Economics*, **31**(3): 221–238.

Ayres, Ian, Sophie Raseman, and Alice Shih. (2013). "Evidence from two large field experiments that peer comparison feedback can reduce residential energy usage." *Journal of Law, Economics, and Organization*, **29**(5): 992–1022.

Baird, Sarah J., Aislinn Bohren, Craig McIntosh, and Berk Özler. (2014). "Designing experiments to measure spillover effects." Penn Institute for Economic Research Working Paper 14-006.

Baker, Erin. (2012). "Option value and the diffusion of energy efficient products." *Energy Journal*, **33**(4): 49–59.

Banerjee, Abhijit V. (1992). "A simple model of herd behavior." *Quarterly Journal of Economics*, **107**(3): 797–817.

Benkard, C. Lanier. (2004). "A dynamic analysis of the market for wide-bodied commercial aircraft." *Review of Economic Studies*, **71**(3): 581–611.

Bento, Antonio M., Shanjun Li, and Kevin Roth. (2012). "Is there an energy paradox in fuel economy? A note on the role of consumer heterogeneity and sorting bias." *Economics Letters*, **115**(1): 44–48.

Bento, Antonio M., Lawrence H. Goulder, Mark R. Jacobsen, and Roger H. von Haefen. (2009). "Distributional and efficiency impacts of increased US gasoline taxes." *American Economic Review*, **99**(3): 667–699.

Berndt, Ernst R., Robert S. Pindyck, and Pierre Azoulay. (2003). "Consumption externalities and diffusion in pharmaceutical markets: Antiulcer drugs." *Journal of Industrial Economics*, **51**(2): 243–270.

Berry, Linda G., and Michael B. Gettings. (1998). "Realization rates of the National Energy Audit." Prepared for the Thermal Performance of the Exterior Envelopes of Buildings VII Conference, Clearwater Beach FL, December 7–11.

Berry, Steven T., and Joel Waldfogel. (2001). "Do mergers increase product variety? Evidence from radio broadcasting." *Quarterly Journal of Economics*, **116**(3): 1009–1025.

Berry, Steven T., and Joel Waldfogel. (2010). "Product quality and market size." *Journal of Industrial Economics*, **58**(1): 1–31.

Berry, Steven T., James Levinsohn, and Ariel Pakes. (1995). "Automobile prices in market equilibrium." *Econometrica*, **63**(4): 841–890.

Berry, Steven T., Samuel Kortum, and Ariel Pakes. (1996). "Environmental change and hedonic cost functions for automobiles." *Proceedings of the National Academy of Sciences*, **93**(23): 12731–12738.

Blasnik, Michael. (1990). "Attic insulation performance, air leakage, and ventilation: Measured results in flat roof rowhouses." ACEEE 1990 Summer Study on Energy Efficiency in Buildings Final Report.

Bloom, Nicholas, Benn Eifert, Aprajit Mahajan, David McKenzie, and John Roberts. (2013). "Does management matter? Evidence from India." *Quarterly Journal of Economics*, **128**(1): 1–51.

Blumstein, Carl, Betsy Krieg, Lee Schipper, and Carl York. (1980). "Overcoming social and institutional barriers to energy conservation." *Energy*, **5**(4): 355–371.

Bordalo, Pedro, Nicola Gennaioli, and Andrei Shleifer. (2013). "Salience and consumer choice." *Journal of Political Economy*, **121**(5): 803–843.

Borenstein, Severin. (2005). "The long-run efficiency of real-time electricity pricing." *Energy Journal*, **26**(3): 93–116.

Borenstein, Severin. (2012). "The redistributional impact of nonlinear electricity pricing." *American Economic Journal: Economic Policy*, **4**(3): 56–90.

Borenstein, Severin, and Lucas W. Davis. (2012). "The equity and efficiency of two-part tariffs in U.S. natural gas markets." *Journal of Law and Economics*, **55**(1): 75–128.

Boyes, William J. (1976). "An empirical examination of the Averch-Johnson effect." *Economic Inquiry*, **14**(1): 23–35.

Bradford, David, Charles Courtemanche, Garth Heutel, Patrick McAlvanah, and Christopher Ruhm. (2014). "Time preferences and consumer behavior." National Bureau of Economic Research Working Paper 20320.

Brounen, Dirk, and Nils Kok. (2011). "On the economics of energy labels in the housing market." *Journal of Environmental Economics and Management*, **62**(2): 166–179.

Busse, Meghan R., Christopher R. Knittel, and Florian Zettelmeyer. (2013). "Are consumers myopic? Evidence from new and used car purchases." *American Economic Review*, **103**(1): 220–256.

Caird, Sally, Robin Roy, and Horace Herring. (2008). "Improving the energy performance of UK households: Results from surveys of consumer adoption and use of low- and zero-carbon technologies." *Energy Efficiency*, **1**(2): 149–166.

Camilleri, Adrian R., and Richard P. Larrick. (2014). "Metric and scale design as choice architecture tools." *Journal of Public Policy and Marketing*, **33**(1): 108–125.

Carrico, Amanda R., and Manuel Riemer. (2011). "Motivating energy conservation in the workplace: An evaluation of the use of group-level feedback and peer education." *Journal of Environmental Psychology*, **31**(1): 1–13.

Case, Anne C., and Lawrence F. Katz. (1991). "The company you keep: The effects of family and neighborhood on disadvantaged youths." National Bureau of Economic Research Working Paper 3705.

Chetty, Raj, Adam Looney, and Kory Kroft. (2009). "Salience and taxation: Theory and evidence." *American Economic Review*, **99**(4): 1145–1177.

Chetty, Raj, John N. Friedman, Søren Leth-Petersen, Torben Heien Nielsen, and Tore Olsen. (2014). "Active vs. passive decisions and crowd-out in retirement savings accounts: Evidence from Denmark." *Quarterly Journal of Economics*, **129**(3): 1141–1219.

Choi, Jay Pil. (1997). "Herd behavior, the 'penguin effect,' and the suppression of informational diffusion: An analysis of informational externalities and payoff interdependency." *RAND Journal of Economics*, **28**(3): 407–425.

Choi, Seok Joon, and Sangsin Kim. (2012). "Why do landlords include utilities in rent? Evidence from the 2000 Housing Discrimination Study (HDS) and the 2002 American Housing Survey (AHS)." *Journal of Housing Economics*, **21**(1): 28–40.

Cicala, Steve. (2015). "When does regulation distort costs? Lessons from fuel procurement in US electricity generation." *American Economic Review*, **105**(1): 411–444.

Clements, Benedict, *et al.* (2013). *Energy Subsidy Reform: Lessons and Implications*. Washington, DC: International Monetary Fund.

Coase, Ronald H. (1946). "The marginal cost controversy." *Economica*, **13**(51): 169–182.

Conley, Timothy G., and Christopher R. Udry. (2010). "Learning about a new technology: Pineapple in Ghana." *American Economic Review*, **100**(1): 35–69.

Conlisk, John. (1996). "Why bounded rationality?" *Journal of Economic Literature*, **34**(2): 669–700.

Coscelli, Andrea, and Matthew Shum. (2004). "An empirical model of learning and patient spillovers in new drug entry." *Journal of Econometrics*, **122**(2): 213–246.

Costa, Dora L., and Matthew E. Kahn. (2013). "Energy conservation 'nudges' and environmentalist ideology: Evidence from a randomized residential electricity field experiment." *Journal of the European Economic Association*, **11**(3): 680–702.

Crawford, Gregory S., and Matthew Shum. (2005). "Uncertainty and learning in pharmaceutical demand." *Econometrica*, **73**(4): 1137–1173.

Davis, Lucas W. (2012). "Evaluating the slow adoption of energy efficient investments: Are renters less likely to have energy efficient appliances?" In Don Fullerton and Catherine Wolfram, Eds.. *The Design and Implementation of US Climate Policy*, 301–318. Chicago and London: University of Chicago Press.

Davis, Lucas W., and Erich Muehlegger. (2010). "Do Americans consume too little natural gas? An empirical test of marginal cost pricing." *RAND Journal of Economics*, **41**(4): 791–810.

Davis, Lucas W., and Gilbert E. Metcalf. (2014). "Does better information lead to better choices? Evidence from energy-efficiency labels." National Bureau of Economic Research Working Paper 20720.

Davis, Lucas W., Alan Fuchs, and Paul Gertler. (2014). "Cash for coolers: Evaluating a large-scale appliance replacement program in Mexico." *American Economic Journal: Economic Policy*, **6**(4): 207–238.

De Almeida, Edmar Luiz Fagundes. (1998). "Energy efficiency and the limits of market forces: The example of the electric motor market in France." *Energy Policy*, **26**(8): 643–653.

DeCanio, Stephen J. (1993). "Barriers within firms to energy-efficient investments." *Energy Policy*, **21**(9): 906–914.

DellaVigna, Stefano. (2009). "Psychology and economics: Evidence from the field." *Journal of Economic Literature*, **47**(2): 315–372.

DellaVigna, Stefano, and Ulrike Malmendier. (2006). "Paying not to go to the gym." *American Economic Review*, **96**(3): 694–719.

Diederen, Paul, Frank van Tongeren, and Hennie van der Veen. (2003). "Returns on investments in energy-saving technologies under energy price uncertainty in Dutch greenhouse horticulture." *Environmental and Resource Economics*, **24**(4): 379–394.

Dixit, Avinash K., and Robert S. Pindyck. (1994). *Investment under Uncertainty*, Princeton and Oxford: Princeton University Press.

Dubin, Jeffrey A., and Daniel L. McFadden. (1984). "An econometric analysis of residential electric appliance holdings and consumption." *Econometrica*, **52**(2): 345–362.

Dubin, Jeffrey A., and Steven E. Henson. (1988). "An engineering/econometric analysis of seasonal energy demand and conservation in the Pacific Northwest." *Journal of Business and Economic Statistics*, **6**(1): 121–134.

Dubin, Jeffrey A., Allen K. Miedema, and Ram V. Chandran. (1986). "Price effects of energy-efficient technologies: A study of residential demand for heating and cooling." *RAND Journal of Economics*, **17**(3): 310–325.

Duflo, Esther, and Emmanuel Saez. (2002). "Participation and investment decisions in a retirement plan: The influence of colleagues' choices." *Journal of Public Economics*, **85**(1): 121–148.

Eichholtz, Piet, Nils Kok, and John M. Quigley. (2010). "Doing well by doing good? Green office buildings." *American Economic Review*, **100**(5): 2492–2509.

Eichholtz, Piet, Nils Kok, and John M. Quigley. (2013). "The economics of green building." *Review of Economics and Statistics*, **95**(1): 50–63.

Emerick, Kyle. (2014). "The efficiency of trading in social networks: Experimental measures from India." UC Berkeley. Unpublished.

Fama, Eugene F., and Kenneth R. French. (2004). "The Capital Asset Pricing Model: Theory and evidence." *Journal of Economic Perspectives*, **18**(3): 25–46.

Faruqui, Ahmad, and Sanem Sergici. (2011). "Dynamic pricing of electricity in the mid-Atlantic region: Econometric results from the Baltimore Gas and Electric Company experiment." *Journal of Regulatory Economics*, **40**(1): 82–109.

Fischer, Carolyn. (2010). "Imperfect competition, consumer behavior, and the provision of fuel efficiency in light-duty vehicles." Resources for the Future Discussion Paper 10-60.

Fisher, Anthony C., and Michael H. Rothkopf. (1989). "Market failure and energy policy: A rationale for selective conservation." *Energy Policy*, **17**(4): 397–406.

Fleiter, Tobias, Joachim Schleich, and Ploypleарn Ravivanpong. (2012). "Adoption of energy-efficiency measures in SMEs — an empirical analysis based on energy audit data from Germany." *Energy Policy*, **51**: 863–875.

Foster, Andrew D., and Mark R. Rosenzweig. (1995). "Learning by doing and learning from others: Human capital and technical change in agriculture." *Journal of Political Economy*, **103**(6): 1176–1209.

Foster, Andrew D., and Mark R. Rosenzweig. (2010). "Microeconomics of technology adoption." *Annual Review of Economics*, **2**: 395–424.

Fowlie, Meredith. (2010). "Emissions trading, electricity restructuring, and investment in pollution abatement." *American Economic Review*, **100**(3): 837–869.

Fowlie, Meredith, Michael Greenstone, and Catherine Wolfram. (2015a). "Are the non-monetary costs of energy efficiency investments large? Understanding low take-up of a free energy efficiency program." *American Economic Review*, **105**(5): 201–204.

Fowlie, Meredith, Michael Greenstone, and Catherine Wolfram. (2015b). "Do energy efficiency investments deliver? Evidence from the Weatherization Assistance Program." National Bureau of Economic Research Working Paper 21331.

Gabaix, Xavier. (2014). "A sparsity-based model of bounded rationality." *Quarterly Journal of Economics*, **129**(4): 1661–1710.

Gabaix, Xavier, David Laibson, Guillermo Moloche, and Stephen Weinberg. (2006). "Costly information acquisition: Experimental analysis of a boundedly rational model." *American Economic Review*, **96**(4): 1043–1068.

Gately, Dermot. (1980). "Individual discount rates and the purchase and utilization of energy-using durables: Comment." *Bell Journal of Economics*, **11**(1): 373–374.

Gilbert, Richard J., and David M. Newbery. (1994). "The dynamic efficiency of regulatory constitutions." *RAND Journal of Economics*, **25**(4): 538–554.

Gillingham, Kenneth, and Karen Palmer. (2014). "Bridging the energy efficiency gap: Policy insights from economic theory and empirical evidence." *Review of Environmental Economics and Policy*, **8**(1): 18–38.

Gillingham, Kenneth, Matthew Harding, and David Rapson. (2012). "Split incentives in residential energy consumption." *Energy Journal*, **33**(2): 37–62.

Gillingham, Kenneth, Richard G. Newell, and Karen Palmer. (2009). "Energy efficiency economics and policy." *Annual Review of Resource Economics*, **1**: 597–620.

Giraudet, Louis-Gaëtan, and Sébastien Houde. (2014). "Double moral hazard and the energy efficiency gap." Evidence for Action on Energy and Efficiency (E2e) Working Paper 009.

Goldberg, Pinelopi Koujianou. (1998). "The effects of the Corporate Average Fuel Efficiency Standards in the US." *Journal of Industrial Economics*, **46**(1): 1–33.

Graff Zivin, Joshua S., Matthew J. Kotchen, and Erin T. Mansur. (2014). "Spatial and temporal heterogeneity of marginal emissions: Implications for electric cars and other electricity-shifting policies." *Journal of Economic Behavior and Organization*, **107**(Part A): 248–268.

Granade, Hannah Choi, Jon Creyts, Anton Derkach, Philip Farese, Scott Nyquist, and Ken Ostrowski. (2009). "Unlocking energy efficiency in the U.S. economy." McKinsey & Company.

Greene, David L. (2010). "How customers value fuel economy: A literature review." U.S. Environmental Protection Agency EPA-420-R-10-008.

Greene, David L., David H. Evans, and John Hiestand. (2013). "Survey evidence on the willingness of U.S. consumers to pay for automotive fuel economy." *Energy Policy*, **61**: 1539–1550.

Greening, Lorna A., David L. Greene, and Carmen Difiglio. (2000). "Energy efficiency and consumption — the rebound effect — a survey." *Energy Policy*, **28**(6–7): 389–401.

Griliches, Zvi. (1957). "Hybrid corn: An exploration in the economics of technological change." *Econometrica*, **25**(4): 501–522.

Griliches, Zvi. (1992). "The search for R&D spillovers." *Scandinavian Journal of Economics*, **94**(Supplement): S29–S47.

Grubb, Michael D. (2009). "Selling to overconfident consumers." *American Economic Review*, **99**(5): 1770–1807.

Hall, Bronwyn H., and Nathan Rosenberg, Eds. (2010). *Handbook of the Economics of Innovation: Volume 1*. Amsterdam and Boston: Elsevier, North-Holland.

Hall, Bronwyn H., Jacques Mairesse, and Pierre Mohnen. (2010). "Measuring the returns to R&D." In Bronwyn H. Hall and Nathan Rosenberg Eds., *Handbook of the Economics of Innovation: Volume 1*, 1033–1082. Amsterdam and Boston: Elsevier, North-Holland.

Hall, Robert E. (1997). "The inkjet aftermarket: An economic analysis." Available at: https://web.stanford.edu/~rehall/Inkjet%20Aftermarket%201997.pdf.

Harding, Matthew, and Alice Hsiaw. (2014). "Goal setting and energy conservation." *Journal of Economic Behavior and Organization*, **107**(Part A): 209–227.

Hardisty, David J., Kirstin C. Appelt, and Elke U. Weber. (2013). "Good or bad, we want it now: Fixed-cost present bias for gains and losses explains magnitude asymmetries in intertemporal choice." *Journal of Behavioral Decision Making*, **26**(4): 348–361.

Hassett, Kevin A., and Gilbert E. Metcalf. (1993). "Energy conservation investment: Do consumers discount the future correctly?" *Energy Policy*, **21**(6): 710–716.

Hausman, Jerry A. (1979). "Individual discount rates and the purchase and utilization of energy-using durables." *Bell Journal of Economics*, **10**(1): 33–54.

Hausman, Jerry A., and Paul L. Joskow. (1982). "Evaluating the costs and benefits of appliance efficiency standards." *American Economic Review*, **72**(2): 220–225.

Heath, Chip, Richard P. Larrick, and George Wu. (1999). "Goals as reference points." *Cognitive Psychology*, **38**(1): 79–109.

Helfand, Gloria, and Ann Wolverton. (2011). "Evaluating the consumer response to fuel economy: A review of the literature." *International Review of Environmental and Resource Economics*, **5**(2): 103–146.

Heutel, Garth, and Erich Muehlegger. (2015). "Consumer learning and hybrid vehicle adoption." *Environmental and Resource Economics*, **62**(1): 125–161.

Hirst, Eric. (1986). "Actual energy savings after retrofit: Electrically heated homes in the Pacific Northwest." *Energy*, **11**(3): 299–308.

Hoffman, Ian M., *et al.* (2015). "The total cost of saving electricity through utility customer-funded energy efficiency programs: Estimates at the national, state, sector and program level." Berkeley Lab Technical Brief.

Hossain, Tanjim, and John Morgan. (2006). "...Plus shipping and handling: Revenue (non) equivalence in field experiments on eBay." *Advances in Economic Analysis and Policy*, **5**(2).

Houde, Sébastien. (2014a). "Bunching with the stars: How firms respond to environmental certification." Unpublished.

Houde, Sébastien. (2014b). "How consumers respond to environmental certification and the value of energy information." National Bureau of Economic Research Working Paper 20019.

Houde, Sébastien, and Joseph E. Aldy. (2014). "Belt and suspenders and more: The incremental impact of energy efficiency subsidies in the presence of existing policy instruments." National Bureau of Economic Research Working Paper 20541.

Howarth, Richard B., and Bo Andersson. (1993). "Market barriers to energy efficiency." *Energy Economics*, **15**(4): 262–272.

Howarth, Richard B., Brent M. Haddad, and Bruce Paton. (2000). "The economics of energy efficiency: Insights from voluntary participation programs." *Energy Policy*, **28**(6–7): 477–486.

Howell, Sabrina T. (2017). "Financing innovation: Evidence from R&D grants." *American Economic Review*, **107**(4): 1136–1164.

Huntington, Hillard G. (2011). "The policy implications of energy-efficiency cost curves." *Energy Journal*, **32**(1): 7–21.

International Energy Agency. (2007). *Mind the Gap: Quantifying Principal-Agent Problems in Energy Efficiency*, Paris: IEA Publications.

Irwin, Douglas A., and Peter J. Klenow. (1994). "Learning-by-doing spillovers in the semiconductor industry." *Journal of Political Economy*, **102**(6): 1200–1227.

Ito, Koichiro. (2014). "Do consumers respond to marginal or average price? Evidence from nonlinear electricity pricing." *American Economic Review*, **104**(2): 537–563.

Ito, Koichiro, and James M. Sallee. (2014). "The economics of attribute-based regulation: Theory and evidence from fuel-economy standards." National Bureau of Economic Research Working Paper 20500.

Ito, Koichiro, Takanori Ida, and Makoto Tanaka. (2015). "The persistence of moral suasion and economic incentives: Field experimental evidence from energy demand." National Bureau of Economic Research Working Paper 20910.

Jaffe, Adam B., and Robert N. Stavins. (1994a). "The energy-efficiency gap: What does it mean?" *Energy Policy*, **22**(10): 804–810.

Jaffe, Adam B., and Robert N. Stavins. (1994b). "The energy paradox and the diffusion of conservation technology." *Resource and Energy Economics*, **16**(2): 91–122.

Jaffe, Adam B., and Robert N. Stavins. (1995). "Dynamic incentives of environmental regulations: The effects of alternative policy instruments on technology diffusion." *Journal of Environmental Economics and Management*, **29**(3): S43–S63.

Jaffe, Adam B., Richard G. Newell, and Robert N. Stavins. (2002). "Environmental policy and technological change." *Environmental and Resource Economics*, **22**(1–2): 41–70.

Jaffe, Adam B., Richard G. Newell, and Robert N. Stavins. (2005). "A tale of two market failures: Technology and environmental policy." *Ecological Economics*, **54**(2–3): 164–174.

Janakiraman, Ramkumar, Catarina Sismeiro, and Shantanu Dutta. (2009). "Perception spillovers across competing brands: A disaggregate model of how and when." *Journal of Marketing Research*, **46**(4): 467–481.

Jessoe, Katrina, and David Rapson. (2014). "Knowledge is (less) power: Experimental evidence from residential energy use." *American Economic Review*, **104**(4): 1417–1438.

Jessoe, Katrina, David Rapson, and Jeremy B. Smith. (2014). "Towards understanding the role of price in residential electricity choices: Evidence from a natural experiment." *Journal of Economic Behavior and Organization*, **107**(Part A): 191–208.

Joskow, Paul L., and Catherine D. Wolfram. (2012). "Dynamic pricing of electricity." *American Economic Review*, **102**(3): 381–385.

Joskow, Paul L., and Donald B. Marron. (1993). "What does utility-subsidized energy efficiency really cost?" *Science*, **260**(5106): 281–370.

Jovanovic, Boyan. (1982). "Truthful disclosure of information." *Bell Journal of Economics*, **13**(1): 36–44.

Kahn, Matthew E., and Nils Kok. (2014). "The capitalization of green labels in the California housing market." *Regional Science and Urban Economics*, **47**: 25–34.

Kahneman, Daniel, and Amos Tversky. (1979). "Prospect theory: An analysis of decision under risk." *Econometrica*, **47**(2): 263–292.

Kamien, Morton, and Nancy L. Schwartz. (1982). *Market Structure and Innovation.* Cambridge and New York: Cambridge University Press.

Kellogg, Ryan. (2014). "The effect of uncertainty on investment: Evidence from Texas oil drilling." *American Economic Review*, **104**(6): 1698–1734.

Klier, Thomas, and Joshua Linn. (2012). "New-vehicle characteristics and the cost of the Corporate Average Fuel Economy Standard." *RAND Journal of Economics*, **43**(1): 186–213.

Kőszegi, Botond, and Matthew Rabin. (2006). "A model of reference-dependent preferences." *Quarterly Journal of Economics*, **121**(4): 1133–1165.

Laibson, David. (1997). "Golden eggs and hyperbolic discounting." *Quarterly Journal of Economics*, **112**(2): 443–478.

Langer, Ashley, and Nathan H. Miller. (2013). "Automakers' short-run responses to changing gasoline prices." *Review of Economics and Statistics*, **95**(4): 1198–1211.

Larrick, Richard P., and Jack B. Soll. (2008). "The MPG illusion." *Science*, **320**(5883): 1593–1594.

Levinson, Arik, and Scott Niemann. (2004). "Energy use by apartment tenants when landlords pay for utilities." *Resource and Energy Economics*, **26**(1): 51–75.

Levitt, Steven D., John A. L., and Chad Syverson. (2013). "Toward an understanding of learning by doing: Evidence from an automobile assembly plant." *Journal of Political Economy*, **121**(4): 643–681.

Lewis, Gregory. (2011). "Asymmetric information: Adverse selection and online disclosure: The case of eBay Motors." *American Economic Review*, **101**(4): 1535–1546.

Lieberman, Marvin B. (1984). "The learning curve and pricing in the chemical processing industries." *RAND Journal of Economics*, **15**(2): 213–228.

Lim, Claire S. H., and Ali Yurukoglu. (2015). "Dynamic natural monopoly regulation: Time inconsistency, moral hazard, and political environments." Available at: http://web.stanford.edu/~ayurukog/main_infrastructure.pdf.

Loewenstein, George, and Richard H. Thaler. (1989). "Anomalies: Intertemporal choice." *Journal of Economic Perspectives*, **3**(4): 181–193.

Löfgren, Åsa, Katrin Millock, and Céline Nauges. (2008). "The effect of uncertainty on pollution abatement investments: Measuring hurdle rates for Swedish industry." *Resource and Energy Economics*, **30**(4): 475–491.

Manski, Charles F. (1993a). "Dynamic choice in social settings: Learning from the experiences of others." *Journal of Econometrics*, **58**(1–2): 121–136.

Manski, Charles F. (1993b). "Identification of endogenous social effects: The reflection problem." *Review of Economic Studies*, **60**(3): 531–542.

Manski, Charles F. (2004). "Measuring expectations." *Econometrica*, **72**(5): 1329–1376.

Maruejols, Lucie, and Denise Young. (2011). "Split incentives and energy efficiency in Canadian multi-family dwellings." *Energy Policy*, **39**(6): 3655–3668.

Mau, Paulus, Jimena Eyzaguirre, Mark Jaccard, Colleen Collins-Dodd, and Kenneth Tiedemann. (2008). "The 'neighbor effect': Simulating dynamics in consumer preferences for new vehicle technologies." *Ecological Economics*, **68**(1–2): 504–516.

McDonald, Robert, and Daniel Siegel. (1986). "The value of waiting to invest." *Quarterly Journal of Economics*, **101**(4): 707–727.

Metcalf, Gilbert E. (1994). "Economics and rational conservation policy." *Energy Policy*, **22**(10): 819–825.

Metcalf, Gilbert E., and Donald Rosenthal. (1995). "The 'new' view of investment decisions and public policy analysis: An application to green lights and cold refrigerators." Journal of Policy Analysis and Management. **14**(4): 517–531.

Metcalf, Gilbert E., and Kevin A. Hassett. (1999). "Measuring the energy savings from home improvement investments: Evidence from monthly billing data." *Review of Economics and Statistics*, **81**(3): 516–528.

Muller, Nicholas Z., and Robert Mendelsohn. (2009). "Efficient pollution regulation: Getting the prices right." *American Economic Review*, **99**(5): 1714–1739.

Munley, Vincent G., Larry W. Taylor, and John P. Formby. (1990). "Electricity demand in multi-family, renter-occupied residences." *Southern Economic Journal*, **57**(1): 178–194.

Murphy, Rose, and Mark Jaccard. (2011). "Energy efficiency and the cost of GHG abatement: A comparison of bottom-up and hybrid models for the US." *Energy Policy*, **39**(11): 7146–7155.

Murtishaw, Scott, and Jayant Sathaye. (2006). "Quantifying the effect of the principal-agent problem on US residential energy use." Lawrence Berkeley National Laboratory 59773.

Myers, Erica. (2015). "Asymmetric information in residential rental markets: Implications for the energy efficiency gap." Energy Institute at Haas Working Paper 246R.

Nadel, Steve, and Kenneth Keating. (1991). "Engineering estimates vs. impact evaluation results: How do they compare and why?" American Council for an Energy-Efficient Economy Research Report U915.

Narayanan, Sridhar, and Harikesh S. Nair. (2013). "Estimating causal installed-based effects: A bias-correction approach." *Journal of Marketing Research*, **50**(1): 70–94.

National Research Council. (2010). *Hidden Costs of Energy: Unpriced Consequences of Energy Production and Use*. Washington, DC: National Academies Press.

Naughton, Michael C. (1986). "The efficiency and equity consequences of two-part tariffs in electricity pricing." *Review of Economics and Statistics*, **68**(3): 406–414.

Newell, Richard G., and Juha Siikamäki. (2014). "Nudging energy efficiency behavior: The role of information labels." *Journal of the Association of Environmental and Resource Economists*, **1**(4): 555–598.

Newell, Richard G., and Juha Siikamäki. (2015). "Individual time preferences and energy efficiency." *American Economic Review*, **105**(5): 196–200.

Newell, Richard G., Adam B. J., and Robert N. Stavins. (1999). "The induced innovation hypothesis and energy-saving technological change." *Quarterly Journal of Economics*, **114**(3): 941–975.

Nordhaus, William. (2011). "Designing a friendly space for technological change to slow global warming." *Energy Economics*, **33**(4): 665–673.

O'Donoghue, Ted, and Matthew Rabin. (2006). "Optimal sin taxes." *Journal of Public Economics*, **90**(10–11): 1825–1849.

Ostertag, Katrin. (2003). *No-regret Potentials in Energy Conservation: An Analysis of Their Relevance, Size and Determinants*. Heidelberg and New York: Physica-Verlag.

Pakes, Ariel, Steven Berry, and James A. Levinsohn. (1993). "Applications and limitations of some recent advances in empirical industrial organization: Price indexes and the analysis of environmental change." *American Economic Review*, **83**(2): 240–246.

Palmer, Karen L., Margaret A. Walls, and Todd Gerarden. (2012). "Borrowing to save energy: An assessment of energy-efficiency financing programs." Resources for the Future Report.

Palmer, Karen L., Margaret A. Walls, Hal Gordon, and Todd Gerarden. (2013). "Assessing the energy-efficiency information gap: Results from a survey of home energy auditors." *Energy Efficiency*, **6**(2): 271–292.

Papineau, Maya. (2015). "Energy codes and the landlord-tenant problem." Carleton Economic Paper 15-03.

Parry, Ian W. H., and Kenneth A. Small. (2005). "Does Britain or the United States have the right gasoline tax?" *American Economic Review*, **95**(4): 1276–1289.

Parry, Ian W. H., Margaret Walls, and Winston Harrington. (2007). "Automobile externalities and policies." *Journal of Economic Literature*, **45**(2): 373–399.

Petrin, Amil. (2002). "Quantifying the benefits of new products: The case of the minivan." *Journal of Political Economy*, **110**(4): 705–729.

Phillips, Yvonne. (2012). "Landlords versus tenants: Information asymmetry and mismatched preferences for home energy efficiency." *Energy Policy*, **45**: 112–121.

Popp, David, Richard G. Newell, and Adam B. Jaffe. (2010). "Energy, the environment, and technological change." In Bronwyn H. Hall and Nathan Rosenberg Eds., *Handbook of the Economics of Innovation: Volume 2*, 873–937. Amsterdam and Boston: Elsevier, North-Holland.

Price, Michael. (2015). "Using field experiments to address environmental externalities and resource scarcity: Major lessons learned and new directions for future research." National Bureau of Economic Research Working Paper 20870.

Puller, Steven L., and Jeremy West. (2013). "Efficient retail pricing in electricity and natural gas markets." *American Economic Review*, **103**(3): 350–355.

Rapson, David. (2014). "Durable goods and long-run electricity demand: Evidence from air conditioner purchase behavior." *Journal of Environmental Economics and Management*, **68**(1): 141–160.

Rohdin, P., and P. Thollander. (2006). "Barriers to and driving forces for energy efficiency in the non-energy intensive manufacturing industry in Sweden." *Energy*, **31**(12): 1836–1844.

Sallee, James M. (2014). "Rational inattention and energy efficiency." *Journal of Law and Economics*, **57**(3): 781–820.

Sallee, James M., and Joel Slemrod. (2012). "Car notches: Strategic automaker responses to fuel economy policy." *Journal of Public Economics*, **96**(11–12): 981–999.

Sallee, James M., Sarah West, and Wei Fan. (2015). "Do consumers recognize the value of fuel economy? Evidence from used car prices and gasoline price fluctuations." National Bureau of Economic Research Working Paper 21441.

Sanstad, Alan H., Carl Blumstein, and Steven E. Stoft. (1995). "How high are option values in energy-efficiency investments?" *Energy Policy*, **23**(9): 739–743.

Sanstad, Alan H., and Richard B. Howarth. (1994). "Consumer rationality and energy efficiency." *Proceedings of the ACEEE*, **1**: 175–183.

Sanstad, Alan H., W. Michael Hanemann, and Maximilian Auffhammer. (2006). "End-use energy efficiency in a 'post-carbon' California economy: Policy issues and research frontiers." In W. Michael Hanemann and Alexander E. Farrell Eds., *Managing Greenhouse Gas Emissions in California*, 6-1–6-32. Berkeley: California Climate Change Center.

Schleich, Joachim. (2009). "Barriers to energy efficiency: A comparison across the German commercial and services sector." *Ecological Economics*, **68**(7): 2150–2159.

Schultz, P. Wesley, Jessica M. Nolan, Robert B. Cialdini, Noah J. Goldstein, and Vladas Griskevicius. (2007). "The constructive, destructive, and reconstructive power of social norms." *Psychological Science*, **18**(5): 429–434.

Sebold, Frederick D., and Eric W. Fox. (1985). "Realized savings from residential conservation activity." *Energy Journal*, **6**(2): 73–88.

Sorrell, Steve. (2004). "Understanding barriers to energy efficiency." In Steve Sorrell, Eoin O'Malley, Joachim Schleich, and Sue Scott (Eds.). *The Economics of Energy Efficiency: Barriers to Cost-Effective Investment*, 25–93. Cheltenham: Edward Elgar.

Shaked, Avner, and John Sutton. (1987). "Product differentiation and industrial structure." *Journal of Industrial Economics*, **36**(2): 131–146.

Shama, Avraham. (1983). "Energy conservation in US buildings: Solving the high potential/low adoption paradox from a behavioural perspective." *Energy Policy*, **11**(2): 148–167.

Sharma, Dhruv N. (2011). "Economic efficiency and distributional impacts of policies for increasing U.S. residential insulation." Ph.D. dissertation, Stanford University.

Sorrell, Steve, John Dimitropoulos, and Matt Sommerville. (2009). "Empirical estimates of the direct rebound effect: A review." *Energy Policy*, **37**(4): 1356–1371.

Sorrell, Steve, Eoin O'Malley, Joachim Schleich, and Sue Scott. (2004). "Standing on a burning platform: Barriers to energy efficiency in the UK brewing industry." In *The Economics of Energy Efficiency: Barriers to Cost-Effective Investment*. Cheltenham, UK and Northampton, MA: Edward Elgar Publishing.

Spann, Robert M. (1974). "Rate of return regulation and efficiency in production: An empirical test of the Averch-Johnson thesis." *Bell Journal of Economics and Management Science*, **5**(1): 38–52.

Spence, A. Michael. (1975). "Monopoly, quality, and regulation." *Bell Journal of Economics*, **6**(2): 417–429.

Spence, A. Michael. (1976). "Product selection, fixed costs, and monopolistic competition." *Review of Economic Studies*, **43**(2): 217–235.

Spence, A. Michael. (1981). "The learning curve and competition." *Bell Journal of Economics*, **12**(1): 49–70.

Suri, Tavneet. (2011). "Selection and comparative advantage in technology adoption." *Econometrica*, **79**(1): 159–209.

Sutherland, Ronald J. (1991). "Market barriers to energy-efficiency investments." *Energy Journal*, **12**(3): 15–34.

Ternes, Mark P., and Michael B. Gettings. (2008). "Analyses to verify and improve the accuracy of the manufactured home energy audit (MHEA)." Available at: http://weatherization.ornl.gov/pdfs/ORNL_CON-506.pdf.

Thaler, Richard. (1985). "Mental accounting and consumer choice." *Marketing Science*, **4**(3): 199–214.

Thollander, Patrik, and Mikael Ottosson. (2008). "An energy efficient Swedish pulp and paper industry — exploring barriers to and driving forces for cost-effective energy efficiency investments." *Energy Efficiency*, **1**(1): 21–34.

Thollander, Patrik, Maria Danestig, and Patrik Rohdin.(2007). "Energy policies for increased industrial energy efficiency: Evaluation of a local energy programme for manufacturing SMEs." *Energy Policy*, **35**(11): 5774–5783.

Thornton, Rebecca Achee and Peter Thompson. (2001). "Learning from experience and learning from others: An exploration of learning and spillovers in wartime shipbuilding." *American Economic Review*, **91**(5): 1350–1368.

Tietenberg, Tom. (2009). "Reflections — energy efficiency policy: Pipe dream or pipeline to the future?" *Review of Environmental Economics and Policy*, **3**(2): 304–320.

Train, Kenneth. (1985). "Discount rates in consumers' energy-related decisions: A review of the literature." *Energy*, **10**(12): 1243–1253.

Trianni, A., and E. Cagno. (2012). "Dealing with barriers to energy efficiency and SMEs: Some empirical evidences." *Energy*, **37**(1): 494–504.

Turrentine, Thomas S., and Kenneth S. Kurani. (2007). "Car buyers and fuel economy?" *Energy Policy*, **35**(2): 1213–1223.

Tversky, Amos, and Daniel Kahneman. (1981). "The framing of decisions and the psychology of choice." *Science*, **211**(4481): 453–458.

Tversky, Amos, and Daniel Kahneman. (1991). "Loss aversion in riskless choice: A reference-dependent model." *Quarterly Journal of Economics*, **106**(4): 1039–1061.

Tversky, Amos, and Daniel Kahneman. (1992). "Advances in prospect theory: Cumulative representation of uncertainty." *Journal of Risk and Uncertainty*, **5**(4): 297–323.

UK Department of Energy and Climate Change. (2013). "Removing the hassle factor associated with loft insulation: Results of a behavioural trial." Available at: https://www.gov.uk/government/uploads/system/uploads/attachment_data/file/236858/DECC_loft_clearance_trial_report_final.pdf.

Ungemach, Christoph, Adrian R. Camilleri, Eric J. Johnson, Richard P. Larrick, and Elke U. Weber. (Forthcoming). "Translated attributes as choice architecture: Aligning objectives and choices through decision signposts." *Management Science*.

US Department of Energy. (1991/1992). *National Energy Strategy: Powerful Ideas for America*, First edition. Washington, DC: US Government Printing Office.

US Environmental Protection Agency. (2015). "Learn about the fuel economy label." Available at: https://www.epa.gov/greenvehicles/learn-about-fuel-economy-label.

US Environmental Protection Agency and US Department of Transportation, National Highway Traffic Safety Administration. (2011). "Greenhouse gas emissions standards and fuel efficiency standards for medium- and heavy-duty engines and vehicles; final rule." *Federal Register*, **76**(179): 57105–57513.

Verboven, Frank. (2002). "Quality-based price discrimination and tax incidence: Evidence from gasoline and diesel cars." *RAND Journal of Economics*, **33**(2): 275–297.

Walls, Margaret, Karen Palmer, Todd Gerarden, and Xian Bak. (2013). "Is energy efficiency capitalized into home prices? Evidence from three US cities." Resources for the Future Discussion Paper 13-18.

Weber, Elke U., and Eric J. Johnson. (2009). "Mindful judgment and decision making." *Annual Review of Psychology*, **60**: 53–85.

Weber, Elke U., Eric J. Johnson, K. F. Milch, H. Chang, J.C. Brodscholl, and D. G. Goldstein. (2007). "Asymmetric discounting in intertemporal choice: A query-theory account." *Psychological Science*, **18**(6): 516–523.

West, Sarah E., and Roberton C. Williams, III. (2007). "Optimal taxation and cross-price effects on labor supply: Estimates of the optimal gas tax." *Journal of Public Economics*, **91**(3–4): 593–617.

Whitefoot, Kate S., Meredith Fowlie, and Steven J. Skerlos. (2017). "Compliance by design: Influence of acceleration trade-offs on CO_2 emissions and costs of fuel economy and greenhouse gas regulations." *Environmental Science and Technology*, **51**(18): 10307–10315.

Wood, Gavin, Rachel Ong, and Clinton McMurray. (2012). "Housing tenure, energy consumption and the split-incentive issue in Australia." *International Journal of Housing Policy*, **12**(4): 439–469.

https://doi.org/10.1142/9789811292415_0005

Chapter 5

Climate Negotiators Create an Opportunity for Scholars*

Joseph E. Aldy[†,‖] and Robert N. Stavins[†,‡,§,¶]

[†]*John F. Kennedy School of Government, Harvard University, Cambridge, MA, USA*

[‡]*Resources for the Future, Washington, DC, USA*

[§]*National Bureau of Economic Research, Cambridge, MA, USA*

[‖]*joseph_aldy@hks.harvard.edu*

[¶]*robert_stavins@harvard.edu*

The 1992 United Nations Framework Convention on Climate Change (UNFCCC) launched a process to confront risks posed by global climate change. It has led to a dichotomy between countries with serious emission-reduction responsibilities and others with no responsibilities whatsoever. This has prevented progress, but recent talks suggest the prospect for a better way forward and an openness to outside-the-box thinking. Scholars and practitioners have a new opportunity to contribute innovative proposals for a future international climate policy architecture.

---

*This chapter was originally published in *Science*, **337**(6098), 1043–1044, August 2013.

Beyond a Dichotomous Distinction

Article 3 of the 1992 UNFCCC established a key principle: "The Parties should protect the climate system … on the basis of equity and in accordance with their common but differentiated responsibilities and respective capabilities. Accordingly, the developed country Parties should take the lead. …" (United Nations, 1992a). As a result, the UNFCCC explicitly recognized that developed countries should "take immediate action" as "a first step towards comprehensive strategies" to address climate change (United Nations, 1992b). This differentiation in action dates back, in some form, at least to the 1972 Stockholm Declaration on the Human Environment and was incorporated in the 1992 Rio Declaration on Environment and Development.

In the first decision of the first Conference of the Parties (COP-1) of the UNFCCC, the global community agreed to the Berlin Mandate, which interpreted "common but differentiated responsibilities" in which "developed country Parties" (also known as Annex I countries) alone are to take on emission-reduction responsibilities. The Berlin Mandate, codified with numerical national targets and timetables for Annex I countries in the 1997 Kyoto Protocol, produced a dramatic gap between rhetoric and reality. By the time of the Berlin Mandate, non-Annex I countries' annual greenhouse gas emissions surpassed those of Annex I countries (World Resources Institute, 2012). By 2005, when the Kyoto Protocol entered into force, per capita fossil fuel carbon dioxide emissions of nearly 50 non-Annex I countries exceeded those of the Annex I country with the lowest per capita measure (United States Energy Information Administration, 2012) (see the Chart 1). Further, the six largest

Chart 1: Negotiating political architecture. Both developed and developing countries need to be engaged in emission reduction initiatives.

greenhouse gas emitters are not constrained by the Kyoto Protocol, because of lack of commitments (China, Indonesia, Brazil, and India), the nonbinding nature of its emission commitment (Russia), or failure to ratify the agreement (United States).

The dichotomous structure effectively quadruples the global cost of emission abatement necessary to stabilize atmospheric concentrations of greenhouse gases relative to a cost-minimizing scenario that includes emission abatement by all nations (Nordhaus, 2008). The Kyoto Protocol provides no means for developing countries to take on emission targets and engage in international emission trading, because some of the largest developing countries actively opposed a voluntary accession mechanism at the 1997 Kyoto negotiations. Argentina offered to take on an emission target in 1999 but could not even secure agreement to have this discussed on the negotiating agenda. Thus, the Kyoto Protocol severely limited opportunities for developed countries to leverage finance of low-cost emission abatement in developing countries (e.g., domestic cap-and-trade, fossil fuel subsidy reform, and building codes) through international emission trading under emission targets.

But prospects for change emerged in 2009. Leaders of the seventeen largest developed and developing countries, at the Major Economies

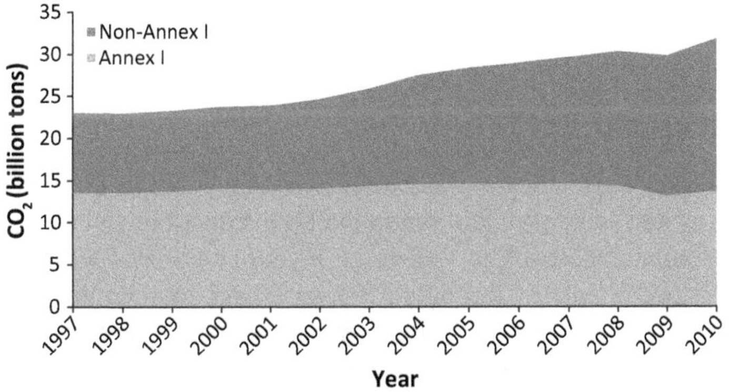

Annex I and non-Annex I: Fossil fuel carbon dioxide emissions, 1997–2010. Since the 1997 Kyoto Conference, Annex I countries' emissions of fossil fuel-based carbon dioxide have remained level while non-Annex I countries' emissions have nearly doubled and stood nearly one-third greater than developed countries' emissions in 2010. This gap is likely wider when accounting for all greenhouse gas emissions. Data from U.S. Energy Information Administration (4). See supplementary materials for details.

Forum on Energy and Climate, agreed that they would need to reduce their greenhouse gas emissions. Leaders of these economies and many more nations negotiated the Copenhagen Accord later in 2009, followed a year later by the Cancun Agreements (December 2010), which together blurred the distinction between Annex I and non-Annex I. Under Copenhagen and Cancun, developed countries pledged economy-wide emission targets, and nearly 50 developing countries pledged emission mitigation policies and actions.

An even greater departure from the Annex I/non-Annex I dichotomy took place at the most recent negotiations in Durban, South Africa, in December, 2011. At the COP-17 talks in Durban, the international community agreed to a negotiating process focused on long-term participation of all parties in the effort to mitigate greenhouse gas emissions (United Nations, 2011). The Durban Platform for Enhanced Action (DPEA) calls for a comprehensive legal regime by 2020 that essentially eliminates the Annex I versus non-Annex I distinction.

We ought not to overestimate the importance of a nonbinding agreement to reach a future agreement, especially as some developing countries have considered stepping back from this agreement. Nonetheless, this is a significant departure from the past. It is of vast potential importance, but only "potential," because just as the Kyoto Protocol's targets and timetables fulfilled the Berlin Mandate's promise, future COPs must deliver on the DPEA with a new post-Kyoto agreement by 2015.

Architectural Evolution

Many international policy architectures exist that could be consistent with the process and principles laid out in the DPEA and the UNFCCC. A top-down formulaic approach to reforming Kyoto could set 5-year emission targets for all countries through 2100 based on four equity principles (Bosetti & Frankel, 2011): "progressivity," adjusting emissions targets based on per capita income; "latecomer catch-up," helping close the gap between 1990 emissions (the Kyoto baseline) and the starting points for latecomers (e.g., Canada, China, and the United States); "equalization," aligning targets with global average per capita emissions by the end of this century (Aldy & Stavins, 2010); and an economic feasibility constraint that costs should not exceed a particular share of Gross Domestic Product.

Emissions targets for major developing countries could be set at "business-as-usual" (BAU) emissions levels but become more stringent as countries become wealthier. Keeping poor countries near BAU emissions prevents carbon leakage, an increase in emissions in one country resulting from a decrease in another country. Combining BAU targets with an international emission-trading program could provide direct economic incentive (export revenues and foreign direct investment) for developing-country participation. By taking on BAU targets, developing countries could create a new export industry by reducing emissions below BAU and exporting emission allowances to developed countries. Developing countries could fully participate without incurring prohibitive costs, addressing cost effectiveness and distributional equity concerns.

Greenhouse gas cap-and-trade systems are in place or under development in the European Union, Australia, Japan, Korea, New Zealand, California (USA), and several Canadian provinces; a global emission reduction credit scheme, the Clean Development Mechanism, has supporters in developing countries. There is interest in linking cap-and-trade systems to allow the use of allowances or credits across systems to meet compliance obligations. Linking increases liquidity and functioning of markets and can greatly reduce abatement costs (Ranson *et al.*, 2010). However, direct linkage of cap-and-trade systems will propagate certain cost-containment design elements from one system to another, so advanced harmonization could be required, akin to bilateral trade agreements that were a precursor to today's multilateral trade regime.

However, when cap-and-trade systems link with a common emission reduction–credit system (which does not have a cap, but issues credits when emissions are reduced below some agreed baseline), indirect links among cap-and-trade systems are created but without propagation of those design elements of concern. Such indirect linkages can thus achieve many of the benefits that direct links achieve but without the need for advanced harmonization. Bottom-up, indirect international linkage has begun to emerge, and may be part of the *de facto* international climate-policy architecture.

Finally, the UNFCCC regime for measurement, reporting, and verification is inadequate. For example, China's most recent greenhouse gas emissions report submitted to the UNFCCC is for the 1994 calendar year (Aldy, 2012). In contrast, under the Montreal Protocol, China has reported annual detailed ozone-depleting substances consumption inventory data over 1990–2010. A rigorous system of surveillance — of policies, actions, and outcomes — could support a more robust international climate-policy regime. Conditioning international finance on participation in surveillance could increase the transparency of and trust in the global climate regime for all participants.

The Path Ahead

The outcome of the Durban negotiations has increased the likelihood that a sound foundation for meaningful long-term action can be developed. With the DPEA, there is a mandate for change. Governments around the world need fresh ideas, and they need those ideas over the next 2 to 3 years. Indeed, they have begun to solicit such ideas as the negotiators begin to frame the implementation of the DPEA.

How can an international agreement facilitate meaningful emission mitigation in developed and developing countries while meeting the UNFCCC's principle of "common but differentiated responsibilities and respective capabilities?" How can an agreement best leverage public and private finance for investment in climate-friendly technologies and climate adaptation? How can market mechanisms broaden participation and deepen emission mitigation? How can an agreement improve transparency, improve trust, and thereby increase both participation and compliance among nations?

This is a time for innovative proposals for future international climate-policy architecture, not for incremental adjustments to the old pathway. We hope this call will be heard by researchers in universities, think tanks, and advocacy groups around the world.

References

United Nations. (1992a). United Nations Framework Convention on Climate Change, Article 3, paragraph 1. New York: UN.

United Nations. (1992b). United Nations Framework Convention on Climate Change, Preamble. New York: UN.

World Resources Institute. (2012). Climate Analysis Indicators Tool. Washington, DC: WRI. Retrieved from www.wri.org/project/cait/.

United States Energy Information Administration. (2012). International Energy Statistics. Washington, DC: U.S. Department of Energy. Retrieved from www.eia.gov/cfapps/ipdbproject/IEDIndex3.cfm.

Nordhaus, W. D. (2008). A Question of Balance. New Haven, CT: Yale University Press.

United Nations. (2011). Establishment of an Ad Hoc Working Group on the Durban Platform for Enhanced Action, Decision 1/CP.17. New York: UNFCCC.

Bosetti, V., and Frankel, J. (2011). Sustainable cooperation in global climate policy: Specific formulas and emission targets to build on Copenhagen and Cancun (Discussion Paper 2011-46). Cambridge, MA: Harvard Project on Climate Agreements, Harvard Kennedy School. Retrieved from http://belfercenter.ksg.harvard.edu/project/56/harvard_project_on_climate_agreements.html.

Aldy, J. E., and Stavins, R. N. (2010). Post-Kyoto International Climate Policy: Implementing Architectures for Agreement. New York: Cambridge University Press.

Ranson, M., Jaffe, J., and Stavins, R. (2010). *Ecological Law Quarterly*, **36**(2009): 789–808.

Aldy, J. E. (2012). Designing a Bretton Woods institution to address climate change (Working Paper). Cambridge, MA: Harvard Kennedy School. Retrieved from web.hks.harvard.edu/publications/getFile.aspx?Id=792.

Supplementary Materials

www.sciencemag.org/cgi/content/full/337/6098/1043/DC1.

Part II

Policy Instruments

https://doi.org/10.1142/9789811292415_0006

Chapter 6

The Promise and Problems of Pricing Carbon: Theory and Experience*

Joseph E. Aldy[†,‖] and Robert N. Stavins[†,‡,§,¶]

[†]*John F. Kennedy School of Government, Harvard University, Cambridge, MA, USA*

[‡]*Resources for the Future, Washington, DC, USA*

[§]*National Bureau of Economic Research, Cambridge, MA, USA*

[‖]*joseph_aldy@hks.harvard.edu*

[¶]*robert_stavins@harvard.edu*

Introduction

In a modern economy, nearly all aspects of economic activity affect greenhouse gas — in particular, carbon dioxide (CO_2) — emissions, and hence the global climate. To be effective, climate change policy must affect decisions regarding these activities. This can be done in one of three ways: (a) mandate businesses and individuals to change their behavior regarding technology choice and emissions; (b) subsidize businesses and individuals to invest in

*This chapter was originally published in *Journal of Environment & Development*, **21**(2), 152–180, 2012. DOI: 10.1177/1070496512442508.

and use lower emitting goods and services; or (c) price the greenhouse gas externality, so that decisions take account of this external cost.

By internalizing the externalities associated with CO_2 emissions, carbon pricing can promote cost-effective abatement, deliver powerful innovation incentives, and ameliorate rather than exacerbate government fiscal problems. By pricing CO_2 emissions (or, equivalently, by pricing the carbon content of the three fossil fuels — coal, petroleum, and natural gas), governments defer to private firms and individuals to find and exploit the lowest cost ways to reduce emissions and invest in the development of new technologies, processes, and ideas that could further mitigate emissions. A range of policy instruments can facilitate carbon pricing, including carbon taxes, cap-and-trade, emission reduction credits, clean energy standards, and fossil fuel subsidy reduction.

Some of these instruments have been used with success in other environmental domains as well as for pricing CO_2 emissions. The U.S. sulfur dioxide (SO_2) cap-and-trade program cut U.S. power plant SO_2 emissions more than 50 percent after 1990 and resulted in compliance costs one half of what they would have been under conventional regulatory mandates (Carlson, Burtaw, Cropper, & Palmer, 2000).[1] The success of the SO_2 allowance trading program motivated the design and implementation of the European Union's Emission Trading Scheme (EU ETS), the world's largest cap-and-trade program, focused on cutting CO_2 emissions from power plants and large manufacturing facilities throughout Europe (Ellerman & Buchner, 2007). The U.S. lead phase-down of gasoline in the 1980s, by reducing the lead content per gallon of fuel, served as an early, effective example of a tradable performance standard (Stavins, 2003). These positive experiences provide motivation for considering market-based instruments as potential approaches to mitigating greenhouse gas emissions. This chapter focuses on the experience in industrialized countries that have implemented these instruments extensively. We hope that our summary of relevant theory and survey of experience from industrialized nations may be helpful to those who wish to examine the potential applicability of carbon pricing for developing countries.

---

[1] In the developing country context, refer to Coria and Sterner (2010) and Coria, Löfgren, and Sterner (2010) for an assessment of air pollutant emission trading in Chile.

Climate Change Policy Instruments for the Regional, National, or Subnational Level

We consider five generic policy instruments that could conceivably be employed by regional, national, or even subnational governments for carbon pricing, including carbon taxes, cap-and-trade, emission reduction credits, clean energy standards, and fossil fuel subsidy reduction. First, however, we examine the possibility of relying on conventional environmental policy approaches, namely, command-and-control instruments, which have dominated environmental policy in virtually all countries over the past four decades.[2]

Command-and-Control Regulations

Conventional approaches to environmental policy employ uniform standards to protect environmental quality. Such command-and-control regulatory standards are either *technology based* or *performance based.* Technology-based standards typically require the use of specified equipment, processes, or procedures. In the climate policy context, these could require firms to use particular types of energy-efficient motors, combustion processes, or landfill-gas collection technologies.

Performance-based standards are more flexible than technology-based standards, specifying allowable levels of pollutant emissions or allowable emission rates, but leaving the specific methods of achieving those levels up to regulated entities. Examples of uniform performance standards for greenhouse gas abatement would include maximum allowable levels of CO_2 emissions from combustion (e.g., the grams-of-CO_2-per-mile requirement for cars and light-duty vehicles recently

---

[2]Where market-based policy instruments have been employed, they have typically complimented rather than substituted for command-and-control regulations. Green taxes have been employed in some contexts for the purpose of raising revenue, with little concern for their impacts on environmental outcomes. The OECD (2001) provides an assessment of environmental taxes in a variety of pollution contexts. Beyond the OECD, Máca, Melichar, and Ščasný (in press) evaluate environmental taxes and subsidies in central and eastern European countries, Cao, Ho, and Jorgenson (2009) assess green taxes in China, and Blackman (2010) and Sterner and Coria (2012) review a variety policy instruments in developing countries.

promulgated as part of U.S. tailpipe emission standards) and maximum levels of methane emissions from landfills.

Uniform technology and performance standards can — in principle — be effective in achieving some environmental purposes. But, given the ubiquitous nature of green-house gas emissions from diverse sources in an economy, it is unlikely that technology or ordinary performance standards could form the centerpiece of a meaningful climate policy.

Furthermore, these command-and-control mechanisms lead to non-cost-effective outcomes in which some firms use unduly expensive means to control pollution. Since performance standards give firms some flexibility in how they comply, performance-based standards will generally be more cost-effective than technology-based standards, but neither tends to achieve the cost-effective solution.

Beyond considerations of static cost-effectiveness, conventional standards would not provide dynamic incentives for the development, adoption, and diffusion of environmentally and economically superior control technologies. Once a firm satisfies a performance standard, it has little incentive to develop or adopt cleaner technology. Regulated firms may fear that if they adopt a superior technology, the government may tighten the performance standard. Technology standards are worse than performance standards in inhibiting innovation since, by their very nature, they constrain the technological choices available.

The substantially higher cost of a standards-based policy may undermine support for such an approach, and securing political support may require a weakening of standards and hence lower environmental benefits.[3]

The key limitations of command-and-control regulations can be avoided through the use of market-based policy instruments. In the context of climate change, this essentially means carbon pricing.

Carbon Taxes

In principle, the simplest approach to carbon pricing would be through government imposition of a carbon tax (Metcalf, 2007). The government could set a tax in terms of dollars per ton of CO_2 emissions (or CO_2-equivalent on greenhouse gas emissions) by sources covered by the tax,

[3]However, in special cases where emission monitoring and enforcement is particularly costly — such as for methane emissions in agriculture — a standards-based approach may be appropriate.

or — more likely — a tax on the carbon content of the three fossil fuels (coal, petroleum, and natural gas) as they enter the economy. To be cost-effective, such a tax would cover all sources, and to be efficient, the carbon price would be set equal to the marginal benefits of emission reduction, represented by estimates of the social cost of carbon (Interagency Working Group on Social Cost of Carbon, 2010). Over time, an efficient carbon tax would increase to reflect the fact that as more greenhouse gas emissions accumulate in the atmosphere, the greater is the incremental damage from one more ton of CO_2. Imposing a carbon tax would provide certainty about the marginal cost of compliance, which reduces uncertainty about returns to investment decisions, but would leave uncertain economy-wide emission levels (Weitzman, 1974).

The government could apply the carbon tax at a variety of points in the product cycle of fossil fuels, from fossil fuel suppliers based on the carbon content of fuel sales ("upstream" taxation/regulation) to final emitters at the point of energy generation ("downstream" taxation/regulation). Under an upstream approach, refineries and importers of petroleum products would pay a tax based on the carbon content of their gasoline, diesel fuel, or heating oil. Coal-mine operators would pay a tax reflecting the carbon content of the tons extracted at the mine mouth. Natural-gas companies would pay a tax reflecting the carbon content of the gas they bring to surface at the wellhead or import via pipelines or liquefied natural gas (LNG) terminals. Focusing on the carbon content of fuels would enable the policy to capture about 98 percent of U.S.

CO_2 emissions, for example, with a relatively small number of covered firms — on the order of a few thousand — as opposed to the hundreds of millions of smokestacks, tailpipes, and so forth, that emit CO_2 after fossil fuel combustion.

A carbon tax would be administratively simple and straightforward to implement in most industrialized countries, since the tax could incorporate existing methods for fuel-supply monitoring and reporting to the regulatory authority. Some developing countries with effective tax systems, including monitoring and enforcement regimes to minimize tax evasion, could also implement carbon taxes in a relatively straight-forward manner. Given the molecular properties of fossil fuels, monitoring the physical quantities of these fuels yields a precise estimate of the emissions that would occur during their combustion.

In the event that carbon capture and storage technologies become commercially available, a crediting system for downstream sequestration could complement the emission tax system. A firm that captures and stores CO_2 through geological sequestration, thereby preventing the gas from entering the atmosphere, could generate tradable CO_2 tax credits and sell these to firms that would otherwise have to pay the emission tax.[4]

As fuel suppliers face the emission tax, they will increase the cost of the fuels they sell. This will effectively pass the tax down through the energy system, creating incentives for fuel-switching and investments in more energy-efficient technologies that reduce CO_2 emissions.

The effects of a carbon tax on emission mitigation and the economy will depend in part on the amount and use of the tax revenue. For example, an economy-wide U.S. carbon tax of US$20 per ton of CO_2 would likely raise more than US$100 billion per year. The carbon tax revenue could be put toward a variety of uses. It could allow for reductions in existing distortionary taxes on labor and capital, thereby stimulating economic activity and offsetting some of a policy's social costs (Goulder, 1995; Goulder & Parry, 2008). Other socially valuable uses of revenue include reduction of debt, and funding desirable public programs, such as research and development of climate-friendly technology. The tax receipts could also be used to compensate low-income households for the burden of higher energy prices as well as compensating others bearing a disproportionate cost of the policy.

The implementation of a carbon tax (or any other meaningful climate policy instrument) will increase the cost of consuming energy and could adversely affect the competitiveness of energy-intensive industries. This competitiveness effect can result in negative economic and environmental outcomes: firms may relocate facilities to countries without meaningful climate change policies, thereby increasing emissions in these new locations and offsetting some of the environmental benefits of the policy. Such "emission leakage" may actually be relatively modest, because a majority of the emissions in developed countries occur in nontraded sectors, such as electricity, transportation, and residential buildings. However, energy-intensive manufacturing industries that produce goods competing in international markets may face incentives to relocate and advocate for a variety of policies to mitigate these impacts (Aldy & Pizer, 2011).

[4]Similar approaches could be undertaken to promote biological sequestration in forestry and agriculture and potentially emission-reduction projects ("offsets") in other countries. See discussion of Emission Reduction Credit programs below.

Additional emission leakage may occur through international energy markets — as countries with climate policies reduce their consumption of fossil fuels and drive down fuel prices, those countries without emission mitigation policies increase their fuel consumption in response to the lower prices. Since leakage undermines the environmental effectiveness of any unilateral effort to mitigate emissions, international cooperation and coordination becomes all the more important. These competitiveness impacts on energy-intensive manufacturing could be mitigated through policy designs we discuss below. Also, it is important to keep in mind that these emission leakage effects exist with any meaningful climate policy, whether carbon pricing or command-and-control.

Real-world experience with energy pricing demonstrates the power of markets to drive changes in the investment and use of emission-intensive technologies. The run-up in gasoline prices in 2008 resulted in a shift in the composition of new cars and trucks sold toward more fuel-efficient vehicles, while reducing vehicle miles traveled by the existing fleet (Ramey & Vine, 2010). Likewise, electric utilities responded to the dramatic decline in natural gas prices (and decline in the relative gas-coal price) in 2009 and 2010 by dispatching more electricity from gas plants that resulted in lower carbon dioxide (CO_2) emissions and the lowest share of U.S. power generation by coal in some four decades (U.S. Energy Information Administration, 2009). Longer term evaluations of the impacts of energy prices on markets have found that higher prices have induced more innovation — measured by frequency and importance of patents — and increased the commercial availability of more energy-efficient products, especially among energy-intensive goods such as air conditioners and water heaters (Newell, Jaffe, & Stavins, 1999; Popp, 2002).

Cap-and-Trade Systems

A cap-and-trade system constrains the aggregate emissions of regulated sources by creating a limited number of tradable emission allowances — in sum equal to the overall cap — and requiring those sources to surrender allowances to cover their emissions (Stavins, 2007). Faced with the choice of surrendering an allowance or reducing emissions, firms place a value on an allowance that reflects the cost of the emission reductions that can be avoided by surrendering an allowance. Regardless of the initial allowance distribution, trading can lead allowances to be put to their highest valued use: covering those emissions that are the most costly to reduce and providing the incentive to undertake the least costly reductions (Hahn & Stavins, in press; Montgomery, 1972). Cap-and-trade sets an aggregate quantity, and through trading, yields a price on emissions, and is effectively the dual of a carbon tax that prices emissions and yields a quantity of emissions as firms respond to the tax's mitigation incentives. Uncertainty in the costs of abatement leads to uncertainty regarding the allowance price in a cap-and-trade system and uncertainty regarding emissions under a tax. This has potentially important economic and political implications, which we discuss below.

In developing a cap-and-trade system, policy makers must decide on several elements of the system's design. Policy makers must determine how many allowances to issue — the size or level of the emission cap. Policy makers must determine the scope of the cap's coverage: identify the types of greenhouse gas emissions and sources covered by the cap, including whether to regulate upstream (based on carbon content of fuels) or downstream (based on monitored emissions).

After determining the amount of allowances and scope of coverage, policy makers must determine whether to freely distribute or sell (auction) allowances. Free allocation of allowances to firms could reflect some historical record ("grandfathering"), such as recent fossil fuel sales. Such grandfathering involves a transfer of wealth, equal to the value of the allowances, to existing firms, whereas, with an auction, this same wealth is transferred to the government. With an auction, the government would, in theory, collect revenue identical to that from a tax producing the same amount of emission abatement. As with tax receipts, auction revenues could be used to reduce distortionary taxes or finance other programs.

In an emission trading program, cost uncertainty — unexpectedly high or volatile allowance prices — can undermine political support for climate policy and discourage investment in new technologies and research and development. Therefore, attention has turned to incorporating "cost-containment" measures in cap-and-trade systems, including offsets, allowance banking and borrowing, safety valves, and price collars.

An offset provision allows regulated entities to offset some of their emissions with credits from emission reduction measures lying outside the cap-and-trade system's scope of coverage. An offset provision can link a cap-and-trade system with an emission-reduction-credit system (see below). Allowance banking and borrowing effectively permit emission trading across time. The flexibility to save an allowance for future use (banking) or to bring a future period allowance forward for current use (borrowing) can promote cost-effective abatement. Systems that allow banking and borrowing redefine the emission cap as a cap on cumulative emissions over a period of years, rather than a cap on annual emissions. This makes sense in the case of climate change, because it is a function of cumulative emissions of gases that remain in the atmosphere for decades to centuries.

A safety valve puts an upper bound on the costs that firms will incur to meet an emission cap by offering the option of purchasing additional allowances at a predetermined fee (the safety valve "trigger price"). This effective price ceiling in the emission allowance market reflects a hybrid approach to climate policy: a cap-and-trade system that transitions to a tax in the presence of unexpectedly high mitigation costs. When firms exercise a safety valve, their aggregate emissions exceed the emission cap. A price collar combines the ceiling of a safety valve with a price floor created by a minimum price in auction markets or a government commitment to purchase allowances at a specific price.

Increasing certainty about mitigation cost — through a carbon tax, safety valve, or price collar — reduces certainty about the quantity of emissions allowed.[5] Smoothing allowance prices over time through banking and borrowing reduces the certainty over emissions in any given year, but maintains certainty of aggregate emissions over a longer time period. A cost-effective policy with a mechanism insuring against unexpectedly high costs — either through cap-and-trade or a carbon tax — increases the likelihood that firms will comply with their obligations and can facilitate a country's participation and compliance in a global climate agreement.

In a similar fashion as under a carbon tax, domestic cap-and-trade programs could include some variant of a border tax to mitigate some of the adverse competitiveness impacts of a unilateral domestic climate policy and encourage trade partners to take on mitigation policies with comparable stringency. In the case of a cap-and-trade regime, the border adjustment would take the form of an import allowance requirement, so that imports would face the same regulatory costs as domestically produced goods. However, border measures under a carbon tax or cap-and-trade raise questions about the application of trade sanctions to encourage broader and more extensive emission mitigation actions

[5]From a political perspective, environmentalists have expressed concerns about "emission certainty," as an alternative to "cost certainty." From an economic welfare perspective, cost certainty is more important than emission certainty if the slope of estimated marginal abatement costs is relatively steeper than the slope of estimated marginal benefits of abatement (Pizer, 2002; Weitzman, 1974).

globally as well as questions about their legality under the World Trade Organization (Brainard & Sorking, 2009; Frankel, 2010).

Emission-Reduction-Credit Systems

An emission-reduction-credit (ERC) system delivers emission mitigation by awarding tradable credits for "certified" reductions. Generally, firms that are not covered by some set of regulations — be they command-and-control or market-based — may voluntarily participate in such systems, which serve as a source of credits that entities facing compliance obligations under the regulations may use. Individual countries can implement an ERC system without having a corresponding cap-and-trade program.

For example, as we discuss below, the Clean Development Mechanism (CDM) under the Kyoto Protocol provides credits used by firms covered by the EU ETS. A firm earns credits for projects that reduce emissions relative to a hypothetical "no project" baseline. In determining the number of credits to grant a firm for a project, calculation of the appropriate baseline is therefore as important as measuring emissions. Dealing with this unobserved and fundamentally unobservable hypothetical baseline is at the heart of the so-called "additionality" problem.

While ERC systems can be self-standing, as in the case of the CDM, governments can also establish them as elements of domestic cap-and-trade or other regulatory systems. These ERC systems — often referred to as offset programs — serve as a source of credits that can be used by regulated entities to meet compliance obligations under the primary system. For example, the Regional Greenhouse Gas Initiative (RGGI) in the northeast United States, which regulates CO_2 emissions from electric power plants (and which we discuss below), recognizes offsets from activities such as landfill methane capture and destruction, reductions in emissions of sulfur hexafluoride from the electric power sector, and afforestation. Electricity generators covered by RGGI can use these offset credits to cover part of their emissions. Other cap-and-trade systems that we discuss below also contain offset provisions.

Clean Energy Standards

The purpose of a clean energy standard is to establish a technology-oriented goal for the electricity sector that can be implemented cost-effectively (Aldy, 2011). Under such standards, power plants generating electricity with technologies that satisfy the standard create tradable credits that they can sell to power plants that fail to meet the standard, thereby minimizing the costs of meeting the standard's goal in a manner analogous to cap-and-trade.

In the United States, for example, state renewable electricity standards (RESs), a restricted type of a clean energy standard, typically establish the objective of the standard as a specific renewable share of total power generation that increases over time (U.S. Congressional Budget Office, 2011). A few states have implemented alternative energy standards in their power sector that target renewables, new nuclear power generating capacity, and advanced fossil fuel power generating technologies.

The European Union and China have promoted renewable power through renewable electricity mandates that include tradable renewable energy credits.

Clean energy standards that focus on technology targets do not explicitly price the greenhouse gas externality and thus impose a higher cost for a given amount of emission reductions than a carbon tax or cap-and-trade program. A renewable man-date treats coal-fired power, gas-fired power, and nuclear power as equivalent — none of these technologies create credits necessary for compliance — despite the fact that a natural gas combined cycle power plant typically produces a unit of generation with half the CO_2 emissions of a conventional coal power plant, and a nuclear plant produces zero-emission power, as do wind, solar, and geothermal. Thus, mandating power from a limited portfolio of technologies can result in higher costs by providing no incentive to switch from emission-intensive coal to emission-lean gas or emission-free nuclear.

A more cost-effective approach to a clean energy standard would employ a technology-neutral performance standard, such as tons of CO_2 per megawatt hour of generation. All power sources, from fossil fuels to renewables, could be eligible under such a performance standard. This has the advantage over the portfolio approach of providing better innovation incentives and of enabling all possible ways of reducing the emissions intensity of power generation. The Canadian province of Alberta has employed such a tradable carbon performance standard for most large sources of CO_2 emissions and has required a 12 percent improvement in the emission intensity of these sources since 2007.

Power plants would be awarded credits for generating cleaner (less emission-intensive) electricity than the standard. These clean power plants could sell credits to other power plants or save them for future use.

Tradable credits promote cost-effectiveness by encouraging the greatest deployment of clean energy from those plants that can lower their emission intensity at lowest cost. Those power plants could then sell their extra credits to other power plants that face higher costs for deploying clean energy. The creation and sale of clean energy credits would provide a revenue stream that could conceivably enable the financing of low- and zero- emission power plant projects.

Eligible technologies for the standard could extend beyond generation technologies and also permit improvements in energy efficiency, or a broad set of emission offset activities, to create tradable credits. Extending the price on carbon to a broader set of activities could improve cost-effectiveness, but allowing for energy efficiency and other offsets poses risks. As emphasized above, estimating offsets is complex, requires extensive review and monitoring by third parties or regulatory agencies, and risks undermining the objective of a policy because of the additionality problem.

Monitoring and enforcement could be relatively straightforward under either a portfolio or performance standard approach. For example, in the United States, electricity generation, generating technology type, and CO_2 emissions are already tracked at power plants by state and Federal regulators.

A clean energy standard represents a de facto free allocation of the right to emit greenhouse gases to the power sector. Suppose that the U.S. government created a clean energy performance standard of 0.5 tons of CO_2 per megawatt hour (the 2010 U.S. power sector emission intensity was 0.56 tons of CO_2/MWh); this is roughly comparable to a 50 percent clean energy standard that allows all technologies with lower emission intensity than conventional coal to qualify (with partial crediting for low- but non-zero- emitting facilities). As a result, a clean energy standard could not generate the revenues that a carbon tax or a cap-and-trade program with an allowance auction could.

Eliminating Fossil Fuel Subsidies

Phasing out fossil fuel subsidies can represent significant progress toward "getting prices right" for fossil fuel consumption, especially in some developing countries, where subsidies are particularly large. Imposing a carbon price on top of a fuel subsidy will not lead to the socially optimal price for the fuel, but removing such subsidies can deliver incentives for efficiency and fuel switching comparable to implementing an explicit carbon price. In sharp contrast with our discussion above of other policy instruments, in which we focused on ways to price externalities to correct a market failure, our overview of eliminating fossil fuel subsidies addresses the removal of policy interventions that represent "government failures" and thereby exacerbate a market failure.

At the 2009 G20 Summit in Pittsburgh, Pennsylvania, the leaders of 20 of the largest developed and developing countries agreed to phase out fossil fuel subsidies over the "medium term," and encouraged all other nations to eliminate such subsidies. The agreement called for phasing out these subsidies while targeting support for the poor, and noted that "inefficient fossil fuel subsidies encourage wasteful consumption, reduce our energy security, impede investment in clean energy sources and undermine efforts to deal with the threat of climate change" (G20 Leaders, 2009). Soon thereafter, leaders of the APEC nations[6] reached agreement on fossil fuel subsidy elimination at the 2009 Singapore Summit.

The economic and climate benefits of fossil fuel subsidy reform could be significant. In 2008, fossil fuel consumption subsidies exceeded US$500 billion globally and could exceed US$660 billion by 2020 without policy reforms (International Energy Agency [IEA], 2011). In at least 10 countries, fossil fuel subsidies exceeded 5 percent of GDP, and constituted substantial fractions of government budgets (IEA, 2010). Eliminating fossil fuel subsidies could reduce global oil consumption by about 4.7 million barrels per day by 2020, representing a decline of about 5 percent of current consumption. The International Energy Agency (2010) estimates that eliminating all fossil fuel subsidies would reduce global CO_2 emissions by about two gigatons per year by 2020. To put this in perspective, the UN Environmental Programme (2010) estimates that the Copenhagen Accord emission pledges will reduce green-house gas emissions by three to seven gigatons relative to business as usual in 2020.

The vast majority of fossil fuel subsidies suppress the prices for petrol, diesel, electricity, natural gas, and coal that consumers face, primarily in developing countries.[7] Some developing country governments have

---

[6]The 21 "member economies" of APEC (Asia-Pacific Economic Cooperation) are Australia, Brunei, Canada, Chile, China, Hong Kong, Indonesia, Japan, Korea, Malaysia, Mexico, New Zealand, Papua New Guinea, Peru, Philippines, Russia, Singapore, Taipei, Thailand, United States, and Viet Nam.

[7]Refer to Badiani, Jessoe, and Plant (in press) for a detailed discussion of electricity subsidies in the agricultural sector in India.

been historically reticent to let fuel and electricity prices rise to market-determined levels because of concerns of public opposition. For example, protests over reducing petrol subsidies contributed to President Suharto's downfall in Indonesia in 1998 (Beaton & Lontoh, 2010). Interestingly, Indonesia successfully reduced their fossil fuel subsidies — doubling consumers' prices for petrol and diesel and tripling consumers' prices for kerosene — in 2005 by coupling the change in the fuel price regime with a targeted, means-tested program to transfer government resources from fuel subsidies to income support. Before its late 2010 subsidy reform that significantly raised petrol and diesel prices in exchange for lump-sum cash transfers, Iran priced diesel fuel at about 10 cents per gallon (Coady *et al.*, 2010).

Critics of subsidy reform claim it will harm low-income households, but most fossil fuel subsidies disproportionately benefit the relatively wealthy in developing countries. Indeed, about 40 percent of the benefits of petroleum subsidies accrue to the wealthiest quintile, while the lowest income quintile enjoys less than 10 percent of the subsidy benefits, on average globally (Coady *et al.*, 2010).[8]

To promote implementation and cooperation on the G20 fossil fuel subsidies commitment, the leaders established two processes that enable a de facto "pledge and review" process. First, the leaders tasked their energy and finance ministers to compile a list of their own country's fossil fuel subsidies and present their strategies for eliminating them. After a series of staff-and ministerial-level consultations among the G20, the energy and finance ministers presented their plans in 2010 (G20 Leaders, 2010a). Second, the leaders tasked the Organization of Economic Cooperation and Development (OECD), International Energy Agency (IEA), World Bank, and the Organization of Petroleum Exporting Countries (OPEC) to evaluate fossil fuel subsidies (G20 Leaders, 2009). These international organizations subsequently produced joint reports that serve as independent benchmarks of fossil pricing policies by which countries may evaluate others' subsidy elimination plans (IEA, OPEC, OECD, & World Bank, 2010).

---

[8]The G20 agreement permits exclusion for subsidies that are explicitly targeted to low-income households. For example, the U.S. government has indicated that it considers the Low Income Home Energy Assistance Program to be exempt from the subsidy elimination commitment for this reason.

In 2010, the G20 leaders explicitly called on these international organizations to "further assess and review the progress made in implementing the Pittsburgh and Toronto commitments" (G20 Leaders, 2010b). While the G20 has no formal compliance mechanism to explicitly enforce the leaders' commitment, it does establish a goal, an implementation process, and what can effectively be a third-party expert review. This combination provides transparency for governments and stakeholders to assess whether nations are delivering on their leaders' commitments. This can promote credibility and trust for future international cooperation and may provide some lessons for the design of bottom-up international climate policy (see more on this below in our discussion of international coordination of carbon pricing policies).

Regional, National, and Subnational Experiences With Carbon Pricing

We briefly examine the few explicit carbon pricing policy regimes that are currently in place: the European Union's Emission Trading Scheme; New Zealand's cap-and-trade system; the Kyoto Protocol's Clean Development Mechanism; northern European carbon tax policies; British Columbia's carbon tax; and Alberta's tradable carbon performance standard (similar to a clean energy standard).[9]

European Union Emission Trading Scheme

By far the world's largest carbon pricing regime is the European Union Emission Trading Scheme (EU ETS), a cap-and-trade system of CO_2 allowances. Adopted in 2003 with a pilot phase that became active in 2005, the EU ETS covers about half of EU CO_2 emissions in 30 countries in a region of the world that accounts for about 20 percent of global GDP and 17 percent of world energy-related CO_2 emissions

[9]In addition to the EU ETS and the New Zealand cap-and-trade system, the Japanese Voluntary Emissions Trading System has operated since 2006, and Norway operated its own emissions trading system for several years before joining the EU ETS in 2008. Legislation to establish cap-and-trade systems is under debate in Australia (combined with a carbon tax for an initial 3-year period) and in the Canadian provinces of Ontario and Quebec. Japan is considering a compulsory emissions trading system.

(Ellerman & Buchner, 2007).[10] The 11,500 emitters regulated by the *downstream* program include large sources such as oil refineries, combustion installations over 20 MWth, coke ovens, cement factories, ferrous metal production, glass and ceramics production, and pulp and paper production. Up until now, the program has not covered sources in the transportation, commercial, or residential sectors (Ellerman & Buchner, 2007) although the EU plans to extend the ETS to cover aviation sector emissions starting in 2012.

The EU ETS was designed to be implemented in phases: a pilot or learning phase from 2005 to 2007, a Kyoto phase from 2008 to 2012,[11] and a series of subsequent phases. Penalties for violations increase from 40 Euros per ton of CO_2 in the first phase to 100 Euros in the second phase. Although the first phase allowed trading only in carbon dioxide, the second phase broadened the program to include other GHGs, such as nitrous oxide emissions.

The process for setting caps and allowances in member states was initially decentralized (Kruger, Oates, & Pizer, 2007), with each member state responsible for proposing its own national carbon cap, subject to review by the European Commission. This created incentives for individual countries to try to be generous with their allowances to protect their economic competitiveness (Convery & Redmond, 2007). Not surprisingly, the result was an aggregate cap that exceeded business-as-usual emissions.

In the spring of 2006, it became clear that the allocation of allowances in 2005 on net had exceeded emissions by about 4 percent of the overall cap. This led, as would be anticipated, to a dramatic fall in allowance prices. In January, 2005, the price per ton was approximately €8/tCO_2; by early 2006, it exceeded €30/tCO_2, then fell by about half in one week of April, 2006, before fluctuating and returning to about €8/tCO_2 (Convery & Redmond, 2007). This volatility was attributed to the absence of transparent, precise emissions data at the beginning of the program, a surplus of allowances, energy price volatility, and a program feature that *prevents banking* of allowances from the first phase to the second phase (Market Advisory Committee, 2007). In truth, the "overallocation" was

[10]The EU ETS covers all 27 member states plus Iceland, Liechtenstein, and Norway.

[11]This is the first commitment period of the Kyoto Protocol, 2008–2012.

concentrated in a few countries, particularly in Eastern Europe, and in the nonpower sectors (Ellerman & Buchner, 2007).

The first and second phases of the EU ETS require member states to distribute almost all of the emissions allowances (a minimum of 95 percent and 90 percent, respectively) freely to regulated sources, but beginning in 2013, member states will be allowed to auction larger shares of their allowances. The initial free distribution of allowances led to complaints from energy-intensive industrial firms about "windfall profits" among electricity generators, when energy prices increased significantly in 2005. But the higher electricity prices were only partly due to allowance prices, higher fuel prices also having played a role; and it is unclear whether the large profits reported by electricity generators were due mainly to their allowance holdings or to having low-cost nuclear or coal generation in areas where the (marginal) electricity price was set by higher cost natural gas (Ellerman & Buchner, 2007).

The system's cap was tightened for Phase 2 (2008–2012), and its scope expanded to cover new sources in countries that participated in Phase 1 plus sources in Bulgaria and Romania, which acceded to the European Union in 2007. Liechtenstein, Iceland, and Norway joined the EU ETS in 2008 although sources in Iceland are not yet subject to an emissions cap. Allowance prices in Phase 2 increased to over €20/tCO_2 in the first half of 2008, averaged €22/tCO_2 in the second half of 2008, and then fell to €13/tCO_2 in the first half of 2009, and down to €10/tCO_2 in the fall of 2011, as the economic recession brought decreased demand for allowances due to reduced output in the energy-intensive sectors and lower electricity consumption.

The European Union plans to extend the EU ETS through Phase 3, 2013–2020, with a centralized cap becoming increasingly stringent (20 percent below 1990 emissions), a larger share of the allowances subject to auctioning, tighter limits on the use of offsets, and unlimited banking of allowances between Phases 2 and 3.

Regional Greenhouse Gas Initiative

The Regional Greenhouse Gas Initiative (RGGI) is a *downstream* cap-and-trade program that was originally intended to limit CO_2 emissions in the United States from power sector sources in 10 northeastern states (Connecticut, Delaware, Maine, Maryland, Massachusetts, New Hampshire,

New Jersey,[12] New York, Rhode Island, and Vermont).[13] The system is both narrow in its sectoral coverage and unambitious in terms of its emissions reduction objectives.

The program took effect in 2009, after approval by individual state legislatures, and set a goal of limiting emissions from regulated sources to then current levels in the period from 2009 to 2014. Beginning in 2015, the emissions cap is set to decrease by 2.5 percent each year until it reaches an ultimate level 10 percent below 2009 emissions in 2019. It was originally anticipated that meeting this goal would require a reduction approximately 35 percent below business-as-usual emissions (13 percent below 1990 emissions levels). However, due to the combined effects of the economic recession and drastic declines in natural gas prices relative to coal prices, the program is no longer binding and is unlikely to become binding through 2020, unless the targets are revised.[14]

Because RGGI only limits emissions from the power sector, incremental monitoring costs are low, because U.S. power plants are already required to report their hourly CO_2 emissions to the Federal government (under provisions for continuous emissions monitoring as part of the SO_2 allowance trading program). The system sets standards for certain categories of CO_2 offsets, and limits the number and geographic distribution of offsets. The program requires participating states to auction at least 25 percent of their allowances and to use the proceeds for energy efficiency and consumer-related improvements.[15] The remaining 75 percent

[12] In May of 2011, New Jersey Governor Chris Christie announced that his state would withdraw from the system.

[13] In addition to RGGI, other regional and state efforts to limit GHGs in the United States have begun. One of the most prominent is California's enactment of the Global Warming Solutions Act of 2006, which set a statewide GHG emissions limit for 2020 equal to California's 1990 emissions level. In 2008, the California Air Resources Board proposed the use of a cap-and-trade program as a primary policy for achieving this target. The cap initially would cover electric generators and large industrial facilities, and its scope would later be expanded to include smaller facilities and the transportation sector. The cap-and-trade system is scheduled to commence operations in 2012.

[14] Allowance prices have reflected these realities, falling from approximately US$3 per ton of CO_2 at the first auction in September, 2008, to the floor price of US$1.89 per ton in 2011.

[15] Three states have used some of their auction revenue to help balance their overall state budgets.

of allowances may be auctioned or distributed freely. In practice, states have auctioned virtually all allowances.

Several problems with the program's design can be noted. First is the leakage problem, which is potentially severe for any state or regional program, particularly given the interconnected nature of electricity markets (Burtraw, Kahn, & Palmer, 2005). Second, the program is downstream for just one sector of the economy and so very limited in scope. Third, despite considerable cost uncertainty, a true firm safety valve mechanism was not adopted. Instead, there are trigger price that allow greater reliance on offsets and external credits in the expectation that these can increase supply. The program does impose a price floor in the allowance auctions, without which the allowance prices would have approached zero (when the combined forces of the economic recession and lower natural gas prices caused emissions to fall below the declining cap). Fourth, as mentioned above, the program limits the number and geographic origin of offsets.

New Zealand Emissions Trading Scheme

In January, 2008, the New Zealand Emissions Trading Scheme (NZ ETS) was launched. Under this system, the intention is to include all sectors of the economy and all greenhouse gases by 2015, using free allocation of allowances, with special protections (output-based updating allocations) for emission-intensive, trade-sensitive sectors. The forestry sector entered the program first, in 2008; and stationary energy, industrial, and liquid fuel fossil fuel sectors joined in 2010. The waste (landfills) sector is scheduled to enter in 2013, and agriculture — which accounts for nearly half of New Zealand's gross emissions — is scheduled to enter in 2015.

Covered sources have the option of paying a fixed fee of NZUS$25 per ton of emissions, and until 2013, all sectors other than forestry require only one unit of allowances for each two units of emissions. Thus, although the NZ allowances are indirectly linked with the EU ETS through the CDM, the current effective price is very low while the system becomes established. Early evidence suggests that the forestry component has deterred deforestation and may be encouraging new planting, although international policy and consequent price uncertainty are major problems for investment (Karpas & Kerr, 2010).

The Climate Change Response Act of 2002, which provided for the creation of the emissions trading scheme for the purpose of meeting the country's Kyoto obligations, required a review of the NZ ETS by an independent review panel every 5 years. The first review (Emissions Trading Scheme Review Panel, 2011) was released by the government in September, 2011. While most of the scheme was upheld, it recommended that the agriculture sector face a lower price as it enters the system and that the government should review the wisdom of allowing offsets from HFC-23 destruction projects under the Clean Development Mechanism (see below). The government hopes to link with Australia's emissions trading program, scheduled to be launched in 2015.

Clean Development Mechanism

The most significant GHG emission-reduction-credit system to date is the Kyoto Protocol's Clean Development Mechanism (CDM). Under the CDM, certified emission reduction (CER) credits are awarded for voluntary emission reduction projects in non-Annex I countries (largely, developing countries) that ratified the Protocol, but are not among the Annex I countries subject to the Protocol's emission limitation commitments — also known as the Annex B countries.[16] CDM projects can potentially take the form of building new wind farms, investing in more energy efficient equipment in a manufacturing facility, and capturing methane from landfills. While CERs can be used by the Annex I countries to meet their emission commitments, they could also be used for compliance purposes by entities covered by other cap-and-trade systems, including systems in countries that are not Parties to the Protocol, such as the United States.

From the perspective of the industrialized countries, the CDM provides a means to engage developing countries in the control of GHG emissions, while from the perspective of the developing countries, the CDM

[16]Parties include 37 industrialized countries and emerging market economies of central and eastern Europe. Like the CDM, Joint Implementation (JI) was established as a project-based flexibility mechanism under the Kyoto Protocol. Unlike the CDM, JI applies to emission reduction projects carried out in an Annex I country (the host country) that has a national emissions target under the Protocol. JI projects generate credits, referred to as emission reduction units (ERUs), which can be used to cover increased emissions in other countries.

provides an avenue for the financing of "sustainable development." Essentially, the purchase of CERs by industrialized country entities to offset their own emissions can reduce the aggregate cost of compliance with the Kyoto Protocol, because it tends to be much less expensive to construct new low-carbon energy infrastructure in developing nations than to modify or replace existing infrastructure in industrialized countries (Wara, 2007).

Of the six GHGs covered by the Kyoto Protocol,[17] approximately 38 percent of projects in the CDM pipeline as of 2007 were for CO_2, 28 percent for HFC-23, 23 percent for methane, and 11 percent for nitrous oxide (Wara, 2007). In terms of CO_2-equivalent reductions, the CDM has accounted for annual reductions of 278 million tons, about 1 percent of annual global emissions of CO_2 (U.S. Energy Information Administration, 2011).[18] The largest shares of CERs have been generated in China (52 percent) and India (16 percent), with Latin America and the Caribbean making up another 15 percent of the total, Brazil (at 7 percent) being the largest producer in that region (World Bank, 2010).

Because the CDM is an ERC system, it is subject to concerns about the additionality of emission-reductions associated with its projects (see generic discussion above regarding ERC systems). Empirical analysis has validated these concerns, with estimates that up to 75 percent of claimed reductions would have occurred in the absence of the program (Zhang & Wang, 2011).

A particular concern has centered on the fact that nearly 30 percent of average annual CERs have come from the destruction of HFC-23, a potent GHG that is a by-product of the manufacture of certain refrigerant gases. It is very inexpensive to destroy HFC-23, and companies can earn nearly twice as much from sale of CDM credits as they can from selling respective refrigerant gases. As a result, it has been argued that plants are being built simply for the purpose of generating CERs from destruction of HFC-23. Because of this, beginning in 2013, CERs from HFC-23 destruction will not be valid for purposes of compliance with the EU ETS.

As debate continues regarding a possible second commitment period for the Kyoto Protocol, it appears that the CDM will continue to function,

---

[17]These are CO_2, methane, nitrous oxide, hydrofluorocarbons, perfluorocarbons, and sulfur hexafluoride.

[18]Note that carbon sequestration projects of forestation and reduced deforestation are not included in the CDM under the Kyoto Protocol's first commitment period, 2008–2012.

in any event (Bodansky, 2011). A variety of proposals have been put forward to improve its structure and implementation, many targeted at increasing the additionality of approved projects (Hall, Levi, Pizer, & Ueno, 2010). In the meantime, as we discuss below, the CDM may provide a significant function by facilitating indirect linkages among diverse national cap-and-trade systems.

Northern European Experience With Carbon Taxes[19]

In the 1990s, a number of northern European countries imposed carbon taxes to limit their greenhouse gas emissions. In 1991, Norway implemented a carbon tax that varied in its level across sectors of the economy, despite the fact that cost-effective abatement would call for a uniform tax. In the transportation sector, by 2009, the Norwegian carbon tax had increased to about US\$58/tCO_2 on gasoline, but only US\$34/tCO_2 on diesel (Government of Norway, 2009). Natural gas faced a carbon tax of US\$31/tCO_2 to US\$33/tCO_2 in 2009, depending on use. By 1999, facilities using coal paid US\$24/tCO_2 for coal for energy purposes and US\$19/tCO_2 for coal for coking purposes (Bruvoll & Larsen, 2004), but the Government of Norway exempted these activities from the carbon tax starting in 2003 (Government of Norway, 2009). In 2009, the carbon tax applied to about 55 percent of Norwegian green-house gas emissions, while the emission trading scheme that is linked to the EU ETS covered an additional 13 percent of emissions.[20] In 2003, Norway also introduced a tax of about US\$33/tCO_2-equivalent on HFCs and PFCs, which slowed the growth rate of these potent greenhouse gases (Government of Norway, 2009).

Likewise in 1991, Sweden implemented a carbon tax of about US\$33/tCO_2 as a part of a fiscal reform that lowered high income tax rates (Speck, 2008). The carbon tax has since increased to more than US\$135/tCO_2 by 2009 (Government of Sweden, 2009). At the same time, Sweden reduced its general energy tax on many of the sources bearing the carbon

---

[19]All carbon taxes reported in this subsection are in 2009 U.S. dollars, based on market exchange rates.

[20]Greenhouse gas emissions in the offshore oil sector, representing 24 percent of the nation's emissions, are covered by both a (lower) carbon tax and the emission trading scheme (Government of Norway, 2009).

tax. Refineries, steel, and other primary metal industries received an exemption from the carbon tax (Daugjberg & Pedersen, 2004). In addition, those industries covered by the EU ETS were exempted from the carbon tax (Government of Sweden, 2009). About 33 percent of Sweden's greenhouse gas emissions are covered by the EU ETS, a smaller fraction than the norm in the EU (Government of Sweden, 2009).

In 1992, Denmark implemented a carbon tax of about US\$18/tCO_2, and reduced this tax modestly to a level of about US\$17/tCO_2 in 2005, where it remained through 2009 (Speck, 2008; Government of Denmark, 2009). Manufacturing industries bear discounted tax rates of more than 90 percent depending on their energy intensity and participation in a voluntary agreement (Government of Denmark, 2009). The carbon tax on gasoline amounted to about 16 cents per gallon in 2009.

Since 1997, Finland has imposed a general tax on energy coupled with a surtax based on the carbon content of the energy. Like other northern European nations, Finland reduced its carbon tax for some industries covered by the EU ETS, reflecting concerns about adverse competitiveness impacts on trade-exposed manufacturing. Since 2008, the carbon surtax has been about US\$28/tCO_2 although natural gas faces half this rate (Government of Finland, 2009).

Obviously, implementation of carbon taxes in northern Europe have yielded significant variations in the effective tax per unit CO_2 across fuels and industries within each country, contrary to the cost-effective prescription of a common price on carbon among all sources. In addition, fiscal cushioning to carbon taxes — by adjustments to preexisting energy taxes — and to the EU ETS — by adjustments to then preexisting carbon taxes — was common, especially for those industries expressing concerns about their international competitiveness. Nonetheless, these nations have demonstrated that carbon taxes can deliver greenhouse gas emission reductions and raise revenues to finance government spending and lower income tax rates (OECD, 2001; Government of Denmark, 2009; Government of Finland, 2009; Government of Norway, 2009).

British Columbia Carbon Tax

Since 2008, the Canadian province of British Columbia has had in place a carbon tax as one part of its plan to reduce provincial GHG emissions by 33 percent by 2020 (British Columbia, 2007). The carbon tax is intended to be economy-wide, with a tax of C$10 per ton of CO_2-equivalent emissions in 2008, increasing by C$5 per year for 4 years, and reaching C$30/ton in 2012. The tax is collected "upstream" at the wholesale level (fuel distributors) based on the carbon content of fuels to facilitate administration (Duff, 2008). By law, 100 percent of the tax revenue must be refunded through tax cuts to businesses and individuals, and low-income individuals are further protected through a Low Income Climate Action Tax Credit.

During 2008 and 2009, the tax generated C$846 million in revenue. This was accompanied by reductions in a variety of personal and corporate income taxes, plus tax credits for low-income individuals. These cuts totaled approximately C$1.1 billion, so that the policy yielded significant net tax reductions (Plumer, 2010). A similar pattern occurred in 2010. The government estimates that by 2020, the carbon tax will reduce British Columbia's CO_2 emissions by approximately 3 million tons annually.

Interestingly, another part of the province's Climate Action Plan is a provincial cap-and-trade system, which is to be linked with a similar systems planned in California (under Assembly Bill 32), Ontario, and Quebec through the Western Climate Initiative. The province's plans have not addressed how the carbon tax and cap-and-trade system will be coordinated.[21]

Alberta Tradable Carbon Performance Standard

In 2007, the Canadian province of Alberta designed a market-based policy to reduce the carbon intensity of its large sources of greenhouse gas emissions. This program established a rate-based performance standard for emission sources exceeding 100,000 metric tons of CO_2 annually. Building on emission inventories dating to 2003, each large source covered by the program was required to reduce the emission intensity of its production 12 percent below a base year intensity drawn from the 2003–2006 period.[22] The program covers about 100 sources from the power

---

[21] An important issue for national and subnational climate policies is the potential for interactions — some problematic and some positive — among overlapping policy instruments. On this, see McGuinness and Ellerman (2008); Fischer and Preonas (2010); Levinson (2010); Goulder and Stavins (2011); and Organization for Economic Cooperation and Development (2011).

[22] New sources covered by the program initially bear less stringent performance standards that converge to the 12 percent objective over time (Province of Alberta, 2007).

sector, pulp and paper, cement, and fertilizer industries, and oil sands development. The unit of measure is emissions of CO_2 per unit of physical production from that industry, for example, per barrel of oil from oil sands development (Sass, 2010).

Covered firms have four options for complying with the performance standard. First, they can reduce the emission intensity of production to meet the standard. Second, they may purchase credits from other covered firms with emission intensities below the standard. Third, they may purchase Alberta-based emission offset credits through an emission-reduction credit program. Finally, they may pay the provincial government C$15 for every metric ton they exceed the standard by, which serves as a safety valve on the cost of compliance with the program (Province of Alberta, 2008).

In 2010, covered sources employed all four options to comply with the performance standard. These sources reduced their emissions relative to baseline by about 2.7 million tons of CO_2 (with a majority of this effort traded from low mitigation cost facilities to high mitigation cost facilities), purchased about 3.9 million tons emission offset credits, and satisfied the remaining 4.7 million ton emission reduction obligation through the C$15/t$CO_2$ safety valve. This last option generated about C$70 million of revenue directed to the Climate Change and Emissions Management Fund, which invests in emission-lean technologies and projects (Province of Alberta, 2011).

International Coordination of Carbon Pricing Policies

Climate change is truly a global commons problem: the location of greenhouse gas emissions has no effect on the global distribution of damages. Hence free-riding problems plague unilateral and multilateral approaches. Furthermore, nations will not benefit proportionately from greenhouse gas mitigation policies. Thus mitigation costs are likely to exceed direct benefits for virtually all countries. Cost-effective international policies — insuring that countries get the most environmental benefit out of their mitigation investments — will help promote participation in an international climate policy regime.

In principle, internationally employed market-based instruments can achieve overall cost effectiveness. Three basic routes stand out. First, countries could agree to apply the same tax on carbon (*harmonized domestic taxes*) or adopt a *uniform international tax*. Second, the international policy community could establish a system of *international tradable permits* — effectively a nation-state level cap-and-trade program. In its simplest form, this represents the Kyoto Protocol's Annex B emission targets and the Article 17 trading mechanism. Third, a more decentralized system of internationally linked domestic cap-and-trade programs could ensure internationally cost-effective emission mitigation.

International Taxes and Harmonized Domestic Taxes

In principle, a carbon tax could be imposed on nation states by an international agency. The supporting agreement would have to specify both tax rates and a formula for allocating the tax revenues. Cost-effectiveness would require a uniform tax rate across all countries. It is unclear, however, what international agency could impose and enforce such a tax, and so an alternative more frequently considered has been a set of harmonized domestic carbon taxes (Cooper, 2010). In this case, an agreement would stipulate that all countries are to levy the same domestic carbon taxes and retain their revenues.

The uniformity of tax rates is necessary for cost-effectiveness. But some developing countries may argue that the resulting distribution of costs does not conform to principles of distributional equity and call for significant resource transfers. Under a harmonized tax system, an agreement could include fixed lump-sum payments from developed to developing countries, and under an international tax system, an agreement could specify shares of the total international tax revenues that go to participating countries.

As an alternative to these explicit transfers, developed countries could commit to constrain the use of their tax revenues in ways that produce global benefits. For example, carbon tax revenues in developed countries could, in part, finance major research and development programs on zero-carbon technologies and adaptation efforts in developing countries, while developing countries could freely use their tax revenues in ways that best facilitate their development.

In some developing countries reluctant to implement a carbon tax, an initial cost-effective contribution to combat climate change could take the form of reducing fossil fuel subsidies. For example, a developing country cutting a petrol subsidy equal to 10 percent of its price is approximately equivalent to a rich country imposing a carbon tax on petrol that raises its price 10 percent. Well-planned, broad fossil fuel price reforms in a developing country could deliver substantial emission mitigation just as a carbon tax in a developed country (IEA, 2010). The energy prices are higher in both countries, providing the incentive to invest in energy-efficient technologies and nonfossil energy sources, but the relative prices remain unchanged, so that energy-intensive firms do not face the incentive to relocate to the developing country.

Lowering energy subsidies can free up government revenues that could be directed to other beneficial uses and improve the allocation of resources in the economy to promote faster economic growth. Of course, some energy subsidies in developing countries address pressing, basic energy needs, and efforts to combat climate change may need to account for these social objectives.

International Tradable Permits: Cap-and-Trade and Emission-Reduction-Credits

Under an international tradable permit scheme, all participating countries would be allocated permits for "net emissions," that is, emissions minus sequestration. A permit would define a right to emit a given volume over some time period, such as a year. In each period, countries would be free to buy and sell permits on an international exchange.

Initial permit allocations could reflect a variety of criteria, such as previous emissions, gross domestic product, population, and fossil fuel production. Whatever the initial allocation, subsequent trading can, in theory, lead to a cost-effective outcome (Montgomery, 1972), if transaction costs are not significant (Stavins, 1995). This potential for pursuing distributional objectives while assuring cost-effectiveness is an important attribute of the tradable permit approach.

Providing large initial permits to developing countries (for reasons of distributional equity) implies that they would sell permits primarily to developed countries. Since permit prices represent an implicit tax on all participating countries, the terms of trade within the coalition for countries with the same carbon intensities in production would remain unaffected. From a distributional point of view, developing countries would receive compensation, whereas developed countries would have to pay for their own emission abatement and for permit purchases from abroad to cover the balance of their emissions (Olmstead & Stavins, 2012).

An important obstacle to the successful operation of such a system is that by its very nature, the trading would be among nations (Hahn & Stavins, 1999). Nation-states are hardly simple cost-minimizers, like private firms, so there is no reason to anticipate that competitive pressures would lead to equating of marginal abatement costs across countries. The system would not have the cost-effectiveness property ordinarily associated with a domestic tradable permit system among firms. Even if nations were cost-minimizers, they do not have sufficient information about the marginal abatement costs of firms within their jurisdiction to define their own aggregate marginal costs. The notion of a simple trading program among countries may be more of a metaphor than a practical policy.

If every country participating in such a system were to devolve the tradable permits to firms within its jurisdiction, that is, if each country instituted a domestic tradable permit system as its means of achieving its national target, then the trading could be among firms, not governments, both within countries and internationally (Hahn & Stavins, 1999). Such a system could indeed be cost-effective. In the near term, this trading system could be integrated with an emission-reduction-credit system, such as the CDM, for countries that do not take on emission caps.

The current design of the CDM does not secure all low-cost mitigation opportunities in developing countries. The project basis for credits under the CDM increases transaction costs and excludes policy reforms that undermine the cost-effectiveness of the mechanism. Modifying the CDM along several lines could improve its cost-effectiveness, increase the investment in low-carbon technologies in developing countries, and address concerns about whether CDM activities truly reflect additional emission mitigation effort (Hall *et al.*, 2010).

First, the CDM could be expanded to cover mitigation policies. Some of the potentially low-hanging fruit in developing countries — from reducing energy subsidies to designing and enforcing building codes — do not neatly fall within a "project" under the CDM. A policy-oriented CDM could deliver price signals to a greater share of a developing country's economy that can yield more emission mitigation and reduce the potential for emission leakage. This could also serve as a mechanism for transfers to developing countries that pursue a carbon tax. The obvious challenge lies in setting baseline emissions to assess the emission reduction benefits for any given policy. This effort may be substantial, but when spread over all of the potential emission reductions, the transaction costs may be minor in comparison to the costs of a project-based approach resulting in the same abatement.

Second, the CDM could be expanded to cover sectors as an alternative to projects. A sectoral CDM could establish emission baselines for entire sectors (such as the power sector or the steel sector), and allow countries to implement mitigation policies in those sectors to generate credits. Integrating these policies into the international regime — such as pegging a sectoral carbon tax to the international tradable permit price, or implementing a sectoral cap-and-trade system linked to the international regime — could promote cost-effectiveness. Focusing on the most energy-intensive sectors could also address concerns about competitiveness and emission leakage in developed countries. It would also provide developing countries with the experience to inform their consideration of taking on broader emission or policy commitments in future agreements.[23]

Decentralized, Bottom-Up Architectures

Cap-and-trade systems seem to have emerged as the preferred national and regional instrument for reducing emissions of greenhouse gases throughout much of the industrialized world, and the CDM has developed a substantial constituency, despite concerns about its performance. Because linkage between tradable permit systems (that is, unilateral or bilateral recognition of allowances from one system for use in another) can reduce compliance costs and improve market liquidity, there is great interest in linking cap-and-trade systems with each other.

There are not only benefits but also concerns associated with various types of linkages (Jaffe, Ranson, & Stavins, 2010). A major concern is that when two cap-and-trade systems are directly linked (that is, allow bilateral recognition of allowances in the two jurisdictions), key cost-containment mechanisms, such as safety valves, are automatically propagated from one system to the other. Because some jurisdictions (such as the European Union) are opposed to the notion of a safety valve, whereas other jurisdictions (such as the United States) seem very favorably predisposed to the use of a safety valve, challenging harmonization would be required.

[23] Such an approach could be superior to some calls for sectoral policies that effectively set industry-specific performance standards common across participating developed and developing countries. This standard approach establishes walls between sectors that can increase the total mitigation cost for any given emission goal and eliminates opportunities to raise revenues, either through a carbon tax or an allowance auction, to benefit other social objectives.

This problem can be avoided by the use of indirect linkage, whereby two cap-and-trade systems accept offsets from a common emission-reduction-credit system, such as the Clean Development Mechanism. As a result, the allowance prices of the two cap-and-trade systems converge (as long as the ERC market is sufficiently deep), and all the benefits of direct linkage are achieved (lower aggregate cost, reduced market power, decreased price volatility), but without the propagation from one system to another of cost-containment mechanisms. Such indirect linkage may already be evolving as a key element of the *de facto* post-2012 international climate policy architecture.

Despite the apparent current popularity of cap-and-trade as a national policy approach in many parts of the world, in reality, there are a variety of policy instruments — both market based and conventional command-and-control — that countries can employ to reduce their GHG emissions. Hence it is important to ask whether a diverse set of heterogeneous national, subnational, or regional climate policy instruments can be linked in productive ways. The basic answer is that such a set of instruments can be linked, but the linkage is considerably more difficult than it is with a set of more homogeneous tradable permit systems (Hahn & Stavins, 1999). In fact, the basic approach behind emission reduction credit systems such as the CDM and Joint Implementation (JI) can be extended to foster linkage opportunities among diverse policy instruments, including cap-and-trade, taxes, and certain regulatory systems (Metcalf & Weisbach, 2010).

Another form of coordination can be unilateral instruments of economic protection, that is, border adjustments. In the case of a national carbon tax, this would take the form of a tax on imports that was equivalent to the implicit tax on the same domestically produced goods. In the case of a cap-and-trade system, this would take the form of an import-allowance-requirement. Such border adjustments are found as part of most existing, planned, and proposed national climate policies.

The Future of Carbon Pricing

The political responses to possible market-based approaches to climate policy in most countries have been and will continue to be largely a function of issues and structural factors that transcend the scope of environmental and climate policy. Because a truly meaningful climate policy — whether market based or conventional in design — will have significant impacts on economic activity in a wide variety of sectors (because of the pervasiveness of energy use in a modern economy) and in every region of a country, it is not surprising that proposals for such policies bring forth significant opposition, particularly during difficult economic times.

In the United States, political polarization — which began some four decades ago, and accelerated during the economic downturn — has decimated what had long been the key political constituency in the Congress for environmental (and energy) action, namely, the middle, including both moderate Republicans and moderate Democrats (Stavins, 2011). Whereas Congressional debates about environmental and energy policy had long featured regional politics, they are now fully and simply partisan. In this political maelstrom, the failure of cap-and-trade climate policy in the U.S. Senate in 2010 was essentially collateral damage in a much larger political war.

It is possible that better economic times will reduce the pace — if not the direction — of political polarization. Furthermore, it is also possible that the ongoing challenge of large budgetary deficits in many countries will increase the political feasibility of new sources of revenue. When and if this happens, consumption taxes (as opposed to traditional taxes on income and investment) could receive heightened attention, and primary among these might be energy taxes, which can be significant climate policy instruments, depending on their design.

It is much too soon to speculate on what the future will hold for the use of market-based policy instruments for climate change. It is conceivable that two decades of relatively high receptivity in the United States, Europe, and other parts of the world to cap-and-trade and offset mechanisms will turn out to be no more than a relatively brief departure from a long-term trend of reliance on conventional means of regulation. On the other hand, it is also possible that the recent tarnishing of cap-and-trade in U.S. political dialogue will itself turn out to be a temporary departure from a long-term trend of increasing reliance on market-based environmental policy instruments. It is too soon to say.

References

Aldy, J. E. (2011). "Promoting Clean Energy in the American Power Sector" (The Hamilton Project Discussion Paper 2011–04). Washington, DC: The Hamilton Project.

Aldy, J. E., and Pizer, W. A. (2011, December). "Competitiveness Impacts of Climate Change Mitigation Policies" (National Bureau of Economic Research Working Paper No. 17705). Cambridge, MA: National Bureau of Economic Research.

Badiani, R., Jessoe, K., and Plant, S. (in press). "Development and environmental implications of agricultural electricity subsidies in India." *Journal of Environment and Development*.

Beaton, C., and Lontoh, L. (2010). *Lessons Learned from Indonesia's Attempts to Reform Fossil-Fuel Subsidies*. Winnipeg, Manitoba, Canada: International Institute for Sustainable Development.

Blackman, A. (2010). "Alternative pollution control policies in developing countries." *Review of Environmental Economics and Policy*, **4**, 234–253.

Bodansky, D. (2011). "Whither the Kyoto Protocol? Durban and Beyond." Policy Brief, *Harvard Project on Climate Agreements*, Belfer Center for Science and International Affairs, Harvard Kennedy School.

Brainard, L., and Sorking, I. Eds. (2009). *Climate Change, Trade, and Competitiveness: Is a Collision Inevitable?* Washington, DC: Brookings Institution Press.

British Columbia. (2007). *Climate Action Plan*. Vancouver, British Columbia, Canada.

Bruvoll, A., and Larsen, B. M. (2004). "Greenhouse Gas Emissions in Norway: Do Carbon Taxes Work?" *Energy Policy*, **32**, 493–505.

Burtraw, D., Kahn, D., and Palmer, K. (2005). "*CO_2 Allowance Allocation in the Regional Greenhouse Gas Initiative and the Effect on Electricity Investors*" (Discussion Paper CP 05-55). Washington, DC: Resources for the Future.

Cao, J., Ho, M., and Jorgenson, D. (2009). "The local and global benefits of green tax policies in China." *Review of Environmental Economics and Policy*, **3**, 189–208.

Carlson, C., Burtraw, D., Cropper, M., and Palmer, K. (2000). "SO_2 control by electric utilities: What are the gains from trade?" *Journal of Political Economy*, **108**, 1292–326.

Coady, D., Gillingham, R., Ossowski, R., Pietrowski, J., Tareq, S., and Tyson, J. (2010). *Petroleum Product Subsidies: Costly, Inequitable, and Rising* (IMF Staff Position Note SPN/10/05). Washington, DC: International Monetary Fund.

Convery, F., and Redmond, L. (2007). "Market and price developments in the European union emissions trading scheme." *Review of Environmental Economics and Policy*, **1**, 66–87.

Cooper, R. N. (2010). "The Case for Charges on Greenhouse Gas Emissions." In J. E. Aldy and R. N. Stavins Eds., *Post-Kyoto International Climate Policy: Implementing Architectures for Agreement* (pp. 151–178). New York, NY: Cambridge University Press.

Coria, J., and Sterner, T. (2010). "Tradable permits in developing countries: Evidence from air pollution in Santiago, Chile." *Journal of Environment and Development*, **19**, 145–170.

Coria, J., Löfgren, Å., and Sterner, T. (2010). "Trade or not to trade: An analysis of trading schemes at the firm level." *Journal of Environmental Management*, **91**, 2126–2133.

Daugjberg, C., and Pedersen, A. B. (2004). "New Policy Ideas and Old Policy Networks: Implementing Green Taxation in Scandinavia." *Journal of Public Policy*, **24**, 219–249.

Duff, D. G. (2008). "Carbon Taxation in British Columbia." *Vermont Journal of Environmental Law*, **10**, 85–105.

Ellerman, A. D., and Buchner, B. K. (2007). "The European Union Emissions Trading Scheme: Origins, Allocation, and Early Results." *Review of Environmental Economics and Policy*, **1**(1), 66–87.

Emissions Trading Scheme Review Panel. (2011). "Doing New Zealand's fair share: Emissions trading scheme review 2011, final report." Wellington, New Zealand: Ministry for the Environment.

Fischer, C., and Preonas, L. (2010). "Combining Policies for Renewable Energy: Is the Whole Less than the Sum of Its Parts?" *International Review of Environmental and Resource Economics*, **4**, 51–92.

Frankel, J. (2010). "Global Environment and Trade Policy." In J. E. Aldy and R. N. Stavins Eds., *Post-Kyoto International Climate Policy: Implementing Architectures for Agreement* (pp. 493–529). New York, NY: Cambridge University Press.

G20 Leaders. (2009, September 24–25). "Leaders' statement: The Pittsburgh summit." The third G-20 Summit in Pittsburgh, PA, USA.

G20 Leaders. (2010a, June 26–27). "Annex: G20 initiative on rationalizing and phasing out inefficient fossil fuel subsidies, implementation strategies and timetables." The fourth G-20 Summit in Toronto, Ontario, Canada.

G20 Leaders. (2010b, November 11-12). "The G20 seoul summit leaders' declaration." The fifth G20 Summit in Seoul, Republic of Korea.

Goulder, L. H. (1995, August). "Environmental Taxation and the 'Double Dividend': A Reader's Guide." *International Tax and Public Finance*, **2**(2).

Goulder, L. H., and Parry, I. W. H. (2008). "Instrument Choice in Environmental Policy." *Review of Environmental Economics and Policy*, **2**, 152–174.

Goulder, L. H., and Stavins, R. N. (2011). "Challenges from State-Federal Interactions in U.S. Climate Change Policy." *American Economic Review Papers and Proceedings*, **101**, 253–257.

Government of Denmark. (2009). *Denmark's Fifth National Communication on Climate Change*. Copenhagen, Denmark: Ministry of Climate and Energy.

Government of Finland. (2009). *Finland's Fifth National Communication under the Framework Convention on Climate Change*. Helsinki, Finland: Ministry of the Environment and Statistics.

Government of Norway. (2009). *Norway's Fifth National Communication under the Framework Convention on Climate Change*. Oslo, Norway: Norwegian Ministry of the Environment.

Government of Sweden. (2009). *Sweden's Fifth National Communication on Climate Change*. Stockholm, Sweden: Ministry of the Environment.

Hahn, R. W., and Stavins, R. N. (1999). "What has the kyoto protocol wrought? The real architecture of international tradeable permit markets." Washington, DC: The AEI Press.

Hahn, R. W., and Stavins, R. N. (in press). "The effect of allowance allocations on cap-and-trade system performance." *Journal of Law and Economics*.

Hall, D. S., Levi, M. A., Pizer, W. A., and Ueno, T. (2010). "Policies for Developing Country Engagement." In J. E. Aldy & R. N. Stavins Eds., *Post-Kyoto International Climate Policy: Implementing Architectures for Agreement* (pp. 649–681). New York, NY: Cambridge University Press.

Interagency Working Group on Social Cost of Carbon, U.S. Government. (2010). "Technical support document: Social cost of carbon for regulatory impact analysis under executive order 12866." Washington, DC: Author.

International Energy Agency. (2010). *World Energy Outlook 2010*. Paris, France: IEA.

International Energy Agency. (2011). *World Energy Outlook 2011*. Paris, France: IEA.

International Energy Agency, Organization of Petroleum Exporting Countries, Organisation for Economic Co-operation and Development, & World Bank. (2010, June 26–27). "Analysis of the scope of energy subsidies and suggestions for the G20 initiative" (June 16 version). Prepared for submission to the G-20 Summit Meeting, Toronto, Canada.

Jaffe, J., Ranson, M., and Stavins, R. (2010). "Linking tradable permit systems: A key element of emerging international climate policy architecture." *Ecology Law Quarterly*, **36**, 789–808.

Karpas, E., and Kerr, S. (2010). "Preliminary evidence on responses to the New Zealand forestry emissions trading scheme" (Motu Working Paper 11-09). Wellington, New Zealand: Motu Economic and Public Policy Research.

Kruger, J., Oates, W. E., and Pizer, W. A. (2007). "Decentralization in the EU emissions trading scheme and lessons for global policy." *Review of Environmental Economics and Policy*, **1**, 112–133.

Levinson, A. (2010). "Interactions among climate policy regulations" (NBER Working Paper 16109). Cambridge, MA: National Bureau of Economic Research.

Máca, V., Melichar, J., and Ščasný, M. (in press). "Internalization of External Costs of Energy Generation in Central and Eastern European Countries." *Journal of Environment and Development*.

Market Advisory Committee to the California Air Resources Board. (2007). "Recommendations for designing a greenhouse gas cap-and-trade system for California." Sacramento, CA: California Environmental Protection Agency.

McGuinness, M., and Ellerman, A. D. (2008). "The effects of interactions between federal and state climate policies" (Working Paper WP-2008-004). Cambridge: Massachusetts Institute of Technology Center for Energy and Environmental Policy Research.

Metcalf, G. E. (2007). "A proposal for a U.S. carbon tax swap" (The Hamilton Project Discussion Paper 2007–12). Washington, DC: Brookings Institution.

Metcalf, G. E., and Weisbach, D. (2010). "Linking policies when tastes differ: Global climate policy in a heterogeneous world" (Discussion Paper 2010–38). Cambridge, MA: Harvard Project on International Climate Agreements, Belfer Center for Science and International Affairs, Harvard Kennedy School.

Montgomery, D. W. (1972). "Markets in Licenses and Efficient Pollution Control Programs." *Journal of Economic Theory*, **5**, 395–418.

Newell, R. G., Jaffe, A. B., and Stavins, R. N. (1999). "The Induced Innovation Hypothesis and Energy-Saving Technological Change." *Quarterly Journal of Economics*, **114**, 941–975.

Olmstead, S. M., and Stavins, R. N. (2012). "Three Key Elements of Post-2012 International Climate Policy Architecture." *Review of Environmental Economics and Policy*, **6**(2), 1–22.

Organization for Economic Cooperation and Development. (2001). *Environmentally Related Taxes in OECD Countries: Issues and Strategies*. Paris, France: Author.

Organization for Economic Cooperation and Development. (2011). "Interactions Between Emission Trading Systems and Other Overlapping Policy Instruments." Paris, France: Environment Directorate, OECD.

Pizer, W. A. (2002). "Combining Price and Quantity Controls to Mitigate Global Climate Change." *Journal of Public Economics*, **85**, 409–434.

Plumer, B. (2010, July 27). "B.C.'s carbon-tax experiment seems to be working." *New Republic*. Retrieved from http://www.tnr.com/blog/the-vine/76595/bcs-carbon-tax-experiment-seems-be-working.

Popp, D. (2002). "Induced Innovation and Energy Prices." *American Economic Review*, **92**, 160–180.

Province of Alberta. (2007). *Specified Gas Emitters Regulation* (Alberta Regulation 139/2007). Edmonton, Alberta, Canada: *Alberta Queen's Printer*.

Province of Alberta. (2008). *Alberta's 2008 Climate Change Strategy*. Edmonton, Alberta, Canada: Ministry of Environment and Water.

Province of Alberta. (2011). "2010 Greenhouse Gas Emission Reduction Program Results." Edmonton, Alberta, Canada: Ministry of Environment and Water. Retrieved from http://environment.alberta.ca/03501.html.

Ramey, V. A., and Vine, D. J. (2010). "Oil, Automobiles, and the U.S. Economy: How Much Have Things Really Changed?" (NBER Working Paper 16067). Cambridge, MA: National Bureau of Economic Research.

Sass, B. (2010, November 1). "Inside Alberta's Quiet Carbon Market." *Alberta Oil*. Retrieved from http://www.albertaoilmagazine.com/2010/11/a-homegrown-system-puts-the-brakes-on-runaway-emissions/.

Speck, S. (2008). "The Design of Carbon and Broad-Based Energy Taxes in European Countries." *Vermont Journal of Environmental Law*, **10**, 31–59.

Stavins, R. N. (1995). "Transaction Costs and Tradeable Permits." *Journal of Environmental Economics and Management*, **29**, 133–148.

Stavins, R. N. (2003). "Experience with Market-Based Environmental Policy Instruments." In K.-G. Mäler & J. Vincent Eds., *Handbook of Environmental Economics*, Vol. I (Chap. 9, pp. 355–435). Amsterdam, Netherlands: Elsevier Science.

Stavins, R. N. (2007). "A U.S. Cap-and-Trade System to Address Global Climate Change" (The Hamilton Project Discussion Paper 2007–13). Washington, DC: The Brookings Institution.

Stavins, R. N. (2011). "Polarized Politics Paralyze Policy." *Environmental Forum*, **28**(6), 16.

Sterner, T., and Coria, J. (2012). *Policy Instruments for Environmental and Natural Resource Management* (2nd ed.). Washington, DC: RFF Press, Routledge.

UN Environment Programme. (2010). *The Emissions Gap Report: Are the Copenhagen Accord Pledges Sufficient to Limit Global Warming to 2C or 1.5C?* (A preliminary assessment). Nairobi, Kenya: Author.

U.S. Congressional Budget Office. (2011). "The effects of renewable or clean electricity standards." Washington, DC: Author.

U.S. Energy Information Administration. (2009). *Emissions of Greenhouse Gases in the United States*. Washington, DC: Author.

U.S. Energy Information Administration. (2011). *Annual Energy Outlook 2011*. Washington, DC: Author.

Wara, M. (2007). "Is the Global Carbon Market Working?" *Nature*, **445**, 595–596.

Weitzman, M. L. (1974). "Prices vs. Quantities." *Review of Economic Studies*, **41**, 477–491.

World Bank. (2010). *World Development Report 2010: Development and Climate Change*. Washington, DC: Author.

Zhang, J., and Wang, C. (2011). "Co-Benefits and Additionality of the Clean Development Mechanism: An Empirical Analysis." *Journal of Environmental Economics and Management*, **62**, 140–154.

https://doi.org/10.1142/9789811292415_0007

Chapter 7

The SO_2 Allowance-Trading System and the Clean Air Act Amendments of 1990: Reflections on 20 Years of Policy Innovation*

Gabriel Chan[†,‖], Robert N. Stavins[†,‡,§,¶], Robert Stowe[†,], and Richard Sweeney[†,††]**

[†]*John F. Kennedy School of Government, Harvard University, Cambridge, MA, USA*

[‡]*National Bureau of Economic Research, Cambridge, MA, USA*

[§]*Resources for the Future, Washington, DC, USA*

[‖]*gabe_chan@hksphd.harvard.edu*

[¶]*robert_stavins@harvard.edu*

[**]*robert_stowe@harvard.edu*

[††]*rich_sweeney@hksphd.harvard.edu*

*This chapter was originally published in *National Tax Journal*, **65**(2), 419–452, June 2012.

Introduction

In 2009, the U.S. Congress considered but ultimately failed to enact legislation aimed at limiting U.S. greenhouse-gas (GHG) emissions.[1] Over several months of often contentious debate, millions of Americans were introduced to the phrase "cap-and-trade," a regulatory approach that first came to prominence in the 1990s as the centerpiece of a national program to address the threat of acid rain by limiting emissions of sulfur dioxide (SO_2), primarily from electric power plants.

The 1990 SO_2 cap-and-trade program was conceived by the administration of President George H. W. Bush and was widely viewed as a success. Yet cap-and-trade became a lightning rod for congressional opposition to climate legislation from 2009–2010. Some of that hostility reflected skepticism about whether climate change was real and, if it was, whether humans played a key role in causing it. A larger group of opponents in Congress worried about the proper role of government and the costs of combating climate change, particularly given the lack of commitments for action by the large emerging economies of China, India, Brazil, Korea, South Africa, and Mexico. The congressional debate touched only lightly on the relative merits of various policy options to reduce GHG emissions. Thus, cap-and-trade may not have been defeated on its merits (or demerits), but rather as collateral damage in the larger climate policy wars.

Congress (to the extent it did assess policy alternatives to cap-and-trade), as well as the broader community of analysts and observers in the late 2000s, raised a number of substantive questions about the merits of this policy instrument as a means for responding to a major environmental policy challenge of the sort posed by climate change (Peace and Stavins, 2010):

- Cap-and-trade is part of a larger class of policy approaches to alleviating pollution and managing natural resources that rely on market

[1] The bill under consideration at that time, the American Clean Energy and Security Act of 2009, was the last in a series considered over several years. Sponsored by Representatives Henry Waxman (D-California) and Edward Markey (D-Massachusetts), the bill passed the U.S. House of Representatives but failed to win sufficient support in the Senate. No legislation was enacted, and by 2010, both Congress and the White House had abandoned efforts to pass federal climate legislation. The text of H.R. 2454 (111th Congress): American Clean Energy and Security Act of 2009 and information on the bill and its legislative context are available at www.govtrack.us/congress/bill.xpd?bill=h111-2454.

mechanisms.[2] How do the costs of such a market-based approach compare with traditional regulatory policies to reduce pollution?
- Can market-based policies — and the markets they create — be trusted to reduce emissions? That is, are they environmentally effective?
- What are the distributional impacts of market-based environmental policies — who are the winners and losers?
- How well does a cap-and-trade system stimulate technological innovation, as compared with an environmental policy that sets performance standards, specifies technologies for reducing pollution, or both?

In May 2011, the Harvard Environmental Economics Program hosted a two-day research workshop and policy roundtable in Cambridge, Massachusetts,[3] to reflect on these and other questions in light of twenty years of experience implementing the SO_2 cap-and-trade program, established under Title IV of the Clean Air Act Amendments (CAAA) of 1990.[4] Also known as the Acid Rain Program and the SO allowance-trading system, Title IV represented the first large-scale application of cap-and-trade to control pollution — in the United States or any other country.[5] The May 2011 workshop and roundtable included economists and legal experts who had conducted extensive research on the SO_2 allowance-trading system, as well as leaders of non-governmental organizations and former government officials who had guided the formulation and passage of the CAAA. Drawing on their analysis, and on supplementary evidence, this chapter examines the design, enactment, implementation, and performance of the Acid Rain Program, with an eye toward identifying lessons learned for future efforts to apply cap-and-trade to other environmental challenges, including global climate change.[6]

---

[2]The principal market-based alternative to cap-and-trade is a tax on emissions. Stavins (2003) provides a comprehensive discussion of market-based environmental policy.

[3]For a list of conference participants, see http://www.hks.harvard.edu/m-rcbg/heep/so2-policy-brief.html.

[4]See "Acid Rain Program," Clean Air Markets, U.S. Environmental Protection Agency, Washington, DC.

[5]The largest emissions trading program in the world is now the European Union Emissions Trading System, a GHG cap-and-trade system that was implemented in 2005 and whose design was influenced by the U.S. SO_2 program.

[6]Ellerman *et al.* (2000) and Stavins (1998) provide additional background on and analysis of the SO_2 allowance-trading program.

The organization of the remainder of the chapter is as follows. The first section provides background on the Acid Rain Program and summarizes data and analysis on its benefits. Subsequent sections examine key questions regarding cost, environmental effectiveness, market performance, distributional implications, and effects on technology innovation. We then examine the political context of the formulation, enactment, and implementation of the SO_2 allowance-trading system. Finally, in the conclusion, we briefly reflect on implications for climate change policy.

The Acid Rain Program

Background and Benefits

By the late 1980s, there was growing concern that acid rain was damaging aquatic ecosystems, forests, and buildings in the northeastern United States and southeastern Canada. Acid rain is the result of SO_2 and, to a lesser extent, nitrogen oxides (NO_x) reacting in the atmosphere to form sulfuric and nitric acids, which are deposited on the Earth's surface through either precipitation or dry processes. Flue gas emissions from coal-fired, electric-power plants were (and remain) the primary source of SO_2 emissions and a major source of NO_x emissions in the United States.

The stated purpose of Title IV of the CAAA of 1990 was to reduce total annual SO_2 emissions in the United States by 10 million tons relative to 1980, when total U.S. emissions were about 25.9 million tons.[7] The program mandated an allowance-trading system[8] and specified that this goal would be accomplished in two phases. Phase I (1995–1999) required significant emissions reductions from the 263 most polluting coal-fired electric generating units, almost all located east of the Mississippi River.[9]

---

[7]The legislation itself did not specify a target year. For SO emissions data, see U.S. Environmental Protection Agency, National Emissions Inventory Air Pollutant Emissions Trends Data; "1970–2011 Average annual emissions, all criteria pollutants in MS Excel — October 2011."

[8]We use the phrases "allowance trading" and "cap-and-trade" interchangeably. The CAAA also mandated a smaller quantity of power-sector NOx reductions, but the NOx program did not allow for allowance trading and is not addressed in this chapter.

[9]A number of additional units that were to be regulated only in Phase II opted-in early for Phase I.

Phase II, which began in 2000, placed an aggregate national emissions cap of 8.95 million tons per year on approximately 3,200 electric generating units — nearly the entire fleet of coal-fired plants in the continental United States (Ellerman *et al.*, 2000; National Acid Precipitation Assessment Program (NAPAP), 2005). This cap — affecting almost exclusively the power sector — represented an approximately 50 percent reduction from 1980 levels, when power-sector emissions were about 17.5 million tons. The SO_2 allowance-trading program had a number of features that would subsequently become common to virtually all cap-and-trade systems (see below). At the beginning of the program, the government (freely) allocated allowances, denominated in tons of SO_2 emissions, to power plants covered by the law, according to formulas contained in the legislation and elaborated upon by regulation. If annual emissions at a regulated facility exceeded the allowances allocated to that facility, the facility owner could either buy allowances or reduce emissions, whether by installing pollution controls, changing the mix of fuels used to operate the facility, or by scaling back operations. If emissions at a regulated facility were reduced below its allowance allocation, the facility owner could sell the extra allowances or bank them for future use; these opportunities created incentives to find ways to reduce emissions at the lowest cost.

By contrast, most air pollution regulations prior to the 1990 CAAA took a much more prescriptive approach, either by setting uniform emission limits on classes of emitters or by specifying the type of pollution-control equipment to be installed. Such requirements are relatively inflexible, imposing the same abatement path upon a range of heterogeneous facilities and ignoring the fact that the costs of compliance might vary widely across individual facilities depending on the age, technology characteristics, operating conditions, and quality of fuel used. This type of inflexible environmental regulation came to be known by the somewhat pejorative term "command-and-control," invoking visions of Soviet-style planning.

The environmental objective of the Acid Rain Program was to reduce emissions of SO_2 and NO_x, but its effectiveness in achieving these objectives should be distinguished from the benefits of the program (intended or not). The intended benefits of the program were associated with reduced acidification of aquatic ecosystems, primarily in the Northeast. However, subsequent assessments of the program found that by far the greatest benefits were in the form of avoided health damages from reduced levels of airborne fine particles derived from SO emissions.[10] Estimates of these health benefits vary widely, but they appear to be on the order of $50 billion per year by 2010. This compares with estimated program costs (see below) on the order of $0.5 billion (Burtraw, 1998; NAPAP, 2005; Shadbegian *et al.*, 2005; Office of Air and Radiation, 2000).[11]

What is Cap-and-Trade?

The fundamental motivation for any government policy to reduce emissions is that pollution imposes costs on *society* (related to health and environmental quality) that are not borne by polluters — "external costs." These costs to society must be "internalized" or made the responsibility of the polluter, if the polluter is to have an incentive to abate. A *cost-effective* system of regulation would be one in which the costs incurred are minimized, relative to other systems of regulation with commensurate environmental results.

Several basic features are common to all cap-and-trade programs. First, government decides on the total (aggregate) quantity of emissions to be allowed under the program for a stated time period (usually per year) — that is, the "cap." Next, government creates allowances (or "permits"), denominated in quantities of the pollutant in question. The total number of allowances issued is equal to the cap.

At the start of the program, allowances may be given to the entities subject to the program (firms, facilities) for free or sold for a price (usually through an auction) — or some combination. A regulated entity must hold and surrender to the government at the end of each compliance period

[10]Though the program's SO_2-emissions-reductions targets were achieved, and there has been an observed, significant reduction in acid precipitation in the Northeast, it takes much longer to reverse the acidification of ecosystems, which is the environmental harm that inspired the legislation in the first place (NAPAP, 2005). However, health benefits will dominate ecological benefits regardless of the time required for ecosystem recovery.

[11]Attempts to quantify the benefits of the Acid Rain Program have generally not included all improvements to ecosystems. These are much more difficult to estimate and they are much smaller than human health benefits — by at least an order of magnitude — as discussed in Burtraw (1998). Banzhaf *et al.* (2006) found that the benefits of ecosystem recovery in the Adirondacks alone justified the costs of the acid rain program. Schmalensee and Stavins (2011) provide a detailed analysis of costs and health benefits associated with recent policies intended to replace the SO_2 allowance-trading system.

allowances equivalent to that entity's actual emissions during the period. If a firm does not hold sufficient allowances, it is subject to penalties or other enforcement actions. In the case of the SO_2 program, these penalties were, for the first time, specified in the statute, set at levels significantly higher than the anticipated compliance costs, and imposed automatically, thus providing certainty with regard to consequences for noncompliance.

Firms may buy allowances on the market to meet their compliance obligations, or they may choose to reduce their emissions. For companies holding too few allowances, the choice to abate or buy allowances would depend on the cost of compliance versus the price (or anticipated price) of purchasing allowances. Because each individual company (or facility) has the flexibility to choose the course of action that costs it the least to achieve compliance, investment in abatement technology or procedures would flow to where it was least costly to reduce emissions. Thus the marginal costs of abatement become equalized across all entities. In aggregate, the mandated environmental target is achieved at lowest cost; this is why cap-and-trade is generally considered a cost-effective form of environmental regulation.

Cost

A key question concerns cost — specifically, how the costs of achieving environmental objectives through cap-and-trade compare with those of a "counterfactual" (hypothetical alternative) command-and-control regulatory approach. Indeed, policy makers asked this question during discussions in the late 1980s about a new program for SO emissions reduction. They proceeded on the basis of projections[12] and economic theory suggesting that cap-and-trade would be much less costly, relative to traditional, prescriptive regulatory approaches.[13]

Extensive analysis has demonstrated over the subsequent twenty years that these projections were largely correct. A summary of economic research addressing this question and presented in the workshop identified

[12] These projections were largely the result of modeling conducted by ICF International, a consulting firm retained by the U.S. Environmental Protection Agency; see, for example, the references in Burtraw and Palmer (2003).

[13] Costs referenced in this section include those to industry for complying with the program and to government for administering the program.

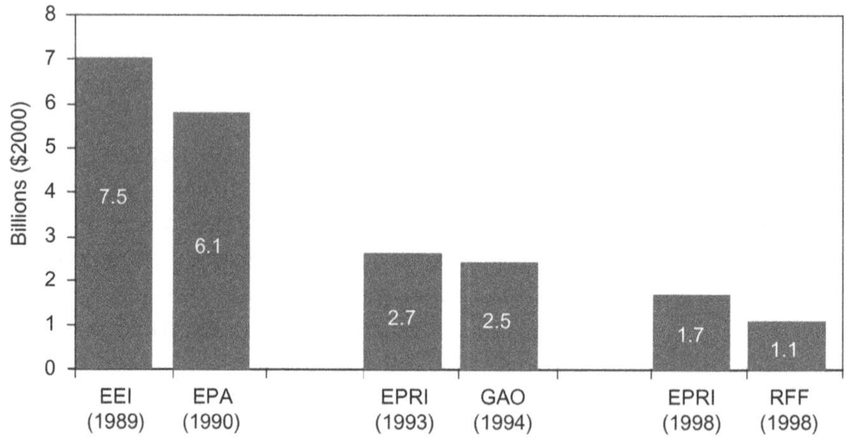

Figure 1. Evolution of cost estimates for implementing Title IV acid rain program in the year 2010.

Source: These estimates are adapted from NAPAP (2005, 13); "EEI": Edison Electric Institute; "GAO": U.S. General Accounting Office (now Government Accountability Office). The other abbreviations are defined in the text.

a range of 15–90 percent savings, compared to counterfactual policies that specified the means of regulation in various ways and for various portions of the program's regulatory period — as discussed in, among others, Carlson *et al.* (2000), Ellerman *et al.* (2000), and Keohane (2003).

In addition to being less costly than traditional command-and-control policies would have been, the program's costs were significantly below estimates generated by government and industry analysts in the debate leading up to the passage of the CAAA. In 1990, the U.S. Environmental Protection Agency (EPA) estimated the cost of implementing the Acid Rain Program (with allowance trading) at $6.1 billion. In 1998, the Electric Power Research Institute (EPRI), an industry organization, and Resources for the Future (RFF), an independent think tank, estimated that total implementation costs would be $1.7 and $1.1 billion respectively (based in part on actual figures for the first few years of the program (NAPAP, 2005), as shown in Figure 1).

Several factors explain the large decline in the cost estimates. Power-plant operators in the eastern states benefited from increased access to — and falling prices of — low-sulfur coal from the Powder River Basin in Wyoming and Montana, due to the deregulation of the railroads in the 1980s, which reduced transportation costs (Ellerman *et al.*, 2000). For many facilities this made fuel switching less expensive than installing scrubbers.[14] The primary technology for reducing SO_2 emissions is flue-gas desulfurization, and equipment employing this technology is commonly known as a "scrubber." Scrubbers remove SO_2 from a boiler's flue gas stream before the gas enters the atmosphere. At the same time, coal mine operators elsewhere in the country responded to Powder River Basin competition and changing fuel demands by exploiting medium-sulfur coal seams. Coal from these seams would produce emissions just above the limit of 1.2 pounds of SO_2 per million BTUs[15] set by the Clean Air Act of 1970 for new plants, but not enough in excess of that limit to be worth scrubbing. Finally, technological innovation in both scrubbers and power plants (some of it prompted by the trading program itself, as discussed below) reduced costs over this time period, primarily through better management of the fuel mix. Taken together, these developments made it possible for electric utilities to achieve greater SO_2 reductions through fuel switching, relative to more expensive investments in new equipment.[16]

While the costs of the SO_2 allowance-trading system were low, other evidence suggests that they were not as low as they could have been, in the sense that they did not achieve the theoretical least-cost abatement solution for a cap-and-trade system. One study suggests that costs remained \$280 million (51 percent) and \$339 million (59 percent) higher than the least-cost solution in 1995 and 1996, respectively (Carlson *et al.*, 2000).

Factors that kept costs above the theoretical minimum[17] were, first, provisions in the CAAA that encouraged early scrubbing to limit impacts

---

[14]Of the 263 Phase I units, 136 (52 percent) pursued fuel switching or blending. These units accounted for 59 percent of Phase I emissions reductions; scrubbers were installed at 27 (10 percent) of the units, accounting for 28 percent of the emissions reduction (Lange and Bellas, 2005).

[15]British Thermal Units (BTUs) are a measure of the quantity of heat.

[16]Some analysts have suggested that because the reduction in fuel costs would have occurred anyway — and would have reduced the costs of a command-and-control SO_2 program as well — then the cost savings attributed to the SO_2 allowance-trading program (relative to a command-and-control system) should be adjusted downward (Carlson *et al.*, 2000). However, a prescriptive regulatory approach (such as a policy that required the installation of scrubbers at all power plants) might have prevented utilities from taking advantage of these alternative compliance options.

[17]That marginal abatement costs still varied across facilities, even after the SO cap-and-trade system was implemented, is evidence that the cap-and-trade system did not always

on high-sulfur coal producers, and second, lack of information about marginal abatement costs and other crucial factors on the part of market participants. In the early years, power-plant operators may have lacked the information (and associated experience and confidence) to take full advantage of the flexibility that the SO_2 allowance-trading system offered. Third, in the early years of the program, utilities were subject to economic regulation at the state level that had the effect of distorting or constraining their responses to market-based federal environmental regulation (Arimura, 2002; Bohi and Burtraw, 1992). In those states that allowed costs to be recovered from electric ratepayers, some faced uncertainty over whether state regulators would approve the inclusion of costs incurred to purchase emissions allowances. Similarly, there were interactions between the SO_2 system and other federal regulations, such as New Source Review and New Source Performance Standards, that may have created inefficiencies in how the program operated. Finally, there was considerable policy uncertainty — particularly in Phase II — when regulators and policy makers were considering further reductions in the national SO_2 cap, as is discussed below.

In sum, the SO_2 allowance-trading system's actual costs, even if they exceeded the cost-effective ideal for a cap-and-trade system, were much lower than would have been incurred with a comparable traditional regulatory approach, and were much lower than the trading system's predicted costs. There is broad agreement that the SO_2 allowance-trading system provided a compelling demonstration of the cost advantages of a market-based approach. It is important to elaborate on this conclusion, however, by examining two ancillary issues that have significant cost implications: uncertainty and the problems of combining policy approaches.

Cost Uncertainty and Cap-and-Trade

Firms desire certainty (low variance) in regulatory requirements and compliance costs, the latter being facilitated by flexibility in the means to comply. A regulatory instrument that offers a predictable compliance

yield cost-effective mitigation outcomes; some utilities ended up paying more on a dollar-per-ton basis to comply with the program than others. Analysts disagree, though, on the significance of these variations, largely depending on whether they are compared with much larger heterogeneity in abatement costs prior to the SO_2 allowance-trading system or with the ideal convergence of marginal costs in a cost-minimizing outcome.

regime and greater cost certainty[18] will usually enable companies to take advantage of longer-term investments that may reduce costs over time. Cost certainty is especially important for the electric power industry, whose capital assets (physical facilities) are long-lived.

Compared with an emissions tax (see below) or technology-standards-based, command-and-control-style regulations, a cap-and-trade system offers individual firms less certainty about abatement costs, because the price of allowances fluctuates with market conditions. Firms that make incorrect predictions about allowance prices (or, alternatively, marginal abatement costs) are less likely than competitors with better foresight to select an optimal compliance strategy. However, ancillary policy-design elements of the SO_2 allowance-trading system mitigated this uncertainty. Banking provisions gave firms the flexibility to save ("bank") allowances from one compliance period for use in a future compliance period, thus effectively smoothing price fluctuations (Burtraw and Mansur, 1999). Another program feature that required EPA to auction small percentages of the total allowance pool "facilitated both the price discovery process and the development of the allowance market," (Schmalensee *et al.*, 1998, p. 66). This allowed firms to forecast allowance prices more accurately.

The difficulty of predicting program costs and benefits suggests that it may have been desirable to build more capacity for adaptation into the SO_2 system — including with regard to the cap. Instead of legislating a fixed cap on emissions in years well beyond the planning horizon of decision makers at the beginning of the program, the 1990 Amendments could have given EPA authority to adjust the SO_2 cap in future years as the science evolved and as better information on real-world control costs became available. Alternatively, the 1990 Amendments could have implemented a rule-based adjustment process that might have been easier for firms to anticipate. For example, Burtraw *et al.* (2010) discuss the role of a reserve price in the revenue-neutral auction that, if triggered, could have tightened the cap automatically when abatement costs turned out to be lower than expected.

Tension exists between providing regulatory certainty over long periods of time (which is desirable from the standpoint of reducing costs) and allowing for flexibility to adjust program goals (which may be desirable

[18] In the case of regulated electric utilities, greater uncertainty may require greater ability to *recover* costs through rate increases.

from the standpoint of maximizing net program benefits over time). In striking that balance, the 1990 Amendments may have leaned too heavily towards providing certainty at the cost of reducing flexibility to adjust the policy as the understanding of both science and markets improved. This preference undoubtedly also reflected a certain amount of distrust of the EPA on the part of Congress, with a corresponding unwillingness to cede to EPA the right to set program requirements in the future without congressional input and approval. The inflexibility of the Acid Rain Program ultimately led to its demise, as is discussed below.

Taxes versus Cap-and-Trade

Emission taxes are a market-based alternative to cap-and-trade (Metcalf, 2007): like cap-and-trade, they create a price signal that provides incentives for emissions reductions while leaving individual firms the flexibility to pursue whatever abatement strategy is least costly for them. Emission taxes have some potentially important advantages over cap-and-trade: first, they do not require the government to track or allocate allowances and thereby avoid questions about how to allocate allowances in the first place. (Ofcourse, calculating tax charges does require monitoring of actual emissions, just as determining compliance with an allowance-trading system does.) Second, taxes provide price certainty — once government sets the tax rate, everyone knows exactly what the cost per ton will be for as long as the tax is in place (Weitzman, 1974). Third, taxes avoid concerns about distortion, manipulation, or excessive price volatility in allowance markets. Finally, in countries that may not have a well-developed institutional infrastructure to support commodity markets, taxes may be a more administratively feasible option.

Taxes also have disadvantages. First, and of particular concern to environmental advocates, is that a tax does not guarantee specific quantities of emissions reduction. Annual emissions-reductions will fluctuate, depending on the cost and availability of abatement options (which cannot be precisely known in advance) relative to the level of the tax. Second, taxes often raise distributional concerns (e.g., the concern that emission taxes are regressive or might fall more heavily on some groups than others), although it is the case that any regulatory policy creates winners and losers. (Distributional issues are discussed in more detail below.)

Third, while concerns about market complexities and failures arise with cap-and-trade, a tax is subject to becoming increasingly complex, to being changed in the future, and to having revenues redirected to other purposes as exemptions, deductions, loopholes, and subsidies are introduced through the interplay of interest-based politics and the legislative process. The most complex aspects of a cap-and-trade system usually involve the distribution of free allowances, but these allocation decisions have no effect on the cost-effectiveness of the system (to a close approximation, Stavins, 1995). In tax legislation, by contrast, complexity arises when tax preferences of various sorts are granted to favored interests. Such preferences *do* adversely affect the cost-effectiveness of the system. In particular, when lower tax rates or exemptions are granted to some parties or interests, the same quantity of emissions will have multiple prices. This detracts from the cost effectiveness of the policy. A cap-and-trade system, on the other hand, preserves a single price per unit of emissions, even when relief is granted to favored interests through free allocation.

Finally, and perhaps decisively, taxes are extremely unpopular. Taxes make the costs of abating emissions highly visible, whereas in an allowance-trading system, these costs are less obvious. Having said this, given the extreme fiscal pressures sure to be faced by the U.S. government over coming years and the unpopularity of cap-and-trade in recent climate debates, it is possible that a carbon tax, in some form, will be among the options considered as lawmakers look for ways to raise needed revenue.

Exclusion of Command-and-Control Add-Ons

An important feature of the SO_2 allowance-trading program was what was *not* included in the program. Despite widespread skepticism about the cost and environmental effectiveness of a cap-and-trade system, the 1990 CAAA largely avoided imposing supplementary mandates for SO_2 abatement, whether through specific pollution control technology requirements or performance standards for individual plants.[19] This enabled the system

[19]More recently, however, new regulations, especially the Clean Air Interstate Rule (CAIR) and the Cross-State Air Pollution Rule, have contained plant-level requirements that have sharply curbed, to the point of virtually eliminating, emissions trading in SO_2. See "Clean Air Interstate Rule," U.S. EPA, and "Cross-State Air Pollution Rule (CSAPR)."

to capture the efficiency gains of allowing flexibility in the *methods* of abatement used by different firms and making it possible for firms with high abatement costs to trade with firms that faced low abatement costs.

When the SO_2 allowance-trading program was introduced, power plants around the country had widely different emissions profiles. Older coal-fired plants in the East tended to have high SO_2 emissions, while the relatively newer power plants in the West and Southwest generally had much lower emissions — in part because they were built after the introduction of stringent EPA standards regulating newly-constructed facilities (New Source Performance Standards), and because they burned primarily lower sulfur coal from mines in the West.

Largely because of this heterogeneity, had the 1990 CAAA included a technology (most likely scrubber) mandate, aggregate compliance costs would have been much greater. Technology mandates would also have constituted an obstacle to firms reducing emissions further than was either required by regulation or was otherwise financially reasonable.[20] Absent a requirement to invest in a specific manner to comply with a technology mandate, plant operators who discovered new, cost-effective abatement opportunities had an incentive to implement them so that they could bank or sell the excess allowances. There is significant evidence of such "over-compliance" under the SO_2 allowance-trading program (as discussed below).

Environmental Effectiveness

Environmental effectiveness refers to the degree to which a policy achieves its objective. In the case of a cap-and-trade program, the question is whether emissions are kept at (or below) the cap. Can cap-and-trade systems (compared with command-and-control regulation) be relied on to produce desired levels of emissions reductions? If the answer were no,

[20]A number of Senators from eastern states that produced high-sulfur coal did insert a provision into the CAAA to award bonus allowances to plant operators who installed scrubbers. These states had an interest in promoting greater reliance on scrubbers, since this abatement option — in contrast to fuel-switching options — allowed for the continued use of the high-sulfur coal that was mined in their states (Ellerman *et al.*, 2000). The provision was of sufficiently small scope that it did not significantly affect the cost effectiveness of the system.

cap-and-trade would probably be a poor policy choice regardless of its cost advantages.

In exploring this question, it is important to make a distinction, relevant to all environmental policy, between the stringency or ambition of the program — that is, whether the goal set for emission reductions is adequate to address the public health or environmental damages that have been identified — and the effectiveness of the policy in achieving whatever goal is set (that is, whether targeted reductions are, in fact, realized). Deciding the stringency of the program — that is, setting the level of the cap — is the first critical step in designing a cap-and-trade system.

Setting the Level of the Cap

The efficient level of pollution abatement occurs when the cost of reducing emissions by one additional unit equals the benefit to society of an additional unit of pollution reduction. In practice, it is usually difficult to determine the efficient level of abatement, both because it is difficult to assess the marginal cost of abatement in advance and because it is difficult to quantify, in monetary terms, the environmental or public health benefit that would result from an additional ton of emissions reduction. Partly because of this uncertainty, political negotiations over program stringency tend to focus on identifying a level of perceived benefits for which costs are acceptable, rather than employing formal benefit-cost analysis to find the level of action at which the difference between benefits and costs is greatest (Arrow *et al.*, 1996). This was the case both for the Title IV program and in more recent climate proposals.

The explicit and implicit analysis carried out by the George H.W. Bush Administration in the context of the 1990 CAAA focused almost exclusively on the cost side. The benefits considered were those associated with reducing the ecological impacts of acid rain. Not surprisingly, analysts failed to foresee either lower-than-expected abatement costs or the substantial human health benefits of reducing fine particulate pollution, which also originates from SO_2 emissions. Had those lower costs and added benefits been fully appreciated, policy makers might have pursued an even lower SO_2 cap. According to workshop participants, formal analysis was neither fully ignored by nor fully incorporated into the decision-making process; rather it was overwhelmed by heuristic ("back of the envelope") sketches of real and perceived costs — to industry, electricity ratepayers, and the economy as a whole — and of potential environmental effectiveness.[21]

That the SO_2 emissions cap was not determined by formal benefit-cost analysis, but instead reflected a qualitative collective judgment about what constitutes an acceptable balance of cost and environmental protection, does not make the decision about the cap any less important to the design or effectiveness of the cap-and-trade program. On the contrary, the level of the cap in the SO_2 allowance-trading system was very important for political and economic reasons and of great concern to electric utilities. There was a sentiment at the workshop that the stand out lesson of the acid rain program was that the main role of government is to set the cap, and to give the market the flexibility to achieve it in a cost effective manner. This view of the central rationale for a cap-and-trade system can be traced to an idea articulated by Baumol and Oates (1971): if it is too difficult to determine what level of pollution control is perfectly efficient in every instance (in the sense that the marginal costs incurred to provide that level of control are exactly offset by the marginal benefits), then government can simply set an acceptable standard and focus on minimizing the costs of achieving it (and perhaps iterating through subsequent adjustments).

Given that decisions about major new environmental policies are — to some degree — determined by political leaders' evaluations of how both costs and environmental effectiveness will be perceived by stakeholders, a cap-and-trade system offered promise on both fronts. Cap-and-trade can reduce costs, and it offers a clear and stable environmental target — the emissions cap. The challenge remained, in the case of acid rain, to convince stakeholders that the cap was low enough.[22] By reducing the costs of regulation relative to conventional prescriptive approaches, cap-and-trade made it politically feasible to reduce emissions more than might otherwise have been the case. Without the cap-and-trade architecture, it is unlikely that a 10 million ton reduction would have been endorsed by the Bush Administration or would have had the votes to pass the Congress. Apparently, the one type of formal economic analysis that White House policy makers *did* consider was the so-called "knee" or "elbow" of the cost curve analysis — that is, identifying the level of pollution control at which the marginal cost of abatement began to increase

[21] Benefit-cost analysis has developed very considerably since 1990 and is now more regularly and systematically deployed in meaningful ways to inform policy decisions.

[22] A second challenge was to show that the market for allowances would work (see below).

sharply. Again, there was considerable uncertainty, but it appeared that the knee was in the range of a seven to eight million ton reduction over the approximate time period envisioned for the program. Adopting cap-and-trade would move the knee up (enabling larger emissions reductions before marginal costs rose sharply), but workshop participants agreed that no one knew by how much. The Bush team eventually chose a 10 million ton reduction policy, which was the most ambitious of the three options presented to the President by the Domestic Policy Council at the time, according to workshop participants. (The other options proposed targeted reductions of six and eight million tons.)[23] This 10-million-ton option presented marketing opportunities: it was a double-digit number, and it represented a 50 percent reduction in emissions, both of which signified that the Bush administration was serious about pollution reductions.

Effectiveness in Achieving the Cap

The SO_2 allowance-trading program was highly effective. SO_2 emissions from electric power plants decreased 36 percent (from 15.9 million to 10.2 million tons) between 1990 and 2004,[24] despite the fact that electricity generation from coal-fired power plants *increased* 25 percent over the same period (growing from 1.59 to 1.98 billion megawatt hours).[25] The program's long-term goal of reducing annual nationwide utility emissions to 8.95 million tons was achieved in 2007; by 2010 emissions had declined further, to 5.1 million tons, in response to the related Clean Air Interstate

[23]The 10 million ton cap also represented the greatest reduction in emissions of the more than 70 legislative proposals offered in the preceding 10 years, and was consistent with reductions advocated by Canada and the environmental community. For example, a bill sponsored by Senator George Mitchell (D-Maine) called for a 12 million ton reduction from projected 2000 emissions, which was consistent with a 10 million ton reduction from actual 1980 levels as contained in President Bush's proposal and the enacted legislation (Jackson, 1987; Joskow and Schmalensee, 1998).

[24]See U.S. EPA, National Emissions Inventory Air Pollutant Emissions Trends Data, "1970–2011 Average annual emissions, all criteria pollutants in MS Excel — October 2011."

[25]See U.S. Energy Information Administration, "Electricity Net Generation: Total (All Sectors), 1949–2010."

Rule (CAIR), which was promulgated in 2005 under the George W. Bush Administration. (CAIR is discussed further in a later section).[26]

The SO_2 allowance-trading program delivered emissions reductions more quickly than expected. Because of its banking provisions, many utility companies — some of which owned plants that were very dirty and had large and relatively inexpensive abatement opportunities — over-complied in the first phase of the program. As a result, actual emissions during Phase I of the program (1995–1999) fell well below the Phase I target. At the workshop it was remarked that this was the most significant, abrupt decline in emissions in the history of air pollution regulation. Again, utilities were not compelled to over-comply in the early years of the program; rather, incentives internal to the program led to the decisions that produced these large, early reductions. On the other hand, in the early years of Phase II (2000–2010), national emissions exceeded the national cap as firms applied excess allowances banked during Phase I.

Effective monitoring and compliance mechanisms played a major role in the SO_2 allowance-trading system's environmental effectiveness, in the view of both environmental advocates and industry stakeholders. One participant noted that while he initially opposed the requirement that regulated units install costly, real-time, continuous emissions monitors, he later came to view this requirement as central to the legitimacy of the program.

Although the specific cap was identified and set in a somewhat *ad hoc* manner, the SO_2 allowance-trading system is widely viewed as having been highly effective. The program achieved its emission-reduction goals with relatively little government intervention (of the traditional type) and with very high levels of compliance among regulated entities (compared with significantly lower levels of compliance for most previous traditional regulatory policies). These results were achieved despite considerable concern that the SO_2 allowance market would fail to function properly — a topic to which we now turn.

Market Performance and Regulatory Complexity

Because a cap-and-trade system for emissions had never been implemented on a large scale prior to 1990, considerable concern arose during

[26]See U.S. EPA, National Emissions Inventory, cited in footnote 24, and U.S. EPA (2011b). On CAIR, see "Clean Air Interstate Rule," cited in footnote 20.

the CAAA debate about how well the SO_2 allowance market would work in practice. One potential problem was that the market would have too few buyers and sellers of allowances — insufficient liquidity — to function well. In that case, utilities needing allowances to comply might not be able to obtain them. A related concern was that incumbent firms might use the allowance market to construct barriers to entry against new entrants. To address these issues, approximately three percent of the allowances allocated to installations were retained by EPA and auctioned annually, with the proceeds (less expenses) returned *pro rata* to those same installations. But these concerns did not materialize, and the allowance auction proved to be largely unnecessary for liquidity purposes.[27]

Other potential problems with the SO_2 market centered on access to information and on transaction costs — specifically, that information about buyer and seller positions might be difficult to access and that transaction costs in the allowance market would be high. Again, these problems did not materialize in practice, and the SO_2 market supported a robust level of trading activity almost from the outset. By March 1998, 20.3 million allowances had been traded between unrelated entities and another 1.3 million allowances had been purchased through EPA auctions (Ellerman *et al.*, 2000). The banking provisions included in the program helped the market adjust to fluctuations in allowance supply and demand over time.

There is broad consensus that the SO_2 allowance market operated transparently and fairly. According to Burtraw and Szambelan (2009, p. 2), "Transparent data systems, public access to information, and strict and certain penalties for noncompliance have led to a virtually perfect compliance record." And evidence suggests that both traders and EPA auctions played valuable roles in the price discovery process during the early years of the SO_2 allowance-trading system (Joskow *et al.*, 1998). Excessive price volatility would be an indicator of potential problems in the allowance market, particularly if volatility were driven by trading behavior rather than by changes in market fundamentals. In general, participants at

[27]The CAAA also included a provision that allowed firms to purchase SO allowances directly from the government at a fixed price of $1,500 per ton. However, SO_2 allowance markets functioned well and allowance prices remained at or below $200 per ton through 2003 — well below prices anticipated prior to implementation of the program. The direct sale provision was nullified in 1997 because it was deemed unnecessary. More information is available at "Acid Rain Program: Auctions and Direct Sale," U.S. EPA, www.epa.gov/airmarkets/progsregs/arp/basic.html#auctions.

the workshop agreed that SO_2 allowance prices had tracked the fundamentals in the market, but there was some discussion about what can be considered a "fundamental" in a market that is created by regulation. For example, it is unclear if expectations of a future policy change should be considered a "fundamental" in the SO_2 emissions-trading market.

A major source of uncertainty with any government-created market is that the government can undo what it created — possibly unintentionally. In essence, this is what has transpired in the SO_2 allowance market. It was recognized by the late 1990s that SO_2 reductions in excess of those resulting from Title IV would be required by other provisions in the Clean Air Act and would otherwise be warranted in any case, given the significant adverse health effects of fine particulates associated with SO_2 emissions. Questions remained about how to accomplish these additional reductions. In 2005, after Congress failed to pass President George W. Bush's Clear Skies Act of 2002, which would have tightened the SO_2 cap, the Administration promulgated CAIR with the same intentions. CAIR lowered the cap on SO_2 emissions — in part by applying more stringent emission requirements on certain "upwind [primarily midwestern] states that were contributing to violations of EPA's primary ambient air quality standards for fine particulates in the eastern United States" (Palmer and Evans, 2009). CAIR attempted to do so while maintaining the nationwide cap-and-trade system (and the allowances) established under Title IV.

SO_2 (Title IV) allowance prices rose in anticipation of CAIR (which one would expect if the cap were to be lowered). Thereafter, an array of factors led to much greater volatility — and reduced liquidity — in the SO_2 allowance market. Among these factors were natural disasters (including Hurricanes Katrina and Rita, which impaired petroleum refining capacity) and developments in broader energy markets. Importantly, in 2008, the Washington, DC Circuit Court of Appeals ruled that Title IV SO_2 allowances could not be limited on the basis of facility location to address the other Clean-Air-Act requirements (ambient air standards) in question (U.S. EPA 2011a). Neither the Bush nor the Barack Obama Administrations appealed that decision, and congressional attempts to affirm the reduction in the cap (which industry had already begun implementing) were unsuccessful. In response to the Court's 2008 decision on CAIR, the Bush and Obama Administrations developed new rules to replace CAIR that employ trading only *within* states and do not employ

Title IV allowances; the Cross-State Air Pollution Rule (CSAPR) was finalized in July 2011. Subsequently, SO_2 (Title IV) allowance prices fell to near zero (Burtraw and Szambelan, 2009).[28]

In sum, the recent history of SO_2 regulation is complex — and that is the point. The allowance-trading system was highly successful in its first decade of operation, in terms of both aggregate cost and environmental effectiveness — and showed every sign of continuing to be so. However, conflicts arose between market-based and traditional regulatory methods, as well as between objectives specified in law and regulation. While the Title IV allowance market itself functioned transparently, effectively, and with great integrity, the broader regulatory environment for this market — to the chagrin of almost all stakeholders — served to end its life prematurely.

Distribution of Allowances and Fairness of Impact

A program that is seen as unfair or inequitable in its distribution of benefits and costs can have difficulty winning political support. Three distributional issues are particularly relevant to the SO_2 allowance-trading system: (1) the method by which emissions allowances were allocated; (2) the geographic distribution of program benefits and costs; and (3) the distribution of benefits and costs across socio-economic groups.

Allowance Allocation

To a close approximation, regulated entities in a cap-and-trade system will face the same incentives to reduce emissions, regardless of how allowances are initially allocated, including, specifically, how many allowances a given firm holds at the outset (Montgomery, 1972). What matters with regard to firms' decisions to trade or abate are marginal abatement costs, and these costs are generally unaffected by the initial allocation of allowances.[29]

---

[28]More information is provided in Belden (2005), Bravender (2009), Palmer and Evans (2009), Schmalensee and Stavins (2011), Spinney (2011), and U.S. EPA (2011a).

[29]Hahn and Stavins (2010) and Stavins (1995) examine the conditions under which this theorem of the independence of the initial allocation from the equilibrium allocation after trading is violated.

Emissions allowances have monetary value as a result of the aggregate cap placed on emissions, combined with the system's enforcement mechanisms. Government, in effect, is creating a new commodity (that is, a new property right in limited supply, in place of a previously unlimited open-access resource) and must decide at the outset how to transfer that commodity to the private entities that will need it to demonstrate compliance. As discussed above, the government has two basic options: allowances can be given away or sold (preferably through an auction, which will facilitate smooth functioning of the market).

The intent of the Acid Rain Program was to cut permitted emissions in half. To achieve this goal, emitters were expected to incur billions of dollars per year in new compliance costs. Congress and the George H.W. Bush Administration judged that it was politically untenable to double the cost of the legislation by requiring SO_2 emitters to pay the government for the emissions they were still allowed under the new policy. In particular, the free allocation of allowances was critical for gaining the support, or at least the acquiescence, of the expected "losers" in the SO_2 allowance-trading program — that is, high-sulfur-coal-intensive power companies in the Midwest and their congressional representatives. (In contrast, some roundtable participants maintained that the Waxman-Markey bill's CO_2 cap-and-trade system was disadvantaged politically because it included an initial auction of 15 percent of allowances, with the percentage rising significantly thereafter.) Free allowances represent a cash transfer to firms and so can be used to compensate firms that face particularly high costs, without changing the cap or distorting the market incentives of the program that lead to a cost-effective solution. Although free allowances can, under some circumstances, constitute a significant windfall, the option to freely allocate some or all allowances nonetheless provides an opportunity to build political support for a nascent cap-and-trade program. Conversely, an auction forces emitters to pay for permitted emissions for which they have previously not had to pay.

Indeed, members of Congress fought intensely to increase the share of freely allocated allowances that would go to utilities in their home districts, as a means to sell the SO_2 allowance-trading program to constituents.[30] In the end, the distribution of free allowances to individual firms

[30] Joskow and Schmalensee (1998) and Ellerman *et al.* (2000) provide detailed quantitative analyses of the political economy of the congressional process that determined allocation methods.

was largely based on prior regulatory benchmarks associated with emissions per unit of heat. This general principle allowed for considerable political horse-trading at the margin, however — that is, awarding a few more allowances to a particular plant in a particular district while maintaining the total cap — to win support for the overall policy.[31]

At the time the CAAA were being debated, consumer advocates, economists, and environmental organizations exerted little pressure to consider alternatives to free allocation, the most significant of which is an auction that would raise public revenues. Economic analyses conducted since then have elucidated the relative merits of free allocation and auctions, with regard to distributional issues and cost-effectiveness. Three conclusions are relevant to the SO_2 allowance-trading program:

1. Unless the overall emissions cap is very stringent, the sum of the market value of allowances is likely to substantially exceed the total abatement costs incurred to meet the cap. Thus, recipients of free allowances are likely to be overcompensated for their actual compliance costs, resulting in a windfall.[32]
2. In competitive markets, free allocation does not reduce firms' incentives to pass the marginal cost of emissions control (as reflected in the market price of allowances) through to customers. Again, this is because the cost to a firm of using an allowance is the same whether the firm already holds the allowance (in which case it is foregoing the opportunity to sell that allowance at the market price) or has to purchase the allowance. This means that a large share of the costs of a cap-and-trade program can be expected to ultimately be borne by consumers. In effect, free allowances amount to a transfer of wealth

---

[31]An important adjustment that was made for political purposes was to allow utilities to select the average annual fuel consumption of a plant in the years 1985–1987, to account for those power plants that were operating at less than capacity or were inoperative for maintenance for all or a portion of the year 1985.

[32]The magnitude of the windfall to emitters could be even more significant in the context of a much larger market for GHG allowances. The experience of the European Union Emissions Trading System provides some evidence for this windfall effect. An approach that would fully compensate emitters (on average, across all sectors) in a U.S. economy-wide CO_2 cap-and-trade system would initially auction 50 percent of the allowances and move gradually to a 100 percent auction over 25 years. This would be roughly equivalent to a 15 percent free allocation in perpetuity (Stavins, 2008).

from consumers to the shareholders of the firms holding the free allowances. However, under cost-of-service regulation of electric-utility companies, which is still in place in many states, regulators are unlikely to allow firms to pass through the market price of allowances if those allowances have been received for free. In these cases, free allocation will lead to lower electricity prices. This will create significant differences in effects in different regions of the country, based on whether markets are competitive or regulated.

3. An allowance auction generates public revenues that can be used to reduce distortionary taxes in the economy (especially taxes on income or investment).[33] In this way, an auction can improve overall economic efficiency and reduce costs to society, even though the private costs incurred for pollution abatement under the policy remain unchanged.

Regional Distribution of SO_2 Program Costs and Benefits

Most of the nation's coal-fired, electric-generating capacity is concentrated east of the Mississippi River, and much of that capacity was built more than a generation ago.[34] Plants in the West tend to be newer. Air pollutants emitted from the tall smokestacks of older plants are transported long distances in the lower atmosphere, causing environmental harm hundreds and even thousands of miles from their sources.[35] Because of prevailing west to east wind patterns, much of the pollution emitted by large coal plants in the upper Midwest and Ohio River Valley is carried to the northeastern and mid-Atlantic states (as well as eastern Canada). Thus, it was reasonable to expect that most of the cost of SO_2 controls would be concentrated in the midwestern states, while most of the benefits would accrue to northeastern states.

However, from the beginning, there were concerns that a cap-and-trade system could not guarantee that emissions reductions would occur

---

[33] This is an application of a more general principle that society would often benefit from shifting the burden of taxation from social "goods" (primarily investment or income) to social "bads" (such as pollution).

[34] In aggregate, coal-fired capacity in the United States (approximately 330 gigawatts in 2000) had an average age of 35 years in 2002 (Massachusetts Institute of Technology, 2007).

[35] The tall stacks employed by coal-fired power plants were themselves a response to earlier Clean Air Act regulations that governed ambient concentrations of SO_2 and other so-called criteria air pollutants.

in the quantities and *at the locations* needed to protect all areas from environmental harm. Indeed, the advantage of cap-and-trade is that it directs abatement to where it is least costly, not necessarily to facilities causing the most geographic-specific damage. Northeastern states worried that the ability to buy allowances in lieu of installing SO_2 controls might leave upwind sources too much latitude to avoid making the actual emissions reductions needed to address downwind impacts.

New York and North Carolina, among other eastern states, implemented their own regulations to direct abatement to where it would produce the most benefits for their residents. New York, in particular, conducted a lengthy legal campaign to maintain its more stringent standards (Palmer *et al.*, 2005; Stavins, 2003; Winebrake *et al.*, 1995). These actions highlight something of a tension between geographically broad-based, cap-and-trade approaches and state and local authorities' desires to limit emissions within a particular area or from a particular set of sources. As suggested in the discussion of regulatory complexity above, extending the allowance-trading program over the largest geographically-relevant area and minimizing (or eliminating) overlapping regulatory requirements was key to realizing its potential to be cost-effective. On the other hand, any source that might be compelled by state or local regulations to implement extra pollution controls would end up with extra allowances under the federal program that could then be sold to other sources in a different jurisdiction.[36] The end result would be no net change in total emissions over the larger region covered by the cap.

Distributional concerns also arose with respect to impacts on electricity rates. To the extent that midwestern utilities implemented the largest share of SO_2 reductions, they (and their ratepayers) also incurred the largest share of SO_2 control costs. Nevertheless, the SO_2 allowance-trading system on the whole did not produce substantial rate differentials across regions, in part because overall compliance costs ended up being quite low, but also because coal hardly ever sets the electricity price in competitive markets. As a result, the effect of the program on marginal electricity prices was small. This was true despite it being common in regulated electricity markets for state regulators, legislators, or both to adopt policies that discouraged the pursuit of least-cost compliance options. For example, a number of states tried to direct in-state utilities toward using

[36] Goulder and Stavins (2010) provide a discussion of parallel concerns about the interaction of federal and state regulations pertaining to greenhouse gases.

in-state coal or installing scrubbers so they could continue using in-state, high-sulfur coal rather than taking advantage of lower cost fuel-switching options from out-of-state sources. The courts struck down such state policies as interference with interstate commerce. These types of policies would have made the national SO_2 trading program more costly. Nonetheless, the rate impacts were still small, particularly since electricity rates in the regulated, coal-intensive areas of the Midwest were generally quite low to begin with (and considerably lower than rates in the downwind northeastern states).

The acid rain experience and subsequent debates about the use of cap-and-trade in other contexts suggest that issues of geographically-specific impacts and state and local control should be considered in light of the type of pollutant being regulated, its behavior in the environment, and the specific harm being addressed. For some pollution problems, particularly those characterized by well-defined relationships between sources and points of damage (receptors) combined with increasing marginal receptor damages, cap-and-trade (or other flexible, market-based mechanisms) can lead to problematic "hot-spots" — or geographically-concentrated damage — which increase total damages and hence may not be appropriate. By contrast, in the case of climate change, the location of the emissions source has no bearing whatsoever on its environmental impact: GHGs are evenly distributed throughout the global atmosphere, thus emissions from any given source have the same warming effect on the atmosphere as GHGs emitted anywhere else. From this perspective, cap-and-trade and other market-based approaches are especially well suited to limiting GHG emissions.

On the spectrum from pollutants with primarily local impacts to pollutants with entirely global impacts, SO_2 falls in the middle: because of its transport and deposition properties, emissions impacts may be dispersed over a very broad region; at the same time there was some heterogeneity in the distribution of benefits across the nation. Concerns about local impacts or potential hot spots were to some extent alleviated by the existence of separate regulatory protections in the form of federally-mandated ambient air quality standards for SO_2.[37] In addition, modeling analyses

[37]Near the opposite end of the spectrum from GHGs, the EPA under the George W. Bush Administration attempted to implement a trading system related to its Clean Air Mercury Rule (CAMR), which was intended to reduce mercury emissions from coal-fired power plants. Mercury is not transported far from its source, and concern about hot spots was one factor (among several) in CAMR not being implemented.

undertaken prior to passage of the 1990 CAAA pointed to the likelihood that the distribution of actual emission cuts would be highly correlated geographically with the distribution of the largest and most damaging emissions sources. Thus, policy makers could be reasonably confident that a single national SO_2 market would drive substantial emissions reductions in the Midwest, where the largest coal plants were concentrated. This confidence was largely borne out as the program was implemented (Ellerman *et al.*, 2000; Swift, 2004).[38] As discussed above, provisions in the Clean Air Act concerning ambient air standards led the EPA under the George W. Bush Administration to develop CAIR, which attempted to reconcile geographically-specific remedies with national allowance trading. The courts determined that this attempt was inconsistent with the Clean Air Act and vacated CAIR. The replacement for CAIR, the Cross-State Air Pollution Rule (CSAPR, initially known as the Clean Air Transport Rule), addresses the concerns of the courts, but in so doing, effectively eliminated national (interstate) allowance trading[39] in favor of more geographically-restricted trading intended to focus the health benefits of emissions reductions on specific downwind states. This will reduce cost-effectiveness in favor of what is intended to be a more equitable distribution of benefits across geographical regions (Belden, 2005; Nelson, 2011; Schmalensee and Stavins, 2011; U.S. EPA, 2011a).

Distribution Across Socio-Economic Groups

Any public policy raises concerns about how the benefits and costs of that policy are distributed across socio-economic groups. As suggested in the foregoing section, the possibility that a facility chooses to purchase allowances rather than reduce emissions could result, under certain conditions, in decreased local air quality. In their study of the SO_2 allowance-trading system, Shadbegian *et al.* (2005) found that low-income groups received slightly lower benefits than people of higher income, but that minority groups received significantly greater benefits, relative to cost, than the

[38]Perhaps further vindicating this approach, later efforts to address acid rain in Europe through smaller, regional cap-and-trade programs illustrated the problems that can arise with thin, regionally differentiated markets.

[39]Interstate allowance trading was previously allowed by the same Court in 2000 when ruling on the NO Budget Trading Program (National Center for Environmental Economics, 2001).

average population. It is likely that this was because minorities are concentrated in cities, where the local health benefits of reduced SO_2 concentrations dominate the benefit-cost analysis.

Evidence indicates that the SO_2 allowance-trading system did not lead to significant hot spots. A number of explanations for this result were offered at the workshop. One explanation is that local and state regulations — including those intended to achieve compliance with National Ambient Air Quality Standards — tended to preclude hot spots; another is that trading in conjunction with a significant overall reduction in emissions (via the cap) tended to lead to reductions at the largest-emitting facilities and to smoothing out emissions over space, rather than concentrating them (Swift, 2004).

Technological Innovation

Advances in technology can expand the menu of abatement options available and substantially reduce the cost of achieving emissions reductions. In choosing among different policy instruments, it is important to consider whether some options are more effective at inducing technology innovation than others (or at least pose fewer impediments to innovation).

On its face, a market-based approach would seem to have advantages over a command-and-control-based approach for at least two reasons. First, the greater flexibility of a market-based approach provides greater latitude for regulated entities to pursue compliance strategies that might not have been anticipated by policy makers at the outset of the program. Second, while a command-and-control system can create incentives for reducing the costs associated with achieving a given environmental standard, it does not provide incentives for out-performing the standard (or "over-complying," as discussed above).[40] A market-based program, by contrast, creates continuous incentives for innovation, since each additional ton of reduction that can be achieved for less than the market price of an allowance creates value for the entity that produces those reductions. In looking at these issues from the standpoint of real-world experience

[40]Under certain conditions, a command-and-control system might even create *disincentives* to further improving on available control technologies — particularly if regulated entities view these improvements as opening the door to ever more stringent pollution control requirements.

with the SO_2 allowance-trading system, workshop participants considered the record of innovation in two areas: improvements in scrubber technologies and the diffusion of a broader set of emissions-reducing practices unrelated to the use of any particular technology.

Scrubbers — as noted, by far the prevalent technology for removing SO_2 from powerplant emissions — were an established technology in 1990. Environmental regulation under the 1970 Clean Air Act had made the use of scrubbers an important compliance option in newly-built coal-fired power plants (Lange and Bellas, 2005). The 1970 legislation had specified an emissions rate that could be met through use of low-sulfur coals found in the East and West, but in response to the 1977 CAAA, regulations were tightened to require a 70–90 percent removal of SO_2 from the emissions of uncontrolled coal. This could only be accomplished through the use of scrubbers. The 1977 bill also required a 90 percent reduction of emissions from new sources relative to the emissions levels that would prevail without mandated control. This further encouraged the use of scrubbers.

More than half of currently installed SO_2 scrubber systems were installed after the 1990 CAAA, but the timing of more recent installations has come in bursts. From 1990–2000, scrubbers were installed at a nearly constant rate; installations slowed early in Phase II of the Acid Rain Program (after 2000), however, as growth in electric-sector demand slowed and as utilities used banked allowances from Phase I to meet their compliance obligations. For utilities subject to Title IV requirements after the passage of the CAAA in 1990, the decision to install scrubber systems involved multiple considerations: the strength of the price signal for SO_2 reductions (as reflected in the market price of SO_2 allowances); the cost and feasibility of other abatement options (such as fuel switching); investment risk (including uncertainty about future allowance prices and about the susceptibility of SO_2 markets to price volatility); cost recovery rules (in the case of regulated utilities); and the effects of state-level or other federal regulatory and financial incentives (Frey, 2008).[41]

[41] One workshop participant pointed out that utilities likely considered another advantage of scrubbers: these systems generally can be shut down or bypassed to increase output during periods of high electricity prices and demand. To compensate for excess emissions released during these periods, utilities can purchase allowances or operate at a more stringent level of emissions control during periods of lower demand.

The wave of scrubber installations (technology diffusion) that occurred in the 1990s was attributable in large part to the incentives created by the SO_2 cap-and-trade program, since the high cost of these systems could only be justified in expectation of non-trivial SO_2 allowance prices. Some evidence also suggests that the program succeeded at inducing innovation in scrubber technology. Scrubber performance has improved over the last two decades, and the costs of achieving a fixed level of scrubber performance have declined (Bellas and Lange, 2011; Popp, 2003; Lange and Bellas, 2005; Burtraw, 2000; Burtraw and Palmer, 2003).[42]

The SO_2 allowance-trading program also appears to have sparked innovation in a range of compliance alternatives that could reduce SO_2 emissions without necessitating the use of add-on pollution controls. One example was the diffusion of mining techniques for extracting lower-sulfur coal seams, a practice that was known before the 1990 CAAA but not in wide use. A related strategy deployed in the 1990s involved blending low-sulfur coal with high-sulfur coal to reduce the aggregate sulfur-intensity of boiler fuel. Prior to 1990, many in the industry believed that existing boilers could accommodate only modest levels of fuel blending unless modifications were made that required large capital investments. After the cap-and-trade program went into effect, this view was disproved, with some plants achieving blend levels of as much as 40 percent without significant modifications. Clearly, fuel switching would not have evolved to become a significant compliance option had the government pursued a more prescriptive regulatory policy that required all emissions sources to install add-on controls.

The SO_2 allowance-trading program also stimulated non-technological innovations in the electric utility industry. These included strategies for managing allowance trading within a firm and creating the appropriate financial management and brokerage capacities needed to exploit new market opportunities. More generally, the cap-and-trade system, by its nature, granted the flexibility of a performance (as opposed to a technology) standard on individual sources, and then allowed trading. In other words, even without trading, the cap-and-trade system was less costly than an inflexible technology standard would have been. Workshop

[42] Some cost reduction was probably the result of learning through using, as the number of installed scrubbers increased. Also, a market emerged for much cheaper scrubbers that were somewhat less reliable than New Source Performance Standards allowed, which lowered average cost.

participants characterized this as facilitating "cost savings without trading." Along with improvements in SO_2 control technologies, these examples of innovation and knowledge diffusion played some role in reducing overall Acid-Rain-Program costs and were seen by workshop participants as strengthening the innovation case for favoring market-based environmental regulation.

Political Context of the Acid Rain Program

In July 1989, President George H.W. Bush proposed substantial revisions to the Clean Air Act, based in part on earlier congressional proposals and in part on new ideas developed by his Administration. The final bill containing the CAAA of 1990 passed the House of Representatives by nearly a 20 to 1 margin (401-21) and the Senate by a large majority (89-11). A joint conference committee met from July to October of 1990 to resolve differences in the House and Senate bills, and both houses approved the package recommended by the conferees with almost identical majorities.[43] The President signed the resulting bill into law on November 15, 1990. The Amendments contained seven titles, each of which substantially updated an existing portion of the Clean Air Act. In addition to the acid rain title (IV), these included programs related to urban smog, industrial emissions of certain toxic chemicals, automobile emissions, and releases of chemicals that deplete ozone in the upper atmosphere.[44]

Unlike most earlier pieces of landmark environmental legislation, the CAAA of 1990 was not precipitated by a "crisis moment," which may have given policy makers greater latitude to implement a flexible and entrepreneurial policy, rather than resorting to a more rigid traditional approach (Wiener and Richman, 2010). On the other hand, some workshop participants did point out that concern about the environment was rising generally in the summer of 1988, with unusually hot weather contributing to poor air quality (as evidenced by a high level of ambient

---

[43] A legislative chronology is available at "Clean Air Act Amendments at 1990: Legislative Chronology."

[44] A summary of the amendments is available at "Overview — The Clean Air Act Amendments of 1990."

ozone — smog — that summer), and with many reports of ocean pollution in New York and New Jersey.

Some workshop participants asserted that the Acid Rain Program flew "under the radar," in terms of the attention it received both from the public and environmental advocacy groups — perhaps because they were more concerned about changes to other portions of the Act or perhaps because the issue had been debated for more than 10 years, and the levels of control were consistent with what environmental groups had advocated. These factors allowed for a more calm and deliberative debate about the choice of policy instruments than might have been possible under other circumstances. The Bush Administration, the Congress, and policy entrepreneurs were important in these developments and helped facilitate the adoption of the national SO trading program as part of the CAAA of 1990.[45]

The Bush Administration

The administration of President Ronald Reagan had been unfavorably inclined to address public-policy problems — including environmental challenges — through regulation. This approach had served Reagan well, on balance, with regard to public opinion about his stewardship of the economy. But it began to present potential political costs for the subsequent Republican presidential candidate, as environmental issues became increasingly important for key demographic groups in swing states with large suburban populations leading up to the 1988 election.

In 1988, Vice President George H.W. Bush made the environment a key theme of his presidential campaign, explicitly promising to update the Clean Air Act and to cut acid rain by half. On February 9, 1989, three weeks after taking office, President Bush addressed a joint session of Congress and said of acid rain that "the time for study alone has passed, and the time for action is now" (Bush, 1989). Five months later, his administration submitted to Congress a single, comprehensive clean air bill, which included the basic structure of the SO_2 allowance-trading program.

---

[45] Conniff (2009) provides an account of the political and policy process, and Yergin (2011) provides a concise account of the individuals who contributed to the development of the SO_2 allowance-trading program.

Given the confluence of President Bush's ideological preferences and his campaign commitment to reducing SO_2 emissions, it was perhaps not surprising that his administration put forward a market-based approach to SO_2 regulation. The Reagan Administration had deregulated many key sectors of the U.S. economy, including airlines, oil and refined oil products, and trucking.[46] The limits of a command-and-control-style approach to governing had become readily apparent with the collapse of the Soviet Union. With the economic growth of the 1980s beginning to slow, President Bush was concerned about the economic impact of the bill. He wanted to improve air quality at the minimum possible cost to industry and the economy as a whole and believed that a market-based approach could accomplish this.[47]

Congress

Bush came into office confronting large Democratic majorities in both houses of Congress. Thus, all involved knew that legislation could not be enacted without considerable bipartisan support. Congress was, on balance, already strongly inclined toward strengthening air quality protections. The Senate Committee on Environment and Public Works had promoted acid-rain legislation for a decade, but it had never gone anywhere, in part because the Majority Leader of the Senate, Robert Byrd (D-West Virginia), represented a state with a high reliance on the mining of (high-sulfur) coal, and in part because the Committee had a history of reporting legislation not sufficiently centrist to attract filibuster-proof majorities in the Senate. But, in November 1988, George Mitchell

---

[46]However, the Staggers Rail Act, which deregulated railroads and made low-sulfur, Powder River Basin coal more competitive (see above), was passed under President Jimmy Carter in 1980.

[47]Workshop participants noted that President Bush never received much credit for the CAAA from the environmental community or the press, failing to win a single endorsement from an environmental advocacy group in his 1992 reelection bid, despite opposing Bill Clinton, the Governor of Arkansas, a state then ranked 50th in terms of environmental protection. Some of the participants at the workshop who had served in the Bush White House believed that this lack of recognition was a major factor in the Republican Party subsequently giving up on the environmental vote, concluding Republicans would never win support from environmental interest groups no matter what policies they pursued.

(D-Maine) was elected Majority Leader, replacing Byrd; Maine was among the states most affected by acid rain.

While Mitchell enjoyed a Democratic majority in the Senate, his coalition was not sufficient to guarantee the 60 votes necessary to invoke cloture in the event of a filibuster against acid rain legislation, especially given disparate regional views within the Democratic Party itself. Thus, the new Majority Leader knew he had to negotiate with the new Bush Administration in order to secure enough votes to steer clean air legislation to passage in the Senate. In this way, both George H.W. Bush (because of his campaign promise and his concern about the economy) and George Mitchell (because of his need for a 60 vote majority) were motivated to negotiate with each other to win passage of a clean air bill acceptable to both parties. Observers at the time, and in the period since, have attributed passage of the CAAA in 1990 to leadership by "the two Georges."

The seminal moment in the debate came when President Bush sent a letter to the Majority Leader indicating that any clean air bill he would sign would have to meet "five tests of balance and reasonableness," the most important of which was that its compliance costs could not exceed $20 billion annually (plus or minus 5 percent). This led to a protracted negotiation between representatives of the Administration and members of the Senate, led by Senator Mitchell, to craft a bill that could achieve the desired environmental outcomes and pass those tests. After months of negotiation, the Administration and the Senate leadership announced an agreement that withstood challenge from both the political left and the political right on the Senate floor and led to passage of the CAAA in the Senate by the above-noted margin of 89-10, with an equal number of Republicans and Democrats voting against.

In the House, the range of competing interests involved in the acid rain debate was well represented in the Committee on Energy and Commerce, which included representatives from eastern (high-sulfur) coal-producing and coal-using states, several of the northeastern states that were most affected by acid rain, and several western low-sulfur coal-producing and coal-using states. The politics of the electric power industry was divided more along regional lines than along party or ideological lines, with coal-intensive districts in the Midwest concerned about stranded capital investments and districts in the West apprehensive of applying differential regulatory treatment to new and existing capital. On the broader topic of clean air, the Committee also represented a wide range of interests, even within parties. The diversity of views was best represented in the long-standing tension between the Chairman of the Committee, Rep. John Dingell (D-Michigan), who represented areas of Michigan in which the automobile industry was an important employer, and the Chairman of the Subcommittee on Health and the Environment, Rep. Henry Waxman (D-California), whose Los Angeles district suffered from the worst smog in the country.

In the 1970s and 1980s, representatives from the northeastern states and environmental advocates had put forth a steady stream of acid rain bills. But the coalitions needed to pass these bills had never been able to overcome the fault lines that formed on the basis of regional differences in mitigation costs. According to one workshop participant, members of the House Subcommittee on Energy and Power (the subcommittee with initial jurisdiction over the SO_2 trading proposal) were not reflexively opposed to environmental regulation as such, but were genuinely concerned about the impact of higher electricity rates in their districts. These representatives were in principle open to reducing SO_2 emissions as long as they could be confident that their constituents would receive a "fair" deal.

Policy Entrepreneurs

The proposal for what became the SO_2 allowance-trading system was part of a legislative package developed by the George H. W. Bush White House. But where did the White House get its ideas, and how did it develop them? In addition to elected officials, the environmental and academic communities played key roles. In 1960, University of Chicago Professor Ronald Coase laid the intellectual foundation in the *Journal of Law and Economics* (Coase, 1960) for the notion of using markets to solve environmental problems. Then, U.S. economist Thomas Crocker (1966) and Canadian economist John Dales (1968) followed up by arguing that the best way to clean up air and water pollution would be with a market in rights to emit pollution. These arguments were made much more rigorous a few years later when David Montgomery — a workshop participant — demonstrated in the *Journal of Economic Theory* (Montgomery, 1972) precisely how and why an emissions-trading system would be cost-effective. Prominent legal scholars also advocated emissions trading (Ackerman and Stewart, 1985). These and other explorations in the academic world eventually led EPA to experiment with small-scale emissions-credit-trading systems in the 1970s and 1980s, including most importantly the phase out of leaded gasoline in vehicle fuel in the mid-1980s.

The design and implementation of a much larger-scale allowance-trading program required the participation of committed policy entrepreneurs. George H.W. Bush, as already noted, was one. Several of those later involved in the Bush Administration played key roles in formulating President Bush's campaign commitments on the environment. Robert Grady (a workshop participant), chief speechwriter and senior policy adviser on the 1988 campaign, joined the White House staff as Associate Director of the Office of Management and Budget in charge of Natural Resources, Energy, and Science. Robert Zoellick, issues director on the campaign, became Under Secretary of State and later White House Deputy Chief of Staff. C. Boyden Gray (a workshop participant), who had advised Vice President Bush earlier on the White House Competitiveness Council that oversaw the phase out of lead in gasoline, became White House Counsel.

Ironically, in light of the political dynamics of the recent climate debate, the main opposition to market-based environmental policies at the time came from environmental advocacy groups (with an important exception highlighted below) and from Democrats (with a few important exceptions, also highlighted below). Some of these advocates thought that a policy based on the principle that firms could "pay to pollute" was morally bankrupt; they worried that the very creation of tradable allowances implied that firms had a right or an entitlement to emit. In their view, the government should continue to regulate private-sector emissions through command-and-control regulation, in effect setting minimum control standards or technology requirements for each individual emissions source.

Among the major environmental advocacy groups, it was the Environmental Defense Fund (EDF) that set itself apart from its environmental brethren by backing market-based approaches to environmental protection, including for acid rain control. EDF was led then (as now) by Fred Krupp, another workshop participant. When EDF helped the Bush Administration design, and later announced its support of, the trading component of the CAAA, it was a "Nixon-in-China" moment and a turning point in the politics of market-based regulation. Several workshop participants from the Bush White House confirmed that the SO_2 trading program could not have won congressional support had EDF not provided the administration with the necessary credibility from within the environmental community.

Two policy entrepreneurs in the U.S. Senate, Timothy Wirth (D-Colorado, now President of the United Nations Foundation) and the late John Heinz (R-Pennsylvania), together created and chaired Project 88, which developed a compelling economic proposal for a market-based program to reduce SO_2 emissions through a cap-and-trade system (Stavins, 1988).[48] In 1988, shortly after the election and even before inauguration, C. Boyden Gray brought the director of the Heinz-Wirth Project 88 effort, Robert Stavins (then a new assistant professor at the Harvard Kennedy School), to the White House, together with Fred Krupp and key members of the EDF staff. Gray also recruited emissions-trading advocate Richard Stewart, a law professor at Harvard, to serve as the top environmental lawyer at the Justice Department.

The development, adoption, and implementation of the Acid Rain Program — as any major innovation in public policy — can be attributed to a solid base of knowledge, sound strategy, and a certain amount of luck in placing effective policy entrepreneurs in important positions, in this case at the White House, EPA, the Department of Justice, the Congress, and environmental organizations. These entrepreneurs, working together on the Acid Rain Program, made a break with the past with regard to environmental policy.

Conclusion

More than 20 years later, the introduction of the national SO_2 allowance-trading program as part of the CAAA of 1990 remains widely regarded as a landmark step in the worldwide history of environmental regulation. The program, while not without flaws, is viewed as a success by almost all measures. Certainly it demonstrated that broad-based cap-and-trade systems can be used to achieve significant emissions reductions, that firms can navigate and regulators can enforce the compliance requirements of such systems, and that giving the private sector the flexibility to pursue a range of abatement options can simultaneously protect the environment, stimulate innovation and diffusion, and reduce aggregate costs.

[48] Information is available at the Heinz Family Philanthropies' web page for Project 88: "Project 88: Harnessing Market Forces to Protect Our Environment Initiatives for the New President," Heinz Family Philanthropies.

The SO_2 allowance-trading program was enacted with large bipartisan majorities and was successful in reducing SO_2 emissions at a cost much less than a traditional-regulatory approach would have incurred (and less than had been predicted). The program was partially inspired by the belief that the shortcomings of earlier emissions-credit-trading programs could be overcome with a cap-and-trade design and strong monitoring. The program's subsequent success in turn inspired other market-based emissions-reductions programs, including the much larger European Union Emissions Trading System.

The broad political consensus on the CAAA of 1990 was hard-won. A number of influential stakeholders engaged in a decade of often contentious deliberation and negotiation — including intense discussion about the Title IV provisions — before Congress passed the Amendments. Divergent views on the CAAA largely reflected regional differences in the distribution of coal-fired power plants and coal types. But the advent of the proposed allowance-trading program facilitated the consensus that emerged among leaders in the Bush Administration, lawmakers in Congress, and many affected corporations and business associations (Joskow and Schmalensee, 1998). Thus, the SO_2 allowance-trading program made it possible to focus on how one could achieve the agreed public policy goal (in this case, reducing acid rain pollution) in a manner that would simultaneously minimize costs and provide regulated entities with the flexibility embodied in markets.

The recent climate debate has taken place in a political context that is much different than that of the CAAA of 1990. Deep ideological division dominates today's dialogue in Washington; the two major political parties were much less ideologically polarized in 1990. A convergence of the creative vision and the large bipartisan majorities of 1990 appears much less likely today. Recent hostility toward cap-and-trade in U.S. climate legislation may reflect the broader political environment of the climate debate more than it reflects the substantive merits (or demerits) of market-based regulation.[49] In other words, congressional hostility toward GHG cap-and-trade appears to have been collateral damage in a wider set of policy and ideological battles.

Ironically, the cap-and-trade model seems especially well suited to addressing the problem of climate change, in that emitted GHGs are

[49]The design of the Waxman-Markey climate-change bill, including the auctioning of 15 percent of allowances initially, with the percentage rising over time, may have also affected the political outcome.

evenly distributed throughout the world's atmosphere. Emissions reductions anywhere make identical contributions to helping alleviate the problem, and there are no pollutant concentration hot spots. The sheer number and variety of GHG-emissions sources heightens the practical difficulty of developing a comprehensive and effective command-and-control approach and magnifies the cost savings that could be achieved by enlisting the market to find the least costly abatement options.

It is difficult to achieve an international agreement to limit GHG emissions, however, for precisely the same reasons — many countries, hosting many emissions sources, must agree to take action. Given the complexities of either developing a domestic U.S. cap-and-trade system for GHGs or obtaining congressional approval for an international system in which the United States participates, it is likely that at least as much bipartisan collaboration would be required as was evident in the CAAA process. Instead, we have much less.

The stakes for a broad-based GHG policy — economic, political, and environmental — are much higher than they were for SO_2 policy in 1990. While the debate over federal policy to address climate change is currently in hiatus, the lessons of the SO_2 allowance-trading program will prove useful and relevant to future deliberations about climate change policy when the time arrives for serious reflection.

Acknowledgements

We gratefully acknowledge the contributions of participants in an environmental economics research workshop and a policy roundtable sponsored by the Harvard Environmental Economics Program and held at Harvard in May 2011, as well as the comments and edits some participants provided on an earlier draft of this chapter. Their expertise and experience made the project possible. (Comments made by participants in the workshop were not intended for attribution, and specific insights are not referenced in the chapter.) We also thank Marika Tatsutani and Bryan Galcik. This work was partially conducted while Gabriel Chan was a Giorgio Ruffolo Fellow in the Sustainability Science Program at Harvard University. Chan gratefully acknowledges support from Italy's Ministry for Environment, Land, and Sea. Finally, we are grateful to the Alfred P. Sloan Foundation, which provided generous support for the workshop and for the preparation of this study.

References

Aldy, J. E. (2011). "Promoting clean energy in the american power sector" (The Hamilton Project Discussion Paper 2011-04). Washington, DC: The Hamilton Project.

Aldy, J. E., and Pizer, W. A. (2011, December). "Competitiveness impacts of climate change mitigation policies" (National Bureau of Economic Research Working Paper No. 17705). Cambridge, MA: National Bureau of Economic Research.

Badiani, R., Jessoe, K. K., & Plant, S. (2012). Development and the Environment: The Implications of Agricultural Electricity Subsidies in India. *The Journal of Environment & Development*, **21**(2), 244–262.

Beaton, C., and Lontoh, L. (2010). *Lessons Learned from Indonesia's Attempts to Reform Fossil-Fuel Subsidies*. Winnipeg, Manitoba, Canada: International Institute for Sustainable Development.

Blackman, A. (2010). "Alternative pollution control policies in developing countries." *Review of Environmental Economics and Policy*, **4**, 234–253.

Bodansky, D. (2011). "Whither the Kyoto Protocol? Durban and Beyond." Policy Brief, *Harvard Project on Climate Agreements*, Belfer Center for Science and International Affairs, Harvard Kennedy School.

Brainard, L., and Sorking, I. (Eds.). (2009). *Climate Change, Trade, and Competitiveness: Is a Collision Inevitable?* Washington, DC: Brookings Institution Press.

British Columbia. (2007). *Climate Action Plan*. Vancouver, British Columbia, Canada.

Bruvoll, A., and Larsen, B. M. (2004). "Greenhouse gas emissions in norway: Do carbon taxes work?" *Energy Policy*, **32**, 493–505.

Burtraw, D., Kahn, D., and Palmer, K. (2005). "*CO_2 Allowance Allocation in the Regional Greenhouse Gas Initiative and the Effect on Electricity Investors*" (Discussion Paper CP 05-55). Washington, DC: Resources for the Future.

Cao, J., Ho, M., and Jorgenson, D. (2009). "The local and global benefits of green tax policies in China." *Review of Environmental Economics and Policy*, **3**, 189–208.

Carlson, C., Burtraw, D., Cropper, M., and Palmer, K. (2000). "SO_2 control by electric utilities: What are the gains from trade?" *Journal of Political Economy*, **108**, 1292–326.

Coady, D., Gillingham, R., Ossowski, R., Pietrowski, J., Tareq, S., and Tyson, J. (2010). *Petroleum Product Subsidies: Costly, Inequitable, and Rising* (IMF Staff Position Note SPN/10/05). Washington, DC: International Monetary Fund.

Convery, F., and Redmond, L. (2007). "Market and price developments in the European union emissions trading scheme." *Review of Environmental Economics and Policy*, **1**, 66–87.

Cooper, R. N. (2010). "The Case for Charges on Greenhouse Gas Emissions." In J. E. Aldy & R. N. Stavins (Eds.), *Post-Kyoto International Climate Policy: Implementing Architectures for Agreement* (pp. 151–178). New York, NY: Cambridge University Press.

Coria, J., and Sterner, T. (2010). "Tradable permits in developing countries: Evidence from air pollution in Santiago, Chile." *Journal of Environment and Development*, **19**, 145–170.

Coria, J., Löfgren, Å., and Sterner, T. (2010). "Trade or not to trade: An analysis of trading schemes at the firm level." *Journal of Environmental Management*, **91**, 2126–2133.

Daugjberg, C., and Pedersen, A. B. (2004). "New policy ideas and old policy networks: Implementing green taxation in Scandinavia." *Journal of Public Policy*, **24**, 219–249.

Duff, D. G. (2008). "Carbon taxation in British Columbia." *Vermont Journal of Environmental Law*, **10**, 85–105.

Ellerman, A. D., and Buchner, B. K. (2007). "The European union emissions trading scheme: Origins, allocation, and early results." *Review of Environmental Economics and Policy*, **1**(1), 66–87.

Emissions Trading Scheme Review Panel. (2011). "*Doing New Zealand's Fair Share: Emissions Trading Scheme Review 2011, Final Report.*" Wellington, New Zealand: Ministry for the Environment.

Fischer, C., and Preonas, L. (2010). "Combining policies for renewable energy: Is the whole less than the sum of its parts?" *International Review of Environmental and Resource Economics*, **4**, 51–92.

Frankel, J. (2010). "Global Environment and Trade Policy." In J. E. Aldy & R. N. Stavins (Eds.), *Post-Kyoto International Climate Policy: Implementing Architectures for Agreement* (pp. 493–529). New York, NY: Cambridge University Press.

G20 Leaders. (2009). "*Leaders' Statement: The Pittsburgh Summit.*" The third G-20 Summit in Pittsburgh, PA, USA.

G20 Leaders. (2010a, June 26-27). "*Annex: G20 Initiative on Rationalizing and Phasing Out Inefficient Fossil Fuel Subsidies, Implementation Strategies and Timetables.*" The fourth G-20 Summit in Toronto, Ontario, Canada.

G20 Leaders. (2010b). "*The G20 Seoul Summit Leaders' Declaration.*" The fifth G20 Summit in Seoul, Republic of Korea.

Goulder, L. H. (1995, August). "Environmental taxation and the 'double dividend': A reader's guide." *International Tax and Public Finance*, **2**, 157–183.

Goulder, L. H., and Parry, I. W. H. (2008). "Instrument choice in environmental policy." *Review of Environmental Economics and Policy*, **2**, 152–174.

Goulder, L. H., and Stavins, R. N. (2011). "Challenges from state-federal interactions in U.S. climate change policy." *American Economic Review Papers and Proceedings*, **101**, 253–257.

Government of Denmark. (2009). *Denmark's Fifth National Communication on Climate Change*. Copenhagen, Denmark: Ministry of Climate and Energy.

Government of Finland. (2009). *Finland's Fifth National Communication under the Framework Convention on Climate Change*. Helsinki, Finland: Ministry of the Environment and Statistics.

Government of Norway. (2009). *Norway's Fifth National Communication under the Framework Convention on Climate Change*. Oslo, Norway: Norwegian Ministry of the Environment.

Government of Sweden. (2009). *Sweden's Fifth National Communication on Climate Change*. Stockholm, Sweden: Ministry of the Environment.

Hahn, R. W., and Stavins, R. N. (1999). "*What Has the Kyoto Protocol Wrought? The Real Architecture of International Tradeable Permit Markets*." Washington, DC: The AEI Press.

Hahn, R. W., and Stavins, R. N. (2011). "The effect of allowance allocations on cap-and-trade system performance." *Journal of Law and Economics*, **54**, S267–S294.

Hall, D. S., Levi, M. A., Pizer, W. A., and Ueno, T. (2010). "Policies for Developing Country Engagement." In J. E. Aldy & R. N. Stavins Eds., *Post-Kyoto International Climate Policy: Implementing Architectures for Agreement* (pp. 649–681). New York, NY: Cambridge University Press.

Interagency Working Group on Social Cost of Carbon, U.S. Government. (2010). "*Technical Support Document: Social Cost of Carbon for Regulatory Impact Analysis Under Executive Order 12866*." Washington, DC: Author.

International Energy Agency. (2010). *World Energy Outlook 2010*. Paris, France: IEA.

International Energy Agency. (2011). *World Energy Outlook 2011*. Paris, France: IEA.

International Energy Agency, (2010) *Organization of Petroleum Exporting Countries, Organisation for Economic Co-operation and Development, & World Bank. "Analysis of the Scope of Energy Subsidies and Suggestions for the G20 Initiative*" (June 16 version). Prepared for submission to the G-20 Summit Meeting, Toronto, Canada.

Jaffe, J., Ranson, M., and Stavins, R. (2010). "Linking tradable permit systems: A key element of emerging international climate policy architecture." *Ecology Law Quarterly*, **36**, 789–808.

Karpas, E., and Kerr, S. (2010). "Preliminary Evidence on Responses to the New Zealand Forestry Emissions Trading Scheme" (Motu Working Paper 11-09). Wellington, New Zealand: *Motu Economic and Public Policy Research*.

Kruger, J., Oates, W. E., and Pizer, W. A. (2007). "Decentralization in the EU emissions trading scheme and lessons for global policy." *Review of Environmental Economics and Policy*, **1**, 112–133.

Levinson, A. (2010). "Interactions Among Climate Policy Regulations" (NBER Working Paper 16109). Cambridge, MA: *National Bureau of Economic Research*.

Máca, V., Melichar, J., and Ščasný, M. (in press). "Internalization of external costs of energy generation in central and eastern european countries." *Journal of Environment and Development.*

Market Advisory Committee to the California Air Resources Board. (2007). "*Recommendations for Designing a Greenhouse Gas Cap-and-Trade System for California.*" Sacramento, CA: California Environmental Protection Agency.

McGuinness, M., and Ellerman, A. D. (2008). "*The Effects of Interactions Between Federal and State Climate Policies*" (Working Paper WP-2008-004). Cambridge: Massachusetts Institute of Technology Center for Energy and Environmental Policy Research.

Metcalf, G. E. (2007). "*A Proposal for a U.S. Carbon Tax Swap*" (The Hamilton Project Discussion Paper 2007-12). Washington, DC: Brookings Institution.

Metcalf, G. E., and Weisbach, D. (2010). "*Linking Policies When Tastes Differ: Global Climate Policy in a Heterogeneous World*" (Discussion Paper 2010-38). Cambridge, MA: Harvard Project on International Climate Agreements, Belfer Center for Science and International Affairs, Harvard Kennedy School.

Montgomery, D. W. (1972). "Markets in licenses and efficient pollution control programs." *Journal of Economic Theory*, **5**, 395–418.

Newell, R. G., Jaffe, A. B., and Stavins, R. N. (1999). "The induced innovation hypothesis and energy-saving technological change." *Quarterly Journal of Economics*, **114**, 941–975.

Olmstead, S. M., and Stavins, R. N. (2012). "Three key elements of post-2012 international climate policy architecture." *Review of Environmental Economics and Policy*, **6**(2), 1–22.

Organization for Economic Cooperation and Development. (2001). *Environmentally Related Taxes in OECD Countries: Issues and Strategies.* Paris, France: Author.

Organization for Economic Cooperation and Development. (2011). "Interactions between emission trading systems and other overlapping policy instruments." Paris, France: Environment Directorate, OECD.

Pizer, W. A. (2002). "Combining price and quantity controls to mitigate global climate change." *Journal of Public Economics*, **85**, 409–434.

Plumer, B. (2010, July 27). "B.C.'s carbon-tax experiment seems to be working." *New Republic.* Retrieved from http://www.tnr.com/blog/the-vine/76595/bcs-carbon-tax-experiment-seems-be-working.

Popp, D. (2002). "Induced innovation and energy prices." *American Economic Review*, **92**, 160–180.

Province of Alberta. (2007). *Specified Gas Emitters Regulation* (Alberta Regulation 139/2007). Edmonton, Alberta, Canada: Alberta Queen's Printer.

Province of Alberta. (2008). *Alberta's 2008 Climate Change Strategy*. Edmonton, Alberta, Canada: Ministry of Environment and Water.

Province of Alberta. (2011). "2010 Greenhouse Gas Emission Reduction Program Results." Edmonton, Alberta, Canada: *Ministry of Environment and Water*. Retrieved from http://environment.alberta.ca/03501.html.

Ramey, V. A., and Vine, D. J. (2010). "*Oil, Automobiles, and the U.S. Economy: How Much Have Things Really Changed?*" (NBER Working Paper 16067). Cambridge, MA: National Bureau of Economic Research.

Sass, B. (2010, November 1). "Inside Alberta's Quiet Carbon Market." *Alberta Oil*. Retrieved from http://www.albertaoilmagazine.com/2010/11/a-homegrown-system-puts-the-brakes-on-runaway-emissions/.

Speck, S. (2008). "The design of carbon and broad-based energy taxes in European countries." *Vermont Journal of Environmental Law*, **10**, 31–59.

Stavins, R. N. (1995). "Transaction Costs and Tradeable Permits." *Journal of Environmental Economics and Management*, **29**, 133–148.

Stavins, R. N. (2003). "Experience with Market-Based Environmental Policy Instruments." In K.-G. Mäler & J. Vincent (Eds.), *Handbook of Environmental Economics*, Vol. I (Chap. 9, pp. 355–435). Amsterdam, Netherlands: Elsevier Science.

Stavins, R. N. (2007). "*A U.S. Cap-and-Trade System to Address Global Climate Change*" (The Hamilton Project Discussion Paper 2007-13). Washington, DC: The Brookings Institution.

Stavins, R. N. (2011, November/December). "Polarized politics paralyze policy." *Environmental Forum*, **28**(6), 16.

Sterner, T., and Coria, J. (2012). *Policy Instruments for Environmental and Natural Resource Management* (2nd edn.). Washington, DC: RFF Press, Routledge.

UN Environment Programme. (2010). *The Emissions Gap Report: Are the Copenhagen Accord Pledges Sufficient to Limit Global Warming to 2C or 1.5C?* (A preliminary assessment). Nairobi, Kenya: Author.

U.S. Congressional Budget Office. (2011). "The effects of renewable or clean electricity standards." Washington, DC: Author.

U.S. Energy Information Administration. (2009). *Emissions of Greenhouse Gases in the United States*. Washington, DC: Author.

U.S. Energy Information Administration. (2011). *Annual Energy Outlook 2011*. Washington, DC: Author.

Wara, M. (2007, February). "Is the global carbon market working?" *Nature*, **445**, 595–596.

Weitzman, M. L. (1974). "Prices vs. Quantities." *Review of Economic Studies*, **41**, 477–491.

World Bank. (2010). *World Development Report 2010: Development and Climate Change*. Washington, DC: Author.

Zhang, J., and Wang, C. (2011). "Co-benefits and additionality of the clean development mechanism: An empirical analysis." *Journal of Environmental Economics and Management*, **62**, 140–154.

https://doi.org/10.1142/9789811292415_0008

Chapter 8

The SO_2 Allowance Trading System: The Ironic History of a Grand Policy Experiment[*]

Richard Schmalensee[†,‖,¶] and Robert N. Stavins[‡,§,‖,]**

[†]*Massachusetts Institute of Technology, Cambridge, MA, USA*

[‡]*John F. Kennedy School of Government, Harvard University, Cambridge, MA, USA*

[§]*Resources for the Future, Washington, DC, USA*

[‖]*National Bureau of Economic Research, Cambridge, MA, USA*

[¶]*rschmal@mit.edu*

[**]*robert_stavins@harvard.edu*

In the late 1980s, there was growing concern in the United States and other countries that acid precipitation — the result of emissions of sulfur dioxide (SO_2) and, to a lesser extent, nitrogen oxides (NO_x) reacting in the atmosphere to form sulfuric and nitric acids — was damaging forests and aquatic ecosystems, particularly in the US Northeast and Southern Canada. In the United States, flue gas emissions from coal-fired, electric generating plants were the primary source of SO_2 emissions and a major source of NO_x emissions. In response to this and other concerns, the US Congress

[*]This chapter was originally published in *Journal of Economic Perspectives*, **27**(1), 103–122, Winter 2013. http://dx.doi.org/10.1257/jep.27.1.103.

passed and President George H. W. Bush signed into law the Clean Air Act Amendments of 1990. Title IV of this law (which took up only 16 percent of its total pages) launched a grand experiment in market-based environmental policy: the path-breaking SO_2 allowance trading program.

The concept of allocating permits to emit a certain quantity of pollution that would phase down over time, while allowing permit-holders to trade their permits, is now broadly familiar. But two decades ago, this cap-and-trade approach to environmental protection was quite novel. Many in the environmental community — with the prominent exception of the Environmental Defense Fund — were hostile to the notion of trading "rights to pollute"; others doubted the workability of such a scheme. Nearly all pollution regulations took a much more prescriptive "command-and-control" approach, either by setting uniform emission rate limits on classes of emitters or by specifying the type of pollution-control equipment to be installed. Of course, such inflexible regulations impose the same abatement path upon a range of heterogeneous facilities and ignore the fact that the costs of compliance might vary widely across individual facilities depending on their age, technology characteristics, operating conditions, and characteristics of fuel used.

By the close of the twentieth century, the SO_2 allowance trading system had come to be seen as both innovative and successful (for discussion in this journal, see Schmalensee *et al.*, 1998; Stavins, 1998). It has become exceptionally influential, leading to a series of policy innovations in the United States and abroad to address a range of environmental challenges, including the threat of global climate change (Stavins, 2003). Most prominent among these innovations has been the European Union Emission Trading System, a carbon dioxide (CO_2) cap-and-trade system adopted in 2003 that is by far the world's largest environmental pricing regime (European Commission, 2012).

However, the design and implementation of the landmark SO_2 cap-and-trade system have led to a number of striking ironies, which are the focus of this essay. First, subsequent research indicates that in enacting an ambitious — and successful — policy to reduce SO_2 emissions in order to curb acid rain, the government essentially did the right thing for the wrong reason. Second, although the program appears to have been successful, a substantial source of its cost-effectiveness was an unanticipated consequence of the deregulation of railroad rates in the late 1970s and early 1980s. Third, market-based, cost-effective policy innovation in environmental regulation — in particular, cap-and-trade — was championed and implemented by Republican administrations from that of President Ronald Reagan to that of President George W. Bush, but in recent years Republicans have led the way in demonizing cap-and-trade (as an approach to limiting carbon emissions). Fourth and finally, court decisions and subsequent regulatory responses have led to the virtual collapse of the SO_2 market, demonstrating that what the government gives, the government can take away. In order to explore these four ironies, we first briefly review highlights of the system's design and performance.

A fifth, long-recognized irony deserves brief mention. Acid rain itself was largely a consequence of compliance with national ambient air quality standards set in the 1970s for SO_2 and other localized pollutants. In order to reduce local concentrations of these pollutants, electric utilities built more than 400 tall smokestacks, many greater than 500 feet in height (Regens and Rycroft, 1988), which successfully dispersed the stack gases, but did so by injecting them high enough into the atmosphere that they precipitated out tens or hundreds of miles downwind as acidified rain, snow, or particles.

Design

Any cap-and-trade policy must face two basic decisions, the level of pollution to be permitted over time and how the initial allocation of permits will be set. The objective of the SO_2 trading program was to reduce total annual US SO_2 emissions by 10 million tons relative to 1980. Phase I (1995–1999) of the trading program required significant emissions reductions from the 263 most-polluting coal-fired electric generating units, almost all located east of the Mississippi River. Phase II, which began in 2000, placed an aggregate national emissions cap on approximately 3,200 electric generating units — nearly the entire fleet of fossil-fueled plants in the continental United States (Ellerman *et al.*, 2000). This cap — affecting almost exclusively the power sector — represented a 50 percent reduction from 1980 levels. The permits were demarcated by vintage, with the total number decreasing for successive vintages, thereby achieving a declining cap. (The discussion in this section draws on Chan *et al.*, 2012; also see Ellerman *et al.*, 2000.)

How was this target selected? When the policy was enacted, no credible estimates of economic benefits of alternative target levels were available. (Actually, this is true of most environmental policies.) Instead, the target was selected largely based on what was believed to be the "elbow" of the abatement cost curve — that is, a level of abatement that was possible at relatively low costs, and above which the marginal costs of reducing emissions would climb dramatically. This process was consistent with the Baumol and Oates (1971) model of policy making, whereby a politically acceptable target is chosen with an eye toward avoiding regions of steep change in the policy's impact on social welfare. Also, there was a political desire to choose a target level of reductions that was big enough to gain the support of the environmental community and to be seen as satisfying a campaign pledge of newly elected President George H. W. Bush.

The government *gave* permits to emit called "allowances" — denominated in tons of SO_2 emissions — to power plants covered by the law. (The term "permit," which is standard in the economics literature, had another long-established meaning in US environmental law, so the new term "allowance" was coined and used instead.) If annual emissions at a regulated facility exceeded the allowances allocated to that facility, the owner could buy allowances or reduce emissions, whether by installing pollution controls, changing the mix of fuels used to operate the facility, or scaling back operations. If emissions at a regulated facility were reduced below its allowance allocation, the facility owner could sell the extra allowances or, since damages were understood to reflect cumulative emissions over time rather than annual emissions, bank them for future use. EPA's role was essentially to keep score by monitoring emissions on a continuous basis, tracking the ownership of all outstanding allowances (that is, recording initial allocations and subsequent trades), and withdrawing allowances corresponding to each facility's emissions from its account annually. As opposed to a command-and-control regulatory scheme that would have specified an across-the-board timeline for reductions in emissions or dictated specific technologies for pollution control, a cap-and-trade system created incentives to find ways to reduce SO_2 emissions at the lowest cost and to take advantage of low-cost abatement options as soon as they became available.

The free allocation of allowances posed some tradeoffs. After all, government auctioning of allowances would have generated revenue that could, in principle, have been used to reduce distortionary taxes, thereby reducing the program's social cost (Goulder, 1995). But this efficiency argument was not advanced at the time; and the affected utilities and their customers' representatives would have strongly opposed auctioning.

The case for free allocation rested on several arguments. Because cost-of-service regulation characterized the entire investor-owned electric utility industry in 1990, it was assumed that the value of free allowances would be passed on to consumers and would not generate windfall profits for providers. (The use of any allowance involves an opportunity cost because the allowance could be sold instead of used. Absent regulation, output prices would be expected to increase to reflect these opportunity costs, and because the allowances were in fact freely allocated, windfall profits would result.) As important, the political value of being able to allocate free allowances to address differential economic impacts across regions, states, and Congressional districts as well as other concerns was substantial (Joskow and Schmalensee, 1998). This was possible because the equilibrium allocation of pollution permits, after trading has occurred, is independent of the initial allocation (Coase, 1960; Montgomery, 1972) — at least barring particularly problematic types of transaction costs (Stavins, 1995; Hahn and Stavins, 2011). This means that the initial allocation of allowances could be designed to ensure the greatest political support without fear that this would jeopardize the system's environmental performance or economic cost.

Performance

Beginning in 1995 and over the subsequent decade, the SO_2 allowance trading program performed exceptionally well along all relevant dimensions. SO_2 emissions from electric power plants decreased 36 percent — from 15.9 million to 10.2 million tons — between 1990 and 2004 (US Environmental Protection Agency, 2011b), even though electricity generation from coal-fired power plants *increased* 25 percent over the same period (US Energy Information Administration, 2012). The program's long-term annual emissions goal was achieved in 2006, and by 2010, SO_2 emissions had declined further, to 5.1 million tons, as shown in Figure 1.

Overall, the program delivered emissions reductions more quickly than expected, as utilities, particularly Phase I units, took advantage of the freedom to bank allowances for future use. (Phase I units were expected, in aggregate, to have lower costs of emissions reduction than Phase II units). Hence, emissions from Phase I units fell well below their cap from 1995 to 1999 and then total emissions temporarily exceeded their cap as banked allowances were used for compliance. After 2006, total emissions (from all units combined) dropped to well below the aggregate cap because of other regulations that imposed tighter restrictions, as we discuss later. With the program's $2,000/ton statutory fine for any emissions

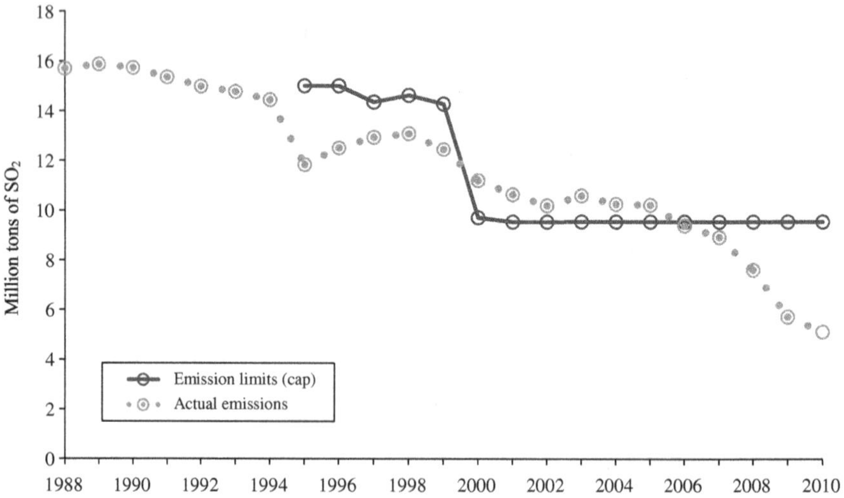

Figure 1. SO_2 caps and emissions, 1988–2010.

Notes: The emission limits shown for the period 1995–1999 are equal to the Phase 1 units' cap plus Phase 2 units' emissions. Actual emissions shown for all years are the sum of emissions from Phase 1 and Phase 2 units.

Source: Ellerman (2003) and US Environmental Protection Agency (2012).

exceeding allowance holdings and continuous emissions monitoring, compliance was nearly 100 percent.

The costs of achieving these environmental objectives with cap-and-trade were significantly less than they would have been with a command-and-control regulatory approach. Cost savings were at least 15 percent, and perhaps as much as 90 percent, compared with counterfactual policies that specified the means of regulation in various ways and for various portions of the program's regulatory period (Carlson *et al.*, 2000; Ellerman *et al.*, 2000; Keohane, 2003). In addition to static cost effectiveness, there is evidence that the program brought down abatement costs over time by providing incentives for innovation and diffusion that were generally much stronger than those provided by traditional command-and-control regulation. Utilities learned how to burn cost-effective mixtures of different types of coal,[1] how to take allowance prices into account in operating

[1]Coal is often divided into three categories: anthracite, bituminous, and lignite. Anthracite is the highest-quality coal, burning with the most energy. Much eastern coast coal is

decisions, and how to build more cost-effective flue gas desulfurization devices, called "scrubbers" (Ellerman *et al.*, 2000, pp. 235–248; Popp, 2003; Bellas and Lange, 2011; Frey, 2013).

While the SO_2 trading program was less costly than a conventional approach, the costs may or may not have been as low as they could have been. There was significant trading — about 20.3 million tons of allowances were bought and sold by March 1998 (Ellerman *et al.*, 2000, p. 176) — but the implications of this large amount of trade are not obvious. The efficient volume of trade depends on the difference between the initial allocation of allowances and the efficient distribution of emissions among regulated entities, thus very low volumes of trading could also be consistent with overall cost minimization. That said, marginal abatement costs did vary significantly across facilities, at least in the program's first two years (Carlson *et al.*, 2000).

There is evidence that the intertemporal allocation of abatement cost (via allowance banking) was at least approximately efficient (Ellerman and Montero, 2007), with greater-than-required emissions reductions in Phase I used (via banking) to delay more expensive reductions by Phase II units. In addition, the pattern of voluntary compliance was consistent with cost-effective compliance strategies (Montero, 1999). Finally, it is worth noting that the volume of trading grew substantially during the program's early years as utilities gained experience, from 1.5 million tons in the April 1994 to March 1995 period, to 8.4 million tons in the April 1997 to March 1998 period (Ellerman *et al.*, 2000, p. 176).

The following factors could have kept costs above the theoretical minimum, though their influence has been debated: (1) certain provisions in the 1990 legislation that encouraged early use of scrubbers instead of switching to low-sulfur coal, provisions included in an attempt to limit effects of the legislation on high-sulfur coal producers (Ellerman *et al.*, 2000, pp. 301–302); (2) lack of information about marginal abatement costs on the part of market participants, particularly in the early years; (3) state regulations intended to protect domestic high-sulfur coal interests that, particularly in the early years of the program, had the effect of distorting or constraining utilities' responses to federal environmental regulation (Arimura, 2002; Bohi and Burtraw, 1992; Ellerman *et al.*, 2000, pp. 190–195); (4) interactions between the SO_2 program and other federal

---

bituminous, and is of intermediate quality. Much of the Powder River Basin coal is "subbituminous." Lignite is the lowest quality.

regulations, such as New Source Review and New Source Performance Standards, which constrained the program's operation (Gruenspecht and Stavins, 2002); and (5) policy uncertainty when regulators and policy makers subsequently considered further reductions in the national SO_2 cap, as we discuss later.

The program can also be evaluated based on the geographic distribution of impacts. Recall that the program came into being mainly in response to concerns about acid rain in the US Northeast. Although it was clear at the time the program was enacted that emissions from different plants had different impacts, the Title IV emissions trading scheme ignored this fact. Most coal-fired power plants were located east of the Mississippi, and model-based analyses predicted that the largest share of cost-effective emissions reductions would come from plants having the greatest impact on lakes and forests in the Northeast. Nonetheless, some worried that emissions would end up disproportionately concentrated and would produce "hot spots" of unacceptably high SO_2 concentrations. Despite these concerns, the geographic pattern of emissions reductions was broadly consistent with model predictions, and the program did not generate significant hot spots (Ellerman *et al.*, 2000, pp. 130–131; Swift, 2004).[2]

In sum, the SO_2 allowance trading system's actual costs, even if they exceeded the cost-effective ideal for a cap-and-trade system, were much lower than would have been incurred with a comparable traditional regulatory approach. The program's goals were achieved with less litigation (and thus less uncertainty) than is typical for traditional environmental programs, both because firms that found it particularly costly to reduce emissions had the option of buying allowances and because firms could not complain about the exercise of administrative discretion by the US Environmental Protection Agency, as the law gave it essentially no discretion. Overall, there is broad agreement that the SO_2 allowance trading system provided a compelling demonstration of the advantages of a market-based approach to environmental protection. With this background on design and performance, we turn to four significant ironies.

[2]Muller and Mendelsohn (2009) suggest that the use of damage-based trading ratios, where allowances might be adjusted for the marginal environmental damage each source of emissions would do, rather than using a single allowance price, could have been welfare-improving. Of course, the practical challenges of setting such ratios — particularly in a political environment — would be serious.

Doing the Right Thing for the Wrong Reason

The central purpose of the SO_2 allowance trading program was to reduce the acidification of forest and aquatic ecosystems by cutting precursor SO_2 emissions, primarily in the Northeastern United States (National Acid Precipitation Assessment Program, 1998). The goal of reducing SO_2 emissions was met and exceeded. However, it turns out that the ecological benefits of the program have been relatively small, largely because it takes much longer than thought to reverse the acidification of ecosystems (National Acid Precipitation Assessment Program, 2005). On the other hand, other completely unanticipated benefits of the program have been massive.

Whereas some studies at the time of the program's enactment predicted that its benefits would be approximately equal to its costs (Portney, 1990), more recent estimates suggest annual benefits of between \$59 and \$116 billion, compared with annual costs of \$0.5 to \$2 billion, as shown in Table 1. However, more than 95 percent of these benefits are associated not with ecological impacts — including acidification of aquatic ecosystems — but instead with human health impacts of reduced levels of airborne fine sulfate particles less than 2.5 micrometers in diameter ($PM_{2.5}$), particles which derive from SO_2 emissions. Epidemiological evidence of the harmful human health effects of these fine particulates

Table 1. Estimated annual US benefits and costs of the SO_2 allowance trading program; Title IV, Clean Air Amendments of 1990 (billions of US 2000 Dollars).

Benefits	
Mortality	50–100
Morbidity	3–7
Recreational visibility	2–3
Residential visibility	2–3
Ecosystem effects	0.5
Total	**59–116**
Costs	**0.5–2.0**
Net benefits	**58–114**

Sources: Burtraw *et al.* (1998), Burtraw (1999), Chestnut and Mills (2005), and Banzhaf *et al.* (2006).

mounted rapidly in the decade *after* the CAAA was enacted (Chestnut and Mills, 2005).

Estimates of these health benefits vary widely, but they appear to be on the order of $50 billion to more than $100 billion per year (Burtraw *et al.*, 1998; Burtraw, 1999; Chestnut and Mills, 2005; National Acid Precipitation Assessment Program, 2005; Shadbegian *et al.*, 2005; US Environmental Protection Agency, 2011a).[3] As Table 1 shows, strict ecosystem benefits are probably considerably less than program costs, though at least one study (Banzhaf *et al.*, 2006) suggests that ecosystem benefits alone have exceeded costs. But estimated human health benefits of the program may have exceeded annual costs by a factor of more than fifty! With its mandated 50 percent cut in SO_2 emissions, the government did what turned out to be the right thing for the wrong reason.

An Unanticipated Consequence of Deregulation

The realized costs of the SO_2 allowance trading program were substantially less than forecasts made prior to implementation (National Acid Precipitation Assessment Program 2005).[4] Part of this discrepancy was due to technological innovation and the speed with which the allowance market matured. But another major factor in low realized compliance costs was the emergence of input substitution, from high- to low-sulfur coal, as a cost-effective strategy for reducing SO_2 emissions. Indeed, the attractiveness of switching to low-sulfur coal was increasing *before* the program even went into effect due to a public policy change *unrelated to the environment* and initiated long before 1990.

The three major coal deposits in the United States are located in the Powder River Basin of Wyoming and Montana, the Illinois Basin, and Central Appalachia. Of these, Powder River Basin coal is cheapest to mine and has the lowest sulfur content (though considerable low-sulfur coal was also produced in the East, particularly after the acid rain program

[3]The lower end of this range of benefit estimates is linked with the possibly nonlinear relationship between cuts in SO_2 emissions and reductions in $PM_{2.5}$ deposition (West *et al.*, 1999).

[4]A revolutionary aspect of the cap-and-trade approach was that for the first time regulators had instantaneous information in a summary statistic (the allowance price) of the marginal cost of compliance, but the program's design did not allow for any response to that information, such as changing the cap.

took effect). However, the majority of coal-fired power plants in the United States are located along or east of the Mississippi River, making Powder River Basin the most distant option for major sources of demand.

Prior to 1976, the Interstate Commerce Commission set rates for freight rail, which is the main way in which coal is transported. The Railroad Revitalization and Regulatory Reform Act of 1976 and the Staggers Rail Act of 1980 gave rail carriers the ability to set their own rates and legalized private railroad-shipper contracts. As a result, shipping rates for coal (and other products) declined significantly (Winston, 2005; US Government Accountability Office, 2007). The cost of bringing coal from the Powder River Basin to centers of high demand east of the Mississippi River fell dramatically (Ellerman *et al.*, 2000) — even though the existence of only two major rail lines kept shipping costs above competitive levels (Busse and Keohane, 2007).

Deregulation gave the freight carriers flexibility and incentive to contract with eastern utilities, and, as noted above, these same utilities developed cost-effective ways to burn sub-bituminous coal (which had lower energy content as well as lower sulfur content) (Ellerman *et al.*, 2000, pp. 243–245). The average sulfur content of coal burned at electric generating units began to fall. In fact, SO_2 emissions at units covered by the allowance trading program were actually falling from 1985 to 1993, *before* the acid rain program took effect (Ellerman and Montero, 1998). The main source of this decline was the increased use of Powder River Basin coal, with average rail rates of shipping that coal from Wyoming and Montana to Midwest generators falling by over 50 percent from 1979 to 1993 (Gerking and Hamilton, 2008).

For some power plants, fuel-switching from high- to low-sulfur coal was cost-effective even without acid rain legislation; and for many other eastern power plants, rail deregulation made fuel-switching less expensive than installing scrubbers in response to the legislation. Of the 263 units regulated in Phase I of the allowance trading program, 52 percent primarily pursued fuel-switching or blending low-sulfur coal with higher-sulfur coal, accounting for 59 percent of emissions reductions; and scrubbers were installed at about 10 percent of the units, accounting for 28 percent of emissions reduction (US Energy Information Administration, 1997).[5]

[5] In addition, 32 percent of the units complied by obtaining additional allowances as well as switching to lower-sulfur coal, accounting for 9 percent of emissions reductions; 3 percent of the units were retired, accounting for 2 percent of emissions reductions; and

About one-third of SO_2 emissions reductions in the early years of the program were due to prior railroad deregulation and two-thirds to the SO_2 allowance trading program (Ellerman *et al.*, 2000, p. 122).

It could be argued that because these reductions in delivered fuel costs would have occurred in the absence of the SO_2 allowance trading program and would have reduced the costs of a command-and-control SO_2 program as well, the cost savings attributed to the SO_2 allowance trading program (relative to a command-and-control system) should be adjusted downward (Carlson *et al.*, 2000). This point has some validity, but it is also true that a prescriptive regulatory approach — say, a policy that required installing scrubbers at all power plants — might have prevented electricity companies from taking advantage of some of these alternative compliance options. In any event, it is clear that significant shares of the emissions reduction — about one-third in the early years — and of the cost savings associated with the SO_2 allowance trading system were actually an unanticipated consequence of an earlier, unrelated public policy change.

Conservatives Demonize Their Own Innovation

For a long time, market-based approaches to environmental protection, such as cap-and-trade, bore a Republican label. In the 1980s, President Ronald Reagan's Environmental Protection Agency put in place a trading program to phase out leaded gasoline. It produced a more rapid elimination of leaded gasoline from the marketplace than had been anticipated, and at a savings of some $250 million per year compared with a conventional no-trade, command-and-control approach (Stavins, 2003). Not only did President George H. W. Bush successfully propose the use of cap-and-trade to cut US SO_2 emissions, his administration advocated in international forums the use of emissions trading to cut global CO_2 emissions, a proposal initially resisted but ultimately adopted by the European Union. In 2005, President George W. Bush's EPA issued the Clean Air Interstate Rule, aimed at reducing SO_2 emissions by a further 70 percent from their 2003 levels. Cap-and-trade was again the policy instrument of choice. (More about this rule below.)

3 percent of the units used other compliance methods, accounting for 2 percent of emissions reductions (US Energy Information Administration, 1997).

When the Clean Air Act Amendments were being considered in the US Congress in 1989–1990, political support was not divided on partisan lines. Indeed, environmental and energy debates from the 1970s through much of the 1990s typically broke along geographic, rather than partisan, lines,[6] with key parameters being degree of urbanization and reliance on specific fuel types, such as coal versus natural gas. Thus, the Clean Air Act Amendments of 1990 passed the US Senate by a vote of 89–11 with 87 percent of Republican members and 91 percent of Democrats voting yea, and the legislation passed the House of Representatives by a vote of 401–421 with 87 percent of Republicans and 96 percent of Democrats voting in support.

However, 20 years later when climate change legislation was receiving serious consideration in Washington, environmental politics had changed dramatically, with Congressional support for environmental legislation coming mainly to reflect partisan divisions.[7] In 2009, the US House of Representatives passed the American Clean Energy and Security Act of 2009 (H.R. 2454) — often known as the Waxman–Markey bill — that included an economy-wide cap-and-trade system to cut carbon dioxide (CO_2) emissions. The Waxman–Markey bill passed the House by a narrow margin of 219–212, with support from 83 percent of Democrats, but only 4 percent of Republicans. In July 2010, the US Senate abandoned its attempt to pass companion legislation. In the process of debating this legislation, conservatives (largely Republicans and some coal-state Democrats) attacked the cap-and-trade system as "cap-and-tax,"[8] much as an earlier generation of liberals had denigrated cap-and-trade as "selling licenses to pollute."

Many conservatives in the Congress undoubtedly opposed climate policies because of disagreement about the threat of climate change or the

---

[6]The same was true of trade policy debates until the early 1990s, that is, they were driven by economic impacts on various sectors and populations, which resulted in geographic, not partisan, divisions.

[7]This polarization between the two political parties on environmental issues (Shipan and Lowry, 2001) was and is part of a gradually widening gulf between the parties on virtually all issues (Fleisher and Bond, 2004; Poole and Rosenthal, 1997, 2007). Moderates have been gradually disappearing for decades (Lowry and Shipan, 2002; Theriault, 2008).

[8]They may have been helped by President Obama's February 2009 budget message to Congress, which provided for revenues from an auction of 100 percent of the allowances under such a scheme (Chan *et al.*, 2012).

costs of the policies, but instead of debating those risks and costs, they chose to launch an ultimately successful campaign to demonize and thereby tarnish cap-and-trade as an instrument of public policy, rendering it "collateral damage" in the wider climate policy battle. This scorched-earth approach could come back to haunt conservatives if future environmental initiatives with widespread support are enacted without making use of the power of the marketplace to reduce compliance costs. It is ironic that conservatives chose to demonize their own market-based creation. It is perhaps even more ironic that this tactic seems to have been effective despite their creation's excellent performance.

What the Government Gives, It Can Take Away

A major source of uncertainty about any government-created market is that the government can undo what it created — possibly unintentionally. In essence, this happened in the SO_2 allowance market. Through a series of new Clean Air Act regulations, court rulings, and regulatory responses, the courts affirmed that EPA could not set up a new interstate trading system or modify the Title IV system in the absence of new legislation from Congress. In response, state-level and source-level constraints were put in place that ultimately rendered the SO_2 cap-and-trade system itself non-binding and effectively closed down the allowance market.

Prices for SO_2 allowances were remarkably stable throughout the program's first decade, as shown in Figure 2, and then we see a steep spike. What happened? It was widely recognized by the late 1990s that SO_2 reductions in excess of those resulting from the trading program of Title IV would be required by other provisions in the Clean Air Act dealing with air quality standards because of the significant adverse health effects of fine particulates associated with SO_2 emissions. But the law did not give the EPA authority to adjust the Title IV program, such as by tightening the overall cap, in response to new information about the benefits (or costs) of emissions reductions. This crucial fact drove the chain of events leading to the ultimate collapse of the SO_2 allowance trading program.

In early 2002, President George W. Bush proposed the Clear Skies Act, which would have greatly tightened the SO_2 cap. Prices in the allowance market did not immediately budge, however, which suggests it was no surprise to market participants when this proposal died in March 2005, having failed to move out of committee. The Bush administration then

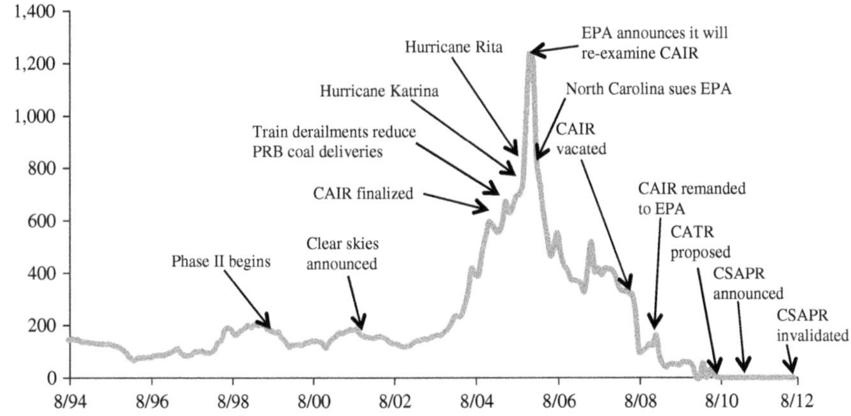

Figure 2. SO_2 allowance prices and the regulatory environment, 1994–2012 (1995 dollars per ton).

Note: CAIR is "Clean Air Interstate Rule." CATR is "Clean Air Transport Rule." CSAPR is "Cross-State Air Pollution Rule."

Source: Data on spot prices compiled by Power & Energy Analytic Resources (PEAR) Inc. from Cantor Fitzgerald until September 11, 2001, and from ICAP United thereafter.

promulgated its Clean Air Interstate Rule in May 2005, with the same purpose of lowering the cap on SO_2 emissions (to 70 percent below the 2003 emissions level). This rule sought to apply more stringent emission requirements on states that were contributing to violations of EPA's primary ambient air quality standards for fine particulates in the eastern United States (Palmer and Evans, 2009). It required sources within those states to surrender two additional allowances for every ton of SO_2 emissions — effectively reducing the cap by two-thirds. Because the Clean Air Interstate Rule provided that firms could bank their existing SO_2 allowances for use in the new program, prices rose further in anticipation of this more stringent cap, with spot prices increasing from \$273 per ton in EPA's 2004 auction to \$703 in the 2005 auction.[9]

[9]An array of other factors contributed to the run-up and eventual spike in SO_2 allowance prices, including Hurricanes Katrina (August 2005) and Rita (September 2005), which impaired petroleum refining and natural gas capacity. In addition, delivery of low-sulfur coal from the Powder River Basin to Midwestern power plants was disrupted by track failures (May 2005) on both the Union Pacific and Burlington Northern Santa Fe railroads, which caused low-sulfur coal prices in the Midwest to peak in December 2005, at a level

After peaking in 2005 at more than $1,200 per ton (see Figure 2), SO_2 allowance prices dropped just as fast as they had risen, aided by an announcement from the US Environmental Protection Agency that it would reexamine the Clean Air Interstate Rule (Samuelsohn, 2005) and speculation about impending legal challenges (Samuelsohn, 2006a; Kruse, 2009).[10] On June 26, 2006, North Carolina and other states and a number of utilities sued the Environmental Protection Agency over the Clean Air Interstate Rule (Samuelsohn, 2006b). The states argued that the interstate trading allowed under the rule was inconsistent with Section 110(a) of the Clean Air Act, which obliges each state to prevent emissions that interfere with any other state's attainment or maintenance of air quality standards. This meant that the EPA could not set up a new trading program built on the SO_2 allowance trading system by regulatory means and would therefore have to focus on source-level or other types of regulation in its efforts to reduce emissions below the limits established in Title IV in order to meet new local-air-quality standards. Because the new, required regulation, rather than Title IV, would become the binding constraint on emissions, trading under the original SO_2 allowance trading system would be rendered unimportant.

Two years later, on July 11, 2008, the Circuit Court of Appeals for the District of Columbia (*State of North Carolina v. Environmental Protection Agency*, 531 F. 3d 896 [D.C. Cir. 2008]) vacated the Clean Air Interstate Rule in its entirety on the grounds that, under the Clean Air Act, the Environmental Protection Agency could not ignore the relationship

three times greater than a year earlier. As a result, some power companies switched to higher-sulfur coal from the east, increasing demand for SO_2 allowances. A final factor was features of the allowance trading program's design that interacted with the tax system and utility regulation to restrict the number of allowances actually available for trading at any time (the "float"), thus compounding the price impacts of the other factors (Parsons *et al.*, 2009).

[10] Also contributing to the fall in allowances prices from their peak was a drop in natural gas prices, the restoration of refining and gas capacity in the Gulf of Mexico following Hurricanes Katrina and Rita, and the realization of a likely adequate supply of allowances and installed scrubber capacity to comply with the Clean Air Interstate Rule (Burtraw and Szambelan, 2009). In addition, many expected an economy-wide CO_2 cap-and-trade system, which all three major Presidential candidates — John McCain, Hillary Clinton, and Barack Obama — in 2007 supported and which would have led to an exogenous, long-run decline in coal usage and thus in SO_2 emissions, and hence to a decline in the value of banked allowances.

between sources and receptors in matters involving air quality standards (US Environmental Protection Agency, 2011a). Thus, without new legislation, the Title IV program, with interstate trading at its core, could not be modified to drive further reductions in SO_2 emissions to meet air quality standards. On that single day, the SO_2 allowance price fell from \$315 to \$115 (Burtraw and Szambelan, 2009). The Bush administration, followed by the subsequent Obama administration, chose not to appeal that ruling. The court allowed the Clean Air Interstate Rule to remain in effect while the EPA devised a replacement that addressed its concerns, but it remained clear that unlimited interstate trading was doomed. Prices continued to fall, returning to the range of their pre-2004 levels. At the 2009 auction, spot allowances (which could be used in 2009 or later) sold for \$70 per ton, compared with \$390 a year earlier (Burtraw and Szambelan, 2009).

In July 2010, the Obama administration proposed an alternative rule to limit annual SO_2 (and NO_x) emissions in 28 states, as a replacement for the Clean Air Interstate Rule. The proposed rule established state-specific emissions caps for power plant SO_2 emissions, thereby limiting interstate trading. The rule was finalized in July 2011 as the Cross-State Air Pollution Rule, allowing only intrastate trading and limited trading between two groups of states. Predictably, this rule too was challenged in court, by 27 states and 18 other parties; in August 2012, the US Court of Appeals for the D.C. Circuit invalidated the rule (*EME Homer City Generation, L.P. vs. Environmental Protection Agency, et al.*, No. 11-1302).

While the SO_2 allowance market functioned well, the broader regulatory environment served to end its effective life. The allowance market remains nominally in place, but the imposition of state-level and source-specific prescriptive regulation has virtually eliminated the demand for federal SO_2 allowances. By the time of the Environmental Protection Agency's 2012 auction, market-clearing prices had fallen to \$0.56 in the spot auction and \$0.12 in the seven-year advance auction.[11] Those states

[11] When new Mercury and Air Toxics Standards affecting coal-fired power plants take effect — likely in 2015–2016 — they will likely be so stringent that SO_2 constraints under the Cross-State Air Pollution Rule will be rendered nonbinding in one of the two SO_2 trading zones. Further, the Mercury and Air Toxics Standards explicitly do not allow trading, and so assuming these rules are finalized and implemented as expected, there will be only a minimal market for SO_2 (Burtraw *et al.*, 2012).

with binding caps for SO_2 under the Cross-State Air Pollution Rule must still reduce their emissions, whether by mandating the use of scrubbers, retiring coal-fired power plants, or setting up intrastate trading of emission allowances.

In essence, the series of regulations, court rulings, and regulatory responses that followed Congress's rejection of the George W. Bush administration's Clear Skies Act affirmed that: (1) EPA cannot set up an interstate trading system under the Clean Air Act in the absence of specific legislation from Congress (which, of course, it had for the SO_2 allowance trading system under Title IV of the Clean Air Act amendments of 1990); and (2) consequent state-level and source-level constraints following the Clean Air Interstate Rule rendered the SO_2 cap-and-trade system itself nonbinding.

One more irony: the SO_2 program's success may have weakened the case for continuing the allowance market by reducing the heterogeneity of abatements costs across sources, thus reducing potential gains from trade (Newell and Stavins, 2003).

When the government creates a market, it can also destroy it, possibly fostering a legacy of increased regulatory uncertainty and reduced investor confidence in future cap-and-trade regimes, and hence reduced credibility of pollution markets more broadly.

Conclusions

More than 20 years ago, the Clean Air Act amendments of 1990 launched the path-breaking SO_2 allowance trading system, the world's first large-scale market-based environmental initiative. That grand experiment in public policy continues to enjoy its reputation around the world as a great success. Although it is true that the system performed at least as well as its advocates had anticipated through its first decade of operation — reducing emissions cost-effectively — it is also true that reflections from our current perspective yield a considerably more nuanced assessment of performance. The actual costs of compliance turned out to be lower than expected, but this was in substantial part an unintended consequence of other, nonenvironmental policy innovations: specifically, the earlier deregulation of US railroads that allowed less-expensive delivery of low-sulfur coal from the Powder River Basin to the Midwest. The actual benefits turned out to be substantially greater than originally expected but not because of ecological benefits. Rather, reductions in SO_2 emissions resulted in substantial decreases in downwind concentrations of small particulates, thereby producing great benefits to human health.

What appeared in 1990 to be a quintessential moderate Republican approach to environmental protection — cap-and-trade — generated great hostility from conservatives 20 years later. In the process of opposing Congressional climate policy initiatives in 2009–2010, conservatives demonized cap-and-trade proposals as "cap-and-tax" and may have thereby tarnished this market-based approach to environmental protection for years to come. Ironically, an attempt by a Republican administration to use the cap-and-trade approach to reduce the SO_2 emissions cap eventually led, through a series of court cases and regulatory responses, to the virtual closure of the SO_2 allowance market.

What are some lessons of this history of the SO_2 allowance trading program for future market-based and other public policies? First, much is often learned over time regarding any policy's benefits and costs. What may appear to be wise initially may not turn out to be wise in the long term, and what appears to be unwise initially may turn out to be very attractive in the long term. Thus it can be important for policies to be flexible and responsive to changes in knowledge and technology. On the other hand, policy stability encourages efficient investment, so unnecessary changes can be destructive. It can be argued that the SO_2 cap-and-trade system provided valuable stability, but the legislation also made it impossible to make what would have been responsive, effective, and efficient changes in the policy.

Second, unintended consequences of policies are almost inevitable. They can sometimes be beneficial, as in the case of the effects of rail deregulation on the performance of the SO_2 allowance trading system. They can sometimes be negative, as when regulatory responses to invalidation of the Clean Air Interstate Rule led to the virtual collapse of the SO_2 market. But by definition, such changes are almost impossible to predict. The implication is to be very careful and modest with forecasts and assessments. This can be demonstrated by a retrospective review of initial (under)estimates of the consequences of the Staggers Rail Act of 1980 and (overly hopeful) assessments of the promulgation of the Clean Air Interstate Rule in 2005.

Third, in most cases, politics trumps science and economics. The target of Title IV to reduce SO_2 emissions by 50 percent was set neither on the basis of the science, drawing on the findings of the National Acid

Precipitation Assessment Program, nor economics, drawing on a comparison of anticipated benefits and costs. The implication is not to ignore politics but, rather to design policies that are likely to succeed in real-world political settings. Cap-and-trade systems can facilitate sound performance in political settings because of their ability to build constituencies of political support through free allocation of allowances without this negatively affecting the system's aggregate performance, either environmentally or economically.

Fourth, market-based policies have great cost and feasibility advantages, but like any public policy, the government can change or repeal these initiatives, or render them irrelevant. Market-based and other public policies can be constrained by other policies. Economists and other analysts tend to examine policies one at a time, but this misses potential interactions, which can be exceptionally important (Goulder and Stavins, 2011).

Finally, what are the implications for future climate change policy? The bad news seems to be that "cap-and-tax" rhetoric may make it hard to use this approach in the United States to deal with climate change. Emissions of CO_2 from coal-fired power plants will no doubt be reduced by EPA rules on SO_2, NO_x, mercury, coal fly-ash, and cooling-water withdrawals that are working their way through the regulatory process and that will drive up the cost of generating electricity with coal. But these rules, and those likely to be adopted by the Environmental Protection Agency in response to the US Supreme Court decision in *Massachusetts et al. v. Environmental Protection Agency et al.* (549 US 497 [2007] (at http://www.supremecourt.gov/opinions/06pdf/05-1120.pdf) that it regulate CO_2 under the Clean Air Act, are unlikely to be cost-effective policies for reducing greenhouse gas emissions in the long run. At a time when environmental protection in general and climate policy in particular have become highly partisan in the US Congress, the outlook for an efficient and effective national climate policy is not very promising.

The good news, however, is that cap-and-trade is no longer just a subject for academic seminars and journal articles; it is a proven, viable option for tackling large-scale environmental problems. It is now being used around the world, including for addressing CO_2 emissions linked with global climate change. Even if the SO_2 allowance trading program's performance was enhanced by unanticipated benefits and declines in coal prices, and even if it has been essentially wiped out by later policy changes, the fact is that the allowance trading program achieved its target emissions reductions rapidly and cost-effectively. Few other environmental programs of any sort have performed as well.

Acknowledgements

We thank Richard Sweeney for research assistance, and Dallas Burtraw, Juan-Pablo Montero, Sean Theriault, Tom Tietenberg, and especially Denny Ellerman, as well as the Editor, Co-editors, and Managing Editor of this journal for valuable comments on a previous version of this chapter. Any errors and all opinions are our own.

References

Arimura, Toshi H. (2002). "An empirical study of the SO2 allowance market: Effects of PUC regulations." *Journal of Environmental Economics and Management*, **44**(2): 271–289.

Banzhaf, H. Spencer, Dallas Burtraw, David Evans, and Alan Krupnick. (2006). "Valuation of natural resource improvements in the Adirondacks." *Land Economics*, **82**(3): 445–464.

Baumol, William J., and Wallace E. Oates. (1971). "The use of standards and prices for protection of the environment." *Swedish Journal of Economics*, **73**(1): 42–54.

Bellas, Allen S., and Ian Lange. (2011). "Evidence of innovation and diffusion under tradable permit programs." *International Review of Environmental and Resource Economics*, **5**(1): 1–22.

Bohi, Douglas R., and Dallas Burtraw. (1992). "Utility investment behavior and the emission trading market." *Resources and Energy*, **14**(1–2): 129–153.

Burtraw, Dallas. (1999). "Cost savings, market performance and economic benefits of the U.S. Acid Rain Program. In Steve Sorrell and Jim Skea. Cheltenham Eds., *Pollution for Sale: Emissions Trading and Joint Implementation*, UK: Edward Elgar.

Burtraw, Dallas, and Sarah Jo Szambelan. (2009). "*U.S. Emissions Trading Markets for SO_2 and NO_x*." Discussion Paper 09–40, Resources for the Future.

Burtraw, Dallas, Alan Krupnick, Erin Mansur, David Austin, and Deirdre Farrell. (1998). "Cost and benefits of reducing air pollutants related to acid rain." *Contemporary Economic Policy*, **16**(4): 379–400.

Burtraw, Dallas, Karen L. Palmer, Anthony Paul, Blair Beasley, and Matthew Woerman. (2012). "*Reliability in the Electricity Industry Under New Environmental Regulations*." Discussion Paper 12–18, Resources for the Future.

Busse, Meghan R., and Nathaniel O. Keohane. (2007). "Market effects of environmental regulation: Coal, railroads, and the 1990 Clean Air Act." *RAND Journal of Economics*, **38**(4): 1159–1179.

Carlson, Curtis, Dallas Burtraw, Maureen L. Cropper, and Karen Palmer. (2000). "Sulfur dioxide control by electric utilities: What are the gains from trade?" *Journal of Political Economy*, **108**(6): 1292–1326.

Chan, Gabriel, Robert Stavins, Robert Stowe, and Richard Sweeney. (2012). *The SO2 Allowance Trading System and the Clean Air Act Amendments of 1990: Reflections on Twenty Years of Policy Innovation*. Cambridge, MA: Harvard Environmental Economics Program.

Chestnut, Lauraine G., and David M. Mills. (2005). "A fresh look at the benefits and costs of the U.S. Acid Rain Program." *Journal of Environmental Management*, **77**(3): 252–266.

Coase, Ronald H. (1960). "The problem of social cost." *Journal of Law and Economics*, **3**(October): 1–44.

Ellerman, A. Denny. (2003). "Ex post evaluation of tradable permits: The U.S. SO_2 cap-and-trade program." Working Paper CEEPR 03-003, Massachusetts Institute of Technology.

Ellerman, A. Denny, and Juan-Pablo Montero. (1998). "The declining trend in sulfur dioxide emissions: Implications for allowance prices." *Journal of Environmental Economics and Management*, **36**(1): 26–45.

Ellerman, A. Denny, and Juan-Pablo Montero. (2007). "The efficiency and robustness of allowance banking in the U.S. Acid Rain Program." *Energy Journal*, **28**(4): 47–71.

Ellerman, A. Denny, Paul L. Joskow, Richard Schmalensee, Juan-Pablo Montero, and Elizabeth M. Bailey. (2000). *Markets for Clean Air: The U.S. Acid Rain Program*. Cambridge, UK: Cambridge University Press.

European Commission. (2012). Emissions Trading System (EU ETS). Available at https://climate.ec.europa.eu/eu-action/eu-emissions-trading-system-eu-ets_en.

Fleisher, Richard, and John R. Bond. (2004). "The shrinking middle in the U.S. Congress." *British Journal of Political Science*, **34**(3): 429–451.

Frey, Elaine. (2013). "Technology diffusion and environmental regulation: The adoption of scrubbers by coal-fired plants." *Energy Journal*, **34**(1): 177–205.

Gerking, Shelby, and Stephen F. Hamilton. (2008). "What explains the increased utilization of Powder River Basin coal in electric power generation?" *American Journal of Agricultural Economics*, **90**(4): 933–950.

Goulder, Lawrence H. (1995). "Environmental taxation and the 'double dividend': A reader's guide." *International Tax and Public Finance*, **2**(2): 157–183.

Goulder, Lawrence H., and Robert N. Stavins. (2011). "Challenges from state–federal interactions in US climate change policy." *American Economic Review*, **101**(3): 253–257.

Gruenspecht, Howard K., and Robert N. Stavins. (2002). "New source review under the Clean Air Act: Ripe for reform." *Resources*, (147), 19–23.

Hahn, Robert W., and Robert N. Stavins. (2011). "The effect of allowance allocations on cap-and-trade system performance." *Journal of Law and Economics*, **54**(4): S267–S294.

Joskow, Paul L., and Richard Schmalensee. (1998). "The political economy of market-based environmental policy: The U.S. Acid Rain Program." *Journal of Law and Economics*, **41**(1): 37–83.

Keohane, Nathaniel O. (2003). "What did the market buy? Cost savings under the U.S. tradeable permits program for sulfur dioxide." Working Paper YCELP-01-11-2003, Yale Center for Environmental Law and Policy.

Kruse, Elizabeth. (2009). "North Carolina v. Environmental Protection Agency." *Harvard Environmental Law Review*, **33**(1): 283–296.

Lowry, William R., and Charles R. Shipan. (2002). "Party differentiation in Congress." *Legislative Studies Quarterly*, **27**(1): 33–60.

Montero, Juan-Pablo. (1999). "Voluntary compliance with market-based environmental policy: Evidence from the U.S. Acid Rain Program." *Journal of Political Economy*, **107**(5): 998–1033.

Montgomery, W. David. (1972). "Markets in licenses and efficient pollution control programs." *Journal of Economic Theory*, **5**(3): 395–418.

Muller, Nicholas Z., and Robert Mendelsohn. (2009). "Efficient pollution regulation: Getting the prices right." *American Economic Review*, **99**(5): 1714–1739.

National Acid Precipitation Assessment Program. (1998). *Biennial Report to Congress: An Integrated Assessment*. Washington, DC: National Science and Technology Council, Committee on Environment and Natural Resources.

National Acid Precipitation Assessment Program. (2005). *National Acid Precipitation Assessment Program Report to Congress: An Integrated Assessment*. Washington, DC: National Science and Technology Council, Committee on Environment and Natural Resources.

Newell, Richard G., and Robert N. Stavins. (2003). "Cost heterogeneity and the potential savings from market-based policies." *Journal of Regulatory Economics*, **23**(1): 43–59.

Palmer, Karen, and David A. Evans. (2009). "The evolving SO2 allowance market: Title IV, CAIR, and beyond." *Resources for the Future Weekly Policy Commentary*, July 13.

Parsons, John E., A. Denney Ellerman, and Stephen Feilhauer. (2009). "Designing a U.S. market for CO2." *Journal of Applied Corporate Finance*, **21**(1): 79–86.

Poole, Keith T., and Howard Rosenthal. (1997). *Congress: A Political-Economic History of Roll Call Voting*. New York: Oxford University Press.

Poole, Keith T., and Howard Rosenthal. (2007). *Ideology and Congress*. New Brunswick: Transaction Publishers.

Popp, David. (2003). "Pollution control innovations and the Clean Air Act of 1990." *Journal of Policy Analysis and Management*, **22**(4): 641–660.

Portney, Paul R. (1990). "Policy watch: Economics of the Clean Air Act." *Journal of Economic Perspectives*, **4**(4): 173–181.

Regens, James L, and Robert W. Rycroft. (1988). *The Acid Rain Controversy.* University of Pittsburgh Press.

Samuelsohn, Darren. (2005). "EPA agrees to re-examine CAIR power plant standard." *Greenwire*, November 23.

Samuelsohn, Darren. (2006a). "Bush regs facing a year of legal challenges." *Greenwire*, January 6.

Samuelsohn, Darren. (2006b). "North Carolina sues EPA over upwind emissions." *Greenwire*, June 27.

Schmalensee, Richard, Paul L. Joskow, A. Denny Ellerman, Juan-Pablo Montero, and Elizabeth M. Bailey. (1998). "An interim evaluation of sulfur dioxide emissions trading." *Journal of Economic Perspectives*, **12**(3): 53–68.

Shadbegian, Ronald J., Wayne B. Gray, and Cynthia L. Morgan. (2005). "Benefits and costs from sulfur dioxide trading: A distributional analysis." Working Paper 05–09. U.S. Environmental Protection Agency, National Center for Environmental Economics.

Shipan, Charles R., and William R. Lowry. (2001). "Environmental policy and party divergence in Congress." *Political Research Quarterly*, **54**(2): 245–263.

Stavins, Robert N. (1995). "Transaction costs and tradeable permits." *Journal of Environmental Economics and Management*. **29**(2): 133–148.

Stavins, Robert N. (1998). "What can we learn from the grand policy experiment? Lessons from SO2 allowance trading." *Journal of Economic Perspectives*, **12**(3): 69–88.

Stavins, Robert N. (2003). "Experience with market-based environmental policy instruments." Chap. 9, In Karl-Göran Mäler and Jeffrey Vincent Eds., *Handbook of Environmental Economics*, Vol. I, pp. 355–435. Amsterdam: Elsevier Science.

Swift, Byron. (2004). "Emissions trading and hot spots: A review of the major programs." *Environment Reporter*, **35**(19): 1–16.

Theriault, Sean M. (2008). *Party Polarization in the Congress*. New York: Cambridge University Press.

US Energy Information Administration. (1997). *The Effects of Title IV of the Clean Air Act Amendments of 1990 on Electric Utilities: An Update*. http://www.eia.gov/cneaf/electricity/clean_air_upd97/exec_sum.html.

US Energy Information Administration. (2012). "Electricity net generation: Total (All Sectors), 1949–2011." Table 8.2a in *Annual Energy Review 2011*. http://www.eia.gov/totalenergy/data/annual/pdf/aer.pdf.

US Environmental Protection Agency. (2011a). *Clean Air Interstate Rule, Acid Rain Program, and Former NOx Budget Trading Program 2010 Progress Report*. Washington, DC: U.S. Environmental Protection Agency.

US Environmental Protection Agency. (2011b). "National Emissions Inventory (NEI) Air Pollutant Emissions Trends Data: 1970–2011."

US Environmental Protection Agency. (2012). "Air Markets Program Data." https://echo.epa.gov/resources/echo-data/about-the-data (accessed December 8, 2012.)

US Government Accountability Office. (2007). *Freight Railroads: Updated Information on Rates and Other Industry Trends*. Publication No. GAO07-291R.

West, J. Jason, Asif S. Ansari, and Spyros N. Pandis. (1999). "Marginal PM2.5: Nonlinear aerosol mass response to sulfate reductions in the eastern United States." *Journal of the Air & Waste Management Association*, **49**(12): 1415–1424.

Winston, Clifford. (2005). "The success of the Staggers Rail Act of 1980." Related Publication 05-24, AEI-Brookings Joint Center for Regulatory Studies.

https://doi.org/10.1142/9789811292415_0009

Chapter 9

Lessons Learned from Three Decades of Experience with Cap and Trade*

Richard Schmalensee[†,¶] and Robert N. Stavins[‡,§,‖,]**

[†]*MIT Sloan School of Management, Massachusetts Institute of Technology, Cambridge, MA, USA*

[‡]*John F. Kennedy School of Government, Harvard University, Cambridge, MA, USA*

[§]*Resources for the Future, Washington, DC, USA*

[‖]*National Bureau of Economic Research, Cambridge, MA, USA*

[¶]*rschmal@mit.edu*

[**]*robert_stavins@harvard.edu*

Introduction

Thirty years ago, many environmental advocates argued that government allocation of rights to emit pollution inappropriately legitimized environmental degradation, while others questioned the feasibility of such an approach (Mazmanian and Kraft, 2009). At the time, virtually all pollution

*This chapter was originally published in *Review of Environmental Economics and Policy*, **11**(1), 59–79, Winter 2017. doi: 10.1093/reep/rew017.

regulations took a command-and-control approach, either specifying the type of pollution control equipment to be installed or setting uniform limits on emission levels or rates. Today, it is widely recognized that because emission reduction costs can vary greatly, the aggregate abatement costs under command-and-control approaches can be much higher than under market-based approaches, which establish a price on emissions — either directly through taxes or indirectly through a market for tradable emissions rights (called permits or allowances) established under a cap-and-trade policy. Market-based approaches tend to equate marginal abatement costs rather than emissions levels or rates across sources. This means that in theory, market-based approaches can achieve aggregate pollution control targets at minimum cost. In this chapter, we examine the design and performance of seven of the most prominent emissions trading systems that have been implemented over the past 30 years in order to distill key lessons for future applications of this environmental policy instrument. We focus on systems that are important environmentally and/or economically and whose performance is well documented. We exclude emission reduction credit (i.e., offset) systems, which offer credits for emissions reductions from some counterfactual baseline, because while emissions can generally be measured directly, emissions reductions are unobservable and often ill-defined. It is worth noting, however, that offset systems have been fairly widely used, notably in the Clean Development Mechanism (CDM), an international offset system that is part of the Kyoto Protocol.

The seven emissions trading systems we examine are the U.S. Environmental Protection Agency's (EPA's) phasedown of leaded gasoline in the 1980s, the U.S. sulfur dioxide (SO_2) allowance trading program under the Clean Air Act Amendments of 1990, the Regional Clean Air Incentives Market (RECLAIM) in southern California; the trading of nitrogen oxides (NO_x) in the eastern United States, the Regional Greenhouse Gas Initiative (RGGI) in the northeastern United States, California's cap-and-trade system under Assembly Bill 32, and the European Union (EU) Emissions Trading System (ETS). All these programs except the first are textbook cap-and-trade systems.[1] We review the design, performance, and lessons learned from each of the seven systems, and then briefly discuss several other cap-and-trade systems. In the final section we summarize key lessons for designing and implementing new

[1]See Table A1 in Appendix for a brief overview of these programs.

cap-and-trade systems and present our thoughts about the potential role of cap-and-trade in global climate change policy.

Experience with U.S. National Cap-and-Trade Programs

Beginning in the 1980s, the first emissions trading systems were developed and implemented at the federal level in the United States.

The Phasedown of Leaded Gasoline

In the 1970s, there was growing concern about the use of lead as an additive in gasoline. Although it was later documented that lead oxide emissions were a serious human health threat, the original concern was that these emissions were fouling catalytic converters, which were required in new U.S. cars (starting in 1975) to reduce emissions of carbon monoxide and hydrocarbons. In the early 1980s, in response to this concern, the EPA began a phasedown of lead in gasoline to 10 percent of its original level.

In 1982, the EPA launched a trading program aimed at reducing the burden on smaller refineries, which faced significantly higher compliance costs than large refineries. Unlike a textbook cap-and-trade program, in which a fixed quantity of permits is given or sold to compliance entities, there was no explicit allocation of permits. Instead, the system implicitly awarded property rights on the basis of historical levels of gasoline production (Hahn, 1989). More specifically, if a refiner produced gasoline with a total lead content that was lower than the amount allowed, it earned lead "credits" that the EPA allowed the refiner to sell. Under the program's banking provision, lead credits could also be saved for later use. This created an incentive for refineries to make early reductions in lead content to help them meet the lower limits that took effect over time.

Performance

Overall, the trading program was successful in meeting its environmental targets, although it may have produced some temporary geographic shifts in use patterns (Anderson *et al.*, 1990; Newell and Rogers, 2007), and it resulted in leaded gasoline being removed from the market faster than anticipated. In each year of the program (until the lead phasedown was completed and the program was terminated at the end of 1987), more than 60 percent of the lead added to gasoline was associated with traded lead credits (Hahn and Hester, 1989). This high level of trading far surpassed levels observed in earlier environmental offset markets under the EPA's Emissions Trading Program in the 1970s. The level of trading and the rate at which refiners reduced their production of leaded gasoline suggest that the program was also relatively cost effective (Hahn and Hester, 1989; Kerr and Mare, 1997; Nichols, 1997). The EPA estimated that the lead trading program resulted in savings of approximately 20 percent relative to approaches that did not include trading (U.S. Environmental Protection Agency, 1985). In addition, the program provided significant incentives for cost-saving technology diffusion (Kerr and Newell, 2003).

Lessons

Three major lessons emerge from the design and implementation of this program. First, as the first environmental program in which trading played a central role, the program served as proof of the concept that a tradable emission rights system could be both environmentally effective and economically cost effective.

Second, the program demonstrated that transaction costs in such a system could be small enough to permit substantial trade. In contrast, in the 1970s, the EPA's Emissions Trading Program (a set of emissions reduction credit systems) required prior government approval of individual trades, which hampered trading activity. The lack of such requirements was an important factor in the success of trading in the lead phasedown program (Hahn and Hester, 1989). Third, as in later programs, banking played a very important role. By enabling intertemporal substitution, provisions that allowed firms to bank permits contributed a significant share of the gains from trade.

The Sulfur Dioxide Allowance Trading Program

During the 1980s, there was growing concern that acid precipitation — due mainly to emissions of SO_2 from coal-fired power plants — was damaging forests and aquatic ecosystems (Glass *et al.*, 1982). However, because the costs of emissions reductions differed dramatically among existing plants, legislative proposals to use command-and-control approaches failed to attract significant support.

Title IV of the Clean Air Act Amendments of 1990 addressed this issue by launching the SO_2 allowance trading program. Phase 1 (1995–1999) required emissions reductions from the 263 most polluting coal-fired electric generating units (larger than 100 MW), almost all of which were located east of the Mississippi River. Phase 2, which began in 2000, placed an aggregate national emissions cap on approximately 3,200 electric generating units (larger than 25 MW), nearly the entire fleet of fossil-fueled plants in the continental United States (Ellerman *et al.*, 2000). This cap represented a 50 percent reduction from 1980 levels.

The government gave power plants permits to emit (called "allowances") specific tonnages of SO_2 emissions; allocations were based primarily on actual fuel use during the 1985–1987 period.[2] If annual emissions at a regulated facility exceeded its allowance allocation, the owner could comply by buying additional allowances or reducing emissions by installing pollution controls, shifting to a fuel mix with less sulfur, or reducing production. If emissions at a regulated facility were below its allowance allocation, the facility owner could sell the extra allowances or bank them for future use. The EPA monitored emissions on a continuous basis and verified ownership of the allowances submitted for compliance.

This cap-and-trade system created incentives for facilities to reduce their SO_2 emissions at the lowest cost. Although government auctioning of allowances would have generated revenue that could have been used — in principle — to reduce distortionary taxes, thereby reducing the program's social cost (Goulder, 1995), this efficiency argument was not advanced at the time. Because the entire investor-owned electric utility industry was subject to cost-of-service regulation in 1990, it was assumed that the value of free allowances would be passed on to consumers and thus not generate windfall profits for generators. Just as important, the ability to allocate free allowances helped to build significant political support for the program (Joskow and Schmalensee, 1998). Since the equilibrium allocation of pollution permits (after trading has occurred) is independent of the initial allocation (Montgomery, 1972) — barring particularly problematic types of transaction costs (Hahn and Stavins, 2012) — the initial allocation of allowances could be designed to

---

[2] In addition, the statute required the EPA to withhold about 2.8 percent of all allocated allowances each year, sell them at an annual auction, and return the proceeds in proportion to firms from which allowances had been withheld (Ellerman *et al.*, 2000).

maximize political support without compromising the system's environmental performance or raising its cost.

Performance

The program performed exceptionally well across all relevant dimensions. SO_2 emissions from electric power plants decreased 36 percent between 1990 and 2004 (U.S. Environmental Protection Agency, 2011), even though electricity generation from coal-fired power plants increased 25 percent over the same period (U.S. Energy Information Administration, 2012). The program delivered emissions reductions more quickly than expected, as utilities made substantial use of the ability to bank allowances for future use. With continuous emissions monitoring and a $2,000 per ton statutory fine for any emissions exceeding allowance holdings, compliance was nearly 100 percent (Burtraw and Szambelan, 2010).

Some worried that the geographic pattern of emissions would change so as to produce "hot spots" of unacceptably high SO_2 concentrations. However, the pattern of emissions reductions was broadly consistent with model predictions, and no significant hot spots were produced (Ellerman *et al.*, 2000; Swift, 2004).

The cost of the program was significantly reduced after the substantial deregulation of railroads in 1980, which caused rail rates to fall and thus reduced the cost of burning low-sulfur Western coal in the East (Keohane, 2003; Ellerman and Montero, 1998; Schmalensee and Stavins, 2013). That being said, cost savings were at least 15 percent and perhaps as great as 90 percent of the costs of various alternative command-and-control policies (Carlson *et al.*, 2000; Ellerman *et al.*, 2000; Keohane, 2003). In addition, there is evidence that the program reduced costs over time by providing incentives for innovation (Ellerman *et al.*, 2000; Popp, 2003; Bellas and Lange, 2011). However, for a variety of reasons, the program's costs were likely not as low as they could have been (Schmalensee and Stavins, 2013).

Nevertheless, the SO_2 allowance trading program's actual costs were much lower than under command-and-control regulation — if such an approach had been politically feasible. The program's goals were achieved with less litigation (and thus less uncertainty) than is typical for traditional environmental programs, because firms that found it particularly costly to reduce emissions had the option to buy allowances instead. Moreover, firms could not complain about the EPA's exercise of administrative discretion since the law gave the EPA very little discretion. However, subsequent regulatory actions, court decisions, and regulatory responses led to the virtual elimination of the SO_2 market by 2010 (Schmalensee and Stavins, 2013).

The SO_2 reductions achieved benefits that were a substantial multiple of the program's costs (Burtraw *et al.*, 1998; Chestnut and Mills, 2005). However, the program's benefits were due mainly to the positive human health impacts of decreased local SO_2 and small particulate concentrations, not the ecological benefits of reduced acid deposition that were expected when the program was enacted (Schmalensee and Stavins, 2013). Nevertheless, there were also significant ecological benefits (Banzhaf *et al.*, 2006).

Lessons

Even though the conclusion of the leaded gasoline phasedown trading program preceded the beginning of the SO_2 allowance trading program by a decade, the SO_2 system was, and still is today, often celebrated as the first important cap-and-trade program. Some of the lessons from the SO_2 program reinforce lessons from the lead phasedown program.

First, putting final rules in place well before the beginning of the first compliance period provides regulated entities with some degree of certainty, which facilitates their planning and limits price volatility in early years. In the case of the SO_2 allowance trading program, this was done 2 years prior to the implementation of phase 1.

Second, as with the lead trading program, the absence of requirements for prior approval of trades reduced both the uncertainty for utilities and the administrative costs for government, and it contributed to low transaction costs and substantial trading (Rico, 1995).

Third, as with the lead trading program, banking of allowances was extremely important, accounting for more than half of the program's cost savings (Carlson *et al.*, 2000; Ellerman *et al.*, 2000).

Fourth, when combined with unrestricted trading and banking, a robust allowance market can be fostered through a cap that is significantly below business-as-usual (BAU) emissions.

Fifth, allocation of free allowances can be very useful in building political support.

Sixth, intrasector emissions leakage from regulated to unregulated entities can be minimized, as it was in this program, by regulating all nontrivial sources.

Finally, high levels of compliance can be ensured through rigorous monitoring of emissions and significant penalties for noncompliance.

U.S. Regional and State Programs

Over time, action on emissions trading in the United States has shifted to subnational programs, including the Regional Clean Air Incentives Market in southern California, NO_x trading in the eastern United States, the Regional Greenhouse Gas Initiative in the northeast, and California's cap-and-trade system.

The Regional Clean Air Incentives Market

The South Coast Air Quality Management District, which is responsible for controlling emissions in a four-county area of southern California, launched the Regional Clean Air Incentives Market (RECLAIM) in 1993 to reduce NO_x emissions and in 1994 to reduce SO_2 emissions from 350 affected sources, including power plants and industrial sources in the Los Angeles area that emitted four or more tons per year of either pollutant. RECLAIM replaced command-and-control regulations that were scheduled to bring the region into compliance with national ambient air quality standards (Ellerman *et al.*, 2003).

RECLAIM Trading Credits (RTCs) were allocated for free, with initial allocations of NO_x and SO_2 RTCs based on historical peak production levels and set at 40–60 percent above actual emissions until the year 2000. The NO_x and SO_2 caps declined annually by 8.3 percent and 6.8 percent, respectively, until 2003, when the market reached its overall goal of a 70 percent emissions reduction (Ellerman *et al.*, 2003; Hansjürgens, 2011). The compliance period was a single year and banking was not allowed. An interesting aspect of this program's design was its zonal nature: trades were not permitted from downwind to upwind sources.

Performance

RECLAIM was predicted to achieve significant cost savings via trade (Johnson and Pekelney, 1996; Anderson, 1997). And, by June 1996, 353 program participants had traded more than 100,000 tons of NO_x and SO_2 credits, with a value of more than $10 million (South Coast Air Quality Management District, 2016). Studies have found that emissions at RECLAIM facilities were some 20 percent lower than at facilities regulated with parallel command-and-control regulations, that hotspots did not appear, and that substantial cost savings were achieved (Burtraw and Szambelan, 2010; Fowlie *et al.*, 2012).

In the program's early years, allowance prices remained in the expected range of $500 to $1,000 per ton of NO_x. During California's electricity crisis in 2000–2001, however, some sources of electricity were eliminated, which required generation at some RECLAIM generating facilities to increase dramatically. This caused emissions to exceed permit allocations at those facilities and, in the absence of a pool of banked allowances, resulted in a dramatic spike in allowance prices — to more than $60,000 per ton in 2001 (Fowlie *et al.*, 2012). The program was temporarily suspended and prices returned to normal levels (less than $2,000 per ton) by 2002, with all sources rejoining the program by 2007. As of December 2015, the 12-month moving average of NO_x prices was $1,642 per ton (South Coast Air Quality Management District, 2016).

Lessons

Three lessons emerge from the RECLAIM program. First, because the RECLAIM system included an upwind and a downwind zone, with trades allowed in only one direction, the program demonstrated that appropriate design can accommodate a nonuniformly mixed pollutant and attendant concerns about potential hot spots.

A second lesson from RECLAIM, which later became important for several carbon dioxide (CO_2) cap-and-trade systems, is that an overallocation of allowances eliminates a functioning spot allowance market. Third, provisions for the banking of allowances (along with other cost-containment elements, such as price caps) can be crucial for regulated entities to achieve compliance at a reasonable cost in years in which unanticipated circumstances cause emissions to be greater than expected.

NO_x Trading in the Eastern United States

Under EPA guidance, and enabled by the Clean Air Act Amendments of 1990, in 1999 eleven northeastern states and the District of Columbia developed and implemented the NO_x Budget Program, a regional NO_x cap-and-trade system. Given the significant adverse health effects of ground-level ozone (i.e., smog formed by the interaction of NO_x and volatile organic compounds in the presence of sunlight), the goal of the program was to reduce summertime ground-level ozone by more than 50 percent relative to 1990 levels (U.S. Environmental Protection Agency, 2004). Some 1,000 electric generating and industrial units were required to demonstrate compliance each year during the summer ozone season (May–September).

The region covered by the program was divided into upwind and downwind zones and allowances were given to states to distribute to instate sources. Sources could buy, sell, and bank allowances within limits reflecting the seasonal nature of the ozone problem. Upwind states were given less generous allowance allocations as percentages of 1990 emissions. However, trading across zones was permitted on a one-for-one basis, and the two zones made similar reductions from baseline emissions levels (Ozone Transport Commission, 2003).

In 1998, the EPA issued the NO_x State Implementation Plan (SIP) Call, which required 21 eastern states to submit plans to reduce their NO_x emissions from more than 2,500 sources. The call included a model rule, which, if adopted by a state, would enable it to meet its emission reduction obligations by participating in an interstate cap-and-trade program, known as the NO_x Budget Trading Program. All affected states adopted the model rule and the trading program went into effect in 2003, replacing the NO_x Budget Program. As in the earlier program, states were given allowances to allocate to instate sources. In 2009 the NO_x Budget Trading Program was effectively replaced by the Clean Air Interstate Rule (CAIR), and in January 2015, CAIR was replaced by the Cross-State Air Pollution Rule (CSAPR).

Performance

At the outset, the NO_x Budget Program market was characterized by uncertainty, because some trading rules were not in place when trading commenced. This resulted in high price volatility during the program's first year, although prices stabilized by the program's second year (Farrell, 2000). Overall, under the NO_x Budget Program and the NO_x Budget Trading Program, NO_x emissions declined from about 1.9 million tons in 1990 to less than 500,000 tons by 2006, with 99 percent compliance (Butler *et al.*, 2011; Deschenes *et al.*, 2012). For the 1999–2003 period, abatement cost savings were estimated at 40 to 47 percent relative to conventional regulation, which did not include trading or banking (Farrell, 2000).

Lessons

Four lessons stand out from the NO_x trading program. First, in order to avoid unnecessary price volatility, which imposes unnecessary risk on affected sources and thus raises costs, all of the components of an emissions trading program should be in place well before the program takes effect.

Second, a well-designed multistate process with federal guidance can be effective in coordinating what are legally state-level goals.

Third, the history of NO_x trading in the eastern United States provides a precedent and model for expanding the coverage of a cap-and-trade system over time to include additional jurisdictions, such as neighboring states.

Fourth, states can be given the flexibility to allocate allowances among instate sources without necessarily compromising environmental goals.

The Regional Greenhouse Gas Initiative

Nine northeastern U.S. states participate in the RGGI, the first U.S. cap-and-trade system to address CO_2 emissions. The RGGI is a downstream program that focuses only on the power sector. It began in 2009 with the goal of limiting emissions from regulated sources to 2009 levels through 2014. The emissions cap was then set to decrease by 2.5 percent each year from 2015 to 2019, when the cap would have declined to 10 percent below 2009 emissions. It was originally anticipated that meeting this goal would require a reduction of approximately 35 percent below BAU emissions (13 percent below 1990 emissions).

Due to the recession and the drastic decline in natural gas prices relative to coal prices, the emissions cap quickly ceased to be binding, and it appeared unlikely to become binding through 2020. In response, in 2012, in a preplanned review of the program, the RGGI states agreed to establish a lower cap for 2014, with 2.5 percent annual cuts thereafter to 2019.

Reflecting these economic and policy changes, allowance prices fell from approximately \$3 per ton of CO_2 at the first auction in 2008 to the floor price of \$1.86 per ton in 2010, and rose to \$5.50 per ton in 2015.

Under the RGGI program, participating states must auction at least 25 percent of their allowances and use the proceeds to invest in energy efficiency, renewable energy, and related efforts. Auctioning was required mainly to avoid the windfall profits that would generally result from free allocation of allowances in deregulated electricity markets (Sijm *et al.*, 2006). In practice, states have auctioned virtually all allowances.

There is a ceiling on allowance prices via a cost containment reserve, from which additional allowances were sold when auction prices reach specified levels. There is also a price floor below which allowances are not sold at auction. Any unsold allowances are permanently retired after 3 years, thus automatically tightening the cap if there is a chronic allowance surplus. This combination of a price ceiling and a price floor serves as a price collar, thus making the RGGI program somewhat of a hybrid of a cap-and-trade system and a carbon tax.

Performance

Because the cap was not binding during the program's first compliance period (2009–2011), and has been barely binding since then, the direct impact of the RGGI program on power sector CO_2 emissions has been small, at best. However, the program's auctions have generated more than \$1 billion in revenues for the participating states. Some of this revenue has been used to finance government programs aimed at reducing energy demand and hence CO_2 emissions and the demand for allowances (Hibbard *et al.*, 2011).

Monitoring costs have been very low because U.S. power plants were already required to report their hourly CO_2 emissions under the federal SO_2 allowance trading program. The penalty for noncompliance is that entities must submit three allowances for each allowance they are short.

Because of the geographically limited scope of the RGGI system, combined with interconnected electricity markets, emissions leakage has been a significant concern (Burtraw *et al.*, 2006). One study found that if the program were fully binding, power imports from Pennsylvania to New York could result in emissions leakage of as much as 50 percent (Sue Wing and Kolodziej, 2008).

Lessons

Three lessons have emerged from this program. The first, which has not been lost on policymakers, is that a cap-and-trade system that auctions its allowances can generate substantial revenue for government, whether or not the system has much effect on emissions.

Second, the leakage problem is potentially severe for any subnational program, particularly a power sector program, because of the interconnected nature of electricity markets (Burtraw *et al.*, 2006).

Third, a changing economy can render a cap nonbinding (causing allowance prices to fall) or drive allowance prices to excessive levels. This suggests an important role for price collars. In the case of the RGGI, an effective price floor was established through the use of a reservation price in allowance auctions. The price ceiling has not been tested, however, and may be less effective because of the limited size of the cost containment reserve.

California's Cap-and-Trade System

In 2006, California enacted Assembly Bill 32 (AB-32), which required the California Air Resources Board to establish a program to cut the state's greenhouse gas (GHG) emissions to 1990 levels by the year 2020. The program includes energy efficiency standards for vehicles, buildings, and appliances; renewable portfolio standards that increase renewables' share of electricity supply from 20 to 33 percent; a low-carbon fuel standard that requires refineries to reduce the carbon content of motor vehicle fuels; and a cap-and-trade system (California Environmental Protection Agency, 2014).

The AB-32 cap-and-trade system began in 2013, covering all electricity sold in California, no matter where it was generated,[3] and large-scale manufacturing. The program was expanded to include fuels in 2015, thereby covering 85 percent of the state's emissions. The cap declines annually until 1990 emission levels are achieved in 2020. Initially, most allowances were distributed for free, with greater use of auctions over time. Banking is allowed, and regulated entities may use approved offsets

[3] California imports much of its electricity from out of state. The possibility of reshuffling the contracts involved may enable substantial leakage (Bushnell *et al.*, 2008).

of emissions reductions from forestry, dairy digestion, and ozone-depleting substances reduction to account for up to 49 percent of their emissions reductions.

A price ceiling is established by releasing allowances from a reserve when auction prices reach specified levels. A price floor is created through an auction reservation price, with unsold allowances held until the reservation price is exceeded for six consecutive months. This combination produces an effective price collar, creating a hybrid cap-and-trade and carbon tax system. In addition, the program addresses competitiveness concerns in energy-intensive, trade-exposed (EITE) industries by granting free allowances in proportion to production levels in previous periods.

In 2014, California's system was linked to a very similar system in Quebec (Kroft and Drance, 2015), with mutual recognition of allowances for trading and compliance and joint allowance auctions.

Performance and Lessons

Because California's cap-and-trade system was only launched in 2013, it is too early to assess its performance, other than to note that the auction mechanisms and other design features have functioned as anticipated. Thus the lessons from the AB-32 cap-and-trade system are related to its design rather than its performance.

First, the California system has demonstrated that using an initial free allowance allocation to build political support can transition over time to greater auctioning of allowances.

Second, the California experience is a reminder of the political pressures not to use auction revenues to reduce distortionary taxes. As of May 2015, the AB-32 auctions had generated more than $2 billion and were expected to generate nearly $4 billion by the end of 2016 (California Legislative Analyst's Office, 2015). Assembly Bill 1532 (2012) requires that these funds "be used to reduce GHG emissions and, to the extent feasible, achieve co-benefits such as job creation, air quality improvements, and public health benefits."

Third, as the first CO_2 (or GHG) cap-and-trade system to be essentially economy-wide,[4] California's AB-32 system has demonstrated that

[4]Since 2010, New Zealand has had an economy-wide (except for agriculture) CO_2 emissions trading system linked to international allowance markets under the Kyoto Protocol, but domestic emissions are not capped.

this approach is as feasible as less efficient approaches that treat different sectors differently.

Fourth, the AB-32 system greatly limits price volatility by employing an effective price collar. As noted earlier, although emissions levels are less certain under such hybrid systems, lower price volatility reduces compliance costs.

Fifth, California has employed an effective mechanism to address concerns about competitive impacts on EITE sectors. Granting free allowances to firms in specific sectors in proportion to their production levels in a previous time period subsidizes production and thus directly affects competitiveness. Of course, this subsidy of EITE sectors introduces its own inefficiencies. On the other hand, simply granting extra allowances to firms in EITE sectors (as in the EU's ETS) has no effect on competitiveness because marginal production costs are not affected.[5]

Sixth, California's strong interest in linking its cap-and-trade system with those in other jurisdictions (including its recent linkage with Quebec) illustrates the desirability of using such linkages to reduce abatement costs, price volatility, and market power (Ranson and Stavins, 2013).

Finally, although policies that address energy-related market failures can reduce costs, California's AB-32 system illustrates that some "complementary policies" are more likely to increase costs with no effect on emissions. For example, the state's low-carbon fuel standard (LCFS) requires that California refineries produce fuel with, on average, no more than a set amount of lifecycle carbon content. But refineries and transportation fuels are already covered by the cap-and-trade system, so the LCFS cannot reduce emissions in the short run unless it makes the allowance price floor binding. Because the LCFS is a binding constraint on refiners, refiners achieve additional CO_2 emission reductions beyond what would be achieved through the cap-and-trade system alone. However, unless the price floor becomes binding, this "complementary" policy — the LCFS — will produce 100 percent leakage to other sectors when allowances are sold. In any case, marginal abatement costs are not equated across sectors and sources,[6] so aggregate abatement costs will increase.

[5]For a review of the literature on the competitiveness benefits and the efficiency costs of output-based updating of allowance allocations, see Fowlie (2012).

[6]As of January 2016, LCFS credits were selling for an average of $105 per ton of CO_2 (California Environmental Protection Agency, 2016), while the cap-and-trade allowances were selling for about $13 per ton of CO_2 (Climate Policy Initiative, 2016).

In addition, allowance prices will be depressed, raising concerns about the ability of the cap-and-trade system to encourage technological change — except in the refinery sector. In short, the LCFS is a "complementary" policy that mainly increases abatement costs and lowers allowance prices (Goulder and Stavins, 2011). Many other so-called complementary policies have similar perverse effects.[7]

THE EU Emissions Trading System

The EU ETS, a cap-and-trade system focused on CO_2, is the world's largest and first multicountry emissions trading system (European Commission, 2012). The EU ETS was adopted in 2003 and covers about half of EU CO_2 emissions in 31 countries[8] (Ellerman and Buchner, 2007). More than 11,000 entities are regulated, including electricity generators and large industrial sources. Competitiveness concerns were largely addressed by the allocation of free allowances to a long list of selected sectors. The EU ETS excludes most sources in the transportation, commercial, and residential sectors, although some aviation sector emissions were brought under the cap in 2012.

The EU ETS was designed to be implemented in phases: a pilot phase 1 from 2005 to 2007, a Kyoto phase 2 from 2008 to 2012, and a series of subsequent phases that are now being extended through 2030. Penalties for violations increased from e40 per ton of CO_2 in the first phase to e100 in the second phase. The first phase allowed trading only in CO_2, but the second phase broadened the program to include some other GHGs.

The allocation process was initially decentralized (Kruger *et al.*, 2007), with each member state responsible for proposing its own national cap, subject to approval by the European Commission. This created incentives for member states to set high caps (Convery and Redmond, 2007).

Performance

The EU ETS has performed as might have been anticipated. In January 2005, the phase 1 allowance price per ton of CO_2 was approximately e8;

---

[7] In fact, the requirement that auction revenues from the cap-and-trade system be used to further the goals of the statute (AB-32) virtually guarantees this perverse interaction between "complementary policies" and the cap-and-trade system.

[8] All 28 EU countries plus Iceland, Lichtenstein, and Norway.

by early 2006, it exceeded e30, reflecting anticipated increases in demand. However, once it became clear that the generous allocation of allowances in 2005 had exceeded actual emissions, the allowance price fell by about half during one week in April 2006, fluctuated and soon returned to about e8, and then collapsed to zero in 2007 (Convery and Redmond, 2007). This volatility was attributed to the absence of good emissions data at the beginning of the program, a surplus of allowances, and energy price volatility; the collapse was attributed to the inability to bank allowances from phase 1 to phase 2 (Market Advisory Committee, 2007).

The first and second phases of the EU ETS required member states to distribute almost all of the emissions allowances for free. However, since 2013, member states have been required to auction increasing shares of their allowances. The initial free distribution of allowances led to complaints about "windfall profits" for electricity generators when electricity prices increased significantly in 2005. But higher fuel prices also played a role in the electricity price increases, and some generators' profits reflected their ownership of low-cost nuclear or coal generation in areas where the market electricity price was set by higher-cost natural gas plants (Ellerman and Buchner, 2007).

The system's cap was tightened for phase 2 (2008–2012) and its scope was expanded to cover new sources in countries that had participated in phase 1 as well as countries that joined the EU in 2007 and 2013. In addition, three nonmember states — Norway, Iceland, and Liechtenstein — joined the EU ETS in 2008. Allowance prices in phase 2 increased to more than e20 in 2008 and then fell when the recession reduced energy demand, thus reducing demand for allowances. Demand also declined because of the heavy use of offsets produced under the Kyoto Protocol's CDM. By the fall of 2011, prices had fallen to e10 and have remained in the e5 to e10 range since then.

The EU ETS has been extended through its phase 3 (2013–2020) with a more stringent, centrally determined cap (20 percent below 1990 emissions), auctioning of a larger share of allowances, tighter limits on the use of offsets, and unlimited banking of allowances between phases 2 and 3. Free allocation of allowances continues in phase 3 for EITE sectors (Sartor *et al.*, 2015).

There continues to be concern in the EU regarding low allowance prices (Löfgren *et al.*, 2015). These prices reflect the weak European economic recovery and the lack of a price floor. In addition, other binding EU policies, particularly renewable generation and energy efficiency standards, reduce emissions under the cap. As noted earlier, in the absence of a binding price floor, such "complementary" policies raise costs and reduce allowance prices without affecting total emissions.

Lessons

Five main lessons have emerged from our experience with the EU ETS thus far. First, the availability of good data is important for sound allowance allocation and cap-setting decisions. Had such data been available in phase 1 of the EU ETS, it might have been possible to avoid the overallocation that occurred.

Second, to avoid an artificial price collapse at the end of a compliance period, it is necessary to allow for banking from one period to the next. Because the EU ETS did not allow banking in phase 1, it was hardly surprising that phase 1 allowance prices fell to zero at the end of phase 1. Third, like the AB-32 California system, the EU ETS illustrates the perverse outcomes that result when "complementary" policies are applied to reduce emissions that are also covered under the cap, particularly in the absence of a price floor. Unless such complementary policies apply to sources outside the cap or address other market failures, they relocate emissions, drive up aggregate abatement costs, and depress allowance prices.

Fourth, although granting free allowances can help address distributional concerns as well as serving other political purposes, it is ultimately insufficient for dealing with international competitiveness concerns, because unless allocations are linked to production, they do not affect marginal production costs.

Finally, the history of the EU ETS shows that it is possible to move over time from a regime of generally free allowances to one in which most allowances are auctioned.

Other Cap-and-Trade Systems

Other cap-and-trade systems have been implemented, planned, or at least contemplated in many nations. Under the 1987 Montreal Protocol, several countries implemented systems of tradable rights for ozone depleting substances (ODS) during the ODS phasedown from 1991 to 2000 (Klaassen, 1999; U.S. Environmental Protection Agency, 2014). In addition, an international CO_2 cap-and-trade system has nominally operated since 2008: countries with emissions reduction commitments under the Kyoto Protocol (the "Annex I countries") that have ratified the protocol can, in effect, sell emission reductions that go beyond their compliance obligations to other Annex I parties that have outstanding compliance obligations. However, because the trading agents are nations rather than firms, not surprisingly there has been little activity (Hahn and Stavins, 1999). There has been more international private sector activity in emissions offsets under the Kyoto Protocol's CDM.

Currently, there are CO_2 cap-and-trade systems at various stages of development in a number of countries around the world, including Japan (Sopher and Mansell, 2014a), South Korea (Park and Hong, 2014), Kazakhstan (Kossoy *et al.*, 2014), and Switzerland (Sopher and Mansell, 2014b). Most importantly, China began municipal and provincial pilot trading systems in 2013 (Kossoy *et al.*, 2014), and on September 25, 2015, President Xi Jinping announced that in 2017 China will launch a national CO_2 cap-and-trade system covering key industries (Cunningham, 2015).

Cap-and-trade systems have also been proposed in other countries at levels of governance that range from submunicipal to national (Kossoy *et al.*, 2014; Organization for Economic Cooperation and Development and World Bank Group, 2015). Notably, the government of Ontario (Canada) recently announced a CO_2 cap-and-trade system to be linked to Quebec's system, and thus to California's system (Government of Ontario, 2015). Finally, in August 2015, the United States finalized the Clean Power Plan (CPP), which is aimed at CO_2 emissions from electricity generators and both enables and encourages state-level and multistate emissions trading (U.S. Environmental Protection Agency, 2015). However, on February 9, 2016, the U.S. Supreme Court halted implementation of the CPP, pending the resolution of legal challenges to it, and thus its ultimate fate is unclear.

Summary and Conclusions

This chapter has examined 30 years of experience with emissions trading systems. Overall, we have found that cap-and-trade systems, if well designed and appropriately implemented, can achieve their core objective of meeting targeted emissions reductions cost-effectively. But the devil is in the details, and design as well as the economic environment in which systems are implemented are very important. Moreover, as with any policy instrument, there is no guarantee of success.

Based on the lessons we have identified in our discussion, several design and implementation features of cap-and-trade programs appear critical to their performance.

Key Features for System Design and Implementation

First, it is important not to require prior approval of trades. In contrast to early U.S. experience with emissions offset systems, transaction costs can be low enough to permit considerable efficiency-enhancing trade if prior approval of trades is not required. Second, it is clear from both theory and experience that a robust market requires a cap that is significantly below BAU emissions. Third, to avoid unnecessary price volatility, it is important for final rules (including those for allowance allocation) to be established and accurate data supplied well before commencement of a system's first compliance period. Fourth, high levels of compliance in a down-stream system can be achieved by ensuring there is accurate emissions monitoring combined with significant penalties for noncompliance. Fifth, provisions for allowance banking have proven to be very important for achieving maximum gains from trade, and the absence of banking provisions can lead to price spikes and collapses. Sixth, price collars are important. A changing economy can reduce emissions below a cap, rendering it nonbinding, or a growing economy can increase emissions and drive allowance prices to excessive levels. Price collars reduce price volatility by combining an auction price floor with an allowance reserve. The resulting hybrid systems will generally have lower costs (as more stable prices facilitate investment planning) at the expense of less certain emissions reductions. Finally, economy-wide systems are feasible, although downstream, sectoral programs have been more commonly employed.

Political Considerations That Affect Cap-and-Trade Design

Thirty years of experience with cap-and-trade also indicates the importance of political considerations for the design of cap-and-trade programs. First, because of the potentially large distributional impacts involved, the allocation of allowances is inevitably a major political issue. Free allowance allocation has proven to help build political support. And, under many circumstances, the equilibrium allowance distribution, and hence the aggregate abatement costs of a cap-and-trade system, are independent of the initial allowance allocation (Montgomery, 1972; Hahn and Stavins, 2012). This means that the allowance allocation decision can be used to build political support and address equity issues without concern about impacts on overall cost-effectiveness.

Free allowance allocation does forego the opportunity to cut overall social costs by auctioning allowances and using the proceeds to cut distortionary taxes. On the other hand, experience has shown that political pressures exist to use auction revenue not to cut such taxes, but to fund new or existing environmental programs or relieve deficits. Indeed, cap-and-trade allowance auctions can and have generated very significant revenue for governments.

Second, the possibility of emissions leakage and adverse competitiveness impacts has been a prominent political concern in the design of cap-and-trade systems. Of course, virtually any meaningful environmental policy will increase production costs and thus could raise these concerns, but this issue has been more prominent in the case of cap-and-trade instruments. In practice, leakage from cap-and-trade systems can range from nonexistent to potentially quite serious. It is most likely to be significant for programs of limited geographic scope,[99] particularly in the power sector because of interconnected electricity markets. Attempts to reduce leakage and competitiveness threats through free allocation of allowances does not per se address the problem, but an output-based updating allocation can do so.

Third, although carbon pricing (through cap-and-trade or taxes) may be necessary to address climate change, it is surely not sufficient. In some cases, abatement costs can be reduced through the use of complementary policies that address other market failures, but the types of "complementary policies" that have emerged from political processes have instead addressed emissions under the cap, thereby relocating rather than reducing emissions, driving up abatement costs, and suppressing allowance prices.

Identifying New Applications

Cap-and-trade systems are now being seriously considered for a wide range of environmental problems. Past experience can offer some guidance as to when this approach is most likely to be successful (Stavins, 2007).

[9]For this and other reasons, linkage between cap-and-trade systems and other types of policies in other jurisdictions is likely to become increasingly important in the future because such linkage can reduce abatement costs, leakage, price volatility, and market power.

First, the greater the differences in the cost of abating pollution across sources, the greater the likely cost savings from a market-based system — whether cap-and-trade or tax — relative to conventional regulation (Newell and Stavins, 2003). For example, it was clear early on that SO_2 abatement cost heterogeneity was great, because of differences in the ages of plants and their proximity to sources of low-sulfur coal (Carlson *et al.*, 2000).

Second, the greater the degree of mixing of pollutants in the receiving airshed (or watershed), the more attractive a market-based system, because when there is a high degree of mixing, local hot spots are not a concern and the focus can thus be on cost-effective achievement of aggregate emissions reductions. Most cap-and-trade systems have been based on either the reality or the assumption of uniform mixing of pollutants. However, even without uniform mixing, well-designed cap-and-trade systems can be effective (Montgomery, 1972), as illustrated by the two-zone trading system under RECLAIM, at the cost of greater complexity.

Finally, since Weitzman's (1974) seminal analysis of the effects of cost uncertainty on the relative efficiency of price versus quantity instruments, it has been well known that in the presence of cost uncertainty, the relative efficiency of these two types of instruments depends on the pattern of costs and benefits. Subsequent literature has identified additional relevant considerations (Stavins, 1996; Newell and Pizer, 2003). Perhaps more importantly, theory (Roberts and Spence, 1976) and experience have shown that there are efficiency advantages of hybrid systems that combine price and quantity instruments in the presence of uncertainty.

Implications for Climate Change Policy

Two lessons from 30 years of experience with cap-and-trade systems stand out. First, cap-and-trade has proven itself to be environmentally effective and economically cost effective relative to traditional command-and-control approaches. Moreover, less flexible systems would not have led to the technological change that appears to have been induced by market-based instruments (Keohane, 2003; Schmalensee and Stavins, 2013) or the induced process innovations that have resulted (Doucet and Strauss, 1994). Second, and equally important, the performance of cap-and-trade systems depends on how well they are designed. In particular, we have emphasized the importance of reducing unnecessary price volatility and argued that hybrid designs offer an attractive option if some variability of emissions can be tolerated, since substantial price volatility generally raises costs.

These lessons suggest that cap-and-trade merits serious consideration when regions, nations, or subnational jurisdictions are developing policies to reduce GHG emissions. And, indeed, this has happened. However, because any meaningful climate policy will have significant impacts on economic activity in many sectors and regions, proposals for such policies have often triggered significant opposition.

In the United States, the failure of cap-and-trade climate policy in the Senate in 2010 was essentially collateral damage from a much larger political war that has decimated the ranks of both moderate Republicans and moderate Democrats (Schmalensee and Stavins, 2013). Nevertheless, political support for using cap-and-trade systems to reduce GHG emissions has emerged in many other nations. In fact, in the negotiations leading up to the Paris conference in late 2015, many parties endorsed key roles for carbon markets, and broad agreement emerged concerning the value of linking those markets (codified in Article 6 of the Paris agreement).

It is certainly possible that three decades of high receptivity to cap-and-trade in the United States, Europe, and other parts of the world will turn out to have been only a relatively brief departure from a long-term trend toward reliance on command-and-control environmental regulation. However, in light of the generally positive experience with cap-and-trade reported here, we remain optimistic that the recent tarnishing of cap-and-trade in U.S. political debates will itself turn out to be a temporary departure from a long-term trend of increasing reliance on market-based environmental policy instruments.

Acknowledgements

The authors acknowledge research assistance from Megan Bailey and Jennifer Austin and valuable comments on a previous version of the manuscript by Dallas Burtraw, Denny Ellerman, Robert Hahn, Suzi Kerr, two referees, and the editors.

Appendix

Table A1. Summary of major cap-and-trade systems.

System	Geographic scope	Coverage and sectors	Time period	Allowance allocation method	Cost containment mechanisms	Environmental and economic performance
Leaded gasoline phasedown	USA	Gasoline from refineries	1982–1987	Free	Banking	Phasedown completed successfully, faster than anticipated, with cost savings of $250 million per year
Sulfur dioxide allowance trading	USA	SO_2 from electric power	1995–2010	Free	Banking	Cut SO_2 emissions by half, with cost savings of $1 billion per year, but market closed due to judicial actions
Regional Clean Air Incentives Market (RECLAIM)	South Coast Air Quality Management District, CA	NO_x and SO_2 from electric power and industrial sources	1993–present	Free	—	Emissions lower than with parallel regulations; unquantified cost savings; electricity crisis caused allowance price spike and temporary suspension of the market
NO_x trading in the eastern United States	12–21 U.S. states electric power and industrial	NO_x from sources	1999–2008	Free	—	Significant price volatility in the first year; NO_x emissions declined from 1.9 (1990) to 0.5 million tons (2006); cost savings 40 to 47 percent
Regional Greenhouse Gas Initiative	Nine northeastern U.S. states	CO_2 from electric power	2009–present	Nearly 100 percent auction	Banking, cost containment reserve, auction reservation price	Cap nonbinding, then barely binding due to low natural gas prices; has generated more than $1 billion for participating states
AB-32 cap-and-trade	California	CO_2 from electric power, industrial, and fuels	2013–2020	Transitions from free to auction	Banking, allowance price containment reserve, auction reservation price	Covers 85 percent of emissions; reduces competitiveness effects with output-based updating (OBU) allocation; linked with Quebec cap-and-trade system
European Union Emissions trading system	27 EU Member states plus Iceland, Lichtenstein, & Norway	CO_2 from electric power, large industrial, and aviation	2005–present	Transitions from free to increased use of auctions	Banking after 2008, previous use of offsets from CDM	Overallocation by member states in pilot phase; suppressed allowance prices due to "complementary policies," CDM glut, slow economic recovery

References

Anderson, R. (1997). *The U.S. Experience with Economic Incentives in Environmental Pollution Control Policy*. Washington, DC: Environmental Law Institute.

Anderson, R. C., Hofmann, L. A., and Rusin, M. (1990). *The Use of Economic Incentive Mechanisms in Environmental Management*. Research Paper 51. Washington, DC: American Petroleum Institute.

Banzhaf, H. Spencer, Burtraw, Dallas, Evans, David, and Krupnick, Alan. (2006). "Valuation of natural resource improvements in the adirondacks." *Land Economics*, **82**(4), 445–464.

Bellas, Allen S., and Lange, Ian. (2011). "Evidence of innovation and diffusion under tradable permit programs." *International Review of Environmental and Resource Economics*, **5**(1), 1–22.

Burtraw, Dallas, Kahn, Danny, and Palmer, Karen. (2006). "CO_2 Allowance allocation in the regional greenhouse gas initiative and the effect on electricity investors." *Electricity Journal*, **19**(2), 79–90.

Burtraw, Dallas, and Szambelan, Sarah Jo. (2010). "U.S. Emissions Trading Markets for SO2 and NO_x." In B. Hansjürgens, R. Antes, and M. Strunz (Eds.), *Permit Trading in Different Applications* (Chap. 2). New York: Routledge.

Burtraw, Dallas, Krupnick, Alan J., Mansur, Erin, Austin, David, and Farrell, Alan. (1998). "The costs and benefits of reducing air pollution related to acid rain." *Contemporary Economic Policy*, **16**, 379–400.

Bushnell, James, Peterman, Carla, and Wolfram, Catherine. (2008). "Local solutions to global problems: Climate change policy and regulatory jurisdiction." *Review of Environmental Economics and Policy*, **2**, 175–193.

Butler, T. J., Vermeylen, F. M., Rury, M., Likens, G. E., Lee, B., Bowker, G. E., and McCluney, L. (2011). "Response of ozone and nitrate to stationary source NO_x emission reductions in the eastern USA." *Atmospheric Environment*, **45**(5), 1084–1094.

California Environmental Protection Agency. (2014). *Assembly Bill 32 Overview*. Sacramento, CA: California Air Resources Board.

California Environmental Protection Agency. (2016). *LCFS Credit Transfer Activity Report, January 2016*. Sacramento, CA: California Air Resources Board.

California Legislative Analyst's Office. (2015). *Governor's May Revision: 2015–16 Cap-and-Trade Expenditure Plan*. Sacramento, CA: Author.

Carlson, Curtis, Burtraw, Dallas, Cropper, Maureen, and Palmer, Karen. (2000). "SO2 Control by electric utilities: What are the gains from trade?" *Journal of Political Economy*, **108**, 1292–1326.

Chestnut, Lauraine G., and Mills, David M. (2005). "A fresh look at the benefits and costs of the US acid rain program." *Journal of Environmental Management*, 77(3), 252–266.

Climate Policy Initiative. (2016). *California Carbon Dashboard.* Retrieved from http://calcarbondash.org/.

Convery, Frank, and Redmond, Luke. (2007). "Market and price developments in the european union emissions trading scheme." *Review of Environmental Economics and Policy*, **1**, 66–87.

Cunningham, Edward A. (2015). "China's new plans for a cap and trade system just might work." *Foreign Policy*, October 6.

Deschenes, Olivier, Greenstone, Michael, and Shapiro, Joseph S. (2012). *Defensive Investments and the Demand for Air Quality: Evidence from the NO_x Budget Program and Ozone Reductions*. Working Paper 18267. Cambridge, MA: National Bureau of Economic Research.

Doucet, Joseph A., and Strauss, Todd. (1994). "On the bundling of coal and sulfur dioxide emissions allowances." *Energy Policy*, **22**(9), 764–770.

Ellerman, A. Denny, and Buchner, Barbara K. (2007). "The european union emissions trading scheme: Origins, allocation, and early results." *Review of Environmental Economics and Policy*, **1**, 66–87.

Ellerman, A. Denny, and Buchner, Barbara K. (2008). "Over-allocation or abatement? A preliminary analysis of the EU ETS based on the 2005–06 emissions data." *Environmental and Resource Economics*, **41**(2), 267–287.

Ellerman, A. Denny, and Montero, Juan-Pablo. (1998). "The declining trend in sulfur dioxide emissions: Implications for allowance prices." *Journal of Environmental Economics and Management*, **36**, 26–45.

Ellerman, A. Denny, Joskow, Paul L., and Harrison, David. (2003). *Emissions Trading in the U.S.: Experience, Lessons and Considerations for Greenhouse Gases*. Arlington, VA: Pew Center on Global Climate Change.

Ellerman, A. Denny, Joskow, Paul L., Schmalensee, Richard, Montero, Juan-Pablo, and Bailey, Elizabeth M. (2000). *Markets for Clean Air: The U.S. Acid Rain Program*. Cambridge: Cambridge University Press.

European Commission. (2012). *Emissions Trading System.* Retrieved from http://ec.europa.eu/clima/policies/ets/index_en.htm.

European Commission. (2016). *EU ETS Handbook*. Retrieved from http://aeaep.com.ua/en/wp-content/uploads/2015/07/ets_handbook_en.pdf.

Farrell, Alan. (2000). "The NO_x Budget: A Look at the First Year." *Electricity Journal*, **13**(2), 83–93.

Fowlie, Meredith. (2012). "Updating the Allocation of Greenhouse Gas Emissions Permits in a Federal Cap-and-Trade Program." In D. Fullerton and C. Wolfram (Eds.), *The Design and Implementation of US Climate Policy* (Chap. 10). Chicago: University of Chicago Press.

Fowlie, Meredith, Holland, Stephen P., and Mansur, Erin T. (2012). "What do emissions markets deliver and to whom? Evidence from Southern California's NO_x trading program." *American Economic Review*, **102**(2), 965–993.

Glass, Norman R., Glass, Gary E., and Rennie, Peter J. (1982). "Effects of acid precipitation." *Environmental Science and Technology*, **16**(3), 162A–169A.

Goulder, Lawrence H. (1995). "Environmental taxation and the 'double dividend': A reader's guide." *International Tax and Public Finance*, **2**(2), 157–183.

Goulder, Lawrence H., and Stavins, Robert N. (2011). "Challenges from state-federal interactions in US climate change policy." *American Economic Review*, **101**(3), 253–257.

Government of Ontario. (2015). *Cap and Trade System to Limit Greenhouse Gas Pollution in Ontario*. News Release, April 13. Retrieved from http://news.ontario.ca/opo/en/2015/04/cap-and-trade-system-to-limit-greenhouse-gas-pollution-in-ontario.html.

Hahn, Robert W. (1989). "Economic prescriptions for environmental problems: how the patient followed the doctor's orders." *Journal of Economic Perspectives*, **3**, 95–114.

Hahn, Robert W., and Hester, Gordon L. (1989). "Marketable permits: Lessons for theory and practice." *Ecology Law Quarterly*, **16**, 361–406.

Hahn, Robert W., and Stavins, Robert N. (1999). *What Has the Kyoto Protocol Wrought? The Real Architecture of International Tradeable Permit Markets*. Washington, DC: *AEI Press*.

Hahn, Robert W., and Stavins, Robert N. (2012). "The effect of allowance allocations on cap-and-trade system performance." *Journal of Law and Economics*, **54**(S4), S267–S294.

Hansjürgens, B. (2011). "Markets for SO_2 and NO_x — What can we learn for carbon trading?" *Wiley Interdisciplinary Reviews: Climate Change*, **24**, 635–646.

Hibbard, Paul J., Tierney, Susan F., Okie, Andrea M., and Darling, Pavel G. (2011). *The Economic Impacts of the Regional Greenhouse Gas Initiative on Ten Northeast and Mid-Atlantic States*. Boston: Analysis Group.

Johnson, Scott Lee, and Pekelney, David M. (1996). "Economic assessment of the regional clean air incentives market: A new emissions trading program for Los Angeles." *Land Economics*, **72**(3), 277–297.

Joskow, Paul L., and Schmalensee, Richard. (1998). "The political economy of market-based environmental policy: The U.S. acid rain program." *Journal of Law and Economics*, **41**(1), 37–84.

Keohane, Nathaniel O. (2003). *What Did the Market Buy? Cost Savings Under the U.S. Tradeable Permits Program for Sulfur Dioxide*. Working Paper YCELP-01-11-2003. New Haven, CT: Yale Center for Environmental Law and Policy.

Kerr, Suzi, and Maré, David. (1997). *Efficient Regulation Through Tradeable Permit Markets: The United States Lead Phasedown*. Working Paper 96-06. College Park, MD: Department of Agricultural and Resource Economics, University of Maryland.

Kerr, Suzi, and Newell, Richard. (2003). "Policy-induced technology adoption: Evidence from the U.S. lead phasedown." *Journal of Industrial Economics*, **51**(3), 317–343.

Klaassen, G. (1999). "Emissions Trading in the European Union: Practice and Prospects." In S. Sorrell and J. Skea (Eds.), *Pollution for Sale: Emissions Trading and Joint Implementation* (pp. 83–100). Cheltenham, UK: Edward Elgar.

Kossoy, A., Opperman, K., Platanova-Oquab, A., Suphachalasai, S., Höhne, N., Klein, N., ... Wong, L. (2014). *State and Trends of Carbon Pricing 2014.* Washington, DC: World Bank.

Kroft, P. Jason, and Drance, Jonathan. (2015). *Examining California's and Quebec's Cap-and-Trade Systems.*

Kruger, Joseph, Oates, Wallace E., and Pizer, William A. (2007). "Decentralization in the EU emissions trading scheme and lessons for global policy." *Review of Environmental Economics and Policy*, **1**, 112–133.

Löfgren, Asa, Burtraw, Dallas, Wråke, Markus, and Malinovskaya, Anna. (2015). *Architecture of the EU Emissions Trading System in Phase 3 and the Distribution of Allowance Asset Values.* Discussion Paper 15-45. Washington, DC: Resources for the Future.

Market Advisory Committee. (2007). *Recommendations for Designing a Greenhouse Gas Cap-and-Trade System for California.* Sacramento, CA: California Air Resources Board.

Mazmanian, Daniel A., and Kraft, Michael E. (2009). "The Three Epochs of the Environmental Movement." In D. A. Mazmanian and M. E. Kraft (Eds.), *Toward Sustainable Communities: Transition and Transformations in Environmental Policy* (pp. 3–32). Cambridge, MA: MIT Press.

Montgomery, David W. (1972). "Markets in licenses and efficient pollution control programs." *Journal of Economic Theory*, **5**(3), 395–418.

Newell, Richard G., and Pizer, William. (2003). "Regulating stock externalities under uncertainty." *Journal of Environmental Economics and Management*, **45**, 416–432.

Newell, Richard G., and Rogers, K. (2007). "The Market-Based Lead Phasedown." In J. Freeman and C. Kolstad (Eds.), *Moving to Markets in Environmental Regulation: Lessons from Twenty Years of Experience* (pp. 173–193). Oxford: Oxford University Press.

Newell, Richard G., and Stavins, Robert N. (2003). "Cost heterogeneity and the potential savings from market-based policies." *Journal of Regulatory Economics*, **23**(1), 43–59.

Nichols, Albert L. (1997). "Lead in Gasoline." In R. D. Morgenstern (Ed.) *Economic Analyses at EPA: Assessing Regulatory Impact* (pp. 49–86). Washington, DC: Resources for the Future.

Organization for Economic Cooperation and Development and World Bank Group. (2015). *The FASTER Principles for Successful Carbon Pricing: An Approach Based on Initial Experience.* Washington, DC: OECD and World Bank.

Ozone Transport Commission. (2003). *NO_x Budget Program: 1999–2002 Progress Report*. Retrieved from http://www2.epa.gov/sites/production/files/2015-08/documents/otcreport.pdf.

Park, Hojeong, and Hong, Won Kyung. (2014). "Korea's emission trading scheme and policy design issues to achieve market-efficiency and abatement targets." *Energy Policy*, **75**, 73–83.

Popp, David. (2003). "Pollution control innovations and the clean air act of 1990." *Journal of Policy Analysis and Management*, **22**(4), 641–660.

Ranson, Matthew, and Stavins, Robert N. (2013). "Post-Durban climate policy architecture based on linkage of cap-and-trade systems." *Chicago Journal of International Law*, **13**, 403–438.

Rico, Renee. (1995). "The U.S. allowance trading system for sulfur dioxide: An update of market experience." *Environmental and Resource Economics*, **5**(2), 115–129.

Roberts, Mark, and Spence, Michael. (1976). "Effluent charges and licenses under uncertainty." *Journal of Public Economics*, **5**(3–4), 193–208.

Sartor, Oliver, Lecourt, Stephen, and Palliere, Clement. (2015). "Benchmark-Based Free Allocations in EU ETS Phase III: How Much Better than Phase II?" In M. Gronwald and B. Hintermann (Eds.), *Emissions Trading as a Policy Instrument*. Cambridge, MA: MIT Press.

Schmalensee, Richard, and Stavins, Robert N. (2013). "The SO_2 allowance trading system: The ironic history of a grand policy experiment." *Journal of Economic Perspectives*, **27**(1), 103–122.

Sijm, Jos, Neuhoff, Karsten, and Chen, Yihsu. (2006). "CO_2 cost pass through and windfall profits in the power sector." *Climate Policy*, **6**(1), 49–72.

Sopher, P., and Mansell, A. (2014a). "Japan." *The World's Carbon Markets: A Case Study Guide to Emissions Trading*. Washington, DC: Environmental Defense Fund and International Emissions Trading Association.

Sopher, P., and Mansell, A. (2014b). "Switzerland." *The World's Carbon Markets: A Case Study Guide to Emissions Trading*. Washington, DC: Environmental Defense Fund and International Emissions Trading Association.

South Coast Air Quality Management District. (2016). "RECLAIM Trading Credits (RTCs) Trade Information." Retrieved from http://www.aqmd.gov/home/programs/business/about-reclaim/reclaim-trading-credits.

Stavins, Robert N. (1996). "Correlated uncertainty and policy instrument choice." *Journal of Environmental Economics and Management*, **30**, 218–232.

Stavins, Robert N. (2007). "Market-Based Environmental Policies: What Can We Learn from U.S. Experience (and Related Research)?" In J. Freeman and C. Kolstad (Eds.), *Moving to Markets in Environmental Regulation: Lessons from Twenty Years of Experience* (pp. 19–47). New York: Oxford University Press.

Sue Wing, Ian, and Kolodziej, Marek. (2008). *The Regional Greenhouse Gas Initiative: Emission Leakage and the Effectiveness of Interstate Border Adjustments*. Working Paper RPP-2008-03. Cambridge, MA: Mossavar-Rahmani Center for Business and Government, John F. Kennedy School of Government, Harvard University.

Swift, Byron. (2004). "Emissions trading and hot spots: A review of the major programs." *Environment Reporter*, **35**(19), 1–16.

U.S. Energy Information Administration. (2012). "Electricity Net Generation: Total (All Sectors), 1949–2011." Table 8.2a. In *Annual Energy Review 2011*. Washington, DC: Department of Energy.

U.S. Environmental Protection Agency. (1985). *Costs and Benefits of Reducing Lead in Gasoline, Final Regulatory Impact Analysis*. Washington, DC: Author.

U.S. Environmental Protection Agency. (2004). *Evaluating Ozone Control Programs in the Eastern United States: Focus on the NO_x Budget Trading Program*. Washington, DC: Author.

U.S. Environmental Protection Agency. (2011). *National Emissions Inventory (NEI) Air Pollutant Emissions Trends Data: 1970–2011*. Retrieved from http://www3.epa.gov/ttnchie1/trends/.

U.S. Environmental Protection Agency. (2014). *Chlorofluorocarbon Taxes and Allowance Trading*. Retrieved from http://yosemite1.epa.gov/EE/epa/eed.nsf/dcee735e22c76aef85257662005f4116/86a2750ed83fe1d88525774200597f3a!

U.S. Environmental Protection Agency. (2015). *Carbon Pollution Emission Guidelines for Existing Stationary Sources: Electric Utility Generating Units*. Retrieved from http://www2.epa.gov/cleanpowerplan.

Weitzman, Martin. (1974). "Prices vs. Quantities." *Review of Economic Studies*, **41**, 477–491.

Part III

Domestic Policy

https://doi.org/10.1142/9789811292415_0010

Chapter 10

Policy Evolution under the Clean Air Act*

Richard Schmalensee[†,¶] and Robert N. Stavins[‡,§,‖,]**

[†]*Massachusetts Institute of Technology Sloan School of Management, Cambridge, MA, USA*

[‡]*John F. Kennedy School of Government, Harvard University, Cambridge, MA, USA*

[§]*Resources for the Future, Washington, DC, USA*

[‖]*National Bureau of Economic Research, Cambridge, MA, USA*

[¶]*rschmal@mit.edu*

[**]*robert_stavins@harvard.edu*

Nearly half a century has elapsed since 1970, when the first Earth Day was celebrated, the US Environmental Protection Agency (EPA) was established, and the US Clean Air Act passed with unanimous bipartisan support in the Senate and only a single negative vote in the House of Representatives. It was not the first federal law to deal with air pollution — that was the Air Pollution Control Act of 1955 — and it was technically only an amendment to the original Clean Air Act of 1963 (Stern, 1982). But the 1970 Clean Air Act established the basic architecture of the US air pollution control system, it was the first environmental law to give the

*This chapter was originally published in *Journal of Economic Perspectives*, **33**(4), 27–50, Fall 2019. https://doi.org/10.1257/jep.33.4.27.

federal government a serious regulatory role, and it became a model for many subsequent environmental laws in the United States and abroad. In this chapter, we describe the evolution of air pollution control policy under this legislation with particular attention to the types of policy instruments used.

While the Clean Air Act evolved over time, so too did the area of scholarship that came to be known as "environmental economics." For almost a half century after Pigou (1920) advanced the abstract notion of taxing pollution, economists paid very little attention to environmental protection. In the late 1960s, Crocker (1966), Dales (1968), Ayres and Kneese (1969), and a few others began serious study of environmental policy, but economists were not engaged in the design of the US Clean Air Act. The *Journal of Environmental Economics and Management* was launched in 1974, and environmental protection received increasing attention from economists throughout the late 1970s and 1980s, leading to the area's emergence as a distinct field during the 1990s. The National Bureau of Economic Research held its first Conference on Economics of the Environment in 1991, and in 2007 it launched its Environment and Energy Economics Program.

We begin our analysis by outlining the key provisions of the 1970 act and its main changes over time. We then turn to our main focus, which is to trace and assess the historical evolution of the policy instruments used by the Environmental Protection Agency in its clean air regulations. This evolution has been driven at various times by the emergence on the policy agenda of new air quality problems, by innovation and experimentation by the agency, and by changes in the Clean Air Act itself. Until roughly 2000, EPA made increasing use of market-based instruments, enabled in part by major amendments to the Clean Air Act in 1977 and 1990 that passed with overwhelming bipartisan support. In recent years, however, environmental policy has become a partisan battleground. So far, it has not been possible to provide an efficient response to climate change or to address other new and evolving air quality problems.

The Evolution of the Clean Air Act: 1970–1990

The 1970 Clean Air Act was a national-level response to environmental concerns. For environmental activists, this national approach addressed the fears that states would compete by lowering their environmental standards. For industries operating across states, it addressed the fear of facing a multitude of state-level mandates. This law, only 24 pages in length, gave the Environmental Protection Agency considerable discretion and authority to set and change regulations and to enforce compliance. Under the Administrative Procedure Act of 1946 (Pub. L. 79-404, 60 Stat. 237), EPA is required to publish proposals for major changes in regulation and to take public comments into account in the final versions. Its compliance with provisions of the Clean Air Act and the Administrative Procedure Act can be reviewed by federal courts. In addition, because EPA is an Executive Branch agency, since the Reagan administration its major regulatory proposals have been required to pass a benefit-cost test administered by the Office of Management and Budget (for discussion, see Copeland, 2009). A key part of the process is submission of a Regulatory Impact Analysis that compares the benefits and costs of the proposal.

The 1970 law contained four key provisions. First, the Environmental Protection Agency was charged with identifying pollutants that are produced by numerous or diverse sources and have "an adverse effect on public health or welfare" and with promulgating a system of National Ambient Air Quality Standards for these "criteria air pollutants" to protect public health and welfare. The six criteria air pollutants are carbon monoxide, lead, ground-level ozone, nitrogen dioxide, particulate matter, and sulfur dioxide.

Second, states were tasked with developing State Implementation Plans, to which the Environmental Protection Agency could require modification, to bring areas under their jurisdiction into attainment with the National Ambient Air Quality Standards.

Third, the Environmental Protection Agency was to develop national New Source Performance Standards for power plants and other stationary pollution sources, and emissions standards for new motor vehicles. It was empowered, but not required, to regulate motor vehicle fuels. Imposing requirements only on *new* stationary and mobile sources had the perverse effect of encouraging firms to retain their existing capital stock, slowing turnover of the capital stock and thereby retarding environmental progress (Stavins, 2006). However, states retained the authority to regulate existing stationary sources if necessary to bring areas into attainment with air quality standards.

Fourth, the Environmental Protection Agency was to develop National Emission Standards for Hazardous Air Pollutants, also known as air toxics, to protect public health. These air toxics, such as benzene, are mainly produced by manufacturing plants and other isolated sources and have localized effects.

The first major set of amendments to the Clean Air Act, 112 pages in length, passed in 1977 by a voice vote in the Senate and a vote of 273–109 in the House of Representatives. A regime of Prevention of Significant Deterioration was established, which limited the worsening of air quality in areas that were already in compliance with the National Ambient Air Quality Standards. This regime permitted new stationary sources of air pollution to be built in nonattainment areas if, through modifications of existing sources, overall emissions were reduced. This regime enabled the Environmental Protection Agency to extend its experiments with emissions trading, which began in 1974 (and are discussed below). Also, EPA was empowered to issue technology-based control standards for air toxics instead of emission or performance standards, where the latter were deemed impractical. Finally, EPA was given authority to regulate substances likely to deplete stratospheric ozone.

Unsurprisingly, the 1977 legislation included some politically driven provisions. For example, one stipulation was that the New Source Performance Standards for sulfur dioxide from coal-fired power plants must require that some of the sulfur in the coal burned be removed from the plants' flue gas. This "scrubber" requirement was a political victory for producers of high-sulfur Eastern coal (Ackerman and Hassler, 1981) over the producers of low-sulfur Western coal, which would otherwise have been favored for meeting standards for reduced sulfur emissions.

In the 1980s, acid rain caused by emissions of sulfur dioxide (SO_2) from coalfired power plants emerged as a significant problem. In 1988, the United States ratified the Montreal Protocol to protect the ozone layer. In response to these developments and others, Congress passed the 314-page 1990 amendments, which included four main provisions: (1) the establishment of the path-breaking sulfur dioxide cap-and-trade program, intended to cut acid rain to half of 1980 levels (discussed in this journal in Schmalensee *et al.*, 1998; Stavins, 1998; Schmalensee and Stavins, 2013); (2) regulation of a number of aspects of motor vehicle fuels, including volatility (that is, how easily a fuel vaporizes)[1]; (3) authority for the Environmental Protection Agency to ensure that the United States

[1]The volatility standard was explicitly relaxed if corn-based ethanol was used. The Senate minority leader in 1990, Robert Dole (R-Kansas), represented a large, corn-producing state.

would meet its obligations under the Montreal Protocol, and direction to use a cap-and-trade system to do so; and (4) instructions to EPA to issue technology standards for each of 189 listed air toxics, providing the maximum degree of emissions reduction, taking into account costs and non-air-quality effects. Economists inside and outside the administration were engaged in the design of the acid rain program (Chan *et al.*, 2012). This final provision reflected the fact that developing harm-based standards for air toxics had proven to be unworkable: only seven such standards had been issued since 1970. The 1990 amendments were passed by large bipartisan majorities: over 90 percent of Democrats voted in favor in both houses of Congress, as did 87 percent of Republicans.

Beginning in the late 1980s, climate change emerged as a significant issue. Then-candidate George H. W. Bush promised in 1988 to use the "White House Effect" to address the emerging problem of the greenhouse effect, and the Senate ratified the UN Framework Convention on Climate Change in October 1992 without a roll-call vote. By the time legislation to deal with climate change received serious consideration in 2009, however, environmental policy had become a partisan issue, and polarization between the parties had increased.

In June 2009, the House of Representatives passed legislation (the American Clean Energy and Security Act of 2009, also known as the Waxman–Markey bill) that included an economy-wide emissions trading system to cut carbon dioxide (CO_2) emissions linked with global climate change. Despite bipartisan support for emissions trading in the 1990 amendments, many Republicans and some coal-state Democrats attacked the proposed emissions trading system as "cap-and-tax." The legislation passed the House by a vote of 219–212, with support from 83 percent of Democrats but only 4 percent of Republicans. Five of the eight Republicans who supported the legislation were from heavily Democratic states, where a "nay" vote would have been highly visible and attracted opposition, and 25 of the 44 Democrats who did not support it were from heavily Republican states. The legislation would have had its greatest impact on coal, the most carbon-intensive fossil fuel, and 25 of the 44 Democrats who opposed the legislation were from states in which more than half of electricity was generated from coal. In July 2010, the Senate abandoned its attempt to pass companion legislation.

This polarization between the two political parties in regard to environmental policy — well documented by political scientists (for example, Shipan and Lowry, 2001) — was part of a gradually widening gulf between the parties on virtually all issues (Fleisher and Bond, 2004).[2] The Clean Air Act, and federal air pollution legislation generally, ceased to evolve after 1990, although regulatory actions authorized by existing legislation and judicial oversight continued.

Policy Instruments Used under the Clean Air Act

Three major types of policy instruments have been employed under the authority of the Clean Air Act: technology standards, which specify the equipment or process to be used for compliance; performance standards, which specify the maximum quantity of emissions (typically in rate-based units, such as grams of pollutant per mile driven) or maximum atmospheric concentrations that are allowed; and emissions trading systems, either in the form of emissions-reduction credit (offset) systems or cap-and-trade. In addition, taxes have sometimes been employed, although their use under the Clean Air Act has been peripheral.[3]

As panel A of Table 1 indicates, three types of instruments have been used for the control of criteria air pollutants. Hazardous air pollutants have been controlled only by standards; emissions trading and taxes have been used to address the protection of stratospheric ozone; and cap-and-trade has been employed to reduce SO_2 emissions as a precursor of acid rain. As we discuss below, the Obama administration proposed a hybrid standard/trading regulation under the Clean Air Act to reduce CO_2 emissions in the electricity sector, but the Trump administration has proposed replacing it with a standards regime.

---

[2]Polarization, and a corresponding gradual disappearance of moderates, has been taking place for decades (Lowry and Shipan, 2002; Theriault, 2008). It has shown up in studies by political scientists employing a diverse set of measures (Poole and Rosenthal, 1997, 2007). The rise of the Tea Party movement within the Republican Party and the nomination and election in 2016 of Donald Trump are only the most recent episodes in a much longer story.

[3]The 1990 amendments to the Clean Air Act allowed states to tax regulated air pollutants to recover administrative costs of state programs, and allowed areas in extreme noncompliance to charge higher rates. Under this structure, the South Coast Air Quality Management District in Los Angeles implemented the highest permit fees in the country (US Congress, Office of Technology Assessment, 1995). As we discuss below, Congress imposed a tax, outside the Clean Air Act, on ozone-depleting chemicals that took effect in 1990.

Table 1. Major categories of pollutants and sectors regulated by the clean air act.

	Policy instrument used			
	Technology standards	**Performance standards**	**Emissions trading**	**Taxes**
A: Pollutant categories				
Criteria pollutants	*	*	*	
Toxic/hazardous pollutants	*	*		
Stratospheric ozone depletion			*	*
Acid rain			*	
Greenhouse gases		Proposed	Proposed	
B: Regulated sectors				
Electricity generation	*	*	*	
Other stationary sources	*	*	*	*
Mobile sources	*	*		

Panel B of Table 1 examines the use of the four types of policy instruments across regulated sectors of the economy: electricity generation, other stationary sources, and mobile sources. The command-and-control mainstays of the original 1970 act — technology standards and performance standards — have been used in all domains, while emissions trading has been applied only to stationary sources.

Most economists would agree that economic efficiency — achieved when the difference between benefits and costs is maximized — ought to be a fundamental criterion for evaluating environmental protection efforts (Pareto, 1896; Hicks, 1939; Kaldor, 1939).[4] However, discussions in the environmental policy realm have frequently employed the criterion of cost effectiveness — that is, minimizing the costs of reducing emissions to a specified level. Of course, cost effectiveness is not the same as economic efficiency, but measuring the benefits of environmental protection is challenging. Reducing emissions to a level determined by noneconomic considerations, but at the lowest cost, offers an empirically easier alternative. Using this approach (and assuming equal effectiveness of enforcement), performance standards for reduced emissions are at least as

[4]This criterion is considered in the companion article by Janet Currie and Reed Walker in this issue.

cost effective as technology standards in meeting a given emissions standard, because they provide greater flexibility to minimize compliance costs.

When emissions from multiple sources are *well mixed*, so that emissions from all sources produce the same damages per unit of pollution, cost effectiveness requires that all sources that exercise some degree of emissions control experience the same marginal abatement cost (Baumol and Oates, 1988). In principle, governments could employ nonuniform performance standards to bring about the cost-effective allocation of control responsibility among emissions sources with heterogeneous control costs, but to develop such a set of standards, the government would need to know the marginal abatement cost functions of all sources. Costs are generally heterogeneous, and the government rarely, if ever, knows the relevant cost functions of pollution sources. As a consequence, such detailed command-and-control methods are rarely, if ever, cost effective.

In principle, government has two methods for achieving the cost-effective reduction of pollution across sources when it lacks detailed information about source-level control costs: a tax on pollutant emissions and an emissions trading system. In theory, the tax on each unit of pollution should equal the marginal social damages at the efficient level of control (Pigou, 1920). Even if damages cannot be measured, imposing the same tax rate on all sources will lead them to reduce emissions to the point where their marginal abatement costs are equal to the common tax rate, thereby satisfying the necessary condition for cost effectiveness. But such pollution taxes have never been implemented under the Clean Air Act.

Why have Pigouvian taxes not been much used, despite their theoretical advantages (Kneese and Schultz, 1975)? First, it is difficult to identify the appropriate tax rate. Although for efficiency the tax should be set equal to the marginal benefits of cleanup at the efficient level of cleanup, policymakers are much more likely to focus on a desired level of cleanup, and there is uncertainty about how firms will respond to a given level of taxation. A more important political problem is that tax systems are likely to be more costly for regulated firms than command and control, because firms both incur abatement costs and pay taxes on their residual emissions (Buchanan and Tullock, 1975). In practice, some of these costs will be passed on to consumers, but many firms may still be worse off under a tax.

The work of Coase (1960) pointed to an alternative way that the government could achieve its pollution-control targets cost effectively, without the abatement uncertainty inherent in the tax approach, and without the tax burden on regulated firms. Coase described the issue of how to address pollution as a problem of poorly defined property rights. If resources such as clean air could be recognized as a form of property, with corresponding rights that could be traded in a market, private actors could allocate the use of this property in a cost-effective way.

Not long after Coase's work appeared, Crocker (1966) and Dales (1968) proposed emissions trading systems based on property rights. Such systems are of two basic types: credit programs and cap-and-trade systems. Under credit programs, credits are assigned (or created) when a source reduces emissions below the level required by existing, source-specific limits; these credits can enable the same or another firm to meet its control target. Under a cap-and-trade system, an allowable overall level of pollution is established and allocated among firms in the form of allowances. Firms that keep their emissions below their allotted level may sell their surplus allowances to other firms or, in many systems, bank them for later use. Each source has an incentive to abate emissions up to the point where its marginal control costs are equal to the market-determined price of tradable allowances. Hence, the environmental constraint is satisfied, and marginal abatement costs are equated across sources, satisfying the condition for cost effectiveness. Although the specified overall level of pollution abatement is certain under cap-and-trade regimes, the price at which pollution allowances will be traded is not assured in advance.

Under a cap-and-trade system, the unique cost-effective equilibrium can usually be achieved independent of the initial allocation of allowances (Montgomery, 1972; Hahn and Stavins, 2011). This independence property is a key reason why cap-and-trade systems have been preferred to pollution tax systems in representative democracies. The government can set the overall emissions cap and then allocate the available (and valuable) allowances among regulated sources to maximize support for the initiative, without either reducing the system's environmental performance or driving up its cost. In some cap-and-trade systems, most allowances are auctioned off, notably in the Regional Greenhouse Gas Initiative in the northeastern United States (Burtraw *et al.*, 2006) and the California cap-and-trade program (California Legislative Analyst's Office, 2017), but auctioning of allowances has not played an important role under the Clean Air Act.

Even when the assumption that emissions are well mixed is only approximately correct, taxes or emissions trading may be more cost effective than command and control if marginal abatement costs differ substantially across sources. If source-specific damages differ too much, however, command and control may be superior. If sources are relatively isolated, trading may produce "hot spots," areas of unacceptably high concentrations, without further policy protections. Further, neither taxes nor emissions trading has been used to regulate mobile sources, although tradable performance standards have been employed, as we discuss below.

The Evolution of Air Quality Policy Instruments

Under the original 1970 Clean Air Act, all federal air pollution regulation involved either technology standards or performance standards. At that time, some environmental advocates argued that implementing greater flexibility through tradable rights to emit pollution would inappropriately legitimize environmental degradation, while others questioned the feasibility of such an approach (Mazmanian and Kraft, 2009). But over time, as the Clean Air Act was amended and as the interpretation of its provisions by the Environmental Protection Agency evolved, air pollution regulation evolved from sole reliance on conventional, command-and-control regulations to greater use of emissions trading.[5] This evolution has come to a halt in the past decade.

First Experiments with Emissions Trading in the 1970s

Beginning in 1974, the Environmental Protection Agency experimented with emissions trading among stationary sources through four programs: netting, bubbles, offsets, and banking. Under netting or bubbles, firms that reduced emissions below the level required by law received credits usable against higher emissions elsewhere within the firm, so long as total, combined emissions did not exceed an aggregate limit (Tietenberg, 1985; Hahn, 1989; Foster and Hahn, 1995). Bubbles allowed firms to treat multiple sources within a plant as a single source, whereas netting extended the practice to multiple firms. These may be thought of as basic forms of intrafirm and interfirm emissions trading, respectively. By the mid-1980s, EPA had approved more than 50 bubbles, and states had authorized many

[5]A report from the Environmental Protection Agency (2001) provides a comprehensive discussion of the use of economic incentives in all US environmental protection programs through 2000, but command-and-control regulations were still the norm (Hahn, 2000).

more under EPA's framework rules. Estimated compliance cost savings from these bubble programs exceeded $430 million (Korb, 1998). The offset program, as explicitly authorized by the 1977 amendments, allowed trades between firms. Firms wishing to establish new sources in areas that were not in compliance with National Ambient Air Quality Standards could offset their new emissions by reducing existing emissions through internal sources or through agreements with other firms. Finally, under the banking program, firms could store earned emission credits for future use, allowing for either internal expansion or sale of credits to other firms.

The Environmental Protection Agency codified all four programs in its Emissions Trading Program in 1986, but the programs were not widely used. States were not required to use the programs, and uncertainties about their future course may have made firms reluctant to participate (Liroff, 1986). In addition, individual trades between firms were subject to administrative approval, and trades were required to produce significant net emissions reductions, all of which raised transactions costs. Nevertheless, companies such as Armco, DuPont, USX, and 3M did trade emissions credits, and a market for transfers developed. Even this limited degree of participation in EPA's post-1974 trading programs may have saved between $5 billion and $12 billion over the life of the programs (Hahn and Hester, 1989).

The Leaded Gasoline Phasedown in the 1980s

Starting in 1975, new US car models were required to be built with catalytic converters to reduce emissions of carbon monoxide and hydrocarbons. However, lead in gasoline fouls catalytic converters, so the Environmental Protection Agency required that only unleaded gasoline could be used in new cars.

There was also concern about the threat of lead emissions to human health, and the Environmental Protection Agency began to set rules for reducing the quantity of lead in gasoline beginning in 1979. However, smaller refineries found it difficult to meet the requirements, even though the rules for reducing lead were less stringent for smaller operations (Newell and Rogers, 2007). In late 1982, EPA launched a lead emissions trading program aimed at reducing the burden of the phasedown on the smaller refineries. Unlike a textbook cap-and-trade program, in which a fixed quantity of allowances is given or sold to potential emitters, there was no explicit allocation of allowances (Hahn, 1989). Instead, if a refiner produced gasoline with a total lead content that was lower than the amount allowed, it earned lead "credits" that EPA allowed it to trade. This structure is sometimes called a "tradable performance standard." In 1985, EPA promulgated rules for an accelerated phaseout of lead. These new rules included a "banking" provision, so that lead credits could be saved for later use. This created an incentive for refineries to make early reductions in lead content, which in turn would help them meet the lower limits that took effect over time.

Taken together, these tradable and bankable lead "credits" resulted in leaded gasoline being removed from the market faster than anticipated (Anderson *et al.*, 1990; Newell and Rogers, 2007). In each year of the program before it was terminated in 1987, more than 60 percent of the lead added to gasoline was associated with traded lead credits (Hahn and Hester, 1989). This high level of trading far surpassed levels observed earlier under the Emissions Trading Program in the 1970s. The level of trading and the rate at which the production of leaded gasoline was reduced suggest that the program was relatively cost effective (Kerr and Maré, 1997; Nichols, 1997). The program resulted in savings of approximately 20 percent relative to approaches that did not include trading (Environmental Protection Agency, 1985). In addition, the program provided significant incentives for diffusion of cost-saving technology (Kerr and Newell, 2003). By 1988, when uniform performance standards were imposed for reductions in lead at oil refineries of all sizes, very little leaded gasoline was produced in the United States. The 1990 amendments to the Clean Air Act banned all leaded gasoline beginning in 1996.

The phasedown of leaded gasoline was the first environmental program in which trading played a central role, and it demonstrated that a trading system could reduce emissions in an economically cost-effective manner. Moreover, it demonstrated that transaction costs in such a system could be low enough to permit substantial trade. The lack of a prior approval requirement, as had existed in the preceding Emissions Trading Program, was an important factor in the success of lead trading (Hahn and Hester, 1989). Also, the ability to bank credits enabled significant cost savings and early reductions.

Stratospheric Ozone Protection

Following US ratification of the Montreal Protocol in 1988, Congress imposed an excise tax on chemicals that deplete stratospheric ozone that took effect in 1990 (Omnibus Budget Reconciliation Act of 1989, Pub. L. 101-239, 103 Stat. 2106, §7506 [1989]). Beginning in 1989, the Environmental Protection Agency set up an emissions trading system for ozone-depleting chemicals, which was then expanded after the 1990 amendments (Hahn and McGartland, 1989). Limits were placed on both the production and the use of ozone-depleting chemicals by issuing allowances to producers. Different types of ozone-depleting chemicals have different effects on ozone depletion, and each ozone-depleting chemical was assigned a weight on the basis of its depletion potential. Through mid-1991, there were 34 participants in the market and 80 trades, but we are not aware of any studies that estimate cost savings. The timetable for the phaseout of ozone-depleting chemicals was subsequently accelerated, and the tax on ozone-depleting chemicals was raised over time (Reitze, 2001). It effectively served as a windfall-profits tax, to prevent firms that held emissions permits benefitting from higher prices created by the quantity restrictions (Merrill and Rousso, 1990; Environmental Protection Agency, 2001). There was considerable debate regarding the extent to which the pollution taxes or the emissions trading system should be credited with the ultimately successful reduction in the use of ozone-depleting chemicals, for which US production ceased in 1995 (Cook, 1996).

Sulfur Dioxide Allowance Trading

There was concern starting in the early 1980s (for example, see Glass *et al.*, 1982) that emissions of SO_2 from coal-fired power plants leading to greater acidity in precipitation was damaging forests and aquatic ecosystems. Because costs of reducing these emissions differed dramatically across sources, command-and-control instruments for specifying levels of emissions failed to attract congressional support. However, the path-breaking 1990 amendments to the Clean Air Act required the Environmental Protection Agency to launch the SO_2 allowance trading program, eventually covering all nontrivial power plants with a declining cap achieving a 50 percent reduction below 1980 levels (Ellerman *et al.*, 2000).

The government allocated allowances to power plants to emit specific quantities of SO_2 at zero cost, based primarily on actual fuel use during the 1985–1987 period. In addition, because of concerns about barriers to entry for new generating plants, the statute required the Environmental Protection Agency to withhold about 2.8 percent of all allowance allocations each year, sell them at an annual auction, and return the proceeds to firms from which allowances had been withheld (Ellerman *et al.*, 2000). If annual emissions at a regulated facility exceeded its allowance allocation, the owner could comply by buying additional allowances or reducing emissions — which in turn could be accomplished by installing pollution controls, shifting to a fuel mix with less sulfur, or reducing production. If emissions at a regulated facility were below its allowance allocation, the facility owner could sell the extra allowances or bank them for future use.

Although government auctioning of allowances would have generated revenue that could have been used — in principle — to reduce distortionary taxes, thereby reducing the program's social cost (Goulder, 1995), this efficiency argument was not advanced at the time. Because the entire investor-owned electric utility industry was subject to cost-of-service regulation in 1990, it was assumed that the value of free allowances would be passed on to consumers and thus not generate windfall profits for utilities. Just as important, the ability to allocate *free* allowances helped to build significant political support for the program (Joskow and Schmalensee, 1998). Because of the independence property associated with cap-and-trade systems, the initial allocation of allowances could be designed to maximize political support without compromising the system's environmental performance or increasing its cost.

The program performed well, with SO_2 emissions from electric power plants decreasing 36 percent between 1990 and 2004 (Environmental Protection Agency, 2011), even though electricity generation from coal-fired power plants *increased* 25 percent over the same period (Table 8.2a in Energy Information Administration, 2012). The program delivered emissions reductions more quickly than expected, as utilities made substantial use of the ability to bank allowances for future use. Although the program's costs, at least initially, were likely not as low as they ideally could have been (Schmalensee and Stavins, 2013), cost savings overall were eventually at least 15 percent and perhaps as great as 90 percent of the costs of various alternative command-and-control policies (Carlson *et al.*, 2000; Ellerman *et al.*, 2000; Keohane, 2003).

The SO_2 reductions achieved benefits that were a substantial multiple of the program's costs (Burtraw *et al.*, 1998; Chestnut and Mills, 2005), although these benefits were due mainly to what have been termed "co-benefits" — in this case, human health impacts of decreased local SO_2 and small particulate concentrations — rather than primarily arising from the ecological benefits of reduced acid deposition that motivated the program's establishment (Schmalensee and Stavins, 2013).

One concern was that trading might produce "hot spots" of unacceptably high SO_2 concentrations. However, computer models had predicted that plants that had the most impact on ecosystems had the lowest costs of reducing emissions. The pattern of emissions reductions was broadly consistent with those predictions, and no significant hot spots emerged (Ellerman *et al.*, 2000; Swift, 2004).[6]

In retrospect, there are number of reasons this program worked so well. First, a key feature was putting final rules in place well before the beginning of the first compliance period, which provided regulated entities with some degree of certainty, thereby facilitating their planning and limiting allowance price volatility in early years (Schmalensee and Stavins, 2017). Second, as with the lead trading program, the absence of requirements for prior approval of trades contributed to low transaction costs and substantial trading (Rico, 1995). Third, banking of allowances was again important, accounting for more than half of the program's cost savings (Carlson *et al.*, 2000; Ellerman *et al.*, 2000). Fourth, the program may have reduced costs over time by providing incentives for technology innovation (Ellerman *et al.*, 2000; Popp, 2003; Bellas and Lange, 2011). Fifth, the emissions reduction goals were achieved with less litigation (and thus less uncertainty) than was typical for environmental programs, because firms that found it particularly costly to reduce emissions had the option to buy allowances instead. Sixth, with continuous emissions monitoring and a $2,000 per ton statutory fine for any excess emissions, enforcement was stringent and compliance was nearly perfect (Burtraw and Szambelan, 2010).

Finally, the cost of the SO_2 reduction program was significantly reduced by an external factor: the substantial deregulation of railroads in 1980, which caused rail rates to fall and thus reduced the cost of burning low-sulfur Western coal in the East (Ellerman and Montero, 1998; Keohane, 2003; Schmalensee and Stavins, 2013). A command-and-control policy that required the use of certain technologies to reduce sulfur dioxide emissions would not have provided the flexibility to take advantage of the fall in rail rates (Schmalensee and Stavins, 2017).

Although subsequent regulatory actions, court decisions, and regulatory responses led to the virtual elimination of the SO_2 allowance market

[6]Chan *et al.* (2018) argue that the actual SO_2 emissions had worse health impacts than emissions under a hypothetical uniform performance standard with the same total emissions. Of course, given very heterogeneous costs of compliance, that hypothetical program had been a political nonstarter.

by 2010 (Schmalensee and Stavins, 2013), the SO_2 trading program is widely regarded as a success story of cost-effective environmental regulation.

Regional Programs under Clean Air Act Authority

Two other market-oriented environmental programs that merit attention were regional programs executed under the authority of the Environmental Protection Agency and the Clean Air Act: the Regional Clean Air Incentives Market in the Los Angeles area, and NO_x trading among eastern states.[7]

The REgional CLean Air Incentives Market (RECLAIM) was launched in 1993 by the South Coast Air Quality Management District, which is responsible for controlling emissions in a four-county area of Southern California. It sought to replace command-and-control regulations and find a more cost-effective way of reducing emissions of nitrogen oxides (NO_x) and sulfur dioxide (SO_2) from 350 sources, including power plants and industrial sources in the Los Angeles area. RECLAIM Trading Credits were allocated for free, with the NO_x and SO_2 caps declining annually until 2003, when the market reached its overall goal of a 70 percent reduction in emissions (Ellerman *et al.*, 2003). Banking of unused credits from one year to the next was not allowed. A unique aspect of this program's design was that trades were not permitted from downwind to upwind sources, reflecting differences in marginal source-specific damages.

The program was predicted to achieve significant cost savings via trade (Johnson and Pekelney, 1996; Anderson, 1997). By June 1996, 353 program participants had traded more than 100,000 tons of credits, with a value of over $10 million (South Coast Air Quality Management District, 2018). Emissions at facilities covered by the program were some 20 percent lower than at facilities regulated with parallel command-and-control regulations, hot spots did not appear, and substantial cost savings were achieved (Burtraw and Szambelan, 2010; Fowlie *et al.*, 2012).

[7]A systematic study of the evolution of environmental policy instrument use at the state level is beyond the scope of this article. It is worth noting, however, that some states have made significant use of market-based instruments. The California cap-and-trade system for greenhouse gases is a notable example (Borenstein *et al.*, 2018).

In the program's early years, allowance prices remained in the expected range of \$500 to \$1,000 per ton of NO_x. During California's electricity crisis in 2000–2001, however, some sources of electricity were taken offline, which required dramatic increases in generation at some RECLAIM facilities. This caused emissions to exceed permit allocations at those facilities, and, in the absence of a pool of banked allowances, it resulted in a dramatic spike in allowance prices — to more than \$60,000 per ton in 2001 (Fowlie *et al.*, 2012). The program was temporarily suspended. Prices returned to normal levels (about \$2,000 per ton) by 2002, with all sources rejoining the program by 2007. As of July 2018, the twelve-month moving average of NO_x prices was \$2,530 per ton (South Coast Air Quality Management District, 2018).

Another regional program of particular interest is NO_x trading in the eastern United States, which was enabled by the 1990 Clean Air Act amendments. In 1999, eleven northeastern states and the District of Columbia developed and implemented the NO_x Budget Program, a regional NO_x cap-and-trade system. The goal of the program was to reduce summertime ground-level ozone — that is, smog formed by the interaction of NO_x and volatile organic compounds in the presence of sunlight — by more than 50 percent relative to 1990 levels (Environmental Protection Agency, 2004). Some 1,000 electric generating and industrial units were required to demonstrate compliance each year during the summer ozone season.

The region covered by the program was divided into upwind and downwind zones, reflecting differences in source-specific damages, and allowances were given to states to distribute to in-state sources. Sources could buy, sell, and bank allowances within limits reflecting the seasonal nature of the ozone problem. Upwind states were given less generous allowance allocations. However, trading across zones was permitted on a one-for-one basis, and the upwind and downwind zones made similar reductions from baseline emissions levels (Ozone Transport Commission, 2003).

At the outset, the NO_x Budget Program market was characterized by uncertainty because some trading rules were not in place when trading commenced. This resulted in high price volatility during the program's first year, although prices stabilized by the program's second year (Farrell, 2000). For the 1999–2003 period, abatement cost savings were estimated at 40 to 47 percent relative to conventional regulation that did not include trading or banking (Farrell, 2000).

In 1998, the Environmental Protection Agency had issued a call for State Implementation Plans, which required 21 eastern states to submit plans to reduce their NO_x emissions from more than 2,500 sources. The result was an interstate cap-and-trade program, known as the NO_x Budget Trading Program, which went into effect in 2003, replacing the earlier NO_x Budget Program. Overall, under the NO_x Budget Program and the NO_x Budget Trading Program, NO_x emissions declined from about 1.9 million tons in 1990 to less than 500,000 tons by 2006, with 99 percent compliance (Butler *et al.*, 2011; Deschenes *et al.*, 2017).

Overall, this experience demonstrated that in order to avoid unnecessary price volatility, all of the components of an emissions trading program should be in place well before the program takes effect, and that a well-designed multistate process with federal guidance could be effective in coordinating what were legally state-level goals.

In 2005, the NO_x Budget Trading Program was effectively replaced by the Clean Air Interstate Rule, which reduced allowance allocations under the acid rain program. In July 2008, however, an appeals court ruled that the Clean Air Act did not give authority to the Environmental Protection Agency to amend the acid rain program (*North Carolina v. Environmental Protection Agency*, No. 05-1244), while an appellate court decision in December of the same year left the policy in place while EPA developed a new approach. In 2015, the Clean Air Interstate Rule was replaced by the Cross State Air Pollution Rule, which does not allow interstate trading.

Climate Change Policies

The single greatest air pollutant emissions issue facing the United States and the world is the emissions of greenhouse gases. For a time, it was unclear whether this topic fell under the purview of the Clean Air Act. Early in the 2000s, the Environmental Protection Agency considered whether it had the authority to regulate emissions of carbon dioxide and other greenhouse gases, noting that during the major amendments to the Clean Air Act in 1990, Congress had not specified that such emissions should be treated as a pollutant.

Obama Administration Climate Policies

In response to a lawsuit brought by twelve states and several cities, the US Supreme Court ruled in *Massachusetts et al. v. Environmental Protection*

Agency et al. (549 US 497 [2007]) that if the Environmental Protection Agency was to find that emissions of greenhouse gases endanger public health or welfare, it would be obligated (on the basis of authority in the 1970 act) to regulate those emissions. In December 2009, the Obama administration EPA issued an "Endangerment Finding," which found that current and projected levels of six greenhouse gases endangered public health and welfare. When attempts to address climate change via new legislation (the American Clean Energy and Security Act of 2009, commonly known as the Waxman–Markey bill) failed in 2010, the focus of addressing green-house gas emissions thus turned to the possibility of regulatory approaches under existing authority of the Clean Air Act. EPA proceeded to issue regulations covering greenhouse gas emissions from mobile and then stationary sources. Treating CO_2 as a criteria air pollutant under the Clean Air Act may have been cumbersome and represented a "stretch," but it was a stretch the administration was essentially required to make by the 2007 Supreme Court decision combined with the administration's 2009 Endangerment Finding.

In September 2009, the Obama administration finalized a rule with two main steps: to increase fuel efficiency under the Corporate Average Fuel Economy (CAFE) program and to establish national greenhouse gas emissions standards under the Clean Air Act (Broder, 2009). The rule increased the required average fuel efficiency in model year 2016 to 35.5 miles per gallon, with a second phase announced in 2012 increasing the standard to 54.5 miles per gallon for model year 2025. Notably, this rule enabled manufacturers for the first time to earn, bank, and trade credits for exceeding these performance standards (Leard and McConnell, 2017).

The second part of the Obama administration's regulatory action on climate change began quietly in 2013, with a proposal for New Source Performance Standards to limit CO_2 emissions from all new coal and natural gas power plants built in the United States. The proposed rule would essentially have made it impossible to build new traditional coal plants, but since there were no new coal plants planned or likely to be built, due to the relative prices of coal and natural gas, the rule had no real impacts and was not particularly controversial.

However, a subsequent rule — the Clean Power Plan — announced in June 2014 had considerably more bite. This rule sought to reduce CO_2 emissions from existing sources in the electricity-generating sector. The proposal listed specific targets for each state but gave the states many ways to meet their targets: increasing the efficiency of fossil fuel power plants, switching electricity generation from coal-fired plants to natural gas–fired plants, developing new low-emissions generation (including renewable and nuclear generation), fostering more efficient end-use of electricity, and others. States were also given flexibility to employ any of a wide variety of policy instruments, including market-based trading systems. Furthermore, states could work together to submit multistate plans. The regulation was to be finalized in June 2015 and implemented in 2020.

The state-by-state approach in the Clean Power Plan did not guarantee cost effectiveness, because marginal abatement costs would vary greatly across states. However, encouragement was given to states to employ cap-and-trade systems, and the Environmental Protection Agency emphasized its willingness to consider and facilitate multistate implementation plans. EPA was not guaranteeing cost effectiveness, but it was allowing for it and, indeed, attempting to facilitate it.

A difficult challenge for climate change policies is that global damages are unaffected by the location of emissions. Thus, any jurisdiction taking action will incur the direct costs of its actions, but the direct climate benefits will be distributed globally. Hence, the direct climate benefits a jurisdiction reaps from its actions will almost certainly be less than the costs it incurs, even if global climate benefits from emissions reductions are much greater than global costs. Despite this logic, the central estimate of annual net benefits (benefits minus costs) of the Clean Power Plan in 2030 in the Environmental Protection Agency's Regulatory Impact Analysis submitted to the Office of Management and Budget was $67 billion (Environmental Protection Agency, 2014). How could this be?

Table 2 emphasizes two key underlying assumptions. First, the estimate of climate benefits was not limited to benefits received by the United States, but rather was an estimate of global climate benefits. Second, the estimate of benefits included (the much larger) benefits of human health impacts associated with reductions in correlated air pollutants that were not themselves greenhouse gases.

It would certainly be inappropriate to use a global measure of benefits in analysis of all US regulations (Gayer and Viscusi, 2016). Doing so could imply that a labor policy that increased US employment, but led to lower employment in competitor economies, would have zero benefits! On the other hand, it can be argued that counting only domestic benefits is not appropriate for a global commons problem (National Academy of Sciences, 2017). In a global commons problem, every jurisdiction will find itself in a situation where the benefits of its actions spill over to other jurisdictions, and the direct climate benefits it reaps from reducing greenhouse

Table 2. Estimated benefits and costs of clean power plan rule in 2030 (Environmental Protection Agency's Regulatory Impact Analysis, midpoint estimates, billions of dollars).

	Climate change impacts from CO_2		**Domestic health impacts from correlated pollutants plus . . .**	
	Domestic	**Global**	**Domestic climate impacts**	**Global climate impacts**
Climate change benefits	3	31	3	31
Health co-benefits	—	—	45	45
Total benefits	3	31	48	76
Total compliance costs	9	9	9	9
Net benefits (benefits minus costs)	−6	22	39	67

Sources: Authors' calculations, based on table ES-7 (p. ES-19) and table ES-10 (p. ES-23) of June 2014 Regulatory Impact Analysis of proposed Clean Power Plan Rule (Environmental Protection Agency, 2014), adopting midpoint estimates, using 3 percent discount rate, and domestic shares of global climate benefits from the Interagency Working Group on Social Cost of Carbon (2010).

gas emissions within its own jurisdiction will be less than the costs it incurs. One can also imagine trying to argue that a US climate policy would increase the probability of other countries taking similar actions, but trying to quantify this effect would be speculative at best.

In addition to counting climate benefits outside the US, the Environmental Protection Agency under President Obama counted health benefits from reductions of other pollutants, the emissions of which are correlated with those of CO_2. For example, the Clean Power Plan was expected to reduce the burning of coal, leading to decreased emissions of sulfur dioxide (SO_2), nitrogen oxides (NO_x), particulate matter, and mercury. These pollutants — especially particulate matter less than 2.5 microns across — have very significant human health impacts; indeed, the estimated benefits from reducing their emissions dwarf the domestic climate benefits. According to the Regulatory Impact Analysis, whereas the US climate change benefits from CO_2 reductions due to the proposed rule in 2030 would probably be less than \$3 billion per year,[8] the domestic

[8] Suppose a domestic US climate benefits number were used in this analysis, rather than a global number. EPA estimated global climate benefits of the rule in 2030 using a midrange 3 percent discount rate to be \$31 billion. According to the Obama administration's Interagency Working Group on Social Cost of Carbon (2010), US benefits from reducing

health benefits from reduced concentrations of correlated non-greenhouse gas air pollutants would amount to some $45 billion per year! Thus, 94 percent of estimated domestic benefits of this climate policy were due to reductions of non-greenhouse gas air pollutants. In turn, these estimates of health benefits are driven heavily by predicted reductions in morbidity and mortality, and those in turn are driven by the dose-response assumptions EPA employs.

The inclusion of these human health co-benefits is the key argument that climate policies provide a near-term or medium-term increase in US welfare. If the global estimate of climate benefits ($31 billion per year) is employed instead, then the Clean Power Plan Rule looks even better, with total annual benefits of $76 billion, leading to the Environmental Protection Agency's bottom-line estimate of positive net benefits of $67 billion per year in 2030. The Obama administration's proposed Clean Power Plan thus offered the flexibility to be cost effective, and if one accepts the estimates of benefits and costs, it could also have been welfare enhancing.

Trump Administration Climate Policies

Both of the main Obama administration climate change regulatory initiatives — the Corporate Auto Fuel Economy standards for motor vehicles and the Clean Power Plan for the electricity sector — were reversed by the Trump administration. In August 2018, the Environmental Protection Agency and the National Highway Traffic Safety Administration proposed a rule that would have the federal government freeze the motor vehicle standards at their 2020 levels going forward (Environmental Protection Agency, 2018a).

When the final version of the Clean Power Plan was published in October 2015 (40 C.F.R. 60), it immediately faced lawsuits from a number of states. They argued, among other things, that the Clean Air Act gave authority to the Environmental Protection Agency only to issue technical

---

greenhouse gas emissions would be, on average, about 7–10 percent of global benefits. If benefits within the United States were thus 8.5 percent of global benefits, they would amount to about $2.6 billion, considerably less than the $8.8 billion in total annual compliance costs estimated by the Regulatory Impact Analysis.

and performance standards for power plants (some argued that only the states could regulate *existing* plants), and that by allowing flexibility, the Clean Power Plan went well beyond that authority. In February 2016, the US Supreme Court issued a stay in the implementation of the Clean Power Plan while that litigation proceeded (Liptak and Davenport, 2016).

In August 2018, with implementation of the Clean Power Plan still suspended, the Trump administration announced the Affordable Clean Energy Rule as a replacement for the Clean Power Plan Rule (Friedman, 2018; Environmental Protection Agency, 2018c). The new rule instructs the states to set standards for efficiency improvements in existing coal-fired power plants, subject to guidance from the Environmental Protection Agency regarding technologies to be used as well as EPA approval. (It seems that states could require no improvements at all, if EPA agreed.) It also changes the rules on what constitutes a new source, subject to very strict standards, so that old plants can increase efficiency without becoming subject to new source standards. It does not provide incentives for changing the mix of methods used for generating electricity or even allow such methods for compliance. Without such flexibility, there is no possibility of cost effectiveness in reducing air pollution. However, it is interesting to note that by issuing the revised regulation, the Trump administration implicitly accepted the 2009 finding by EPA that greenhouse gas emissions do cause harm (Friedman, 2018).

The Regulatory Impact Analysis for the Affordable Clean Energy Rule compares it with the Clean Power Plan and finds it superior (Environmental Protection Agency, 2018d), although the same report estimates that it would have lower costs, greater coal use, greater greenhouse gas emissions, and greater adverse health effects.[9] The different conclusion is based on different underlying assumptions. This Regulatory Impact Analysis uses a US-only social cost of carbon to value those emissions increases. Whereas, with a 3 percent discount rate, the global social cost of carbon in 2030 used by the Obama administration was $50 per ton, the US-only cost used by the Trump administration was $7 per ton. With a

[9]It is not clear how fully this analysis of the Affordable Clean Energy Rule takes into account the so-called rebound effect: if coal-fired power plants are made more efficient, their marginal costs will be reduced, and it will be economic to use them more intensively. The impact of this effect on human health may be substantial (Keyes *et al.*, 2019).

7 percent discount rate, the US-only social cost for a ton of carbon emissions was $1 per ton.

The same US-only social cost of carbon was also used in the Regulatory Impact Analysis for the Trump Administration's revised CAFE standards. In several tables that take the loss of health benefits into account, the Affordable Clean Energy Rule is found to have lower net benefits than the Clean Power Plan. But the presentation in the Regulatory Impact Analysis de-emphasizes these health co-benefits and focuses on "net benefits associated with the targeted pollutant (CO_2)." On that metric, and considering only domestic climate benefits, the cost savings from moving from the Clean Power Plan to the Affordable Clean Energy Rule outweigh the foregone benefits.

Conclusions

The supporters of the 1970 Clean Air Act no doubt hoped that it would produce major environmental benefits. They would surely be pleased that despite the fact that real US GDP more than tripled between 1970 and 2017, aggregate emissions of the six criteria pollutants declined by 73 percent (Environmental Protection Agency, 2018a). On the other hand, the original supporters of the 1970 Clean Air Act might well be surprised by some of the twists and turns of clean air regulation since then. For example, it is difficult to imagine that any of the supporters of the 24-page 1970 act imagined how complex air pollution regulation would become over the subsequent half century. In addition, we suspect that the evolution toward more intensive use of market-based environmental policy would also have been a surprise to those involved in passage of the 1970 act.

But those involved in the strongly bipartisan passage of the 1970 Clean Air Act would surely be disappointed that environmental policy has become a partisan battleground. It has seemingly become impossible to amend the Clean Air Act or to pass other legislation to address climate change in a serious and economically efficient manner. Regulation under the Clean Air Act has not ceased, but addressing new problems such as climate change has become exceedingly difficult, partly because the existing legislation provides no simple vehicle for doing so. The climate effects of CO_2 emissions are predicted to last for many centuries (Stocker *et al.*, 2013). If US inaction slows global reductions of greenhouse gas emissions, the environmental damage is likely to be both profound and long lasting.

A great deal has been learned over the 50 years since the Clean Air Act was signed into law in 1970. The 1977 and 1990 amendments reflect some of that learning, including the practical difficulty of regulating a myriad of air toxics. Much has also been learned about the design and implementation of emissions trading systems (Schmalensee and Stavins, 2017). Most importantly, we now know from experience that cap-and-trade systems can be environmentally effective and economically cost effective. Provisions for the banking of permits have proven to be very important for achieving maximum gains from trade, and the absence of such provisions has led to price spikes and market collapses.

Another implication of these five decades of experience may be that policies to address climate change and other new environmental problems should be designed to make them more acceptable in the real world of politics. This could mean, for example, giving greater attention to suboptimal, second-best designs of carbon-pricing regimes (Stavins, 2019). Examples might include earmarking revenues from taxes or allowance auctions to finance additional climate mitigation, rather than optimizing the system via cuts in distortionary taxes, and/or using such revenues for fairness purposes, such as with lump-sum rebates or rebates targeted to low-income and other particularly burdened constituencies (Goulder and Hafstead, 2017; Stavins, 2019). Economists might also be more effective by sometimes working to catch up with the political world by examining better design of second-best nonpricing climate policy instruments, such as clean energy standards, subsidies for green technologies, and other approaches. At some point the politics may change, of course, which is why ongoing economic research on climate policy instruments of all kinds is important.

Acknowledgements

We acknowledge valuable comments on a previous version of the manuscript by Dallas Burtraw, Robert Hahn, Amelia Keyes, Alan Krupnick, Al McGartland, and Paul Portney, as well as comments from the editorial team — Gordon Hanson, Enrico Moretti, Heidi Williams, and especially Timothy Taylor.

References

Ackerman, Bruce A., and William T. Hassler. (1981). *Clean Coal/Dirty Air*. New Haven, CT: Yale University Press.

Anderson, Robert C., and Andrew Q. Lohof. (1997). "The United States experience with economic incentives in environmental pollution control policy." Environmental Protection Agency Paper EE-0126A.

Anderson, Robert C., Lisa A. Hofmann, and Michael Rusin. (1990). "The use of economic incentive mechanisms in environmental management." American Petroleum Institute Research Paper 51.

Ayres, Robert U., and Allen V. Kneese. (1969). "Production, consumption, and externalities." *American Economic Review*, **59**(3): 282–297.

Baumol, William J., and Wallace E. Oates. (1988). *The Theory of Environmental Policy*. Cambridge: Cambridge University Press.

Bellas, Allen S., and Ian Lange. (2011). "Evidence of innovation and diffusion under tradable permit programs." *International Review of Environmental and Resource Economics*, **5**(1): 1–22.

Borenstein, Severin, James Bushnell, Frank A. Wolak, and Matthew Zaragoza-Watkins. (2018). "Expecting the unexpected: Emissions uncertainty and environmental market design." University of California, Berkeley, Energy Institute at Haas Working Paper 274.

Broder, John. (2009). "Obama to toughen rules on emissions and mileage." *New York Times*, May 18, 2009, A1.

Buchanan, James M., and Gordon Tullock. (1975). "Polluters' profits and political response: Direct controls versus taxes." *American Economic Review*, **65**(1): 139–147.

Burtraw, Dallas, Danny Kahn, and Karen Palmer. (2006). "CO2 allowance allocation in the Regional Greenhouse Gas Initiative and the effect on electricity investors." *Electricity Journal*, **19**(2): 79–90.

Burtraw, Dallas, Alan Krupnick, Erin Mansur, David Austin, and Dierdre Farrell. (1998). "Costs and benefits of reducing air pollution related to acid rain." *Contemporary Economic Policy*, **16**(4): 379–400.

Burtraw, Dallas, and Sarah Jo Szambelan. (2010). "US emissions trading markets for SO_2 and NO_x." In Bernd Hansjürgens, Ralf Antes, and Marianne Strunz Eds., *Permit Trading in Different Applications*, 15–45. New York: Routledge.

Butler, Thomas J., Francoise M. Vermeylen, Melissa Rury, Gene E. Likens, Brian Lee, George E. Bowker, and Lance McCluney. (2011). "Response of ozone and nitrate to stationary source NO_x emission reductions in the eastern USA." *Atmospheric Environment*, **455**(5): 1084–1094.

California Legislative Analyst's Office. (2017). "The 2017–18 budget: Cap-and-trade." https://lao.ca.gov/reports/2017/3553/cap-and-trade-021317.pdf.

Carlson, Curtis, Dallas Burtraw, Maureen Cropper, and Karen L. Palmer. (2000). "Sulfur dioxide control by electric utilities: What are the gains from trade?" *Journal of Political Economy*, **108**(6): 1292–1326.

Chan, Gabriel, Robert Stavins, Robert Stowe, and Richard Sweeney. (2012). "The SO_2 allowance-trading system and the Clean Air Act Amendments of 1990: Reflections on 20 years of policy innovation." *National Tax Journal*, **65**(2): 419–452.

Chan, H. Ron, B. Andrew Chupp, Maureen L. Cropper, and Nicholas Z. Muller. (2018). "The impact of trading on the costs and benefits of the Acid Rain Program." *Journal of Environmental Economics and Management*, **88**(1): 180–209.

Chestnut, Lauraine G., and David M. Mills. (2005). "A fresh look at the benefits and costs of the US Acid Rain Program." *Journal of Environmental Management*, **77**(3): 252–266.

Coase, Ronald. (1960). "The problem of social cost." *Journal of Law and Economics*, **3**(1): 1–44.

Cook, Elizabeth, Ed. (1996). *Ozone Protection in the United States: Elements of Success*. Washington, DC: World Resources Institute.

Copeland, Curtis W. (2009). "Federal rulemaking: The role of the Office of Information and Regulatory Affairs." Congressional Research Service Report for Congress RL32397.

Crocker, Thomas D. (1966). "The structuring of atmospheric pollution control systems." In Harold Wolozin Ed., *The Economics of Air Pollution*, 61–86. New York: W. W. Norton.

Dales, J. H. (1968). "Land, water, ownership." *Canadian Journal of Economics*, **1**(4): 791–804.

Deschenes, Olivier, Michael Greenstone, and Joseph S. Shapiro. (2017). "Defensive investments and the demand for air quality: Evidence from the NOx Budget Program." *American Economic Review*, **107**(10): 2958–2989.

Ellerman, A. Denny, and Juan-Pablo Montero. (1998). "The declining trend in sulfur dioxide emissions: Implications for allowance prices." *Journal of Environmental Economics and Management*, **36**(1): 26–45.

Ellerman, A. Denny, Paul L. Joskow, and David Harrison Jr. (2003). "Emissions trading in the U.S.: Experience, lessons, and considerations for greenhouse gases." Prepared for the Pew Center on Global Climate Change. http://web.mit.edu/globalchange/www/PewCtr_MIT_Rpt_Ellerman.pdf.

Ellerman, A. Denny, Paul L. Joskow, Richard Schmalensee, Juan-Pablo Montero, and Elizabeth M. Bailey. (2000). *Markets for Clean Air: The U.S. Acid Rain Program*. Cambridge: Cambridge University Press.

Energy Information Administration. (2012). *Annual Energy Review 2011*. Washington, DC: Energy Information Administration.

Environmental Protection Agency. (1985). *Costs and Benefits of Reducing Lead in Gasoline: Final Regulatory Impact Analysis*. Washington, DC: Office of Policy Analysis, Environmental Protection Agency.

Environmental Protection Agency. (2001). "The United States experience with economic incentives for protecting the environment." National Center for Environmental Economics Report EPA-240-R-01-001.

Environmental Protection Agency. (2004). "Evaluating ozone control programs in the eastern United States: Focus on the NOx Budget Trading Program, 2004." Environmental Protection Agency Report EPA454-K-05-001.

Environmental Protection Agency. (2011). *National Emissions Inventory (NEI) Air Pollutant Emissions Trends Data: 1970–2011*. Washington, DC: Environmental Protection Agency.

Environmental Protection Agency. (2014). "Regulatory impact analysis for the proposed carbon pollution guidelines for existing power plants and emission standards for modified and reconstructed power plants." Environmental Protection Agency Report EPA-452/R-14-002.

Environmental Protection Agency. (2018a). "Air pollution trends show cleaner air, growing economy." News Release, July 31, 2018. https://www.epa.gov/newsreleases/air-pollution-trends-show-cleaner-air-growing-economy.

Environmental Protection Agency. (2018b). "The Safer and Affordable Fuel Efficient (SAFE) vehicles proposed rule for model years 2021–2026." https://www.epa.gov/regulations-emissions-vehicles-and-engines/safer-and-affordable-fuel-efficient-vehicles-proposed.

Environmental Protection Agency. (2018c). "Proposal: Affordable Clean Energy (ACE) rule." https://www.epa.gov/stationary-sources-air-pollution/proposal-affordable-clean-energy-ace-rule.

Environmental Protection Agency. (2018d). "Regulatory impact analysis for the proposed emissions guidelines for greenhouse gas emissions from existing electric utility generating units; revisions to emission guideline implementing regulations; revisions to new source review program." Environmental Protection Agency Report EPA-453/R-18-006.

Farrell, Alex. (2000). "The NOx budget: A look at the first year." *Electricity Journal*, **13**(2): 83–93.

Fleisher, Richard, and John R. Bond. (2004). "The shrinking middle in the US Congress." *British Journal of Political Science*, **34**(3): 429–451.

Foster, Vivien, and Robert W. Hahn. (1995). "Designing more efficient markets: Lessons from Los Angeles smog control." *Journal of Law and Economics*, **38**(1): 19–48.

Fowlie, Meredith, Stephen P. Holland, and Erin T. Mansur. (2012). "What do emissions markets deliver and to whom? evidence from Southern California's NOx trading program." *American Economic Review*, **102**(2): 965–993.

Friedman, Lisa. (2018). "Trump's plan for coal emissions: Let coal states regulate them." *New York Times*, August 18, 2018, 1A.

Gayer, Ted, and W. Kip Viscusi. (2016). "Determining the proper scope of climate change policy benefits in U.S. regulatory analyses: Domestic versus global approaches." *Review of Environmental Economics and Policy*, **10**(2): 245–263.

Glass, Norman R., Dean E. Arnold, James N. Galloway, George R. Hendrey, Jeffrey J. Lee, William W. McFee, Stephen A. Norton, Charles F. Powers, Danny L. Rambo, and Carl L. Schofield. (1982). "Effects of acid precipitation." *Environmental Science and Technology*, **16**(3): 162A–169A.

Goulder, Lawrence H. (1995). "Environmental taxation and the double dividend: A reader's guide." *International Tax and Public Finance*, **2**(2): 157–183.

Goulder, Lawrence H., and Mark A. C. Hafstead. (2017). *Confronting the Climate Challenge: U.S. Policy Options*. New York: Columbia University Press.

Hahn, Robert W. (1989). "Economic prescriptions for environmental problems: How the patient followed the doctor's orders." *Journal of Economic Perspectives*, **3**(2): 95–114.

Hahn, Robert W. (2000). "The impact of economics on environmental policy." *Journal of Environmental Economics and Management*, **39**(3): 375–399.

Hahn, Robert W., and Albert M. McGartland. (1989). "The political economy of instrument choice: An examination of the U.S. role in implementing the Montreal Protocol." *Northwestern University Law Review*, **83**(3): 592–611.

Hahn, Robert W., and Gordon L. Hester. (1989). "Where did all the markets go? an analysis of EPA's emissions trading program." *Yale Journal on Regulation*, **6**(1): 109–153.

Hahn, Robert W., and Robert N. Stavins. (2011). "The effect of allowance allocations on cap-and-trade system performance." *Journal of Law and Economics*, **54**(4): S267–S294.

Hicks, John R. (1939). "The foundations of welfare economics." *Economic Journal*, **49**(196): 696–712.

Interagency Working Group on Social Cost of Carbon. (2010). "Technical support document: Social cost of carbon for regulatory impact analysis under Executive Order 12866." https://www.epa.gov/sites/production/files/2016-12/documents/scc_tsd_2010.pdf.

Johnson, Scott Lee, and David M. Pekelney. (1996). "Economic assessment of the Regional Clean Air Incentives Market: A new emissions trading program for Los Angeles." *Land Economics*, **72**(3): 277–297.

Joskow, Paul L., and Richard Schmalensee. (1998). "The political economy of market-based environmental policy: The U.S. Acid Rain Program." *Journal of Law and Economics*, **41**(1): 37–83.

Kaldor, Nicholas. (1939). "Welfare propositions of economics and interpersonal comparisons of utility." *Economic Journal*, **49**(195): 549–552.

Keohane, Nathaniel O. (2003). “What did the market buy? cost savings under the U.S. tradeable permits program for sulfur dioxide.” Yale Center for Environmental Law and Policy Working Paper YCELP-01-11-2003.

Kerr, Suzi, and David Maré. (1997). “Efficient regulation through tradeable permit markets: The United States lead phasedown.” Department of Agricultural and Resource Economics, University of Maryland, College Park, Working Paper 96-06.

Kerr, Suzi, and Richard G. Newell. (2003). “Policy-induced technology adoption: Evidence from the U.S. lead phasedown.” *Journal of Industrial Economics*, **51**(3): 317–343.

Keyes, Amelia T., Kathleen F. Lambert, Dallas Burtraw, Jonathan J. Buonocore, Johathan I. Levy, and Charles T. Driscoll. (2019). “The Affordable Clean Energy rule and the impact of emissions rebound on carbon dioxide and criteria air pollutant emissions.” *Environmental Research Letters*, **14**(1): 044018.

Kneese, Allen V., and Charles L. Schultz. (1975). *Pollution, Prices, and Public Policy*, Washington, DC: The Brookings Institution.

Korb, Barry. (1998). “U.S. Experience with Economic Incentives for Emissions Trading.” In *Applying Market-Based Instruments to Environmental Policies in China and OECD Countries*, 99–115. Paris: Organisation for Economic Cooperation and Development.

Leard, Benjamin, and Virginia McConnell. (2017). “New markets for credit trading under US automobile greenhouse gas and fuel economy standards.” Resources for the Future Report.

Liptak, Adam, and Coral Davenport. (2016). “Supreme Court deals blow to Obama’s efforts to regulate coal emissions.” *New York Times*, February 10, 2016, A1.

Liroff, Richard A. (1986). *Reforming Air Pollution Regulations: The Toil and Trouble of EPA’s Bubble*. Washington, DC: Conservation Foundation.

Lowry, William R., and Charles R. Shipan. (2002). “Party differentiation in Congress.” *Legislative Studies Quarterly*, **27**(1): 33–60.

Mazmanian, Daniel A., and Michael E. Kraft. (2009). “The three epochs of the environmental movement.” In Daniel A. Mazmanian and Michael E. Kraft Eds., *Toward Sustainable Communities: Transition and Transformations in Environmental Policy*, 3–32. Cambridge, MA: MIT Press.

Merrill, Peter R., and Ada S. Rousso. (1990). “Federal environmental taxation.” In *Proceedings of the Annual Conference on Taxation Held under the Auspices of the National Tax Association — Tax Institute of America*, **83**:191–198. Washington, DC: National Tax Association.

Montgomery, W. David. (1972). “Markets in licenses and efficient pollution control programs.” *Journal of Economic Theory*, **5**(3): 395–418.

National Academy of Sciences. (2017). *Valuing Climate Damages*. Washington, DC: National Academies Press.

Newell, Richard G., and Kenneth Rogers. (2007). "The market-based lead phase-down." In Jody Freeman and Charles Kolstad Eds., *Moving to Markets in Environmental Regulation: Lessons from Twenty Years of Experience*, 173–193. Oxford: Oxford University Press.

Nichols, Albert L. (1997). "Lead in gasoline." In Richard D. Morgenstern Ed., *Economic Analyses at EPA: Assessing Regulatory Impact*, 49–86. Washington, DC: Resources for the Future.

Ozone Transport Commission. (2003). "NOx budget program: 1999–2002 progress report." http://www2.epa.gov/sites/production/files/2015-08/documents/otcreport.pdf.

Pareto, Vilfredo. (1896). *Cours d'économie politique*. Vol. 2. Lausanne: F. Rouge.

Pigou, Arthur C. (1920). *The Economics of Welfare*. London: Macmillan.

Poole, Keith T., and Howard Rosenthal. (1997). *Congress: A Political-Economic History of Roll Call Voting*. New York: Oxford University Press.

Poole, Keith T., and Howard Rosenthal. (2007). *Ideology and Congress*. New Brunswick, NJ: Transaction Publishers.

Popp, David. (2003). "Pollution control innovations and the Clean Air Act of 1990." *Journal of Policy Analysis and Management*, **22**(4): 641–660.

Reitze, Arnold W. Jr. (2001). "Stratospheric ozone." Chap. 13 in *Air Pollution Control Law: Compliance and Enforcement*. Washington, DC: Environmental Law Institute.

Rico, Renee. (1995). "The U.S. allowance trading system for sulfur dioxide: An update on market experience." *Environmental and Resource Economics*, **5**(2): 115–129.

Schmalensee, Richard, Paul L. Joskow, A. Denny Ellerman, Juan-Pablo Montero, and Elizabeth M. Bailey. (1998). "An interim evaluation of sulfur dioxide emissions trading." *Journal of Economic Perspectives*, **12**(3): 53–68.

Schmalensee, Richard, and Robert N. Stavins. (2013). "The SO2 allowance trading system: The ironic history of a grand policy experiment." *Journal of Economic Perspectives*, **27**(1): 103–122.

Schmalensee, Richard, and Robert N. Stavins. (2017). "Lessons learned from three decades of experience with cap and trade." *Review of Environmental Economics and Policy*, **11**(1): 59–79.

Shipan, Charles R., and William R. Lowry. (2001). "Environmental policy and party divergence in Congress." *Political Research Quarterly*, **54**(2): 245–263.

South Coast Air Quality Management District. (2018). "July 2018 quarterly report to Stationary Source Committee." http://www.aqmd.gov/docs/default-source/Agendas/ssc/ssc-agenda-7-20-18.pdf.

Stavins, Robert N. (1998). "What can we learn from the grand policy experiment? lessons from SO2 allowance trading." *Journal of Economic Perspectives*, **12**(3): 69–88.

Stavins, Robert N. (2006). "Vintage-differentiated environmental regulation." *Stanford Environmental Law Journal*, **25**(1): 29–63.

Stavins, Robert N. (2019). "The future of U.S. carbon-pricing policy." NBER Working Paper 25912.

Stern, Arthur C. (1982). "History of air pollution legislation in the United States." *Journal of the Air Pollution Control Association*, **32**(1): 44–61.

Stocker, Thomas F., Dahe Qin, Gian-Kasper Plattner, Melinda M. B. Tignor, Simon K. Allen, Judith Boschung, Alexander Nauels, Yu Xia, Vincent Bex, and Pauline M. Midgley, Eds. (2013). *Climate Change 2013: The Physical Science Basis. Contribution of Working Group I to the Fifth Assessment Report of the Intergovernmental Panel on Climate Change*. Cambridge: Cambridge University Press.

Swift, Byron. (2004). "Emissions trading and hot spots: A review of the major programs." *Environment Reporter*, **35**(19): 1–16.

Theriault, Sean M. (2008). *Party Polarization in Congress*. New York: Cambridge University Press.

Tietenberg, Tom. (1985). *Emissions Trading: An Exercise in Reforming Pollution Policy*. Washington, DC: Resources for the Future.

US Congress, Office of Technology Assessment. (1995). "Environmental policy tools: A users guide." Office of Technology Assessment Report OTA-ENV-634.

https://doi.org/10.1142/9789811292415_0011

Chapter 11

The Future of US Carbon-Pricing Policy*

Robert N. Stavins

John F. Kennedy School of Government, Harvard University, Cambridge, MA, USA

Resources for the Future, Washington, DC, USA

National Bureau of Economic Research, Cambridge, MA, USA

robert_stavins@harvard.edu

In this chapter, I will compare the two major approaches to carbon pricing — carbon taxes and cap-and-trade — in the context of a possible future US climate policy, and to do so by treating both instruments in a balanced manner, examining their merits and challenges, without necessarily favoring one or the other.[1] I try to follow the principle that when

*This chapter was originally published in "The Future of U.S. Carbon-Pricing Policy." *Environmental and Energy Policy and the Economy*, Volume 1, pp. 8–64. University of Chicago Press, 2020.

[1]In 2007, I was asked to write a paper for the Brookings Institution's Hamilton Project proposing a national ETS to reduce US CO_2 emissions. I said I would prefer to write about what I considered to be the two symmetric carbon-pricing instruments — a carbon tax and a carbon trading program. But the Hamilton Project leaders said they would find someone else to write about carbon taxes (Metcalf, 2007), and I should make the strongest case possible for what is today called cap-and-trade. I did my best, and in the process I came to be identified — and to some degree may have become — an advocate for CO_2 cap-and-trade.

making normative comparisons of policy instruments, it is most valuable to compare either idealized versions of two instruments or realistic (likely to be implemented) versions of both, thereby avoiding a comparison of an idealized version of one instrument with a less-than-ideal but realistic version of another (Hahn and Stavins, 1992).[2]

In the next section, "Setting the Stage: Major Premises", I describe the key premises I adopt, including the importance of global climate change, the current reality of US inaction at the federal level, and my view that in the long term, a truly meaningful, economy-wide US climate policy will likely need to have carbon pricing at its core, either in the form of a carbon tax or a cap-and-trade system. Then, in section "Normative Theory of Policy Instrument Choice", I examine the normative theory of policy instrument choice as it applies to US climate change policy, with brief reviews of the major options and particular attention to what normative theory suggests about the choice between price and quantity instruments for abating CO_2 emissions. In section "Positive Theory of Policy Instrument Choice", I turn to the positive theory of instrument choice as it applies to US climate policy and assess what positive theory can tell us about this choice of climate policy instruments.

In section "Empirical Evidence: What Experience Suggests about Future US Climate Policy", I examine empirical evidence, that is, what experience can tell us, first with regard to empirical evidence bearing on normative instrument choice, including lessons learned from experience with taxes and cap-and-trade, and then with regard to empirical evidence about positive instrument choices. In section "Conclusions: The Path Ahead", I offer some conclusions from the normative and positive analyses — both theoretical and empirical — and comment on the path ahead.

During the Obama administration transition, the design recommendations in my Hamilton Project paper (Stavins, 2007) became the starting point in efforts to structure the administration's proposed CO_2 cap-and-trade system that became part of the failed Waxman-Markey legislation, H.R. 2454, the American Clean Energy and Security Act of 2009.

[2]Normative assessment refers to the merits of the instruments, such as in terms of: quantitative emissions reductions, aggregate abatement costs, and distributional impacts. Positive (political economy) prognosis refers to identifying which instrument is more likely to be enacted and implemented.

Setting the Stage: Major Premises

Gradually, over the 25 years since the US Senate ratified the United Nations Framework Convention on Climate Change, scientific assessments of the risk of global climate change have become increasingly compelling (Intergovernmental Panel on Climate Change, 2013, 2018), and economic analyses supporting the wisdom of policy action have gained considerable prominence, if not influence (Nordhaus, 2015).[3] Although China's annual emissions have surpassed those of the United States since 2006, the United States remains the largest contributor to the accumulated atmospheric stock of anthropogenic greenhouse gases (GHGs) (Boden *et al.*, 2017).

Countries around the world — including nearly all the industrialized countries and large emerging economies — have launched or are in the process of launching national policies aimed at reducing their emissions of GHGs. Of the 169 Parties to the Paris Climate Agreement that have submitted specific pledges (known as Nationally Determined Contributions [NDCs]), more than half (88) refer to the use of carbon pricing in their NDCs. To date, some 51 carbon-pricing policies have been implemented or are scheduled for implementation worldwide, including 26 carbon taxes and 25 emissions trading systems (ETS) (Table 1).[4] Together, these carbon-pricing initiatives will cover about 20 percent of global GHG emissions (World Bank Group, 2018), and many of these systems may eventually be linked with one another under the auspices of Article 6 of the Paris Agreement (Bodansky *et al.*, 2015; United Nations, 2015; Mehling *et al.*, 2018).

In the midst of these global and national developments, the current US administration stands out for its rejection of the science of climate change, its decision to withdraw from the Paris Agreement, and its comprehensive

[3] The phrase, "wisdom of policy action," refers to the global dynamic efficiency of cost-effective actions taken to reduce global emissions, without suggesting that the direct climate change benefits to a single country — in particular, the United States — would exceed the costs it incurs through unilateral actions (i.e., without being part of effective international cooperation). However, if domestic co-benefits of US climate policies are taken into account, such as the health impacts of reductions in fine particulates due to decreased coal combustion, then a unilateral US climate policy can be welfare improving for the United States (Stavins, 2014).

[4] Most of the ETSs are cap-and-trade, but one very important one is a tradable performance standard, namely China's system, officially launched in December 2017 and likely to be implemented in 2020.

Table 1. Implemented and scheduled carbon-pricing initiatives, 1990–2020.

Initiative	Type	Status	Type of jurisdiction	Jurisdiction	Year	GHG emissions ($MtCO_2e$)
Alberta Carbon Competitiveness Incentive Regulation	Trading	Implemented	Subnational	Alberta	2007	120
Alberta Carbon Tax (repealed, May 2019)	Tax	Implemented	Subnational	Alberta	2017	109
Argentina Carbon Tax	Tax	Scheduled	National	Argentina	2019	79
Australia Emissions Reduction Fund Safeguard Mechanism	Trading	Implemented	National	Australia	2016	381
BC Greenhouse Gas Industrial Reporting and Control Act	Trading	Implemented	Subnational	BC	2016	0
BC Carbon Tax	Tax	Implemented	Subnational	BC	2008	42
Beijing ETS	Trading	Implemented	Subnational	Beijing	2013	85
California AB-32/AB-398 Cap-and-Trade System	Trading	Implemented	Subnational	California	2012	378
Canada Federal Output-Based Pricing System	Trading	Scheduled	National	Canada	2019	?
Canada Federal Carbon Tax	Tax	Scheduled	National	Canada	2019	?
Chile Carbon Tax	Tax	Implemented	National	Chile	2017	47
China National ETS	Trading	Scheduled	National	China	2020	3,232
Chongqing ETS	Trading	Implemented	Subnational	Chongqing	2014	97
Colombia Carbon Tax	Tax	Implemented	National	Colombia	2017	42

Denmark Carbon Tax	Tax	Implemented	National	Denmark	1992	22
European Union ETS	Trading	Implemented	Regional	European Union plus Nor., Ice., and Lich.	2005	2,132
Estonia Carbon Tax	Tax	Implemented	National	Estonia	2000	1
Finland Carbon Tax	Tax	Implemented	National	Finland	1990	25
France Carbon Tax	Tax	Implemented	National	France	2014	176
Fujian ETS	Trading	Implemented	Subnational	Fujian	2016	200
Guangdong ETS	Trading	Implemented	Subnational	Guangdong	2013	366
Hubei ETS	Trading	Implemented	Subnational	Hubei	2014	162
Ireland Carbon Tax	Tax	Implemented	National	Ireland	2010	31
Japan Carbon Tax	Tax	Implemented	National	Japan	2012	999
Kazakhstan ETS	Trading	Implemented	National	Kazakhstan	2013	183
Korea ETS	Trading	Implemented	National	Korea	2015	453
Latvia Carbon Tax	Tax	Implemented	National	Latvia	2004	2
Liechtenstein Carbon Tax	Tax	Implemented	National	Liechtenstein	2008	0
Massachusetts Cap-and-Trade System	Trading	Implemented	Subnational	RGGI States	2018	10
Mexico Carbon Tax	Tax	Implemented	National	Mexico	2014	307
New Zealand ETS	Trading	Implemented	National	New Zealand	2008	40
Norway Carbon Tax	Tax	Implemented	National	Norway	1991	40
Poland Carbon Tax	Tax	Implemented	National	Poland	1990	16
Portugal Carbon Tax	Tax	Implemented	National	Portugal	2015	21

(Continued)

Table 1. (*Continued*)

Initiative	Type	Status	Type of jurisdiction	Jurisdiction	Year	GHG Emissions ($MtCO_2e$)
Quebec Cap-and-Trade System	Trading	Implemented	Subnational	Quebec	2013	67
Regional Greenhouse Gas Initiative	Trading	Implemented	Subnational	RGGI States	2009	94
Saitama ETS	Trading	Implemented	Subnational	Saitama	2011	7
Shanghai ETS	Trading	Implemented	Subnational	Shanghai	2013	170
Shenzhen ETS	Trading	Implemented	Subnational	Shenzhen	2013	61
Singapore Carbon Tax	Tax	Scheduled	National	Singapore	2019	42
Slovenia Carbon Tax	Tax	Implemented	National	Slovenia	1996	5
South Africa Carbon Tax	Tax	Scheduled	National	South Africa	2019	360
Spain Carbon Tax	Tax	Implemented	National	Spain	2014	9
Sweden Carbon Tax	Tax	Implemented	National	Sweden	1991	26
Switzerland ETS	Trading	Implemented	National	Switzerland	2008	6
Switzerland Carbon Tax	Tax	Implemented	National	Switzerland	2008	18
Tianjin ETS	Trading	Implemented	Subnational	Tianjin	2013	118
Tokyo Cap-and-Trade System	Trading	Implemented	Subnational	Tokyo	2010	14
UK Carbon Price Floor	Tax	Implemented	National	United Kingdom	2013	136
Ukraine Carbon Tax	Tax	Implemented	National	Ukraine	2011	287
Washington State Clean Air Rule	Trading	Implemented	Subnational	Washington	2017	58

Notes: GHG = greenhouse gas; $MtCO_2e$ = metric tons of carbon dioxide equivalent; BC = British Columbia; ETS = emissions trading system.
Source: World Bank Group (2018).

moves to reverse climate policy initiatives of the previous administration. In this context, it is of value to assess the long-term future of US climate policy — both normatively and positively.

There is widespread agreement among economists — and a diverse set of other policy analysts — that at least in the long term, economy-wide carbon pricing will be an essential element of any policy that can achieve meaningful reductions of CO_2 emissions cost-effectively in the United States, as well as in many other industrialized countries (Metcalf, 2009; Kaplow, 2010; Borenstein *et al.*, 2018).[5] The ubiquitous nature of energy generation and use and the diversity of CO_2 sources in a modern economy mean that conventional technology and performance standards would be infeasible, and — in any event — excessively costly (Newell and Stavins, 2003). The cost advantage of carbon pricing exists because of the flexibility it provides and the incentive it fosters for all sources to control at the same marginal abatement cost, thereby achieving cost-effectiveness in aggregate. In addition, in the long term, pricing approaches can reduce abatement costs further by inducing carbon-friendly technological change (Newell *et al.*, 1999).[6]

---

[5]Carbon pricing may be necessary, but it would not be sufficient because other market failures limit the impacts of price signals (Jaffe *et al.*, 2005). One example is the well-known principal-agent problem that constrains incentives for energy-efficiency investments by either landlords or tenants in renter-occupied properties. Another is the public-good nature of R&D, whereby firms capture only a share of the benefits of the information their research produces. Both argue for specific policies that would complement a carbon-pricing regime (Stavins, 2010).

There is a prominent minority view that carbon pricing is little more than a sideshow, due to the fact that sufficiently high carbon prices are politically unattainable and that the only politically feasible path is making carbon-free energy cheaper (not making carbon-intensive energy more costly). The thinking from private industry representatives in the renewables sector tends to be that government subsidies are the answer, although the response from some policy analysts is that government-funded research initiatives should be the prime focus (Stepp and Trembath, 2013; Sachs, 2018). Others recognize that carbon pricing may be the first-best policy for the long term but argue that the best set of approaches for the short term may be those that are politically achievable (Gillis, 2018; Goulder, 2019a). For a comparison of US carbon pricing (carbon taxes and cap-and-trade) with use of a national clean energy standard and a gasoline tax increase, see Goulder and Hafstead (2018).

[6]Two additional advantages of carbon-pricing instruments are that they encourage demand-side conservation, and can raise revenues for governments, which through

There is less agreement among economists regarding the choice of specific carbon-pricing policy instruments, with some supporting carbon taxes (Mankiw, 2006; Nordhaus, 2007) and others cap-and-trade mechanisms (Ellerman *et al.*, 2003; Keohane, 2009). That prompts two questions: How do the two major approaches to carbon pricing compare on relevant dimensions, including but not limited to efficiency, cost-effectiveness, and distributional equity? And which of the two approaches is more likely to be adopted in the future in the United States? Much has been written by academic economists about the first question, and the second question has been addressed from a number of disciplinary perspectives by social scientists, as well as by commentators in the broader policy community.

Among many findings from this survey and synthesis, two major conclusions stand out. One is that the specific designs of carbon taxes and cap-and-trade systems may be more consequential than the choice between the two instruments. The two approaches to carbon pricing are perfectly or nearly equivalent in regard to some issues and attributes while significantly different in regard to some others. But many of these differences fade with specific implementations, as elements of design foster greater symmetry. Indeed, what appears at first to be the dichotomous choice between two distinct policy instruments often turns out to be a choice of design elements along a policy continuum. A second major conclusion is that issues of positive political economy — such as the probability that a particular instrument will actually be adopted and implemented — frequently have normative dimensions, as well. Likewise, normative attributes — ranging from cost-effectiveness to distributional equity — have important implications for any political prognosis.

Normative Theory of Policy Instrument Choice

For much of the past 100 years, economists have considered environmental pollution to be a classic — indeed, textbook — example of a negative externality, an unintentional consequence of production or consumption that reduces another agent's profits or utility (Pigou, 1920). A separate but

judicious use of those revenues, can lower social costs of the policies (Goulder and Hafstead, 2018; Metcalf, 2019b).

related strand of literature, stemming from Ronald Coase's work (1960), has identified environmental pollution essentially as a public-good problem — that is, a problem of incomplete property rights. These two perspectives can lead to different policy prescriptions for climate change: carbon taxes versus tradable carbon rights.[7]

For some 40 years prior to Coase (1960), the literature focused on a single economic response to the problem of externalities: taxing the externality in question. In principle, a regulator could ensure that emitters would internalize the damages they caused by charging a tax on each unit of pollution equal to the marginal social damages at the efficient level of pollution control (Pigou, 1920). Such a system makes it worthwhile for firms to reduce emissions to the point where their marginal abatement costs are equal to the common tax rate. Hence, marginal abatement costs will be equated across sources, satisfying the necessary condition for cost-effectiveness. In theory, this will hold both in the short term and in the long term by providing incentives for diffusion (Jaffe and Stavins, 1995) and innovation (Newell *et al.*, 1999) of low-cost abatement technologies. Following Coase (1960), it became possible to think about solving the problem of pollution as one of clarifying poorly defined property rights. If resources such as clean air and water could be recognized as a form of property, whose corresponding rights could be traded in a market, private actors could allocate the use of this property in a cost-effective way. Some 50 years ago, Thomas D. Crocker (1966) and J. H. Dales (1968) each proposed a system of transferable discharge permits that could provide such a market solution: the regulator need only designate the total quantity of emissions allowed (the cap), distribute rights corresponding to this total, and allow individual sources of emissions to trade the permits until an optimal allocation had been reached. This was the fundamental thinking behind what is known as cap-and-trade.[8]

Under this approach, an allowable overall level of pollution is established by the government (not necessarily at the efficient level) and allocated among firms in the form of tradable allowances. Firms that keep their emissions below their allotted level may sell their surplus allowances

[7]Both the Pigouvian (externality) and Coasian (property rights) approaches are examples of missing markets (Arrow, 1969).

[8]Cap-and-trade systems should not be confused with emission-reduction-credit systems or offset systems, whereby permits are assigned when a source reduces emissions below some baseline, which may or may not be readily observable (Stavins, 2003).

to other firms or use them to offset excess emissions in other parts of their operations. Under these conditions, it is in the interest of each source to carry out abatement up to the point where its marginal control costs are equal to the market-determined price of tradable allowances. Hence, the environmental constraint is satisfied, and marginal abatement costs are equated across sources, satisfying the condition for cost-effectiveness.[9]

Although the two instruments — carbon taxes and carbon cap-and-trade — may be said to derive respectively from the externality (Pigou, 1920) and property-rights (Coase, 1960) perspectives, the two approaches are more similar than different. A carbon tax would directly place a price on carbon (most likely upstream, where fossil fuels [coal, petroleum, and natural gas] enter the economy), with quantities of carbon use and CO_2 emissions adjusting in response. An upstream carbon cap-and-trade system would constrain the quantity of carbon entering the economy through allowances on the carbon content of the three fossil fuels, with prices emerging indirectly from the market for allowances.

In some cases, what may at first appear to be key differences between the two instruments fade on closer inspection, whereas other apparent differences survive such inspection. I first explore symmetries between carbon taxes and cap-and-trade, and then I turn to significant differences.

Equivalence, Similarities, and Symmetries

To a significant degree, a carbon tax and a commensurate cap-and-trade system are functionally similar, with differences in specific design elements dominating fundamental differences between the instruments themselves (Stavins, 1997; Goulder and Schein, 2013). I examine six areas of symmetry: (1) emissions reductions, (2) abatement costs, (3) possibilities for raising revenue, (4) costs to regulated firms (with respective

[9]In theory, as I discuss later, a number of factors can adversely affect the performance of a cap-and-trade system, including: concentration in the permit market (Hahn, 1984); concentration in the related product market (Malueg, 1990); transaction costs (Stavins, 1995); nonprofit-maximizing behavior, such as sales or staff maximization (Tschirhart, 1984); the preexisting regulatory environment (Bohi and Burtraw, 1992); and the degree of monitoring and enforcement (Montero, 2007). Some of these also affect the performance of pollution taxes.

revenue-raising instruments), (5) distributional impacts, and (6) competitiveness effects. The findings that emerge in regard to these six areas are summarized in Table 2, where I characterize the symmetries between carbon taxes and cap-and-trade as being perfectly equivalent, nearly equivalent, or similar.

Emission Reductions

In the absence of uncertainty, by setting the respective time paths of the tax rate or the emissions cap, commensurate tax and trading instruments can achieve the same emissions reductions. Both instruments can employ an upstream, midstream, or downstream point of regulation (distinct from the point of allocation of allowances). This does not affect aggregate cost in either case, but it can affect decisions about the scope of coverage, and therefore can affect environmental effectiveness, as well as cost-effectiveness. With either carbon tax or cap-and-trade, focusing on the carbon content of fossil fuels upstream could enable a policy to capture up to 98 percent of US CO_2 emissions with a relatively small number of compliance entities — on the order of a few thousand — as opposed to the hundreds of millions of smokestacks, tailpipes, and other sources that emit CO_2 after fossil-fuel combustion (Metcalf, 2007; Stavins, 2007).

Abatement Costs

If firms subject to a policy are operating in a competitive market, they have strong incentives with either instrument to minimize their total costs, which include the sum of abatement costs and tax liability, or the sum of abatement costs and cost of allowance purchases (or net of allowance sales revenue).[10] In both cases, there is an incentive to abate emissions up to the point where each source's marginal abatement cost is equal to the tax rate or the market-determined allowance price. All firms control at the same marginal cost, so the same (minimized) aggregate cost is experienced across the scope of the policy.

[10] Whether firms receive allowances for free (sometimes called "grandfathering") in a cap-and-trade system or via auction, they face the same marginal opportunity cost for emissions.

Table 2. Similarities and differences between carbon taxes and carbon cap-and-trade.

Perfectly equivalent	Nearly equivalent	Similar	Some distinctions	Differences	Significant differences
Incentives for emission reductions					
Aggregate abatement costs					
Effects on competitiveness	Possibilities for raising revenue				
		Costs to regulated firms			
		Distributional impacts			
			Transaction costs		
				Performance in presence of uncertainty	
				Ease of linkage with other jurisdictions	
					Effects on carbon price volatility Interactions with complementary policies
					Potential for market manipulation Complexity and administrative requirements

Considering the temporal dimension of the respective policies, an important question is the relative effect of the two approaches on technological innovation. Here, a series of theoretical explorations have found that a tax and a cap-and-trade system (with auctioned allowances) are equivalent in their incentives for carbon-saving innovation (Milliman and Prince, 1989; Jung *et al.*, 1996), or at least that neither system dominates (Fischer, Parry, and Pizer 2003).[11]

Finally, in principle, offsets for emissions reductions outside of the respective programs can be used with either tax or trading regimes, bringing about additional abatement cost savings (Goulder and Schein, 2013).

Possibilities for Raising Revenue

An important attribute of a carbon tax is that it raises revenue for the government, which can be used for a variety of beneficial public purposes, including but not limited to using the revenue to enable cuts in the rates of distortionary taxes, thereby lowering the net social cost of the overall policy (Bovenberg and Goulder, 1996). More broadly, given the need for government revenues for other purposes as well, this is indeed an important attribute of taxes.

An auction mechanism in a cap-and-trade system can, in principle, accomplish the same outcome (Goulder and Schein, 2013). In this regard, of various cap-and-trade designs, it has been estimated that auctioning and recycling revenue via income tax cuts would be the least costly, although the most costly would be recycling revenue through lump-sum dividends or freely allocated allowances (Parry and Williams, 2010). The results are similar for the use of revenue from a tax.

Because the systems are theoretically equivalent in their abilities to raise revenue, any differences in this regard would be in terms of

---

[11]Throughout this chapter, I frequently include the caveat of considering cap-and-trade systems that include auctioning of allowances, because it is with this design that the symmetry of these price and quantity instruments is greatest.

A related temporal issue is that carbon prices — and, for that matter, performance standards — that devalue existing carbon-intensive capital can have the effect of fostering stranded assets (Rozenberg *et al.*, 2019), which could create political resistance to policies. This can be avoided with policies that target only new investments, as opposed to the existing capital stock, but this would introduce the problems created by vintage-differentiated regulation (Stavins, 2006).

implementation. One possible difference is that given the committee jurisdictions in the US Congress, it could be more difficult to link revenue recycling with a cap-and-trade system than it would be to link revenue recycling with a carbon tax (Metcalf, 2007). This is because in the cap-and-trade case, committees with environmental jurisdiction and those with financial jurisdiction would need to be involved in the legislative process, whereas for a revenue-neutral carbon tax only the financial committees would be necessary. Whether or not this causal chain is the real explanation, there is empirical support for the overall point from global experience, where about 70 percent of cap-and-trade auction revenue has been earmarked for green spending, and 72 percent of carbon tax revenue has been recycled or dedicated to general funds (Carl and Fedor, 2016).

Costs to Regulated Firms (with Revenue-Raising Instruments)

The cost of a carbon tax or cap-and-trade system that includes auctioning greatly depends on the use of the revenue. Compared with a lumpsum redistribution of revenue (rebates), recycling through rate cuts in payroll taxes, individual income taxes, or corporate income taxes may have net costs (after accounting for the benefits of eliminating the excess burden of distortionary taxes) that are 15 percent, 26 percent, and 67 percent lower, respectively (Goulder and Hafstead, 2018).[12]

The results with a cap-and-trade system with complete auctioning of allowances are similar. With a lump-sum rebate, the cost is identical to the rebate paired with a carbon tax. According to one set of estimates, if auction revenue is recycled via cuts in tax rates, then there are "slight differences" in costs, compared with respective cuts in the same tax rates (above) with a carbon tax (Goulder and Hafstead, 2018). If allowances are not auctioned, but given out for free, then the costs are considerably greater than with auctioning: at best, 8 percent higher than if lump-sum rebates are employed, and 200 percent higher than if revenue is recycled through corporate tax rate cuts (Goulder and Haftstead, 2018).

If the comparison is between a cap-and-trade system with freely allocated allowances and an ordinary carbon tax, then the cost differential is

[12]All the numerical estimates in this chapter are from analyses carried out prior to implementation of the Tax Cuts and Jobs Act of 2017. One effect of that set of tax reforms would be to lessen the magnitude of the efficiency gains that could be achieved from further cuts in corporate tax rates (Metcalf, 2019b).

significant. Free allocation could increase regulatory costs of carbon cap-and-trade enough that the sign of the efficiency impact could conceivably be reversed from positive to negative net benefits (Parry *et al.*, 1999). On the other hand, as I discuss later, free allocation of allowances would meet with much less political resistance.

It might appear that cap-and-trade systems offer greater opportunities to protect the profits of regulated firms (through free allocation of allowances), but, as I discuss later, the same can be accomplished under a tax regime through inframarginal tax exemptions for emissions below a specified level.

Distributional Impacts

In principle, either instrument can be designed to be roughly equivalent to the other in distributional terms. If allowances are auctioned, a cap-and-trade system looks much like a carbon tax from the perspective of regulated firms. Likewise, if a carbon tax system includes tradable tax exemptions for a specified quantity of emissions (i.e., the tax is levied only on emissions above a specified amount), then a carbon tax can resemble a cap-and-trade system with freely allocated allowances (Goulder and Schein, 2013).[13] This is because inframarginal tax exemptions have the same effect as freely allocated allowances in a cap-and-trade system: they allow a specified quantity of emissions for which a compliance entity need not pay.

Goulder and Haftstead (2018) and others have examined minimum free allocations that could make firms whole in terms of fully compensating them for their compliance costs. In general, these turn out to be a relatively small share of allowances yet produce significant decreases in overall costs (with auctioning and recycling of the remainder of allowances). In theory, a similar approach is conceivable with a carbon tax system, namely tradable exemptions to the carbon tax for emissions up to some threshold where the tax begins (Goulder and Hafstead, 2018). Household distributional impacts also can be identical, depending on two elements of design — the extent of free emissions, and the use of revenue. This emerges from an assessment of two components of household

[13] A compliance entity that receives more exemptions than needed may sell the exemptions to other entities.

impacts of a carbon price. One of these has been termed "use-side impacts," reflecting how a policy affects relative prices of goods and services purchased by households, in other words, impacts that take place through household expenditures. The other has been termed "source-side impacts" reflecting how the policy affects nominal wages, capital, and transfers, in other words, impacts that take place through household income (Goulder and Hafstead, 2018; Goulder *et al.*, 2018; Metcalf, 2019a, 2019b). On the use side, carbon pricing is generally regressive (ignoring the return of tax revenue), due to changes in the prices of goods and services. Although the degree of regressivity can be altered by the use of the revenue, this effect remains regressive (Goulder and Hafstead, 2018).[14]

However, on the source side, changes in wage and capital income (as well as government transfers) are generally progressive.[15] Lump-sum recycling of the revenue makes this very progressive. Using the revenue instead for cuts in corporate tax rates, the effect is still progressive, although somewhat less so. Most important, in most cases (in the models employed by Goulder and Hafstead, 2018, and others), the overall (useside plus source-side) impact tends to be progressive. Because source-side impacts dominate use-side impacts for most cases where there is revenue recycling (tax rate cuts in payroll or individual income taxes), the overall impact of carbon taxes — or cap-and-trade with 100 percent auctioning of allowances and the same recycling through tax rate cuts — is progressive. Using the tax or auction revenue for lump-sum rebates is even more progressive. Hence, there is a trade-off, namely that by using approaches that are more cost-effective (tax rate cuts), the progressivity is less than it is with lump-sum rebates (most progressive, but most costly because distortionary taxes are unaffected).

[14]This discussion abstracts from the fact that there can be a mix of winners and losers in any group, which is missed by focusing on averages.

[15]This reflects the fact that carbon-intensive industries (which face the greatest burden from a carbon tax) tend to be relatively capital-intensive. As a result, the burden of a carbon tax falls more on capital than on labor and tends to reduce returns to capital more than returns to labor. Because capital income represents a larger share of total income for wealthier households than for poorer households, the impacts from reduced returns to capital are progressive.

Competitiveness Effects

A frequently expressed concern about new proposals for carbon-pricing policies is their impact on competitiveness. The concern is that by increasing the costs of producing carbon-intensive goods and services within a jurisdiction, there will be a shift in comparative advantage to the production of those same goods and services in other jurisdictions that do not face commensurate climate policy compliance costs. In theory, this can produce "leakage" of economic activity and of related emissions.

In reality, such leakage may be relatively modest, particularly if the emissions occur in nontraded sectors, such as electricity generation, transportation, and residential buildings, but energy-intensive manufacturing industries could face incentives to relocate (Aldy and Pizer, 2015). Additional emissions leakage may occur through international energy markets because countries with climate policies reduce their consumption of fossil fuels and drive down fuel prices, and those countries without such policies may increase their fuel consumption in response to the lower prices (Aldy and Stavins, 2012).

These impacts on competitiveness would be anticipated equally with either type of carbon-pricing policy instrument (and with virtually any meaningful CO_2-limiting policy, for that matter). The impacts on energy-intensive manufacturing can be mitigated — in theory — through specific elements of policy design with either instrument. With a carbon tax, border adjustments — a tax on imports of products from countries without commensurate climate policies — can be employed. With a cap-and-trade system, an allowance requirement can be employed for those same imports, together with an output-based updating allocation of allowances (Goulder and Schein, 2013), although leakage through international energy markets may remain.

Differences and Distinctions

In theory, there are also some significant differences and distinctions between the two main approaches to carbon pricing. I examine eight such areas: (1) performance in the presence of uncertainty about benefits and costs, (2) price volatility, (3) interactions with complementary policies, (4) potential market manipulation, (5) transaction costs, (6) ease of linkage with policies in other jurisdictions, (7) complexity and administration, and (8) political resistance to the simplest forms of both instruments.[16] The findings that emerge in regard to these eight areas are summarized in Table 2, where I characterize the comparison between carbon taxes and cap-and-trade as representing significant differences, differences, or some distinctions.

Uncertainty about Benefits and Costs

Significant uncertainty characterizes the benefits and the costs of environmental protection. For two decades following Weitzman's (1974) classic paper, "Prices vs. Quantities," it was generally acknowledged that benefit uncertainty on its own has no effect on the identity of the efficient policy instrument, but that cost uncertainty could have significant effects, depending on the relative slopes of the marginal benefit (damage) and marginal cost functions.[17] In particular, in the presence of cost uncertainty when (the absolute value of) the marginal cost function exceeds that of the marginal benefit function, then — in expected value terms — a price instrument, such as a tax, is likely to be more efficient (smaller deadweight loss due to mistaken predictions of future costs) than a quantity instrument, such as a cap-and-trade system. When the opposite is the case — slope of the marginal benefit function exceeds slope of the marginal cost function — then a cap-and-trade instrument would be more efficient.[18]

---

[16]An additional difference, noted by Goulder and Schein (2013), is the potential for wealth transfers to oil-exporting nations (that have market power) if those countries choose to behave strategically in response to the imposition of a cap-and-trade system in the United States, with the result that policy-generated rents can be transferred in part from the domestic economy to the oil-exporting countries. In theory, the same phenomenon would not arise in response to the imposition of a US carbon tax.

[17]Weitzman's (1974) model assumed uncertainty regarding the level (intercept), but not the slope of the marginal abatement cost function, and assumed no correlation between benefit uncertainty and cost uncertainty. Also, the original analysis considered a situation where the regulator makes a one-time choice of instrument. Subsequent work (as discussed later), relaxed these assumptions.

[18]Intuition for this result is that a steep marginal benefit function suggests large gains or losses in the benefits of abatement with relatively small changes in abatement levels. A tax fixes the emissions price but allows the quantity of emissions to vary, whereas a quantity instrument fixes the emissions (abatement) level and allows the price to vary. Hence, the quantity instrument is favored when the marginal benefit function is steeper than the

In the Weitzman (1974) analysis, benefit uncertainty has no effect on the relative efficiency of the two instruments. However, 20 years after Weitzman's work, it was noted that when there is simultaneous and correlated uncertainty about marginal benefits and marginal costs, and marginal benefits are positively correlated with marginal costs, then it is more likely than it is solely on the basis of the usual relative slopes analysis to favor the relative efficiency of the quantity instrument (Stavins, 1996). The opposite result holds if there is a negative correlation between benefit and cost uncertainty.[19]

It would take another two decades (Karp and Traeger, 2018) before any use was made in the climate policy context of the findings from Stavins (1996), which drew on an important insight in Weitzman's original analysis. Much sooner than that, however, Newell and Pizer (2003) and others (Hoel and Karp, 2002) applied the Weitzman analysis to the circumstances of climate change. Newell and Pizer reasoned that because GHGs accumulate in the atmosphere (with CO_2 remaining in the atmosphere in excess of 100 years), changes in emissions in a specific period of time do not significantly alter atmospheric concentrations. Furthermore, climate change is itself a stock externality; that is, climate change is a function of the atmospheric stock of GHGs, not the emissions *per se* at any point in time.

Newell and Pizer (2003) and others found that this implies that the marginal damage function (for any period) is relatively flat, which means that the marginal benefit function (of emissions reductions for that period)

---

marginal cost function. On the other hand, a steep marginal cost function suggests that large increases in the costs of abatement take place with relatively small changes in abatement levels. Hence, a price instrument is favored.

[19] Intuition for this result is that if emission taxes are used to control pollutant emissions, firms will respond to unexpectedly high marginal control costs by reducing their control efforts. But if there is a positive correlation between uncertain benefits and uncertain costs, then at the same time that firms are reducing their control efforts, the marginal benefits of those efforts will be unexpectedly great. Hence, the firms' natural response to the emission tax will be less appropriate than indicated by the simple relative slopes rule. On the other hand, if there is a negative correlation between the marginal benefits and marginal costs of control, then unexpectedly high marginal control costs will be associated with unexpectedly low marginal benefits, meaning that a tax instrument will lead firms to reduce their control efforts (because of high control costs) at times at which the marginal benefits of those efforts are unusually low; hence, the tax instrument will lead to particularly appropriate actions.

is also relatively flat, whereas the costs of emissions reductions are a function of contemporaneous policies. Hence, the current-period marginal benefits would have a smaller slope (in absolute value) than current-period marginal costs. Hence, the standard Weitzman analysis would suggest that the more efficient climate policy instrument under conditions of uncertainty about abatement costs will be a price instrument, such as a carbon tax, rather than a quantity instrument, such as cap-and-trade.[20]

This comparison refers to the relative slopes of marginal benefits and marginal costs in a given time period, but the marginal damages of a unit of emissions during some time period (such as the current period) are equivalent to the present discounted value of the future stream of marginal damages, otherwise known as the social cost of carbon (Weitzman, 2014, 2017; Interagency Working Group on Social Cost of Carbon, 2016). In other words, with a stock pollutant, the marginal benefit of reducing emissions in the current period equals the present discounted value of the stream of reductions of current and future marginal damages. This is the appropriate comparison in the climate change context (Pizer and Prest, 2019).

In a recent analysis, Karp and Traeger (2018) utilize this comparison of the slopes of the current marginal cost of CO_2 emissions reduction and the marginal benefits (avoided social cost of carbon) of a current unit of CO_2 emissions reduction. They do this by applying to climate change policy the earlier analysis of the relative efficiency of price and quantity instruments in the presence of simultaneous and correlated benefit and cost uncertainty (Stavins, 1996). They note that an important source

[20]At about the same time the paper by Newell and Pizer (2003) appeared, Hoel and Karp (2002) independently came to the same conclusion regarding stock externalities, but with a different analytical model. In their framework, the ranking of price versus quantity instruments also depends on the discount rate and the rate of decay of the stock, with higher discount and decay rates favoring price instruments. They examined both open-loop policy (as did Newell and Pizer, 2003), where price and quantity are set by the regulator and unchanged, and closed-loop (feedback) policy, where the price and quantity can be adjusted over time by the regulatory authority in response to new information. In the latter case, the relative efficiency of the two instruments also depends on the length of intervals between adjustments of prices and quantities by the regulator. They parameterized their models to examine the control of GHGs and found — like Newell and Pizer (2003) — that prices (carbon taxes) are preferred to quantities (cap-and-trade). Also see Hoel and Karp (2001).

of uncertainty is technological change, which brings about positive correlation between uncertainty of abatement costs and uncertainty of (stock-related) damages, because technological change lowers current abatement costs, as well as future abatement costs, due to the persistence of the technology effect. Then, in their closed-loop (feedback) model, future policymakers will take these lower costs into account, and reduce future targeted emissions, and lower the expected future pollution stock in the atmosphere.

Hence, today's marginal damage function shifts downward, because the damages of emissions now are the discounted present value of the future stream of damages. On this basis, they find a positive correlation between uncertain benefits and uncertain costs. And, as previously demonstrated (Stavins, 1996), such a positive correlation tends to favor a quantity instrument, compared with the finding from the usual relative slopes comparison, which considers only cost uncertainty and ignores correlated benefit and cost uncertainty.

This analysis does not lead to an unambiguous finding favoring the quantity or the price instrument. Rather, the implication of the analysis by Karp and Traeger (2018) is that what was thought to be an unambiguous result from the stock externality application (Newell and Pizer, 2003) of the Weitzman (1974) relative slopes rule becomes ambiguous; that is, it becomes an empirical question of the magnitude of the effect from Stavins (1996), compared with the basic effect of the relative slopes (Weitzman, 1974; Hoel and Karp, 2002; Newell and Pizer, 2003), where the slopes compare current marginal costs with current marginal damages measured as the avoided social cost of carbon. The simple ranking of price over quantity instruments for the stock externality of climate change no longer holds.[21]

Karp and Traeger (2018) calibrate their dynamic model, drawing largely on the DICE model (Nordhaus, 2015), and find that in many cases, the quantity instrument is superior to the price instrument. At a minimum,

---

[21] In a distinct, but related analysis, Pizer and Prest (2019) find that with policy updating (closed-loop model), if firms have expectations regarding future policy updates and if the quantity instrument is tradable over time, the quantity instrument can be preferred on efficiency grounds to the price instrument, although their "main finding" is that the comparative advantage of one instrument versus the other depends more on firms' information and expectations about policy updates than on the relative slopes of marginal benefits and marginal costs.

their analysis suggests that quantities can be (but are not necessarily) superior on efficiency grounds to price instruments for addressing climate change. In other words, the case for carbon taxes compared with cap-and-trade in the presence of uncertainty "is much weaker than widely believed" (Karp and Traeger, 2018, 24).[22]

Carbon Price Volatility

Putting aside the issue of long-term benefit and cost uncertainty, another issue is short-term price volatility. It is straightforward that the tax approach eliminates the potential for short-term price volatility, which can surely exist under a cap-and-trade system. This is essentially an issue of two different types of endogeneity. Whereas prices are endogenous (and hence subject to fluctuation and volatility) under a cap-and-trade mechanism, emissions are endogenous under a carbon tax (Goulder and Schein, 2013). Greater certainty about mitigation cost via a carbon tax (or a price collar in a cap-and-trade system — see later sections) reduces the certainty about the quantity of emissions allowed (Aldy and Stavins, 2012).

Such cost uncertainty (price volatility) in a cap-and-trade system can be an impediment to capital investment (Pindyck, 2017; Metcalf, 2019b) and could undermine political support for climate policy and discourage investment in new technologies, as well as research and development (R&D) (Aldy and Stavins, 2012). From an economic perspective, it makes sense to allow emissions (of a stock pollutant) to vary from year to year with economic conditions that affect aggregate abatement costs.

This happens automatically with a carbon tax, but with a cap-and-trade system, such temporal flexibility needs to be built in through provisions for banking and borrowing of allowances, which redefines the cap as a limit on cumulative emissions over a period of years, rather than a cap on annual emissions (Aldy and Stavins, 2012). Conversely, a carbon tax can employ measures to automatically adjust to meet some quantity target (Hafstead *et al.*, 2017; Metcalf, 2019b), as I consider next when examining hybrid policy instruments.

---

[22] Given the very recent vintage of the analysis by Karp and Traeger (2018), I have placed the issue — performance in the presence of benefit and cost uncertainty — within the section on differences rather than the previous section on similarities.

Interactions with Complementary Policies

It is rarely, if ever, the case that carbon-pricing instruments are considered as the sole policy to be used to address climate change. More often, carbon pricing — whether a carbon tax or cap-and-trade — is considered as one of a suite of policy measures. If there are other market failures present, such as the principal-agent problem that affects decisions regarding adoption of thermal insulation in renter-occupied buildings or the public-good nature of information produced by carbon-friendly R&D activities, then there are solid economic arguments in favor of complementing a carbon-pricing regime with other regulatory policies (Schmalensee and Stavins, 2017b). But if such additional market failures are not present (and if the complementary policies are not targeting sources outside of the scope of the carbon-pricing regime), then differences emerge between carbon taxes and cap-and-trade.

With a cap-and-trade regime, there are two possibilities of concern. One is that a complementary regulatory policy targets sources under the cap of the cap-and-trade system. The other is that a policy (of any type) is geographically nested within the area of a cap-and-trade system. In either of these situations, the results are threefold (Schmalensee and Stavins, 2017b): (1) if the complementary policy is binding, there is no additional reduction in emissions due to the complementary policy, but rather a relocation of emissions to other sectors under the overall cap (100 percent leakage), unless the complementary policy renders the allowance price floor binding; (2) with the binding complementary policy, marginal abatement costs are no longer equated among all sources, and so aggregate abatement costs are greater than without the additional policy; and (3) allowance prices are suppressed, raising concerns about the ability of the cap-and-trade system to encourage technological change (except in the sector directly regulated by the complementary policy). Under these circumstances, the addition of a "complementary" policy increases abatement costs and lowers allowance prices but does not — on net — reduce emissions (Goulder and Stavins, 2011).

When a carbon tax is paired with complementary policies, the emissions-leakage effect (and allowance price suppression) does not occur, and the complementary policy will serve to reduce emissions below the level that the tax alone would achieve. However, the combination of carbon tax and complementary policy is, like in the cap-and-trade case, not cost-effective, because marginal abatement costs are no longer identical for all sources. It would cost less to abandon the complementary policies and rely instead on a boosted carbon tax rate to achieve the same degree of aggregate emissions reduction.

Corruption and Market Manipulation

With any policy there is a possibility of various kinds of corruption, including attempts by private firms to manipulate the market. For this reason, cap-and-trade systems require regulatory oversight. In the large European Union Emissions Trading System (EU ETS) for GHG control, there was a single and quite significant case of theft of allowances in 2011 in the Czech Republic, as well as hacking of allowance accounts in a number of other countries (Metcalf, 2019b).

The parallel concern with a carbon tax system would presumably be tax evasion of one kind or another, a significant problem in many countries, but not of sufficient magnitude in the United States to present a major concern for a carbon tax (Metcalf, 2019b). However, much the same can be said of concerns for market manipulation in cap-and-trade systems within this country, because there has been only a single case of fraudulent activity reported (in the Regional Clean Air Incentives Market [RECLAIM] program), which was successfully prosecuted by the US Department of Justice. In the large and ambitious California cap-and-trade system and the electricity-sector system in the Northeast (Schmalensee and Stavins, 2017b), there have been no reported cases of attempted fraud. That said, it is difficult to contest the judgment of one analyst that in the United States "the risk of cybertheft from electronic registries in a cap and trade system is likely to present a greater problem than the risk of tax evasion in a carbon tax" (Metcalf, 2019b, 82).

Transaction Costs

A cap-and-trade system is likely to involve the trading of allowances among firms (unless the initial allocation matches the cost-effective-equilibrium allocation), and, therefore, there is the possibility of transaction costs, which increase aggregate compliance costs. More important, if transaction costs take the form of volume discounts, then with such decreasing marginal transaction costs, the equilibrium allocation through market activity is no longer independent of the initial allocation, removing a key political attraction of cap-and-trade (Stavins, 1995). But historically, transaction costs — of any form — have not been empirically significant in implemented systems (Schmalensee and Stavins, 2017b). The sulfur dioxide (SO_2) allowance trading system demonstrated that in properly designed systems, private markets can render transaction costs minimal (Schmalensee and Stavins, 2013).

Ease of Linkage with Policies in Other Jurisdictions[23]

Linkage of policies across jurisdictions — connections among policy systems that allow emission reduction efforts to be redistributed across systems — is of great potential value because it: (1) can facilitate cost savings by allowing firms to take advantage of lower-cost abatement opportunities in other jurisdictions; (2) may improve the functioning of individual markets by reducing market power by enlarging the trading market and reduce total price volatility by thickening markets; (3) can provide political benefits to linking parties by conveying a sign of momentum as political jurisdictions band together; (4) provides administrative economies of scale; and (5) allows for distributional equity among nations under existing international climate agreements (United Nations, 2015) without sacrificing cost-effectiveness (Bodansky *et al.*, 2015; Mehling *et al.*, 2018).

Cap-and-trade systems generate a natural unit of exchange for linkage — allowances denominated in units of carbon content of fossil fuels or CO_2 emissions. Hence, it would appear to be easier to link a domestic US cap-and-trade system with other countries, particularly if they employ cap-and-trade approaches (Jaffe *et al.*, 2010). Recent research has found that through appropriate mechanisms, it is possible that linkage could be carried out between a domestic US carbon tax system and certain other policy instruments in other jurisdictions, although linkage of such heterogeneous policy instruments is considerably more challenging than the standard variety of linking two cap-and-trade regimes (Metcalf and Weisbach, 2012; Bodansky *et al.*, 2015; Mehling *et al.*, 2018).

[23]Also in the international domain, Weitzman (2014, 2017) has argued that negotiating a specific, single carbon price (if nations have already agreed to hold such a negotiation and abide by the negotiated price, where each country has one vote and accepts majority rule) is easier than negotiating a set of quantity limits.

Complexity and Administration

The simplest cap-and-trade system will involve greater complexity than the simplest carbon tax. But more important than the relative complexity of the two approaches is the fact that greater complexity in design elements frequently translates into greater administrative burden for the system's implementation.

A cap-and-trade system requires government to track allowances (at the end of compliance periods), possibly hold auctions, and develop other necessary rules. These include rules to prevent fraud and abuse, although as noted previously, issues of fraud have been rare with previous cap-and-trade applications. In contrast, a carbon tax is administratively simple and relatively straightforward to implement, given that the tax could incorporate existing methods for fuel-supply monitoring and reporting to the regulatory authority. It is reasonable to conclude that textbook applications of carbon taxes and cap-and-trade would yield greater administrative costs with the latter instrument (Goulder and Schein, 2013).

Two possibly minor caveats are warranted. First, experience with cap-and-trade systems has demonstrated that the actual (marginal) costs of trading institutions have not been significant (Schmalensee and Stavins, 2017b), although the fixed costs of setting up such institutions would presumably be greater than the fixed costs of setting up a carbon tax, because the latter could build on existing fossil fuel excise taxes. Second, experience also suggests that a simple tax proposal might become considerably more complex as it passes through the legislature. Whether a policy as important as a national carbon tax would turn out to be "simple" in its design and implementation is at least open to question. That said, it is also true that the simplest cap-and-trade regimes become more complex as they work their way through legislative processes.

Political Resistance and Support for the Two Instruments

A common thread throughout this chapter is the endorsement of the principle that realistic versions of alternative policies should be analyzed and compared (Hahn and Stavins, 1992). In a recent presentation, Goulder (2019a, 2019b) goes further by suggesting that when comparing proposed climate policy instruments in an ex ante net present value analysis, it would be appropriate and desirable to weight the net benefits of each alternative by the probability of it being implemented within some period of time.

These probabilities would presumably be dependent on current and future political factors.[24] In any event, this suggestion recognizes that issues of positive political economy may have normative dimensions, as well.

In summary, Table 2 characterizes carbon taxes and cap-and-trade as being perfectly equivalent in regard to three attributes — incentives for emission reductions, aggregate abatement costs, and effects on competitiveness; nearly equivalent in regard to possibilities for raising revenue; similar in regard to costs to regulated firms, and distributional impacts; exhibiting some distinctions in regard to transaction costs; different in regard to performance in presence of uncertainty; and significantly different in regard to effects on carbon price volatility, interactions with complementary policies, potential for market manipulation, and complexity and administrative requirements.

Hybrid Policy Instruments and a Policy Continuum

Some remaining differences between carbon taxes and cap-and-trade can diminish with implementation because hybrid policies that combine specific features of tax and cap-and-trade instruments can blur distinctions between the two. As already noted, the government can auction allowances in a cap-and-trade system, thereby reproducing many of the properties of a tax approach. In addition, mechanisms that reduce short-term price volatility and/or long-term price uncertainty in a cap-and-trade system bring it closer to a tax approach (Roberts and Spence, 1976). These design elements include cost-containment mechanisms that place a cap or collar on allowance prices, banking that creates a floor under prices, and borrowing that provides flexibility similar to a tax. Hence, elements of design can foster symmetry of the two carbon-pricing instruments.

[24] In simple terms, as David Leonhardt (2019) has written in the *New York Times*, policies "are not efficient if they never pass." However, making this analytical approach operational would require quantifying the probability of a specific policy being implemented (or rather, implementable) over some period of time, which would be a function of current and future political factors. It is possible that quantifying those probabilities in a regulatory impact analysis could render the overall analysis less useful because of the degree of uncertainty that would inevitably be associated with the respective politically determined implementation probabilities.

The use of a safety valve (hard price ceiling) or a price floor in a cap-and-trade system would appear to eliminate the key attribute that is strongly favored by environmental advocates, namely, lack of uncertainty regarding the quantity of emissions (Metcalf, 2019b), because a price ceiling is achieved through the provision of additional allowances, whereas a binding price floor results in fewer emissions than the stated cap level (Goulder and Schein, 2013). However, in principle, the additional allowances the government offers for sale at the safety-valve price can come from an allowance reserve set aside for this purpose, or there can be borrowing from future allocations, so that total allowed emissions over time are unchanged, which is appropriate for the stock externality of climate change (Stavins, 2008). Of course, the use of borrowing in a cap-and-trade regime raises a set of concerns that have prevented the adoption of this element in previous applications.

Likewise in a carbon tax system, certain elements of design can bring it closer to the properties of cap-and-trade. For example, emissions uncertainty with a tax can be reduced through a variety of means (Aldy *et al.*, 2017), including a formula for adjusting the tax (Hafstead *et al.*, 2017), periodic government review (Aldy, 2018), or dedicating some tax revenue for emission mitigation activities (Goulder and Schein, 2013; Murray, Pizer, and Reichert 2017). Some of these approaches may be thought of as rendering a pure carbon tax a hybrid instrument, just as a price collar may be said to render a pure cap-and-trade system a hybrid instrument. Thus, the dichotomous choice between carbon taxes and cap-and-trade can be a choice of design elements along a policy continuum (Weisbach, 2010). Ultimately, the design of either instrument is very consequential, possibly more important than the choice between the two (Stavins, 1997; Keohane *et al.*, 1998; Goulder and Schein, 2013; Goulder and Hafstead, 2018).

Positive Theory of Policy Instrument Choice

To examine the most likely future choice in the United States between the two types of carbon-pricing instruments, this part of the chapter applies the positive theory of policy instrument choice in the environmental realm to the choice between carbon taxes and cap-and-trade. First, I review the major components of positive theory in this realm, and then I turn to an application of the model to the choice between taxes and trading.

Components of Positive Theory

Drawing on the metaphor of a political market, we can identify three components of a positive theory of policy instrument choice: political demand for a particular policy instrument, political supply of that policy instrument, and the equilibrium outcome in a legislature (Keohane *et al.*, 1998).

Political Demand for Policy Instruments

The effective demand for policy instruments comes largely from firms and interest groups (Stigler, 1971; Peltzman, 1976; Becker, 1983). Firms tend to demand those policy instruments that promise the highest profits — or lowest losses — from regulation, and some instruments augment profits through the generation of rents and the erection of entry barriers (Buchanan and Tullock, 1975; Maloney and McCormick, 1982). In addition, individual firms may support policy instruments that impose costs, as long as those costs are less than the industry average, giving them some competitive advantage (Oster, 1982).

Environmental interest groups tend to exercise demand for policy instruments that provide high confidence of low pollutant emissions levels; make benefits visible and may hide costs; offer lower compliance costs, if those lower costs mean more aggressive emissions targets; and keep congressional authority in committees that are typically dominated by pro-environment members (Kelman, 1981).

Political Supply of Policy Instruments

The political supply of policy instruments emanates from legislators (Kalt and Zupan, 1984; Shepsle and Weingast, 1984). In theory, legislators may start from a strong position of status quo bias (Kneese and Schulze, 1975) but favor those policy instruments that provide (visible) benefits but not (visible) costs to their constituents (McCubbins and Sullivan, 1984). Because politicians are risk averse, they prefer control over outcomes, particularly if their constituents are affected (Shepsle and Weingast, 1984). But because constituents typically have very limited information, politicians may engage in symbolic politics or exhibit demands that are consistent with their ideology, rather than their constituents' interests (Kalt and Zupan, 1984).

Political Equilibrium

The equilibrium of these forces of political supply and demand plays out in what may be thought of as a political market. Policy instrument choice takes place in the legislature, where the key commodity is effective support, and the political currency is the accumulation of resources necessary for a legislator's reelection (Keohane *et al.*, 1998). Exchanges occur among legislators, constituents, and interest groups, with the equilibrium yielding the legislative outcome.

Positive Theory of the Choice between Carbon Taxes and Cap-and-Trade

Consistent with the theory, we can separate out demand-and supply-side implications for the choice between carbon taxes and cap-and-trade.[25]

Political Demand

The historical opposition of private industry to pollution taxes results in part from the fact that with the simplest form of taxes, firms pay not only their compliance costs but also the costs associated with tax payments for residual emissions (Buchanan and Tullock, 1975), which will be some amount less than the full amount of tax payments, because some share is passed on to consumers. This also explains the historical and ongoing opposition of private industry to auctioning of allowances in cap-and-trade systems.

Rent generation and the erection of entry barriers helps explain why for many years when market-based instruments were used they most frequently took the form of cap-and-trade systems with freely allocated allowances, where scarcity rents are conveyed to firms, and also provide entry barriers, because new entrants must purchase allowances from incumbent firms, making the rents sustainable (Keohane *et al.*, 1998). On a global basis, this may help explain the ongoing preference from private industry for cap-and-trade mechanisms in the climate context.

[25]For a very different approach to a theory of positive political economy of instrument choice in the context of climate change (which can help explain the recent prominence of the Green New Deal), see Driesen (2019).

Turning to the demand from environmental interest groups, there continues to be a strong preference for cap-and-trade over taxes, in part because these interest groups prefer policies that help obscure the costs but make benefits transparent and visible (Stavins, 1998), although in the United States this political difference has been significantly lessened, due to the successful tarnishing of the Obama administration's CO_2 cap-and-trade proposal as "cap-and-tax" by Republican conservatives and coal-state Democrats.[26] In addition, environmental interest groups may favor cap-and-trade over carbon taxes, because the former keeps the authority in environmental congressional committees, where the advocacy groups have considerable influence, as opposed to the tax and finance committees, which are typically more conservative, and where the environmental groups typically have less influence (Kelman, 1981; Metcalf, 2019b).

Political Supply

For politicians in the legislature, freely allocated allowances in a cap-and-trade system are typically favored over auctioned allowances or a tax, because no money is exchanged at the time of the initial allocation. On the other hand, the revenue from a tax or from auctioned allowances is attractive to the government (Stavins, 1998) and may come to be a major political force on behalf of a future US carbon tax.

A cap-and-trade policy gives legislators considerable control over the outcome for their constituents through the initial free allocation of allowances, because a cost-effective equilibrium is likely to be achieved independently of the initial allocation of allowances (Montgomery, 1972), except under specific, limited circumstances.[27] This independence property is of central political importance and is the primary reason why cap-and-trade systems have been employed in representative democracies, where distributional issues are of paramount importance in mustering support for a policy. In principle, the government can set the overall emissions cap,

---

[26]The cap-and-tax moniker may have derived from the fact that the Obama administration included in its first budget proposal revenue to be obtained from a CO_2 cap-and-trade program with auctioning of 100 percent of allowances.

[27]This property can be violated under specific, but relatively uncommon conditions (Hahn and Stavins, 2012), as well as in the presence of imperfect competition (Fowlie *et al.*, 2016).

whether on the basis of economic efficiency or, more likely, some other grounds, and then leave it up to the legislature to allocate the available number of allowances among sources to build a constituency of support for the initiative without reducing the system's environmental performance or driving up its cost (Joskow and Schmalensee, 1998). This should be contrasted with most public policy proposals — environmental or otherwise — for which the normal course of events is that the political machinations that are necessary to develop sufficient legislative support reduce the effectiveness of the policy and/or drive up its costs.

Thus, cap-and-trade leaves distributional issues up to politicians and provides a straightforward means to compensate burdened sectors and other constituencies. Of course, this political advantage can be an economic disadvantage if it invites particularly harmful rent-seeking behavior. In any event, the compensation associated with free distribution of allowances based on historical emissions can be mimicked under a tax regime through the assignment of specific tax exemptions (Goulder and Schein, 2013), as noted previously.

Although there is a propensity of political processes under cap-and-trade to compensate sectors through free allowance allocations, a carbon tax would be sensitive to the same political pressures, and succumb in other ways, namely through sectoral or other tax exemptions that may reduce environmental achievement or drive up costs. Instead, a cap-and-trade system may be anticipated to lead to battles over the allowance allocation, but these do not raise the overall cost of the program nor affect its climate impacts (Montgomery, 1972).

In terms of symbolic politics, policymakers working in the environmental realm seem to think in terms of pollution quantities, not prices. However, the political process may no longer favor announcing quantity goals (with conventional standards, cap-and-trade, or some other quantity-based approach), as it once did.

Empirical Evidence: What Experience Suggests about Future US Climate Policy

In this section, I turn to an exploration of empirical evidence regarding first the normative aspects and then the positive aspects of the choice between carbon taxes and cap-and-trade. In other words, I seek to identify lessons that can be learned from previous and current applications of these two carbon-pricing instruments.

Empirical Evidence for Normative Assessment of Carbon Taxes and Cap-and-Trade

Although more than 50 carbon-pricing policies have been implemented or are scheduled for implementation worldwide, including 26 carbon taxes and 25 ETSs (Figure 1), I focus on a few of the more prominent examples of taxes and cap-and-trade that can offer the most useful lessons.

Lessons from Experience with Cap-and-Trade Policies

Among the most important applications of cap-and-trade in the United States have been the leaded gasoline phasedown (1982–1987), the sulfur dioxide (SO_2) allowance trading system (1994–2010), NO_x trading (1998–2009), and the RECLAIM (1993–present).[28] In addition, two prominent US cap-and-trade systems address CO_2 emissions — the Regional Greenhouse Gas Initiative (RGGI, 2009–present) and California's system (2013–present); and the world's largest carbon-pricing initiative is the EU ETS (2008–present). Table 3 summarizes the geographic scope, sectoral coverage, time duration, allowance allocation method, cost-containment mechanisms, and environmental and economic performance of these seven important ETSs.

There has also been rights trading for ozone-depleting substances (ODS) in several countries during the ODS phasedown from 1991 to 2000 under the 1987 Montreal Protocol (Klaassen, 1999; Stavins, 2003; US Environmental Protection Agency, 2014), as well as CO_2 cap-and-trade systems in New Zealand, Japan, South Korea, Kazakhstan, Quebec, and other jurisdictions. Also, an international CO_2 cap-and-trade system has been in place since 2008 under Article 17 of the Kyoto Protocol, but because the trading agents are nations, rather than firms, there has been little significant activity, an outcome that was anticipated (Hahn and Stavins, 1999). As I discuss later, cap-and-trade systems are under development, planned, or proposed in many other jurisdictions (Schmalensee and Stavins, 2017a).

Turning to lessons from these experiences, first, in terms of the basics, cap-and-trade has long since proven to be environmentally effective and

[28]The program was a tradable performance standard rather than a textbook cap-and-trade system.

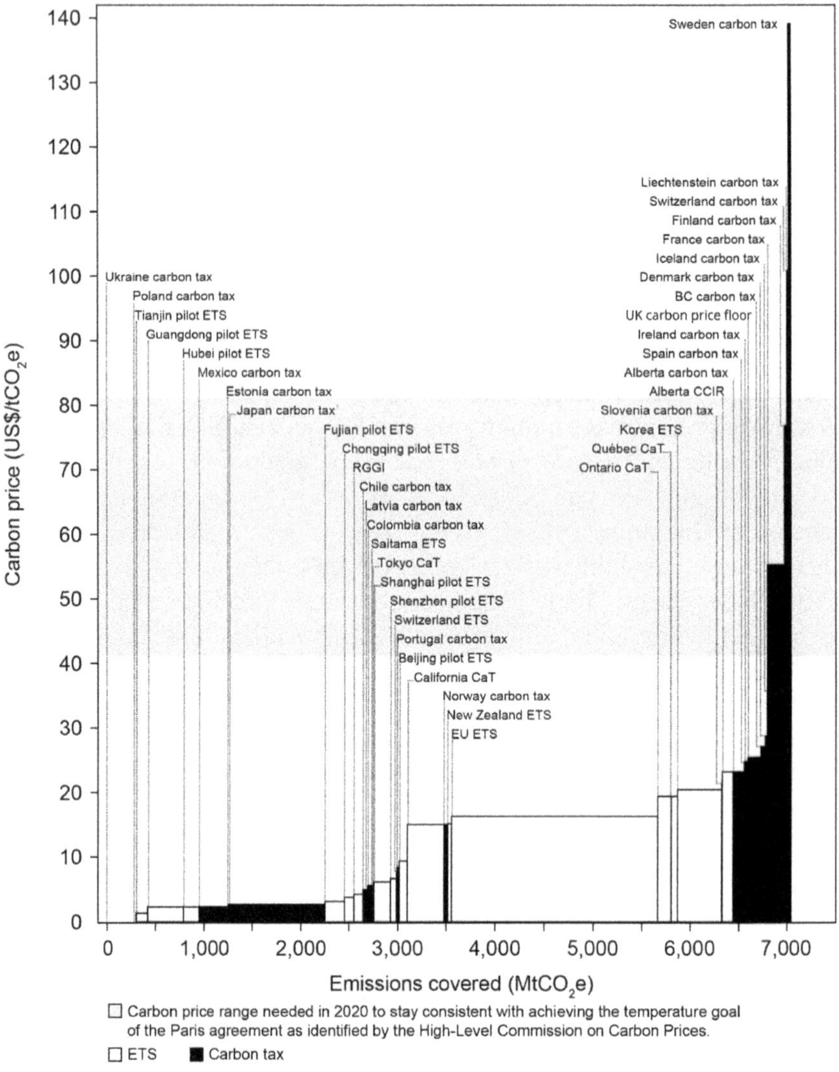

Figure 1. Carbon price and emissions coverage of implemented carbon-pricing initiatives.

Notes: The Australia Emissions Reduction Fund Safeguard Mechanism, British Columbia Greenhouse Gas Industrial Reporting and Control Act, Kazakhstan emissions trading systems, and Washington Clean Air Rule are not shown in this graph as price information is not available for those initiatives. The carbon tax rate applied in Mexico and Norway varies with the fossil-fuel type and use. The carbon tax rate applied in Denmark varies with the greenhouse gas type. The graph shows the average carbon tax rate weighted by the amount of emissions covered at the different tax rates in those jurisdictions.

Source: World Bank Group (2018).

Table 3. Most important cap-and-trade systems.

System	Geographic scope	Coverage and sectors	Time period	Allowance allocation method	Cost-containment mechanisms	Environmental and economic performance
Leaded Gasoline Phasedown	USA	Gasoline from refineries	1982–1987	Free	Banking	Phasedown completed successfully, faster than anticipated, with cost savings of 20 percent or $250 million/year
Sulfur Dioxide Allowance Trading	USA	SO_2 from electric power	1995–2010	Free	Banking	Cut SO_2 emissions by half, with cost savings of $1 billion/year; but market closed due to judicial actions
Regional Clean Air Incentives Market	South Coast Air Quality Management District, CA	NO_x and SO_2 from electric power and industrial sources	1993–present	Free	. . .	Emissions lower than with parallel regulations; unquantified cost savings; electricity crisis caused allowance price spike and temporary suspension of market

(*Continued*)

Table 3. (*Continued*)

System	Geographic scope	Coverage and sectors	Time period	Allowance allocation method	Cost-containment mechanisms	Environmental and economic performance
NO_x Trading in the Eastern United States	12–21 US states	NO_x from electric power and industrial sources	1999–2008	Free	. . .	Significant price volatility in first year; NO_x emissions declined from 1.9 (1990) to .5 million tons (2006); cost savings 40–47 percent
Regional Green-house Gas Initiative	Nine northeastern US states	CO_2 from electric power	2009–present	Nearly 100 percent auction	Banking, cost containment reserve, auction reservation price	Cap nonbinding then barely binding due to low natural gas prices; has generated more than $1 billion for participating states
AB-32 and AB-398 California Cap-and-Trade	California, USA	CO_2 from electric power, industrial, and fuels	2013–2020 2021–2030	Transitions from free to auction	Banking, allowance price containment reserve, auction reservation price	Covers 85 percent of emissions, reduced 40 percent below 1990 by 2030; reduces competitiveness effects without output-based updating allocation; linked with Quebec cap-and-trade system

European Union Emissions Trading System	27 European Union member states plus Iceland, Lichtenstein, and Norway	CO_2 from electric power, large industrial, and aviation	2005–	Transitions from free to increased use of auctions	Banking after 2008, previous use of offsets from CDM	Covers half of emissions, has cut abatement costs by about 50 percent compared with no trading; overallocation by member states in pilot phase; suppressed allowance prices due to "complementary policies," CDM glut, slow economic recovery

Note: CDM = Clean Development Mechanism.

Sources: Adapted from Schmalensee and Stavins (2017b). Sources include: Carlson *et al.* (2000), Cludius *et al.* (2019), Ellerman *et al.* (2000), Ellerman and Buchner (2007), Fowlie, Holland, and Mansur (2012), Keohane (2003), Schmalensee and Stavins (2013, 2017a, 2017b), and US Environmental Protection Agency (1985).

economically cost-effective (lead phasedown, SO_2 allowance trading).[29] For example, it has been estimated that SO_2 trading reduced aggregate abatement costs by more than half, compared with a commensurate, well-designed command-and-control approach (Metcalf, 2019b). The world's most important CO_2 cap-and-trade system — EU ETS — had its share of problems in its pilot phase (Metcalf, 2019b), but it has functioned essentially as anticipated since then (Ellerman *et al.*, 2010). Relatively low allowance prices were a function of: (1) the degree of ambition of the cap; (2) the perverse effect of EU and member state "complementary policies," including those targeting renewable sources of energy and energy efficiency; and (3) the 2008–2009 recession, which reduced energy demand. Of course, the lower allowance prices and fewer emissions reductions that occur with cap-and-trade during a recession are an economic virtue, that is, they are countercyclical, and do not unduly burden industry when it is fundamentally unnecessary and unwise to do so. As with the EU ETS and RGGI, downstream, sectoral programs have been commonly employed, although economy-wide systems have been shown to be feasible (AB-32).

Transaction costs have turned out to be low to trivial, particularly when compliance entities have been homogeneous (lead phasedown, SO_2 allowance trading). In particular, the SO_2 allowance trading system demonstrated that in properly designed systems, private markets can render transaction costs minimal (Schmalensee and Stavins, 2013). In the context of climate policy, CO_2 emissions trading programs have been limited in scope of coverage, in contrast with textbook, upstream trading of rights associated with the carbon content of fossil fuels (World Bank Group, 2016).

It is clear from basic theory and validated by experience that a robust market requires a cap that is significantly below business-as-usual emissions (SO_2 allowance trading, RECLAIM).[30] Likewise, high levels of

---

[29]Lessons learned from experiences in industrialized countries are emphasized, both because these contexts are more relevant to the United States and because of the greater availability of reliable evaluations.

The policy experiences listed in parentheticals in this part of the chapter refer to the sources of evidence for respective lessons.

[30]For an analysis of how other government regulations (and some related judicial decisions) essentially eliminated the SO_2 market beginning in 2006, see Schmalensee and Stavins (2013).

compliance require monitoring, reporting, and verification combined with significant penalties for noncompliance (SO_2 allowance trading). Also, it has been shown to be important for final rules to be established well before commencement of a system's first compliance period to avoid unnecessary price volatility (SO_2 allowance trading, NO_x budget, EU ETS). Turning to specific elements of design, experience argues for systems that allow for a broad set of compliance alternatives, in terms of both timing and technological options. One of the most significant benefits of using carbon pricing — whether tax or cap-and-trade — is simply that technology and uniform performance standards are thereby avoided. Less flexible systems would not have led to the technological change that appears to have been induced by market-based instruments (Bohi and Burtraw, 1992; Ellerman and Montero, 1998; Keohane, 2003; Schmalensee and Stavins, 2013; Calel and Deschezlepretre, 2016), or the induced process innovations that have resulted (Doucet and Strauss, 1994) in previous applications.

Provisions for banking of allowances have proven to be exceptionally important, as such intertemporal trading has represented a large share of the realized gains from trade (lead phasedown, SO_2 allowance trading). In contrast, the absence of banking provisions can lead to price spikes (RECLAIM) and price collapses (EU ETS). More broadly, a changing economy can render a cap nonbinding (RGGI, EU ETS) or drive prices to excessive levels (RECLAIM). Hence, there is a distinct role in cap-and-trade systems for price collars, which reduce the risk of unanticipated allowance price changes and price volatility by combining an auction price floor with an allowance reserve (RGGI, AB-32), a topic to which I return later.[31] On the other hand, excessive constraints on offset use can lead to a thin market that fails to be effective for cost-containment purposes (RGGI, AB-32).

Simplicity is important, and transparent formulae — including for allowance allocations — are difficult to contest or manipulate, particularly if rules are clearly defined up front, without ambiguity. By avoiding any requirements for prior government approval of individual trades,

[31]A laboratory experiment by Holt and Shobe (2016), which compared price collars, as used in RGGI and AB-32, with quantity collars (modeled after the EU ETS Market Stability Reserve), found that the price collar was superior to the quantity collar in terms of reducing allowance price volatility and increasing efficiency.

uncertainty and transaction costs are decreased (lead phasedown, SO_2 allowance trading).

The allocation of allowances is inevitably a major political issue, because of the large distributional impacts that can be involved. A striking and important experience has been that free allowance allocation has proven to foster political support, although it means that the opportunity is foregone to cut the program's overall social cost by refunding revenues from auctioning allowances through cuts of distortionary taxes (SO_2 allowance trading, AB-32). However, empirical experience has revealed that political pressures exist to use auction revenue not for the economist's favorite purpose of cutting distortionary taxes but to fund new or existing government programs or relieve deficits (AB-32, RGGI). Cap-and-trade allowance auctions can and have generated very significant revenue for governments (RGGI, AB-32).

Another prominent political concern with cap-and-trade systems has been the possibility of emissions and economic leakage and related competitiveness impacts. In practice, leakage from cap-and-trade systems can range from nonexistent (lead phasedown) to potentially quite serious (RGGI). It is most likely to be significant for programs of limited geographic scope, particularly in the power sector because of interconnected electricity markets (RGGI, AB-32). Attempts to reduce leakage and competitiveness threats through free allocation of allowances do not address the problem (EU ETS), but an output-based updating allocation — in principle — can do so (AB-32).

Carbon pricing (through cap-and-trade or taxes) may be said to be necessary to address climate change, but it is surely not sufficient, due to the limited sectoral scope of some carbon-pricing regimes, and — more broadly — due to the presence of other market failures that inhibit the perfect functioning of markets. Hence, there can be an appropriate role for complementary policies. But actual suites of so-called complementary policies have frequently conflicted rather than complemented by addressing emissions under the cap, thereby relocating rather than reducing emissions, driving up abatement costs, and suppressing allowance prices (Organization for Economic Cooperation and Development, 2011). This perverse situation has characterized two of the most prominent applications of cap-and-trade in the climate policy context (AB-32, EU ETS).

The degree of perverse interaction of a complementary policy with a cap-and-trade system within which it is nested can be characterized by the difference in marginal abatement costs between the cap-and-trade system and the complementary policy. In the case of California, these marginal costs are known because they are represented by the allowance price in the AB-32 cap-and-trade system, and by a separate allowance price under a distinct trading system that operates in the state's refinery-based Low Carbon Fuel Standard (LCFS). In February 2019, AB-32 allowances were trading at about $16/ton, whereas LCFS allowances were trading at approximately $200/ton (Lithgow, 2019a), representing a dramatic departure from an overall system of cost-effective emissions reduction.

These perverse interactions, frequently characterized as the "waterbed effect" in the European context (Fankhauser *et al.*, 2010; Perino, 2018), may be partially alleviated by planned reforms employing "market stability reserves" in the EU ETS, California, and RGGI (Edenhofer *et al.*, 2017; Perino *et al.*, 2019).

Lessons from Experience with Carbon Taxes

In contrast with the history of cap-and-trade systems, the lion's share of implemented pollution taxes has been focused on CO_2 (or related energy generation), including 26 carbon taxes identified by the World Bank as of 2018. As with cap-and-trade, I focus on the most prominent applications — carbon taxes that are set at particularly high levels in several northern European countries, and the more recent carbon tax in British Columbia.

Northern European Carbon Taxes. European carbon taxes have frequently been elements of broader energy and excise tax reform initiatives, as opposed to a singular focus on reducing CO_2 emissions (Murray and Rivers, 2015). The systems have had different scopes of coverage, different tax rates, and many are coincident with — if not linked with — the EU ETS, making it difficult to assess impacts (Murray and Rivers, 2015). In the 1990s, several northern European countries imposed carbon taxes to limit their GHG emissions as part of broader tax policies.

Norway implemented a carbon tax in 1991 that varied in its level across sectors of the economy, despite the fact that cost-effective abatement would call for a uniform tax. By 1999, facilities using coal paid $24/ton of CO_2 for coal for energy purposes and $19/ton for coal for coking purposes (Bruvoll and Larsen, 2004), but these activities were completely exempted from the carbon tax beginning in 2003. In the transportation sector, by 2009, the Norwegian carbon tax was $58/ton of CO_2 on gasoline and \$34/ton on diesel. In 2009, the carbon tax applied to about 55 percent of Norwegian GHG emissions, whereas an emission-trading scheme linked to the EU ETS covered an additional 13 percent of emissions.[32] In 2003, Norway also introduced a tax of \$33/ton of CO_2 equivalent on hydrofluorocarbons and perfluorocarbons, to slow the growth rate of these potent GHGs. Sweden implemented a carbon tax of \$33/ton of CO_2 in 1991 as a part of a fiscal reform that cut high income tax rates (Speck, 2008). The carbon tax has since increased to approximately \$120/ton of CO_2 (based on the February 2019 exchange rate). When the carbon tax was implemented, Sweden — as a relatively small, open economy — reduced its general energy tax on many of the sources bearing the carbon tax, and refineries, steel, and other primary metal industries received exemptions from the carbon tax (Daugjberg and Pedersen, 2004). In addition, those industries covered by the EU ETS were exempted from the carbon tax, but in 2018, these exemptions were relaxed.[33] The tax has generated considerable revenue for the general budget, as there is no earmarking of tax revenues in Sweden (Government Offices of Sweden, 2019). However, because of its (fully intended) impacts, revenues from the tax on heating fuels, for example, have fallen due to decreased use and consequent erosion of the tax base.

Denmark implemented a carbon tax of about \$18/ton of CO_2 in 1992 and reduced the tax to \$17/ton of CO_2 in 2005, where it has remained (Speck, 2008; World Bank Group, 2018). Manufacturing sectors face lower tax rates, up to 90 percent below the standard rate, depending on their energy intensity.

Finland has imposed a general tax on energy coupled with a surtax based on the carbon content of the energy since 1997. Like other northern European nations, Finland lowers its carbon tax for industries covered by

---

[32] Greenhouse gas emissions in the offshore oil sector, representing 24 percent of Norway's emissions, are covered by both a (lower) carbon tax and the emission-trading scheme.

[33] Since January 1, 2018, previously exempted emissions from combined heat and power plants that are also covered by the EU ETS are being taxed at 11 percent of the full tax rate. The tax level for other heat production covered by the EU ETS increased from 80 to 91 percent of the full rate, whereas industrial facilities covered by the EU ETS are still entirely exempt from the carbon tax. In addition, since January 1, 2018, the carbon tax rate on industrial facilities not covered by the EU ETS became aligned with the general tax rate. Prior to this date, a lower tax rate was applied to these facilities (World Bank Group, 2019).

the EU ETS. Since 2008, the carbon surtax has been about $28/ton of CO_2, although natural gas faces half this rate (World Bank Group, 2018).

Some of the carbon taxes in northern Europe are at the highest levels of any carbon prices worldwide (Figure 1), although implementation has yielded significant variations in the effective tax per unit of CO_2 across fuels and industries within each country, contrary to the cost-effective prescription of a common price on carbon. In addition, fiscal cushioning to the carbon taxes — by adjustments to preexisting energy taxes — and to the EU ETS — by adjustments to preexisting carbon taxes — is common, especially for those industries expressing concerns about their international competitiveness (Aldy and Stavins, 2012). Nevertheless, these countries were the first to demonstrate that carbon taxes could be employed to reduce GHG emissions while raising revenue to finance government spending or lower other tax rates (Organization for Economic Cooperation and Development, 2001). Unfortunately, there is little empirical evidence of the emissions impacts of these taxes.

British Columbia Carbon Tax. The Canadian province of British Columbia has had in place since 2008 a carbon tax that comes closest to the version of an ideal carbon tax typically recommended by economists (Metcalf, 2019b). As such, it has been characterized — like the US SO_2 allowance trading system — as "a grand policy experiment" (Stavins, 1998; Murray and Rivers, 2015). The tax is one part of British Columbia's plan to reduce provincial GHG emissions by 33 percent by 2020 (British Columbia, 2007). The carbon tax is intended to be economy-wide (covering approximately 70–75 percent of emissions).

It began at $7.50/ton of CO_2-equivalent emissions in 2008, increasing by $3.75 per year, and now amounts to $27/ton, but it is scheduled to reach $38/ton in 2021.[34] The tax is collected upstream at the wholesale level (fuel distributors), based on the carbon content of fuels (Duff, 2008), and, according to Metcalf (2019b, 50), covers "carbon emissions of all hydrocarbon fuels burned in the province." Exemptions from the tax include: fuels exported from British Columbia; fuels used by aviation and shipping into or out of the province; operations and fuels used in agriculture (since 2012); all nonfossil–fuel GHG emissions, including from industrial processes, landfills, forestry, and agriculture; and methane

[34]The April 2019 exchange rate has been used to convert Canadian dollars to US dollars.

emissions from the production and transmission of fossil fuels.[35] Originally, by law, 100 percent of the tax revenue was to be refunded through tax cuts to businesses and individuals, with low-income individuals further protected through a targeted tax credit. But, over time, the policy has evolved from using revenues to cut distortionary taxes to more focused use of specific tax cuts for specific sectors and locations (Murray and Rivers, 2015). That said, combining general tax cuts and those targeted to specific sectors, companies, and locations, the current disposition of tax revenues is: 50 percent to business tax rate reductions and corporate income tax credits, 23 percent to personal income tax cuts, and 25 percent to equal lumpsum rebates to households (Goulder and Hafstead, 2018). According to an analysis by Beck *et al.* (2015), when taking into account both its use-and source-side impacts (see earlier), the British Columbia carbon tax turns out to be progressive in its distributional impacts, even before considering the consequences of specific uses of revenue.

In terms of its performance, empirical evidence is unclear. One estimate is that the tax policy has reduced the province's CO_2 emissions by 5–10 percent, with little negative impact on the economy (Metcalf, 2019b), but unknown emissions leakage (Murray and Rivers, 2015). But other research has questioned whether emissions have been reduced (Pretis, 2019). On the other hand, the government has estimated that by 2020, the carbon tax will reduce British Columbia's CO_2 emissions by approximately 3 million tons annually.

Lessons from Experience with Hybrid Policy Instruments

As discussed previously, hybrid policies that combine features of tax and cap-and-trade can blur distinctions between the two. Empirical experiences with cap-and-trade systems suggest a trend of greater use over time of auctioning of allowances, as in the California AB-32/398 system, the RGGI, and the EU ETS.

The blurring of the two approaches can become even more pronounced with the use of cost-containment elements in cap-and-trade systems, which reproduce many of the properties of a tax approach, as do mechanisms that reduce short-term price volatility and/or long-term price

---

[35]Note that virtually all the coal mined in British Columbia is exported (Murray and Rivers, 2015). About 90 percent of the province's coal production is steel-producing coking coal. The province does not use coal for power generation.

uncertainty in a cap-and-trade system. Banking provisions have been common in all CO_2 cap-and-trade systems (and nearly all cap-and-trade systems for other pollutants), but borrowing provisions have only been present implicitly in the form of compliance periods that have ranged from 1 to 5 years.

The California system and RGGI have employed safety-valve prices, $10 in the case of RGGI, and greater than $50 in the California system. Both systems now employ price collars, combining an auction price floor with a price that triggers availability from an allowance reserve. However, these approaches provide a "soft ceiling" on prices (or a soft price collar), because there is a finite supply of allowances in the reserve. Going forward, California's post-2020 system will include a hard ceiling on prices, in which there will be no limit on the supply of allowances available at a specified, escalating price level (Schatzki and Stavins, 2018b).

Empirical Evidence for Positive Assessment of Carbon Taxes and Cap-and-Trade

Some analysts have contended that because the differences in outcomes with the two approaches need not be very great, the key questions to address in deciding between these two policy approaches are which is more politically feasible and which is more likely to be well designed (Furman *et al.*, 2007). To some degree, responses to the first question could be provided by the political revealed preference of individual countries. The number of CO_2 cap-and-trade and carbon tax systems around the world is about the same (World Bank Group, 2018).

Cap-and-Trade Experience

Rather than counting the number of systems, the relative significance of the two approaches can be assessed to some degree by observing the relative mass exhibited in Figure 1, which provides a sense of scope of coverage multiplied by stringency (carbon price).[36] The world's most significant carbon-pricing regime is surely the EU ETS.

---

[36]In addition to these existing cap-and-trade systems, there are other systems in various stages of planning (or at least proposing) in Canada, Chile, China, Costa Rica, Japan, Mexico, Taiwan, Thailand, Turkey, Ukraine, and Vietnam (Schmalensee and Stavins,

A major factor behind the choice of that instrument by the European Commission was the perceived success of the US SO_2 allowance trading program. However, another factor said to have influenced the choice of cap-and-trade over a tax approach was the fact that fiscal measures — such as a carbon tax — require unanimity in the Council of the European Union, whereas most other measures — including cap-and-trade — require only a majority (Metcalf, 2019b). It is for this same reason that an upstream (and hence, economy-wide) system was not employed, because it was thought that since it would appear downstream like a tax, it might require unanimity in the EU Council.

Going forward, other evidence of politically revealed preference for emissions trading comes from China, where after much reflection on cap-and-trade and carbon tax theory, as well as the experience of its six pilot provincial and municipal ETSs, the government chose to proceed with a national ETS, although it should be noted that it is not cap-and-trade per se, but rather a national set of sectoral tradable performance standards (Goulder and Morgenstern, 2018; Pizer and Zhang, 2018).[37]

In December 2018, nine northeastern states plus the District of Columbia announced the Transportation and Climate Initiative, intended to reduce GHG emissions from the transportation sector, with the design of the mechanism to be completed by the end of 2019. The announcement referred to the development of a "market-based policy," with much of the original thrust emphasizing the potential use of a tax mechanism for

---

2017a), as well as at the subnational level in the United States, including New Mexico (Lithgow, 2019d), New Jersey, Oregon (Lithgow, 2019e), and Washington (Lithgow, 2019f). There are carbon tax proposals at various stages in Brazil, Ivory Coast, and the Netherlands (World Bank Group, 2018), plus subnational proposals in Maine (Lithgow, 2019b), Massachusetts, New Hampshire (Lithgow, 2019c), and Washington.

[37]China's new Ministry of Ecology and Environment circulated a work plan in April 2019 for its ETS, originally "launched" in December 2017. A trial ETS for the electricity-generation sector is scheduled to commence in November 2019, with the actual market — covering 80 percent of China's generators, which emit about 3–3.5 billion tons of CO_2 annually — expected to start in 2020. Over the subsequent 5 years, the plan is to bring petrochemicals, chemicals, building materials, steel, nonferrous metals, paper production, and aviation sectors under the system. Initially, allowances will be distributed freely, with auctioning commencing sometime between 2020 and 2025. If China meets this plan, the ETS will cover about 7 billion tons of CO_2 emissions annually, making the system more than four times the size of the EU ETS, currently the world's largest (Reklev, 2019). In the longer term, it is anticipated that the TPS system will evolve into a mass-based cap-and-trade system sometime after 2025.

transportation fuels, to complement the cap-and-trade instrument used by the RGGI states in the electricity sector. However, by early February 2019, indications were that "officials will gravitate towards a cap-and-trade programme for the final design, as all jurisdictions except Pennsylvania and Washington, D.C. have experience with that structure via RGGI" (McGraw, 2019, 1).

At the same time, Oregon is poised to enact in 2019 an economy-wide CO_2 cap-and-trade system, patterned after the California system, with which it would link via the Western Climate Initiative (Schatzki and Stavins, 2018a; Burtraw *et al.*, 2019). The system lays out in a 98-page "Clean Energy Jobs" bill how the system — beginning in 2021 — would achieve emission reduction goals of 45 percent by 2035 and 80 percent by 2050, relative to 1990 levels (Climate Xchange, 2019). Electricity generators and importers, natural gas utilities, petroleum-product distributors (including gasoline and diesel fuel), and large point sources will be included under the declining cap. Emissions from energy used out of state, as well as aviation, watercraft, and rail transportation, will be exempted. An increasing share of allowances is to be auctioned over time, starting with 60 percent at the program's launch in 2021, with most funds directed to climate-related programs. Emissions-intensive trade-exposed industries receive allowances through an output-based updating allocation. In addition, New Jersey is preparing to join RGGI.

The Limits of Cap-and-Trade Experience and the Promise of a US Carbon Tax

Past may not be prologue, at least not in the United States. What has been the dominant politically revealed preference for emissions trading over pollution taxes may not hold for future applications at the national level to GHG emission reductions.[38] Since the successful demonization in 2009 of cap-and-trade as cap-and-tax by opponents of the Waxman-Markey

[38] However, at the subnational level in the United States, the only two significant carbon-pricing systems are the cap-and-trade policies in California and the northeast.

In the state of Washington, the Senate blocked a cap-and-trade bill in 2015. Then voters rejected carbon tax ballot initiatives in 2016 with revenues directed to cutting other tax rates, and in 2018 with revenues directed to environmental programs and projects. None of three climate bills introduced early in 2019 in Washington involve carbon pricing of any kind (Kagubare, 2019), although a cap-and-trade proposal is again circulating in the state Senate (Lithgow, 2019f).

legislation (H.R. 2454, the American Clean Energy and Security Act of 2009), the political advantage held by this instrument (namely, doing a better job of obscuring cost than did a tax) may have been lost, at least for the foreseeable future for national climate legislation (Schmalensee and Stavins, 2013, 2017b).

Beyond that, as I discuss later, there is clearly increasing interest within the policy community — and even within Congress — in the possibility of using a federal carbon tax to reduce CO_2 emissions. This heightened activity includes: the Market Choice Act of July 2018, which would have imposed a \$24/ton carbon tax, with 70 percent or the revenue going to infrastructure projects; the Energy Innovation and Carbon Dividend Act of November 2018, which provided a \$15/ton carbon "fee," with the revenue rebated to households; and the even more prominent bipartisan proposal from the Climate Leadership Council, endorsed by some leading Republican economists and former senior government officials (Akerloff *et al.*, 2019). On the other hand, the most prominent climate proposal in the current Congress is surely the "Green New Deal," which is noticeably silent about, if not hostile toward any kind of carbon-pricing initiative.[39] In the meantime, there may be positive political economy lessons to be learned from British Columbia's experience with its carbon tax system.[40]

Political Economy of the British Columbia Carbon Tax

The successful enactment in British Columbia of its carbon tax has been attributed to the "confluence of political conditions ripe for carbon taxation" (Harrison, 2013; Datla and Lee, 2016), including: (1) availability of

---

[39]The Green New Deal proposal includes a set of economic stimulus objectives and programs intended to address climate change and economic inequality (US House of Representatives, 2019). A political advantage of noncarbon–pricing approaches is that — like cap-and-trade in the past — they can hide the economic costs of the policies (Leonhardt, 2019).

[40]The unusually high carbon taxes that exist in Sweden — and to lesser degrees in the other Scandinavian countries — may have less to offer for relevant political economy lessons for the United States, because in Sweden, high taxes exist, in general, and are well accepted, with citizens enjoying state-funded access to services such as child care and education. High taxes may work in the region because the notion of state welfare is so deeply rooted in the culture. Therefore, I focus on potential positive political economy lessons for the United States from the British Columbia experience.

untapped hydroelectric potential as an important source of electrical power; (2) a strongly environmentalist electorate combined with a surge in public concern about climate change (as with California's move to a CO_2 cap-and-trade system); (3) a right-center majority government that had the trust of the business community (as with the George H. W. Bush administration's push for the SO_2 allowance trading program); and (4) a committed leader with the institutional capacity to pursue his personal policy preferences — the premier made the decision about a carbon tax (Harrison, 2013).[41]

The political economy of this carbon tax has changed over time. Public opinion was opposed to the tax when it was introduced in 2008, with 60 percent somewhat or strongly opposed. But by 2015, only 45 percent of the surveyed population was somewhat or strongly opposed (Murray and Rivers, 2015). This increased public acceptance may partly have been due to the perception that emissions had been reduced without severe economic impacts (Harrison, 2013). In addition, the British Columbia government had become reliant on the revenue.

Over time, political pressures have caused the system to evolve from one where revenues were used broadly to cut distortionary taxes to a system that was considerably more focused on the use of tax cuts to favor specific sectors (including the motion picture industry), and for payments and tax cuts for northern rural households and low-income populations (Murray and Rivers, 2015). "What began as use of carbon tax revenues for general tax reform to reduce distortions and promote economic growth (straight out of the economist's playbook) appears to have evolved into a system with some 'industrial policy' objectives for promoting certain sectors" (Murray and Rivers, 2015, 7).

Interestingly, the policy is no longer revenue-neutral. From 2008 through 2015, the carbon tax generated \$4.6 billion of revenue, with tax cuts exceeding \$5.3 billion over the same period (Plumer, 2010; Murray and Rivers, 2015). The tax reached \$27 in April 2018 and is scheduled to increase annually by \$3.75 until the rate reaches \$38/ton of CO_2 equivalent in 2021. However, according to one analysis, there is likely to be continuing political pressure for exemptions for trade-exposed industries

[41]To a degree not frequently recognized by academic studies, successful policy initiatives can at least partly be attributed to healthy doses of chance that have placed specific persons at critical moments into key positions in government and the broader policy community (Stavins, 1998).

(Harrison, 2013). Experience with concessions that have been granted to local governments, rural voters, and farmers may be cause for concern in this regard (Harrison, 2013).

It is fair to say that political pressures can drive up the social costs of both carbon-pricing instruments, with incentives sometimes working against auctioning of allowances in cap-and-trade systems, and a variety of pressures working against employing cost-effective cuts of distortionary taxes in carbon tax systems.[42]

Conclusions: The Path Ahead

At the outset, I posed two questions: How do the two major approaches to carbon pricing compare on relevant dimensions? And which of the two approaches is more likely to be adopted in the future in the United States?

Does Either Carbon-Pricing Instrument Dominate in Normative or Positive Terms?

In principle, either carbon-pricing instrument could be used in a national system to achieve meaningful reductions of CO_2 emissions, such as the 2025 target of 26–28 percent below the 2005 level, expressed in the US NDC under the Paris Agreement (Chen and Hafstead, 2018). When carbon taxes and carbon cap-and-trade systems are designed in ways that make them truly comparable, their characteristics and outcomes are similar, and in some cases fully equivalent (normatively), in terms of their: emission reductions, abatement costs, possibilities for raising revenue, costs to regulated firms when revenue-raising instruments are employed, distributional impacts, and effects on competitiveness.

On some other dimensions, there can be real differences between the performance of these two approaches. Some of these dimensions favor carbon taxes and some cap-and-trade, and most depend on respective

[42] It is possible that additional carbon-pricing systems will be forthcoming at the provincial level in Canada. Four provinces that had resisted the federal government's carbon-pricing mandate — Ontario, Saskatchewan, Manitoba, and New Brunswick — became subject to the federal government's backstop carbon tax on April 1, 2019. The mandate is now being subjected to legal challenge, but all of this may become moot, depending on the outcome of the national general election on October 21, 2019.

design elements. In particular, the tax approach is clearly favored by three elements: complexity and administrative requirements; interactions with complementary policies; and effects on carbon price volatility. Cap-and-trade is favored by its ease of linkage with policies in other jurisdictions; and possibly by its anticipated performance in the presence of uncertainty. However, neither transaction costs nor the potential for market manipulation with cap-and-trade appear to be particularly important in the US context.

Thus, the available evidence supports the normative conclusion that neither approach dominates the other, and any overall ranking would depend on the weights given to the various dimensions of difference (Goulder and Schein, 2013; Goulder and Hafstead, 2018), as well as the relative probability of good design.

Much the same can be said in the positive political economy domain: there is decidedly mixed evidence regarding which of the two carbon-pricing approaches (if either) is more likely to be adopted at the national level in the United States in the future. Thus, there is not a strong case for the superiority of taxes or trading, normatively or positively, and differences in performance that are a function of specific design of the two instruments dominate differences in the performance of the instruments themselves. Two major conclusions therefore stand out. One is that the specific designs of carbon taxes and cap-and-trade systems may be more consequential than the choice between the two instruments. Many differences fade with specific implementations, and what appears to be the dichotomous choice between two distinct policy instruments often turns out to be a choice of design elements along a policy continuum. The other conclusion that stands out is that issues of positive political economy frequently have normative dimensions, and normative attributes have important implications for political prognosis.

All of this serves as a reminder of the importance of avoiding comparisons of two policy instruments where one is idealized and the other realistic; rather, comparisons are best made between idealized versions of two instruments, or — better yet — realistic versions of both (Hahn and Stavins, 1992). This is consistent with the notion of comparing proposed climate policy instruments by weighting the net benefits of each by the probability of it being implemented within some time period, an approach which would essentially merge the normative and positive domains. National policy instruments that appear impeccable from the vantage point of Berkeley, Cambridge, Madison, or New Haven, but consistently prove infeasible in Washington, DC, can hardly be considered "optimal" (Stavins, 2012).

The Virtue of Simplicity and the Challenge of Politics

It may be reasonable to stipulate (as the lawyers say) that in regard to relative simplicity, carbon taxes have the upper hand over cap-and-trade. But real carbon taxes "are among the least used climate policy instruments" (Carattini *et al.*, 2017, 1), with only 20 countries and 2 Canadian provinces having implemented carbon taxes as of 2018, with South Africa now having delayed implementation. Also, carbon tax proposals have been undone, reversed, or simply failed — sometimes at very advanced stages politically — such as in France and Switzerland in 2000, Australia in 2014, and the State of Washington in 2016 and 2018 (Carattini *et al.*, 2017; Anderson *et al.*, 2018). Cap-and-trade has not fared much better (Figure 1), having failed at the national level in the United States during the Obama administration (although at the subnational level, cap-and-trade systems are poised to be launched in 2019 in three states).

This track record can be compared with the 176 countries that had renewable energy policies and/or energy-efficiency standards, and another 110 national and subnational jurisdictions with feed-in tariffs, as of 2016 (Carattini *et al.*, 2017). Thinking about how to make carbon taxes or cap-and-trade more politically acceptable may be a critical step for more effective climate policy action.

Can Carbon Pricing Be Made More Politically Acceptable?

Can carbon taxes or cap-and-trade be made more acceptable by designing them in ways that respond to voter concerns? This is a particularly important question, given the considerable ambiguity regarding the normative superiority of either of these instruments, and the reality that specific elements of design can minimize, if not eliminate, remaining differences.

Survey and other evidence indicate that a set of public perceptions — at least some of which are inaccurate — are primary factors behind an aversion to carbon taxes, including: the personal costs are too great, the policy is regressive, it could damage the economy, it will not discourage carbon intensive behavior, and governments just want to increase their revenues (Carattini *et al.*, 2017).[43] This suggests that one way to improve public acceptability could be through better informing the public about the real nature and consequences of carbon-pricing policies.

Another way to increase public acceptability could be through judicious policy design. Several routes might be employed to make carbon taxes or cap-and-trade more politically acceptable while departing from what may be first-best design. One approach would be to phase in taxes or caps over time, because a lower carbon price is presumably more politically acceptable, and as aversion may abate over time, prices can be increased (Carattini *et al.*, 2017). This is the route that California and British Columbia have taken with their respective carbon-pricing policies. A gradual phase in also reduces the stranded asset problem (Rozenberg *et al.*, 2019), even if the outcome is less effective in the short run and hence less efficient. There is a risk that the carbon price would become stuck at too low a level, so a commitment device may be appropriate, such as making the emissions cap or tax rate trajectory part of legislation, as was done with the SO_2 allowance trading program and the British Columbia and Swedish carbon taxes.

A second, very important design modification that would frequently depart from the first-best (most efficient) design would be to earmark carbon tax or auctioned allowance revenue to finance additional climate mitigation (Amdur *et al.*, 2014; Carattini *et al.*, 2017; Kotchen *et al.*, 2017). This is in contrast to economists' first-best use of treating carbon tax proceeds as part of general revenues, so that the tax system as a whole can be optimized, such as through cutting distortionary taxes. There is, in fact, substantial evidence of voter preference for such earmarked use of revenues, with particular attraction to using revenue for low-carbon R&D, and subsidies to promote deployment.

The former, at least, can be part of an efficient portfolio of complementary climate policies, due to the separate market failure of the public good nature of information. In principle, earmarking could be phased down over time.

[43] This list of factors as well as the potential means of addressing these through modifications of carbon tax design I subsequently describe are drawn from Carattini *et al.* (2017), and a large number of other studies cited therein.

A third and final design modification that departs from a first-best approach is to use revenues for fairness purposes, such as with a progressive revenue-neutral carbon tax or cap-and-trade system with lump-sum rebates of tax (or auction) revenue or rebates more targeted to cushion impacts on low-income or other particularly burdened constituencies (Amdur *et al.*, 2014; Carattini *et al.*, 2017), rather than recycling carbon tax revenue through cuts in distortionary taxes (Goulder and Hafstead, 2018; Metcalf, 2019b). A diverse set of surveys indicate voter support for using carbon-pricing revenue to ease impacts on low-income households (Carattini *et al.*, 2017). Proposals from very different political perspectives have favored this approach, using so-called carbon dividends with carbon taxes or as part of a "cap-and-dividend" trading system (Boyce and Riddle, 2007; Sedor, 2015; US House of Representatives, 2018; Akerloff *et al.*, 2019; Harder, 2019).

Survey evidence does not indicate support from the general public for using revenue to cut distortionary taxes. Surveys in Denmark, Germany, the United Kingdom, and other countries have found cutting other taxes to be the least popular strategy for the use of revenues (Carattini *et al.*, 2017). Why might this be? It could be that voters do not understand the logic of the "double dividend" (Goulder, 1995), which can come from cutting these other taxes. Or it may be a simple lack of trust of politicians and government; that is, doubt that governments will actually cut the other taxes, or fear that the "wrong people" would benefit. In general, survey evidence indicates that public support both for carbon taxes and for carbon cap-and-trade is linked with proposed uses of revenue (Amdur *et al.*, 2014; Mills *et al.*, 2015; Kotchen *et al.*, 2017).

Can the Rejection of National Carbon Cap-and-Trade Help Carbon Tax Proposals?

Political polarization in the United States, which began some five decades ago and accelerated after 1990, has decimated what had long been the key source of political support in the Congress for environmental and energy action, namely, the middle, including both moderate Republicans and moderate Democrats (Stavins, 2011; Schmalensee and Stavins, 2013). Whereas congressional debates about environmental and energy policy had long featured regional politics, they are now fully and simply partisan. In this political maelstrom, the failure of cap-and-trade climate policy in the US Senate in 2010 was essentially collateral damage in a much larger political war.

The successful political battle against the Obama administration's CO_2 cap-and-trade legislation featured the demonization of that instrument as cap-and-tax. Does the consequent reputational loss for cap-and-trade present an opening for serious consideration of the other carbon-pricing instrument — a carbon tax? The ongoing challenge of large budgetary deficits may increase the political feasibility of new sources of revenue. When and if that happens, consumption taxes (as opposed to traditional taxes on income and investment) could receive heightened attention, and primary among these might be energy or carbon taxes.

Surely this opening already exists in the broader policy community, with support not only from the usual Democratic sources but also from prominent Republican academic economists and former high government officials. The January 16, 2019, economists' statement on a carbon dividend plan in the *Wall Street Journal* (Akerloff *et al.*, 2019) and support from the Niskanen Center provide evidence of the diversity of bipartisan support for a carbon tax (typically in the form of a carbon dividend plan) in the broader policy community.

Do such openings also exist in the real political world of those currently holding elective office in the federal government? A carbon tax is not cap-and-trade; that may help with the political messaging. But if conservatives were able to label cap-and-trade as cap-and-tax, it surely will not be very difficult to label a tax (or a fee) as a tax. In addition to opposition from the right, it is — as of now — questionable whether the new left of the Democratic Party in the Congress will want a carbon tax to be part of its promoted Green New Deal. So, for the short term, national carbon pricing of either type may continue to face an uphill battle in the United States. Therefore, in addition to economic research on judicious design of second-best carbon-pricing policies, economists can be effective by working to catch up with the political world by examining better design of second-best nonpricing climate policy instruments, such as clean energy standards.[44] But at some point the politics will change, and it is important to be ready, which is why — for the long term — ongoing research on carbon-pricing instruments is very much warranted, particularly if it is

[44]For example, the Clean Energy Standard Act of 2019, Senate Bill 1359, introduced on May 8, 2019, would establish a standard for clean generation of electricity with a market-oriented credit trading program.

carried out in the context of real-world politics and focuses on policies that are likely at some point to prove feasible.

Acknowledgements

He acknowledges valuable comments on a previous version of the manuscript by Lawrence Goulder, Larry Karp, Gilbert Metcalf, William Pizer, Richard Schmalensee, and the organizers of the NBER conference on Environmental and Energy Policy and the Economy, as well as comments on his presentation at the conference. The author, who is responsible for all remaining errors, can be reached at robert_stavins@harvard.edu. For acknowledgments, sources of research support, and disclosure of the author's material financial relationships, if any, please see https://www.nber.org/chapters/c14285.ack.

References

Akerloff, George, Robert Aumann, Martin Baily, Ben Bernanke, Michael Boskin, Angus Deaton, Peter Diamond, Robert Engle, *et al.* (2019). "Economists' statement on carbon dividends." Opinion/Commentary. *Wall Street Journal*, January 16.

Aldy, Joseph E. (2018). "Carbon tax review and updating." Unpublished paper, John F. Kennedy School of Government, Harvard University, Cambridge, MA.

Aldy, Joseph E., and William A. Pizer. (2015). "Competitiveness impacts of climate change mitigation policies." *Journal of the Association of Environmental and Resource Economists*, **2**(4): 565–595.

Aldy, Joseph E., and Robert N. Stavins. (2012). "The promise and problems of pricing carbon: Theory and practice." *Journal of Environment and Development*, **21**(2): 152–180.

Aldy, Joseph E., Marc Hafstead, Gilbert E. Metcalf, Brian C. Murray, William A. Pizer, Christina Reichert, and Roberton W. Williams. (2017). "Resolving inherent uncertainty of carbon taxes." *Harvard Environmental Law Review*, **41**: 1–13.

Amdur, David, Barry G. Rabe, and Christopher Borick. (2014). "Public views on a carbon tax depend on the proposed use of revenue." *Issues in Energy and Environmental Policy*, **13**(July): 9–45.

Anderson, Soren, Ioana Marinescu, and Boris Shor. (2018). *Who Joined the Pigou Club? A Postmortem Analysis of Washington State's Carbon Tax Initiative I-732*. June 6.

Arrow, Kenneth J. (1969). "The organization of economic activity: Issues pertinent to the choice of market versus non-market allocation." In Joint Economic Committee of U.S. Congress (Ed.), *The Analysis and Evaluation of Public Expenditures: The PPB System*, 47–64. Washington, DC: US Government Printing Office.

Beck, Marisa, Nicholas Rivers, Randall Wigle, and Hidemichi Yonezawa. (2015). "Carbon tax and revenue recycling: Impacts on households in British Columbia." *Resource and Energy Economics*, **41**: 40–69.

Becker, Gary S. (1983). "A theory of competition among pressure groups for political influence." *Quarterly Journal of Economics*, **98**(3): 371–400.

Bodansky, Daniel, Seth Hoedl, Gilbert Metcalf, and Robert Stavins. (2015). "Facilitating linkage of climate policies through the Paris outcome." *Climate Policy*, August 5.

Boden, T. A., G. Marland, and R. J. Andres. (2017). *National CO2 Emissions from Fossil-Fuel Burning, Cement Manufacture, and Gas Flaring: 1751–2014*. Carbon Dioxide Information Analysis Center, Oak Ridge National Laboratory, US Department of Energy, Washington, DC.

Bohi, Douglas, and Dallas Burtraw. (1992). "Utility investment behavior and the emission trading market." *Resources and Energy*, **14**: 129–153.

Borenstein, Severin, James Bushnell, Frank A. Wolak, and Matthew Zaragoza-Watkins. (2018). *Expecting the Unexpected: Emissions Uncertainty and Environmental Market Design*. Energy Institute at Haas Working Paper 274R (June), University of California, Berkeley.

Bovenberg, A. Lans, and Lawrence H. Goulder. (1996). "Optimal environmental taxation in the presence of other taxes: General equilibrium analyses." *American Economic Review*, **86**: 985–1000.

Boyce, James K., and Matthew Riddle. (2007). *Cap and Dividend: How to Cap Global Warming while Protecting the Incomes of American Families*. Amherst: University of Massachusetts.

British Columbia. (2007). *Climate Action Plan*. Vancouver: BC, Government.

Bruvoll, Annegrete, and Bodil Merethe Larsen. (2004). "Greenhouse gas emissions in Norway: Do carbon taxes work?" *Energy Policy*, **32**: 493–505.

Buchanan, James M., and Gordon Tullock. (1975). "Polluters' profits and political response: Direct control versus taxes." *American Economic Review*, **65**: 139–147.

Burtraw, Dallas, Richard Morgenstern, Amelia Keyes, and Clayton Munnings. (2019). *Carbon Pricing in Oregon: Memoranda for the Oregon Climate Policy Office*. Report 19-01 (January), Washington, DC.

Calel, R., and A. Dechezlepretre. (2016). "Environmental policy and directed technological change: Evidence from the European carbon market." *Review of Economics and Statistics*, **98**(1): 173–191.

Carattini, Stefano, Maria Carvalho, and Sam Fankhauser. (2017). *How to Make Carbon Taxes More Acceptable*. London: Grantham Research Institute on Climate Change and the Environment, and Centre for Climate Change Economics and Policy, London School of Economics and Political Science.

Carl, Jeremy, and David Fedor. (2016). "Tracking global carbon revenues: A survey of carbon taxes versus cap-and-trade in the real world." *Energy Policy*, **96**: 50–77.

Carlson, Curtis, Dallas Burtraw, Maureen Cropper, and Karen Palmer. (2000). "SO2 control by electric utilities: What are the gains from trade?" *Journal of Political Economy*, **108**: 1292–1326.

Chen, Yunguang, and Marc A. C. Hafstead. (2018). "Using a carbon tax to meet U.S. international climate pledges." *Climate Change Economics*, **10**(1): 195002-1–19.

Climate XChange. (2019). "Cap-and-trade could be coming to Oregon — here's what you need to know." *Carbon Pulse*, February 8.

Cludius, Johanna, Vicky Duscha, Nele Friedrichsen, and Katja Schumacher. (2019). "Cost-efficiency of the EU emissions trading system: An evaluation of the second trading period." *Economics of Energy and Environmental Policy*, **8**(1): 145–161.

Coase, Ronald. (1960). "The problem of social cost." *Journal of Law and Economics*, **3**: 1–44.

Crocker, Thomas D. (1966). "The structuring of atmospheric pollution control systems." In H. Wolozin (Ed.), *The Economics of Air Pollution*, 61–86. New York: W.W. Norton.

Dales, J. H. (1968). "Land, water, ownership." *Canadian Journal of Economics*, **1**: 791–804.

Datla, Anjani, and Henry Lee. (2016). *Pricing Carbon: The Birth of British Columbia's Carbon Tax*. Harvard Kennedy School Case Number 2062.0.

Daugjberg, Cartsen, and Anders Branth Pedersen. (2004). "New policy ideas and old policy networks: Implementing green taxation in Scandinavia." *Journal of Public Policy*, **24**(2): 219–249.

Doucet, Joseph A., and Todd Strauss. (1994). "On the bundling of coal and sulfur dioxide emissions allowances." *Energy Policy*, **22**(9): 764–770.

Driesen, David M. (2019). "Toward a populist political economy of climate disruption." *Environmental Law*, **49**(2): 379–406.

Duff, David G. (2008). "Carbon taxation in British Columbia." *Vermont Journal of Environmental Law*, **10**: 85–105.

Edenhofer, Ottmar, Christian Flachsland, Christoph, Lisa Katharina Schmid, Anna Leipprand, Nicolas Koch, Ulrike Kornek, and Michael Pahle. (2017). *Decarbonization and EU ETS Reform: Introducing a Price Floor to Drive Low-Carbon Investments*. Berlin: Mercator Research Institute on Global Commons and Climate Change.

Ellerman, Denny A., and Barbara K. Buchner. (2007). "The European Union emissions trading scheme: Origins, allocation, and early results." *Review of Environmental Economics and Policy*, **1**(1): 66–87.

Ellerman, Denny A., and Juan-Pablo Montero. (1998). "The declining trend in sulfur dioxide emissions: Implications for allowance prices." *Journal of Environmental Economics and Management*, **36**: 26–45.

Ellerman, Denny A., Paul L. Joskow, and David Harrison. (2003). *Emissions Trading in the U.S.: Experience, Lessons, and Considerations for Greenhouse Gases*. Arlington, VA: Pew Center on Global Climate Change.

Ellerman, Denny A., Frank J. Convery, and Christian de Perthuis, (Eds.). (2010). *Pricing Carbon: The European Union Emissions Trading Scheme*. Cambridge: Cambridge University Press.

Ellerman, Denny A., Paul L. Joskow, Richard Schmalensee, Juan-Pablo Montero, and Elizabeth M. Bailey. (2000). *Markets for Clean Air: The U.S. Acid Rain Program*. Cambridge: Cambridge University Press.

Fankhauser, Samuel, Cameron Hepburn, and Jisung Park. (2010). "Combining multiple climate policy instruments: How not to do it." *Climate Change Economics*, **1**(3): 209–225.

Fischer, Carolyn, Ian W. H. Parry, and William A. Pizer. (2003). "Instrument choice for environmental protection when technological innovation is endogenous." *Journal of Environmental Economics and Management*, **45**: 523–545.

Fowlie, Meredith, Mar Reguant, and Stephen P. Ryan. (2016). "Market-based emissions regulation and industry dynamics." *Journal of Political Economy*, **124**(1): 249–302.

Fowlie, Meredith, Stephen P. Holland, and Erin T. Mansur. (2012). "What do emissions markets deliver and to whom? evidence from Southern California's NOx trading program." *American Economic Review*, **102**(2): 965–993.

Furman, Jason, Jason E. Bordoff, Manasi Deshpande, and Pascal J. Noel. (2007). "An economic strategy to address climate change and promote energy security." The Hamilton Project, Strategy Paper, The Brookings Institution, Washington, DC.

Gillis, Justin. (2018). "Forget the carbon tax for now." *New York Times*, December 27.

Goulder, Lawrence H. (1995). "Environmental taxation and the 'double dividend': A reader's guide." *International Tax and Public Finance*, **2**(2): 157–183.

Goulder, Lawrence H. (2019a). "Addressing the urgency of climate-change policy." Working Paper, Stanford University, March.

Goulder, Lawrence H. (2019b). *Presentation at Winter Luncheon and Annual Business Meeting, Association of Environmental and Resource Economists*, Atlanta, GA, January 5.

Goulder, Lawrence H., and Andrew R. Schein. (2013). "Carbon taxes versus cap and trade: A critical review." *Climate Change Economics*, **4**(3): 1–28.

Goulder, Lawrence H., and Richard D. Morgenstern. (2018). "China's rate-based approach to reducing CO2 emissions: Attractions, limitations, and alternatives." *American Economic Review Papers and Proceedings*, **108**: 458–462.

Goulder, Lawrence H., and Robert N. Stavins. (2011). "Challenges from state-federal interactions in U.S. climate change policy." *American Economic Review Papers and Proceedings*, **101**(3): 253–257.

Goulder, Lawrence H., and Mark A. C. Hafstead. (2018). *Confronting the Climate Challenge: U.S. Policy Options*. New York: Columbia University Press.

Goulder, Lawrence H., Marc A. C. Hafstead, GyuRim Kim, and Xianling Long. (2018). *Impacts of a Carbon Tax Across U.S. Household Income Groups: What are the Equity-Efficiency Trade-Offs?* Working Paper No. 25181 (October), NBER, Cambridge, MA.

Government Offices of Sweden. (2019). *Sweden's Carbon Tax*. https://www.government.se/government-policy/taxes-and-tariffs/swedens-carbon-tax.

Hafstead, Marc, Gilbert E. Metcalf, and Roberton C. Williams. (2017). "Adding quantity certainty to a carbon tax: The role of a tax adjustment mechanism for policy pre-commitment." *Harvard Environmental Law Review*, **41**: 41–57.

Hahn, Robert W. (1984). "Market power and transferable property rights." *Quarterly Journal of Economics*, **99**: 753–765.

Hahn, Robert W., and Robert N. Stavins. (1992). "Economic incentives for environmental protection: Integrating theory and practice." *American Economic Review Papers and Proceedings*, **82**: 464–468.

Hahn, Robert W., and Robert N. Stavins. (1999). *What Has the Kyoto Protocol Wrought? The Real Architecture of International Tradeable Permit Markets*. Washington, DC: The AEI Press.

Hahn, Robert W., and Robert N. Stavins. (2012). "The effect of allowance allocations on cap-and-trade system performance." *Journal of Law and Economics*, **54**(4): S267–S294.

Harder, Amy. (2019). "In shadow of Green New Deal, other climate-change bills proliferate." *Axios*, April 10.

Harrison, Kathryn. (2013). *The Political Economy of British Columbia's Carbon Tax*. OECD Environment Working Paper No. 63. OECD, Paris.

Hoel, Michael, and Larry Karp. (2001). "Taxes and quotas for a stock pollutant with multiplicative uncertainty." *Journal of Public Economics*, **82**: 91–114.

Hoel, Michael, and Larry Karp. (2002). "Taxes versus quotas for a stock pollutant." *Resource and Energy Economics*, **24**: 367–384.

Holt, C. A., and W. M. Shobe. (2016). "Price and quantity collars for stabilizing emission allowance prices: Laboratory experiments on the EU ETS market stability reserve." *Journal of Environmental Economics and Management*, **76**: 32–50.

Interagency Working Group on Social Cost of Carbon. (2016). *United States Government Update of the Social Cost of Carbon for Regulatory Impact Analysis under Executive Order 12866*. Washington, DC.

Intergovernmental Panel on Climate Change. (2013). *Climate Change 2013: The Physical Science Basis*. Cambridge: Cambridge University Press.

Intergovernmental Panel on Climate Change. (2018). *Global Warming of 1.5°C, IPCC Special Report, Summary for Policymakers*. Geneva: World Meteorological Organization and United Nations Environment Program.

Jaffe, Adam B., and Robert N. Stavins. (1995). "Dynamic incentives of environmental regulation: The effects of alternative policy instruments on technology diffusion." *Journal of Environmental Economics and Management*, **29**: S43–S63.

Jaffe, Adam B., Richard G. Newell, and Robert N. Stavins. (2005). "Tale of two market failures: Technology and environmental policy." *Ecological Economics*, **54**: 164–174.

Jaffe, Judson, Matthew Ranson, and Robert N. Stavins. (2010). "Linking tradable permit systems: A key element of emerging international climate policy architecture." *Ecology Law Quarterly*, **36**: 789–808.

Joskow, Paul L., and Richard Schmalensee. (1998). "The political economy of market-based environmental policy: The U.S. Acid Rain Program." *Journal of Law and Economics*, **41**: 81–135.

Jung, Chulho, Kerry Krutilla, and Roy Boyd. (1996). "Incentives for advanced pollution abatement technology at the industry level: An evaluation of policy instruments." *Journal of Environmental Economics and Management*, **30**: 95–111.

Kagubare, Ines. (2019). "Legislators Roll Out Climate Bills as Session Opens." *Climate Wire*, January 15.

Kalt, Joseph P., and Mark A. Zupan. (1984). "Capture and ideology in the economic theory of politics." *American Economic Review*, **74**(3): 279–300.

Kaplow, Louis. (2010). *Taxes, Permits, and Climate Change*. Working Paper No. 16268 (August), NBER, Cambridge, MA.

Karp, Larry, and Christian Traeger. (2018). *Prices Versus Quantities Reassessed.* CESifo Working Paper 7331 (November), Munich Society for the Promotion of Economic Research.

Kelman, Steven P. (1981). *What Price Incentives?* Boston: Auburn House.

Keohane, Nathaniel O. (2003). *What Did the Market Buy? Cost Savings Under the U.S. Tradeable Permits Program for Sulfur Dioxide.* Working Paper YCELP 01-11-2003, Yale Center for Environmental Law and Policy, New Haven, CT.

Keohane, Nathaniel O. (2009). "Cap and trade, rehabilitated: Using tradable permits to control U.S. greenhouse gases." *Review of Environmental Economics and Policy*, **3**: 42–62.

Keohane, Nathaniel O., Richard L. Revesz, and Robert N. Stavins. (1998). "The choice of regulatory instruments in environmental policy." *Harvard Environmental Law Review*, **22**(2): 313–367.

Klaassen, Ger. (1999). "Emissions Trading in the European Union: Practice and Prospects." In S. Sorrell and J. Skea (Eds.), *Pollution for Sale: Emissions Trading and Joint Implementation*, 83–100. Cheltenham: Edward Elgar Publishing.

Kneese, Allen V., and Charles L. Schultze. (1975). *Pollution, Prices, and Public Policy*. Washington, DC: Brookings Institution.

Kotchen, Matthew J., Zachary M. Turk, and Anthony A. Leiserowitz. (2017). "Public willingness to pay for a U.S. carbon tax and preferences for spending the revenue." *Environmental Research Letters*, **12**(9): 094012.

Leonhardt, David. (2019). "The problem with putting a price on the end of the world." *New York Times Magazine*, April 9.

Lithgow, Matt. (2019a). "LCFS market: California prices near return to $200 as PG&E fears pass." *Carbon Pulse*, February 8.

Lithgow, Matt. (2019b). "Maine legislator proposes state-wide carbon tax without RGGI exemption." *Carbon Pulse*, January 25.

Lithgow, Matt. (2019c). "New Hampshire legislators propose $20 carbon tax bill." *Carbon Pulse*, January 30.

Lithgow, Matt. (2019d). "New Mexico governor calls for market-based programme in climate order." *Carbon Pulse*, January 29.

Lithgow, Matt. (2019e). "Renewed Oregon cap-and-trade push underway as bill released." *Carbon Pulse*, February 1.

Lithgow, Matt. (2019f). "Washington State senator circulates WCI-modelled cap-and-trade outline." *Carbon Pulse*, January 17.

Maloney, Michael T., and Robert E. McCormick. (1982). "A positive theory of environmental quality regulation." *Journal of Law and Economics*, **25**: 99–123.

Malueg, David A. (1990). "Welfare consequences of emission credit trading programs." *Journal of Environmental Economics and Management*, **18**: 66–77.

Mankiw, L. Gregory. (2006). *The Pigou Club Manifesto*. Greg Mankiw's Blog. https://gregmankiw.blogspot.com/2006/10/pigou-club-manifesto.html.

McCubbins, Matthew, and Terry Sullivan. (1984). "Constituency influences on legislative policy choice." *Quality and Quantity*, **18**: 299–319.

McGraw, Dan. (2019). "U.S. Jurisdictions Working on TCI Carbon Pricing Game Plan." *Carbon Pulse*, February 8.

Mehling, Michael A., Gilbert E. Metcalf, and Robert N. Stavins. (2018). "Linking climate policies to advance global mitigation." *Science*, **359**(6379): 997–998.

Metcalf, Gilbert E. (2007). *A Proposal for a U.S. Carbon Tax Swap: An Equitable Tax Reform to Address Global Climate Change*. The Hamilton Project, Discussion Paper 2007-12, The Brookings Institution, Washington, DC.

Metcalf, Gilbert E. (2009). "Market-based policy options to control U.S. greenhouse gas emissions." *Journal of Economic Perspectives*, **23**(2): 5–27.

Metcalf, Gilbert E. (2019a). "The distributional impacts of U.S. energy policy." *Energy Policy*, **129**(C): 926–929.

Metcalf, Gilbert E. (2019b). *Paying for Pollution: Why a Carbon Tax Is Good for America*. New York: Oxford University Press.

Metcalf, Gilbert E., and David Weisbach. (2012). "Linking policies when tastes differ: Global climate policy in a heterogeneous world." *Review of Environmental Economics and Policy*, **6**(1): 110–129.

Milliman, Scott R., and Raymond Prince. (1989). "Firm incentives to promote technological change in pollution control." *Journal of Environmental Economics and Management*, **17**: 247–265.

Mills, Sarah B., Barry G. Rabe, and Christopher Borick. (2015). "Cap-and-trade support linked to revenue use." *Issues in Energy and Environmental Policy*, **23**(June).

Montero, Juan-Pablo. (2007). "Tradable Permits with Incomplete Monitoring: Evidence from Santiago's Particulate Permits Program." In J. Freeman and C. Kolstad (Eds.), *Moving to Markets in Environmental Regulation: Lessons from Twenty Years of Experience*, 147–170. New York: Oxford University Press.

Montgomery, David W. (1972). "Markets in licenses and efficient pollution control programs." *Journal of Economic Theory*, **5**: 395–418.

Murray, Brian, and Nicholas Rivers. (2015). "British Columbia's revenue-neutral carbon tax: A review of the latest 'grand experiment' in environmental policy." *Energy Policy*, **86**: 674–683.

Murray, Brian, William A. Pizer, and Christina Reichert. (2017). "Increasing emissions certainty under a carbon tax." *Harvard Environmental Law Review*, **41**: 14–27.

Newell, Richard G., and Robert N. Stavins. (2003). "Cost heterogeneity and the potential savings from market-based policies." *Journal of Regulatory Economics*, **23**: 43–59.

Newell, Richard G., and William A. Pizer. (2003). "Regulating stock externalities under uncertainty." *Journal of Environmental Economics and Management*, **45**: 416–432.

Newell, Richard G., Adam B. Jaffe, and Robert N. Stavins. (1999). "The induced innovation hypothesis and energy-saving technological change." *Quarterly Journal of Economics*, **114**: 941–975.

Nordhaus, William D. (2007). "To tax or not to tax: Alternative approaches to slowing global warming." *Review of Environmental Economics and Policy*, **1**: 26–44.

Nordhaus, William D. (2015). *The Climate Casino: Risk, Uncertainty, and Economics for a Warming World*. New Haven, CT: Yale University Press.

Organization for Economic Cooperation and Development. (2001). *Environmentally Related Taxes in OECD Countries: Issues and Strategies*. Paris: OECD.

Organization for Economic Cooperation and Development. (2011). *Interactions between Emission Trading Systems and Other Overlapping Policy Instruments*. Paris: OECD.

Oster, Sharon. (1982). "The strategic use of regulatory investment by industry sub-groups." *Economic Inquiry*, **20**: 604–618.

Parry, Ian W. H., and Roberton C. Williams. (2010). "What are the costs of meeting distributional objectives for climate policy?" *B.E. Journal of Economic Analysis and Policy*, **10**(2): 1–35.

Parry, Ian W. H., Roberton Williams C., and Lawrence H. Goulder. (1999). "When can carbon abatement policies increase welfare? The fundamental role of distorted factor markets." *Journal of Environmental Economics and Management*, **37**: 52–84.

Peltzman, Sam. (1976). "Toward a more general theory of regulation." *Journal of Law and Economics*, **19**: 211–240.

Perino, Grischa. (2018). "New EU ETS Phase 4 rules temporarily puncture waterbed." *Nature Climate Change*, **8**(4): 262–264.

Perino, Grischa, Robert Ritz A., and Aruthur van Benthem. (2019). *Understanding Overlapping Policies: Internal Carbon Leakage and the Punctured Waterbed*. Working Paper no. 25643 (March), NBER, Cambridge, MA.

Pigou, Arthur C. (1920). *The Economics of Welfare*. London: Macmillan.

Pindyck, Robert S. (2017). "Coase lecture — taxes, targets, and the social cost of carbon." *Economica*, **84**: 345–364.

Pizer, William A., and Brian C. Prest. (2019). "Prices versus quantities with policy updating." Working Paper No. 22379 (June, Revised January 6, 2019), NBER, Cambridge, MA.

Pizer, William A., and Xiliang Zhang. (2018). "China's new national carbon market." *American Economic Review Papers and Proceedings*, **108**: 463–467.

Plumer, Bradford. (2010). "B.C.'s carbon-tax experiment seems to be working." *New Republic*, July 27.

Pretis, Felix. (2019). "Does a carbon tax reduce CO2 emissions? Evidence from British Columbia." February 8. https://ssrn.com/abstract=3329512.

Reklev, Stian. (2019). "China aims for 2020 ETS start, quick expansion — sources citing govt plan." *Carbon Pulse*, April 12.

Roberts, Marc J., and Michael Spence. (1976). "Effluent charges and licenses under uncertainty." *Journal of Public Economics*, **5**: 193–208.

Rozenberg, Julie, Adrien Vogt-Schilb, and Stephane Hallegatte. (2019). "Instrument choice and stranded assets in the transition to clean capital." *Journal of Environmental Economics and Management*, **39**(1): 67–96.

Sachs, Jeffrey D. (2018). "For climate safety, call in the engineers." *Project Syndicate*, December 20.

Schatzki, Todd, and Robert N. Stavins. (2018a). *GHG Cap-and-Trade: Implications for Effective and Efficient Climate Policy in Oregon*. Harvard Project on Climate Agreements Discussion Paper 18-92 (November), Harvard University, Cambridge, MA.

Schatzki, Todd, and Robert N. Stavins. (2018b). *Key Issues Facing California's GHG Cap-and-Trade System for 2021–2030*. Discussion Paper (July), Harvard University, Cambridge, MA.

Schmalensee, Richard, and Robert N. Stavins. (2013). "The SO2 allowance trading system: The ironic history of a grand policy experiment." *Journal of Economic Perspectives*, **27**(1): 103–122.

Schmalensee, Richard, and Robert N. Stavins. (2017a). "The design of environmental markets: What have we learned from experience with cap and trade?" *Oxford Review of Economic Policy*, **33**(4): 572–588.

Schmalensee, Richard, and Robert N. Stavins. (2017b). "Lessons learned from three decades of experience with cap and trade." *Review of Environmental Economics and Policy*, **11**(1): 59–79.

Sedor, Noelle. (2015). "Why fee and dividend is better than cap and trade at fighting climate change." *Los Angeles Times*, March 5.

Shepsle, Kenneth A., and Barry R. Weingast. (1984). "Political solutions to market problems." *American Political Science Review*, **78**: 417–434.

Speck, Stefan. (2008). "The design of carbon and broad-based energy taxes in European countries." *Vermont Journal of Environmental Law*, **10**: 31–59.

Stavins, Robert N. (1995). "Transaction costs and tradeable permits." *Journal of Environmental Economics and Management*, **29**: 133–146.

Stavins, Robert N. (1996). "Correlated uncertainty and policy instrument choice." *Journal of Environmental Economics and Management*, **30**: 218–232.

Stavins, Robert N. (1997). "Policy instruments for climate change: How can national governments address a global problem?" *University of Chicago Legal Forum*, **1997**: 293–329.

Stavins, Robert N. (1998). "What can we learn from the grand policy experiment? positive and normative lessons from SO2 allowance trading." *Journal of Economic Perspectives*, **12**(3): 69–88.

Stavins, Robert N. (2003). "Experience with Market-Based Environmental Policy Instruments." In Karl-Göran Mäler and Jeffrey Vincent (Eds.), *Handbook of Environmental Economics*, Vol. 1, 355–435. Amsterdam: Elsevier Science.

Stavins, Robert N. (2006). "Vintage-differentiated environmental regulation." *Stanford Environmental Law Journal*, **25**(1): 29–63.

Stavins, Robert N. (2007). *A U.S. Cap-and-Trade System to Address Global Climate Change*. The Hamilton Project, Discussion Paper 2007-13, The Brookings Institution, Washington, DC.

Stavins, Robert N. (2008). "A meaningful U.S. cap-and-trade system to address climate change." *Harvard Environmental Law Review*, **32**(2): 293–371.

Stavins, Robert N. (2010). *Both are Necessary, but Neither is Sufficient: Carbon-Pricing and Technology R&D Initiatives in a Meaningful National Climate Policy*. An Economic View of the Environment [Blog], October 21.

Stavins, Robert N. (2011). "Polarized politics paralyze policy." *Environmental Forum*, **28**(6): 16.

Stavins, Robert N. (2012). *Cap-and-Trade, Carbon Taxes, and My Neighbor's Lovely Lawn*. An Economic View of the Environment [Blog], October 24.

Stavins, Robert N. (2014). *What are the Benefits and Costs of EPA's Proposed CO_2 Regulation?* An Economic View of the Environment [Blog], June 19.

Stepp, Matthew, and Alex Trembath. (2013). "A climate policy that would actually work." *The Hill*, October 11.

Stigler, George J. (1971). "The theory of economic regulation." *Bell Journal of Economics*, **2**: 3–21.

Tschirhart, John T. (1984). "Transferable discharge permits and the control of stationary source air pollution: A survey and synthesis." In Thomas D. Crocker (Ed.), *Economic Perspectives on Acid Deposition Control*, Boston: Butterworth.

United Nations. (2015). *Paris Agreement*. Adopted December 12; entered into force November 4, 2016.

US Environmental Protection Agency. (1985). *Costs and Benefits of Reducing Lead in Gasoline, Final Regulatory Impact Analysis*. Washington, DC: Office of Policy Analysis.

US Environmental Protection Agency. (2014). *Regulatory Impact Analysis for the Proposed Carbon Pollution Guidelines for Existing Power Plants and Emission Standards for Modified and Reconstructed Power Plants*. EPA-452/R-14-002 (June), Research Triangle Park, NC.

US House of Representatives. (2018). *Energy Innovation and Carbon Dividend Act of 2018*, H.R. 7173, 115th Congress, introduced November 27.

US House of Representatives. (2019). *Resolution 109 Recognizing the Duty of the Federal Government to Create a Green New Deal*. Washington, DC: 116th Congress, 1st Session, introduced by Ms. Ocasio-Cortez, February 7.

Weisbach, David. (2010). "Instrument choice is instrument design." In Gilbert E. Metcalf (Ed.), *U.S. Energy Tax Policy*, 113–158. Cambridge: Cambridge University Press.

Weitzman, Martin L. (1974). "Prices vs. quantities." *Review of Economic Studies*, **41**(4): 477–491.

Weitzman, Martin L. (2014). "Can negotiating a uniform carbon price help to internalize the global warming externality?" *Journal of the Association of Environmental and Resource Economists*, **1–2**: 29–49.

Weitzman, Martin L. (2017). "On a world climate assembly and the social cost of carbon." *Economica*, **84**: 559–586.

World Bank Group. (2016). *Emissions Trading in Practice: Handbook on Design and Implementation*. Partnership for Market Readiness and International Carbon Action Partnership. Washington, DC: World Bank.

World Bank Group. (2018). *State and Trends of Carbon Pricing*. Washington, DC: World Bank.

World Bank Group. (2019). *Carbon Pricing Platform*. Washington, DC: World Bank.

https://doi.org/10.1142/9789811292415_0012

Chapter 12

The Relative Merits of Carbon Pricing Instruments: Taxes versus Trading*

Robert N. Stavins

John F. Kennedy School of Government, Harvard University, Cambridge, MA, USA

Resources for the Future, Washington, DC, USA

National Bureau of Economic Research, Cambridge, MA, USA

robert_stavins@harvard.edu

Introduction

In 2007, the Brookings Institution's Hamilton Project asked me to write a paper proposing a trading system to reduce US emissions of carbon dioxide (CO_2). I replied that I preferred to write about what I considered to be two symmetric carbon pricing instruments: a carbon tax and a carbon trading program. The Hamilton Project leaders said that they would find someone else to write about carbon taxes (Metcalf, 2007) and that I should instead focus on making the strongest possible case for what is today called "cap-and-trade." I did my best and, in the process, came to be identified as an advocate for emissions trading to address global

*This chapter was originally published in *Review of Environmental Economics and Policy*, **16**(1), Winter 2022. https://doi.org/10.1086/717773.

climate change.[1] In this chapter, I approach the issue as I wished to more than a decade ago, treating both pricing instruments in a balanced manner and examining their advantages and disadvantages without favoring one over the other.

Nearly all industrialized countries and most large emerging economies have launched or are launching policies aimed at reducing greenhouse gas (GHG) emissions. Of the 169 parties to the Paris climate agreement that have submitted pledges to reduce their emissions, more than half indicate that they will use carbon pricing instruments. To date, 61 carbon pricing policies, including 30 carbon taxes and 31 emissions trading systems (ETS), have been implemented or are scheduled for implementation worldwide. Most of the trading systems are cap-and-trade, but an important one — China's system, implemented in 2021 — is a tradable performance standard. Together, these carbon pricing initiatives will cover about 22 percent of global GHG emissions (World Bank Group, 2020).

There is widespread agreement among most economists that economy-wide carbon pricing will be a necessary (although not sufficient) component of any effective policy that can achieve meaningful and cost-effective CO_2 reductions in large and complex economies (Metcalf, 2009; Kaplow, 2010; Borenstein *et al.*, 2019). Given the diversity of CO_2 sources in such economies, conventional technology and performance standards would be infeasible and, in any event, excessively costly (Newell and Stavins, 2003). The key advantages of pricing instruments are their flexibility and the incentives they provide for achieving overall cost-effectiveness (Knittel, 2019). Moreover, pricing approaches can reduce long-term abatement costs by inducing climate-friendly technological change (Newell *et al.*, 1999).

There is less agreement among economists regarding which is the better pricing instrument. Some support carbon taxes (Mankiw, 2006; Nordhaus, 2007), while others favor cap-and-trade (Ellerman *et al.*, 2003; Keohane, 2009). A carbon tax places a price on carbon directly — ideally upstream, where fossil fuels enter the economy. By contrast, an upstream cap-and-trade system assigns scarce permits (allowances) for quantities of

[1]The design recommendations in my Hamilton Project paper (Stavins, 2007) served as the starting point for early efforts by the Obama administration to design a CO_2 cap-and-trade proposal. That proposal became part of the failed Waxman-Markey legislation, the American Clean Energy and Security Act of 2009.

carbon where they enter the economy, with the market for the allowances generating a carbon price.

How do these pricing approaches compare in terms of their anticipated and actual performance? I review and synthesize theory and experience concerning carbon taxes and cap-and-trade and find that they are equivalent — or nearly equivalent — along some important dimensions but significantly different along others. However, many of these differences fade with implementation. Indeed, what appears at first glance to be a dichotomous choice between two distinct instruments can turn out to be a choice of specific design elements along a policy continuum.

In the next two sections, I explore the theoretical similarities and differences between carbon taxes and cap-and-trade. Next, I examine the theoretical possibility and empirical reality of hybrid policy instruments that combine features of the two approaches. I then consider some of the key lessons that can be learned from experience with implementation of both types of policies. I offer a summary and some conclusions in the final section.

Similarities between Carbon Taxes and Cap-and-Trade

In theory, carbon taxes and cap-and-trade can be designed to be perfectly equivalent in terms of three attributes (incentives for achieving emission reductions, aggregate abatement costs, and effects on competitiveness), nearly equivalent in terms of potential for raising revenue, and similar in terms of costs to regulated firms and distributional impacts.

Incentives for Achieving Emission Reductions

In the absence of uncertainty, tax and trading instruments can achieve the same emission reductions, whether the point of regulation is upstream (carbon content of fossil fuels), midstream (electricity generation), or downstream (electricity use). While the point of regulation does not affect either instrument's aggregate cost, it can affect decisions about the scope of coverage (ranging from a single sector to economy-wide), which in turn has implications for environmental effectiveness as well as cost-effectiveness. Indeed, by focusing on the carbon content of fossil fuels upstream (at the mine mouth, the wellhead, and the point of import), either a tax or a cap-and-trade program could cover up to 98 percent of US CO_2 emissions. This would also limit the number of compliance entities (on the order of a few thousand), versus regulating the hundreds of millions of individual smokestacks, tailpipes, and other downstream sources that emit CO_2 (Metcalf, 2007; Stavins, 2007).

Aggregate Abatement Costs

If firms operate in a competitive market, either pricing instrument provides strong incentives for them to minimize their costs, which include the costs to abate emissions plus either their tax liability under a carbon tax or their costs to purchase any needed allowances (net of revenues from allowance sales) under a cap-and-trade system. Each firm faces incentives to abate emissions up to the point where the firm's marginal abatement cost is equal to the tax rate or the market-determined allowance price. Because all firms abate emissions at the same marginal cost, both instruments lead to the same (minimized) aggregate abatement cost. In principle, additional cost savings could be realized with either approach by allowing regulated sources to use offsets for emission reductions achieved outside the program to reduce tax liability or allowance requirements (Goulder and Schein, 2013).[2]

Consideration of the relative effects of the two approaches on technology innovation adds a temporal dimension to the comparison. Several theoretical explorations of this issue have found that taxes and cap-and-trade (with auctioned allowances)[3] are equivalent in their ability to incentivize carbon saving innovation (Milliman and Prince, 1989; Jung *et al.*, 1996), although under particular market conditions, carbon taxes could be superior because of their impacts on related energy prices (Scotchmer, 2011).

---

[2] Offsets refer to emission reduction credits generated when an entity reduces emissions below what they otherwise would have been. However, this raises concerns about environmental efficacy because it requires comparison with a fundamentally unobservable counterfactual.

[3] Throughout the chapter, I focus on cap-and-trade systems in which allowances are auctioned, both because this design maximizes the symmetry between price and quantity instruments and because most trading systems appear to be evolving in that direction.

Effects on International Competitiveness

By increasing the cost of producing carbon-intensive goods and services within a jurisdiction, a climate policy may shift comparative advantage to the production of those goods and services in jurisdictions where comparable climate policies do not exist. In theory, this can cause "leakage" of economic activity and related emissions. Such leakage may be relatively modest, particularly in internationally nontraded sectors, such as transportation and electricity production.[4] However, some energy-intensive manufacturing industries could face incentives to relocate (Aldy and Pizer, 2015). Additional emissions leakage may occur through international energy markets, specifically when reduced fossil fuel consumption in countries with climate policies reduces demand and drives down fuel prices, and countries without such policies respond by increasing consumption (Aldy and Stavins, 2012).

Such leakage would be equally likely to occur with either type of pricing instrument (and indeed with nearly any meaningful CO_2-limiting policy). Moreover, such leakage impacts can be mitigated, in theory, through program design. For example, border adjustments — a tax on imports of products from countries without equivalent climate policies — can be implemented together with a carbon tax (Flannery *et al.*, 2018; Cosbey *et al.*, 2019). In cap-and-trade systems, the imposition of an allowance requirement on imports, together with an allowance allocation that is periodically updated on the basis of product output levels, can help address competitiveness concerns (Stavins, 2007; Goulder and Schein, 2013). However, such allocations can have perverse effects because they tend to subsidize carbon-intensive production (Bushnell and Chen, 2012).

Possibilities for Raising Revenue

An important attribute of a carbon tax is that it raises revenue for government. This revenue can be used to achieve various objectives, including reducing other distortionary taxes, which lowers the net social cost of the overall policy (Bovenberg and Goulder, 1996). Of course, auctioning allowances in a cap-and-trade system can, in principle, accomplish the same objective (Goulder and Schein, 2013). Although both pricing

[4]However, if the relevant jurisdiction is subnational, interconnected electricity markets can foster leakage with either instrument.

mechanisms can be nearly equivalent in their ability to raise revenue, in practice, there has been more variation in allowance prices in cap-and-trade auctions than in emission quantities in carbon tax systems, which means that tax systems may well offer greater certainty regarding government revenue (Carl and Fedor, 2016).

Social Costs

The social cost of a carbon tax or a cap-and-trade system with allowance auctioning depends on how program revenues are used. Relative to a lump-sum redistribution (e.g., through direct rebates to taxpayers), recycling revenue through rate cuts in payroll taxes, individual income taxes, or corporate income taxes has been estimated to reduce the net cost of a carbon tax (after accounting for the benefits of eliminating the excess burden of distortionary taxes) by 15, 26, or 67 percent, respectively (Goulder and Hafstead, 2018).

The social costs for a cap-and-trade system with complete auctioning of allowances are similar. If revenue is redistributed via a lump-sum rebate, the social cost of the policy is identical to the social cost of a carbon tax paired with a rebate. Goulder and Hafstead (2018) find that recycling auction revenue through cuts in tax rates produces "slight differences" in costs relative to making the same tax cuts using revenue from a carbon tax. But if the comparison is between a cap-and-trade system with free allowance allocation (which generates no revenue for government) and an ordinary carbon tax, then the difference in social costs is significant (Parry *et al.*, 1999).

Distributional Impacts

From the perspective of regulated firms, a carbon tax looks much like a cap-and-trade system if allowances are auctioned. Similarly, a carbon tax that includes tradable exemptions for a specified quantity of emissions (i.e., the tax is levied only on emissions above a certain threshold) can resemble a cap-and-trade system with free allowance allocation (Goulder and Schein, 2013).

The distributional impacts can also be identical for households, but they depend on two design elements: the extent of "free" emissions and the use of revenue. This finding is based on an assessment of how carbon pricing affects household expenditures ("use-side" impacts) and household income (source-side impacts; Goulder and Hafstead, 2018; Goulder *et al.*, 2018; Metcalf, 2019a, 2019b). Use-side impacts occur through changes in the relative prices of goods and services purchased by households, while source-side impacts occur through changes in nominal wages, capital, and transfers, which in turn affect household income.

On the use side, the effects of carbon pricing are generally regressive (ignoring the return of any revenue) because of price increases, but the degree of regressivity can be altered depending on how the revenue is used (Goulder and Hafstead, 2018). On the source side, changes in wage and capital income (as well as government transfers) are generally progressive, reflecting the fact that carbon-intensive industries also tend to be relatively capital-intensive. This means that the burden of a carbon price tends to fall more on capital than on labor, and since capital income represents a larger share of income for wealthier households, the impacts are generally progressive. If revenue from a carbon tax or allowance auction is used to lower corporate tax rates, the over-all effect is still progressive, although to a somewhat lesser extent. Because source-side impacts are larger than use-side impacts for most cases in which carbon pricing is paired with revenue recycling, the overall impact of either policy — a tax or cap-and-trade with 100 percent allowance auctioning — is likely to be progressive.

Differences between Carbon Taxes and Cap-and-Trade

In terms of differences, carbon taxes and cap-and-trade are, in theory, somewhat different in terms of transaction costs, different in terms of performance in the presence of uncertainty and linkage with other jurisdictions, and significantly different in terms of carbon price volatility, interactions with complementary policies, potential for corruption and market manipulation, and complexity and administrative requirements.

Transaction Costs

Because cap-and-trade systems involve allowance trading (unless, of course, the initial allocation matches the cost-effective equilibrium), there may be transaction costs that increase aggregate compliance costs.[5]

[5] Clearly, this is not an issue with carbon taxes.

Importantly, if transaction costs take the form of volume discounts (e.g., brokers charging smaller commissions for larger trades), then decreasing marginal transaction costs may cause the equilibrium allocation achieved through market activity to depend on the initial allocation (Stavins, 1995). This removes a key political advantage of cap-and-trade: the ability to make initial allocation decisions without affecting the equilibrium outcome (Hahn and Stavins, 2012). However, market design can minimize transaction costs through, for example, provision of public clearinghouses for trading (Schmalensee and Stavins, 2013), and evidence from implemented programs indicates that these costs have generally not been significant (Schmalensee and Stavins, 2017b).

Performance in the Presence of Uncertainty

Significant uncertainty characterizes the benefits and costs of environmental protection. In the two decades following the publication of Weitzman's (1974) classic "Prices vs. Quantities" article, it was generally acknowledged that cost uncertainty could significantly affect which policy instrument was more efficient for addressing a given externality because the preferred instrument would depend on the relative slopes of the marginal benefit (damage) and marginal cost (abatement) functions. In particular, Weitzman (1974) showed that in the presence of cost uncertainty, a pure price instrument (such as a tax) is more efficient than a quantity instrument (such as cap-and-trade) when (the absolute value of) the slope of the marginal cost function is greater than (the absolute value of) the slope of the marginal benefit function. This is because there is a smaller deadweight loss due to mistaken predictions of future costs. Conversely, when the slope of the marginal benefit function is greater than the slope of the marginal cost function, cap-and-trade is more efficient.

In Weitzman's (1974) analysis, benefit uncertainty on its own has no effect on the relative efficiency of the two instruments because in neither case is the abatement response affected by abatement benefits. However, building on Weitzman (1974), Stavins (1996) found that when there is simultaneous and positively correlated uncertainty about both marginal benefits and marginal costs, it is more likely that a quantity instrument will be more efficient than would be the case in the standard relative slopes analysis. The opposite result will occur if there is negative correlation between benefit and cost uncertainty (i.e., a price instrument is more likely to be more efficient than in the standard analysis).

This finding regarding correlated benefit and cost uncertainty (Stavins, 1996) has only recently been applied in the specific context of climate policy (Karp and Traeger, 2018), although the original Weitzman (1974) analysis has been used to examine the merits of different carbon pricing strategies since the early 2000s (Hoel and Karp, 2002; Newell and Pizer, 2003). Newell and Pizer (2003) argued that because GHGs accumulate in the atmosphere (CO_2 can remain in the atmosphere for hundreds of years), changes in emissions at a specific point in time do not significantly alter atmospheric concentrations. Moreover, because climate change is a function of the atmospheric stock of GHGs, the marginal damage function (for any period) is relatively flat. This means that the marginal benefit function is also relatively flat. In contrast to damages, the costs to abate emissions are a function of current policies. This implies that current period marginal costs will have a steeper slope (in absolute value) than current period marginal benefits and that the more efficient policy will be a price instrument (Newell and Pizer, 2003).[6]

With a stock pollutant like CO_2, the marginal benefit of reducing emissions in the current period equals the present discounted value of the stream of reductions in current and future marginal damages — also known as the social cost of carbon (Interagency Working Group on Social Cost of Carbon, 2016; Aldy *et al.*, 2021). Karp and Traeger (2018) compare the slopes of the current marginal cost and marginal benefits curves (which indicate the avoided social cost of carbon) for a current unit of CO_2 reduction and employ Stavins's (1996) findings regarding the relative efficiency of price and quantity instruments in the presence of simultaneous and correlated uncertainty about benefits and costs.

Technological change is a key source of uncertainty. By reducing both current and future abatement costs (due to the persistence of technology effects), technological change creates a positive correlation between uncertainty about abatement costs and (stock-related) damages. This is because future policy makers will take lower abatement costs into account and adopt more stringent emissions targets and thereby reduce the expected future stock of GHGs in the atmosphere. Thus, Karp and Traeger (2018) find a positive correlation between uncertain benefits and uncertain costs that would — as shown by Stavins (1996) — favor a quantity instrument. It is important to note that Karp and Traeger's (2018) theoretical

[6]Using a different analytical model, Hoel and Karp (2002) independently reached the same conclusion regarding stock externalities.

analysis does not unambiguously support either a quantity or price instrument. Rather, what Newell and Pizer (2003) found to be an unambiguous result for a stock externality becomes ambiguous; that is, it becomes an empirical question, including the effect of correlated uncertainty (Stavins, 1996), rather than being solely a question of the relative slopes of the marginal cost versus marginal damages curves. When they adopt empirical estimates of key parameters from Nordhaus's (2013) DICE model, Karp and Traeger (2018) find that in many cases, a quantity instrument is superior to a price instrument. They conclude that at a minimum, in the presence of uncertainty, the case for a carbon tax over cap-and-trade "is much weaker than widely believed" (Karp and Traeger, 2018, 24).[7] In other words, the clear ranking of price over quantity instruments for the stock externality of climate change no longer holds. Given that the instruments may differ in their performance in the presence of uncertainty but that one instrument is not clearly and consistently superior to the other, I include performance in the presence of uncertainty as an area of difference but not significant difference.

Linkage with Other Jurisdictions

Linking policies across jurisdictions such that emission reductions can be redistributed across jurisdictions facilitates cost savings by allowing firms to take advantage of lower-cost abatement opportunities in other jurisdictions. In the international domain, linkage can allow for distributional equity among nations under existing international climate agreements (United Nations, 2015) without sacrificing cost-effectiveness (Bodansky *et al.*, 2015; Mehling *et al.*, 2018).

Cap-and-trade systems generate a natural unit of exchange for linkage: allowances, typically denominated in units of carbon content (for fossil fuels) or CO_2 emissions (Jaffe *et al.*, 2010). Linkage is also possible between heterogeneous instruments, such as a carbon tax in one jurisdiction and a performance standard in others (Metcalf and Weisbach, 2012), although this is more challenging to implement than linkage between two

[7] In a separate but related analysis, Pizer and Prest (2019) find that the comparative advantage of one instrument over the other depends more on firms' information and expectations about future policy than on the relative slopes of their marginal benefit and marginal cost curves.

cap-and-trade regimes (Bodansky *et al.*, 2015; Mehling *et al.*, 2018). Furthermore, either a carbon tax or a cap-and-trade system can be linked with policies in other jurisdictions via a carbon border adjustment mechanism (CBAM).[8]

Effects on Carbon Price Volatility

Under a cap-and-trade mechanism, carbon prices are endogenous (and hence subject to fluctuation and volatility), while under a carbon tax, emissions are endogenous (Goulder and Schein, 2013). This means that policies that provide greater certainty about carbon prices and hence mitigation cost, such as taxes or cap-and-trade systems with a "price collar" (i.e., an upper and lower limit on allowance prices), provide less certainty about future emissions (Aldy and Stavins, 2012). Typically, the price collar combines an auction price floor with a price that triggers the availability of additional allowances from a reserve. On the other hand, a carbon tax that is vulnerable to change for political reasons may offer less predictability than cap-and-trade in terms of the long-term price signal (Rabe, 2018). Of course, the "cap" in a cap-and-trade system may also be subject to change for political reasons.

Turning to short-term price volatility, price movements in a cap-and-trade system can discourage capital investment (Pindyck, 2017; Metcalf, 2019b), which may undermine political support and reduce investment in new technologies and research and development (Aldy and Stavins, 2012). From an economic perspective, it makes sense to allow emissions of a stock pollutant to vary from year to year with changes in economic conditions that affect aggregate abatement costs. This occurs automatically with a carbon tax, but with cap-and-trade, temporal flexibility must be incorporated through provisions for allowance banking (and possibly borrowing). In effect, this redefines the cap as a limit on cumulative emissions over a period of years, rather than a limit on annual emissions (Aldy and Stavins, 2012). Conversely, a tax can be designed to automatically adjust to meet some quantity target (Hafstead *et al.*, 2017; Metcalf, 2019b).

---

[8]For example, in 2023, the European Union plans to link a CBAM to the allowance price in its ETS.

Interactions with Complementary Policies

In jurisdictions where carbon taxes or cap-and-trade systems have actually been implemented, they have invariably been part of a larger set of climate policies. Strong economic arguments can be made for complementing a carbon pricing regime with additional policies when other market failures are present; such market failures include the principal-agent problem that affects incentives for energy efficiency improvements in renter-occupied buildings and information spillovers from research and development activities (Schmalensee and Stavins, 2017b). But when these types of market failures do not exist (and if the complementary policies target CO_2 sources that are covered by a carbon pricing regime), problems can arise, as well as differences in the consequences of a carbon tax versus a cap-and-trade system.

Under cap-and-trade, a threefold problem can arise when a complementary policy targets sources that fall under the cap (Schmalensee and Stavins, 2017b). First, if the complementary policy is binding, then it achieves no additional emission reductions beyond what is achieved by the cap-and-trade system; instead, emissions simply shift to other sectors under the overall cap (100 percent leakage), unless the complementary policy renders the allowance price floor binding. Second, marginal abatement costs are no longer equalized across sources, which means that aggregate abatement costs are higher than without the additional policy. Third, allowance prices are suppressed, which may diminish incentives for technological change. Thus, the overall effect of the complementary policy is to increase abatement costs and lower allowance prices without further reducing emissions (Goulder and Stavins, 2011).

By contrast, pairing a carbon tax with a complementary policy neither creates emissions leakage nor suppresses allowance prices. In fact, the complementary policy can serve to reduce emissions below the level that would be achieved by the tax alone. Nevertheless, combining a tax with other policies affecting the same sources will not be cost-effective because marginal abatement costs will not be identical across all sources. It would be cheaper to achieve the same aggregate emissions reduction by abandoning the complementary policy and increasing the carbon tax rate.

Potential for Corruption and Market Manipulation

Any policy can create the potential for corruption and attempts by firms to manipulate the market. Indeed, although the EU ETS has experienced just one case of allowance theft (in the Czech Republic in 2011), it was quite significant, and allowance accounts have been hacked in a number of countries (Metcalf, 2019b). Thus, cap-and-trade systems require regulatory oversight.

With a carbon tax, the parallel concern is tax evasion, which is a significant problem in many countries. In the US context, however, tax evasion is infrequent and does not present major challenges (Metcalf, 2019b). In contrast, market manipulation in cap-and-trade systems could be a problem in the United States, although only one case of fraudulent activity has been reported, and it was successfully prosecuted by the US Department of Justice.[9] No cases of fraud have been reported in California's large and ambitious cap-and-trade system or in the northeastern states' electric sector trading program (Schmalensee and Stavins, 2017b). That said, it is difficult to contest the conclusion that, at least in the United States (and probably other industrialized countries), "the risk of cybertheft from electronic registries in a cap-and-trade system is likely to present a greater problem than the risk of tax evasion in a carbon tax" (Metcalf, 2019b, p. 82).

Complexity and Administrative Requirements

The simplest cap-and-trade system is likely to involve greater design complexity than the simplest carbon tax, and greater complexity can mean higher administrative costs. At a minimum, under a cap-and-trade system, the regulatory authority must track allowances (at the end of compliance periods), possibly hold auctions, and develop necessary rules. In contrast, a carbon tax can be implemented using existing methods for monitoring and reporting fuel supplies. Thus, administrative costs are likely to be higher for cap-and-trade than for a carbon tax (Goulder and Schein, 2013).

However, it is important to note two caveats. First, the actual (marginal) administrative costs of cap-and-trade systems have not been significant (Schmalensee and Stavins, 2017b), although the fixed costs of establishing trading institutions are presumably greater than the fixed costs of establishing a carbon tax, especially where the latter can build on existing fossil fuel excise taxes. Second, experience suggests that simple tax proposals can become considerably more complex as they are passed

[9] This occurred in California's REgional CLean Air Incentives Market (RECLAIM).

into law. It is not clear whether a policy as important as a national carbon tax would turn out to be "simple" in both its design and implementation.

Hybrid Policy Instruments and a Policy Continuum

An important theme that emerges from the discussion thus far is that some differences between carbon taxes and cap-and-trade diminish with implementation. Indeed, some potential design elements of taxes and cap-and-trade systems result in what could be described as hybrids of price and quantity approaches. For example, auctioning allowances and adding mechanisms such as a price cap or price collar in order to reduce short-term price volatility and/or long-term price uncertainty can make a cap-and-trade system more like a tax (Roberts and Spence, 1976). Of course, including a ceiling on allowance prices eliminates an attribute of cap-and-trade that is important to environmental advocates — namely, certainty regarding future emissions (Goulder and Schein, 2013). However, any additional allowances the government offers for sale to contain costs could come from an allowance reserve set aside for this purpose or could be borrowed from future allocations, which means that there would be no change in the total quantity of emissions allowed over time (Stavins, 2008).

Similarly, a carbon tax can be designed to include features that make it more like cap-and-trade. To provide greater emissions certainty, for example, policy makers could employ various strategies (Aldy *et al.*, 2017). Such strategies could include a formula for adjusting the tax (Hafstead *et al.*, 2017), requiring periodic government review (Aldy, 2018), or dedicating some tax revenue to mitigation activities (Murray *et al.*, 2017). Such features can turn a pure carbon tax into a hybrid instrument, just as adding a price collar can be viewed as turning a pure cap-and-trade system into a hybrid instrument (Borenstein *et al.*, 2019). This suggests that the two carbon pricing instruments — taxes and cap-and-trade — do not present a dichotomous policy choice. Rather, each presents a choice of design elements along a policy continuum (Weisbach, 2010). This means that ultimately, the design details themselves are highly consequential, regardless of which of the two instruments is used; indeed, these details can actually be more important than the choice between the two instruments (Stavins, 1997; Keohane *et al.*, 1998; Goulder and Hafstead, 2018).

Lessons Learned from Experience with Carbon Pricing Policies

As noted in the introduction, more than 60 carbon pricing policies have been implemented or are scheduled for implementation worldwide. In this section, I discuss a few prominent examples that offer the most useful lessons for policy makers considering and possibly designing carbon pricing systems.

Lessons from Experience with Cap-and-Trade Policies

Major emissions trading programs in the United States have included the leaded gasoline phasedown (1982–1987), the sulfur dioxide (SO_2) allowance trading system (1994–2010), a trading program for nitrogen oxides (NO_x; 1998–2009), and RECLAIM in California (1993–present). All of these have been true cap-and-trade programs, except for the leaded gasoline phasedown, which involved a tradable performance standard. In addition, two prominent US trading systems specifically address CO_2 emissions: the Regional Greenhouse Gas Initiative (RGGI), implemented by a group of northeastern states (2009–present), and California's AB-32/398 system (2013–present). The world's largest carbon pricing initiative is the EU ETS (2008–present). Details on the performance of all of these systems can be found in Schmalensee and Stavins (2017a, 2017b) and Haites *et al.* (2018).

Environmental and Economic Performance

Programs such as the US lead phasedown and SO_2 allowance trading have demonstrated that cap-and-trade can be environmentally effective and economically cost-effective. For example, SO_2 trading is estimated to have reduced aggregate abatement costs by more than half relative to a well-designed command and control approach (Metcalf, 2019b). RGGI has been credited with achieving roughly half of the region's CO_2 reductions observed since the program was launched, with the remaining reductions attributed to low natural gas prices, economic recession, and other policies (Murray and Maniloff, 2015). The EU ETS had a number of problems in its pilot phase (Metcalf, 2019b) but has since functioned as anticipated (Ellerman *et al.*, 2010), producing significant emission reductions (Bayer and Aklin, 2020) and inducing climate-friendly technological change (Calel, 2020), with no observable negative impact on the economic performance of regulated firms (Dechezleprêtre *et al.*, 2018).

To date, the scope of coverage in most CO_2 trading programs has been limited. This is due to the common use of downstream sector-specific programs (e.g., that target the electricity sector), although economy-wide systems have been shown to be feasible in California. This downstream sector-specific focus contrasts with the textbook approach of trading carbon rights upstream based on fuel carbon content (World Bank Group, 2016).

Transaction Costs, Monitoring, and Enforcement

Overall, transaction costs have been small to trivial, particularly when compliance entities are homogeneous, as in the lead phasedown and SO_2 trading programs. Experience confirms the importance of establishing a cap that is well below business as usual emissions to ensure a robust allowance market (SO_2 trading, RECLAIM). Indeed, other government regulations and judicial decisions eventually eliminated the SO_2 market (Schmalensee and Stavins, 2013). High levels of compliance require a combination of strict monitoring, reporting, and verification and significant penalties for noncompliance (SO_2 trading). In addition, setting final rules well before the first compliance period can avoid unnecessary price volatility (SO_2 trading, NO_x trading, EU ETS).

Experience shows that simplicity and transparency are also important. For example, transparent rules can make allowance allocations difficult to contest or manipulate, particularly if rules are clearly defined up front. Avoiding requirements for prior regulatory approval of individual trades can also help limit uncertainty and reduce transaction costs (lead phasedown, SO_2 trading).

Flexibility Mechanisms

Experience also indicates the importance of flexible systems that allow for a broad set of compliance alternatives, in terms of timing and technology options. Studies have shown that under less flexible systems, market-based instruments would not have induced as much technological change (Ellerman and Montero, 1998; Keohane, 2003; Schmalensee and Stavins, 2013) or process innovation (Doucet and Strauss, 1994).

Provisions for allowance banking have been important and account for a large share of realized gains from trade (lead phasedown, SO_2 trading). In contrast, the absence of banking provisions can lead to allowance price spikes (RECLAIM) and collapses (EU ETS). More broadly, a changing economy can render a cap nonbinding (RGGI, EU ETS) or drive allowance prices to excessive levels (RECLAIM). Thus, there is a key role for mechanisms that establish both a floor and a ceiling on allowance prices (RGGI, AB-32/398). A comparison of such price collars (used in RGGI and AB-32/398) with quantity collars (modeled after the EU ETS Market Stability Reserve)[10] found that price collars were superior to quantity collars in terms of reducing price volatility and increasing efficiency (Holt and Shobe, 2016). However, excessive constraints on the use of offsets can render this mechanism ineffective for cost containment (RGGI, AB-32/398).

Allowance Allocations

Free allowance allocation has been used to gain initial political support for trading programs, although this strategy forgoes the opportunity to reduce overall social cost by using revenues from auctions to cut distortionary taxes (SO_2 trading, AB-32/398). Where allowances have been auctioned, the revenues have more often been used to fund new or existing government programs, not to cut distortionary taxes as economists would recommend (AB-32/398, RGGI). In fact, allowance auctions have generated very significant revenue for governments (RGGI, AB-32/398).

Over time, there has been a trend toward greater use of allowance auctioning in cap-and-trade systems (AB-32/398, RGGI, EU ETS), which has resulted in more systems that can be characterized as hybrids of price and quantity instruments. Other design elements aimed at containing costs or reducing short-term price volatility and/or long-term price uncertainty have further blurred the distinction between cap-and-trade systems and a tax.

The increasing use of price collars has reinforced the trend toward hybrid systems. Although the price ceiling in the California cap-and-trade system has been "soft" in the sense that the reserve supply was finite, the state's post-2020 system includes a hard cap on prices by making an unlimited number of allowances available at a specified, escalating price level

[10]The Market Stability Reserve adjusts the number of allowances available at auction.

(Schatzki and Stavins, 2018), further reinforcing the trend toward truly hybrid systems.

Competitiveness Impacts

The competitiveness impacts of cap-and-trade systems have been a prominent political concern. In practice, leakage from cap-and-trade systems has ranged from nonexistent (lead phasedown) to potentially serious, as in the case of RGGI (Fell and Maniloff, 2018). Free allowance allocation will not address these problems per se (EU ETS), but an output-based updating allowance allocation can provide an effective response (AB-32/398).

Complementary Policies

Although complementary policies can play a constructive role in a carbon pricing regime, in practice, such policies have frequently conflicted with trading programs, causing emissions to be relocated rather than reduced, driving up abatement costs, and suppressing allowance prices (Organization for Economic Cooperation and Development, 2011). This perverse outcome has occurred in two of the most prominent applications of cap-and-trade for climate mitigation purposes (AB-32/398, EU ETS).

The extent of such perverse interactions between a complementary policy and the cap-and-trade system within which it is nested can be measured by the difference in marginal abatement costs between the two policies. For example, in spring 2021, allowances in California's two distinct trading systems — the AB-32/398 program and the state's refinery-based Low Carbon Fuel Standard — were trading at about \$19 per ton of CO_2 and nearly \$200 per ton, respectively. This very large gap indicates a dramatic departure from cost-effective policy design. Such perverse policy interactions (Fankhauser *et al.*, 2010) may be partially addressed through reforms such as the market stability reserves introduced in the EU, California, and RGGI trading systems (Perino *et al.*, 2019).

Lessons from Experience with Carbon Taxes

In contrast to cap-and-trade, most pollution taxes, including the 30 carbon taxes (as of 2020) identified by the World Bank (World Bank Group, 2020), thus far have focused on CO_2 (or closely related energy generation).

The high carbon taxes adopted by several northern European countries and a more recent carbon tax implemented in British Columbia are the most prominent applications of this instrument.

Northern European Carbon Taxes

In the 1990s, several northern European countries implemented carbon taxes as part of broader tax policy changes, frequently as excise tax reforms (Murray and Rivers, 2015). These policies have differed in the scope of their coverage and their tax rates, and many have been in place simultaneously (or even linked) with the EU ETS, making it difficult to assess their impacts (Murray and Rivers, 2015). Some of these countries, such as Sweden, now impose the highest carbon prices in the world, although there are significant variations in the effective tax per unit of CO_2 across fuels and industries within each country (Bruvoll and Larsen, 2004; Daugjberg and Pedersen, 2004). Provisions to cushion fiscal impacts have been common, especially where industries have raised concerns about international competitiveness (Aldy and Stavins, 2012). As a result, carbon taxes have typically not provided uniform price signals across emission sources. Unfortunately, there is only limited empirical evidence on the emissions impacts of these carbon taxes. In 1991, Sweden implemented a CO_2 tax of $33 per ton as a part of fiscal reforms that cut income tax rates (Speck, 2008). The tax, which has since increased to about $120 per ton, has generated considerable revenue for Sweden's general budget, as the government does not earmark tax revenues (Government Offices of Sweden, 2019). One recent analysis indicates that transport sector CO_2 emissions fell after the country implemented both carbon and value-added taxes on transport fuel (Andersson, 2019).

In 1991, Norway implemented a carbon tax that applied different rates to different sectors. In 2009, the tax covered about 55 percent of the country's GHG emissions, while a trading scheme linked to the EU ETS covered an additional 13 percent of emissions. Denmark's tax began at about $18 per ton of CO_2 in 1992 and reached $28 per ton by 2020, but with a lower rate for manufacturers (Speck, 2008; World Bank Group, 2020). Finland has imposed a general tax on energy, coupled with a carbon-based fuel surtax, since 1997. The tax on CO_2 ranges from about $58 to $68 per ton, depending on the sector (World Bank Group, 2020).

British Columbia's Carbon Tax

Established in 2008, British Columbia's carbon tax comes closest to the "ideal" form recommended by economists (Metcalf, 2019b). The tax, which is part of a broader plan to cut provincial GHG emissions by a third (British Columbia, 2021), was intended to be economy-wide, covering approximately 70–75 percent of GHG emissions. It is collected upstream at the wholesale level (from fuel distributors) on the basis of fuel carbon content (Duff, 2008). The tax does not apply to non-fossil fuel GHG emissions (including from industrial processes, landfills, forestry, and agriculture) or methane. In addition, fuel exports, including virtually all of the coal mined in the province (Murray and Rivers, 2015), fuels used by aviation and shipping into or out of the province, and operations and fuels used in agriculture (since 2012), are exempt.

British Columbia's tax began at \$7.50 per ton of CO_2 in 2008 and increased gradually thereafter; it is now \$32 per ton and is scheduled to increase to \$40 in 2022 (British Columbia, 2021). Originally, all of the revenue was to be refunded through tax cuts to businesses and individuals, with low-income individuals protected through a targeted tax credit. Over time, the policy has evolved to provide additional tax cuts to specific sectors and locations (Murray and Rivers, 2015; Goulder and Hafstead, 2018). Considering both use-side and source-side impacts, the tax appears to be progressive, even without accounting for revenue use (Beck *et al.*, 2015). However, empirical evidence on the policy's environmental impacts is unclear. One study estimates province-wide CO_2 reductions of 5–10 percent, with little negative economic impact (Metcalf, 2019b) but with unknown emissions leakage (Murray and Rivers, 2015). Other research questions whether emissions have been reduced at all (Pretis, 2019).

Summary and Conclusions

This chapter has identified the theoretical and empirical similarities and differences between carbon taxes and cap-and-trade, examined their advantages and disadvantages, and highlighted some of the key lessons learned from experience with these policies. I find that when carbon taxes and carbon cap-and-trade systems are designed in ways that make them truly comparable, their characteristics and outcomes are similar and, in some respects, fully equivalent, particularly concerning key dimensions such as emission reductions, abatement costs, possibilities for raising revenue, costs to regulated firms, distributional impacts, and effects on competitiveness. However, the two approaches can perform quite differently in terms of other dimensions, sometimes favoring taxes and sometimes favoring cap-and-trade. In terms of complexity and administrative requirements, interaction with complementary policies, and effects on carbon price volatility, a tax has clear advantages. On the other hand, cap-and-trade may have advantages in terms of ease of linkage with policies in other jurisdictions and, possibly, anticipated performance in the presence of uncertainty. The major differences between the two approaches depend on the details of program design. Indeed, I argue that what appears at first glance to be a dichotomous choice between two distinct instruments can end up being a choice of specific design elements along a policy continuum.

I find that neither approach clearly dominates in terms of anticipated performance, and any ranking of the two instruments in a specific context would likely depend on the weight given to different policy considerations (Goulder and Hafstead, 2018). When there are relatively minor differences in impacts, a key question becomes which of the two approaches is more politically feasible and which is more likely to be well designed (Furman *et al.*, 2007). Judgments about political feasibility might be informed by the revealed preference of jurisdictions that have adopted carbon pricing strategies, but thus far carbon tax and CO_2 cap-and-trade systems have been introduced in roughly equal numbers around the world (World Bank Group, 2020). A more informative comparison of the two approaches might be to focus instead on the combination of the scope of coverage and program stringency (measured by allowance price or tax level), in which case cap-and-trade stands out as the more important approach worldwide, at least for the present time.

An examination of which type of system is more likely to be better designed is consistent with the notion that a policy's net benefits should be weighted by the probability that the policy will be implemented in the first place (Pizer *et al.*, 2020). Indeed, even if carbon pricing is the first-best policy for the long term, other strategies may be more politically achievable in the short term (Gillis, 2018; Goulder, 2019). To illustrate this point, while 61 jurisdictions have carbon taxes or cap-and-trade policies, fully 176 countries have adopted renewable energy policies or energy efficiency standards, and another 110 jurisdictions have implemented feed-in tariffs (Carattini *et al.*, 2017). This highlights that building political acceptance for pricing instruments more broadly could be a key step toward more effective climate policy action.

Public perceptions — some of them inaccurate — appear to be a primary reason for aversion to carbon pricing (Carattini *et al.*, 2017). Hence, one approach might be to improve public understanding of such policies through better media coverage, not to mention broader educational initiatives. But careful policy design would be another and perhaps more effective approach. For example, departing from first-best design may make carbon emission taxes or caps more palatable (Jaccard, 2012), as suggested by the gradual phased approach in California and British Columbia. Of course, this could lead to a carbon price becoming stuck at a level that is too low to achieve the environmental objective, in which case a commitment device, such as a trajectory of tax levels or caps over time, may be helpful. For example, the legislation that established the US SO_2 trading program and the British Columbia and Swedish carbon taxes included such trajectories for future caps and tax rates.

Another departure from first-best design would be to earmark revenues to finance additional mitigation (Kotchen *et al.*, 2017) or to address equity concerns. Either pricing instrument can be designed to be revenue neutral by including lump-sum rebates of tax (or auction) revenue or by using revenue to cushion impacts on low-income or other burdened constituencies (Amdur *et al.*, 2014; Carattini *et al.*, 2017). But as surveys in several countries suggest, there is a distinct lack of public support for using revenue to cut distortionary taxes (Carattini *et al.*, 2017). Perhaps voters do not understand the logic of the "double dividend" (Goulder, 1995), or perhaps they simply harbor doubts that governments will actually follow through on cutting other taxes. In contrast, in many countries, there is support for using carbon pricing revenue to ease impacts on low-income households (Carattini *et al.*, 2017). In fact, proposals from across the US political spectrum have featured carbon dividend or cap-and-dividend systems, which return revenues directly to citizens (Boyce and Riddle, 2007; Sedor, 2015; US House of Representatives, 2018; Akerlof *et al.*, 2019).

Is there now a political opening for well-designed carbon taxes in the United States? The successful demonization of the Obama administration's CO_2 cap-and-trade proposal as "cap-and-tax" (Wall Street Journal, 2009) might present such an opening for more serious consideration of a carbon tax in this country. In particular, large budget deficits may heighten interest in new sources of revenue, with consumption taxes — such as energy or carbon taxes — likely to be particularly attractive in this regard. The past few years have witnessed support for such strategies, not only in the broader policy community and among the usual Democratic sources of support but also among prominent Republican academic economists and former high-level government officials (Akerlof *et al.*, 2019).

However, the prospects for support among current elected US officials are decidedly less clear. Indeed, if it was possible to rally opposition to cap-and-trade by calling it "cap-and-tax," it will be that much easier to label a carbon tax a "tax." Even the progressive politicians who authored the Green New Deal in the United States did not make a carbon tax central to their proposal. Given that any national carbon pricing policy appears likely to continue to face an uphill battle in the United States, it may be more productive for economists to redirect some of their attention to designing better second-best nonpricing policies, such as better performance standards. At some point, however, the politics surrounding climate policy will change. Thus, it is important that research on carbon pricing instruments continues, particularly if it is focused on policies that are likely (sooner or later) to be politically feasible, whether in the United States or other countries.

Acknowledgments

This chapter draws in part from Stavins (2019). Valuable comments on that working paper were provided by Lawrence Goulder, Larry Karp, Gilbert Metcalf, William Pizer, and Richard Schmalensee. I am grateful to Marika Tatsutani, two anonymous referees of this journal, and Suzanne Leonard, who provided exceptionally helpful comments and suggestions for this chapter. I am responsible for all remaining errors.

References

Akerlof, G., R. Aumann, A. Deaton, P. Diamond, R. Engle, E. Fama, L. P. Hansen, *et al.* (2019). "Economists' statement on carbon dividends." *Wall Street Journal*, January 16.

Aldy, J. E. (2018). "Carbon tax review and updating." Unpublished Paper, John F. Kennedy School of Government, Harvard University, Cambridge, MA.

Aldy, J. E. and W. A. Pizer. (2015). "Competitiveness impacts of climate change mitigation policies." *Journal of the Association of Environmental and Resource Economists*. **2**(4): 565–595.

Aldy, J. E. and R. N. Stavins. (2012). "The promise and problems of pricing carbon: Theory and practice." *Journal of Environment and Development*. **21**(2): 152–180.

Aldy, J. E., M. J. Kotchen, R. N. Stavins, and J. H. Stock. (2021). “Keep climate policy focused on the social cost of carbon.” *Science*. **373**(6557): 850–852.

Aldy, J. E., M. Hafstead, G. E. Metcalf, B. C. Murray, W. A. Pizer, C. Reichert, and R. W. Williams. (2017). “Resolving inherent uncertainty of carbon taxes.” *Harvard Environmental Law Review*. **41**: 1–13.

Amdur, D., B. G. Rabe, and C. Borick. (2014). “Public views on a carbon tax depend on the proposed use of revenue.” *Issues in Energy and Environmental Policy*. **13**: 1–9.

Andersson, J. J. (2019). “Carbon taxes and CO2 emissions: Sweden as a case study.” *American Economic Journal*. **11**(4): 1–30.

Bayer, P. and M. Aklin. (2020). “The European Union emissions trading system reduced CO2 emissions despite low prices.” *Proceedings of the National Academy of Sciences of the USA*. **117**(16): 8804–8812.

Beck, M., N. Rivers, R. Wigle, and H. Yonezawa. (2015). “Carbon tax and revenue recycling: Impacts on households in British Columbia.” *Resource and Energy Economics*. **41**: 40–69.

Bodansky, D., S. Hoedl, G. Metcalf, and R. Stavins. (2015). “Facilitating linkage of climate policies through the Paris outcome.” *Climate Policy*. **16**(8): 956–972.

Borenstein, S., J. Bushnell, F. A. Wolak, and M. Zaragoza-Watkins. (2019). “Expecting the unexpected: Emissions uncertainty and environmental market design.” *American Economic Review*. **109**(11): 3953–3977.

Bovenberg, A. L. and L. H. Goulder. (1996). “Optimal environmental taxation in the presence of other taxes: General equilibrium analyses.” *American Economic Review*. **86**(4): 985–1000.

Boyce, J. K. and M. Riddle. (2007). *Cap and Dividend: How to Cap Global Warming While Protecting the Incomes of American Families*. Working Paper 150, Political Economy Research Institute, University of Massachusetts, Amherst.

British Columbia. (2021). “British Columbia’s carbon tax.” https://www2.gov.bc.ca/gov/content/environment/climate-change/clean-economy/carbon-tax.

Bruvoll, A. and B. M. Larsen. (2004). “Greenhouse gas emissions in Norway: Do carbon taxes work?” *Energy Policy*. **32**: 493–505.

Bushnell, J. and Y. Chen. (2012). “Allocation and leakage in regional cap-and-trade markets for CO2.” *Resource and Energy Economics*. **34**: 647–668.

Calel, R. (2020). “Adopt or innovate: Understanding technological responses to cap-and-trade.” *American Economics Journal*. **12**(3): 170–201.

Carattini, S., M. Carvalho, and S. Fankhauser. (2017). *How to Make Carbon Taxes More Acceptable*. Policy Report, Grantham Research Institute on Climate Change and the Environment and Centre for Climate Change Economics and Policy, London School of Economics and Political Science, London.

Carl, J. and D. Fedor. (2016). "Tracking global carbon revenues: A survey of carbon taxes versus cap-and-trade in the real world." *Energy Policy*. **96**: 50–77.

Cosbey, A., S. Droege, C. Fischer, and C. Munnings. (2019). "Developing guidance for implementing border carbon adjustments: Lessons, cautions, and research needs from the literature." *Review of Environmental Economics and Policy*. **13**(1): 3–22.

Daugjberg, C. and A. B. Pedersen. (2004). "New policy ideas and old policy networks: Implementing green taxation in Scandinavia." *Journal of Public Policy*. **24**(2): 219–249.

Dechezleprêtre, A., D. Nachtigall, and F. Venmans. (2018). *The Joint Impact of the European Union Emissions Trading System on Carbon Emissions and Economic Performance*. OECD Economics Department Working Papers No. 1515, Organization for Economic Cooperation and Development, Paris.

Doucet, J. A. and T. Strauss. (1994). "On the bundling of coal and sulfur dioxide emissions allowances." *Energy Policy*. **22**(9): 764–770.

Duff, D. G. (2008). "Carbon taxation in British Columbia." *Vermont Journal of Environmental Law*. **10**: 85–105.

Ellerman, A. D. and J.-P. Montero. (1998). "The declining trend in sulfur dioxide emissions: Implications for allowance prices." *Journal of Environmental Economics and Management*. **36**: 26–45.

Ellerman, A. D., F. J. Convery, and C. de Perthuis (eds.). (2010). *Pricing Carbon: The European Union Emissions Trading Scheme*. Cambridge: Cambridge University Press.

Ellerman, A. D., P. L. Joskow, and D. Harrison. (2003). *Emissions Trading in the U.S.: Experience, Lessons, and Considerations for Greenhouse Gases*. Arlington, VA: Pew Center on Global Climate Change.

Fankhauser, S., C. Hepburn, and J. Park. (2010). "Combining multiple climate policy instruments: How not to do it." *Climate Change Economics*. **1**(3): 209–225.

Fell, H. and P. Maniloff. (2018). "Leakage in regional environmental policy: The case of the Regional Greenhouse Gas Initiative." *Journal of Environmental Economics and Management*. **87**: 1–23.

Flannery, B., J. Hillman, J. Mares, and M. Porterfield. (2018). *Framework Proposal for a US Upstream Greenhouse Gas Tax with WTO-Compliant Border Adjustments*. RFF Report, Resources for the Future, Washington, DC, October.

Furman, J., J. E. Bordoff, M. Deshpande, and P. J. Noel. (2007). "An economic strategy to address climate change and promote energy security." Strategy Paper, Hamilton Project, Brookings Institution, Washington, DC.

Gillis, J. (2018). "Forget the carbon tax for now." *New York Times*, December 27.

Goulder, L. H. (1995). "Environmental taxation and the 'double dividend': A reader's guide." *International Tax and Public Finance*. **2**(2): 277–313.

Goulder, L. H. (2019). *Addressing the Urgency of Climate-Change Policy*. Working Paper, Stanford University, Stanford, CA, March.

Goulder, L. H. and M. A. C. Hafstead. (2018). *Confronting the Climate Challenge: U.S. Policy Options*. New York: Columbia University Press.

Goulder, L. H. and A. R. Schein. (2013). "Carbon taxes versus cap and trade: A critical review." *Climate Change Economics*. **4**(3): 1–28.

Goulder, L. H. and R. N. Stavins. (2011). "Challenges from state-federal interactions in U.S. climate change policy." *American Economic Review Papers and Proceedings*. **101**(3): 253–257.

Goulder, L. H., M. A. C. Hafstead, G. Kim, and X. Long. (2018). *Impacts of a Carbon Tax Across U.S. Household Income Groups: What are the Equity-Efficiency Trade-Offs?* NBER Working Paper No. 25181, National Bureau of Economic Research, Cambridge, MA, October.

Government Offices of Sweden. (2019). "Sweden's carbon tax."

Hafstead, M., G. E. Metcalf, and R. C. Williams. (2017). "Adding quantity certainty to a carbon tax: The role of a tax adjustment mechanism for policy pre-commitment." *Harvard Environmental Law Review*. **41**: 41–57.

Hahn, R. W. and R. N. Stavins. (2012). "The effect of allowance allocations on cap-and-trade system performance." *Journal of Law and Economics*. **54**(4): S267–S294.

Haites, E., D. Maosheng, K. Sims Gallagher, S. Mascher, E. Narassimhan, K. Richards, and M. Wakabayashi. (2018). "Experience with carbon taxes and greenhouse gas emissions trading systems." *Duke Environmental Law and Policy Forum*. **29**: 109–182.

Hoel, M. and L. Karp. (2002). "Taxes versus quotas for a stock pollutant." *Resource and Energy Economics*. **24**: 367–384.

Holt, C. A. and W. M. Shobe. (2016). "Price and quantity collars for stabilizing emission allowance prices: Laboratory experiments on the EU ETS market stability reserve." *Journal of Environmental Economics and Management*. **76**: 32–50.

Interagency Working Group on Social Cost of Carbon. (2016). *Technical Update of the Social Cost of Carbon for Regulatory Impact Analysis Under Executive Order 12866*. Technical Support Document, US Government, Washington, DC.

Jaccard, M. (2012). "The political acceptability of carbon taxes: Lessons from British Columbia." In *Handbook of Research on Environmental Taxation*, J. E. Milne and M. S. Andersen (eds.), pp. 175–191. Cheltenham, UK: Edward Elgar.

Jaffe, J., M. Ranson, and R. N. Stavins. (2010). "Linking tradable permit systems: A key element of emerging international climate policy architecture." *Ecology Law Quarterly*. **36**: 789–808.

Jung, C., K. Krutilla, and R. Boyd. (1996). "Incentives for advanced pollution abatement technology at the industry level: An evaluation of policy instruments." *Journal of Environmental Economics and Management*. **30**: 95–111.

Kaplow, L. (2010). *Taxes, Permits, and Climate Change*. NBER Working Paper No. 16268, National Bureau of Economic Research, Cambridge, MA.

Karp, L. and C. Traeger. (2018). *Prices versus Quantities Reassessed*. CESifo Working Paper 7331, Munich Society for the Promotion of Economic Research, Munich, November.

Keohane, N. O. (2003). *What Did the Market Buy? Cost Savings Under the U.S. Tradeable Permits Program for Sulfur Dioxide*. Working Paper YCELP-01-11-2003, Yale Center for Environmental Law and Policy, New Haven, CT.

Keohane, N. O. (2009). "Cap and trade, rehabilitated: Using tradable permits to control U.S. greenhouse gases." *Review of Environmental Economics and Policy*. **3**: 42–62.

Keohane, N. O., R. L. Revesz, and R. N. Stavins. (1998). "The choice of regulatory instruments in environmental policy." *Harvard Environmental Law Review*. **22**(2): 313–367.

Knittel, C. R. (2019). *Diary of a Wimpy Carbon Tax: Carbon Taxes as Federal Climate Policy*. CEEPR WP 2019-013, August, MIT Center for Energy and Environmental Policy Research, Cambridge, MA.

Kotchen, M. J., Z. M. Turk, and A. A. Leiserowitz. (2017). "Public willingness to pay for a U.S. carbon tax and preferences for spending the revenue." *Environmental Research Letters*. **12**: 094012.

Mankiw, L. G. (2006). "The Pigou Club manifesto." *Greg Mankiw's Blog*. http://gregmankiw.blogspot.com/2006/10/pigou-club-manifesto.html.

Mehling, M. A., G. E. Metcalf, and R. N. Stavins. (2018). "Linking climate policies to advance global mitigation." *Science*. **359**(6379): 997–998.

Metcalf, G. E. (2007). *A Proposal for a U.S. Carbon Tax Swap: An Equitable Tax Reform to Address Global Climate Change*. Discussion Paper 2007-12, Hamilton Project, Brookings Institution, Washington, DC.

Metcalf, G. E. (2009). "Market-based policy options to control U.S. greenhouse gas emissions." *Journal of Economic Perspectives*. **23**(2): 5–27.

Metcalf, G. E. (2019a). "The distributional impacts of U.S. energy policy." *Energy Policy*. **129**(June): 926–929.

Metcalf, G. E. (2019b). *Paying for Pollution: Why a Carbon Tax Is Good for America*. New York: Oxford University Press.

Metcalf, G. E. and D. Weisbach. (2012). "Linking policies when tastes differ: Global climate policy in a heterogeneous world." *Review of Environmental Economics and Policy*. **6**(1): 110–129.

Milliman, S. R. and R. Prince. (1989). "Firm incentives to promote technological change in pollution control." *Journal of Environmental Economics and Management*. **17**: 247–265.

Murray, B. and P. Maniloff. (2015). "Why have greenhouse gas emissions in RGGI states declined? an econometric attribution to economic, energy market, and policy factors." *Energy Economics*. **51**: 581–589.

Murray, B. and N. Rivers. (2015). "British Columbia's revenue-neutral carbon tax: A review of the latest 'grand experiment' in environmental policy." *Energy Policy*. **86**: 674–683.

Murray, B., W. A. Pizer, and C. Reichert. (2017). "Increasing emissions certainty under a carbon tax." *Harvard Environmental Law Review*. **41**: 14–27.

Newell, R. G. and W. A. Pizer. (2003). "Regulating stock externalities under uncertainty." *Journal of Environmental Economics and Management*. **45**: 416–432.

Newell, R. G. and R. N. Stavins. (2003). "Cost heterogeneity and the potential savings from market-based policies." *Journal of Regulatory Economics*. **23**: 43–59.

Newell, R. G., A. B. Jaffe, and R. N. Stavins. (1999). "The induced innovation hypothesis and energy-saving technological change." *Quarterly Journal of Economics*. **114**: 941–975.

Nordhaus, W. D. (2007). "To tax or not to tax: Alternative approaches to slowing global warming." *Review of Environmental Economics and Policy*. **1**: 26–44.

Nordhaus, W. D. (2013). *The Climate Casino: Risk, Uncertainty, and Economics for a Warming World*. New Haven, CT: Yale University Press.

Organization for Economic Cooperation and Development. (2011). *Interactions Between Emission Trading Systems and Other Overlapping Policy Instruments*. General Distribution Document, Environment Directorate, Organization for Economic Cooperation and Development, Paris.

Parry, I. W. H., R. C. Williams, and L. H. Goulder. (1999). "When can carbon abatement policies increase welfare? the fundamental role of distorted factor markets." *Journal of Environmental Economics and Management*. **37**: 52–84.

Perino, G., R. A. Ritz, and A. van Benthem. (2019). *Understanding Overlapping Policies: Internal Carbon Leakage and the Punctured Waterbed*. NBER Working Paper No. 25643, March, National Bureau of Economic Research, Cambridge.

Pindyck, R. S. (2017). "Coase lecture — taxes, targets, and the social cost of carbon." *Economica*. **84**: 345–364.

Pizer, W. A. and B. C. Prest. (2019). *Prices versus Quantities with Policy Updating*. NBER Working Paper No. 22379, June, National Bureau of Economic Research, Cambridge, MA.

Pizer, W. A., R. N. Stavins, and D. N. Stuart. (2020). "Incorporating political feasibility into economic analysis: The expected net benefits of alternative climate change policy instruments." Harvard Environmental Economics Program, Cambridge, MA.

Pretis, F. (2019). "Does a carbon tax reduce CO2 emissions? evidence from British Columbia." *SSRN*. https://ssrn.com/abstract=3329512.

Rabe, B. (2018). *Can We Price Carbon?* Cambridge, MA: MIT Press.

Roberts, M. J. and M. Spence. (1976). "Effluent charges and licenses under uncertainty." *Journal of Public Economics*. **5**: 193–208.

Schatzki, T. and R. N. Stavins. (2018). *Key Issues Facing California's GHG Cap-and-Trade System for 2021–2030*. M-RCBG Faculty Working Paper Series No. 2018-02, Mossavar-Rahmani Center for Business and Government, Harvard Kennedy School, Cambridge, MA.

Schmalensee, R. and R. N. Stavins. (2013). "The SO2 allowance trading system: The ironic history of a grand policy experiment." *Journal of Economic Perspectives*. **27**(1): 103–122.

Schmalensee, R. and R. N. Stavins. (2017a). "The design of environmental markets: What have we learned from experience with cap and trade?" *Oxford Review of Economic Policy*. **33**(4): 572–588.

Schmalensee, R. and R. N. Stavins. (2017b). "Lessons learned from three decades of experience with cap and trade." *Review of Environmental Economics and Policy*. **11**(1): 59–79.

Scotchmer, S. (2011). "Cap-and-trade, emissions taxes, and innovation." *Innovation Policy and the Economy*. **11**: 29–54.

Sedor, N. (2015). "Why fee and dividend is better than cap and trade at fighting climate change." *Los Angeles Times*, March 5.

Speck, S. (2008). "The design of carbon and broad-based energy taxes in European countries." *Vermont Journal of Environmental Law*. **10**: 31–59.

Stavins, R. N. (1995). "Transaction costs and tradeable permits." *Journal of Environmental Economics and Management*. **29**: 133–146.

Stavins, R. N. (1996). "Correlated uncertainty and policy instrument choice." *Journal of Environmental Economics and Management*. **30**: 218–232.

Stavins, R. N. (1997). "What can we learn from the grand policy experiment? positive and normative lessons from SO2 allowance trading." *Journal of Economic Perspectives*. **12**(3): 69–88.

Stavins, R. N. (2007). *A U.S. Cap-and-Trade System to Address Global Climate Change*. Discussion Paper 2007-13, Hamilton Project, Brookings Institution, Washington, DC.

Stavins, R. N. (2008). "A meaningful U.S. cap-and-trade system to address climate change." *Harvard Environmental Law Review*. **32**(2): 293–371.

Stavins, R. N. (2019). *The Future of U.S. Carbon-Pricing Policy*. NBER Working Paper No. 25912, National Bureau of Economic Research, Cambridge, MA.

United Nations. (2015). "Paris agreement." December 12.

US House of Representatives. (2018). *Energy Innovation and Carbon Dividend Act of 2018*. H.R. 7173, November 27.

Wall Street Journal. (2009). "The cap and tax fiction." June 26.

Weisbach, D. (2010). "Instrument choice is instrument design." In *U.S. Energy Tax Policy*, G. E. Metcalf (ed.), pp. 113–158. Cambridge: Cambridge University Press.

Weitzman, M. L. (1974). "Prices vs. quantities." *Review of Economic Studies*. **41**(4): 477–491.

World Bank Group. (2016). *Emissions Trading in Practice: Handbook on Design and Implementation*. Washington, DC: Partnership for Market Readiness and International Carbon Action Partnership.

World Bank Group. (2020). *State and Trends of Carbon Pricing*. Washington, DC: World Bank Group.

https://doi.org/10.1142/9789811292415_0013

Chapter 13

Keep Climate Policy Focused on the Social Cost of Carbon: A Proposed Shift away from the SCC is Ill Advised*

Joseph E. Aldy[†,‡,§,], Matthew J. Kotchen[‡,‖,††], Robert N. Stavins[†,‡,§,‡‡], and James H. Stock[†,‡,§,¶,§§]**

[†]*John F. Kennedy School of Government, Harvard University, Cambridge, MA, USA*

[‡]*National Bureau of Economic Research, Cambridge, MA, USA*

[§]*Resources for the Future, Washington, DC, USA*

[‖]*School of the Environment, Yale University, New Haven, CT, USA*

[¶]*Department of Economics, Harvard University, Cambridge, MA, USA*

[**]*joseph_aldy@hks.harvard.edu*

[††]*matthew.kotchen@yale.edu*

[‡‡]*robert_stavins@harvard.edu*

[§§]*james_stock@harvard.edu*

In the context of climate change, the application of cost-benefit analysis to inform mitigation policies can help to achieve the best outcomes and avoid

*This chapter was originally published in *Science*, **373**(6557), 20 August 2021. doi: 10.1126/science.abi7813.

the worst: spending trillions of dollars but failing to get the job done (Arrow, 1996). The costs of a climate policy are the abatement costs of reducing emissions of carbon dioxide (CO_2) (or other greenhouse gases). The standard measure of the benefits of a climate policy is the social cost of carbon (SCC), which measures the avoided economic damages associated with a metric ton of CO_2 emissions. Recently, however, there have been calls for an alternative approach to policy evaluation that ignores the benefits of avoided climate damages and instead focuses only on minimizing the compliance costs of a given, politically determined climate objective (Stern and Stiglitz, 2021; Kaufman *et al.*, 2020). We argue here that a shift from use of the SCC and cost-benefit analysis to an alternative approach for evaluating policy that focuses on costs alone would be misguided. Rather than advocate for alternative approaches, now is the time to support efforts to update the SCC and its application to official climate policy evaluation.

The SCC

The economic value of a policy's climate benefits is the sum of current and future damages that are avoided. The SCC is the monetized value of these benefits per metric ton of CO_2 abated. Those avoided damages include impacts on agricultural production, reductions in labor productivity, property damage (particularly along coastal areas), mortality and morbidity impacts, and induced migration, among others.

SCC estimations need to integrate climate and economic models, make economic projections into the distant future, and put those damages on a current-day basis by discounting them back to the present (Goulder and Stavins, 2002). And all of this must take place in the context of considerable scientific and economic uncertainty. In the United States, the original federal government estimates of the SCC (Interagency Working Group on Social Cost of Carbon, 2010) used the results of scientific and economic research that were then available to develop initial estimates and subsequent updates. Although the Trump administration asserted an alternative set of assumptions to vastly reduce the value of the SCC, it never questioned the use of the SCC for cost-benefit analysis, nor were its alternative set of assumptions adopted more broadly or supported by the economics community.

From 2008 to 2019, SCC estimates were used in 60 federal regulatory analyses (see supplementary materials). In addition to such analyses, SCC estimates can be used to inform the design of carbon-pricing climate policy instruments, which use price signals to bring about emissions reductions, typically either as a carbon tax or as a CO_2 cap-and-trade system (for example, British Columbia's carbon tax and the European Union's emissions trading system). A substantial number of state governments use the federal SCC to evaluate their own energy and climate policies. In New York and Illinois, the SCC serves as the basis for the value of "zero-emission credits" paid to electric utilities under state clean-energy legislation. In Colorado, Minnesota, and Washington, electric utilities are required to use the federal SCC in their resource planning. And in California, legislation requires regulators to incorporate the SCC in policy analysis. Outside of the United States, the Canadian government has adopted the estimation methodology, and several other national governments as well as the International Monetary Fund have developed their own SCC estimates or drawn on the US experience, including France, Germany, Mexico, and Norway (Aldy *et al.*, 2021).

On his first day in office, President Biden issued an executive order (Biden, 2021) to reestablish the Interagency Working Group on the Social Cost of Greenhouse Gases and directed it to produce within 30 days an "interim SCC" and a final SCC no later than January 2022. The administration recently issued its interim SCC, with a primary value of \$51/ton and ranging from \$14 to \$152/ton (in 2020 US dollars) (Interagency Working Group on Social Cost of Greenhouse Gases, 2021), which is in line with the SCC used under the Obama administration (Interagency Working Group on Social Cost of Carbon, 2010) after adjusting for inflation. These numbers, or any subsequent revisions, are to be used to quantify the climate benefits of federal policies in official cost-benefit analyses (Arrow, 1996). In practice, their use can change an overall assessment from negative to positive net benefits (Pizer *et al.*, 2014). President Biden has also tasked agencies to consider applying the SCC to monetize the climate benefits of budget, procurement, and other government actions (Biden, 2021).

A Target-Consistent Price

Cost-benefit analysis is not the only way economists evaluate policies. An alternative is cost-effectiveness analysis, which is used to compare policies with the same objective. In the case of climate policy, this involves identifying some target, such as a maximum increase in the global average temperature or a date by which zero net emissions of CO_2 is to be achieved, and then comparing the costs of alternative approaches to achieve that target.

With a given target and the cost-effectiveness approach, policy evaluation no longer entails comparing costs to benefits but rather focuses on adopting the lowest cost policy to achieve the target. In practice, the menu of all possible policies is not available, nor are their costs. Still, it is possible to compare the cost of a particular candidate policy with some threshold, which is a modeled estimate of the minimum-cost policy consistent with achieving the given target. In the context of climate policy, the minimum costs are actually a time path of carbon prices equal to the estimated marginal costs of abatement in each future year until the target is met. To be clear, these carbon prices are not equivalent to — and are not intended to reflect — the marginal benefits of lowering emissions, as with the SCC. Instead, they reflect an estimate of the marginal abatement costs of implementing cost-effective policies that align with the target, and they are called target-consistent carbon prices. In practice, the SCC is a tool for cost-benefit analysis, and the target-consistent price is a tool for cost-effectiveness analysis. Also, these target-consistent prices should not be confused with the specific prices used in carbon-pricing policy instruments such as carbon taxes or cap-and-trade.

Although cost-benefit analysis using the SCC has been the dominant approach to climate policy assessment in practice in the United States, there has been some use of cost-effectiveness analysis with target-consistent pricing. For example, since 2009, the United Kingdom has been using a target-consistent price to assess climate policies (Aldy *et al.*, 2021). In the US context, this approach has recently been promoted by a pair of prominent economists, Lord Nicholas Stern and Nobel Laureate Joseph Stiglitz (Stern and Stiglitz, 2021), who argue that for the purpose of policy evaluation, the target-consistent price should replace the SCC as the benchmark for assessment.

The main arguments for relying on cost-effectiveness analysis and a target-consistent price are as follows: Climate policy cost-benefit analysis is fine in theory but cannot be implemented in practice because too little is known to estimate the SCC credibly. Beyond that, it may be argued that climate change raises questions of moral responsibility to future generations and Earth's ecosystem that surpass what economists can monetize, so any SCC will necessarily underestimate damages. Hence, the argument goes, we should be guided by science and moral considerations to identify some goal, such as keeping warming within 1.5°C, and then translate that

Cleanup begins after floods in Bad Münstereifel, North Rhine-Westphalia, Germany, 19 July 2021. Estimating impacts of climate change, such as damages from extreme weather events, that could be averted by curbing carbon emissions is critical for policy analysis.

into a policy target, such as achieving net zero emissions by 2050. If politicians adopt a given policy target, the task of the policy analyst is then simply to help achieve that target as cost-effectively as possible.

Given a target, the technical task is therefore to compute a target-consistent price to use for comparison with the cost of a specific policy. In most climate-economic models, an analyst can estimate a cost-effective emissions time path for achieving a given temperature objective in any future year. Associated with this cost-effective emission time path is an implicit carbon price trajectory, which is the target-consistent price of carbon.

Pitfalls of a Target-Consistent Price

Which to use for evaluating climate policy: an assessment of benefits and costs using the SCC, or cost-effectiveness analysis with a target-consistent price? Some advocates of the target-consistent price call it an alternative estimate of the SCC, which it decidedly is not. Terminology matters. The SCC measures the benefits of reducing CO_2 emissions, whereas the target-consistent price is a cost estimate that takes no account whatsoever of benefits.

Our view is that a push to replace costbenefit analysis and the SCC with cost-effectiveness analysis and a target-consistent price could set back climate policy, just as the United States is poised to take meaningful climate action. Despite the apparently logical appeal of using some politically defined target as an operational, bright-line rule in the face of uncertainty, we find that calls for the target-consistent approach are unwise for four main reasons.

First, the target-consistent approach replaces scientific assessments of damages from storms, floods, fires, and a myriad of other climate impacts with subjective judgments about policy targets and choices. The starting point and necessary condition for the target-consistent price is a political decision about the goal: an emissions objective in a specified future year. Much of the developed world has adopted a target of net zero emissions by 2050, but ultimately that is a political decision. The Trump administration had no such target, so its target-consistent price would have been zero. A future US administration may have a different view on the target from that of the current administration — perhaps more ambitious, perhaps less — resulting in yet another price. The anchor for the target-consistent price is fundamentally political, not scientific, and therefore subject to arbitrary change. This is not to say that the cost-benefit approach using the SCC is completely immune from political interference in its application to policy analysis, but that it is more consistent with how scientific assessments are typically undertaken.

The cost-effectiveness approach to analyzing policies with the target-consistent price involves scientific estimates in regard to future technological change; the benefit-cost approach using the SCC places greater reliance on the science of climate change because the SCC is an estimate of future damages of climate change.

Moreover, as a technical matter, calculating the target-consistent price requires making assumptions about a myriad of complementary policies over the next several decades (Kaufman *et al.*, 2020). Those assumptions matter tremendously. For example, the UK target-consistent price trajectory for achieving an 80 percent reduction in emissions by 2050 (a goal set in a 2008 law) assumed that the UK would purchase emission reductions from other countries after 2030 (Aldy *et al.*, 2021). The analysts were thus able to substantially lower the target-consistent carbon price and thus make the approach more appealing politically, by assuming that policies far from certain will unfold. This illustrates another way that the target-consistent price depends on policies and political projections, not science, in sharp contrast with the SCC.

Second, the target-consistent price calculation depends not only on assumptions about future politically determined public policies but also on critical assumptions about technologies that are not commercially available today. Many energy-economic models that can solve for ambitious climate goals — such as limiting warming to 1.5°C or net-zero emissions by 2050 — do so by assuming aggressive global deployment of bioenergy with carbon capture and storage in the power sector. Uncertainty about this prospect (and uncertainties characterizing other emerging technologies, such as direct air capture) helps explain the large variation in target-consistent prices in the literature for a given goal. The Intergovernmental Panel on Climate Change (IPCC) 2019 special report illustrated that limiting warming to 1.5°C would require carbon prices ranging from \$135 to \$5500/ton (Masson-Delmotte *et al.*, 2019). Such uncertainty is also demonstrated by the broad distribution of target-consistent prices for limiting warming to 2°C in the IPCC fifth assessment report's (AR5) integrated assessment modeling database. A common critique of the SCC is its considerable uncertainty, yet the AR5 target-consistent prices exhibit substantially greater dispersion than the distribution of SCCs estimated through hundreds of thousands of modeling runs in the US Interagency Working Group's Monte Carlo Simulations of the SCC (Aldy *et al.*, 2016).

Third, a target-consistent approach seems unlikely to meet legal requirements, at least in the US context. In 2008, a federal court ruled that fuel economy standards must account for the benefits of reducing CO_2 emissions (Pizer *et al.*, 2014). In addition, the Department of Energy must show that the benefits of appliance efficiency standards exceed their economic burdens (Cornell Law School, n.d.). Under Executive Orders issued by Democratic and Republican presidents since 1981, federal regulatory agencies are required to compare the costs of major regulations with their benefits (Arrow, 1996). Because the target-consistent price is based on costs, with no regard for benefits, it would not fulfill these requirements, posing substantial legal hurdles for officially adopting the approach in the coming years, precisely when meaningful climate action is most needed.

Fourth, the target-consistent approach is entirely inward-looking for any country that adopts it because it is essentially a go-it-alone approach to evaluating domestic climate policy. By contrast, the SCC inherently builds in the notion of reciprocity among countries because it reflects the global damages of emissions. A future in which all countries seek to guide domestic policy by using the SCC can lead to progress on addressing climate change in a globally efficient and least-cost way. The same cannot be said of the alternative approach. Although it is true that signatories of the Paris Agreement have agreed on a global target for temperature changes, vast uncertainty remains on how emissions will be reduced by each country and on what timetable.

The Path Ahead

Over the coming months, the Biden administration intends to complete its update to the SCC. We believe that it is critical that the Interagency Working Group should keep its focus on the SCC rather than commencing work on a target-consistent price. This is important not only for the continued use of cost-benefit analysis in the United States but also for maintaining an objective and defensible basis for climate policy around the world.

Correctly estimating the SCC is by no means an easy task. In 2017, the National Academy of Sciences (NAS) developed a list of needed improvements (National Academies, 2017). Fortunately, research on the NAS list has progressed substantially. In the coming months and beyond, the Biden administration's Interagency Working Group can pull together the large body of new research on damages, uncertainty, discount rates, socioeconomic projections, and other considerations, including those identified by the NAS and others (National Academies, 2017; Carleton and Greenstone, 2021; Wagner *et al*., 2021). In particular, estimates of biophysical and monetized damages have continued to improve, and today's economic environment suggests an update of the discount rate previously used.

Aside from the immediate goal of improving the estimate, a broader goal should be to establish a process by which science drives policy, not the reverse. By establishing a procedural and substantive record, such as periodic peer review through NAS (Pizer *et al.*, 2014; National Academies, 2017), it will be more difficult for a future administration with less ambitious climate goals to undercut the SCC. Although the Trump administration attempted just this (with its inappropriately high discount rate of 7 percent and no consideration of damages outside the United States), it never gained traction because it was out of step with standard and objective economic analysis, and the process for estimating the SCC was originally intended to be separate from political decision-making. The same cannot be said of the target-consistent approach, which hinges on political decisions.

We recognize the value of research that can promote cost-effective ways of achieving climate goals, but this is only one side of the cost-benefit comparison. It is critically important to maintain focus on the benefits of addressing climate change as a means for evaluating and justifying climate policy. With this goal in mind, now is not the time to change lanes and advocate the alternative approach. Instead, we need credible and updated estimates of the SCC.

References

Aldy, J., G. Atkinson, and M. J. Kotchen. (2021). *Environmental Benefit-Cost Analysis: A Comparative Analysis Between the United States and the United Kingdom*. Discussion Paper 21-90, January, Harvard Environmental Economics Program.

Aldy, J., W. Pizer, M. Tavoni, L. A. Reis, K. Akimoto, G. Blanford, C. Carraro, L. E. Clarke, J. Edmonds, G. C. Iyer, H. C. McJeon, R. Richels, S. Rose, and F. Sano. (2016). "Economic tools to promote transparency and comparability in the Paris Agreement." *Nature Climate Change*. **6**: 1000–1004.

Arrow, K. J., M. L. Cropper, G. C. Eads, R. W. Hahn, L. B. Lave, R. G. Noll, P. R. Portney, M. Russell, R. Schmalensee, V. K. Smith, and R. N. Stavins. (1996). "Is there a role for benefit-cost analysis in environmental, health, and safety regulation?" *Science*. 272: 221–222.

Biden, J. R. (2021). "Executive order 13990 of January 20, 2021: protecting public health and the environment and restoring science to tackle the climate crisis." *Federal Register*. **86**: 7037.

Carleton, T. and M. Greenstone. (2021). *Updating the United States Government's Social Cost of Carbon*. Working Paper No. 2021-04, Energy Policy Institute, University of Chicago.

Cornell Law School. (n.d.). 42 U.S. Code § 6295 — Energy Conservation Standards, www.law.cornell.edu/uscode/text/42/6295.

Goulder, L. H. and R. N. Stavins. (2002). "Discounting: An eye on the future." *Nature*. **419**: 673–674 (2002).

Interagency Working Group on Social Cost of Carbon. (2010). *Technical Support Document: Social Cost of Carbon for Regulatory Impact Analysis Under Executive Order 12866 (Plus Technical Updates in 2013, 2015, and 2016)*. US Government.

Interagency Working Group on Social Cost of Greenhouse Gases. (2021). *Technical Support Document: Social Cost of Carbon, Methane, and Nitrous Oxide, Interim Estimates Under Executive Order 13990*. February, US Government.

Kaufman, N., A. R. Barron, W. Krawczyk, P. Marsters, and H. McJeon. (2020). "A near-term to net zero alternative to the social cost of carbon for setting carbon prices." *Nature Climate Change*. **10**: 1010–1014.

Masson-Delmotte, V., *et al.* (eds.) (2019). *Global Warming of 1.5°C*. Special Report, IPCC.

National Academies. (2017). *Valuing Climate Damages: Updating Estimation of the Social Cost of Carbon Dioxide*.

Pizer, W., M. Adler, J. Aldy, D. Anthoff, M. Cropper, K. Gillingham, M. Greenstone, B. Murray, R. Newell, R. Richels, A. Rowell, S. Waldhoff, and J. Wiener. (2014). "Using and improving the social cost of carbon: Regular, institutionalized updating and review are essential." *Science*. **346**: 1189–1190.

Stern, N. and J. E. Stiglitz. (2021). *The Social Cost of Carbon, Risk, Distribution, Market Failures: An Alternative Approach*. Working Paper 28472, National Bureau of Economic Research.

Wagner, G., D. Anthoff, M. Cropper, S. Dietz, K. T. Gillingham, B. Groom, J. P. Kelleher, F. C. Moore, and J. H. Stock. (2021). Eight priorities for calculating the social cost of carbon. *Nature*. **590**: 548–550.

Supplementary Materials

science.sciencemag.org/content/373/6557/850/suppl/DC110.1126/science.abi7813.

https://doi.org/10.1142/9789811292415_0014

Chapter 14

An Economic Perspective on the EPA's Clean Power Plan — Cross-State Coordination Key to Cost-Effective CO_2 Reductions[*]

Meredith Fowlie[†,||], Lawrence Goulder[‡], Matthew J. Kotchen[§,‡‡,¶¶], Severin Borenstein[†], James Bushnell[||], Lucas Davis[†], Michael Greenstone[¶], Charles Kolstad[‡,*], Christopher Knittel[**], Robert N. Stavins[††,‡‡,§§,†††], Michael Wara[‡], Frank Wolak[‡], and Catherine Wolfram[†]**

[†]*University of California Berkeley, Berkeley, CA, USA*

[‡]*Stanford University, Palo Alto, CA, USA*

[§]*Yale University, New Haven, CT, USA*

[||]*University of California, Davis, CA, USA*

[¶]*University of Chicago, Chicago, IL, USA*

[**]*Massachusetts Institute of Technology, Cambridge, MA, USA*

[††]*John F. Kennedy School of Government, Harvard University, Cambridge, MA, USA*

[‡‡]*National Bureau of Economic Research, Cambridge, MA, USA*

---

[*]This chapter was originally published in *Science*, **346**(6211), 14 November 2014. doi: 10.1126/science.1261349.

[§§]*Resources for the Future, Washington, DC, USA*

[||]*fowlie@berkeley.edu*

[¶¶]*matthew.kotchen@yale.edu*

[***]*ckolstad@stanford.edu*

[†††]*robert_stavins@harvard.edu*

In June, the Obama Administration unveiled its proposal for a Clean Power Plan, which it estimates would reduce carbon dioxide (CO_2) emissions from existing U.S. power plants 30 percent below 2005 levels by 2030 (see Figure 1). Power plant emissions have declined substantially since 2005, so the plan is seeking reductions of about 18 percent from current levels. Electricity generation accounts for about 40 percent of U.S. CO_2 emissions.

The Environmental Protection Agency (EPA) is seeking public comment on the proposed plan before issuing a revised and final rule in June 2015. The proposed plan, which of each state's power sector. Third, states are obligated to design and implement plans to reduce their emissions and meet the EPA's designated standard.

There are vast uncertainties associated with estimates of the benefits and costs of the plan. The required Regulatory Impact Analysis accompanying the plan (U.S. EPA, 2014) estimates that, under most scenarios, benefits will exceed costs by a considerable margin. One central estimate puts benefits in the year 2030 at $76 billion, with projected compliance costs of $9 billion. Estimated benefits include avoided climate-related damages in both the United States and other countries. The Administration's rationale for including other countries is that addressing global climate change will require all countries to pursue policies based on consideration of global costs and benefits associated with their own actions.

Also included in the benefits are domestic "nonclimate" effects. To the extent that the plan leads to reductions in CO_2 emissions plan. The denominator is a measure of electricity generation at most existing sources, with an adjustment to account for generation avoided due to demand-side efficiency improvements. The quantity of emissions associated with meeting the standards depends on both the level of emissions (in the numerator) and the level of electricity generation (in the denominator). The Administration's estimate of emissions reductions thus depends on its forecasts of electricity generation.

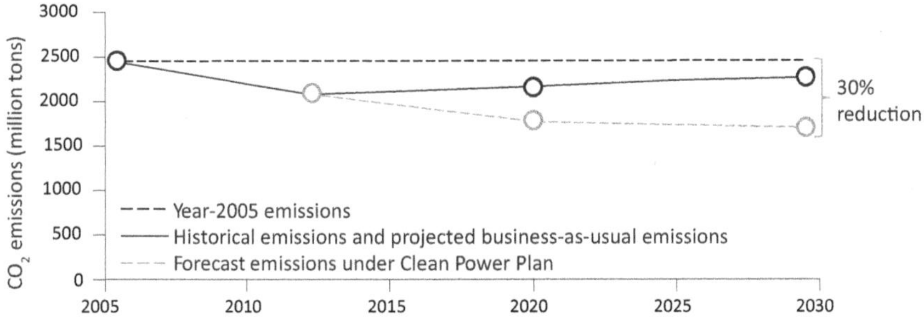

Data from (1).

Figure 1. Projected CO_2 emissions impacts of the proposed power plan.

Each state has the option to convert the ratio-based requirement into a mass-based limit on the quantity (i.e., tons) of CO_2 emitted. In principle, this involves multiplying projected electricity production at affected generating units in the state by the target emissions ratio. In practice, the modeling and assumptions required to make the state-level conversions will be complicated, and many details are unspecified in the proposed plan.

The use of a ratio-based standard makes for a loose connection between meeting the required emissions-output ratio and achieving is likely to undergo substantial revision, has been shaped by a confluence of technical, political, legal, and economic factors. Here, we point out, from an economics perspective, some of the main attractions and potential weaknesses of the current proposal. We focus on key design features that will affect whether the plan achieves its intended emissions reductions and on what can be done to help minimize the economic costs of meeting the plan's requirements.

In the absence of new federal legislation, the main channel for a national climate-change mitigation policy is action by the Executive Branch under authority of the Clean Air Act. The plan seeks to regulate emissions from fossil fuel-fired power plants in three steps. First, the EPA identifies "adequately demonstrated" approaches for reducing emissions in the power sector. Second, the EPA derives state-specific emissions standards based on these demonstrated approaches, taking into account the characteristics from fossil-fuel plants, there will also be reductions in other pollutants, with associated benefits to health and the local environment.

Drawing from existing studies, the EPA considered health benefits from reductions in particulate matter and ground-level ozone. These reductions were estimated to yield about 60 percent of the plan's gross benefits.

Will Intended Reductions Be Achieved?

Although the Administration hopes that the plan will bring about emissions reductions of a given magnitude, the plan does not specify particular levels the Administration's forecast emissions reductions. If a state chooses to maintain a ratio-based standard rather than convert to a mass-based limit, it could potentially meet the EPA's requirement without lowering emissions. A state could bring down its average emission ratio by simply increasing production of low-carbon — but not necessarily no-carbon — electricity. Although the extent to which this will undermine the plan's goal for emission reductions is uncertain, economic analysis of ratio-based standards in other sectors has revealed considerable potential for these unintended effects (Holland *et al.*, 2009).

Another issue with ratio-based standards concerns programs for demand-side energy efficiency improvements (such as programs designed to increase the adoption of more-efficient appliances). These can offer a cost-effective way for states to cut emissions by reducing electricity consumption. To receive credit for energy efficiency improvements under a ratio-based standard, efficiency-induced reductions in electricity demand are added to the denominator in calculating the state's emissions ratio. The problem is that accurately measuring how efficiency investments affect electricity demand is notoriously difficult, and recent studies indicate that savings are frequently overestimated by a wide margin (Allcott and Greenstone, 2012). Overestimation of gains from energy efficiency will in effect reduce the stringency of a ratio-based standard.

Under a mass-based approach, the two concerns discussed above no longer apply. There is no incentive for a state to increase electricity production so as to reduce an emissions ratio. Efficiency measures would contribute directly to compliance under a cap by reducing demand for electricity, and therefore emissions, without any need to estimate savings for compliance purposes. A mass-based approach would also be administratively simpler and would provide greater certainty about the plan's impact on emissions. Moreover, for states that already have mass-based policies limiting greenhouse gas emissions, mass-based standards are more easily integrated into the existing regulatory framework

Despite the various attractions of a mass-based approach, it is far from certain that states will choose this compliance option. Ratio-based standards have more built-in flexibility. While maintaining the same emissions ratio, states can expand and contract emissions in response to changing economic conditions that affect electricity demand and supply.

To ensure that ratio-based standards meet their objective, the EPA should establish detailed protocols and guidance for evaluation, monitoring, and verification of efficiency programs. The EPA should favor field-based savings estimates over engineering estimates and should encourage evaluators to take advantage of state-of-the-art approaches to program evaluation.

Will We Pay too Much for Emissions Reductions?

To reduce emissions cost-effectively, it is critical to adopt a flexible structure in which lower-cost options can be favored over higher-cost ones. Several features of the plan are consistent with this flexibility principle.

The plan offers within-state flexibility in how each state can comply with its standard. When setting the standard for each state, the EPA considered a range of demonstrated methods for reducing emissions, including efficiency improvements at power plants, greater use of natural-gas plants, expansion of renewables, and demand-side energy efficiency programs. Yet states need not employ these approaches. They can choose any approach, taking advantage of changing market conditions, new information, and cost-saving innovations to comply at least cost.

The plan also allows for across-state flexibility in terms of where required emissions reductions occur. Across-state coordination has important cost implications because low-cost abatement options are not evenly distributed across states. Emissions trading is one approach to coordinating emissions abatement cost-effectively across states. Under the proposed plan, states can

> a state … could potentially meet the EPA's requirement without lowering emissions

file multistate implementation plans that allow electricity producers in one state to trade emissions reduction obligations with producers in other states. Plants facing relatively high costs of emission reductions could pay plants with relatively low costs to take on additional emissions reductions on their behalf. Experience in the United States with emissions trading systems has demonstrated that this kind of flexibility within and across states can substantially lower the costs of reducing emissions overall (Schmalensee and Stavins, 2013).

Even if states do not pursue emissions trading, effective interstate coordination on implementation within regional electricity markets will be critical. Electricity production is linked and dispatched through regional grid interconnections that span multiple states. Electricity will be traded among states within a regional power system regardless of whether the states choose to trade emissions. Without interstate coordination, technologically identical power plants located in different states — yet servicing the same electricity customers — could face very different regulatory incentives and operating costs. Such differences would distort the flow of electricity between states and raise the overall cost per ton of emissions reduced under the plan.

At a minimum, states within the same electricity interconnection should coordinate to implement the plan in a way that harmonizes emissions reduction incentives across states. Although coordination of state implementation is certainly possible under the proposed plan, it is by no means guaranteed. The EPA can promote coordination by issuing specific guidelines — "model rules" — in the revised plan that states seeking to coordinate can adopt. The EPA has assumed this coordinating role in past programs to reduce administrative difficulties that impede coordination across state boundaries. Under the proposed plan, the EPA will also need to consider how coordination among states can be achieved between rate-based and mass-based approaches to compliance.

Key Issues Going Forward

The Clean Power Plan is the centerpiece of the Obama Administration's Climate Action Plan. The proposed reductions in power sector emissions may take on strategic importance in an international setting, where other countries are looking to the United States to gauge their own commitments to reduce emissions as part of the next international agreement. Two concerns need to be addressed regarding the ratio-based approach to defining emissions reduction targets. The first is perverse incentives for expanded electricity production in place of reduced emissions. The second is potential overestimation of energy efficiency gains that will effectively weaken the standard. The plan would also benefit from EPA guidance as to how states will be permitted to convert ratio-based targets into mass-based approaches.

The plan's considerable flexibility regarding how and where emission reductions can occur is an important feature because it promotes cost-effectiveness. Whether states will fully capitalize on this flexibility is an open question. Effective coordination among states and within multistate power markets will require state governments to overcome considerable analytical, logistical, and administrative hurdles. As part of the final rule, the EPA can play a facilitating role by providing additional and more concrete guidance on how states choosing to harmonize their implementation plans and/or compliance obligations can do so efficiently. These considerations are critical to meeting emissions reduction goals at the least cost.

References

Allcott, H. and M. Greenstone. (2012). "Is there an energy efficiency gap?" *Journal of Economic Perspectives*. **26**: 3–28.

Holland, S. P., J. E. Hughes, and C. R. Knittel. (2009). "Greenhouse gas reductions under low carbon fuel standards?" *American Economic Journal: Economic Policy*. **1**: 106–146.

Schmalensee, R. and R. N. Stavins. (2013). The SO_2 allowance trading system: The ironic history of a grand policy experiment. *Journal of Economic Perspectives*. **27**: 103–122.

U.S. EPA. (2014). *Regulatory Impact Analysis for the Proposed Carbon Pollution Guidelines for Existing Power Plants and Emission Standards for Modified and Reconstructed Power Plants*. EPA, Washington, DC.

Part IV

International Policy

https://doi.org/10.1142/9789811292415_0015

Chapter 15

The IPCC at a Crossroads: Opportunities for Reform — Increase Focus on Policy-Relevant Research[*]

Carlo Carraro[†,‡,¶], Ottmar Edenhofer[§,∥,¶,§§,*], Christian Flachsland[§,**], Charles Kolstad[††,‡‡‡], Robert N. Stavins[‡‡,§§,∥∥,†††], and Robert Stowe[‡‡,§§§]**

[†]*Fondazione Eni Enrico Mattei, Venice, Italy*

[‡]*Ca' Foscari University of Venice, Venice, Italy*

[§]*Mercator Research Institute on Global Commons and Climate Change, Berlin, Germany*

[∥]*Potsdam Institute for Climate Research, Potsdam, Germany*

[¶]*Technische Universität Berlin, Berlin, Germany*

[**]*Hertie School of Governance, Berlin, Germany*

[††]*Stanford University, Stanford, CA, USA*

[‡‡]*John F. Kennedy School of Government, Harvard University, Cambridge, MA, USA*

[§§]*National Bureau of Economic Research, Cambridge, MA, USA*

[∥∥]*Resources for the Future, Washington, DC, USA*

[*]This chapter was originally published in *Science*, **350**(6256), 2 October 2015. doi: 10.1126/science.aac4419.

¶¶carraro@feem.it

***ottmar.edenhofer@pik-potsdam.de

†††robert_stavins@harvard.edu

‡‡‡ckolstad@stanford.edu

§§§robert_stowe@harvard.edu

The Intergovernmental Panel on Climate Change (IPCC) has proven its value as an institution for large-scale scientific collaboration to synthesize and assess large volumes of climate research for use by policy-makers, as well as for establishing credibility of findings among diverse national governments. But the IPCC has received considerable criticism of both its substance and process. The new IPCC leadership to be elected in October could help guide the IPCC to a clear, shared understanding of future objectives and could shape procedural reforms. We identify key opportunities for reform by addressing two related questions: Is the IPCC doing the right things? Is the IPCC doing things right?

Doing the Right Things?

To remain policy-relevant, the IPCC needs to shift focus and increasingly address response options to climate change. The information base for making decisions on climate stabilization and related public policies is fragmented. Providing clear and integrated information regarding climate impacts and policy options for mitigation and adaptation at various scales (subnational, national, and international) along alternative climate stabilization pathways — and about their respective costs, benefits, and risks — would better inform decision-makers and societies about consequences associated with alternative policy choices. This does not mean that the IPCC should choose among policy options but rather provide the information to facilitate choices by policy-makers.

A major reason for this fragmentation of key information is that IPCC Assessment Reports (ARs) are organized by Working Groups (WGs) focused on the physical science of climate change (WGI), adaptation and impacts (WGII), and mitigation options (WGIII). A different organization might achieve more integrated analysis of policies. For example, one WG could focus on natural-science aspects of climate change, and a second could provide a more integrated perspective on mitigation, adaptation, and the socioeconomic implications of impacts.

IPCC reports could also develop better understanding and assessment of climate impacts, drivers of greenhouse gas emissions, and policy options at subglobal levels. However, the approval session of the WGIII summary for policy-makers (SPM) in Berlin in 2014 revealed that such geographically specific assessments can be difficult for governments to accept (Victor *et al.*, 2014; Dubash *et al.*, 2014; Edenhofer and Minx, 2014).

The architecture of the climate agreement to be concluded at the United Nations Framework Convention on Climate Change (UNFCCC) conference in Paris in December will consist of voluntary pledges by governments that might be compared with one another to provide incentives for increasing levels of ambition over time. In this context, increasing the IPCC's focus on policy assessment, capitalizing on emerging literature in this area (e.g., Koch *et al.*, 2014; Böhringer, 2014; Ranson and Stavins, 2014), would offer two advantages. First, it would facilitate learning and diffusion of lessons from climate policy experiments worldwide. Second, credible *ex post* empirical analysis of policies and comparison with *ex ante* forecasts are critical to building trust between countries continuously involved in policy negotiations (Aldy, 2014). Also, more consideration could be given to alternative options for defining and measuring equity and efficiency in a voluntary, "bottom-up" climate regime — again building trust and possibly prompting increased mitigation ambition over time.

Increased focus on alternative public policies may bring potential for controversy between governments and researchers (Victor *et al.*, 2014; Dubash *et al.*, 2014; Edenhofer and Minx, 2014; Stavins, 2014). Governments hesitate to have their policy programs publicly scrutinized by an intergovernmental panel, and researchers may not be aware of or sensitive to value-laden and politicized questions. Governments and researchers need to carefully execute their roles at the science-policy interface in recognizing and carefully managing diverse viewpoints, without compromising scientific rigor and objectivity (Edenhofer and Minx, 2014; Edenhofer and Kowarsch, 2015). If the IPCC shifts focus along these lines, it will need to actively encourage targeted research on selected topics for which evidence is still lacking. The next leadership of the IPCC should enhance engagement with policy researchers and modelers to help build the necessary knowledge base.

Doing Things Right?

In addition to building a clear, common understanding of its future focus, the IPCC must address practical and procedural problems. The Fifth AR pushed author teams and technical support units (TSUs) to their management limits. Operating single TSUs from multiple geographical locations should be avoided so as not to further complicate management tasks. Also, the high costs of time and travel commitments put at risk the participation of the best researchers. At the least, the IPCC should consider reducing the number and length of lead author meetings and making greater use of remote collaboration. Focusing the initial scoping process on identifying policy-maker questions that the

> Governments and researchers need to carefully execute their roles at the science-policy interface…

AR will respond to (rather than unspecified broad topics) could increase its relevance and usefulness. IPCC rules enable direct interaction between policy-makers, scientists, and other stakeholders only at the start and end of the multiyear assessment process. This limits opportunities to maximize the AR's policy relevance and address potential conflicts between researchers and government representatives. This could be improved by adding a round of interactions during the writing process. Lessons might be learned from the Structured Expert Dialogues organized during the UNFCCC's 2013–2015 review of the 2°C goal, in which government representatives held interactive question-and-answer sessions with experts from the IPCC and other organizations.

The IPCC could strengthen its process of selecting lead authors. Developing-country perspectives must be adequately represented, although scientific skills, capability, and international reputation should remain paramount. These dual goals of quality and diversity can be better achieved by more actively recruiting from the many distinguished scholars from developing countries who are working in the developed world but, nevertheless, can represent developing-country perspectives. This has sometimes been a challenge in the past. New partnerships, including with national and international academies of sciences, could support the author-nomination process.

The SPMs are the most widely referenced element of each WG report, largely because their text is negotiated and formally approved by IPCC-member governments. The politically negotiated nature of the government-approval process at the end of each AR can lead to a dilution of key messages. Yet it would be difficult and possibly undesirable to change the SPM production process; IPCC reports are treated as authoritative partly because governments have formally accepted the SPM text. Instead of trying to change the SPM process and format, increasing the prominence of technical summaries (written solely by lead authors) would be useful. Renaming them "executive summaries" and engaging expert communicators could make them more accessible to policy-makers and the public. More clearly distinguishing between these two types of summaries could facilitate explicit acknowledgment and acceptance of divergent views that sometimes prevail between scientists and governments.

As the IPCC considered in its recent round of self-evaluation, the panel could also emphasize shorter, more-targeted reports that focus on recent research and that respond quickly and flexibly to the expressed needs of policy-makers.

Overcoming Inertia

The new IPCC leadership will require support from governments to ensure success. The lack of government interest in major IPCC reform in the past can suggest satisfaction with its performance, but also reflects resistance to change in an organization prone to bureaucratic inertia. With its current substantive focus and procedural rules, the IPCC will have a difficult time meeting future challenges. After the UNFCCC Paris talks conclude in December, governments may have more appetite — and reason — to reconsider the IPCC's role in light of a new global climate-policy regime based on national implementation of highly heterogeneous, domestically determined policies.

Acknowledgments

The authors acknowledge the Alfred P. Sloan Foundation, the Fondazione Eni Enrico Mattei, and the Mercator Research Institute on Global

Commons and Climate Change for sponsoring a workshop in Berlin, Germany, 18 to 20 February 2015, where these ideas were discussed. We appreciate contributions made by participants.

References

Aldy, J. (2014). "The crucial role of policy surveillance in international climate policy." *Climate Change*. **126**: 279–292.

Böhringer, C. (2014). "Two decades of European climate policy: A critical appraisal." *Review of Environmental Economics Policy*. **8**: 1–17.

Dubash, N. K., M. Fleurbaey, and S. Kartha. (2014). "Political implications of data presentation." *Science*. **345**: 36–37.

Edenhofer, O. and J. C. Minx. (2014). "Climate policy. Mapmakers and navigators, facts and values." *Science*. **345**: 37–38.

Edenhofer, O. and M. Kowarsch. (2015). "Cartography of pathways: A new model for environmental policy assessments." *Environmental Science & Policy*. **51**: 56–64.

Koch, N., S. Fuss, G. Grosjean, and O. Edenhofer. (2014). "Causes of the EUETS price drop: Recession, CDM, renewable policies or a bit of everything?—New evidence." *Energy Policy*. **73**: 676–685.

Ranson, M. and R. N. Stavins. (2014). "Linkage of greenhouse gas emissions trading systems: Learning from experience." *Climate Policy*. **16**: 284–300.

Stavins, R. N. (2014). *Environmental Forum (Washington, DC)*. **31**: 14.

Victor, D. G., R. Gerlagh, and G. Baiocchi. (2014). "Climate policy. Getting serious about categorizing countries." *Science*. **345**: 34–36.

https://doi.org/10.1142/9789811292415_0016

Chapter 16

Reforming the IPCC's Assessment of Climate Change Economics[*]

Gabriel Chan[†,¶¶], Carlo Carraro[‡,§,*], Ottmar Edenhofer[‖,¶,**,†††], Charles Kolstad[††,‡‡‡], and Robert N. Stavins[‡‡,§§,‖‖,§§§]**

[†]*Humphrey School of Public Affairs, University of Minnesota, Minneapolis, MN, USA*

[‡]*Fondazione Eni Enrico Mattei, Isola di San Giorgio Maggiore, Venice, Italy*

[§]*Ca' Foscari University of Venice, Venice, Italy*

[‖]*Mercator Research Institute on Global Commons and Climate Change, Berlin, Germany*

[¶]*Potsdam Institute for Climate Impact Research, Potsdam, Germany*

[**]*Technische Universität Berlin, Berlin, Germany*

[††]*Stanford University, Stanford, CA, USA*

[‡‡]*John F. Kennedy School of Government, Harvard University, Cambridge, MA, USA*

[*]This chapter was originally published in *Climate Change Economics*, 7(1), 1640001, 2016. doi: 10.1142/S2010007816400017.

[§§]*National Bureau of Economic Research, Cambridge, MA, USA*

[||]*Resources for the Future, Washington, DC, USA*

[¶¶]*gabechan@umn.edu*

[***]*carraro@feem.it*

[†††]*ottmar.edenhofer@pik-potsdam.de*

[‡‡‡]*ckolstad@stanford.edu*

[§§§]*robert_stavins@harvard.edu*

Introduction

The Intergovernmental Panel on Climate Change (IPCC), which completed its Fifth Assessment Report (AR5) in 2014, provides the only comprehensive review of climate change science, impacts, and mitigation that draws on a government-sanctioned international body of scholars. Because of its official status as a United Nations body and the key role the IPCC plays in building an accepted consensus around scientific findings, the IPCC enjoys a high degree of legitimacy among policymakers.

The size and scope of the IPCC has grown significantly since its inception in 1988, reflecting the growing body of academic literature on climate change (Grieneisen and Zhang, 2011), but this growth has rendered the IPCC process increasingly cumbersome. In this chapter, we assess the scope of the IPCC and the procedural rules governing the drafting of its reports, which reflect the political complexities underlying many issues in climate policy, and which foster an inefficient process that leads to final products that are far from ideal. Because of the IPCC's public prominence and unique legitimacy among policymakers and the public, improving the IPCC process and its products can be of considerable social value. With the recent completion of AR5, this is a good time to examine opportunities and challenges for reform.

The IPCC's coverage of the literature on climate change mitigation (and economics) has been traditionally concentrated in IPCC Working Group III (WGIII). The authors of this chapter have been involved in nearly all levels of activity of WGIII and in the preparation of AR5.[1] This chapter draws in part on their personal experiences, assessing the literature on climate change economics (and closely related fields), but some observations and recommendations may also be relevant to the IPCC's coverage of other disciplines and broader issues in climate change science, impacts, and mitigation.

The IPCC's Structure and Process

The IPCC was established in 1988 by the World Meteorological Organization and the United Nations Environment Program to assess and synthesize scientific research on climate change, its impacts, and response options.[2] The IPCC has since developed detailed sets of principles and procedures for writing assessment reports (IPCC, 2013, 2015). The IPCC is governed by a Plenary (composed of representatives of member governments), Bureau, Executive Committee, and Secretariat, which have distinct roles to provide oversight, develop procedures, and facilitate operation. Coverage of the scientific literature is divided into three Working Groups that respectively assess climate change science, impacts and adaptation, and mitigation. Authors are nominated by national governments, and selected by the IPCC Bureau. Authors serve as Coordinating Lead Authors (CLAs), with responsibility for leading the writing of a chapter, or as Lead Authors (LAs), who serve on a chapter team and participate in the writing process. CLAs and LAs participate in numerous meetings held at diverse locations around the world. Other experts serve as Contributing Authors (CAs), but the process for nominating these contributors is less formal, and the CAs typically do not participate in meetings and deliberations.

---

[1] Chan was a Chapter Scientist and Contributing Author, Working Group III of the IPCC's Fifth Assessment Report (AR5 WG-III); Carraro was Vice-Chair, AR5 WG-III; Edenhofer was Co-Chair of AR5 WG-III; Kolstad and Stavins were Coordinating Lead Authors, AR5 WG-III. We have drawn, in part, on: Carraro *et al.* (2015), Carraro *et al.* (2015), Stavins (2014a), and Edenhofer and Minx (2014). The authors of the present chapter bear sole responsibility for its content; it is not intended to reflect official positions of the IPCC.

[2] For detailed accounts of the IPCC's history, see Bolin (2007), and Hulme and Mahoney (2010), as well as the references therein.

The assessment cycle for each round of the IPCC begins with a scoping process, wherein government representatives, together with a large group of scholars and other interested parties, draft outlines of each chapter of the IPCC. Following the scoping process, the IPCC Plenary approves the outlines, sometimes after some modification. CLAs and LAs are then nominated and subsequently approved by the IPCC Bureau. CLAs and LAs serve as volunteer labor, though some have their travel expenses reimbursed. In the AR5 WGIII process, Lead Author Meetings (LAMs) were convened four times from July 2011 to July 2013 (in Changwon, Korea; Wellington, New Zealand; Vigo, Spain; and Addis Ababa, Ethiopia). Over the course of the LAMs, CLAs lead their chapter teams to review relevant literature and prepare chapter text, tables, and figures.

At three points during this process, external Expert Reviewers and government representatives submit detailed comments on drafted text. These comments, numbering in the many thousands in AR5, are made public following the assessment cycle, and, are checked by appointed Review Editors, who confirm that authors reply to comments appropriately. After four drafting rounds, the Working Group reports are preliminarily finalized. Towards the end of the assessment cycles, authors of each Working Group, primarily CLAs, engage in writing two summary documents for each report, a Technical Summary (TS) and a Summary for Policymakers (SPM). Finally, concurrent with much of the chapter-drafting process, a subset of CLAs and LAs from all three Working Groups convene to draft the Synthesis Report (SYR) and its SPM.[3]

Reforming the IPCC Process

We propose four reforms of the IPCC process, which would lower costs for the best researchers to participate in the IPCC and would in this and other ways improve the quality of the final products.

Improving Interactions between Governments and Academics

The IPCC is a nearly universal intergovernmental organization that commissions scholars to assess, summarize, and synthesize available

---

[3]Four LAMs for the AR5 SYR were held from June 2012 to June 2014 in Geneva, Switzerland; Oslo, Norway; De Bilt, Netherlands; and Kuala Lumpur, Malaysia.

literature. Academics typically operate with few constraints, beyond those self-imposed by the standards and norms of their academic discipline. For many, working within any convening institution, especially a governmental institution that at times behaves politically, is uncomfortable. The IPCC has worked hard to limit the influence of politics on science, most importantly by formally prescribing that its reports be policy relevant, but not policy prescriptive. However, more can be done to ensure that the IPCC's assessments retain their scientific integrity.

Government representatives play important roles in the IPCC author-selection process. At the beginning of each assessment, selected experts are invited to a Working-Group Scoping Meeting, where outlines and titles for each of the report's chapters are drafted. Following the Scoping Meeting, government representatives convene and may make substantial changes to the drafted chapter titles and outlines, but there is no direct interaction between governments and experts during this process. Following the government approval of chapter outlines, governments engage with the assessment process only when they submit their comments on the "Second Order Draft," typically produced about two years after the Scoping Meeting. These comments must be addressed by authors, but authors are under no obligation to implement any suggested revisions.

Importantly, at the end of the assessment process, governments engage directly with authors during week-long Approval Sessions, which immediately precede the release of reports. At these meetings, governments play a crucial role; they must unanimously approve the SPM of each Working Group, line-by-line.[4] (The Approval Session for AR5 WGIII was held in April 2014, in Berlin.) The underlying chapters of IPCC reports and the TS are *not* approved line-by-line, and require only a blanket (up or down) approval — again unanimous. The SYR and its SPM are also subject to government approval in separate sessions. (The AR5 SYR approval session was held in October 2014 in Copenhagen, Denmark.)

This process of engaging national governments with a large number of experts during the scoping process, receiving nonbinding comments in a one-way dialogue more than halfway through the drafting process, and then negotiating the SPM document at length creates a highly structured engagement of scientists with policymakers. This dialogue could be

[4]An exception to the unanimity rule exists at the IPCC approval session chair's prerogative, whereby individual countries' objections can be acknowledged in footnotes.

improved, in order to make the final IPCC reports of greater policy relevance, while decreasing procedural burdens on IPCC authors.

First, the process used at the Scoping Meetings and prior to the finalization of chapter outlines merits reform. Following the government editing and approval of the outlines and before writing begins, the broad outlines of the IPCC chapters are largely fixed; after the plenary during which outlines are accepted by governments, making amendments to chapter outlines is exceptionally difficult, requiring approval from the IPCC's Bureau. Therefore, developing sound outlines of chapters at the beginning has important implications for the effort authors expend to manage redundancy and the quality of final reports. For example, in AR5, the coverage of climate finance was separated across four chapters during the scoping process with required section headings on climate finance appearing in the three WGIII chapters on mitigation policy in addition to a new independent chapter on "Cross-Cutting Issues on Investment and Finance." The scoping process locked-in this overlapping coverage of the issue of climate finance, making the writing process more challenging for authors who had to repeatedly communicate with authors from other chapters to determine where sub-issues would be covered. It follows that this division also made it more difficult for readers to gain a comprehensive understanding of climate finance, as they must search across four chapters.

The scoping process could engage a small group of scholars with broad disciplinary and substantive expertise prior to the formal Scoping Meeting, in order to facilitate progress during the larger scoping meeting. This process would include authors of previous reports and authors with expertise spanning the scope of the three Working Groups (Griggs, 2014). In particular, economists and other social scientists could participate to highlight issues at the frontiers of their respective fields. However, engaging a broader community of scholars is not sufficient. A more effective scoping process would force deeper engagement and communication between scholars and governments. This could help move the IPCC reports closer to policy-relevant questions, framed in ways that governments will understand, while simultaneously providing an opportunity for scholars to provide checks to government questions by expressing the limitations of what assessments of scholarly literature can reasonably answer.

In addition to reforming the scoping process, difficulties associated with problematic communication between policymakers and authors at the final stage of the process could be remedied by more interactions between policymakers and scientists throughout the writing process. But increasing the frequency of interactions would require careful planning. First, this will inevitably be time consuming. Second, interactions need to be structured to avoid inefficient or ineffective communication. Both authors and governments need to come to the process with clear understanding and agreement regarding their respective roles and responsibilities. One approach could be for governments to pose clear formulations of policy-relevant questions to authors at the earliest stage. These questions could be responded to with drafted text integrated into the chapters or could be made into specific boxes within the report. Authors could then respond with amendments to questions with potential framings of answers. Then, through an iterative process, policymakers and scientists could come to agreement on the key questions they should seek to answer and the format in which they should provide their answers for the greatest policy relevance. Remaining unanswered questions could be included in the final reports as "knowledge gaps" to help shape the scholarly community's research agenda going forward. Third, more frequent interactions could create real or perceived biases in the scientific assessment process. These interactions should be monitored carefully by third parties, such as national academies of science or the InterAcademy Council, who can enforce the primacy of the scientific mission of the IPCC.

Making IPCC Operations More Efficient

Working in the IPCC is an immense time commitment for authors, who are uncompensated, motivated by a commitment to scientific rigor and a desire to better understand and communicate climate change and its implications. The IPCC reports are valuable public goods that can improve policymakers' understanding of climate change, but the burdens placed on authors make many in the climate economics community shy away from becoming LAs or CLAs. The IPCC is in jeopardy of losing the participation of the most competent scholars if it does not reform its operations.

The top scholars in any field do not necessarily make the best IPCC authors, because LAs must have broad knowledge of the literature of a field, as opposed to frontier expertise in a narrow area. Also, in the case of CLAs, the necessary characteristics include organizational skills and leadership ability. That said, the burdens imposed on IPCC authors detract from the institution's ability to attract those most suited to the tasks. A key reform the IPCC could implement to improve its procedural efficiency is to strengthen the roles of the Technical Support Unit (TSU) and its

Chapter Scientists. The TSUs should remain as centralized bodies that provide logistical support to each of the Working Groups, coordinating all logistical issues for the Working Group reports, helping to manage references and data sources, coordinating cross-chapter and cross-Working Group communication, supporting the development of summary documents, and managing relations with IPCC vendors (for example, graphic design, typesetting/publishing, and event organization). A better understanding of the role of the TSU as a support group within the IPCC would reduce the emerging concern that the TSUs were a source of regional bias. Proposals to create multiple TSUs (one in an industrialized country and one in a developing country) for each Working Group report would lead to less, not greater efficiency. Geographic balance in TSUs could be achieved instead through more expansive global recruiting of professional staff, to be housed at a single location.

AR5 implemented a new measure to reduce burdens on CLAs by creating a role for "Chapter Scientists," who assisted chapter teams in a variety of substantive and logistical ways. Funding for Chapter Scientists was very limited but in some cases raised by individual CLAs, leading to additional burdens and potential unfairness across chapters. Moving forward, the IPCC should support and expand the Chapter Scientist program by allocating funding for the program and encouraging them to participate in all meetings. Chapter Scientists could be recruited as graduate student research assistants or professional support staff (Schulte-Uebbing *et al.*, 2015).

A major driver of the great burdens placed on authors is the series of LAMs. The entire set of LAs in AR5 WGIII convened four times for one week each over the course of the writing process. In addition, many CLAs were invited as experts to the Scoping Meeting at the outset of the process and most convened for the Approval Session at the end of the process. IPCC author meeting locations were selected to be in geographically balanced locations (i.e., on a variety of continents and in developed and developing countries) and required the availability of a venue willing to support the large costs of hosting an IPCC meeting. As a result, IPCC leadership found it challenging to identify willing hosts and these meetings were almost all held in cities far from airline hubs, requiring long connecting flights for most participants — further increasing the opportunity cost of time associated with participation.

Chapter teams should be allowed, indeed encouraged to rely on digital collaboration and communication technologies, such as videoconferencing and digital collaborative writing platforms. For developing country authors without reliable access to some of these technologies, UN regional facilities could provide support. This would mean that the LAMs could be shortened to two or three days, and reduced from four in-person meetings to two or three. Further, the IPCC should redouble efforts to host LAMs in conference centers in closer proximity to international travel hubs, thereby reducing travel time and expenses.[5]

In addition, the IPCC should consider complementing the large full assessment reports with short, targeted reports on specific, timely issues, such as the economics of geo-engineering or the promise and challenges of climate clubs as a substitute or a complement to the negotiations carried out under the United Nations Framework Convention on Climate Change (UNFCCC) (Griggs, 2014; Hulme *et al.*, 2010; *Nature*, 2013). Moving towards a structure of targeted reports that could be written and published over much shorter timeframes would reduce the burdens on authors and improve the policy relevance of the IPCC by moving assessment writing closer in time to the discovery of new findings.

Clarifying and Strengthening Conflict of Interest Rules

The author selection criteria employed by the IPCC are subject to the IPCC's Conflict of Interest (COI) policy, which was implemented for the first time with AR5. Prior to AR5, the InterAcademy Council, in its review of the IPCC's processes and procedures, recommended that "the IPCC should develop and adopt a rigorous COI policy that applies to all individuals directly involved in the preparation of IPCC reports" (InterAcademy Council, 2010). In response, the IPCC adopted an official COI policy in November 2011:

> A "conflict of interest" refers to any current professional, financial or other interest which could: (i) significantly impair the individual's objectivity in carrying out his or her duties and responsibilities for the IPCC, or (ii) create an unfair advantage for any person or organization. For the purposes of this policy, circumstances that could lead a reasonable person to question an individual's objectivity, or whether an unfair

[5]The funds saved by reducing the frequency and length of LAMs could be used to support Chapter Scientists and travel for the TSU, which does require in-person collaboration.

> advantage has been created, constitute a potential conflict of interest. These potential conflicts are subject to disclosure. (IPCC, 2011)

This definition from the IPCC closely mirrors the policy of the U.S. National Academies of Science (U.S. National Academies of Sciences, 2003), which was highlighted in the InterAcademy Council report.

COI definitions are complex, particularly with regard to the distinction between COI and bias. The IPCC is explicit on this issue: "Holding a view that one believes to be correct, but that one does not stand to gain from personally is not a conflict of interest" (IPCC, 2011). This clarification does not make it clear whether personal advantages created for an author's affiliated institution or employer are equivalent to personal gains. Further, the ambiguous phrase "other interest" in the IPCC's COI definition poses challenges, particularly with respect to whether "other interests" include political interests of one's employer. Clarifying these ambiguities should be made a priority, as many IPCC authors are employed by organizations (political or otherwise) that aim to influence climate policy. While the IPCC has been criticized for including authors from industry and nongovernmental organizations (Edenhofer, 2011), there is also the issue of authors directly employed by governments and other politically vested organizations.

The IPCC recognizes that authors will not be able to divorce themselves fully from their personal biases. With this recognition, the IPCC has taken the position that the bias of authors can be mitigated by creating author and leadership teams that are balanced in their biases. The IPCC's approach to mitigating bias by creating author teams that represent a wide variety of biases is reflected in its operational practice to create chapter author teams that are balanced in terms of disciplinary fields, professional background (academia, industry, and NGOs), and geographic location. As an operating principle, geographic balance has been taken to mean that chapter teams should be composed of authors who are currently living in a wide range of geographic regions, with particular focus on developed versus developing countries. To more accurately account for the ways in which personal experiences contribute to individual biases, the IPCC could reform implementation of its geographic balance criterion to focus on authors' countries of origin (not current habitation). Further, the IPCC might consider how diversity in authors' locale of education could be incorporated in procedures to create geographic balance (Corbera *et al.*, 2015).

In the face of COI definitional ambiguity and the strong desire to create author teams that are geographically balanced, the IPCC has faced considerable pressure to relax its COI policy. In part motivated by the priority it gives to geographic balance, the IPCC has gone one step further than many research organizations by explicitly adopting the policy of allowing authors with clear COIs to continue participating as LAs under "exceptional circumstances ... where the individual is deemed to provide a unique contribution to an IPCC product and where it is determined that the conflict can be managed such that it will not have an adverse impact on the relevant IPCC report" (IPCC, 2011).

The IPCC has an important role to play in informing climate change policies at the sub-national, national, and international levels. In AR5, the IPCC appointed several authors who also held official government positions, in most cases as members of their respective countries' climate-negotiating teams (in the UNFCCC process). Under the IPCC COI policy, these authors were allowed to participate as LAs of policy chapters, even when those chapters were directly related to their professional responsibilities. This constitutes a COI that should be unacceptable in the IPCC process, and is one with which the IPCC will need to deal urgently moving forward.

Authors currently working for governments in nonobjective positions[6] should be declared to have a COI. Unlike financial COIs, COIs that are rooted in one's institutional affiliation, employer, or political organization are more complex to understand in terms of what types of biases authors will hold, and these biases can more easily infect the writing process. Unfortunately, as indicated above, implementing a strict COI rule based on one's institutional or political affiliation could have the effect of reducing the pool of developing country authors. As a matter of practice, many scholars in developing countries have been appointed to domestic political positions. Because of this, the IPCC should redouble its recruitment of developing country authors (based on national origin, not current location) to maintain author teams that have a balance of geographically originating biases without COI. As an organization that seeks to create policy relevant reports that are not policy prescriptive, the IPCC must attune itself to COIs rooted in institutional and political affiliations.

---

[6]By this we mean government organizations that shape or advocate on behalf of policy positions, not independent government research organizations, such as the National Center for Atmospheric Research.

Expanding Outreach Related to IPCC Products, with Improved Communication of the Merits of Each IPCC Product

Each IPCC assessment produces a number of written products, across which the length and communication style varies. With careful attention to the various purposes of these products, the IPCC could improve its outreach and communication of results and strengthen its impact.

First and foremost among the IPCC assessment outputs are the main reports. Each of the three IPCC working groups (Working Group I — The Physical Science Basis, Working Group II — Impacts, Adaptation and Vulnerability, and Working Group III — Mitigation of Climate Change) produce individual reports. In AR5, the reports of the three working group totaled 1190, 1652, and 1325 pages, respectively. These reports are the main focus of the work of IPCC authors and Review Editors during the assessment process and contain full citations to the underlying literature. The material from the three working group reports are integrated in the SYR (151 pages in length in AR5), which is written by a subset of CLAs from the three working groups.

Authors of the three Working Group reports also contribute to a "TS" of each report. Under current practice, CLAs have primary authorship responsibilities for the Technical Summaries, but LAs can also contribute. The Technical Summaries in AR5 totaled 83, 58, and 75 pages, for the respective three Working Groups.[7] Technical summaries are intended to integrate the chapters into a coherent single document, with citations referring to the underlying reports. Integration across chapters is very challenging, because chapter teams work independently during the report writing process (outside of the structured "cross-cut" process around specific topics) and because the chapters adhere to clearly defined topical boundaries.

In addition to the Technical Summaries, each working group report is summarized even more briefly in its SPM.[8] In AR5, the SPMs were 27, 32, and 30 pages, respectively, for the three working groups. The most important way in which the SPMs differ from the Technical Summaries is

---

[7]Working Group II included "Cross-Chapter Boxes" in its report directly following the Technical Summary. These boxes summarized material that appeared across chapters organized by themes such as "Coral Reefs" and "Gender in Climate Change" and were written at a level of depth comparable to a Technical Summary.

[8]The SYRt has its own SPMs.

the degree to which they are influenced by the national governments which make up the IPCC.

As noted, among all IPCC products, the SPMs are the only documents that governments must approve line-by-line. After the completion of the writing and reviews of the reports by authors and editors, government delegates and authors (primarily CLAs) convene for the Approval Session, where delegates from nearly every country in the United Nations spend a week reviewing a draft of the SPM line-by-line in a large auditorium.[9] During the Approval Session, the underlying chapters and TS are also accepted by delegates, but these approvals are carried out in aggregate, and no substantive review of the material occurs. In contrast, government delegates exert substantial influence on the SPM, though the SPM text remains scientifically accurate. Delegates can suggest text or raise objections to text. Authors are able to propose revisions and can accept or reject delegate suggestions for revised text.

Delegates and authors must collectively reach consensus on every word of the SPM. In some cases of the AR5 coverage of climate change economics, government delegates intervened more heavily in the text. Notably, in several sections, governments chose to remove large portions of text, including nearly all coverage of international cooperation, rather than craft language that would be both substantively meaningful and unanimously agreeable (Clark, 2014; Stavins, 2014a). Together, the various ways in which governments influenced the SPM led some observes to label the SPM, the "Summary *by* Policymakers"(Stavins, 2014b).

The various IPCC products could be presented to IPCC consumers in ways which would render them more useful. The TS could be strongly marketed as *the* IPCC summary document that the IPCC authors themselves have created. Moreover, to reflect its content more accurately, it should be renamed the "Executive Summary," because "TS" suggests that it is not accessible to nonscientists, which is not really the case. However, to make it more accessible, the IPCC could hire expert professional science communicators to facilitate the writing process. The TS could also be summarized further in a short format, of similar length to the SPM.

Behind these proposals to reform the summary documents is the notion that the material of the IPCC should be conveyed to audiences in a manner that is not influenced by governments. This would likely strengthen the credibility of the IPCC process in the view of the media and the general

---

[9]For a first-hand account of the AR5 WGIII SPM Approval Session, see Broome (2014).

public. Due to institutional constraints and its negotiated character, it is unlikely that the IPCC would be willing to jettison the SPM, but it may be feasible to supplement the government-controlled SPM with additional summaries that are immune to political influence and control.[10]

Another important objective is to achieve a better and simpler communication strategy. It is hard to summarize all the facts about climate in just a few easy-to-understand sentences, but it is important for the IPCC itself to make the effort to summarize and simplify: if the IPCC does not do it, others will. Government delegations, NGOs, think tanks, and journalists craft different summaries of the IPCC's products, some more accurate than others. If the IPCC fails to control the chain of communication of the key findings of their reports from the very first link, it will run the risk that some parts may be misrepresented and misunderstood. This is a particular challenge for the communication of the findings of the WGIII report on climate change mitigation and its coverage of climate change economics. Many of the findings from WGIII can be oversimplified and made misleading. Despite AR5's improvements to communication strategies with alternative media (e.g., the public dissemination of presentation slides and videos), more can be done with digital media and 21st century approaches to information dissemination.

Reforming the IPCC's Coverage of Climate Change Economics

Two measures could improve the substantive coverage of climate change economics in scientific assessments. Improving the communication of the economics of global climate change to broad audiences of decision makers could require looking beyond the IPCC and including complementary research outside of economics.

[10] In addition to improving communication through more accessible writing and more clearly designed summary documents, the IPCC could broaden its readership by more closely aligning the timing of its assessments with the political processes it is designed to inform, that is, the negotiations under the United Nations Framework Convention on Climate Change.

Complementing the IPCC with Other Initiatives

The IPCC's role is fundamentally limited, due to its origin and nature as an UN-commissioned body. For example, there is considerable skepticism that the IPCC could ever effectively review the scholarly literature on the economics of international climate cooperation and other politically sensitive climate economics topics in its SPM because of the consensus-based nature of IPCC government deliberations. While the IPCC has effectively highlighted several emerging issues, IPCC documents can frequently be out of date by the time of their publication due to the lengthy review process. More broadly, nonpeer reviewed literature and research in progress are additional sources of scholarly insight but are not readily captured in the IPCC's reports. Because of these limitations, the IPCC's work should be complemented with other assessment processes. These other processes could include work by institutions that review nonpeer-reviewed literature and research in progress, as well as those that can review politically sensitive issues. These complementary review processes could build on existing networks of scientific institutions, such as the Inter-Academy Council, or could be newly established for this purpose. In this way, climate assessment products could collectively offer a more comprehensive survey of knowledge, while individually becoming more flexible under clarified divisions of responsibility. By recognizing the existence of these complementary processes, the IPCC's mission could be clarified and its work made more efficient.

In addition, the IPCC could strengthen its engagement with other relevant scientific bodies and research communities to initiate new research projects, potentially commissioning research to fill identified knowledge gaps. Commissioned research could be evaluated during the assessment process or could fill a complementary role outside of the IPCC's mandate, such as evaluating the Intended Nationally Determined Contributions (INDCs) submitted by nations under the UNFCCC.

Another area in which the IPCC could benefit from greater cooperation with other institutions is in the identification of potential new LAs by leveraging existing networks of other organizations. In most countries, government agencies manage the author nomination process. For example, in the United States, the State Department manages the author selection process. This could be expanded by enticing national academies and professional societies to play a role in the process. To create author teams that are scientifically expert while maintaining geographic balance, national academies further removed from politics could be the locus of the author nomination process within each country. The academies tend to be more familiar than governments with academic communities. Giving them greater authority and input into the author selection process would not only increase the quality and decrease the politicization of the author selection process, but their involvement could also help increase the disciplinary diversity and representativeness of author teams.

Finally, the IPCC could support complementary educational and training organizations that build scholarly capacity in developing countries. The IPCC itself does not have the finances nor mandate to execute this mission, but satisfying the criterion of geographic balance of authors without relying on authors with COI problems will require the development of a greater pool of developing country authors. The IPCC could give its endorsement and nonfinancial support to other institutions that create scientific expertise in developing countries focused on the economics and other social dimensions of climate change.

The IPCC Could Improve the Integration of Economics with Other Disciplines

IPCC coverage of the social sciences requires deeper integration of economics with other social science and natural science disciplines. In the social sciences, such integration is needed prior to the scoping meetings, and could be achieved, in part, by organizing the scoping process around policy-relevant questions. By focusing on practical questions, scholars might be forced out of their disciplinary boundaries to seek appropriate insights from all available sources. The process of designing policy-relevant questions could also assist in identifying which types of questions are not amenable to positive (as opposed to normative) scholarly response, so that these limitations of academic inquiry could be made explicit to policymakers from the outset.

The dividing lines between academic disciplines reflect divisions that exist in most academic organizations. But for a body such as the IPCC, such divides can be problematic when policymakers seek to understand issues organized by policy responses, rather than by disciplinary approach. For example, on the issue of international cooperation, insights from economics, political science, international relations, and law can provide valuable insights. Organizing thinking about international cooperation by discipline can leave an incomplete picture. Integrating social science thinking by policy issues is particularly challenging for the IPCC because some social science disciplines have not organized in a fashion that is supportive of such work. For example, political scientists who study issues of international cooperation have not drawn many explicit links between international relations theory and practice in the sphere of climate change (Victor, 2015). Developing these deeper links across the social sciences will require changes not only in the IPCC process, but also within academic communities.

Greater coordination across the IPCC's working groups would also facilitate improved coverage of key questions. For example, input from natural scientists and economists who study climate damages should mesh with the work of other economists in developing assessments of the literature that consider tradeoffs between mitigation and adaptation, including integrated assessment models. The IPCC Chair and the TSUs should work to enhance this type of coordination across Working Groups at multiple stages of the assessment process. While cross-Working Group coordination was facilitated in AR5 around specific issues, more could be done to force deeper integration, particularly around the issues of mitigation-adaptation tradeoffs and co-benefits.

The IPCC Should Provide Complete Data for Policy Makers to Make Decisions

The IPCC wisely keeps to its charge of being policy relevant but not policy prescriptive. But policymakers should be able to find the relevant information in IPCC documents to facilitate making policy decisions regarding climate change mitigation. Unfortunately, that is not always the case, particularly when it comes to the economics of climate change. Although scenarios and forecasts of future greenhouse gas emissions inform a major part of the WGIII report, basic information on mitigation costs and the costs of inaction was not provided in ways that could best be used by policymakers.

For example, AR5 WGIII uses models to generate aggregate costs associated with different greenhouse gas concentration pathways, but the information that a policymaker from a given country might need to determine the costs to his or her economy from different actions is unavailable. Similarly, AR5 WGII on climate change impacts includes a great deal of information on the physical dimensions of climate change impacts but scant information on the monetary equivalent of these impacts, information many policy makers need to justify taking costly mitigation actions.

Conclusions

It has been more than 25 years since the inception of the IPCC. With the completion of its Fifth Assessment Report, it is time to consider significant reforms for the IPCC's assessment of the growing literature on climate change economics and other social science aspects of climate change. In this chapter, we have proposed seven areas for reform that emerge from our experience at nearly every level of organization in the IPCC's latest assessment round.

We can say — with no reservations — that working for the IPCC was at times enormously frustrating. As an IPCC author, scholars can at times feels as if they were *in* the policy process, being forced to respond directly to critical government comments based on political sensitivity or even directly negotiating text with professional climate negotiators during the SPM Approval Sessions. Nevertheless, despite these distractions, we believe that because of its broad legitimacy, the IPCC remains a critical institution in the communication of scholarly knowledge about climate change. Only after engaging with the IPCC for many years did each of us conclude that the IPCC is an important institution for governments to understand the findings of academics. Engaging governments in often detailed deliberations over climate science, economics, and policy helps build a broadly shared knowledge base. There is a further, deeper value to the IPCC in that it communicates to governments and the general public that all governments party to the UNFCCC have agreed to the IPCC assessments as scientifically valid. The process of consensus-building around the SPM and the work of the underlying chapters plays a key motivating role in driving international climate negotiations (e.g., under the UNFCCC).

Engaging with the IPCC as authors has created new platforms for us to communicate some of the most important findings of our academic field. We took on the responsibility of presenting the best literature of our field in a way that was of greatest policy relevance. But if scholars with a sound and balanced understanding of the literature are deterred from participating as IPCC authors and surrender the process to quasi-academics with political motivations, the potential harm to the policy process and the reputation of academia could be very great. There is a two-part responsibility to prevent this from happening. On the one hand, the IPCC must reform its operational procedures so that some of the more qualified scholars perceive the time investment as authors to be worthwhile. The IPCC must also reform itself on substantive grounds, in part by leveraging the work of complementary institutions. On the other hand, if the IPCC holds up its end of the deal, scholars of climate change economics should not dismiss the opportunity to provide public service by volunteering for the IPCC in its future assessments.

Acknowledgments

The authors thank Robert Stowe and Christian Flaschland for helpful comments on this manuscript. Participants in a workshop entitled "Assessment and Communication of the Social Science of Climate Change: Bridging Research and Policy," discussed many of the ideas in this work and were influential in developing our own thinking. The authors also acknowledge the Alfred P. Sloan Foundation, the Fondazione Eni Enrico Mattei, and the Mercator Research Institute on Global Commons and Climate Change for sponsoring this workshop. All errors are the responsibility of the authors.

References

Bolin, B. (2007). *A History of the Science and Politics of Climate Change: The Role of the Intergovernmental Panel on Climate Change*. Cambridge, NY: Cambridge University Press.

Broome, J. (2014). *At the IPCC*. LRB Blog. http://www.lrb.co.uk/blog/2014/05/08/john-broome/at-the-ipcc/ (Accessed 3 September 2015).

Carraro, C., C. Kolstad, and R. Stavins. (2015). "Assessment and communication of the social science of climate change: Bridging research and policy." *Memorandum from Workshop Conducted 18–20 February*, Berlin, Germany.

Carraro, C., O. Edenhofer, C. Flachsland, C. Kolstad, R. Stavins, and R. Stowe. (forthcoming). "The IPCC at a crossroads: Opportunities for reform." *Science*. **350**: 34–35.

Clark, P. (2014). "Climate change report was watered down says senior economist." *Financial Times*.

Corbera, E., L. Calvet-Mir, H. Hughes, and M. Paterson. (2015). "Patterns of authorship in the IPCC Working Group III report." *Nature Climate Change*. **6**: 94–99.

Edenhofer, O. (2011). "Different views ensure IPCC balance." *Nature Climate Change*. **1**: 229–230.

Edenhofer, O. and J. Minx. (2014). "Mapmakers and navigators, facts and values." *Science*. **345**: 37–38.

Grieneisen, M. L. and M. Zhang. (2011). "The current status of climate change research." *Nature Climate Change*. **1**: 72–73.

Griggs, D. (2014). "Climate policy: Streamline IPCC reports." *Nature*. **508**: 171–173.

Hulme, M. and M. Mahoney. (2010). "Climate change: What do we know about the IPCC?" *Progress Physical Geography*. **34**: 705–718.

Hulme, M., E. Zorita, T. F. Stocker, J. Price, and J. R. Christy. (2010). "IPCC: Cherish it, tweak it or scrap it." *Nature*. **463**: 730–732.

InterAcademy Council. (2010). *Climate Change Assessments Review of the Processes and Procedures of the IPCC*. InterAcademy Council, Amsterdam, The Netherlands.

IPCC. (2011). *IPCC Conflict of Interest Policy*. Kampala, Uganda and Copenhagen, Denmark.

IPCC. (2013). *Principles Governing IPCC Work*.

IPCC. (2015). *IPCC — Organization — Structure*.

Nature. (2013). "The final assessment." *Nature*. **501**: 281–281.

Schulte-Uebbing, L., G. Hansen, A. M. Hernández, and M. Winter. (2015). "Chapter scientists in the IPCC AR5 — experience and lessons learned." *Current Opinion in Environmental Sustainability*. **14**: 250–256.

Stavins, R. (2014a). *Understanding the IPCC's Products*. The Environmental Forum, Environmental Law Institute, Washington, DC.

Stavins, R. (2014b). *Is the IPCC Government Approval Process Broken? An Economic View of the Environment*. http://www.robertstavinsblog.org/2014/04/25/is-the-ipcc-government-approval-process-broken-2/.

U.S. National Academies of Sciences. (2003). *Policy on Committee Composition and Balance and Conflict of Interest for Committees Used in the Development of Reports*.

Victor, D. (2015). "Climate change: Embed the social sciences in climate policy." *Nature*. **520**: 27–29.

https://doi.org/10.1142/9789811292415_0017

Chapter 17

International Climate Change Policy*

Gabriel Chan[†,], Robert N. Stavins[‡,§,‖,††], and Zou Ji[¶,‡‡]**

[†]*Humphrey School of Public Affairs, University of Minnesota, Minneapolis, Minnesota, USA*

[‡]*John F. Kennedy School of Government, Harvard University, Cambridge, MA, USA*

[§]*National Bureau of Economic Research, Cambridge, MA, USA*

[‖]*Resources for the Future, Washington, DC, USA*

[¶]*Energy Foundation, Beijing, China*

[**]*gabechan@umn.edu*

[††]*robert_stavins@harvard.edu*

[‡‡]*zouji@efchina.org*

Introduction

This review synthesizes the scholarly literature on international climate change cooperation, emphasizing the literature published over the last decade. Over this period, international cooperation under the United Nations (UN) has evolved considerably, culminating in the 2015 Paris

---

*This chapter was originally published in *Annual Review of Resource Economics*, **10**(335–360), 2018. https://doi.org/10.1146/annurev-resource-100517-023321.

Agreement. Simultaneously, climate change has become a focal issue in many other UN fora, non-UN multilateral and transnational fora, and nonstate international activities. While the institutional settings for climate policy have become more diverse, so too has the breadth of issues to which international climate policies have been linked.

We begin in section "Framing Concepts and Evaluation Criteria" by identifying key framing concepts and criteria used to evaluate international climate change policies. In section "Policy Design Elements and Proposals for International Climate Policy", we examine the major design elements of existing and proposed forms of international cooperation to address climate change. In section "Existing Forms and Fora of Cooperation", we describe existing fora and realizations of such cooperation, including the Kyoto Protocol and the Paris Agreement, and in section "Advantages and Disadvantages of Different Forms", we provide an assessment of these forms and examples of international cooperation. In section "Other Issues", we identify some additional issues, and in section "Conclusion", we conclude.

Framing Concepts and Evaluation Criteria

Greenhouse gases (GHGs) mix in the atmosphere, and so the benefits of GHG emissions reductions are distributed globally. These benefits are both nonexcludable — meaning an actor cannot be excluded from the benefits of emissions reductions undertaken by other actors — and nonrival — meaning the benefits of mitigation can be simultaneously enjoyed by any individuals without reducing the benefits to others. But the primary costs of climate policies are borne within the jurisdiction taking action. Hence, for virtually any jurisdiction taking action, the direct climate benefits it receives will be less than the direct abatement costs it incurs, creating incentives for countries to free ride on the mitigation actions of others (Stavins, 2011). Because of this, international — if not global — cooperation is necessary to address climate change.

International cooperation can address several key challenges: multiple actors that are diverse in their perceptions of the costs and benefits of collective action, emissions sources that are unevenly distributed, heterogeneous climate impacts that are uncertain and distant in space and time, and heterogeneous mitigation costs. Because there is no world government, countries must consent voluntarily to any form of international cooperation, and compliance must be verified by parties to an agreement or by a legitimate body (Barrett, 2003, 2007; Brousseau *et al.*, 2012).

Following the Intergovernmental Panel on Climate Change (IPCC) (Stavins *et al.*, 2014), we employ four categories of evaluation criteria for international climate policy: environmental effectiveness, aggregate economic performance, distributional impacts, and institutional feasibility. First, environmental effectiveness encompasses the extent to which a cooperative effort reduces the causes or impacts of climate change. This criterion has been formalized in various ways in several international agreements, including the stabilization of GHG concentrations at levels sufficient to "prevent dangerous anthropogenic interference with the climate system" (UN Framework Convention on Climate Change; UNFCCC); emission-reduction targets for developed countries (Kyoto Protocol); and an aspirational goal of limiting global average temperature increases to 2°C above preindustrial levels (Paris Agreement).

Second, aggregate economic performance incorporates both economic efficiency (maximization of social net benefits, including co-benefits and adverse side-effects) and cost-effectiveness (minimization of social costs for a given degree of environmental effectiveness) (Stern, 2007; Nordhaus, 2008). Although economic efficiency makes the trade-off between aggregate costs and benefits explicit, analysis of a policy's cost-effectiveness may be more feasible in the case of climate change, as some social benefits of climate change mitigation are highly uncertain and distant in time, making them difficult to monetize or otherwise compare. Third, the distributional impacts of a cooperative effort refer to the distribution of costs and benefits across space and time. This criterion can be related to principles of distributive justice, historic responsibility, capability and capacity, and sustainable development (Stavins *et al.*, 2014).

Fourth, institutional feasibility refers to the ability of the parties to an agreement to implement and sustain an effort. This criterion can be understood in terms of four components: participation, compliance, legitimacy, and flexibility. Participation refers to the number of parties, geographical coverage, and efforts of cooperating participants. Compliance affects long-term performance (Barrett, 2003) but is often difficult to establish, due to the lack of supranational authority that can impose sanctions. However, incentives for compliance can be created within the regime established by an agreement (Heitzig *et al.*, 2011). Legitimacy refers to whether parties believe that both the decision-making procedures and substantive outcomes fairly represent the collective will of the involved parties. Finally, flexibility refers to the degree to which a cooperative effort can respond to new information, learn from previous experience, and adapt to changing economic and political conditions.

These four criteria may be mutually reinforcing (Cao, 2010), but there may also be conflicts, forcing trade-offs between and among them. Maximizing global net benefits or attaining cost-effectiveness may lead to actions that decrease distributional equity (van Asselt and Gupta, 2009), which could lead to low participation. Increasing flexibility of an agreement may increase participation, but it can come at the cost of regulatory uncertainty that increases the aggregate cost of compliance by reducing incentives to invest in long-term solutions (Brunner *et al.*, 2012). The environmental effectiveness of a cooperative effort largely depends on trade-offs between the ambition of the agreement, the breadth of participation, and effective compliance mechanisms (Barrett, 2003; Bodansky, 2011).

Policy Design Elements and Proposals for International Climate Policy

In this section, design elements of existing and proposed forms of international climate change cooperation are discussed: policy architecture, legal status, and mechanisms for monitoring and verifying mitigation actions.

Policy Architectures for Climate Change Mitigation and Adaptation

Policy architecture refers to the fundamental nature and structure of an international agreement or other climate regime (Aldy and Stavins, 2010). We consider existing and potential policy architectures based on the level of centralized authority and the degree to which authority is conferred on a multilateral institution. Whereas international cooperation arises through negotiations between independent countries, agreed-upon policies vary in the degree to which they confer authority on centralized multilateral institutions. An alternative and closely related framing is of the degree of cooperation, which ranges from shallow coordination to deep cooperation.

Degrees of Centralized Authority

Policy architectures can be viewed along the spectrum of centralized authority within three categories: strong multilateralism, harmonized national policies, and decentralized approaches. The boundaries between these categories are not sharply defined, and the location of proposed and existing policies on the spectrum can depend on specific design elements.

Figure 1 illustrates how some existing and proposed international agreements can be placed on this spectrum of centralized authority. The figure also organizes policies by the degree to which their cooperative effort requires focus on ends, such as emission targets, or on means, such as policy instruments. Several policies shown in the figure span a range in their potential degree of centralized authority; more distinct placement would depend on specific design elements.

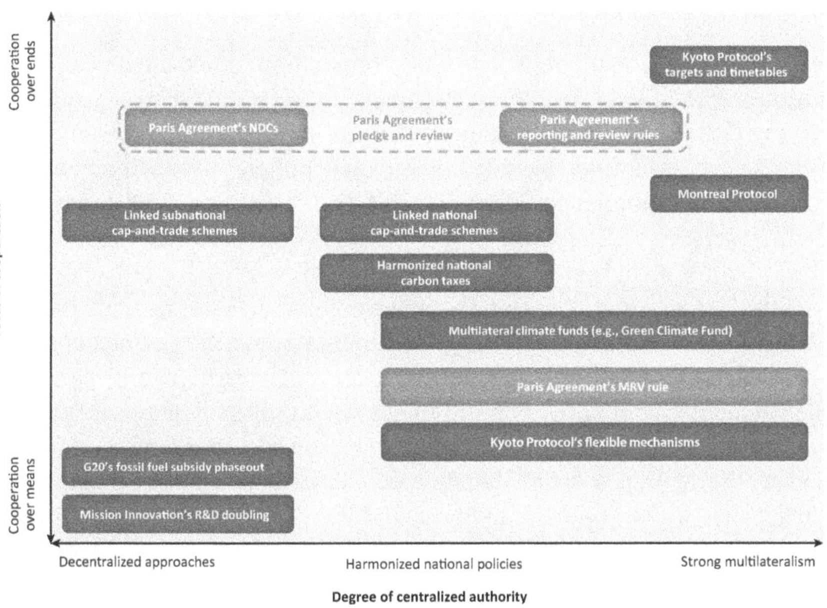

Figure 1. International cooperation over ends/means and degrees of centralized authority. Central elements of the Paris Agreement are highlighted in orange. The degree of centralization indicates the authority an agreement confers on an international institution, not the process of negotiating the agreement.

Notes: Abbreviations: MRV, measurement (or monitoring), reporting, and verification; NDC, nationally determined contribution.

Source: Modified with permission from Stavins *et al.* (2014, Figure 13.2).

Strong Multilateralism

Climate policy architectures based on strong multilateralism, also referred to as centralized or top-down approaches, are characterized by a high degree of coordination of goals or actions among participants (Bodansky, 2007; Aldy and Stavins, 2010). An example would be a global carbon tax or emission trading scheme administered by a single global organization. A prominent example of a centralized architecture is the Kyoto Protocol's emission targets and timetables for participating Annex B countries. Strong multilateralism may also be applied to individual sectors (Meckling and Chung, 2009). While sectoral strong multilateralism may be more difficult to negotiate, these approaches may also have lower leakage rates if sectors can be regulated consistently across countries.

Harmonized National Policies

Harmonized national policies involve cooperation to make the design and ambition of national (or other subglobal) policies similar to one another, relying less on centralized authority than on strong multilateralism. These approaches harmonize the rules of national policies — such as national carbon taxes (Nordhaus, 2008; Metcalf and Weisbach, 2009), emission trading schemes (Ellerman, 2010), technology standards (de Coninck *et al.*, 2008), or hybrid policy approaches (Metcalf and Weisbach, 2012; Mehling *et al.*, 2017) — at the international level. The "pledge and review" mechanism of the Paris Agreement exemplifies elements of the harmonized national policies approach in which participating parties to the agreement voluntarily commit to domestic emission targets or actions. Depending on how national pledges are reviewed (or enforced), a pledge and review approach could also include elements of centralized authority, particularly in the review of pledges, and therefore be considered a hybrid approach (Bodansky, 2016b), which is the case with the Paris Agreement.

Decentralized Approaches

Decentralized approaches, also referred to as bottom-up approaches (Victor *et al.*, 2005; Dubash and Rajamani, 2010), are national and other subglobal policies that are connected to varying degrees (Victor *et al.*, 2005; Hoffmann, 2011). These approaches may link climate policies relying on the same policy mechanism, such as cap-and-trade systems (Jaffe *et al.*, 2009; Metcalf and Weisbach, 2012; Ranson and Stavins, 2013) may link climate policies relying on a heterogeneous set of mechanisms, such as a carbon tax and a cap-and-trade scheme (Metcalf and Weisbach, 2012) or may focus on aspects of technology innovation and transfer (de Coninck *et al.*, 2008; Newell, 2010a). Decentralized approaches may therefore be seen as composed of topically focused building blocks (Falkner *et al.*, 2010; Stewart *et al.*, 2017) or as minilateral cooperation among clubs of countries (Nordhaus, 2015). An example of a decentralized approach is the existing and proposed direct linkages between regional, national, and subnational cap-and-trade systems through the mutual recognition of allowances (Jaffe *et al.*, 2009; Mehling and Haites, 2009; Ranson and Stavins, 2013; Mehling *et al.*, 2017). A related but distinct example of a decentralized approach is the indirect linkage among cap-and-trade systems through mutual recognition of a common emission-reduction credit system, such as the Kyoto Protocol's Clean Development Mechanism (CDM) Certified Emission Reduction (CER) credits.

Legal Frameworks

International agreements exist only by the consent of their parties (Thompson, 2006). Hence, the legal form of an agreement, together with its rules for enforcement, defines how legally binding the agreement is on its parties. The legal character of an international agreement can be understood in four parts: legal type, whether any commitments are mandatory, the specificity of commitments, and the use of enforcement provisions (Bodansky, 2009).

Legal type refers to the range of forms under which an agreement is codified. At the opposite ends of a continuous spectrum are hard law and soft law. Examples of the former include treaties, protocols, and contracts, whereas examples of the latter include declarations, resolutions, and guidelines. The commitments contained in an agreement may be more or less legally binding: They can be expressed in obligatory language (for example, "shall" or "must") or in aspirational language (for example, "should" or "aim"). But the actual bindingness of an agreement may depend on the costs of nonparticipation, noncompliance, withdrawal, and loss of reputation (Hoffmann, 2005, 2011). The specificity of an agreement refers to the degree of detail in which commitments are expressed. Compliance with a vaguely worded commitment is difficult to verify (Abbott and Snidal, 2000). Finally, enforcement refers to an agreement's utilization of procedures, mechanisms, or sanctions, including monitoring and verification of compliance, which can range from inaction to admonishments to trade sanctions to military force (Werksman, 2010).

Legal Forms

Proposed and existing forms of international climate change cooperation can be grouped into five categories that describe their legal bindingness. First, an international agreement may be formalized as mandatory provisions in a legally binding instrument with obligatory language, requisite specificity to assess compliance, and a well-defined enforcement regime. The targets and timetables approach of the Kyoto Protocol and the Marrakech Accords are in this category, with specific emission limits and sanctions for noncompliance.

Second, an agreement can take the form of mandatory provisions in a legally binding instrument but without enforcement mechanisms, relying instead on self-enforcement. An example of such an agreement is Article 4.1 of the UNFCCC, which mandates national emission inventories, measures to mitigate, and measures to facilitate adaptation, but without any enforcement mechanisms.

Third, an agreement can consist of nonmandatory provisions in a legally binding instrument, carrying more weight than a political agreement but without demanding compliance. An example is Article 4.2(a) and (b) of the UNFCCC, in which developed countries commit to adopt policies and measures to limit their net GHG emissions.

Fourth, an agreement can take the form of mandatory provisions in a nonlegally binding instrument, which can induce actions through norms, reputation concerns, or reciprocity. An example of an agreement of this form is the pledges and actions submitted by states under the Copenhagen Accord, Cancún Agreements, and the Paris Agreement.

Fifth and finally, an agreement can be formalized as nonmandatory provisions in a nonlegally binding agreement. Such agreements typically include statements of principles or norms and are expressed as aims or aspirations. An example is the target set in the Noordwijk Declaration at a ministerial summit prior to the 1992 Rio summit.

An agreement's legal form can have important implications for the agreement's effectiveness. Agreements that are more legally binding increase the costs of noncompliance and therefore signal greater seriousness by participating states. But there may be trade-offs between a more legally binding agreement and the ambition of commitments, precisely because greater legal bindingness creates higher costs for failing to achieve commitments. Countries may be more willing to accept ambitious commitments in the context of a less legally binding agreement (Bernstein, 2005; Raustiala, 2005; Guzman and Meyer, 2010).

Legal Remedies and Loss and Damage

Although a scholarly literature exists on the potential use of legal remedies (such as civil liability) to address climate damages (Allen, 2003; Grossman, 2003; Lord *et al.*, 2011), such remedies have not been incorporated in climate agreements, and there would be significant obstacles to doing so, including the lack of a robust international civil liability system. In this context, the notion of "loss and damage" has been discussed in UNFCCC negotiations, but the Paris Agreement removes the possibility of liability or obligatory compensation for climate impacts (Bodansky, 2016a; Lees, 2017). Human rights law could conceivably frame an approach to climate change (Bodansky, 2010; Bell, 2013), as has been acknowledged by the UN Human Rights Council in its Resolution 7/23 and the Office of the UN High Commissioner for Human Rights (Limon, 2009), but this has not moved forward in UNFCCC negotiations.

Frameworks for Monitoring, Reporting, and Verification

Successful compliance is likely to require an effective regime of measurement (or monitoring), reporting, and verification (MRV). Provisions for greater transparency in MRV have been considered with regard to countries' GHG emissions and international financial flows from developed to developing countries for mitigation and adaptation (Breidenich and Bodansky, 2009; Ellis and Moarif, 2009). Lessons regarding effective MRV are available from other multilateral regimes — such as International Monetary Fund (IMF) consultations, Organisation for Economic Co-operation and Development (OECD) economic policy reviews, World Trade Organization (WTO) trade policy reviews, and arms control agreements. Such lessons are in reference to attention to accuracy, evolution over time, self-reporting and third-party verification, independent technical assessment, political or peer review, remote sensing or other technical means, and public domain reporting (Cecys, 2010; Bell *et al.*, 2012; Aldy, 2014).

Existing Forms and Fora of Cooperation

Over the past decade, the landscape of international institutions related to climate policy has become more diverse, as climate change is now addressed in a substantial number of fora across a wide range of scales. Some researchers have described the range of climate policy agreements and institutions as a "regime complex" (Biermann *et al.*, 2009; Keohane and Victor, 2011; Jordan *et al.*, 2015). We review the evolution of international and transnational cooperation on climate change between state and nonstate actors over the past decade. State actors include governments at the international, national, and subnational levels, some of which may be parties to an agreement and others of which may be affected by an agreement to which they are not direct parties. Nonstate actors include nongovernmental organizations (NGOs) and private firms.

Internationally Negotiated Principles and Norms

International cooperation on climate change has been shaped by principles enunciated in several early norm-setting agreements, including the Rio Declaration on Environment and Development and the UNFCCC. The UNFCCC explicitly included principles designed to guide future international agreements: "equity" and "common but differentiated responsibilities and respective capabilities" (CBDR-RC) [Article 3(1)]; relative needs, vulnerability, and burdens in countries of differing wealth [Article 3(2)]; precaution and "cost-effective[ness] so as to ensure global benefits at the lowest possible cost" [Article 3(3)]; "sustainable development" [Article 3(4)]; and cooperation [Article 3(5)].

The UNFCCC established a framework, principles, and goals for the international response to climate change. Under Article 2, the parties agreed to the objective of "prevent[ing] dangerous anthropogenic interference with the climate system," an objective which was not quantified and was subject to caveats. Under Article 4(2)(a), the Annex I parties (largely the industrialized countries as of 1990) committed to adopt measures to limit net emissions (covering both sources and sinks of GHGs not controlled by the Montreal Protocol), "recognizing that the return by the end of the present decade (the year 2000) to earlier levels" would contribute to modifying long-term trends consistent with the treaty's objective. Under Article 4(2)(b), Annex I parties committed to periodically communicate information on their emissions, "with the aim of returning individually or jointly to their 1990 levels."

Cooperation Under the UNFCCC

The UNFCCC's universal membership provides it with a high degree of legitimacy among parties around the world (Karlsson-Vinkhuyzen and McGee, 2013), and steps taken under the Convention have led to more extensive action than under other forms of international cooperation on climate change. Nevertheless, slow progress has been attributed to resistance to costly policies in both developed and developing countries, lack of political will (Keohane and Victor, 2011), and the complexity that characterizes the problem (Hoffmann, 2011). Fragmentation of the climate regime could create opportunities for forum shopping, loss of transparency, and reduced ambition (Biermann *et al.*, 2009).

Although universal participation may be desirable in principle, nations are characterized by great heterogeneity in economic capacity and emissions levels. Variations in both wealth and emissions have evolved over time; for example, many countries classified in the 1992 UNFCCC as developing countries (non-Annex I) have since experienced increased incomes and emissions, in some cases exceeding the incomes and/or emissions of some countries classified in 1992 as developed (Annex I).

The Kyoto Protocol

The first Conference of the Parties (COP-1) of the UNFCCC met in Berlin, Germany, in 1995, and adopted what came to be known as the Berlin Mandate, which interpreted the UNFCCC principle of CBDR-RC as meaning that the Annex I countries alone should take actions to reduce their GHG emissions. This approach was quantified two years later at COP-3 in Kyoto, Japan, where the Kyoto Protocol was developed to include binding quantitative mitigation commitments for developed countries.

The 38 countries listed in the Kyoto Protocol's Annex B, nearly identical to the list of countries in the Convention's Annex I, made aggregate commitments to collectively reduce their GHG emissions by 4.2 percent relative to 1990 levels (5.2 percent relative to the country-specific base years used for establishing national commitments) by the end of the Protocol's first commitment period, 2008–2012 (UNFCCC, 2012). Other parties to the Kyoto Protocol were not constrained but could participate in other ways, in particular, through the CDM.

Negotiations on a second commitment period for the Kyoto Protocol were launched in 2005 and concluded in late 2012 with the establishment of a second commitment period for 2013–2020. However, by that time, several major Annex I countries had decided not to participate in the first commitment period, decided not to participate in the second commitment period, or dropped out altogether (including the United States, Russia, Canada, Japan, and Australia). The remaining Annex I parties (largely the European Union and its member states) adopted quantified emissions reduction commitments covering approximately 13 percent of global GHG emissions (as of 2010) (JRC, 2013).

The aggregate emissions by Annex I countries fell below the Kyoto Protocol's first commitment period collective 5.2 percent reduction target (Shishlov *et al.*, 2016), but much of the reduction was due to factors other than the Protocol. According to UNFCCC GHG inventories, aggregate GHG emissions from all Annex I countries were reduced by 13.6 percent from 1990 to 2011 if land-use and forestry-sector changes are taken into account and 8.5 percent if they are not. Excluding the United States — because it was not a party to the Kyoto Protocol — the reduction from 1990 to 2011 was 22.9 percent if land-use and forestry-sector changes are taken into account and 16.6 percent if they are not. If the economies in transition (EITs) — largely the former countries of the Soviet Union — are excluded, the remaining Annex I countries' aggregate GHG emissions increased by 2.1 percent and 3.2 percent from 1990 to 2011 (with and without changes in land use and forestry, respectively) (UNFCCC 2012). Thus, the fall in aggregate emissions was largely due to the economic restructuring that ensued in the EITs.

The environmental effectiveness of the Protocol's first commitment period was less than it could have been for several reasons. First, only Annex B parties had emissions reduction responsibilities. Second, not all Annex B parties participated. The United States did not ratify the Protocol; Canada withdrew from the Protocol in December, 2011 (effective December, 2012); and Russia, Japan, and New Zealand opted not to participate in the second commitment period (2013–2020). Third, the Annex B EITs were credited for emissions reductions that would have occurred without the Protocol due to their significant economic contraction during the 1990s. But these loose targets may have been necessary to engage them as parties (Stewart and Wiener, 2003).

Since 1990, the Annex B countries' share of global GHG emissions declined significantly, from approximately 56 percent of global emissions in 1990 to about 39 percent in 2010. Simultaneously, overall global GHG emissions have risen significantly; global emissions in 2010 were 31 percent higher than in 1990 (JRC, 2013), with the bulk of this increase coming from the large rapidly growing and emerging economies (notably China, India, Brazil, South Korea, South Africa, Mexico, and Indonesia). Assessments of the efficiency of the Kyoto Protocol depend on respective estimates of the costs and benefits of mitigation, and so some assessments have found the Protocol inefficient (Nordhaus, 2007), whereas some have found it to be cost-effective but insufficient in its ambition (Stern, 2007; Weitzman, 2007). The Kyoto Protocol provides complete flexibility with regard to how parties achieve their targets. One result was the development of emissions trading programs in several countries and regions (Paterson *et al.*, 2014). Regional and national emissions trading programs included those in the European Union (the EU Emission Trading System or EU ETS), Australia, and New Zealand, as well as subnational trading programs in the United States Regional Greenhouse Gas Initiative (RGGI) and in California. In China, seven regional pilot programs were launched in 2013, which were expected to expand to a national program in 2017 (Newell *et al.,* 2013; Ellerman *et al.*, 2016).

Distributional impacts of the Kyoto Protocol have been examined both cross-sectionally (mainly geographically) and temporally. Income patterns and trends as well as distribution of GHG emissions have changed significantly since the 1990s, when the UNFCCC and Kyoto Protocol specified Annex I/Annex B countries; some countries outside these lists have become wealthier and larger emitters than some countries on these lists (Aldy and Stavins, 2012). However, among Annex B countries, the Kyoto Protocol's emissions-target allocation is generally progressive, exhibiting positive correlation between gross domestic product per capita and the degree of targeted emissions reduction below business-as-usual levels (Frankel, 2005).

It is notable that the Kyoto Protocol was ratified (or the equivalent) by 191 countries (plus the European Union), but the high rate of ratification was likely due in part to the lack of emissions reduction commitments asked of non-Annex B countries (Lutter, 2000). Also, allowing Annex B countries the flexibility to choose their own domestic policies to meet their national emissions commitments contributed to institutional feasibility. But compromises made during the negotiation of the Protocol that enabled its institutional and political viability may have reduced its environmental effectiveness (Victor, 2004; Helm, 2010). This serves as an example of a trade-off among ambition, participation, and compliance. Additionally, despite the Kyoto Protocol's compliance system, it was difficult in practice to enforce its targets because of the lack of a legal authority with enforcement powers, and the weakness of possible sanctions relative to the costs of compliance. This is, of course, true of most international agreements (Barrett, 2008).

The Kyoto Protocol's Flexible Mechanisms

The Kyoto Protocol included three flexible mechanisms intended to reduce the aggregate costs of achieving the Protocol's emissions reduction targets by allowing for trading of emission permits between Annex B countries (international emissions trading or IET) and by expanding the scope of emissions reduction opportunities to additional reductions within Annex B countries (joint implementation or JI) and in non-Annex B countries (CDM). Activity under IET and JI was relatively limited.

The CDM aimed to reduce mitigation costs for Annex B countries and contributed to sustainable development in non-Annex B countries. Nearly 1.4 billion emission credits were issued from over 7,300 registered projects by October 2013 (Stavins *et al.*, 2014). The price of CDM credits declined following the 2008 recession, due largely to decreased demand after rule changes in the EU ETS regarding the use of CDM credits. New project registration slowed significantly after late 2013 (UNEP Risoe Cent., 2017).

The environmental effectiveness of the CDM depended on three key factors: whether a credited project actually reduced more emissions than would have been reduced in its absence (additionality); the validity of the baseline from which emissions reductions were calculated; and indirect emissions impacts caused by projects (leakage). The issue of additionality, in particular, generated considerable controversy regarding environmental performance despite increased elaboration of additionality tests used by CDM regulators (Chan, 2015; Chan and Huenteler, 2015; Hayashi and Michaelowa, 2013; Millard-Ball and Ortolano, 2010).

With respect to cost-effectiveness, the Kyoto Protocol's three flexible mechanisms (the CDM, JI, and IET) were intended to lower the cost of the global regime. Although the CDM had the greatest volume of activity, many low-cost opportunities were not taken up by CDM projects (Castro, 2012). However, the long-term contribution of the CDM to cost-effectiveness may have depended on its ability to promote technological change in developing countries (Dechezleprêtre *et al.*, 2008; Seres *et al.*, 2009). IET could, in theory, have reduced abatement costs by as much as 50 percent if trades took place among Annex B countries (Bosetti *et al.*, 2010; Jacoby *et al.*, 2010). But in practice, trading under this mechanism was very limited, with only 0.2 billion tCO_2eq traded through IET as of July 2013 (Stavins *et al.*, 2014). JI also had the potential to improve the costeffectiveness of Annex B countries' activities under the Protocol (Böhringer, 2003), but activity was limited, with a majority of the 0.8 billion emission reduction unit (ERU) credits issued under JI coming in the transition economies.

Negotiations from Kyoto to Paris

Due to the recognition by some parties that the structure of the Kyoto Protocol, including its dichotomous distinction between developed and developing countries, was not consistent with achieving the GHG emissions reduction goals embodied in the UNFCCC, the annual climate negotiations increasingly considered alternative structures for a post-Kyoto period. With the planned conclusion of the First Commitment Period of the Kyoto Protocol in 2012, scholars and practitioners explored a variety of options for new climate policy architectures. Several reviews of alternative international policy architectures have appeared in the literature (Aldy and Stavins, 2010; Moncel *et al.*, 2011; Stavins *et al.*, 2014).

At COP-13, in Bali, Indonesia, in 2007, the blurring of the Annex I/non-Annex I distinction commenced with discussions on long-term cooperative action under the UNFCCC, which led to the Bali Action Plan. Further, under the Copenhagen Accord of 2009 and the Cancún Agreements of 2010, 42 developed countries (including the 27 EU member states) submitted to the UNFCCC absolute emissions reduction commitments against various base years in the form of quantified economy-wide emissions targets for 2020, and 55 developing countries submitted information regarding Nationally Appropriate Mitigation Actions.

COP-17, held in Durban, South Africa, in 2011, produced an important breakthrough in the form of the Durban Platform for Enhanced Action, through which delegates agreed "to launch a process to develop a protocol, another legal instrument or an agreed outcome with legal force under the Convention applicable to all parties" for implementation in 2020. The 2013 Warsaw mechanism established a loose timeline for all parties, without differentiation between developed and developing countries, to offer Intended Nationally Determined Contributions (INDCs), which would represent each country's planned mitigation actions.

The Paris Agreement

At COP-21, held in Paris, France, in December, 2015, the delegates agreed to the Paris Agreement, which formalized the most comprehensive framework for international climate policy since the 1997 Kyoto Protocol. The central component of the Paris Agreement is a pledge and review system of nationally determined contributions (NDCs) that represent roughly 10-year national goals for climate mitigation. In some cases, NDCs also contain pledges concerning adaptation, finance, and other measures (UNFCCC, 2016).

The NDC submissions were compiled in April, 2016. Participation in this first round included NDCs covering nearly all parties to the UNFCCC and countries responsible for 97 percent of global GHG emissions (compared with 13 percent coverage by the Kyoto Protocol's second commitment period). The structure of the mitigation targets in the first round of NDCs varies significantly: 32 percent contain absolute emissions reduction targets; 45 percent contain emissions targets relative to business as usual; 4 percent include emission intensity targets (emissions per unit of GDP); 2 percent specify a year in which emissions will peak; and 20 percent include only strategies, plans, or actions for lowering emissions. In addition, some NDCs also include conditional mitigation pledges that peg domestic targets to the actions of other countries (UNFCCC, 2016).

The legal form of the Paris Agreement is a mix of mandatory (e.g., procedural obligations to prepare and communicate successive NDCs every five years and comply with international transparency requirements) and nonmandatory provisions (e.g., the collective aim to peak global emissions as soon as possible) (Bodansky, 2016a; Oberthür and Bodle, 2016). The combination of top-down centralized elements with the bottom-up voluntary NDCs has led some to characterize the Paris Agreement as having a hybrid structure.

In terms of its eventual environmental performance, the first set of NDC pledges is surely not sufficient to meet the ambition of the Paris Agreement to limit global average temperature to "well below 2°C above preindustrial levels," let alone the Agreement's aspirational reference to 1.5°C (Rogelj *et al.*, 2016; UNFCCC, 2016; UNEP, 2017). Relative to global emissions in 2010, the combined NDC pledges are estimated to result in global emissions that are 13 percent and 16 percent greater by 2025 and 2030, respectively. But, importantly, pre-NDC trajectories suggest that global emissions would have been considerably greater in the absence of the Paris Agreement (UNFCCC, 2016).

Many NDCs endorse domestic and international market-based mechanisms, among various approaches, to improve cost-effectiveness. The Paris Agreement allows for countries to link their mitigation policies, thereby potentially improving aggregate cost-effectiveness (see section "International Linkage Consistent with the Paris Agreement") (Ranson and Stavins, 2015; Bodansky *et al.*, 2016; Mehling *et al.*, 2017).

The distributional equity of the Paris Agreement could be increased through financing of emissions reductions and adaptation in developing countries. Studies have suggested potential approaches to providing financial resources (AGF, 2010; Haites, 2011).

The participation of 169 ratifying parties to the Paris Agreement speaks to the institutional feasibility of the Agreement, but the June 2017 announcement by the United States of its intention to withdraw from the Paris Agreement (effective November 2020) raised concerns about the durability of the Agreement and the future collective ambition of NDCs (Kemp, 2017).

Increasing Ambition under the Paris Agreement

The initial set of NDCs from countries accounting for 97 percent of global GHG emissions was intended only as the first of a series of NDCs with increasing ambition over time. The Paris Agreement establishes a time line for countries to submit revised NDCs every five years. Due to the voluntary nature of the contributions, the ambition of the overall Agreement is fundamentally rooted in national political realities and within an international system of accountability and periodic international review of domestic actions.

At the international level, the so-called "ratchet mechanism" of the Paris Agreement aims to increase the ambition of NDCs over time through five-year cycles of "stocktaking" to report, review, and revise pledges.

The logic of the ratchet mechanism is to leverage soft reciprocity among states, whereby leading states take more ambitious actions with the aim of encouraging other states to reciprocate by raising their own levels of ambition. In the absence of coercive international law, the logic of the Paris Agreement's ratchet mechanism emphasizes political leadership, financial transfers, moral suasion, and norm setting (Falkner, 2016) and could create an expanded role for nonstate actors to influence international policy (van Asselt, 2016).

A significant challenge to conducting the periodic review of NDCs will be developing a common understanding of the effort that country pledges represent. Because NDCs are articulated according to a variety of metrics, no single comprehensive metric can be universally applied. Instead, a set of indicators may be required to compare mitigation efforts (Aldy and Pizer, 2016). Effectively comparing efforts may require additional analytic methods (Aldy *et al.*, 2016; Jacoby *et al.*, 2017; Peters *et al.*, 2017) as well as additional transparency, surveillance, and accounting efforts (Aldy, 2014; Winkler *et al.*, 2017).

International Linkage Consistent with the Paris Agreement

Given concerns regarding the collective ambition of the NDCs submitted under the Paris Agreement, an important pending question is how to provide a structure and incentives that can facilitate increases in ambition over time. Some have argued that international linkage of regional, national, and perhaps subnational policies can be part of the answer by providing a means for parties to receive credit for actions they facilitate in other jurisdictions, thereby reducing aggregate compliance costs and hence facilitating greater ambition over time (Ranson and Stavins, 2015; Bodansky *et al.*, 2016; Mehling *et al.*, 2017). It has been estimated that international linkage could reduce the cost of achieving the emissions reductions specified in the initial set of NDCs under the Paris Agreement by 32 percent by 2030 and by 54 percent by 2050 (World Bank Group, 2016).

Linkage may take different forms. These range from hard linkage, which links systems through formal recognition of programs across jurisdictions to allow for flexibility in where emissions reductions take place (as in the case of the existing link between cap-and-trade systems in California and Quebec), to soft linkage, which can entail a variety of measures to harmonize carbon prices across jurisdictions (e.g., through a mutually agreed upon carbon price collar within a club) (Burtraw *et al.*, 2013; Mehling *et al.*, 2017).

The bottom-up nature of the Paris Agreement has led to great heterogeneity in the set of participating countries' policies in five categories: policy instrument, level of government engaged (regional, national, or subnational), status under the Paris Agreement (party or non-party), type of policy instrument target, and type of NDC target (Ger. Emiss. Trading Auth., 2016a). Heterogeneity per se need not be an impediment to linkage (Metcalf and Weisbach, 2012), but there is a role for guidance on the key provision in the Paris Agreement for linking: Article 6.2 (Mehling *et al.*, 2017). Article 6.2 is a reasonable vehicle to facilitate linkage because this article provides for international transferable mitigation outcomes (ITMOs), which can serve as an accounting mechanism to track international transfers to quantify mitigation targets and outcomes; avoid double-counting of emission reductions; and accommodate different metrics for, and vintages of, targets and outcomes (Ger. Emiss. Trading Auth., 2016b).

Among the accounting rules that could be specified in guidance on Article 6.2 are: standards and procedures for quantifying mitigation outcomes (whether through carbon taxes, cap-and-trade instruments, performance standards, or other policy instruments); registry tracking of the transfer and use of ITMOs; guidance on NDC elements that would increase clarity; and guidance to move NDCs to greater consistency, such as with regard to assumed global warming potential (GWP) values. Guidance could also establish whether and how transfers to or from non-parties (or subnational jurisdictions in parties or non-parties) can be accounted for.

If guidance extends much beyond basic accounting rules, restrictive requirements could impede effective linkage (Mehling *et al.*, 2017). A combination of common accounting rules and absence of restrictive criteria and conditions could accelerate linkage and thereby increase the latitude of parties to scale up the ambition of their NDCs.

Other United Nations Institutions

Acting on climate change may require functions other than negotiation under the UNFCCC, as well as other forms of high-level cooperation, such as analytical support and implementation assistance for mitigation and adaptation efforts. A diverse set of fora both within and outside the

UN system have focused to some degree on climate change over the past several decades (Depledge, 2006).

The UN Environment Program (UNEP) has provided analytical support to the international process, in part through its emissions gap reports (UNEP, 2017), but also through a wide range of other analytical efforts and support for institution building. UN fora beyond the UNFCCC address funding for adaptation and mitigation, but fragmentation of funds may make it difficult for developing countries to access funding (Czarnecki and Guilanpour, 2009). Concerns exist regarding the additionality of official development assistance, that is, how much climate finance is actually new and additional (Smith *et al.*, 2011).

The Montreal Protocol

The Montreal Protocol on Substances that Deplete the Stratospheric Ozone Layer (concluded in 1987 under UN auspices) — and the Protocol's subsequent amendments, adjustments, and decisions — have achieved nearly universal participation and have made significant contributions to reducing GHG emissions (Velders *et al.*, 2007; Molina *et al.*, 2009), as the UNFCCC does not address GHGs already controlled by the Montreal Protocol. In its effort to reduce emissions of ozone-depleting substances (ODSs), the Montreal Protocol initially phased down chlorofluorocarbons (CFCs), which harm the ozone layer and also have very high GWP. In 2007, it accelerated the phasedown schedule for hydrochlorofluorocarbons (HCFCs), an interim replacement for CFCs with a somewhat lower but still significant GWP. The latter decision was affected by climate considerations (Bodansky, 2011). Even before the HCFC decision, the Montreal Protocol's overall net contribution to climate change mitigation may have been five times what the Kyoto Protocol achieved during its first commitment period (Velders *et al.*, 2007, 2012).

Hydrofluorocarbons (HFCs) are being widely adopted as a longer-term substitute for CFCs and HCFCs. Many of these have extremely high GWP, and their use will partially negate climate gains otherwise achieved by the Montreal Protocol. The 2016 Kigali Amendment to the Montreal Protocol would accelerate the phaseout of HFCs, which are not ODSs but are strong GHGs (Velders *et al.*, 2012; Hurwitz *et al.*, 2016).

The Montreal Protocol applied equally stringent emission requirements on all countries but allowed for a 10-year grace period for countries with low per-capita CFC consumption to meet their requirements. The Montreal Protocol also established mechanisms for financing and provided technical support to assist developing countries in reducing their ODS emissions. The most notable mechanism is the Multilateral Fund, which has transferred more than US$3 billion to assist developing-country ODS mitigation (Molina *et al.*, 2009). The experience of the Montreal Protocol illustrates how transfers can engage participation by major developing countries through financial and technological assistance (Andersen *et al.*, 2007).

Non-United Nations International Fora for Climate Change Cooperation

Climate change is increasingly addressed in fora for international cooperation outside of the UN. Some international partnerships have defined themselves as complements to the UNFCCC, rather than as alternatives. For example, the REDD+ Partnership helps coordinate measures for reducing emissions from deforestation and degradation (REDD) in the UNFCCC process. In 2010, more than 50 countries signed a nonbinding agreement to pledge more than $4 billion to REDD+ (Bodansky and Diringer, 2010). In addition, several energy-specific multilateral and plurilateral fora are linked to climate change, including the International Energy Agency (IEA) and the International Renewable Energy Agency (Florini, 2011; Urpelainen and Graaf, 2015).

The United States, during the administrations of Presidents George W. Bush and Barack Obama, organized the Major Economies Forum on Energy and Climate Change (MEF). The MEF provided a forum for informal discussion of policy options and international collaboration with regard to climate and energy. The MEF may have increased the fragmentation of global environmental governance (Biermann and Pattberg, 2008; Biermann, 2010). Activities under the MEF largely halted following the Paris Agreement.

The Group of Twenty (G20) finance ministers from the largest (industrialized and developing) economies could have the capacity to address climate finance, building on the G20's core mission to discuss economic and finance policy. At its meeting in Pittsburgh in 2009, the G20 agreed to "phase out and rationalize over the medium term inefficient fossil fuel subsidies while providing targeted support for the poorest." This effort would significantly affect GHG emissions if countries actually implemented it; by one modeled estimate, a complete phaseout of such subsidies by 2020 could reduce CO_2 emissions by 4.7 percent (IEA, 2011).

A remaining challenge is how pledges to reduce fossil fuel subsidies can be monitored and enforced (Aldy, 2017).

Since 2005, the smaller Group of Eight (G8) heads of state and heads of government have held a series of meetings related to climate change and have affirmed a goal that global average temperature not exceed 2°C above preindustrial levels. At the 2007 G8 summit, member countries agreed (without any binding commitment) to set a goal of a 50 percent reduction in GHG emissions by 2050 (van de Graaf and Westphal, 2011).

Nonstate Forms of International Cooperation

A prominent development over the past several decades has been the emergence of a considerable number of international agreements between and among nonstate entities, often referred to as transnational climate governance initiatives (Biermann and Pattberg, 2008; Pattberg and Stripple, 2008; Andonova *et al.*, 2009; Bulkeley *et al.*, 2012). In the most comprehensive survey, Bulkeley *et al.* documented 60 of these initiatives, which can be grouped into four principal types: public-private partnerships, private sector governance initiatives, NGO transnational initiatives, and subnational transnational initiatives.

The significance of partnerships between the private sector and government depends on their relationship with more traditional state-led governance. Partnerships may work once government regulations send strong signals to investors (Pfeifer and Sullivan, 2008). Rules developed in private sector agreements may then become incorporated in government regulations (Knox-Hayes and Levy, 2011). For example, private carbon market offset standards may be introduced into regulated carbon markets (Hoffmann, 2011).

NGO transnational initiatives have attempted to influence the activities of businesses directly through transnational partnerships, some of which involve collaboration with the private sector. For example, certification schemes for carbon offset credits, such as the Gold Standard, have been established, as have forestry credit schemes, such as the Climate, Community and Biodiversity Alliance standard.

Subnational transnational initiatives have involved subnational actors, such as city-level governments, collaborating at an international scale. One example is the International Council for Local Environmental Initiatives (ICLEI)–Local Governments for Sustainability network, which has taken action through a multicity partnership, the C40 Cities Climate Leadership Group (Román, 2010; Bulkeley *et al.*, 2012). Recognition of subnational and local governments as sources of capacity to meet the goals of the Paris Agreement is reflected in the Agreement's Article 11.

It remains unclear whether agreements among nonstate or subnational actors have been effective in reducing emissions. This is partly because the units of measurement to assess effectiveness are considerably more complex than for interstate agreements (Pinkse and Kolk, 2009). For subnational efforts, the question of attribution requires better disaggregation to understand whether reductions are additional to national efforts or only contribute to delivering national pledges. While these subnational efforts may make a small contribution to climate action, they may be valuable in influencing nation states or helping them meet commitments (Osofsky, 2012). That said, the smaller the geographic jurisdiction, the greater is the likelihood of emissions leakage, which can nullify the impacts of such efforts.

Advantages and Disadvantages of Different Forms

There have been numerous studies of the strengths and weaknesses of negotiating climate policy across multiple fora and institutions. Some have suggested that, in addition to its own action, the UNFCCC effect of catalyzing efforts by others and providing coherence to multiple initiatives may result in greater aggregate impact (Moncel and van Asselt, 2012). Others suggest that regime complexes may emerge from smaller clubs and then expand (Keohane and Victor, 2011). Regimes need external incentives for participation and internal incentives for compliance (Aldy and Stavins, 2010). An advantage of smaller fora (clubs) may be greater efficiency in the negotiation process, but disadvantages are that clubs lack universality and hence legitimacy (Moncel *et al.*, 2011) and that the environmental effectiveness of clubs may be undercut by leakage outside the club (Babiker, 2005). Some have suggested clubs as a way forward outside the UNFCCC, while others suggest they could contribute to the UNFCCC, catalyzing greater ambition (Sabel and Victor, 2016).

The aggregate effectiveness of climate agreements and related institutions could be enhanced by coordination among multiple elements, but coordinating multiple agreements into a coherent whole is challenging in a fragmented world. Coordination may be stimulated by competition among public and private governance regimes (Helfer and Austin, 2011), accountability (Ballesteros *et al.*, 2010), learning (Kolstad and Ulph, 2008), and experimentation (Sabel and Victor, 2016).

In Table 1, we draw on the numerous studies referenced throughout this chapter to summarize assessments of the performance of existing international climate agreements, based on the four criteria introduced in

Table 1. Performance assessment of existing international fora of cooperation on climate change.

	Assessment criteria			
Mode of international cooperation	**Environmental effectiveness**	**Aggregate economic performance**	**Distributional impacts**	**Institutional feasibility**
UNFCCC	Aggregate GHG emissions in Annex I (industrialized) countries declined by 6.0–9.2 percent below 1990 levels by 2000, a larger reduction than the apparent aim of returning to 1990 levels by 2000, but much of the decline is not attributable to the UNFCCC itself.	Authorized the joint fulfillment of commitments, multigas approach, sources and sinks, and domestic policy choice. Cost and benefit estimates depend on baseline, discount rate, participation, leakage, co-benefits, adverse effects, and other factors.	Commitments distinguish between Annex I and non-Annex I countries. Established a principle of common but differentiated responsibilities and commitment to equitable and appropriate contributions by each party.	Ratified (or equivalent) by 195 countries and regional organizations. Compliance depends on national communications.
The Kyoto Protocol	Aggregate emissions in Annex I countries were reduced by 8.5–13.6 percent below 1990 levels by 2011, more than the CP1 collective reduction target of 5.2 percent. Reductions occurred mainly in EITs and emissions increased in some other countries.	Cost-effectiveness improved by flexible mechanisms (JI, CDM, IET) and domestic policy choice. Cost and benefit estimates depend on baseline, discount rate, participation, leakage, co-benefits, adverse effects, and other factors.	Commitments distinguish between developed and developing countries, but dichotomous distinction correlates only partly (and decreasingly) with emissions trends and with changing economic circumstances.	Ratified (or equivalent) by 192 countries and regional organizations but took 7 years to enter into force. Compliance depends on national communications and compliance system. Approaches added to enhance measurement, reporting, and verification.

Table 1. (*Continued*)

Mode of international cooperation	Assessment criteria: Environmental effectiveness	Aggregate economic performance	Distributional impacts	Institutional feasibility
The Kyoto Flexible Mechanisms	Resulted in ~1.4 billion tCO_2eq credits under the CDM, 0.8 billion under JI, and 0.2 billion under IET (through October 2013). Additionality of CDM projects remains an issue.	CDM mobilized some, but not all, low-cost options. Evidence of underperformance of some project types. Some evidence that technology was transferred to non-Annex I countries.	Limited direct investment from Annex I countries. Domestic investment dominates, leading to concentration of CDM projects in several countries.	Helped enable political feasibility of Kyoto Protocol. Yielded largest carbon market to date. Has built institutional capacity in developing countries.
The Paris Agreement	Pledges were made to limit emissions by all emitters, covering 97 percent of global emissions. Goal was set to limit temperature change to 2°C with efforts to reach 1.5°C. Initial NDCs were insufficient for pathway to ultimate goals.	Cost-effectiveness might be improved by market-based policy instruments, policy linkage, and inclusion of a wide set of sectors.	Depends on sources and flows of financing, particularly for actions of developing countries. Preserves national authority.	Resulted in nearly universal participation in NDC framework but more limited participation in finance and technology support mechanisms.
G8, G20, MEF	G8 and MEF have recommended emission reduction by all major emitters. G20 may spur GHG reductions through phaseout of fossil fuel subsidies.	Action by all major emitters may reduce leakage and improve cost-effectiveness if implemented using flexible mechanisms. Potential efficiency gains may occur through subsidy removal.	Has not mobilized climate finance. Removing fuel subsidies would be progressive, but they have negative effects on oil-exporting countries and those with very low incomes, unless other assistance provided.	Led to lower participation of countries compared to UNFCCC but covers 70 percent of global emissions. Opens the possibility for forum-shopping based on issue preferences.

(*Continued*)

Table 1. (*Continued*)

Mode of international cooperation	Assessment criteria: Environmental effectiveness	Aggregate economic performance	Distributional impacts	Institutional feasibility
Montreal Protocol on ODS	Spurred emissions reductions through ODS phaseouts ~5 times the magnitude of Kyoto CP1 targets. Contribution may be negated by high-GWP substitutes, although efforts to phase out HFCs are included in subsequent amendments.	Cost-effectiveness supported by multigas approach. Some countries used market-based mechanisms to implement domestically.	Led to later compliance period for phaseouts by developing countries. Multilateral Fund provided US$3 billion in finance to developing countries.	Led to universal participation, but the timing of required actions varies for developed and developing countries.

Notes: Abbreviations: CDM, clean development mechanism; CP1, first commitment period of Kyoto Protocol; EIT, economy in transition; G8, Group of Eight; G20, Group of Twenty; GHG, greenhouse gas; GWP, global warming potential; HFC, hydrofluorocarbon; IET, international emissions trading; JI, joint implementation; MEF, Major Economies Forum on Energy and Climate Change; NDC, nationally determined contribution; ODS, ozone-depleting substance; UNFCCC, United Nations Framework Convention on Climate Change.
Source: Modified with permission from Stavins *et al.* (2014, Table 13.3).

section "Framing Concepts and Evaluation Criteria". It is important to keep in mind that the performance of any individual policy depends on a wide array of interacting agreements and institutions at the international, national, and subnational levels of the landscape of climate change policy.

Other Issues

A number of cross-cutting issues arise when considering international cooperation to address climate change and related policies at the regional, national, and subnational levels. These include issue linkage, the role of investment and finance in international agreements, technological change and agreements targeting research and development activities, international governance of geoengineering, and the relationship between international cooperation and science policy.

Issue Linkage

Linkages across issues may help encourage participation. Such connections are separate and distinct from the policy instrument linkages considered in section "International Linkage Consistent with the Paris Agreement" in the context of the Paris Agreement. Although some actors may participate in cooperative agreements to a greater degree than self-interest alone would predict, some emissions reductions may be provided without cooperation due to the linkage of climate change with other issues. Participation is likely to increase when otherwise self-beneficial actions on other issues create positive externalities, or co-benefits. For example, actions to reduce energy expenditures, enhance the security of energy supply, and reduce local air pollution can also reduce GHG emissions. However, policies designed to address climate change mitigation may also have negative externalities, reducing incentives for participation. For example, without compensating measures, climate policies may have a disproportionate impact on low-income populations (Hassett *et al.*, 2009).

Investment and Finance in International Agreements

The UNFCCC and subsequent international agreements have created new institutions focused on finance for climate change mitigation and adaptation. Under the 2009 Copenhagen Accord, developed countries made a nonbinding pledge to mobilize \$100 billion per year for climate finance, which may include public and private flows, may be inclusive of bilateral and multilateral funds (multilateral development banks and multilateral climate funds), and may also include grants and loans. A difficulty is that there is no agreement on climate finance definitions and accounting (Stavins *et al.*, 2014). Recently, South-South climate funds have also been established (Hannam *et al.*, 2015).

Several multilateral funds operate under or in coordination with the UNFCCC, including the Adaptation Fund, the Global Environment Facility (GEF), and the Green Climate Fund (GCF). These multilateral climate funds vary in their governance structures. For example, the Adaptation Fund is governed by a majority of developing countries, whereas the GCF is accountable to the Conference of the Parties to the UNFCCC. Contributions to climate funds are voluntary but primarily come from countries classified as Annex I under the Kyoto Protocol. As of early 2018, countries pledged just over \$10 billion to the GCF, of which under 60 percent has been received. By country, the United States pledged $3 billion, and Japan, the United Kingdom, France, and Germany each pledged over $1 billion (GCF, 2018).

Technological Change, R&D Agreements, and International Cooperation

The Technology Mechanism of the UNFCCC, with its subsidiary Climate Technology Centre and Network (CTCN) and Technology Executive Committee (TEC), was established in 2010 to exchange information and implement projects for climate change technology development and transfer. In theory, technology-focused climate agreements can improve the dynamic economic performance of climate mitigation by lowering mitigation costs and increasing environmental effectiveness (Barrett, 2003), but such policies have limited environmental effectiveness in isolation (de Coninck *et al.*, 2008; Newell, 2010b).

International cooperation in clean energy R&D can take several different forms (de Coninck *et al.*, 2008; Newell, 2010a). These range from loosely coordinated pledges for domestic actions, such as the Mission Innovation pledges made during COP-21 to double clean energy R&D in the largest economies; plurilateral technology collaboration platforms, such as the IEA's Technology Collaboration Programmes and the CTCN; and minilateral integrated cooperative R&D centers with pooled resources and shared outputs, such as the US–China Clean Energy Research Center or the ITER fusion demonstration project. International cooperation can increase the efficiency of R&D investments by expanding the base of knowledge for new innovation, creating opportunities for cost sharing to enable R&D projects that are of greater scale and that are less duplicative of domestic efforts, and taking advantage of specialization in specific technology areas or in certain R&D system functions within each geographic region (Malerba and Montobbio, 2003).

In addition to providing opportunities for more efficient R&D investments, international cooperation can, in principle, accelerate the pace at which new energy technologies are deployed, particularly in developing countries (Lema and Lema, 2012; Mallett, 2013). The strength of national intellectual property rights regimes may have significant impacts on the effectiveness of such agreements, particularly those focused on technology transfer (Branstetter *et al.*, 2006; Hall and Helmers, 2010).

International Governance of Geoengineering

Geoengineering refers to approaches to lessen the impacts of climate change that are distinct from emissions mitigation and adaptation. Geoengineering takes two general forms: carbon dioxide removal and solar radiation management. Examination of the economics of these technologies is at an early stage (Heutel *et al.*, 2016). The governance of geoengineering activities remains a challenge for the international regime, partly because there appear to be incentives for unilateral action, which may have negative consequences for other jurisdictions (Bodansky, 2013; Barrett, 2014; Parson, 2014).

International Cooperation and Science Policy

Following the 2015 Paris Agreement, there have been calls to improve the use of scientific inputs in the international climate negotiation process (Kennel *et al.*, 2016). Particular attention has been given to potential reforms of the IPCC to improve its procedures (Chan *et al.*, 2016; Minx *et al.*, 2017) and adjust to the changing demands of the policy process (Beck and Mahony, 2017).

Conclusion

The 2015 Paris Agreement is only the most recent development in a multi-decade history of international cooperation to address climate change, but it represents a significant milestone in the evolution of international cooperation in this realm. As laid out in this review, social science research has helped identify the impacts of past efforts at international cooperation, the trade-offs associated with different institutional design options, and future opportunities. As implementation of the Paris Agreement proceeds in parallel with other activities in an increasingly diverse landscape of loosely coordinated institutions, ongoing research that can inform decision making will become more important. Several key lessons have already arisen in the literature.

First, climate policy has emerged from a complex constellation of institutions and decision-making bodies, a so-called regime complex. The Paris Agreement is notable for its near universal participation, but past international environmental agreements suggest possible trade-offs between level of participation and degree of ambition. While the initial level of ambition in the Paris Agreement's set of NDCs may reflect this relationship, the Paris Agreement has adopted a structure distinct from past agreements in its reliance on authority at regional, national, and subnational levels of governance. Moving forward, as NDCs evolve, ambition can be increased by new climate mitigation and adaptation policies taken by a diffuse set of actors at different scales.

Second, to be environmentally effective, cost-effective, equitable, and institutionally feasible, international cooperative efforts need to take into account the complexity of the regime complex. New cooperative efforts demonstrate an evolution in the shifting authority given to actors at different levels of governance to account for this more complex structure. An example is the set of efforts to pursue bottom-up linkage of national and subnational climate policies consistent with the structure of the multilateral Paris Agreement.

Finally, as climate change has become more salient in international dialogue, it has become linked with other international issues. While these other issues have become more prominent in shaping climate policy, climate has become more salient in the formation of policies in other areas. For example, the World Bank and other multilateral development banks have pursued efforts to "mainstream" climate change in all economic development initiatives. Simultaneously, a broader set of sustainable development issues, such as biodiversity preservation, ocean ecosystem management, human rights, and gender equality, are increasingly considered in the formulation of climate policy. As international policy continues to evolve, these linkages are likely to become deeper, and more opportunities for synergistic progress in multiple domains may emerge.

Acknowledgments

This review draws on work conducted by an international team who contributed to a chapter titled "International Cooperation: Agreements & Instruments" in the Intergovernmental Panel on Climate Change (IPCC) Working Group III Fifth Assessment Report (Stavins *et al.*, 2014). The coordinating lead authors of the chapter were Robert Stavins and Zou Ji, the chapter scientist was Gabriel Chan, and the lead authors were Thomas Brewer, Mariana Conte Grand, Michel den Elzen, Michael Finus, Joyeeta Gupta, Niklas Höhne, Myung-Kyoon Lee, Axel Michaelowa, Matthew

Paterson, Kilaparti Ramakrishna, Gang Wen, Jonathan Wiener, and Harald Winkler. In addition, 13 contributing authors drafted relatively brief text but did not participate in meetings of the chapter team. Two review editors provided support during multiple rounds of extensive review. The IPCC's Working Group III Technical Support Unit provided assistance to the chapter team. Valuable research assistance for this chapter was provided by Alexander Venning. Although this chapter draws significantly on the IPCC chapter, the responsibility for all errors rests exclusively with the authors of the chapter.

References

Abbott, K. W. and D. Snidal. (2000). "Hard and soft law in international governance." *International Organization.* **54**(3): 421–456.

AGF (Advisory Group Finance). (2010). *Report of the Secretary-General's High-Level Advisory Group on Climate Change Financing.* Advisory Group Finance, UN, New York.

Aldy, J. E. (2014). "The crucial role of policy surveillance in international climate policy." *Climatic Change.* **126**(3–4): 279–292.

Aldy, J. E. (2017). "Policy surveillance in the G-20 fossil fuel subsidies agreement: lessons for climate policy." *Climatic Change.* **144**(1): 97–110.

Aldy, J. E. and W. A. Pizer. (2016). "Alternative metrics for comparing domestic climate change mitigation efforts and the emerging international climate policy architecture." *Review of Environmental Economics and Policy.* **10**(1): 3–24.

Aldy, J. E. and R. N. Stavins (eds.). (2010). *Post-Kyoto International Climate Policy: Implementing Architectures for Agreement.* Cambridge, UK: Cambridge University Press.

Aldy, J. E. and R. N. Stavins. (2012). "Climate negotiators create an opportunity for scholars." *Science.* **337**(6098): 1043–1044.

Aldy, J. E., Pizer, W., Tavoni, M., *et al.* (2016). "Economic tools to promote transparency and comparability in the Paris Agreement." *Nature Climate Change.* **6**(11): 1000–1004.

Allen, M. (2003). "Liability for climate change: Will it ever be possible to sue anyone for damaging the climate?" *Nature.* **421**: 891–892.

Andersen, S. O., K. M. Sarma, and K. N. Taddonio. (2007). *Technology Transfer for the Ozone Layer: Lessons for Climate Change.* London: Earthscan.

Andonova, L. B., M. M. Betsill, and H. Bulkeley. (2009). "Transnational climate governance." *Global Environmental Politics.* **9**(2): 52–73.

Babiker, M. H. (2005). "Climate change policy, market structure, and carbon leakage." *Journal of International Economics.* **65**(2): 421–445.

Ballesteros, A., S. Nakhooda, J. Werksman, and K. Hurlburt. (2010). "Power, responsibility, and accountability: Re-thinking the legitimacy of institutions for climate finance." *Climate Law*. **1**: 261–312.

Barrett, S. (2003). *Environment and Statecraft: The Strategy of Environmental Treaty-Making*. Oxford, UK: Oxford University Press.

Barrett, S. (2007). *Why Cooperate? The Incentive to Supply Global Public Goods*. New York: Oxford University Press.

Barrett, S. (2008). "Climate treaties and the imperative of enforcement." *Oxford Review of Economic Policy*. **24**(2): 239–258.

Barrett, S. (2014). "Solar geoengineering's brave new world: Thoughts on the governance of an unprecedented technology." *Review of Environmental Economics and Policy*. **8**(2): 249–269.

Beck, S. and M. Mahony. (2017). "The IPCC and the politics of anticipation." *Nature Climate Change*. **7**(5): 311–313.

Bell, D. (2013). "Climate change and human rights." *Wiley Interdisciplinary Reviews: Climate Change*. **4**(3): 159–170.

Bell, R. G., M. S. Ziegler, B. Blechman, B. Finlay, and M. S. Ziegler. (2012). *Building International Climate Cooperation: Lessons from the Weapons and Trade Regimes for Achieving International Climate Goals*. Washington, DC: World Resources Institute.

Bernstein, S. (2005). "Legitimacy in global environmental governance." *Journal of International Law and International Relations*. **1**(1–2): 139–166.

Biermann, F. (2010). "Beyond the intergovernmental regime: Recent trends in global carbon governance." *Current Opinion in Environmental Sustainability*. **2**(4): 284–288.

Biermann, F. and P. Pattberg. (2008). "Global environmental governance: Taking stock, moving forward." *Annual Review of Environmental Resources*. **33**: 277–294.

Biermann, F., P. Pattberg, H. van Asselt, and F. Zelli. (2009). "The fragmentation of global governance architectures: A framework for analysis." *Global Environmental Politics*. **9**(4): 14–40.

Bodansky, D. (2007). "Targets and timetables: good policy but bad politics." In J. E. Aldy and R. N. Stavins (eds.), *Architectures for Agreement: Addressing Global Climate Change in the Post-Kyoto World*, pp. 57–66. Cambridge, UK: Cambridge University Press.

Bodansky, D. (2009). *Legal Form of a New Climate Agreement*. Report, Pew Center on Global Climate Change, Arlington, VA. https://www.c2es.org/site/assets/uploads/2009/04/new-climate-agreement-legal-form.pdf.

Bodansky, D. (2010). "Introduction: climate change and human rights: Unpacking the issues." *Georgia Journal of International and Comparative Law*. **38**(3): 511–534.

Bodansky, D. (2011). "Tale of two architectures: the once and future U.N. climate change regime." *Arizona State Law Journal*. **43**: 697–712.

Bodansky, D. (2013). "The who, what, and wherefore of geoengineering governance." *Climatic Change*. **121**(3): 539–551.

Bodansky, D. (2016a). "The legal character of the Paris Agreement." *Review of European Comparative and International Environmental Law*. **25**(2): 142–150.

Bodansky, D. (2016b). "The Paris climate change agreement: A new hope?" *American Journal of International Law*. **110**(2): 288–319.

Bodansky, D. and E. Diringer. (2010). The evolution of multilateral regimes: Implications for climate change. In *Advancing the Effort Against Climate Change*. Arlington, VA: Pew Center on Global Climate Change.

Bodansky, D. M., S. A. Hoedl, G. E. Metcalf, and R. N. Stavins. (2016). "Facilitating linkage of climate policies through the Paris outcome." *Climate Policy*. **16**(8): 956–972.

Böhringer, C. (2003). "The Kyoto Protocol: A review and perspectives." *Oxford Review of Economic Policy*. **19**(3): 451–466.

Bosetti, V., C. Carraro, A. Sgobbi, and M. Tavoni. (2010). "Modeling economic impacts of alternative international climate policy architectures: A quantitative and comparative assessment of architectures for agreement." In J. E. Aldy and R. N. Stavins (eds.), *Post-Kyoto International Climate Policy*, pp. 715–752.

Branstetter, L. G., R. Fisman and C. F. Foley. (2006). "Do stronger intellectual property rights increase international technology transfer? Empirical evidence from U.S. firm-level panel data." *Quarterly Journal of Economics*. **121**(1): 321–349.

Breidenich, C. and D. Bodansky. (2009). *Measurement, Reporting and Verification in a Post-2012 Climate Agreement*. Report, Pew Center on Global Climate Change, Arlington, VA.

Brousseau, E., T. Dedeurwaerdere, P.-A. Jouvet, and M. Willinger. (eds.). (2012). *Global Environmental Commons: Analytical and Political Challenges in Building Governance Mechanisms*. Oxford, UK: Oxford University Press.

Brunner, S., C. Flachsland and R. Marschinski. (2012). "Credible commitment in carbon policy." *Climate Policy*. **12**(2): 255–271.

Bulkeley, H., L. B. Andonova, K. Bäckstrand *et al.* (2012). "Governing climate change transnationally: Assessing the evidence from a survey of sixty initiatives." *Environment and Planning C: Politics and Space*. **30**(4): 591–612.

Burtraw, D., K. Palmer, C. Munnings, P. Weber, and M. Woerman. (2013). *Linking by Degrees: Incremental Alignment of Cap-and-Trade Markets*. Report DP 13-04, Resources for the Future, Washington, DC.

Cao, J. (2010). "Reconciling human development and climate protection: A multistage hybrid climate policy architecture." In J. E. Aldy and R. N. Stavins (eds.), *Post-Kyoto International Climate Policy*, pp. 563–598.

Castro, P. (2012). "Does the CDM discourage emission reduction targets in advanced developing countries?" *Climate Policy*. **12**(2): 198–218.

Cecys, K. (2010). "MRV: A survey of reporting and review in multilateral regimes." Brief, Pew Center on Global Climate Change, Arlington, VA. https://www.c2es.org/site/assets/uploads/2010/12/mrv-survey-reporting-review-multilateral-regimes.pdf.

Chan, G. (2015). *Essays on Energy Technology Innovation Policy*. PhD Thesis, Harvard University, Cambridge, MA.

Chan, G. and J. Huenteler. (2015). "Financing wind energy deployment in China through the Clean Development Mechanism." In G. Chan (ed.), *Essays on Energy Technology Innovation Policy*, pp. 145–169. https://dash.harvard.edu/handle/1/17467190.

Chan, G., C. Carraro, O. Edenhofer, C. Kolstad, and R. N. Stavins. (2016). Reforming the IPCC's assessment of climate change economics. *Climate Change Economics*, **7**, 1640001.

Czarnecki, R. and Guilanpour, K. (2009). "The adaptation fund after Poznan." *Carbon and Climate Law Review*. **3**(1): 79–88.

Dechezleprêtre, A., M. Glachant, and Y. Ménière. (2008). "The clean development mechanism and the international diffusion of technologies: An empirical study." *Energy Policy*. **36**(4): 1273–1283.

de Coninck, H., C. Fischer, R. G. Newell, and T. Ueno. (2008). "International technology-oriented agreements to address climate change." *Energy Policy*. **36**(1): 335–356.

Depledge, J. (2006). "The opposite of learning: Ossification in the climate change regime." *Global Environmental Politics*. **6**(1): 1–22.

Dubash, N. K. and L. Rajamani. (2010). "Beyond Copenhagen: Next steps." *Climate Policy*. **10**(6): 593–599.

Ellerman, A. D. (2010). "The EU emission trading scheme: A prototype global system?" In J. E. Aldy and R. N. Stavins (eds.), *Post-Kyoto International Climate Policy*, pp. 88–118.

Ellerman, A. D., C. Marcantonini, and A. Zaklan. (2016). "The European Union emissions trading system: Ten years and counting." *Review of Environmental Economics and Policy*. **10**(1): 89–107.

Ellis, J. and S. Moarif. (2009). *GHG Mitigation Actions: MRV Issues and Options*. Paris: OECD.

Falkner, R. (2016). "The Paris Agreement and the new logic of international climate politics." *International Affairs*. **92**(5): 1107–1125.

Falkner, R., H. Stephan, and J. Vogler. (2010). "International climate policy after Copenhagen: Towards a 'building blocks' approach." *Global Policy*. **1**(3): 252–262.

Florini, A. (2011). "The International Energy Agency in global energy governance." *Global Policy*. **2**: 40–50.

Frankel, J. A. (2005). "You're getting warmer: the most feasible path for addressing global climate change does run through Kyoto." In M. Tamborra and J. Maxwell (eds.), *Trade and the Environment in the Perspective of the EU Enlargement*, pp. 37–58. Cheltenham, UK: Edward Elgar.

GCF (Green Climate Fund). (2018). "Resource mobilization." Incheon, Korea. http://www.greenclimate.fund/how-we-work/resource-mobilization.

German Emissions Trading Authority. (2016a). *Categorization of INDCs in the Light of Art. 6 of the Paris Agreement*. Berlin: German Environmental Agency.

German Emissions Trading Authority. (2016b). *Robust Accounting of International Transfers under Article 6 of the Paris Agreement — Preliminary Findings*. Berlin: German Environmental Agency.

Grossman, D. A. (2003). "Warming up to a not-so-radical idea: Tort-based climate change litigation." *Columbia Journal of Environmental Law*. **28**: 1–62.

Guzman, A. T. and T. L. Meyer. (2010). "International soft law." *Journal of Legal Analysis*. **2**(1): 171–225.

Hall, B. H. and C. Helmers. (2010). "The role of patent protection in (clean/green) technology transfer." *Santa Clara Computer and High Technology Law Journal*. **26**(4): 487–532.

Hannam, P. M., Z. Liao, S. J. Davis, and M. Oppenheimer. (2015). "Developing country finance in a post-2020 global climate agreement." *Nature Climate Change*. **5**(11): 983–987.

Hassett, K. A., A. Mathur, and G. E. Metcalf. (2009). "The incidence of a U.S. carbon tax: A lifetime and regional analysis." *Energy Journal*. **30**(2): 155–177.

Hayashi, D. and A. Michaelowa. (2013). "Standardization of baseline and additionality determination under the CDM." *Climate Policy*. **2**(13): 191–209.

Heitzig, J., K. Lessmann, and Y. Zou. (2011). "Self-enforcing strategies to deter free-riding in the climate change mitigation game and other repeated public good games." *PNAS*. **108**(38): 15739–15744.

Helfer, L. R. and G. Austin. (2011). *Human Rights and Intellectual Property: Mapping the Global Interface*. Cambridge, UK: Cambridge University Press.

Helm, D. (2010). "Climate-change policy: Why has so little been achieved?" In D. Helm and C. Hepburn (eds.), *The Economics and Politics of Climate Change*, pp. 9–35. Oxford, UK: Oxford University Press.

Heutel, G., J. Moreno-Cruz, and K. Ricke. (2016). "Climate engineering economics." *Annual Review of Resource Economics*. **8**: 99–118.

Hoffmann, M. J. (2005). *Ozone Depletion and Climate Change: Constructing a Global Response*. Albany, NY: State University of New York Press.

Hoffmann, M. J. (2011). *Climate Governance at the Crossroads: Experimenting with a Global Response After Kyoto*. Oxford, UK: Oxford University Press.

Hurwitz, M. M., E. L. Fleming, P. A. Newman, F. Li, and Q. Liang. (2016). "Early action on HFCs mitigates future atmospheric change." *Environmental Research Letters*. **11**(11): 114019.

IEA (International Energy Agency). (2011). *World Energy Outlook*. Paris: OECD.

Jacoby, H. D., M. H. Babiker, S. Paltsev, and J. M. Reilly. (2010). "Sharing the burden of GHG reductions." In J. E. Aldy and R. N. Stavins (eds.), *Post-Kyoto International Climate Policy*, pp. 753–785.

Jacoby, H. D., Y.-H. H. Chen, and B. P. Flannery. (2017). "Informing transparency in the Paris Agreement: The role of economic models." *Climate Policy*. **17**(7): 873–890.

Jaffe, J., M. Ranson, and R. N. Stavins. (2009). "Linking tradable permit systems: A key element of emerging international climate policy architecture." *Ecology Law Quarterly*. **36**(4): 789–808.

Jordan, A. J., D. Huitema, M. Hildén, H. van Asselt, T. J. Rayner, J. J. Schoenefeld, J. Tosun, J. Forster, and E.L. Boasson. (2015). "Emergence of polycentric climate governance and its future prospects." *Nature Climate Change*. **5**(11): 977–982.

JRC (Joint Research Centre). (2013). "Emissions Database for Global Atmospheric Research (EDGAR)." European Commission, Brussels. Updated Oct. 30, 2017. http://edgar.jrc.ec.europa.eu/.

Karlsson-Vinkhuyzen, S. I. and J. McGee. (2013). "Legitimacy in an era of fragmentation: The case of global climate governance." *Global Environmental Politics*. **13**(3): 56–78.

Kemp, L. (2017). "US-proofing the Paris Climate Agreement." *Climate Policy*. **17**(1): 86–101.

Kennel, C. F., S. Briggs, and D. G. Victor. (2016). "Making climate science more relevant." *Science*. **354**(6311): 421–422.

Keohane, R. O. and D. G. Victor. (2011). "The regime complex for climate change." *Perspectives on Politics*. **9**(1): 7–23.

Knox-Hayes, J. and D. L. Levy. (2011). "The politics of carbon disclosure as climate governance." *Strategic Organization*. **9**(1); 91–99.

Kolstad, C. and A. Ulph. (2008). "Learning and international environmental agreements." *Climate Change*. **89**(1–2): 125–141.

Lees, E. (2017). "Responsibility and liability for climate loss and damage after Paris." *Climate Policy*. **17**(1): 59–70.

Lema, R. and A. Lema. (2012). "Technology transfer? The rise of China and India in green technology sectors." *Innovation and Development*. **2**(1): 23–44.

Limon, M. (2009). "Human rights and climate change: Constructing a case for political action." *Harvard Environmental Law Review*. **33**: 439–476.

Lord, R., S. Goldberg, L. Rajamani, and J. Brunnée (eds.). (2011). *Climate Change Liability*. Cambridge, UK: Cambridge University Press.

Lutter, R. (2000). "Developing countries' greenhouse emissions: Uncertainty and implications for participation in the Kyoto Protocol." *Energy Journal*. **21**(4): 93–120.

Malerba, F. and F. Montobbio. (2003). "Exploring factors affecting international technological specialization: The role of knowledge flows and the structure of innovative activity." *Journal of Evolutionary Economics*. **13**(4): 411–434.

Mallett, A. (2013). "Technology cooperation for sustainable energy: A review of pathways: technology cooperation for sustainable energy." *Wiley Interdisciplinary Reviews: Energy and Environment*. **2**(2): 234–250.

Meckling, J. O. and G. Y. Chung. (2009). "Sectoral approaches for a post-2012 climate regime: A taxonomy." *Climate Policy*. **9**(6): 652–668.

Mehling, M. and E. Haites. (2009). "Mechanisms for linking emissions trading schemes." *Climate Policy*. **9**(2): 169–184.

Mehling, M., G. Metcalf, and R. N. Stavins. (2017). *Linking Heterogeneous Climate Policies (Consistent with the Paris Agreement)*. Discussion Paper ES 17-6, Harvard Project on Climate Agreements, Harvard University.

Metcalf, G. E. and D. Weisbach. (2009). "The design of a carbon tax." *Harvard Environmental Law Review*. **33**(2): 499–556.

Metcalf, G. E. and D. Weisbach. (2012). "Linking policies when tastes differ: Global climate policy in a heterogeneous world." *Review of Environmental Economics and Policy*. **6**(1): 110–129.

Millard-Ball, A. and L. Ortolano. (2010). "Constructing carbon offsets: The obstacles to quantifying emission reductions." *Energy Policy*. **38**(1): 533–546.

Minx, J. C., M. Callaghan, W. F. Lamb, J. Garard, and O. Edenhofer. (2017). "Learning about climate change solutions in the IPCC and beyond." *Environmental Science and Policy*. **77**: 252–259.

Molina, M., D. Zaelke, K. M. Sarma, S. O. Andersen, V. Ramanathan, and D. Kaniaru. (2009). "Reducing abrupt climate change risk using the Montreal Protocol and other regulatory actions to complement cuts in CO_2 emissions." *PNAS*. **106**(49): 20616–20621.

Moncel, R. and H. van Asselt. (2012). "All hands on deck! Mobilizing climate change action beyond the UNFCCC." *Review of European Community and International Environmental Law*. **21**(3): 163–176.

Moncel, R., P. Joffe, K. McCall, and K. Levin. (2011). *Building the Climate Change Regime: Survey and Analysis of Approaches*. Report, World Resources Institute, UN Environment Programme, Washington, DC.

Newell, R. G. (2010a). "International climate technology strategies." In J. E. Aldy and R. N. Stavins (eds.), *Post-Kyoto International Climate Policy*, pp. 403–438.

Newell, R. G. (2010b). "The role of markets and policies in delivering innovation for climate change mitigation." *Oxford Review of Economic Policy*. **26**(2): 253–269.

Newell, R. G., W. A. Pizer, and D. Raimi. (2013). "Carbon markets 15 years after Kyoto: Lessons learned, new challenges." *Journal of Economic Perspectives*. **27**(1): 123–146.

Nordhaus, W. (2015). Climate clubs: Overcoming free-riding in international climate policy. *American Economic Review*, **105**(4), 1339–1370.

Nordhaus, W. D. (2007). "A review of the Stern review on the economics of climate change." *Journal of Economic Literature*. **45**(3): 686–702.

Nordhaus, W. D. (2008). *A Question of Balance: Weighing the Options on Global Warming Policies*. New Haven, CT: Yale University Press.

Oberthür, S. and R. Bodle. (2016). "Legal form and nature of the Paris outcome." *Climate Law*. **6**(1–2): 40–57.

Osofsky, H. M. (2012). "Climate change and crises of international law: Possibilities for geographic reenvisioning." *Case Western Reserve Journal of International Law*. **44**(1–2): 423–433.

Parson, E. A. (2014). "Climate engineering in global climate governance: Implications for participation and linkage." *Transnational Environmental Law*. **3**(1): 89–110.

Paterson, M., M. Hoffmann, M. Betsill, and S. Bernstein. (2014). "The micro foundations of policy diffusion towards complex global governance: An analysis of the transnational carbon emission trading network." *Comparative Political Studies*. **37**(3–4): 420–449.

Pattberg, P. and J. Stripple. (2008). "Beyond the public and private divide: Remapping transnational climate governance in the 21st century." *International Environmental Agreements: Politics, Law and Economics*. **8**(4): 367–388.

Peters, G. P., R. M. Andrew, J. G. Canadell, S. Fuss, R. B. Jackson, J. I. Korsbakken, C. Le Quéré, and N. Nakicenovic. (2017). "Key indicators to track current progress and future ambition of the Paris Agreement." *Nature Climate Change*. **7**(2): 118–122.

Pfeifer, S. and R. Sullivan. (2008). "Public policy, institutional investors and climate change: A UK case-study." *Climate Change*. **89**(3–4): 245–262.

Pinkse, J. and A. Kolk. (2009). *International Business and Global Climate Change*. Abingdon, UK: Routledge.

Ranson, M. and R. N. Stavins. (2013). "A post-Durban climate policy architecture based on linkage of cap-and-trade systems." *Chicago Journal of International Law*. **13**(2): 403–438.

Ranson, M. and R. N. Stavins. (2015). "Linkage of greenhouse gas emissions trading systems: Learning from experience." *Climate Policy*. **16**(3): 284–300.

Raustiala, K. (2005). "Form and substance in international agreements." *American Journal of International Law*. **99**(3): 581–614.

Rogelj, J., M. den Elzen, N. Höhne, T. Fransen, H. Fekete, H. Winkler, R. Schaeffer, F. Sha, K. Riahi, and M. Meinshausen. (2016). "Paris Agreement climate proposals need a boost to keep warming well below 2°C." *Nature*. **534**(7609): 631–639.

Román, M. (2010). "Governing from the middle: The C40 Cities Leadership Group." *Corporate Governance*. **10**(1): 73–84.

Sabel, C. and D. Victor. (2016). *An Evolutionary Approach to Governing Global Problems: Climate Policy After Paris*. Muscatine, IA: Stanley Foundation.

Seres, S., E. Haites, and K. Murphy. (2009). "Analysis of technology transfer in CDM projects: An update." *Energy Policy*. **37**(11): 4919–4926.

Shishlov, I., R. Morel, and V. Bellassen. (2016). "Compliance of the parties to the Kyoto Protocol in the first commitment period." *Climate Policy*. **16**(6): 768–782.

Smith, J. B., T. Dickinson, J. D. B. Donahue, I. Burton, E. Haites, R. J. T. Klein, and A. Patwardhan. (2011). "Development and climate change adaptation funding: Coordination and integration." *Climate Policy*. **11**(3): 987–1000.

Stavins, R., Z. Ji, T. Brewer, M. Conte Grand *et al.* (2014). "International cooperation: Agreements & instruments." In O. Edenhofer, R. Pichs-Madruga, Y. Sokona, *et al.* (Eds.), *Climate Change 2014: Mitigation of Climate Change. Contribution of Working Group III to the Fifth Assessment Report of the Intergovernmental Panel on Climate Change*, pp. 1001–1082. Cambridge, UK: Cambridge University Press.

Stavins, R. N. (2011). "The problem of the commons: Still unsettled after 100 years." *American Economic Review*. **101**(1): 81–108.

Stern, R. N. (2007). *The Economics of Climate Change: The Stern Review*. Cambridge, UK: Cambridge University Press.

Stewart, R. B. and J. B. Wiener. (2003). *Reconstructing Climate Policy: Beyond Kyoto*. Washington, DC: AEI Press.

Stewart, R. B., M. Oppenheimer, and B. Rudyk. (2017). "Building blocks: A strategy for near-term action within the new global climate framework." *Climate Change*. **144**(1): 1–13.

Thompson, A. (2006). "Management under anarchy: The international politics of climate change." *Climate Change*. **78**(1): 7–29.

UNEP (United Nations Environment Programme). (2017). *The Emissions Gap Report 2017*. Nairobi: UNEP.

UNEP Risoe Centre. (2017). "UNEP DTU CDM/JI pipeline analysis and database." Updated March 1, 2018.

UNFCCC (United Nations Framework Convention on Climate Change). (2012). "Time series — Annex I. UN Climate Change Database." Updated 2014. http://di.unfccc.int/time_series.

UNFCCC (United Nations Framework Convention on Climate Change). (2016). *Aggregate Effect of the Intended Nationally Determined Contributions: An Update*. Report FCCC/CP/2016/2, UNFCCC, Marrakech. http://unfccc.int/resource/docs/2016/cop22/eng/02.pdf.

Urpelainen, J. and T. Van de Graaf. (2015). "The International Renewable Energy Agency: A success story in institutional innovation?" *International Environmental Agreements: Politics, Law and Economics*. **15**(2): 159–177.

van Asselt, H. (2016). "The role of non-state actors in reviewing ambition, implementation, and compliance under the Paris Agreement." *Climate Law*. **6**(1–2): 91–108.

van Asselt, H. and J. Gupta. (2009). "Stretching too far: Developing countries and the role of flexibility mechanisms beyond Kyoto." *Stanford Environmental Law Journal*. **28**(2): 311–380.

van de Graaf, T. and K. Westphal. (2011). "The G8 and G20 as global steering committees for energy: Opportunities and constraints." *Global Policy*. **2**: 19–30.

Velders, G. J. M., S. O. Andersen, J. S. Daniel, D. W. Fahey, and M. McFarland. (2007). "The importance of the Montreal Protocol in protecting climate." *PNAS*. **104**(12): 4814–4819.

Velders, G. J. M., A. R. Ravishankara, M. K. Miller, M. J. Molina, J. Alcamo, J. S. Daniel, D. W. Fahey, S. A. Montzka, and S. Reimann. (2012). "Preserving Montreal Protocol climate benefits by limiting HFCs." *Science*. **335**(6071): 922–923.

Victor, D. G. (2004). *The Collapse of the Kyoto Protocol and the Struggle to Slow Global Warming*. Princeton, NJ: Princeton University Press.

Victor, D. G., J. C. House, and S. Joy. (2005). "A Madisonian approach to climate policy." *Science*. **309**(5742): 1820–1821.

Weitzman, M. L. (2007). "A review of the Stern review on the economics of climate change." *Journal of Economic Literature*. **45**(3): 703–724.

Werksman, J. (2010). "Legal symmetry and legal differentiation under a future deal on climate change." *Climate Policy*. **10**(6): 672–677.

Winkler, H., B. Mantlana, and T. Letete. (2017). "Transparency of action and support in the Paris Agreement." *Climate Policy*. **17**(7): 853–872.

World Bank Group. (2016). *State and Trends of Carbon Pricing*. Report, World Bank Group Climate Change, Washington, DC.

https://doi.org/10.1142/9789811292415_0018

Chapter 18

Three Key Elements of Post-2012 International Climate Policy Architecture*

Sheila M. Olmstead[†] and Robert N. Stavins[‡,§,||,]**

[†]*School of Forestry and Environmental Studies, Yale University Resources for the Future*

[‡]*John F. Kennedy School of Government, Harvard University, Cambridge, MA, USA*

[§]*National Bureau of Economic Research, Cambridge, MA, USA*

[||]*Resources for the Future, Washington, DC, USA*

[**]*robert_stavins@harvard.edu*

Introduction

The nations of the world continue to strive to negotiate what may become the post-2012 (or post-Kyoto) climate regime. This has happened primarily through the United Nations Framework Convention on Climate Change (UNFCCC), but in addition, the key emitting countries of the world have held a series of meetings under the auspices of the Major Economies Forum for Energy and Climate and the G20, and a number of nations have met in

*This chapter was originally published in *Review of Environmental Economics and Policy*, **6**(2), 1–22, Winter 2012.

various bilateral venues. In each of these processes, the goal has been to foster international cooperation to address climate change when the first commitment period of the Kyoto Protocol expires at the end of 2012.

The Kyoto Protocol (United Nations 1997), which came into force in February 2005 and began to bind for ratified countries in 2008, represents the first significant multinational attempt to curb the greenhouse gas (GHG) emissions that are changing the global climate. The Protocol has both strengths and weaknesses that can provide lessons for the design of future international climate policy architecture. The design of such future international policy architecture is the focus of this symposium of four articles.

In this first article, we describe a promising post-2012 international global climate policy architecture with three essential elements: a means to ensure that key industrialized and developing nations are involved in differentiated but meaningful ways; an emphasis on an extended time path of targets; and inclusion of flexible market-based policy instruments to keep costs down and address concerns about international equity.

In the second article, Valentina Bosetti and Jeffrey Frankel (2010) provide an empirical examination of a related architecture which employs negotiated formulas to generate emissions targets for all countries through the end of the 21st century. Their approach — which builds upon political realities and constraints — is designed to limit global carbon dioxide (CO_2) concentrations to 460 parts per million (ppm).

Next, Gilbert Metcalf and David Weisbach (2010) recognize that the *defacto* post-2012 international climate policy architecture may quite possibly rely upon the bottom-up linkage of a diverse set of domestic climate policies. These authors analyze the promise, the mechanics, and the challenges of linking such heterogeneous policies, which might include national or regional cap-and-trade systems, carbon taxes, and some types of regulatory mechanisms.

Finally, Jing Cao (2010) presents the perspective of China, the most important of the emerging economies, by examining an approach which seeks to reconcile fairness, economic development imperatives, and sensible climate policy actions. She takes as her starting point the Copenhagen Accord, the major substantive outcome of the Fifteenth Conference of the Parties (COP-15) of the UNFCCC, in Copenhagen, in December 2009. Cao seeks to identify an international climate policy architecture which has at its heart a burden-sharing rule that countries might consider fair, a flexible structure for countries to choose their own domestic policy approaches, and an overall approach that is politically realistic.

Looking back: The Kyoto Protocol's strengths and weaknesses

Among the Kyoto Protocol's strengths is its inclusion of provisions for market-based approaches intended to lower the cost of the global climate regime: emissions trading among Annex I countries that take on targets under the Protocol; "joint implementation" which allows for project-level trades among the Annex I countries; and the Clean Development Mechanism (CDM), which provides for the use of project-level emission offsets created in non-Annex I (developing) countries to help meet the compliance obligations of firms in Annex I countries. (Annex I of the UNFCCC and Annex B of the Kyoto Protocol are often used interchangeably to represent the industrialized countries that have national emissions targets under the Kyoto Protocol.)

Also, the Kyoto Protocol provides flexibility for nations to meet their national emissions targets — their commitments — in any way they want. By recognizing domestic sovereignty, it provides flexibility at the national level. Further, the Protocol has at least the appearance of fairness in that it focuses on the wealthiest countries and those responsible for the majority of the current stock of anthropogenic GHGs in the atmosphere. This is consistent with the principle enunciated in the UNFCCC of "common but differentiated responsibilities and respective capabilities." Finally, the fact that the Kyoto Protocol was signed by more than 180 countries and subsequently ratified by a sufficient number of Annex I countries for it to come into force speaks to the political viability of the agreement in terms of participation, if not compliance.

The Kyoto Protocol also has some weaknesses. First, some of the world's leading emitters are not constrained. The United States — until recently the country with the largest share of global emissions, about 19 percent (Gregg *et al.*, 2008) — has not ratified and is unlikely to ratify the agreement. Also, some of the largest, most rapidly growing economies in the world do not take on targets, including China, India, Brazil, South Africa, Indonesia, South Korea, and Mexico. The developing world will soon overtake the industrialized world in total emissions. Indeed, China's CO_2 emissions have surpassed those of the United States (Gregg *et al.*, 2008); and China's emissions are expected to continue to grow much faster than U.S. emissions (Blanford, *et al.*, 2008).

Even if all of the Annex I countries, including the United States, were to reduce their CO_2 emissions to zero by 2030, it would be physically impossible for the world to achieve the frequently discussed climate target of stabilizing atmospheric CO_2 concentrations at or below 450 parts per million (ppm) without significant reductions by China and India. The Kyoto Protocol may not be as fair as originally intended, given how dramatically the world has changed since the UNFCCC divided countries into two categories in 1992. Approximately fifty non-Annex I countries now have higher per capita income than the poorest of the Annex I countries.

A second weakness of the Protocol is the relatively small number of countries which have agreed to take action. This "narrow but deep" approach will drive up the costs of producing carbon-intensive goods and services within the coalition of countries taking action. Through the forces of international trade, this approach leads to greater comparative advantage in the production of carbon-intensive goods and services for countries that do not have binding emissions targets, thereby shifting production and emissions from participating nations to non-participating nations — a phenomenon known as "emissions leakage." Leakage will reduce the cost-effectiveness and environmental performance of the agreement, and worse yet, push developing countries onto more carbon-intensive growth paths than they would otherwise have taken, rendering it more difficult for these countries to join the coalition of action later.

A third concern centers on the nature of the Kyoto Protocol's emissions trading elements. The provision in Article 17 for international emissions trading is unlikely to be effective, because the trading would need to be among national governments, not private-sector firms. The cost- effectiveness of cap-and-trade systems depends upon the participants being cost-minimizing entities. This is a reasonable assumption for private firms, because if such firms do not seek to minimize their costs, and indeed succeed in minimizing their costs, they will tend to disappear, given the competitive forces of the market. But nation-states are not simple cost-minimizers — many other objectives affect their decision-making. Furthermore, even if nation-states sought to minimize costs, they do not have sufficient information about marginal abatement costs of the multitude of sources within their borders to carry out cost-effective trades with other countries (Hahn and Stavins 1999).

Also, there is great concern regarding the CDM, an emissions-reduction-credit system. When an individual project results in emissions below what they would have been in the absence of the project, a credit — which may be sold to a source within a cap-and-trade system — is generated. This approach creates a challenge: comparing actual emissions with what they would have been otherwise. The baseline — what would have happened had the project not been implemented — is fundamentally unobservable. In fact, there is a natural tendency, because of economic incentives, to claim credits precisely for those projects that are most profitable, and hence would have been most likely to have been executed without selling credits. This is the "additionality" problem.

Fourth, the Kyoto Protocol, with its five-year time horizon (2008 to 2012), represents a relatively short-term approach for what is fundamentally a long-term problem. GHGs reside in the atmosphere for decades to centuries. And to encourage the magnitude of technological change that will be required to meaningfully address the threat of climate change, it will be necessary to send long-term price signals to the private market to stimulate sustained investment and technological innovation (Newell, 2008).

Finally, the Kyoto Protocol provides insufficient incentives for compliance (Barrett 2008). The Protocol's enforcement mechanism — a requirement that countries make up any deficit in subsequent compliance periods — is unlikely to induce policy responses consistent with targets.

Looking forward

Since the time the Kyoto Protocol was negotiated, scientific consensus regarding the likelihood of future climate change due to anthropogenic emissions of GHGs has grown (Watson, 2001, Pachauri, 2008), and economic analysis increasingly points to the wisdom of policy action (Shogren and Toman, 2000; Kolstad and Toman, 2001; Nordhaus, 2008a, 2008b). However, the Kyoto Protocol's ambitious targets apply only to the short term and only to some industrialized nations. As a result, the agreement imposes relatively high costs and generates minor short-term benefits, while failing to provide a real solution. Some analysts therefore see the agreement as "deeply flawed" (Victor, 2001; Cooper, 2001; McKibbin and Wilcoxen, 2002, 2004), but others see it as an acceptable or good first step (Grubb, 2003; Michaelowa, 2003). Virtually everyone agrees, however, that the current framework is not sufficient to the overall challenge and that further steps will be required.[1]

The negotiation of a post-2012 global climate policy architecture provides an opportunity to consider a significant dilemma. The Kyoto

---

[1]For a summary of critiques of the Kyoto Protocol and some alternatives, see Aldy, Barrett and Stavins (2003). A survey of proposals is provided by Bodansky (2004); and a recent analysis of alternatives is found in Aldy and Stavins, 2010.

Protocol came into force without U.S. participation or meaningful participation by developing countries; its effects on climate change will be trivial; but the economic and scientific consensus points to the need for a credible international approach. Given the global commons nature of the climate problem, a multinational — if not fully global — approach is required. As long as global marginal benefits exceed every nation's own marginal benefits, countries will either want to avoid participating or avoid complying fully if they do participate. Successful international cooperation must change these incentives (Barrett and Stavins, 2003).

Three Key Elements of International Climate Policy Architecture

A post-2012 international global climate policy architecture will need to contain three key elements: a means to ensure that the most important industrialized and developing nations are involved in meaningful ways; an emphasis on an extended time path of action; and inclusion of the flexibility offered by market-based policy instruments.

Expanding participation

The vast majority of the accumulated stock of anthropogenic CO_2 in the Earth's atmosphere was emitted by sources in industrialized countries.[2] Therefore, equity concerns may suggest that industrialized countries should take serious actions to reduce their emissions *before* developing countries are asked to make their own contributions to such efforts. It has therefore been argued that distributional equity favors a narrow coalition of action, like that embodied in Annex I. Efficiency, or more accurately, cost-effectiveness, favors a broader coalition of action, because these criteria focus on the margin, that is, are forward-looking. Indeed, we argue that broad participation — by major industrialized nations and key developing countries — is essential to address this global commons problem effectively.

---

[2]Taking into account land-use change (particularly deforestation), the responsibility for the atmospheric stock of anthropogenic carbon dioxide is more evenly distributed among developed and developing countries (Weisbach, 2010).

Four reasons for employing a broad set of participants

The share of global emissions attributable to developing countries is growing rapidly. China surpassed the United States as the world's largest emitter of CO_2 in 2006. The rate of growth in China's emissions is even more important: China emitted 8 percent of global anthropogenic CO_2 in 1981, and about 21 percent by 2008 (Gregg *et al.*, 2008; Guan *et al.*, 2009). More broadly, developing countries are likely to account for more than half of global emissions by the year 2020, if not before (Nakicenovic and Swart, 2000; Pies and Schröder, 2002; U.S. Energy Information Administration, 2009).

In addition to being an important and growing source of emissions, developing countries provide the greatest opportunities for low-cost emissions reductions (Watson, 2001). Therefore, inclusion of key developing countries in a climate regime can reduce overall costs dramatically. According to one estimate, if the major developing countries were to participate in achieving the Kyoto Protocol's emissions targets, total costs could be cut by 50 percent (Edmonds *et al.*, 1997).

Another reason to include key developing countries in any post-2012 international climate policy architecture is that the United States has signaled its unwillingness otherwise to commit to significant emissions cuts. In the months leading up to Kyoto, the U.S. Senate voted 95-0 in support of the Byrd-Hagel resolution, which stated that the United States Senate would not approve any agreement that did not include major developing countries under binding targets. Other industrialized countries may be willing to agree to more stringent cuts if the United States, China, and other parties are part of the post-2012 architecture. The EU indicated in the run-up to COP-15 in Copenhagen, in December, 2009, that it would increase the stringency of its reduction target from 20 percent to 30 percent below 1990 levels by 2020 if other countries would make commitments to large reductions.

A final reason to include developing countries in a post-2012 global climate policy architecture is to ensure the environmental effectiveness of emissions reductions by participating countries. If developing countries are not included in an agreement, comparative advantage in the production of carbon-intensive goods and services may shift outside the coalition of participating countries, making developing countries' economies more carbon intensive than they otherwise would be, through emissions leakage. Estimates from computable general equilibrium models of potential carbon leakage rates under a global climate regime range from 5 percent to 34 percent (Paltsev, 2001).

Cost-effectiveness and distributional equity

If a post-2012 international climate policy architecture is to be meaningful, the large and rapidly-growing developing countries must be involved, due to the magnitude of their current emissions, their expected rates of growth in emissions, their lower costs of emissions reductions, the increased likelihood of U.S. participation and willingness by other industrialized countries to engage in deeper emissions reductions, and the possibility of carbon leakage. However, it is probably unreasonable to expect developing nations to incur significant emissions-reduction *costs* in the short term, because of consequences for their economic development. Furthermore, it can be argued on an ethical basis that industrialized countries should take the first emission-reduction steps on their own, since they are responsible for the bulk of anthropogenic-based concentrations of GHGs in the atmosphere.

This poses a policy conundrum. On the one hand, for purposes of environmental performance and cost effectiveness, key developing countries must participate in an international effort to reduce GHG emissions, but on the other hand, for purposes of distributional equity and international political pragmatism, they cannot be expected to incur the brunt of the consequent costs. These countries must get on the "global climate policy train" without necessarily paying full fare. How can this be accomplished?

Achieving developing country participation may require a trigger mechanism, imposing binding commitments only when per capita income, emissions per capita, or some other measure of development has reached a predetermined level. But there is no reason to limit action to such a simple, dichotomous instrument. A preferable approach would be continuous "growth targets" that become more stringent for individual counties as they become more wealthy (Lutter, 2000). A growth target is not a number, but essentially an equation or set of equations that relate targeted emissions to per-capita income and other variables. Two necessary characteristics of a growth target formulation are that it not create perverse incentives that would encourage nations to increase their emissions and that it should be relatively simple, so as not to create impediments to negotiation (Aldy, Baron, and Tubiana, 2003).

This is a natural extension of the progressive target allocation present in the Kyoto Protocol from the industrialized world to the developing world and from the cross-sectional dimension to the temporal dimension. The Kyoto Protocol's targets exhibit positive correlation between gross domestic product per capita and the degree of targeted emissions reduction below business-as-usual (BAU) levels. In fact, according to Frankel (1999, 2005), the Kyoto targets exhibit an "income elasticity of reductions" of about 0.14, that is, for a 10 percent increase in per-capita GDP, a country's emissions reduction targets — on average — are about 1.4 percent more stringent.

A formulaic approach to allocating responsibility

In this symposium, Bosetti and Frankel (2010) propose a formulaic approach to generating emissions targets for all key countries for each five-year period remaining in this century. Their formula contains three elements: progressivity, latecomer catch-up, and gradual movement toward equal per capita emissions, while constraining targets so as not to impose costs over the century exceeding an average of 1 percent of GDP per year, or 5 percent of GDP for any country in any period (Frankel, 2008; Bosetti and Frankel, 2010). Game-theoretic analyses suggest that the use of such formulas can render negotiations more likely to succeed (Harstad, 2008).

Their progressivity factor would adjust emissions targets based upon per capita income (applying the income elasticity of reductions implied by the Kyoto targets). "Latecomer catch-up" avoids rewarding countries that failed to curb their emissions after 1990, the Kyoto baseline year. This would include countries such as Canada, which ratified the Protocol but are unlikely to comply; countries such as the United States, which did not ratify the agreement; and countries such as China, which did not take on targets at Kyoto. This would help close the gap between 1990 emissions and the starting points of latecomers to the process. Finally, the "equalization factor" would move all countries in the direction of global average per capita emissions in the second half of the century, asking rich countries to make up, somewhat, for the fact that they previously enjoyed the benefits of unfettered CO_2 emissions, creating an environmental problem for which poor countries bear disproportionate impacts (Frankel, 2008).

In the short term, such indexed targets for major developing countries could be set at BAU emissions levels, but they would become more stringent over time as the countries became wealthier. Whereas the emissions targets of China and the other major emerging economies in the Bosetti and Frankel proposal would be equivalent to BAU emissions from 2010 until 2025, then dropping below BAU, the poorest countries would have targets equal to BAU for the remainder of the century. Keeping even poor countries at or near BAU emissions is an important goal, since it prevents the possibility of significant carbon leakage.

If provision is not made for such a mechanism that includes developing countries at low or no cost to them, then the inevitable result will be a trade-off between cost-effectiveness (or efficiency) and distributional equity (Sugiyama and Deshun, 2004). However, if emissions targets at BAU for the short- to medium-run (or even the long run for some regions) were combined with an appropriate international trading program (discussed below), this could — in principle — provide a direct economic incentive (subsidy) for developing-country participation. Developing countries could fully participate without incurring prohibitive costs (or even any costs in the short term). That is, cost-effectiveness and distributional equity could both be addressed.

An extended time path of targets

Global climate change is a long-term problem, due to the fact that the relevant GHGs remain in the atmosphere for decades to centuries, combined with the reality that significant technological change will be required to bring down costs to levels where greater actions can be taken. The Kyoto Protocol fails to reflect these fundamentally important realities with its short-term targets, an average 5 percent reduction from 1990 levels by the 2008–2012 "first commitment period." However, this apparently modest reduction translates into a severe 25–30 percent cut for the United States from what was its BAU emissions path. The reason for this is that the United States economy grew at an exceptionally rapid rate during the 1990s, exhibiting a remarkable 37 percent increase in real GDP from 1990 to 2000.

This contrasts dramatically with the situation in Europe and elsewhere, where economies grew more slowly or were even stagnant. Furthermore, emissions of CO_2 from the United Kingdom, Germany, and Russia fell significantly subsequent to 1990 (the Kyoto Protocol's baseline year) for reasons having nothing to do with climate policy. Emissions fell in the United Kingdom because of structural changes in the domestic coal industry initiated by Prime Minister Margaret Thatcher's government

(1979–1990); emissions fell in Germany because reunification led to the closure of energy-inefficient plants in the former East Germany; and emissions fell in Russia because of its economic collapse in the 1990s (McKibbin and Wilcoxen, 2002). It has been estimated that up to 80 percent of the European Union's CO_2 reductions under the Kyoto Protocol would be achieved by two countries — Germany and the United Kingdom, facilitated via the EU bubble that is part of the Protocol (Andersen, 2002).

More broadly, the Kyoto Protocol's targets can be characterized as seeking to achieve "too little, too fast." They do little about the problem, but are unreasonable for countries that enjoyed significant economic growth after 1990. Two elements can ameliorate this problem: firm but moderate targets in the short term to avoid rendering large parts of the capital stock prematurely obsolete, and flexible but considerably more stringent targets for the long term to motivate (now and in the future) technological change, which in turn is needed to bring costs down over time (Goulder and Schneider, 1999; Jaffe, Newell, and Stavins, 1999; Pershing and Tudela, 2003; Newell, 2008). Emissions targets ought to start out at BAU levels, and gradually depart from BAU levels, becoming more stringent over time. Globally, the aggregate emissions target should not be monotonically increasing, but should reach a maximum level and then begin to decrease — eventually becoming substantially more severe than the constraints implied by the Kyoto Protocol's short-term targets.

Precise, numerical emissions targets for long time horizons, if they are inflexible, are impractical due to uncertainty over future growth, technological change, and the science of climate change and its effects. Some of the considerable uncertainty throughout the policy-economics-biophysical system will be resolved over time (Richels, Manne, and Wigley, 2004, Mendelsohn, 2008). Thus, long-term targets must retain some flexibility.

In addition, since long-run emissions targets would require that current political leaders (especially elected officials) bind future political leaders to costly commitments, many have pointed out that long-term targets are dynamically inconsistent and must incorporate constraints representing the economic reality that no country is likely to abide by an unenforceable international agreement that causes great economic disruption in any particular year or set of years (Frankel, 2008).

The pattern we suggest is consistent with estimates of the least-cost time path of emissions for achieving long-term greenhouse-gas concentration targets: short-term increases in emissions — just slightly below the

BAU path — and subsequent emission reductions (Wigley, Richels, and Edmonds, 1996; Manne and Richels, 1997).

Such a time path of long-term targets, put in place now, would be consistent with what is often denigrated as "politics as usual." That is, politicians are frequently condemned for the fact that in representative democracies there are strong incentives to place costs on future, not current, voters and, if possible, future generations. It is typically the politically pragmatic strategy. In the case of global climate policy, it can also be the scientifically correct and economically sensible approach.

Market-based policy instruments

The third essential component of post-Kyoto international policy architecture will be necessary to achieve global cost-effectiveness and thereby to render the overall architecture politically achievable: working through the market rather than against it. There is widespread agreement that conventional regulatory approaches cannot do the job, certainly not at acceptable costs. To keep costs down in the short term and bring them down even lower in the long term through technological change, it is essential to embrace market-based instruments (that is, carbon pricing) as the chief means of reducing GHG emissions (Stavins, 1997; Lackner, 2005; Metcalf, 2009).

On a domestic level in some countries, systems of tradable permits — now known as "cap- and-trade" — might be used to achieve national targets. In a cap-and-trade system, sources that have low costs of control have an incentive to take on added reductions, so that they can sell their excess permits to sources that face relatively high control costs and would hence wish to reduce their control efforts (Hockenstein, Stavins, and Whitehead, 1997). This is the same mechanism that was used in the United States to eliminate leaded gasoline from the market in the 1980s at a savings of more than $250 million per year (Stavins, 2003), and the same mechanism being used to cut sulfur dioxide (SO_2) emissions from power plants in the United States by 50 percent, at a savings estimated to be $1 billion per year (Schmalensee, *et al.*, 1998; Stavins, 1998; Ellerman, *et al.*, 2000). The better model for climate change policy is the upstream lead-rights system (analogous to trading based on the carbon content of fossil fuels), rather than the downstream SO_2 emissions-trading system.

For some countries, systems of domestic carbon taxes may be more attractive than cap-and-trade approaches. Rather than imposing a cap on the quantity of pollution, and allowing regulated firms to trade allowances to establish a market price for pollution, a tax imposes a specific price on pollution and allows firms to decide how much to emit in response. A tax has an effect on firms' decisions that is essentially identical to the effect of the permit price created by a cap-and-trade policy; polluters decide, for each ton of emissions, whether to abate that ton (incurring the resulting abatement costs) or pay the tax and continue to emit that ton. Domestic carbon taxes — typically in the form of upstream taxes on the carbon content of fossil fuels — have frequently been recommended by academic economists (Metcalf, 2007; Metcalf and Weisbach, 2009),[3] but have received considerably less support in the policy community.

Another promising market-based approach is a hybrid of tax and tradable-permit systems — that is, an ordinary cap-and-trade system, plus a government promise to sell additional permits at a stated price (Roberts and Spence, 1976; Kopp, *et al.*, 2000; Pizer, 2002; McKibbin and Wilcoxen, 2002). This creates a price (and thereby cost) ceiling, and has hence been labeled a safety-valve system. Likewise, a price floor can be created by a government promise to purchase allowances from the market at a given price. The combination of the two approaches — known as a "price collar" — can have particular attraction (Murray, Newell, and Pizer, 2009).

Among these alternative market-based policy instruments, the one which seems to be emerging as the preferred approach among industrialized countries is cap-and-trade (Jaffe and Stavins, 2010). At the same time, the emission-reduction credit system created under the Kyoto Protocol — the Clean Development Mechanism — enjoys a solid constituency of support in the developing world (Somanathan, 2008).

The promise and problems of international emissions trading

The Kyoto Protocol includes in Article 17 a system whereby the parties to the agreement can engage in trading their "assigned amounts," that is, their reduction targets, translated into quantitative terms of emissions (United Nations, 1997). In theory, such a system of international tradable permits — if implemented only for the industrialized countries (as under the Kyoto Protocol) — could reduce costs by 50 percent. If such a system

---

[3]Others have argued in favor of an international tax regime. See, for example: Cooper (1998, 2008); McKibbin and Wilcoxen (2002); Pizer (2002); Newell and Pizer (2003); and Nordhaus (2008a).

also included major developing countries, costs could be lowered to 25 percent of what they otherwise would be (Edmonds *et al.*, 1997).

An undisputed attraction — in theory — of an international trading approach is that the equilibrium allocation of permits, the market-determined permit price, and the aggregate costs of abatement are independent of the initial allocation of permits among countries. Emerging empirical evidence supports this hypothesis for some domestic trading systems (Fowlie and Perloff, 2008). However, permit allocations and aggregate abatement costs will only be independent as long as particularly perverse types of transaction costs are not prevalent (Stavins, 1995), individual parties — be they nations or firms — do not have market power (Hahn, 1984), and other conditions hold (Hahn and Stavins, 2010). The market-power concern is a real one in the climate change context. In any event, the initial allocation can be highly significant in distributional terms, implying possibly massive international wealth transfers. Some analysts have highlighted this as a major objection to an international carbon trading regime (Cooper, 1998, 2008), but it is essentially because of this feature that a permit system can be used to address cost-effectiveness *and* distributional equity.

If an international trading system were used, it must be designed to facilitate integration with domestic policies that nations use to achieve their respective domestic targets. In the extreme, if all countries were to use domestic cap-and-trade systems to meet their national targets (that is, allocate shares from an international permit system to private domestic parties), then an international system can — in theory — be cost-effective, because a nation-nation trading system then evolves essentially into an international firm-firm trading system. On the other hand, if some countries were to use non-trading approaches, such as GHG taxes or various kinds of regulatory standards — which seems likely — cost minimization is less ensured (Hahn and Stavins, 1999; Metcalf and Weisbach, 2010).

Thus, individual nations' choices of domestic policy instruments to meet their targets can substantially limit the cost-saving potential of an international trading program. A trade-off exists between degree of domestic sovereignty and degree of cost-effectiveness. A possible answer, which we discuss below, is the linkage of independent domestic and regional cap-and-trade systems, and for that matter, domestic carbon taxes and some types of national regulatory systems, thereby facilitating some degree of cost-effective trades among individual sources (firms), both domestically and internationally.

Is the European Union emissions trading scheme a useful model?

When the Kyoto Protocol was signed in 1997, few would have predicted that European countries would employ cap-and-trade systems, given the European Union's strenuous opposition to such approaches. But after some initial flirtations with carbon tax considerations, the EU launched a continent-wide trading system for CO_2 to meet its emissions reduction targets under the Protocol (Kruger and Pizer, 2004).

The Kyoto Protocol establishes a bubble for the European Union, that is, it sets a cap on CO_2 emissions for the EU as a whole, allocated by the EU to its member states. Under this cap, the European Union Emission Trading Scheme (EU ETS) was established in 2005, and after a pilot phase, entered its more meaningful Kyoto phase in January 2008.

The EU ETS is the world's largest emissions trading system, covering some 12,000 facilities in 27 countries as of 2008, and accounting for nearly one-half of EU CO_2 emissions (Ellerman and Buchner, 2007, Ellerman and Joskow, 2008, Ellerman, 2008, Convery and Redmond, 2007). The pilot phase of the EU ETS (2005–2007) was designed to set up the institutional and operating structures necessary for trading. The cap in the EU system in this pilot phase was a very small reduction below expected emissions in the absence of the policy. Given that the system was designed not to begin to bind in meaningful ways until 2008, which turned out to be a time of global recession (and hence falling CO_2 emissions), it is much too soon to determine the impact of this new carbon market on emissions, or the cost savings from the EU ETS over more prescriptive approaches.

The EU ETS could conceivably serve as a prototype for a post-2012 international global climate regime, since the 30 states involved constitute an increasingly diverse set of sovereign countries. Many of the problems encountered and addressed by the EU ETS may be similar to those a fully international architecture would encounter. Indeed, the EU ETS has not been without its conflicts. Nine of the ten East European countries have sued the European Commission over their allotted emissions caps for 2008–2012. But the "club benefits" of continued membership in the European Union, including free labor and capital flows and access to broader markets, have apparently outweighed the costs of the EU ETS for these poorer nations, as they have chosen to remain within the system, rather than dropping out (Ellerman, 2008).

The status of climate cap-and-trade in the United States

Although the U.S. government (Senate) did not ratify the Kyoto Protocol, some states have enacted policies to reduce their GHG emissions. The largest U.S. market-based initiative is the Regional Greenhouse Gas Initiative (RGGI), a cap-and-trade system among 10 northeastern states, initiated in 2003. The trading program, which began in earnest in 2009, covers electricity generators within the region. Allowances under RGGI are auctioned, and firms trade allowances and various financial derivatives (including futures and options contracts) in a secondary market. The RGGI CO_2 emissions cap for 2009–2014 roughly equals the sum of recent emissions among covered generators, then declines by 2.5 percent per year from 2015 through 2018.

California continues to take serious steps toward establishing its own cap-and-trade system for CO_2 emissions to meet the requirements of its Global Warming Solutions Act 2006 (otherwise known as Assembly Bill 32, or AB 32), namely achieving emissions in 2020 equal to those of 1990 (Jaffe and Stavins, 2010).

In June 2009, the Federal government in the United States began to take its most significant steps toward putting in place a national cap-and-trade policy to reduce CO_2 emissions, with the passage in the House of Representatives of the American Clean Energy and Security Act, also known as the Waxman-Markey bill, named for the two Members of Congress who developed the legislation. The legislation would cap national GHG emissions by nearly all significant sources, including coal-fired power plants, factories, natural gas suppliers, and fuels, setting up an economy-wide cap-and-trade system to achieve emissions reductions. The target reductions for covered sources in the bill amount to cuts of 17 percent below 2005 levels by 2020, and progressively steeper cuts as time goes on (42 percent by 2030, and 83 percent by 2050).

In May 2010, companion legislation was introduced in the U.S. Senate by Senators John Kerry and Joseph Lieberman — the American Power Act. Like the House legislation, this proposal features a cap-and-trade system.

Linking national and regional cap-and-trade systems

In addition to the nations of the European Union and the United States, a number of other major countries in the industrialized world are currently considering the adoption of national cap-and-trade systems to reduce their CO_2 emissions, including Australia, Canada, Japan, and New Zealand (Jaffe and Stavins, 2010). The increasing number of existing, planned, and proposed regional, national, and sub-national cap-and-trade policies for CO_2 emissions reduction raises the possibility that the linkage of these systems will be a significant element of future international climate policy architecture. In this context, linkage refers to the recognition of the allowances (permits) from one system for use in meeting compliance requirements of another. The potential benefits of such linkage include cost savings from increasing the scope of the market, greater market liquidity, reduced price volatility, lessened market power, and reduced carbon leakage (Jaffe and Stavins, 2010).

Such linkage of domestic cap-and-trade systems can be initiated by bilateral or multilateral agreements among respective governments, but it leads to trading not among governments, but among firms within the respective countries. This circumvents the problems, mentioned earlier, which are inherent in international emissions trading under Article 17 of the Kyoto Protocol (Hahn and Stavins, 1999).

Domestic cap-and-trade programs could be linked directly, either unilaterally or bilaterally. With a direct bilateral linkage, a pair of domestic cap-and-trade policies would recognize allowances from the other system. Under unilateral linkage, one system recognizes allowances from the other, but the recognition is not mutual. Allowance prices would converge with direct bilateral linkage, so long as there were no constraints on inter-system trades, and with unilateral linkage as long as the buying system's price was higher than the selling system's price – no trading would take place if the opposite were true (Jaffe and Stavins, 2010).

A potential problem is that direct linkage of cap-and-trade systems will lead to the automatic transmission of cost-containment elements — banking, borrowing, safety valves, and price collars — from one system to the other. This raises concerns for some countries, because of the possible loss of control of their domestic systems, and raises the possibility that systems would need to be harmonized in advance of linkage.

This necessity for prior harmonization can be avoided through the substitution of indirect links for direct ones. If each cap-and-trade system links with a common emission-reduction credit system, then all of the cap-and-trade systems will be linked (indirectly), achieving the benefits of cost reduction, greater market liquidity, reduced price volatility, lessened market power, and reduced carbon leakage, but with greatly reduced transmission of cost-containment mechanisms from one system to another, thereby reducing, if not eliminating the need for prior harmonization. With a sufficient supply of credits, prices in all systems will converge, though this may not occur if binding constraints are imposed on the use of credits and allowances from other systems.

This is a rather good description of what appears to be evolving, that is, the emergence of regional and national cap-and-trade systems in the industrialized world, each of which allows offsets to some degree from the clean development mechanism (CDM), the emission-reduction credit system in developing countries that was established under the Kyoto Protocol. Under the CDM, certified emissions reductions (CERs) are awarded for voluntary emission reduction projects in developing countries that ratified the Kyoto Protocol, but are not among the countries subject to emissions limitations. The industrialized countries that did take on emissions targets under the Protocol can use CERs to meet their commitments. The CDM will have generated more than 2.7 billion (tons of) CERs by the end of 2012, the vast majority of them for projects in China, India, and Brazil (Jaffe and Stavins, 2010). The process of indirect linkage has begun, since CERs can be used to meet emissions commitments within the EU ETS and RGGI (under certain circumstances).

A potential concern associated with linking cap-and-trade systems through a common emission-reduction credit systems is "additionality" — credit systems, including the CDM, have been plagued by questions about the actual emissions reductions represented by credits, because of the difficulty of establishing a baseline against which reductions can be measured. Linking credit systems with cap-and-trade system passes this worry along to the latter system, in which it would otherwise not be a significant concern. Thus, there is a trade-off between the potential economic and environmental gains of such a bottom-up system of global indirect linkage, and the potential economic and environmental losses that linkage can bring about if additionality problems are severe.

The role of emissions trading in a future international climate policy architecture

One of the key objections to the efficacy of a post-2012 international climate policy architecture with international emissions trading as a core element is that industrialized countries will not support such a policy, once the cross-border financial flows implied by trading allocations that favor developing countries (in order to prompt their accession to the agreement) become apparent (Victor, 2007, Cooper, 1998). However, despite the significant variation in per capita income across EU ETS member states, this has not turned out to be a point of controversy (Ellerman, 2008). This may be due to the fact that, while trading is active, financial flows from emissions trading represent a very small portion of total imports and exports. For example, the United Kingdom is the largest emissions allowance importer in the ETS, importing 14 percent of its verified emissions, worth about £350 million. But this still represents a very small portion — less than one-tenth of one percent — of its total imports of goods and services, about £415 billion (Ellerman, 2008). Furthermore, it is useful to keep in mind that any viable alternative that engages the major developing countries in an international climate policy architecture will likely involve some form of financial transfers from industrialized to developing countries.

The experience of the EU ETS, the U.S. preference for trading, and support voiced by other countries represent important political arguments for this element of a future international climate policy architecture. International permit trading — not among countries, *per se*, but among firms within and across countries — thus remains a promising approach to achieving global greenhouse targets, despite the challenges that exist. It is probably fair to state that the more one studies international tradable permit systems to address global climate change, the more one comes to believe that this is the worst possible approach — except, of course, for all the others.

Incorporating linkage among a more heterogeneous set of national policies

Although cap-and-trade systems appear as of now to be the preferred approach in most parts of the industrialized world for meaningful GHG emission reductions, it also appears likely that some — perhaps a sizable share of — countries will use other approaches, ranging from other market-based instruments, in particular, carbon taxes, to more conventional types of regulatory instruments, such as performance standards and technology standards. This raises questions about whether bottom-up linkage among a heterogeneous set of national policies is feasible and at what cost.

The short answer is that although bilateral allowance recognition between cap-and-trade systems is the simplest and easiest form of linkage, it is also possible to link carbon tax systems with cap-and-trade systems. For that matter, some types of regulatory standards can also be linked (Hahn and Stavins, 1999; Metcalf and Weisbach, 2010). Direct linkages — and, more likely, indirect linkages through a common emission-reduction-credit system — are possible among a fairly broad, but not unlimited set of national policy instruments. Problems arise with some types of linkages, but some of these can be addressed through *ex ante* harmonization. Rather than saying more here, we direct the reader's attention to the companion paper in this symposium by Metcalf and Weisbach (2010), which focuses on these very questions.

Conclusion

The three elements we have identified are likely to be essential aspects of a future global climate change policy architecture that is meaningful and feasible, and can serve as a successor to the Kyoto Protocol. Key nations have to be involved, including major emerging economies through the use of economic trigger mechanisms such as growth targets. In addition, cost-effective time paths of targets are required: firm, but moderate in the short term, and in the long term, much more stringent and flexible. Finally, to keep costs down, market-based policy instruments need to be part of the package, whether emissions trading, carbon taxes, or hybrids of the two. Most likely, international linkage of regional, national, and even sub-national market-based instruments will be the means through which this third element is implemented.

This overall approach can be made to be scientifically sound, economically rational, and perhaps politically pragmatic. There is no denying that the challenges facing adoption and successful implementation of this climate policy architecture are significant, but they need not be insurmountable, and they are no greater than the challenges facing other approaches to the threat of global climate change.

References

Aldy, J. E., S. Barrett, and R. N. Stavins. (2003). "Thirteen plus one: A comparison of global climate policy architectures." *Climate Policy*. **3**(4): 373–397.

Aldy, J. E. and R. N. Stavins. (2010). *Post-Kyoto International Climate Policy: Implementing Architectures for Agreement*. Cambridge, UK: Cambridge University Press.

Aldy, J. E., R. Baron, and L. Tubiana. (2003). "Addressing cost: The political economy of climate change." In E. Diringer (ed.), *Beyond Kyoto: Advancing the International Effort Against Climate Change*, pp. 85–110. Arlington, VA: Pew Center on Global Climate Change.

Andersen, M. S. (2002). "Regulation or coordination: European climate policy between Scylla and Charybdis." *Paper Presented at 10th Symposium of the Egon Sohmen Foundation*, Dresden, Germany.

Barrett, S. (2008). *A Portfolio System of Climate Treaties*. Discussion Paper 08-13, Harvard Project on International Climate Agreements, Belfer Center for Science and International Affairs, Harvard Kennedy School.

Barrett, S. and R. N. Stavins. (2003). "Increasing participation and compliance in international climate change agreements." *International Environmental Agreements: Politics, Law and Economics*. **3**(4): 349–376.

Blanford, G. J., R. G. Richels, and T. F. Rutherford. (2008). *Revised Emissions Growth Projections for China: Why Post-Kyoto Climate Policy Must Look East*. Discussion Paper 08-06, Harvard Project on International Climate Agreements.

Bodansky, D. (2004). *International Climate Efforts Beyond 2012: A Survey of Approaches*. Arlington, VA: Pew Center on Global Climate Change.

Bosetti, V. and J. Frankel. (2010). "Global climate policy architecture and political feasibility: Specific formulas and emissions targets to attain 460 ppm CO_2 concentrations." *Review of Environmental Economics and Policy*, this issue.

Cao, J. (2010). Beyond Copenhagen: Reconciling international fairness, economic development, and climate protection. *Review of Environmental Economics and Policy*, this issue.

Convery, F. J. and L. Redmond. (2007). "Market and price developments in the European Union Emissions Trading Scheme." *Review of Environmental Economics and Policy*. **1**(1): 88–111.

Cooper, R. (1998). "Toward a real treaty on global warming." *Foreign Affairs*. **77**(2): 66–79.

Cooper, R. (2001). *The Kyoto Protocol: A Flawed Concept*. FEEM Working Paper No. 52.2001.

Cooper, R. (2008). *The Case for Charges on Greenhouse Gas Emissions*. Discussion Paper 08-10, Harvard Project on International Climate Agreements, Belfer Center for Science and International Affairs, Harvard Kennedy School.

Edmonds, J., S. H. Kim, C. N. McCracken, R. D. Sands, and M. A. Wise. (1997). *Return to 1990: The Cost of Mitigating United States Carbon Emissions in the Post-2000 Period*. Washington, DC: Pacific Northwest National Laboratory.

Ellerman, A. D. (2008). *The EU Emission Trading Scheme: A Prototype Global System*? Discussion Paper 2008-02, Harvard Project on International Climate Agreements.

Ellerman, A. D. and B. K. Buchner. (2007). "The European Union Emissions Trading Scheme: Origins, allocation, and early results." *Review of Environmental Economics and Policy*. **1**(1): 66–87.

Ellerman, A. D. and P. L. Joskow. (2008). *The European Union's Emissions Trading System in Perspective*. Washington, DC: Pew Center on Global Climate Change.

Ellerman, A. D., P. Joskow, R. Schmalensee, J. P. Montero, and E. Bailey. (2000). *Markets for Clean Air: The U.S. Acid Rain Program*. Cambridge, UK: Cambridge University Press.

Fowlie, M. and J. M. Perloff. (2008). *Distributing Pollution Rights in Cap-and-Trade Programs: Are Outcomes Independent of Allocation*? Working Paper, University of California, Berkeley.

Frankel, J. (1999). *Greenhouse Gas Emissions*. Policy Brief No. 52. Washington, DC: Brookings Institution.

Frankel, J. (2005). "You're getting warmer: The most feasible path for addressing global climate change does run through Kyoto." In M. Tamborra and J. Maxwell (eds.), *Trade and the Environment in the Perspective of the EU Enlargement*, pp. 37–58. Cheltenham, UK: Edward Elgar.

Frankel, J. (2008). *An Elaborated Proposal for Global Climate Policy Architecture: Specific Formulas and Emission Targets for All Countries in All Decades*. Discussion Paper 2008-08, Harvard Project on International Climate Agreements.

Goulder, L. H. and S. H. Schneider. (1999). "Induced technological change and the attractiveness of CO_2 abatement policies." *Resource and Energy Economics*. **21**(3–4): 211–253.

Gregg, J. S., R. J. Andres, and G. Marland. (2008). "China: Emissions pattern of the world leader in CO_2 emissions from fossil fuel consumption and cement production." *Geophysical Research Letters*. **35**: L08806.

Grubb, M. (2003). "The economics of the Kyoto Protocol." *World Economics*. **4**(3): 143–189.

Guan, D., G. P. Peters, C. L. Weber, and K. Hubacek. (2009). "Journey to the world top emitter: An analysis of the driving forces of China's recent CO_2 emissions surge." *Geophysical Research Letters*. **36**: L04709.

Hahn, R. W. (1984). "Market power and transferable property rights." *Quarterly Journal of Economics*. **99**: 753–765.

Hahn, R. W. and R. N. Stavins. (1999). *What Has the Kyoto Protocol Wrought? The Real Architecture of International Tradable Permit Markets*. Washington, DC: American Enterprise Institute Press.

Hahn, R. W. and R. N. Stavins. (2010). *The Effect of Allowance Allocations on Cap-and-Trade System Performance*. Harvard Kennedy School Faculty Research Working Paper Series RWP10-010, Cambridge, MA.

Harstad, B. (2008). *How to Negotiate and Update Climate Agreements*. Discussion Paper 08-19, Harvard Project on International Climate Agreements, Belfer Center for Science and International Affairs, Harvard Kennedy School.

Hockenstein, J. B., R. N. Stavins, and B. W. Whitehead. (1997). "Crafting the next generation of market-based environmental tools." *Environment*. **39**(4): 12–20, 30–33.

Jaffe, A. B., R. G. Newell, and R. N. Stavins. (1999). *Energy-Efficient Technologies and Climate Change Policies: Issues and Evidence*. Climate Issue Brief No. 19. Washington, DC: Resources for the Future.

Jaffe, J. and R. N. Stavins. (2010). "Linkage of tradable permit systems in international climate policy architecture." In J. E. Aldy and R. N. Stavins (eds.), *Post-Kyoto International Climate Policy: Implementing Architectures for Agreement*, pp. 119–150. Cambridge, UK: Cambridge University Press.

Kolstad, C. D. and M. Toman (2001). *The Economics of Climate Policy*. Discussion Paper 00-40REV. Washington, DC: Resources for the Future.

Kopp, R. J., R. D. Morgenstern, W. A. Pizer, and M. A. Toman. (2000). "A proposal for credible early action in US climate policy." In K. L. Brockmann and M. Stonzik (eds.), *Flexible Mechanisms for Efficient Climate Policy: Cost Saving Policies and Business Opportunities*. Heidelberg, Germany: Physica-Verlag.

Kruger, J. A. and W. A. Pizer. (2004). "Greenhouse gas trading in Europe: The new grand policy experiment." *Environment*. **46**(8): 8–23.

Lackner, K. (2005). "Carbon management technology." *Paper Presented at Global Warming: Looking Beyond Kyoto*, Yale University, New Haven, CT.

Lutter, R. (2000). Developing countries' greenhouse emissions: Uncertainty and implications for participation in the Kyoto Protocol. *The Energy Journal*, **21**(4), 93–120.

Manne, A. and R. Richels. (1997). *On Stabilizing CO2 Concentrations — Cost-Effective Emission Reduction Strategies*. Stanford, CA: Stanford University and Electric Power Research Institute.

McKibbin, W. and P. Wilcoxen. (2002). "The role of economics in climate change policy." *Journal of Economic Perspectives*. **16**(2): 107–129.

McKibbin, W. and P. Wilcoxen. (2004). "Estimates of the costs of Kyoto: Marrakesh versus the McKibbin-Wilcoxen Blueprint." *Energy Policy*. **32**(4): 467–479.

Mendelsohn, R. (2008). "The policy implications of climate change impacts." In E. Zedillo (ed.), *Global Warming: Looking Beyond Kyoto*, pp. 82–88. Washington, DC: Brookings Institution Press.

Metcalf, G. (2007). *A Proposal for a U.S. Carbon Tax Swap: An Equitable Tax Reform to Address Global Climate Change*. Discussion Paper 2007-12, Hamilton Project, Brookings Institution.

Metcalf, G. (2009). "Market-based policy options to control U.S. greenhouse gas emissions." *Journal of Economic Perspectives*. **23**(2): 5–27.

Metcalf, G. and D. Weisbach. (2009). "The design of a carbon tax." *Harvard Environmental Law Review*. **33**(2): 499–506.

Metcalf, G. and D. Weisbach. (2010). "Linking policies when tastes differ: Global climate policy in a heterogeneous world." *Review of Environmental Economics and Policy*, this issue.

Michaelowa, A. (2003). "Global warming policy." *Journal of Economic Perspectives*. **17**(3): 204–205.

Michaelowa, A., M. Stronzik, F. Eckermann, and A. Hunt. (2003). "Transaction costs of the Kyoto mechanisms." *Climate Policy*. **3**(3): 261–278.

Murray, B., R. Newell, and W. Pizer. (2009). "Balancing cost and emissions certainty: An allowance reserve for cap-and-trade." *Review of Environmental Economics and Policy*. **3**(1): 84–103.

Nakicenovic, N. and R. Swart. (eds.). (2000). *Intergovernmental Panel on Climate Change Special Report on Emissions Scenarios*. Cambridge, UK: Cambridge University Press.

Newell, R. G. (2008). *International Climate Technology Strategies*. Discussion Paper 08-12, Harvard Project on International Climate Agreements, Belfer Center for Science and International Affairs, Harvard Kennedy School.

Newell, R. G. and W. A. Pizer. (2003). "Regulating stock externalities under uncertainty." *Journal of Environmental Economics and Management*. **45**(2, Suppl. 1): 416–432.

Nordhaus, W. D. (2008a). "Economic analyses of Kyoto Protocol: Is there life after Kyoto?" In E. Zedillo (ed.), *Global Warming: Looking Beyond Kyoto*, pp. 91–100. Washington, DC: Brookings Institution Press.

Nordhaus, W. D. (2008b). *A Question of Balance: Weighing the Options on Global Warming Policies*. New Haven, CT: Yale University Press.

Pachauri, R. K. (2008). "The IPCC: Establishing the evidence." In E. Zedillo (ed.), *Global Warming: Looking Beyond Kyoto*, pp. 13–20. Washington, DC: Brookings Institution Press.

Paltsev, S. V. (2001). "The Kyoto Protocol: Regional and sectoral contributions to the carbon leakage." *The Energy Journal*. **22**(4): 53–79.

Pershing, J. and F. Tudela. (2003). "A long-term target: Framing the climate effort." In E. Diringer (ed.), *Beyond Kyoto: Advancing the International Effort Against Climate Change*, pp. 11–36. Arlington, VA: Pew Center on Global Climate Change.

Pies, I. and G. Schröder. (2002). *Causes and Consequences of Global Warming: How Rational is Our Policy on Climate Change*. Munich, Germany: Policy Consult.

W. A. Pizer. (2002). "Combining price and quantity controls to mitigate global climate change." *Journal of Public Economics*. **85**(3): 409–434.

Richels, R. G., A. S. Manne, and T. M. L. Wigley. (2004). *Moving Beyond Concentrations — The Challenge of Limiting Temperature Change.* AEI-Brookings Joint Center Working Paper No. 04-11. Washington, DC: AEI-Brookings Joint Center.

Roberts, M. and M. Spence. (1976). "Effluent charges and licenses under uncertainty." *Journal of Public Economics*. **5**(3–4): 193–208.

Schmalensee, R., P. Joskow, D. Ellerman, J. P. Montero, and E. Bailey. (1998). "An interim evaluation of sulfur dioxide emissions trading." *Journal of Economic Perspectives*. **12**(3): 53–68.

Shogren, J. F. and M. A. Toman. (2000). "Climate change policy." In P. R. Portney and R. N. Stavins (eds.), *Public Policies for Environmental Protection*, 2nd ed., pp. 125–168. Washington, DC: Resources for the Future.

Somanathan, E. (2008). *What Do We Expect from an International Climate Agreement? A Perspective from a Low-Income Country*. Discussion Paper 08-27, Harvard Project on International Climate Agreements, Belfer Center for Science and International Affairs, Harvard Kennedy School.

Stavins, R. N. (1995). "Transaction costs and tradeable permits." *Journal of Environmental Economics and Management*. **29**(2): 133–148.

Stavins, R. N. (1997). *Policy Instruments for Climate Change: How Can National Governments Address a Global Problem*? Discussion Paper 97-11, The University of Chicago Legal Forum, pp. 293–329.

Stavins, R. N. (1998). "What can we learn from the grand policy experiment? Lessons from SO2 allowance trading." *Journal of Economic Perspectives*. **12**(3): 69–88.

Stavins, R. N. (2003). "Experience with market-based environmental policy instruments." In K. G. Mäler and J. Vincent (eds.), *Handbook of Environmental Economics*, Vol. 1, pp. 355–435. Amsterdam, Netherlands: Elsevier Science.

Sugiyama, T. and L. Deshun. (2004). "Must developing countries commit [to] quantified targets? Time flexibility and equity in climate change mitigation." *Energy Policy*. **32**(5): 697–704.

United Nations. (1992). *United Nations Framework Convention on Climate Change.*

United Nations. (1997). *Kyoto Protocol to the Convention on Climate Change.*

U.S. Energy Information Administration. (2009). *International Energy Outlook 2009*. Report No. DOE/EIA-0484(2009). Washington, DC: Energy Information Administration.

Victor, D. G. (2001). *The Collapse of the Kyoto Protocol and the Struggle to Slow Global Warming*. Princeton, NJ: Princeton University Press.

Victor, D. G. (2007). "Fragmented carbon markets and reluctant nations: Implications for the design of effective architectures." In J. E. Aldy and R. N. Stavins (eds.), *Architectures for Agreement: Addressing Global Climate Change in the Post-Kyoto World*, pp. 133–172. New York: Cambridge University Press.

Watson, R. T. (ed.). (2001). *Climate Change 2001: Synthesis Report. Contributions of Working Group I, II, and III to the Third Assessment Report of the Intergovernmental Panel on Climate Change*. Cambridge, UK: Cambridge University Press.

Weisbach, D. (2010). *Negligence, Strict Liability, and Responsibility for Climate Change*. Working Paper, The University of Chicago Law School, Chicago, IL.

Wigley, T., R. Richels, and J. Edmonds. (1996). "Economic and environmental choices in the stabilization of atmospheric CO_2 concentrations." *Nature*. **18**: 240–243.

https://doi.org/10.1142/9789811292415_0019

Chapter 19

An Unambiguous Consequence of the Durban Climate Talks*

Robert N. Stavins

John F. Kennedy School of Government, Harvard University, Cambridge, MA, USA

National Bureau of Economic Research, Cambridge, MA, USA

Resources for the Future, Washington, DC, USA

robert_stavins@harvard.edu

In a previous essay — following the 17th Conference of the Parties (COP-17) of the United Nations Framework Convention on Climate Change (UNFCCC), which adjourned on December 11, 2011 — I offered my assessment of the Durban climate negotiations, addressing the frequently- posed question of whether the talks had "succeeded." I took note of three major outcomes from the negotiations: (1) elaboration on several components of the Cancun Agreements; (2) a second five-year commitment period for the Kyoto Protocol; and (3) a non-binding agreement to reach an agreement by 2015 that will bring all countries under the same legal regime by 2020. My conclusion was that this package — in total — represented something

*This chapter was originally published in *Review of Environment, Energy, and Economics*, 1–4, March 9, 2012.

of a "half- full glass of water," that is, an outcome that could be judged successful or not, depending upon one's perspective.

However, something I did not discuss in that previous essay is that this third provision-the "Durban Platform for Enhanced Action" — has opened an important window. To explain what I mean requires a brief review of some key points from twenty years of history of international climate negotiations.

The Rio Earth Summit (1992)

The U.N. Framework Convention on Climate Change, adopted at the U.N. Conference on Environment and Development (the first "Earth Summit") in Rio de Janeiro, Brazil, in 1992, contains what was to become a crucial passage. The first "principle" in Article 3 of the Convention reads as follows: "The Parties should protect the climate system for the benefit of present and future generations of humankind, on the basis of equity and in accordance with their *common but differentiated responsibilities and respective capabilities*. Accordingly, the developed country Parties should take the lead in combating climate change and the adverse effects thereof." [emphasis added] The countries considered to be "developed country Parties" were listed in an appendix to the 1992 Convention — Annex I.

The phrase — common but differentiated responsibilities — has been repeated countless numbers of times since 1992, but what does it really mean? The official answer was provided three years after the Earth Summit by the *first decision* adopted by the *first Conference of the Parties* (COP-1) of the U.N. Framework Convention, in Berlin, Germany, April 7, 1995 — the Berlin Mandate.

The Berlin Mandate (1995)

The Berlin Mandate interpreted the principle of "common but differentiated responsibilities" as:

1. launching a process to commit (by 1997) *the Annex I countries to quantified greenhouse gas emissions reductions within specified time periods* (targets and timetables); and
2. stating unambiguously that the process should "not introduce any new commitments for Parties not included in Annex I."

Thus, the Berlin Mandate established the dichotomous distinction whereby the Annex I countries are to take on emissions-reductions responsibilities, and the non-Annex I countries are to have no such responsibilities whatsoever.

The Kyoto Protocol (1997)

It was in direct response to this Mandate that the U.S. Senate subsequently passed unanimously (95-0) the Byrd-Hagel Resolution in August of 1997 (Senate Resolution 98, 105th Congress, 1st Session) stating that:

> It is the sense of the Senate that the United States *should not be a signatory to any protocol to*, or other agreement regarding, the United Nations Framework Convention on Climate Change of 1992, at negotiations in Kyoto in December 1997, or thereafter, which would mandate *new commitments to limit or reduce greenhouse gas emissions for the Annex I Parties, unless* the protocol or other agreement *also mandates* new specific scheduled commitments to limit or reduce greenhouse gas emissions *for Developing Country Parties* within the same compliance period.

So, in a very real sense, the Berlin Mandate brought about sustained bi-partisan opposition in the United States to the international climate regime and the Kyoto Protocol. This sealed the Protocol's fate in terms of ever being ratified by the U.S. Senate. President Clinton did not submit the Protocol to the Senate for ratification, nor would Al Gore have done so had he been elected to succeed Clinton. Likewise, Senator John Kerry was explicit about his opposition to Kyoto when he ran for President against George W. Bush, and President Bush was subsequently more than explicit about his lack of support for the Protocol and, for that matter, the UNFCCC process. When Barack Obama ran against John McCain for President in 2008, one thing on which they agreed was their opposition to the Kyoto Protocol.

Beyond those decisive impacts on U.S. climate politics, the Berlin Mandate had wide-ranging and worldwide normative consequences, because it became the anchor that prevented and has — until very recently — continued to prevent real progress in international climate negotiations. With 50 non-Annex I countries having greater per capita income than the poorest of the Annex I countries, the distinction is clearly out of whack. But, more important than that, this dichotomous distinction means that:

1. half of global emissions soon will be from nations without constraints;
2. the world's largest emitter — China — is unconstrained;
3. aggregate compliance costs are driven up to be four times their cost-effective level, because many opportunities for low-cost emissions abatement in emerging economies are taken off the table; and
4. an institutional structure is perpetuated that makes change and progress virtually impossible.

Fast Forward to Copenhagen (2009) and Cancun (2010)

The dichotomous Annex I/non-Annex I distinction remained a central — indeed, the central — feature of international climate negotiations ever since COP-1 in Berlin in 1995. Then, at COP-15 in 2009, there were hints of possible change.

The Copenhagen Accord (2009) and the Cancun Agreements (2010) began a process of blurring the Annex I/non-Annex I distinction. However, this blurring was only in the context of the interim pledge-and- review system established at COP-15 in Copenhagen and certified at COP-16 in Cancun, not in the context of an eventual successor to the Kyoto Protocol. Thus, the Berlin Mandate retained its centrality.

Finally, We Arrive in Durban (2011)

The third of the three outcomes of the December 2011 talks in Durban, South Africa, which I mentioned at the beginning of this essay — the Durban Platform for Enhanced Action — completely eliminates the Annex I/non-Annex I (or industrialized/developing country) distinction. In the Durban Platform, the delegates reached a non-binding agreement to reach an agreement by 2015 that will bring all countries under the same legal regime by 2020. That's a strange and confusing sentence, but it's what happened, and it's potentially important.

Rather than adopting the Annex I/non-Annex I (or industrialized/developing country) distinction, the Durban Platform focuses instead on the (admittedly non-binding) pledge to create a system of greenhouse gas reductions including *all Parties* (that is, all key countries) by 2015 that will come into force (after ratification) by 2020. Nowhere in the text of the decision will one find phrases such as "Annex I," "common but differentiated responsibilities," "distributional equity," "historical responsibility," all of which had long since become code words for targets for the richest countries and blank checks for all others.

A Dramatic Departure

Thus, in a dramatic departure from some seventeen years of U.N. hosted international negotiations on climate change, the 17th Conference of the Parties in Durban turned away from the Annex I/non-Annex I distinction, which had been the centerpiece of international climate policy and negotiations since it was adopted at the 1st Conference of the Parties in Berlin in 1995.

Because of this, the international law scholar, Daniel Bodansky, has labeled "the Durban Platform a complete departure from the Berlin Mandate." Likewise, Indian professor of international law, Lavanya Rajamani says that Durban delivered a "new process and with it, a clean slate on differentiation." And Elliot Diringer of the Center for Climate and Energy Solutions, finds the overall Durban deal to be "delicately poised between two eras — the fading age of Kyoto, and a new phase ... with developed and developing countries presumably on a more equal footing."

This is of vast potential importance, but — of course — only "potential" importance, because just as it was the Kyoto Protocol's numerical targets and timetables that fulfilled the Berlin Mandate's promise, it remains for the delegates to the UNFCCC to meet this Durban mandate with a new post- Kyoto agreement by 2015 (to come into force by 2020). Only time will tell whether the Durban Platform delivers on its promise, or turns out to be another "Bali Roadmap," leading nowhere.

So, with such uncertainty, what's the "unambiguous consequence" of Durban that I refer to in the title of this essay?

An Unambiguous Outcome: The Platform Opens a Window

The Durban Platform — by replacing the Berlin Mandate — has opened an important window. It is this. The national delegations from around the world now have a challenging task before them: to identify a new international climate policy architecture that is consistent with the process, pathway, and principles laid out in the Durban Platform, namely to find a way to include all key countries (such as the 20 largest national and regional economies that together account for upwards of 80 percent of global carbon dioxide emissions) in a structure that brings about meaningful emissions reductions on an appropriate timetable at acceptable cost.

Having broken the old mold, a new one must be forged. There is a mandate for change. Governments around the world now need fresh, outside-of-the-box ideas from the best thinkers, and they need those ideas over the next few years. This is a time for new proposals for future international climate policy architecture, not for incremental adjustments to the old pathway. I trust that this call will be heard by a diverse set of universities, think tanks, and — for that matter — advocacy and interest groups around the world. With research initiatives worldwide, the Harvard Project on Climate Agreements and the FEEM Research Programme on Climate Change and Sustainable Development are prepared to contribute to this effort.

https://doi.org/10.1142/9789811292415_0020

Chapter 20

Post-Durban Climate Policy Architecture Based on Linkage of Cap-and-Trade Systems*

Matthew Ranson[†] **and Robert N. Stavins**[‡,§,‖,¶]

[†]*Abt Associates Inc., Cambridge, MA, USA*

[‡]*John F. Kennedy School of Government, Harvard University, Cambridge, MA, USA*

[§]*Resources for the Future, Washington, DC, USA*

[‖]*National Bureau of Economic Research, Cambridge, USA*

[¶]*robert_stavins@harvard.edu*

*This chapter was originally published in *The Chicago Journal of International Law*, **13**(2), 403–438, Winter 2013. https://chicagounbound.uchicago.edu/cjil/vol13/iss2/7.

The second section of the chapter draws upon Jaffe, Ranson, and Stavins (2009), while the fourth section draws — in part — upon Aldy and Stavins (Cambridge 2009). We are grateful for comments we received from Blair Beasley, Dallas Burtraw, Denny Ellerman, Robert Hahn, Sheila Olmstead, William Pizer, Robert Stowe, Tom Tietenberg, and participants in the Conference on Climate Change Justice held at The University of Chicago Law School. The authors are responsible for all remaining errors.

Introduction

Twenty years ago, with the signing of the 1992 United Nations Framework Convention on Climate Change (UNFCCC) in Rio de Janeiro, the nations of the world agreed to launch a process aimed at taking action against the risks posed by global climate change. Some limited progress has been made toward that goal: cap-and-trade systems for greenhouse gases are in place or under development in the European Union (EU), Switzerland, Australia, New Zealand, South Korea, Mexico, California, the northeastern United States, and several Canadian provinces; Japan and several Chinese cities and provinces are considering implementing such systems; and a global emission reduction credit scheme — the Clean Development Mechanism — has an important constituency in the world's developing countries. However, despite these initial steps, international negotiations have not achieved their central objective: developing a climate policy architecture that is capable of delivering broad international participation and significant global CO_2 emissions reductions at reasonable cost.[1]

The recent UNFCCC talks held in Durban, South Africa, in 2011, provide an important opportunity to frame a new approach to this exceptionally difficult global commons problem. A key product of the Durban negotiations is the "Durban Platform for Enhanced Action," a non-binding agreement that calls for a new climate treaty to be reached by 2015 that brings all countries under the same legal regime by 2020.[2] Because this agreement departs from the long-standing UNFCCC division of the world's countries into those with serious emissions-reduction responsibilities (the Annex I countries) and those with no responsibilities whatsoever, it opens up the negotiation process to new thinking about international climate policy architecture.

In this Article, we evaluate one important component of international architecture for the post-Durban era: links among regional, national, and sub-national tradable permit systems for greenhouse gases. Because linkage allows emitters in high-cost cap-and-trade systems to meet their compliance obligations by purchasing allowances or credits from systems with lower marginal abatement costs, it reduces the overall cost of

[1] See generally Posner, E. A. and D. Weisbach. (2010). *Climate Change Justice*. Princeton.

[2] UN Framework Convention on Climate Change (UNFCCC), *Establishment of an Ad Hoc Working Group on the Durban Platform for Enhanced Action* (Nov 2011), Decision 1/CP.17.

achieving a given global emissions target.[3] Due to this reduction in aggregate costs, there is tremendous interest — indeed pressure — to link existing and planned cap-and-trade systems, and in fact, a number of links already or will soon exist.

Based on recent political and economic experience with linkage between tradable permit systems, we draw several preliminary conclusions about the near-term and long-term roles that linkage may play in post-Durban climate policy architecture. Because the outline of a decentralized system of direct and indirect linkages is already emerging, it is possible that in the absence of a top-down international agreement, such a collection of linkages will become the *de facto* near-term architecture for post-Durban international climate policy. Such a system has considerable promise for improving market stability while a broader international climate agreement is being negotiated. However, because direct linkages are currently planned only between systems in highly developed nations, and because most cap-and-trade systems have placed limits on the use of emissions reduction credits (which allow access to inexpensive abatement opportunities in developing countries), the near-term cost savings from this ad hoc system of links may be modest. Nonetheless, this system of linkages could still play an important near-term role by providing the institutional and political foundation for a future climate architecture. Additionally, in the longer term, linkage could provide substantial cost savings while serving as either the decentralized framework for an organic, bottom-up architecture, or as a component of a larger top-down climate architecture.

---

[3] See Jaffe, J. and R. N. Stavins. (2010). "Linkage of tradable permit systems in international climate policy architecture." In J. E. Aldy and R. N. Stavins. (Eds.), *Post-Kyoto International Climate Policy: Implementing Architectures for Agreement*, pp. 119, 129. Cambridge. As Metcalf and Weisbach explain, international links can also be established among national policies (such as carbon taxes, performance standards, and technology standards) that do not involve direct trading of emissions allowances or credits. See Metcalf, G. and D. Weisbach. (2012). "Linking policies when tastes differ: Global climate policy in a heterogeneous world!" *Review of Environmental Economics and Policy*. **6**: 110, 122, 124. However, as Metcalf and Weisbach and Hahn and Stavins argue, such non-trading links are more challenging; and current political and business interest focuses mainly on linking tradable permit systems. See Metcalf and Weisbach, *Linking Policies When Tastes Differ* at 123; Hahn, R. W. and R. N. Stavins. (1999). *What Has the Kyoto Protocol Wrought? The Real Architecture of International Tradable Permit Markets*. Washington, DC: AEI. Therefore, our exclusive focus in this paper is on linkage among trading instruments in the wake of the Durban Platform.

The remainder of this chapter is organized as follows. The second section reviews the basic economic theory of linkage between tradable permit systems. The third section describes existing and proposed links among the world's cap-and-trade systems. The fourth section discusses the Durban Platform and its implications for future linkage, and the fifth section assesses how linkage may contribute to future climate policy architecture. Finally, the last section concludes.

Theory of Linkage

We begin by describing different types of international linkages and explaining how these can affect policy considerations such as cost effectiveness, distribution of cost burdens, and national sovereignty and control.[4]

Types of linkage

The economic and environmental effects of linking different systems depend on the form of the link. One key distinction is between direct and indirect linkage.[5]

Direct linkage

Direct linkage between two systems occurs when one or both systems allow regulated entities to meet their compliance obligations by surrendering allowances or credits obtained from the other system. These direct links can be two-way (bilateral or multilateral) or one-way (unilateral).

Two-way direct linkage occurs when two cap-and-trade systems choose to recognize each other's allowances. Because of the arbitrage opportunity posed by different allowance prices, regulated entities in the

[4]See generally Jaffe, J., M. Ranson, and R. N. Stavins. (2009). "Linking tradable permit systems: A key element of emerging international climate policy architecture." *Ecology Law Quarterly*. **36**: 789. (presenting a more comprehensive treatment of the theory of linkage).

[5]*Id.* at 795–796.

system with the higher allowance price will purchase allowances from the lower-price system. As a result, emissions in the higher-price system will increase, but emissions from the lower-price system will decrease by the same amount. This flow of allowances will cause allowance prices to increase in the lower-price system and to decrease in the higher-price system until, in principle, they converge to a common intermediate price.

One-way direct linkage occurs when a cap-and-trade (CAT) system recognizes credits from an emissions-reduction-credit (ERC) system[6] or from another CAT system. In the former case, if the price of allowances is higher than the price of credits, then regulated entities in the CAT system have an incentive to purchase credits. This will increase the price of credits and reduce the price of allowances, leading prices in the two systems to converge. However, if the initial allowance price is lower than the credit price, then CAT participants will not have any reason to purchase credits, and the one-way link will have no effect on prices or the distribution of emissions. Thus, a one-way link between a cap-and-trade system and a credit system ensures that the CAT system's allowance price never exceeds the price of credits.

One-way direct linkage can also occur when one CAT system recognizes allowances from a different CAT system. As in the case described above, this type of one-way linkage ensures that allowance prices in the first CAT system never exceed allowance prices in the CAT system whose allowances it recognizes.

Governments may place limits on inter-system trading that prevent full convergence of allowance prices. For example, a government may limit the quantity of external allowances that can be used to demonstrate compliance in its own system. Alternatively, an "exchange rate" may be applied to the price of allowances or credits from other systems. Such a requirement might be used to reduce inter-system trading or to ensure that trading with other systems leads to a net reduction in emissions.

---

[6]An ERC system awards saleable credits to firms that implement voluntary projects that reduce greenhouse gas emissions relative to what emissions would have been under a counterfactual business-as-usual scenario. A prominent example of an ERC system is the Clean Development Mechanism, described in the third section.

Indirect linkages

Indirect linkages occur when two systems link directly to a common third system. Even though neither system directly links to the other, the indirect linkage created by trading with the common system allows differences in the supply and demand for allowances to propagate between the original two systems.

An important type of indirect linkage occurs when two cap-and-trade systems both create direct one-way links to the same ERC system. As a result of these links, entities in the two CAT systems will compete for the ERC system's credits. If the price of credits is lower than the price of allowances in both systems, then this indirect linkage can lead prices in all three systems to converge. As a result, developments in the market in one of the CAT systems can affect the allowance price and emissions level in the other CAT system.

A series of bilateral (two-way) linkages between several CAT systems will also result in indirect linkage. Such a system will have the same effects as direct multilateral linkage among all of the systems. For example, if System A has a two-way link with System B, which has a two-way link with System C, then trading will — again, in principle — lead allowance prices to converge across all three systems, despite the fact that A and C are not directly linked.

Implications of linking

Linkage can affect overall cost-effectiveness, the distribution of economic impacts, national control over policy design, and the incentives that nations face in setting domestic emissions reduction targets. Each of these factors has implications for the role that linkage may play in a post-Durban international policy architecture.[7]

Cost effectiveness

The most important benefit of linkage is to lower the aggregate costs of emissions reductions by allowing firms in high-cost systems to pay for less expensive abatement opportunities in lower-cost systems. The improvement in cost-effectiveness will be greatest when the two systems

---

[7] See Jaffe, Ranson, and Stavins, 36 *Ecology Law Quarterly* at 799 (cited in note 4).

face very different marginal abatement costs. Furthermore, by enlarging the scope of the relevant market, linking can improve market liquidity, reduce volatility in prices, and lessen concerns about market power.

However, linkage can also have detrimental effects on the effectiveness of domestic climate policies. A key concern is the problem of "additionality": whether purchasing credits from an emissions-reduction-credit system truly reduces overall emissions.[8] This problem arises from the difficulty of defining a counterfactual baseline against which to measure the effects of projects intended to reduce greenhouse gas (GHG) emissions. If linkage allows regulated firms in a cap-and-trade system to purchase ERC credits from emissions reduction projects that would have occurred anyway, then linkage may actually cause aggregate emissions to increase (or to decrease less than they otherwise would have).

Distribution of policy impacts

Linkage can also change the distributional impacts of GHG policies on regulated firms and the consumers that they serve. Whether a firm benefits or suffers from a new link depends on: (1) whether the firm is a net seller or net buyer of allowances, and (2) whether the firm is located in the higher- or lower- price system. For example, after a link to a system with a higher price, net sellers in the lower-price system will benefit from the opportunity to sell more allowances, and to sell them at the higher post-linkage price. However, net buyers in the lower-price system will have to pay a higher price after linking, making them worse off. Thus, although linkage improves aggregate welfare in both systems, it can also create individual winners and losers in both systems.

The distributional effects of linkage also depend on the type of systems that are linked. For example, the creation of a one-way link between a cap-and-trade system and an emissions-reduction-credit system can only benefit participants in the credit system, since these participants do not face mandatory emissions targets and thus can only benefit from the opportunity to sell emissions credits at higher prices. Hence, there is enthusiastic support for the Clean Development Mechanism from the UNFCCC's non-Annex I countries.[9]

---

[8]See Metcalf and Weisbach, 6 *Review of Environmental Economics and Policy* at 116 (cited in note 3).

[9]See Wara, M. (2007). "Is the global carbon market working?" *Nature*. **445**: 595.

National control

Because linkage exposes a domestic system to the design features and market developments of any system to which it is linked, linkage can reduce national control over the economic and environmental impacts of domestic climate change policies. However, the degree to which domestic systems lose control depends on whether links are two-way or one-way. For example, cost-containment measures — such as banking, borrowing, offsets, or safety-valve provisions — will propagate completely across a two-way link between two cap-and-trade systems. In contrast, under a one-way linkage, cost-containment measures will propagate only to the system that accepts the other's allowances.[10]

Incentives for setting caps

An additional concern about linkage is that it changes the incentives that jurisdictions face when setting their respective emissions caps.[11] Because a link can affect the allowance price within a linked jurisdiction, it can alter the fundamental tradeoff a government faces between the value it can create by issuing additional allowances and the marginal environmental damage that can arise from issuing such allowances. By expanding the scope of the allowance market, linkage can reduce the impact that the issuance of additional allowances has on allowance prices and therefore on the value of existing allowances. Further, by allowing nations with high domestic emission reduction costs to purchase less expensive emission reductions from other systems, linking can reduce the costs that such nations would face in committing to more stringent caps, thereby partially offsetting some of these effects.

For example, when a small cap-and-trade system establishes a direct link with a larger cap-and-trade system, the administrator of the smaller system may be tempted to issue a larger number of allowances in order to raise government revenues or benefit domestic firms. Alternatively, linkage to the larger allowance market may allow the smaller system to

---

[10]Technically speaking, some price effects of cost-containment measures do propagate in both directions of a one-way linkage, via supply and demand effects in the linking and target systems.

[11]See Helm, C. (2003). "International emissions trading with endogenous allowance choices." *Journal of Public Economics*. **87**: 2737–2738.

tighten its cap dramatically, achieving its targets by displacing costs onto foreign firms in the linked system.

Characteristics of Existing and Proposed Linkages

Despite the hiatus in the US of serious consideration of a national CO_2 cap-and-trade system, such systems are in place or under development in the European Union, Switzerland, Australia, New Zealand, South Korea, Mexico, California, the northeastern US, and several Canadian provinces, and are under consideration in Japan and parts of China.[12] Additionally, a global emissions-reduction-credit scheme (the Clean Development Mechanism) has an important constituency of supporters in the world's developing countries.[13] In this section, we review these systems and describe existing and proposed links among them.

Linkage among existing trading systems

Because governments face strong economic and political incentives to link to other systems, there are already a number of links established or proposed between existing tradable GHG (mostly CO_2) permit systems.

Emissions trading under Article 17 of the Kyoto Protocol

Under the Kyoto Protocol, each Annex I country took on a quantitative emissions target for the 2008 to 2012 compliance period. These emissions targets are expressed in Assigned Amount Units (AAUs). Under Article 17 of the protocol, AAUs may be bought and sold by national governments, with the condition that each government must have a sufficient number of AAUs at the end of the compliance period to cover its actual emissions.[14] When two governments exchange AAUs, they create an implicit link between their domestic climate policies.

---

[12] See Guoyi Han *et al.*, *China's Carbon Emission Trading: An Overview of Current Development* 10 (*Fores* 2012).

[13] See Wara, 445 *Nature* at 595 (cited in note 9).

[14] See Kyoto Protocol to the United Nations Framework Convention on Climate Change Art 3 §10 (1997), 37 ILM 22 (1998).

An important obstacle to the successful operation of such a system is that by its very nature, the trading is among nations.[15] Unlike private firms, nation-states are not simple cost-minimizers, and so there is no reason to anticipate that competitive pressures will lead to equating of marginal abatement costs across countries. Furthermore, even if nations did try to minimize costs, they would not have sufficient information about the marginal abatement costs of domestic firms to define their own national aggregate marginal cost functions.[16] Thus, such a system does not have the cost-effectiveness property ordinarily associated with tradable permit systems among firms, and the notion of linkage via trading between countries may be more of a metaphor than a practical policy. To date, sales of AAUs have been modest relative to sales of other types of credits.[17]

Clean development mechanism

The Kyoto Protocol's Clean Development Mechanism (CDM) is the world's largest emissions-reduction-credit system.[18] Under the CDM, firms and other entities in non-Annex I (developing) countries can be awarded certified emission reduction (CER) credits for conducting voluntary projects that reduce greenhouse gas emissions.[19] These projects can take a variety of possible forms, such as building new wind farms, installing more energy efficient equipment in manufacturing facilities, or capturing methane from landfills.[20] CERs can then be purchased by regulated emitters in Annex I countries for use in meeting their domestic emissions commitments.[21] CERs could also be used for entities covered

---

[15] See Hahn and Stavins, *What Has the Kyoto Protocol Wrought?* at 10 (cited in note 3).

[16] *Id.* at 9.

[17] See Marton Kruppa, *Slovakia Eyes AAU Sales to Spain: PointCarbon* (*Reuters* December 21, 2011), online at http://www.reuters.com/article/2011/12/21/us-carbon-slovakia-aau-idUSTRE7BK17V20111221 (visited October 16, 2012); US Energy Information Administration, *Annual Energy Outlook 2011,* DOE/EIA-0383 (April 2011).

[18] See Wara, 445 Nature at 595 (cited in note 9). Anja Kollmuss, Helge Zink, and Clifford Polycarp, *Making Sense of the Voluntary Carbon Market: A Comparison of Carbon Offset Standards* *93 (WWF Germany 2008), online at assets.panda.org/downloads/vcm_report_final.pdf (visited November 4, 2012).

[19] See UNFCCC, *CDM Fact Sheet: General* (May 2012), online at http://cdm.unfccc.int/press/docs/CDM_fact_sheet.pdf (visited November 1, 2012).

[20] *Id.*

[21] *Id.*

by cap-and-trade systems in countries that are not parties to the protocol (in particular, the US).[22]

From the perspective of the developing countries, the CDM provides a mechanism for financing "sustainable development."[23] From the perspective of the industrialized countries, the CDM provides a means to engage developing countries in the control of GHG emissions while simultaneously reducing the costs of achieving domestic emissions targets.[24] Because it tends to be much less expensive to construct new low-carbon energy infrastructure in developing nations than to modify or replace existing infrastructure in industrialized countries,[25] international trading in CERs could significantly reduce the aggregate cost of compliance with the Kyoto Protocol.

A number of cap-and-trade programs explicitly allow the use of CDM credits, including existing systems in the European Union, Switzerland, and New Zealand, as well as a future system in Australia.[26] Most CDM projects have been funded by European parties: Investors in the United Kingdom have sponsored 31 percent of all CDM projects, Swiss investors have sponsored 21 percent, Japanese investors 10 percent, Dutch 9 percent, Swedish 7 percent, and German 5 percent.[27]

---

[22] See Lecocq, F. and P. Ambrosi, "The clean development mechanism: History, status, and prospects." *Review of Environmental Economics and Policy*. **1**: 134, 139.

[23] See Kyoto Protocol, Art 12 §2.

[24] *Id.*

[25] See Wara, 445 *Nature* at 595 (cited in note 9).

[26] See *Directive 2004/101/EC of the European Parliament and of the Council* 18, European Parliament, L338 Official J EU (October 27, 2004); Swiss Federal Office for the Environment, *Emissions, Credits, Offsetting and Trading* (Nov 2007), Referenz/Aktenzeichen: G452-1577; *Guidance on the Use of CERs in the NZ ETS*, New Zealand Ministry for the Environment (2012), online at http://climatechange.govt.nz/emissions-trading-scheme/building/regulatory-updates/guidance-identifying-banned-restriction-cers.pdf (visited October 16, 2012); Australian Clean Energy International Unit Surrender Charge Act 2011, No. 158 §8 (2011); European Commission, *EU Action Against Climate Change: The EU Emissions Trading Scheme* 23 (2008).

[27] See UNFCCC, *Registered Projects by AI and NAI Investor Parties* (September 2012).

The CDM has accounted for annual CO2-equivalent reductions of 278 million tons, about 1 percent of annual global emissions of CO_2.[28] The largest shares of CERs have been generated in China (55 percent) and India (15 percent), with Latin America and the Caribbean making up another 14 percent of the total. Brazil, at 6 percent, is the largest CER producer in that region.[29] Of the CERs expected to be generated by projects in the CDM pipeline by 2012, 35 percent are for renewables, 29 percent are for HFC and N_2O reduction, 19 percent are for methane reduction, and the remaining 17 percent are for electricity generation, fuel switching, and other projects.[30]

As an ERC system, the CDM raises important concerns about additionality (the problem of whether basing credits on an unobservable hypothetical baseline leads to credits being granted for emission reductions that would have occurred in any case). Empirical analysis has validated these concerns, with estimates that many claimed reductions would have occurred even m the absence of the program.[31]

An additional concern has centered on the fact that nearly 30 percent of average annual CERs have come from the destruction of HFC-23, a potent GHG that is a byproduct of the manufacture of certain refrigerant gases.[32] It is very inexpensive to destroy HFC-23, and companies can earn nearly twice as much from the sale of CDM credits as they can from selling respective refrigerant gases.[33] As a result, it has been argued that plants were being built simply for the purpose of generating CERs from destruction of HFC-23. Because of this, beginning in 2013, CERs from HFC-23 destruction will not be valid for purposes of compliance with the EU Emissions Trading System.[34]

---

[28] See Wara, 445 *Nature* at 595 (cited in note 9). Note that carbon sequestration projects of forestation and reduced deforestation are not included in the CDM under the Kyoto Protocol's first commitment period, 2008–2012.

[29] See UN Environment Programme, *CDM Projects by Host Region* (September 2012).

[30] See UN Environment Programme, *CDM Projects Grounded in Type* (Sept 2012).

[31] See Zhang, J. and C. Wang. (2011). "Co-benefits and additionality of the clean development mechanism: An empirical analysis." *Journal of Environmental Economics and Management*. **62**: 140, 142.

[32] See UN Environment Programme, *Growth of Total Expected Accumulated 2012* CERs (September 2012).

[33] Wara, 445 *Nature* at 596 (cited in note 9).

[34] See European Commission, *Emissions Trading: Commission Welcomes Vote to Ban Certain Industrial Gas Credits* (January 2011), online at http://europa.eu/rapid/pressReleasesAction.do?reference=IP/11/56 (visited October 16, 2012).

As negotiations continue regarding the details of a second commitment period for the Kyoto Protocol, the CDM will most likely continue to function in any case.[35] However, a variety of proposals have been put forward to improve its structure and implementation, many targeted at increasing the additionality of approved projects.[36] There have also been discussions of alternative mechanisms for engaging developing countries, such as "new market mechanisms" for sectoral crediting.[37]

Joint implementation

Joint Implementation (JI) is another Kyoto Protocol flexibility mechanism. It allows entities in Annex I countries to generate and sell offset credits — known as Emission Reduction Units (ERUs) — to one another.[38] Like the COM, JI is a project-based ERC system whose credits raise concerns about additionality, although the concerns are somewhat different since countries that can participate in JI projects have caps under the Kyoto Protocol.

The market for ERUs has been less robust than the market for CERs. As of April 2012, host countries had issued 233 million ERUs.[39] Of the 612 approved projects, 194 were based in Ukraine, 178 in Russia, 59 in the Czech Republic, 39 in Bulgaria, and 25 in Poland, with the remainder primarily in Europe.[40]

---

[35] See Daniel Bodansky, *W[h]ither the Kyoto Protocol? Durban and Beyond*, Viewpoints 1, 6 (Harvard Project on Climate Agreements August 2011), online at http://belfercenter.ksg.harvard.edu/files/Bodansky_Viewpoint-Final.pdf (visited Nov 22, 2012).

[36] See Daniel S. Hall, *et al.*, *Policies for Developing Country Engagement*, in Aldy and Stavins, eds., *Post-Kyoto International Climate Policy* 649, 660 (cited in note 3).

[37] See International Emissions Trading Association, *IETA Response to the AWG-LCA Call for Input Regarding New Market-Based Mechanisms* *1 (February 2011), online at https://ieta.memberclicks.net/assets/EUWG/ieta-awg-lca-subrnission-on-market-based-mechanisms-feb-2011-3-web.pdf (visited October 16, 2012).

[38] See Joseph Aldy and Robert N. Stavins, *The Promise and Problems of Pricing Carbon: Theory and Experience*, Belfer Center Discussion Paper *17 n 16 (Harvard University November 2011), online at http://live.belfercenter.org/files/Aldy%20Stavins%20Pricing%20Carbon%20ENRP.pdf (visited November 1, 2012).

[39] See United Nations Environment Programme, *Status of JI Projects*, (September 1, 2012), online at http://cdmpipeline.org/ji-projects.htm (visited October 16, 2012).

[40] *Id.*

European Union Emissions Trading System

The European Union Emissions Trading System (EU ETS) is a downstream CO_2 cap-and-trade system that is by far the world's largest carbon pricing regime.[41] This system, which was adopted in 2003, covers about half of CO emissions from thirty European countries.[42] The EU ETS has been implemented in phases: a first (pilot) phase from 2005 to 2007, a second (Kyoto) phase from 2008 to 2012, and a scheduled third phase from 2013 to 2020. Although the first phase allowed trading only in carbon dioxide, the second phase broadened the program to include some other GHGs from certain industrial sectors, such as nitrous oxide emissions from nitric acid production. The 11,500 regulated sources include large sources such as oil refineries, combustion installations over twenty megawatts thermal, coke ovens, cement factories, and pulp and paper producers.[43] Although EU ETS allowance prices averaged €22 in the second half of 2008, prices had fallen to €7 in 2012 as the economic recession brought reduced economic activity and decreased demand for allowances.[44]

The European Commission's Linking Directive allowed EU ETS participants to use CERs from the CDM beginning in 2005 and ERUs from the JI program beginning in 2008, although certain types of projects, such as land use change, forestry, and nuclear power, have not been eligible for credits,[45] and industrial gas destruction projects will cease to be eligible

---

[41] See European Commission, *Emissions Trading System (EU ETS)* (2010), online at http://ec.europa.eu/clima/policies/ets/index_en.htm (visited October 16, 2012).

[42] *Id.* The EU ETS covers all 27 EU member states plus Iceland, Liechtenstein, and Norway. Iceland, Liechtenstein, and Norway joined the EU ETS in 2008, although sources in Iceland are not yet subject to an emissions cap.

[43] See Ellerman, A. D. and B. K. Buchner. (2007). "The European Union emissions trading scheme: Origins, allocation, and early results." *Review of Environmental Economics and Policy*. **1**: 66, 68, 72 n 9.

[44] In addition, a set of "complementary policies," such as those aimed at increasing the use of renewable sources of energy, have had the effect of reducing emissions in one sector only to see them increase in other sectors under the EU ETS umbrella, thereby accomplishing no additional net emissions reductions, but increasing aggregate costs (decreasing cost effectiveness) by maintaining heterogeneous marginal abatement costs, and reducing allowance prices in the EU ETS.

[45] See *Directive 2004/101/EC of the European Parliament and of the Council* at 18; European Commission, *EU Action Against Climate Change: The EU Emissions Trading Scheme* at 23 (cited in note 26).

after 2013.[46] Because of these links, CER and ERU prices are heavily dependent on EU ETS allowance prices.[47]

During the first and second trading periods, EU ETS member nations each set national limits on the use of credits as a percentage of total allowances, with limits ranging from 0 percent in Estonia to 20 percent in Lithuania and Spain.[48] In future trading periods, the European Commission has mandated that no more than half of the EU ETS overall emissions reductions target may be achieved through credits. Furthermore, for projects initiated in 2013 or later, the EU ETS will recognize CERs only from nations on the UN's list of Least Developed Countries (LDCs) (most of which are in Africa), thereby eliminating projects from the countries that currently dominate the supply, most notably China and India. CERs flowing from projects begun prior to 2013 in more developed non-Annex I countries will continue to be allowed.[49]

To some degree, the EU ETS can itself be viewed as a large multilateral linkage among its member counties, in which each country recognizes allowances issued by all other members.[50] This was particularly true in the first and second trading periods, during which each country proposed its own individual emissions cap for review by the European Commission.[51] This created incentives for individual countries to try to be generous with

---

[46] See European Commission, *Emissions Trading: Commission Welcomes Vote to Ban Certain Industrial Gas Credits* (cited in note 34).

[47] See, for example, Oliver Sartor, *The EU ETS Carbon Price: To Intervene, or Not to Intervene?* 12 Climate Brief CDC Climate Research 1 (February 2012); *CER Market Steadies After Price Hit* (CarbonPositive, November 10, 2008), Point Carbon Advisory Services, *Issues in the International Carbon Market, 2008–2012 and Beyond* 3–4 (Study for New Zealand Emissions Trading Group, October 2007); *CER Prices Ease with EU Carbon,* (CarbonPositive, February 15, 2007).

[48] See European Commission, *Emissions Trading: Commission Adopts Decisions on Amendments to Five National Allocation Plans for 2008–2012* 2 (July 2007), IP/07/1094.

[49] See European Commission, *Questions and Answers on Use of International Credits in the Third Trading Phase of the EU ETS* (November 14, 2011), online at http://ec.europa.eu/clima/policies/ets/linking/docs/q_a_20111114_en.pdf (visited October 16, 2012).

[50] See Denny Ellerman, *The EU Emission Trading Scheme: A Prototype Global System?* in Aldy and Stavins, eds., *Post-Kyoto International Climate Policy* 88, 88, 90 (cited in note 3).

[51] See Kruger, J., W. Oates, and W. Pizer. (2007). "Decentralization in the EU Emissions Trading Scheme and lessons for global policy." *Review of Environmental Economics and Policy*. **1**: 112, 115–116.

their allowances to protect their economic competitiveness.[52] Not surprisingly, the result was an aggregate cap that-at least in Phase I-exceeded business-as-usual emissions.[53] However, for future trading periods, caps have been determined through a more centralized process at the EU level.[54]

Norwegian Emissions Trading Scheme

From 2005 to 2007, Norway operated an Emissions Trading Scheme, which covered 10 percent to 15 percent of national CO2 emissions and imposed a cap equal to 95 percent of 1998–2001 levels.[55] The system included a one-way linkage with the EU ETS, which allowed Norwegian firms to meet their compliance obligations by purchasing emissions permits from the EU ETS.[56] In 2007, the three non-EU member countries of the European Economic Area — Norway, Iceland, and Liechtenstein — joined the EU ETS through the adoption of the EU ETS Directive[57] into the

[52] See Convery, F. and L. Redmond. (2007). "Market and price developments in the European Union Emissions Trading Scheme." *Review of Environmental Economics and Policy*. **1**: 88, 94.

[53] Due to a variety of factors, including the economic recession and the ability of regulated entities to bank allowances into Phase III, it is difficult to assess the system's performance in Phase II.

[54] See *Directive 2009/ 29/ EC of the European Parliament and of the Council*, European Parliament, L140 Official J EU 63 (May 9, 2009); European Commission, *Allocation 2005–2012* (November 15, 2010), online at http://ec.europa.eu/clima/policies/ets/allocation/index_en.htm (visited October 16, 2012).

[55] The Norwegian ETS was designed to be compatible with the EU ETS. See M.J. Mace, *et al., Analysis of the Legal and Organisational Issues Arising in Linking the EU Emissions Trading Scheme to Other Existing and Emerging Emissions Trading Schemes* 6 (Study Commissioned by the European Commission Directorate General–Environment, Climate Change, and Air, May 2008).

[56] Annegrete Bruvoll and Hanne Marit Dalen, *Pricing of CO_2 Emissions in Norway: Documentation of Data and Methods Used in Estimations of Average CO_2 Tax Rates in Norwegian Sectors in 2006*, Statistics Norway 1, 18 (2009).

[57] *Directive 2003/87/EC of the European Parliament and of the Council*, European Parliament (Oct 13, 2003), online at http://eur-lex.europa.eu/LexUriServ/LexUriServ.do?uri=CONSLEG:2003L0087:20090625:EN:PDF (visited November 4, 2012), as amended.

European Economic Area (EEA) agreement.[58] With this agreement, Norway and the other EEA members agreed to follow the same process for setting national caps as the EU member states.

Swiss CO_2 Act

Since 2008, Switzerland has operated a quasi-voluntary cap-and-trade system based on the authority of its CO_2 Act. Under this program, companies can be exempted from a mandatory CO_2 tax on fossil fuels in exchange for taking on a legal commitment under the cap-and-trade system.[59] Under the Swiss system, companies may meet up to 8 percent of their emissions targets using CDM and JI credits.[60] Although Swiss and EU participants cannot currently use each other's allowances, the Swiss government has begun negotiations with the European Commission to create a link between the Swiss trading program and the EU ETS, mostly likely starting in 2014.[61]

New Zealand Emissions Trading Scheme

In January 2008, the New Zealand Emissions Trading Scheme (NZ ETS) was launched. The forestry sector entered the program first, in 2008, and stationary energy, industrial, and liquid fossil fuel sectors joined in 2010. Early evidence suggests that the forestry component has deterred

---

[58] See European Commission, *Emissions Trading: Commission Announces Linkage EU ETS with Norway, Iceland, and Liechtenstein* (October 26, 2007), online at http://europa.eu/rapid/pressReleasesAction.do?reference=IP/07/1617 (visited October 16, 2012); Norwegian Ministry of the Environment, *Norway's Fifth National Communication Under the Framework Convention on Climate Change: Status Report as of December 2009* 36–37 (December 2009). Iceland and Liechtenstein did not previously have cap-and-trade systems.

[59] See Mace, *et al.*, *Analysis of the Legal and Organisational Issues Arising in Linking the EU Emissions Trading Scheme* at 7–8 (cited in note 55).

[60] See Swiss Federal Office for the Environment, *Emissions, Credits, Offsetting and Trading* 3 (November 2007).

[61] See Council of the European Union, *EU to Link Its Greenhouse Gas Emissions Trading System with Switzerland* (December 20, 2010), 18085/10 PRESSE 353; *Switzerland sees EU ETS Link in 2014* (Point Carbon, May 11, 2012).

deforestation, although international policy and consequent price uncertainty are major problems for investment.[62] The waste (landfills) sector is scheduled to enter in 2013, and agriculture — which accounts for nearly half of New Zealand's gross emissions — is scheduled to enter in 2015.[63] Thus, the intention of the system is to include all sectors of the economy and all greenhouse gases by 2015.[64] The NZ ETS features free allocation of allowances, with special protections (output-based updating allocations) for emission-intensive, trade-sensitive sectors, as well as a safety valve that allows participants to meet their obligations by paying a fee of NZ$25 per ton.[65] Additionally, a recent five-year government review recommended that the agriculture sector face a lower price as it enters the system.[66]

Currently, the NZ ETS allows participants to use an unlimited number of credits from the CDM and JI programs, as well as AAU allowances converted from other UNFCCC signatories.[67] Preliminary emissions registry data suggest that 20 percent of New Zealand emissions have been covered using relatively inexpensive AAUs from Hungary.[68] However, certain categories of offset credits are not eligible, such as those based on HFC-23 and N_2O industrial gas destruction.[69] The ETS also includes several features intended to protect participants from the potential price

---

[62] See Eric Karpas and Suzi Kerr, *Preliminary Evidence on Responses to the New Zealand Forestry Emissions Trading Scheme* *36–38 (Motu Working Paper 11-09, June 2011).

[63] See generally NZ Ministry for the Environment, *The New Zealand Emissions Trading Scheme*.

[64] See Emissions Trading Scheme Review Panel, *Doing New Zealand's Fair Share: Emissions Trading Scheme Review 2011: Final Report* 6 (Wellington: Ministry for the Environment, June 30, 2011).

[65] *Id.* at 29; New Zealand Climate Change Response Act, Pub Act 2002 No 40§ 222C (November 18, 2005).

[66] See Emissions Trading Scheme Review Panel, *Doing New Zealand's Fair Share* at 8 (cited in note 64).

[67] See Ministry for the Environment and the Treasury, *The Framework for a New Zealand Emissions Trading Scheme* 46–48 (September 2007), Pub No. ME 810.

[68] *Recent Global Carbon Politics*, 7:34 Carbon Market North America 5 (*Reuters* 2012).

[69] See New Zealand Ministry for the Environment, *Guidance on the Use of CERs in the NZ ETS* (February 2012).

effects of international demand for its allowances (known as New Zealand Units, or NZUs). The establishing legislation prohibits export of NZUs if the total number of NZUs held within the country falls below 90 percent of the initial allocation for that trading period. Additionally, in response to the recession, in 2009 the New Zealand government prohibited participants in all sectors except forestry from exporting any allowances until 2013.[70]

Some features of the New Zealand ETS, particularly the way that allowances are allocated, were chosen for compatibility with Australia's previously proposed Carbon Pollution Reduction Scheme (CPRS). Although the CPRS never became law, the possibility of linking to a future Australian system was — and is — an important consideration for the New Zealand ETS, especially in light of the close trade relationship between the two countries.[71] In 2011, the New Zealand government announced plans to establish a two-way linkage with Australia's forthcoming emissions trading program,[72] beginning in 2015.[73] The details of this linkage have not yet been finalized.

Establishing a direct linkage between the New Zealand ETS and the EU ETS poses greater challenges. Because forest sink credits are a major part of the New Zealand ETS but are not allowed by the EU ETS, the creation of a direct link between the two systems is unlikely in the near future.[74] However, as a result of its direct link to the CDM, the New Zealand ETS does have an indirect linkage to the EU ETS. Because non-forestry New Zealand sources are required to surrender only one allowance per two units of emissions until 2013, the current effective price of NZ allowances is very low.[75]

---

[70] See New Zealand Climate Change Response Act, Pub Act 2002 No 40 at §222G.

[71] See Emissions Trading Scheme Review Panel, *Doing New Zealand's Fair Share* at 28 (cited in note 64).

[72] Australia Clean Energy Act, No 131, ComLaw Authoritative Act C2011A00131 (2011).

[73] See Greg Combet and Tim Graser, *Joint Media Release: Australia and New Zealand Advance Linking of Their Emissions Trading Schemes,* 333/11 GC 1 (December 5, 2011).

[74] See Brian Fallow, *NZ–Europe ETS Link a Long Way Off, Says Official,* NZ Herald (March 30, 2011).

[75] See New Zealand Climate Change Response Act, Pub Act 2002 No 40 at §222B; Karpas and Kerr, *Preliminary Evidence* at *26 (cited in note 62).

Regional Greenhouse Gas Initiative

The Regional Greenhouse Gas Initiative (RGGI) is a downstream cap-and-trade program that limits CO_2 emissions from power sector sources in nine northeastern US states (Connecticut, Delaware, Maine, Maryland, Massachusetts, New Hampshire, New York, Rhode Island, and Vermont).[76] Like the EU ETS, RGGI can be envisioned, to some degree, as a linked set of state-level cap-and-trade programs.

The system is both narrow in its sectoral coverage and unambitious in terms of its emissions reduction objectives. RGGI took effect in 2009 after approval by individual state legislatures and set a goal of lowering emissions to 10 percent below 2009 levels by 2019.[77] It was originally anticipated that meeting this goal would require a reduction of approximately 35 percent below business-as-usual emissions levels.[78] However, due to the combined effects of the economic recession and drastic declines in natural gas prices relative to coal prices, the cap is no longer binding and is unlikely to become binding through 2020, unless the cap trajectory is adjusted.[79]

The Model Rule governing RGGI's implementation allows for two types of one-way linkages. First, covered sources may meet up to 3.3 percent of their compliance obligations using allowances generated by certain types of offset CO_2 projects located in one of the RGGI states or in

[76] See Regional Greenhouse Gas Initiative (RGGI), *About the Regional Greenhouse Gas Initiative (RGGI)*. In May of 2011, New Jersey Governor Chris Christie announced that his state would withdraw from the system. See Mireya Navarro, *Christie Pulls New Jersey From 10-State Climate Initiative, New York Times* A20 (May 27, 2011).

[77] See Aldy and Stavins, *The Promise and Problems of Pricing Carbon* at *15 (cited in note 38).

[78] *Id.*

[79] See id; RGGI, *About the Regional Greenhouse Gas Initiative (RGGI)* (cited in note 76). Allowance prices have reflected these realities, falling from approximately $3 per ton of CO_2 at the first auction in September 2008, to the floor price of $1.93 per ton in 2012. See RGGI CO_2 Allowance Tracking Report, *Transaction Price Report* (2012), online at https://rggi-coats.org/eats/rggi/index.cfm?fuseaction=reportsv2.price_rpt&%20clearfuseatt%20ribs=true (visited October 16, 2012). In response, RGGI states are considering lowering the emissions cap for the 2014 to 2020 period. See *RGGI Officials to Weigh Lower CO_2 Caps* (Point Carbon, March 5, 2012).

another US jurisdiction that has completed a memorandum of understanding with the RGGI states.[80] The 3.3 percent limitation was chosen so that no more than half of all emissions reductions between 2009 and 2020, relative to projected baseline emissions at the time the Model Rule was written, would be achieved using offsets.[81] To address uncertainty about future abatement costs, the rule includes price triggers that allow greater use of offsets if average annual allowance prices exceed certain thresholds. If the price exceeds \$7 (in 2005 dollars), sources may use offsets for up to 5 percent of their compliance obligations, and if the price exceeds a "stage two threshold price" that begins at \$10 in 2005 and increases by about 2 percent each subsequent year, then sources may use offsets for up to 10 percent of their compliance obligations.[82]

The second type of linkage allowed by RGGI is one-way linkage to other international CAT and ERC systems. If annual allowance prices exceed the "stage two threshold price," then RGGI sources may satisfy their compliance obligations using CERs from UNFCCC emissions-reduction-credit programs or allowances from any other cap-and-trade system outside the United States.[83]

As of the spring of 2012, no applications for approval for offset projects have ever been submitted to RGGI[84] because of the low RGGI allowance price.[85] Furthermore, because RGGI prices have remained far below

---

[80] See RGGI, *Part XX CO_2 Budget Trading Program,* 63, 105 (January 5, 2007), online at http://rggi.org/docs/model_rule_corrected_1_5_07.pdf (visited October 16, 2012). The Revised Memorandum of Understanding among the RGGI states also allows offset credits from non-RGGI US states with cap-and-trade systems. See RGGI, *Amendment to Memorandum of Understanding* 2 (August 8, 2006). However, this provision was not included in the Model Rule that serves as the basis for the state regulations.

[81] See RGGI, *Analysis Supporting Offsets Limit Recommendation* (May 1, 2006).

[82] See RGGI, *Part XX CO_2 Budget Trading Program* at 17–18, 63 (cited in note 80).

[83] *Id.* at 105–06.

[84] See RGGI CO_2 Allowance Tracking System, *Public: Offset Projects* (2012), online at https://rggi-coats.org/eats/rggi/index.cfm?fuseaction=search.project_offset&clearfuse%20attribs=true (visited October 16, 2012).

[85] See RGGI, *Fact Sheet: RGGI CO_2 Allowance Auctions* (2010), RGGI CO_2 Allowance Tracking System, *Transaction Price Report* (cited in note 79).

the $10 stage two threshold price, RGGI sources have never been permitted to use CERs or other CAT systems' allowances.[86]

Possible linkage among future trading systems

Several new cap-and-trade systems will come into effect in the near future. Although details of these systems remain to be determined through promulgation of specific regulations, the respective authorizing legislation provides insights into the likely future role of linkage in each system.[87]

Australia's Clean Energy Act of 2011

In 2011, Australia's government passed its Clean Energy Act, which imposes a carbon tax of approximately AUD$25/ton for the period from 2012 to 2015, after which the tax is to be replaced by a cap-and-trade system.[88] The Act includes a number of features directed at possible linkage with other systems. Import and export of allowances is allowed,[89] although the government may set charges on international allowances and credits of up to AUD$15 in 2015, AUD$16 in 2016, and AUD$17.05 in 2017.[90]

Furthermore, the government is tasked specifically with developing regulations on the use of foreign allowances that take into account Australia's international objectives and obligations as well as the environmental integrity of Australia's system.[91] As discussed above, Australia and New Zealand have announced plans to link their trading systems beginning in 2015, once Australia's carbon tax converts to a cap-and-trade system.[92] Additionally, Australian and European Commission officials have announced plans to allow Australian cap-and-trade participants to use EU ETS allowances to cover up to 50 percent of their liabilities starting in 2015, via a one-way linkage. By 2018, the EU and Australia have agreed to establish a full two-way linkage between their emissions trading

---

[86] See RGGI, *Part XX CO_2 Budget Trading Program* at 17–18, 63 (cited in note 80).

[87] We exclude some systems from our analysis. As of early 2012, British Columbia, Manitoba, and Ontario have not yet finalized cap-and-trade regulations.

[88] See Australia Clean Energy Act, No. 131 §100.

[89] *Id.* at §§108–09.

[90] See Australian Clean Energy International Unit Surrender Charge Act 2011, No. 158 §8.

[91] See Australia Clean Energy Act, No. 131 §123.

[92] See Combet and *Groser, Joint Media Release* (cited in note 73).

systems. To facilitate this connection, Australia has agreed to drop its plans for a carbon price floor and to limit the use of Kyoto credits (such as CERs and ERUs) to no more than 12.5 percent of total emissions.[93]

California's Global Warming Solutions Act of 2006

California's Global Warming Solutions Act of 2006 directed the California Air Resources Board (CARB) to promulgate regulations to achieve the goal of reducing the state's greenhouse gas emissions to 1990 levels by the year 2020, a very ambitious target by North American standards. In 2011, CARB finalized a rule that establishes a cap-and-trade system as the primary mechanism by which the state will achieve this goal, beginning in 2013.[94] The regulation includes several cost-containment measures, including banking of allowances and a strategic allowance reserve, as well as allowing for linkage to other systems.[95]

Two types of links are allowed by current regulations governing the cap-and-trade system. First, facilities may use offsets (of any approved type) for up to 8 percent of their compliance obligations.[96] Initially, credit will only be given for offsets from US based projects involving forestry, dairy digesters, and destruction of ozone-depleting substances. However, the regulations create a framework for possible future linkage to CDM, JI, and other international ERC programs,[97] and California has completed a joint memorandum of understanding with Chiapas, Mexico, and Acre, Brazil, that could allow the use of avoided deforestation offsets from these two states as soon as 2015.[98] Second, the regulations allow for unrestricted

---

[93] See European Commission, *Australia and European Commission Agree on Path1JJqys Towards Fully Linking Emissions Trading Systems* (August 28, 2012), online at http://europa.eu/rapid/pressReleasesAction.do?reference=IP/12/916&format=HTML&aged=O&language=EN&guiLanguage=en (visited October 16, 2012).

[94] See California Environmental Protection Agency, *Overview of ARB Emissions Trading Program* (October 20, 2011).

[95] *Id.*

[96] See California Cap on Greenhouse Gas Emissions and Market-Based Compliance Mechanisms, Cal Code Reg 10-5 §95854.

[97] See California Environmental Protection Agency, *Overview of ARB Emissions Trading Program* (cited in note 94).

[98] See Daniel F. Morris, Nathan Richardson, and Anne Riddle, *Importing Climate Mitigation: The Potential and Challenges of International Forest Offsets in California Climate Policy* 1 (Resources for the Future 2011).

use of allowances from directly linked cap-and-trade systems.[99] In March 2012, regulations were proposed that would create a two-way direct link with Quebec's cap-and-trade system, although this linkage was delayed by a legislative subcommittee in 2012.[100] Links with other US states and Canadian provinces may come later via the Western Climate Initiative.[101]

Quebec's cap-and-trade system

In 2011, the Quebec government adopted regulations establishing a cap-and-trade system for industrial facilities emitting more than 25,000 tons of CO2 per year.[102] This system, which will begin capping emissions starting in 2013, is explicitly based on design criteria established by the Western Climate Initiative.[103] Indeed, the regulation allows for linkage with other cap-and-trade systems with which the government of Quebec has concluded an agreement, and Québec plans to link to California's cap-and-trade system.[104] However, the Québec system restricts facilities from using domestic offsets to cover more than 8 percent of their emissions and

---

[99] See Cal *Code Reg* 10-5 §§95821, 95941–42.

[100] See California Air Resources Board, *Discussion Draft--March 30, 2012 Amendments to the California Cap on Greenhouse Gas Emissions and Market-Based Compliance Mechanisms to Allow for the Use of Compliance Instruments Issued by Linked Jurisdictions* §95943 (2012); *California Lawmakers Seek Delay to Quebec ETS Link* (Point Carbon, May 24, 2012).

[101] See Western Climate Initiative, *Design for the WCI Regional Program* 22 (July 2010). The Western Climate Initiative originally was to include eleven western US states and Canadian provinces, and now is likely to begin with California, Ontario, and Québec, which are contemplating linking their developing state/provincial CO_2 cap-and-trade systems beginning in 2013.

[102] See Québec Department of Sustainable Development, Environment, and Parks, *Carbon Market in North America — Adoption of Regulations for the Cap-and-Trade GHG Emission* (December 15, 2011), online at http://www.mddep.gouv.qc.ca/infuseur/communique.asp?no=2012 (visited October 16, 2012).

[103] See International Emissions Trading Association, *Summary of Quebec's Regulation Respecting a Cap-and-Trade System for Greenhouse Gas Emission Allowance* 1 (February 23, 2012).

[104] See Québec Environmental Quality Act, *Regulation Respecting a Cap-and-Trade System for Greenhouse Gas Emission Allowances,* c. Q-2, r. 46.1 at III.I.37(3) (2012).

does not currently allow linking with international sources of offset credits, such as the CDM.[105]

China's emissions trading system pilots

In late 2010, the Chinese government released its Twelfth Five-Year-Plan, which calls for the establishment of a national carbon emission trading system by 2015. The government has begun work to establish pilot cap-and-trade programs in the cities of Beijing, Tianjin, Shanghai, Chongqing, and Shenzhen, and the provinces of Hubei and Guangdong, by 2013 or 2014.[106] Because the basic characteristics of these pilot systems (such as whether they will be mandatory or voluntary, whether the caps will be absolute or intensity-based, and what industries will be included) remain to be determined,[107] it is not clear whether or how these trading programs might link to other cap-and-trade or credit systems.

South Korea's cap-and-trade system

In May of 2012, South Korea's parliament voted to establish a cap-and-trade program that will take effect in 2015. The program will apply to companies whose annual emissions are greater than 125,000 metric tons of CO_2, as well as to some smaller factories, buildings, and livestock producers.[108] The government has not yet promulgated regulations governing offsets or linkage to other systems.

Mexico's cap-and-trade system

In June of 2012, Mexico passed climate change legislation to establish a voluntary cap-and-trade system. Companies who opt in to the system

---

[105] *Id.* at LIII.20(5), III.I.37; International Emissions Trading Association, *Summary of Quebec's Regulation* at 11 (cited in 103).

[106] See Han, *et al.*, *China's Carbon Emission Trading: An Overview of Current Development* at 10 (cited in note 12).

[107] See Petherick, A. (May 2012). "Sweetening the Dragon's breath." *Nature Climate Change*. **2**: 309–311.

[108] See Sangim Han, *South Korean Parliament Approves Carbon Trading System* (*Bloomberg*, May 3, 2012).

would be able to sell their allowances in international markets.[109] Although the details of the system remain to be worked out, Californian officials have already expressed interest in exploring a future linkage between California's system and the Mexican system.[110]

American Clean Energy and Security Act of 2009

In 2009, the US House of Representatives passed the American Clean Energy and Security Act (also known as the Waxman-Markey Bill), which would have established a national CO_2 cap-and-trade system in the US. Although the bill never became law, it offers some insight into US political preferences regarding linkage with other systems. The bill would have allowed US firms to use emissions allowances from foreign cap-and-trade systems, such as the EU ETS, but would have given the US Environmental Protection Agency the option of establishing a limit on the percentage of a firm's emissions that could be covered by such foreign allowances.[111] The bill would also have allowed the use of both domestic and foreign (such as CDM) offset credits, with a combined quantitative limit of up two billion tons per year (compared with a total emissions cap of approximately five billion tons). Starting in 2018, the bill would have applied an exchange rate of 1.25:1 when redeeming foreign offsets.[112]

The Durban Platform and Its Implications for Linkage

A considerable number of linkages have been established or are likely to be established among regional, national, and sub-national tradable permit

---

[109] See *Mexico's President Enacts Climate Change Legislation* (*BBC News*, June 6, 2012), online at http://www.bbc.co.uk/news/world-latin-america-18345079 (visited October 16, 2012); Patrick Rucker and Miguel Angel Gutierrez, *Mexican Senate Clears Way for Climate Bill* (*Reuters*, April 19, 2012), online at http://www.reuters.com/article/2012/04/19/us-mexico-carbon-idUSBRE83I1N020120419 (visited October 16, 2012).

[110] See *Correa Holds Hearing on Merits of California-Mexico "Cap-and-Trade" Partnership* (May 7, 2012), online at http://sd34.senate.ca.gov/news/2012-05-07-correa-holds-hearing-merits-california-mexico-cap-and-trade-partnership (visited November 1, 2012).

[111] See American Clean Energy and Security Act of 2009, H.R. 2454 §§722(d)(3), 728(d).

[112] *Id.* at §§21(e), 722(d)(1).

systems. For better or worse, these linkages have been heavily influenced by the longstanding UNFCCC distinction between Annex I and non-Annex I responsibilities. In particular, because the UNFCCC institutional framework has not encouraged developing countries to establish cap-and-trade systems, all links to developing countries have been through the CDM — an emission-reduction-credit system with flaws related to lack of full additionality. However, the Durban talks have opened up an opportunity for a new international framework that could employ linkage to engage developing countries, reduce the global costs of emissions reductions, and develop an institutional framework for a future top-down or bottom-up international climate policy architecture.

The UNFCCC, the Berlin Mandate, and the Kyoto Protocol

Article 3 of the 1992 UNFCCC established a key principle

> The Parties should protect the climate system for the benefit of present and future generations of humankind, on the basis of equity and in accordance with their *common but differentiated responsibilities and respective capabilities.* Accordingly, the *developed country Parties should take the lead* in combating climate change and the adverse effects thereof.[113]

The countries considered to be "developed country Parties" were listed in an appendix to the 1992 Convention (Annex I) which included the members of the Organisation for Economic Co-operation and Development (OECD) plus most of the emerging market economies of eastern Europe and the former Soviet Union.

Three years after the Rio conference, at the first Conference of the Parties of the Framework Convention (COP-1) in Berlin, the global community agreed to the "Berlin Mandate."[114] This agreement developed a specific interpretation of "common but differentiated responsibilities" by establishing the dichotomous distinction whereby the Annex I countries

---

[113] See United Nations Framework Convention on Climate Change Art 3 (1992), 1771 UN Treaty Ser 107, 169 (1994) (emphasis added).

[114] See UNFCCC, *Reports of the Conference of the Parties on its First Session, Held at Berlin from 28 March to 7 April 1995* (June 6, 1995), FCCC/CP/1995/7/ Add.1.

are to take on emission-reduction responsibilities and the non-Annex I countries are to have no such responsibilities whatsoever.

The Berlin Mandate, subsequently codified in the 1997 Kyoto Protocol via numerical national targets for a limited set of countries, had wide-ranging, worldwide consequences. The dichotomous structure has driven up aggregate compliance costs to as much as four times their cost-effective level, because many opportunities for low-cost emissions abatement in emerging economies are taken off the table.[115] More problematic, an institutional structure was thereby put in place that makes change and progress exceptionally difficult, if not virtually impossible.

A new approach requiring participation of all parties

At the December 2011 UN talks in Durban, South Africa (COP-17), the international community agreed to a negotiating process focused on the long-term participation of all parties in the effort to mitigate greenhouse gas emissions and combat climate change.[116] In particular, they adopted the goal of reaching an agreement by 2015 that will bring all nations under the same legal regime by 2020.

This Durban Platform for Enhanced Action completely eliminates the Annex I/non-Annex I (or industrialized/developing country) distinction. Nowhere in the text of the decision will one find phrases such as "Annex I" or "historical responsibility," which had long since become code words for emission targets applied exclusively to the richest countries.

Negotiators from around the world now have a challenging task before them: to identify a new international climate policy architecture that is consistent with the process, pathway, and principles laid out in the Durban Platform, while still being consistent with the UNFCCC. In other words, the challenge is to find a way to include all countries (or at least, the twenty largest national and regional economies that together account for upwards of 80 percent of global GHG emissions) in a structure that brings about meaningful emission reduction on an appropriate timetable at acceptable cost, while recognizing the different circumstances of nations in a way that is more subtle and sophisticated than the simple dichotomous distinction of years past.

---

[115] See generally Nordhaus, W. D. (2008). *A Question of Balance*. Yale.

[116] See generally UNFCCC, *Establishment of an Ad Hoc Working Group on the Durban Platform for Enhanced Action* (cited in note 2).

Although the Durban Platform opens up a window to a variety of promising international policy architectures,[117] its implications for architectures based on linkage are particularly important. By lessening a key obstacle to the most meaningful international linkages — the absence of cap-and-trade systems in developing countries — the Durban Platform has improved the chances of future direct linkages among tradable permit systems in developed and developing countries. Such linkages could serve a variety of roles in international climate policy architecture.

Linkage as a Climate Policy Architecture

We consider the role that linkage could play in international climate policy architecture. Our examination is informed both by political interest in and economic experience with linkage. The existing and planned links among regional, national, and sub-national climate change policies — as documented in the third section — provide preliminary evidence regarding both the near-term and long-term roles that linkage may play in global climate policy architecture.

Near-term role

In the years since the ratification of the 1997 Kyoto Protocol, a patchwork system of linkages has evolved among independent regional, national, and sub-national climate policies. As described above, the current set of existing and planned international links includes a number of direct connections: links between trading systems in Europe, including the EU ETS, the EEA countries, and (most likely in 2014) Switzerland; the planned links among the members of the Western Climate Initiative, including the recently-announced linkage between California and Québec; and the planned link between Australia's forthcoming cap-and-trade system and the New Zealand ETS, as well as between Australia's system and the EU ETS (a development that could create an indirect linkage between the EU ETS and New Zealand's ETS). Furthermore, the CDM and JI offset markets provide a strong indirect linkage between the European systems and

[117] See generally Aldy and Stavins (Eds.), *Post-Kyoto International Climate Policy* (cited in note 3); Posner and Weisbach, *Climate Change Justice* (cited in note 1).

the New Zealand ETS, and, depending on future allowance prices, could provide an indirect linkage to RGGI.

This sample of existing and planned links hints at the outline of a near-term "system" that combines several regional, directly linked cap-and-trade systems, with some level of indirect connection via a common credit system; such as the CDM or a sectoral crediting program. Until a specific international agreement is realized, such a bottom-up, decentralized system may become the *de facto* structure for near-term to medium-term international climate policy architecture.[118]

Such a *de facto* near-term system could play two roles. First, it could provide economic benefits such as cost savings and market liquidity while (presumably) a future climate agreement is being negotiated. Second, by helping to build an institutional framework of coordination among different systems, near-term linkage could help with the political transition to a robust long-term international climate policy architecture. We discuss these roles in more detail in the following subsections.

Can linkage provide near-term cost savings and market liquidity?

In the short term, linkage may provide two main economic contributions: creating cost savings, and improving market liquidity and stability. As discussed in the second section, the key economic rationale for linking two systems is to lower the aggregate costs of emissions reductions. Because GHG emissions have the same effect on climate change regardless of where in the world they originate, linkage allows firms in high-cost systems to pay for less expensive abatement opportunities in lower-cost systems while still achieving the same overall environmental benefit. Furthermore, because linkage increases the number of market participants available to buy and sell allowances and credits, it can thicken markets and reduce problems with price volatility.

Experience suggests that direct linkages between cap-and-trade systems do in fact help to improve market functioning. The best example of the economic benefits of direct linkage comes from the EU ETS. Although allowance markets during the EU ETS trial phase showed signs of

[118]The Durban Platform calls for an agreement to be reached by 2015 for implementation in 2020.

thinness, more recent trading periods have had higher volumes and greater efficiency.[119]

However, although linkage can help with market functioning, the near-term cost savings from direct links between cap-and-trade systems may be modest. Because two-way links are currently planned primarily between systems in highly developed nations, direct links may not be able to help regulated firms take advantage of very low-cost abatement opportunities (such as those available in developing countries). Furthermore, direct linkages suffer from a climate policy irony: the links that are most attractive for economic reasons — those between systems with very different allowance prices (such as RGGI and the EU ETS) — may be politically the most difficult to establish because of the large international capital flows that such links would generate.

Links with a credit system can also contribute to the near-term goals of cost-minimization and market liquidity. In principle, a near-term set of indirect links could yield much of the cost savings and other advantages of a broad set of multilateral links. This system of indirect links would preserve a high level of national control over domestic carbon markets, thus allowing countries to tailor policies to fit their specific political and economic circumstances.

In practice, the ability of credit systems-in particular, the CDM-to create meaningful indirect links between cap-and-trade systems has been mixed. On the positive side, allowance prices in the New Zealand ETS, which allows unlimited purchase of CDM offset credits, have been strongly influenced by developments in the CDM and the EU ETS.[120] However, despite the potential cost-savings from linking to a credit system, some cap-and-trade systems (such as in California and Québec) have chosen to allow only selected external credits.[121] Others have imposed quantity limits on the use of external credits, have designed application procedures that make it difficult to receive approval for new offset projects, or have implemented trigger mechanisms that only allow the use of

[119] See Montagnoli, A. and F. de Vries. (2010). "Carbon trading thickness and market efficiency." *Energy Economics*. **32**: 1331, 1335.

[120] See Stian Reklev and Naomi Tajitsu, *NZ Spot Carbon Prices Recover from Sell-Off* (*Reuters*, March 2, 2012), online at http://af.reuters.com/article/commoditiesNews/idAF-L4E8E171W20120302 (visited October 16, 2012).

[121] See Section III.B.2-3.

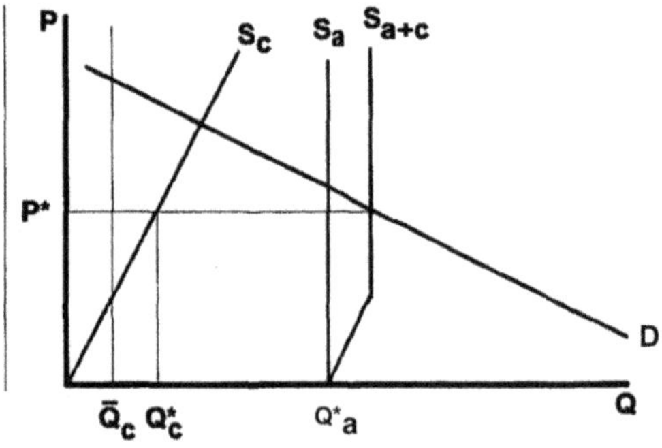

Figure 1. Allowance market with binding limit on offsets.

Notes: **D** represents demand for emissions permits. $\mathbf{S_a}$ and $\mathbf{S_c}$ represent the supply of domestic allowances and offset credits, respectively. $\mathbf{Q_c}$ represents the (binding) limit on offset sales. $\mathbf{S_{a+c}}$ represents aggregate supply of allowances and offset credits. **Q*a** and **Q*c** represent the number of allowances and credits that would be supplied at the market price **P***.

foreign offsets if domestic allowance prices exceed some pre-determined level.[122] This general reluctance to allow links with credit systems (in particular, with the CDM) is motivated by concerns about additionality, as well as an emphasis on achieving domestic emissions reductions. Therefore, whether indirect links can improve the stability and cost-effectiveness of domestic carbon markets will depend largely on broader acceptance and use of credit systems such as the CDM.

Although indirect linkage has clear benefits, it could also have destabilizing effects on offset markets in developing countries. Such a situation could arise as the result of limits that many systems are placing on the use of external offset credits. Consider a simple example, depicted in Figure 1, in which the world economy contains only two systems: a cap-and-trade system and an emission-reduction-credit system. Suppose that the cap-and-trade system limits the number of offset credits that domestic entities can use for compliance, and that this limit is binding. As a result, the ERC system will have an oversupply of emission reduction opportunities that would be profitable at current allowance prices, and the market for credits will fail to clear. The situation is potentially even worse when there are two or more cap-and-trade systems with binding limits on the use of external offsets. Because the market for offset credits

[122] See Section III.A.

will fail to clear, there will be multiple prices for credits, with prices depending on the allowance price in each separate cap-and-trade system. In either case, the markets would face problems with transparency, and the resulting uncertainty could create substantial business risks that might drive up the costs of emissions reductions. In particular, companies that make investments in offset projects would face the risk that they would be unable to sell their CERs at any price due to the binding limits on offset sales.

How likely is such a scenario? Table 1 summarizes limits on the use of offsets and credits for compliance in existing and planned systems. The table shows, for example, that after 2013, credits may make up no more than half of aggregate EU ETS emissions reductions. Other systems have also imposed limits. If nations pursue substantial emissions reduction goals while maintaining limits on offset credits, it is possible that limits on offsets will increasingly bind. The current (May 2012) discount of CER prices relative to EU ETS allowance prices[123] suggests that this may already be happening.

Can linkage provide a foundation for a future policy architecture?

Although most of the ongoing discussions about potential linkages focus on the economic benefits of linking systems with different marginal abatement costs, linkage may provide an additional set of benefits, which are fundamentally political. By helping to build an institutional framework of coordination among different systems, near-term linkage could help create a pathway to a robust long-term international climate policy architecture.

In the short term there will probably be several regional sets of directly linked systems, with some indirect linkage through the CDM or other offset/sectoral crediting programs. Based on the limited political evidence available to date, this system may transition toward a system with greater numbers of two-way and multilateral direct links. Such a network of linked cap-and-trade systems would preserve some national autonomy while requiring increased coordination of legislation, regulation, and institutions. Thus, in the same way that the General Agreement

[123] For an example of the performance of CER prices, see http://www.bloomberg.com/quote/BNSCER:IND (visited November 1, 2012).

Table 1. Summary of limits on the use of offset credits.

System	Period	Limit as percentage of cap	Notes
EUETS	2013–	TBD	(a)
EU ETS: Austria	2008–2012	10	
EU ETS: Belgium	2008–2012	8.4	
EU ETS: Czech Republic	2008–2012	10	
EU ETS: Estonia	2008–2012	0	
EU ETS: Finland	2008–2012	10	
EU ETS: France	2008–2012	13.5	
EU ETS: Hungary	2008–2012	10	
EU ETS: Germany	2008–2012	12	
EU ETS: Greece	2008–2012	9	
EU ETS: Ireland	2008–2012	10	
EU ETS: Italy	2008–2012	14.99	
EU ETS: Latvia	2008–2012	10	
EU ETS: Lithuania	2008–2012	20	
EU ETS: Luxembourg	2008–2012	10	
EU ETS: Netherlands	2008–2012	10	
EU ETS: Poland	2008–2012	10	
EU ETS: Slovakia	2008–2012	7	
EU ETS: Slovenia	2008–2012	15.76	
EU ETS: Spain	2008–2012	20	
EU ETS: Sweden	2008–2012	10	
EU ETS: United Kingdom	2008–2012	8	
Swiss ETS	2008–	8	
New Zealand ETS	2008–	unlimited	
Australia's Clean Energy Act	2012–	12.5	(b)
RGGI	2009–	3.3	(c)
California's CAT system	2013–	8 or 0	(d)
Québec's CAT system	2013–	8 or 0	(d)

Notes: (a) The European Commission will choose a limit that allows credits to make up no more than 50 percent of emissions reductions. (b) From 2012 to 2015, the government may impose a fee of AUD$15 to AUD$17 per credit. The 12.5 percent limit applies to [0oto credits (ERUs and CERs). (c) RGGI's limit rises to 5 percent if allowance prices exceed $7, and to 10 percent if allowance prices exceed approximately $10. (d) Neither California nor Québec recognize offsets from UNFCCC flexibility mechanisms such as the CDM, although California has recently completed an MOU to allow deforestation credits from the states of Acre, Brazj4 and Chiapas, Mexico.

Sources: See text above, and European Commission, Emissions Trading: Commission Adopts Decisions on Amendments to Five National Allocation Plans for 2008–2012 (July 13, 2007).

on Tariffs and Trade transitioned into the World Trade Organization, a bottom-up system of links could, in principle, provide the basic institutional framework for a broader climate agreement. The creation of a broad set of links could generate not only experience but also some degree of mutual trust among nations, and could supply at least a natural starting point for diplomatic negotiations.

Of course, linkage could also create political and regulatory obstacles to a future agreement. Creating a linkage between two systems requires agreement about a variety of design characteristics, including the stringency of the cap in each system. Because linkage can make it difficult for countries to change such design characteristics, it might make it more difficult for countries to make the adjustments necessary to support some future climate agreement.

Linkage could help to support a future climate agreement in another way: by providing participation incentives for nations to adopt market-based climate policies. Major developed countries with cap-and-trade systems may be expected to attempt to use offset programs as both a carrot and stick to stimulate developing country participation.

The best example of this may be EU ETS policy toward CDM offsets from developing countries. Whereas between 2008 and 2012 the EU ETS allowed regulated entities to use CDM credits originating in any developing country, beginning in 2013 new CDM credits will only be allowed for projects originating in LDCs (thus excluding China and India).[124] This policy shift is deliberate; recent EU documents state that "[w]hile initially the use of international credits was allowed for cost-effective compliance, this has been complemented with the objective of actively using the leverage the EU possesses as the by far most important source of demand for international credits."[125] Furthermore, the EU ETS website states that the "EU has set out a vision for the development of an international carbon market: the market is expected to develop through bottom-up linking of compatible domestic cap-and-trade systems."[126] An OECD-wide carbon market is expected by 2015, which would be extended to include economically more advanced developing countries by 2020 and "[n]ew

---

[124] See European Commission, *Questions and Answers on Use of International Credits in the Third Trading Phase of the EU ETS* 1 (cited in note 49).

[125] *Id.*

[126] See European Commission, *International Carbon Market* (November 2012), online at http://ec.europa.eu/clima/policies/ets/linking/index_en.htm (visited November 22, 2012).

sectoral crediting mechanisms would be a stepping stone towards establishing cap and trade systems in these developing countries."[127] Whether or not this EU linkage strategy will be effective is difficult to predict.

Obstacles to near-term linkage

It is important to keep in mind that a variety of political, institutional, and economic factors will determine the types of links that are formed in the near future. Recent political experience suggests that it has not been difficult to establish direct linkages between existing and planned cap-and-trade systems in developed countries. However, these direct linkages are occurring primarily between jurisdictions that already have strong economic, political, and/or geographic ties.

One obstacle to the establishment of additional direct links between cap-and-trade systems is the need to harmonize cost-containment measures and reach mutual agreement about emissions caps. This may prove to be a particular challenge for a direct link between the EU ETS and North American cap-and-trade systems. For example, because California's system includes an allowance reserve and RGGI's system includes an allowance price trigger for the use of additional offset credits, links to the EU ETS would result in automatic propagation of these cost control measures.

An additional obstacle to direct linkage is the diversity of stringency across systems. For example, a link between RGGI and the EU ETS is unlikely in the near future, given the current difference in allowance prices in the two systems ($1.93 per allowance in RGGI versus $8.53 per allowance in the EU ETS).[128] Such a link would result in large capital flows from Europe to the United States, and could be perceived as Europeans subsidizing lackluster US ambition.

Although the idea of linkage to a common credit system is also appealing, given that such a mechanism would not require systems to harmonize design features, such linkage also faces some practical obstacles. First, most existing and planned cap-and-trade systems have placed

---

[127] *Id.*

[128] See RGGI CO_2 Allowance Tracking System, *Transaction Price Report* (cited in note 79). For a useful source of market news, visit European Commission, *International Carbon Market*, online at http://ec.europa.eu/clima/policies/ets/linking/index_en.htm (cited in note 126).

restrictions on the use of offset credits. Table 1 summarizes these restrictions. The table shows, for example, that although many EU ETS participants have had relatively generous limits on credits for the 2008 to 2012 compliance period, future limits will allow credits to make up no more than half of aggregate EU ETS emissions reductions after 2013. Other systems have also imposed relatively low limits.

Second, although the CDM is currently the world's most important supplier of offset credits, it is not clear that it will continue in this role in the future. Beginning in 2013, the EU ETS — the largest source of demand for offset credits — will only accept new offsets from CDM projects in LDCs. This requirement implies that China and India, which together have produced 68 percent of CDM offsets to date, will no longer be eligible to sell CERs into the European market. What program or institution might replace the CDM is unknown. Recent UN discussions have centered on the possibility of "new market mechanisms," a vaguely defined set of sectoral crediting mechanisms that would require host country engagement and possibly emissions reduction commitments.[129] Other jurisdictions, such as California's AB 32 system, have begun developing other protocols for certifying emissions reduction credits from international sources.

A third set of obstacles to indirect linkage via a credit system are the policy goals — espoused by many European countries — of achieving domestic emissions reductions and promoting investment in renewable energy sources. Because allowing the use of credits has the effect of reducing allowance prices, linkage to a credit system (or even to a cap-and-trade system with a lower allowance price) reduces incentives for domestic firms to invest in renewable energy and other "green" technologies. The desire to achieve this separate policy goal may create political opposition to linkage. For example, European Commission documents reflect a clear concern that most emissions reductions be achieved domestically.[130] Such emphasis was also exhibited in the Kyoto Protocol: "The acquisition of emission reduction units shall be supplemental to domestic actions for the purposes of meeting commitments."[131]

[129] See International Emissions Trading Association, *IETA Response to the AWG-LCA Call for Input Regarding New Market-Based Mechanisms* at *1 (cited in note 37).

[130] See *Directive 2004/101 /EC of the European Parliament and of the Council* at 18–19 (cited in note 26); Kruger, Oates, and Pizer, *Decentralization in the EU Emissions Trading Scheme*. 1 *Review of Environmental Economics and Policy* at 118 (cited in note 51).

[131] See Kyoto Protocol, Art 6 §l(d).

Long-term role

In the long term, linkage could contribute to international climate policy architecture in at least two ways.[132] First, linkage could serve as an element of a broader international climate architecture. In such a system, linkage might play several different roles. In the short term, indirect linkages via a common credit system might serve as an implicit framework that would provide market liquidity and some cost savings, while still allowing nations to maintain control over domestic allowance markets. In the longer term, nations might successfully negotiate a top-down climate agreement that specifies targets and timetables for emissions reductions. Such an architecture might include a more comprehensive set of multilateral linkages between industrialized and developing countries that would allow nations to achieve more stringent emissions targets at lower aggregate cost.

A second possibility is that a set of unilateral emissions commitments in a pledge-and-review system combined with a decentralized set of links could serve as a stand-alone, bottom-up architecture.[133] As discussed above, the near-term outlines of such an architecture may already be emerging, with regional trading partners choosing to link directly with each other, with broader indirect linkages via the CDM or new sectoral crediting mechanisms, and with the Copenhagen Accord[134] and the Cancun Agreements[135] providing a pledge-and-review system of essentially voluntary national targets. As more jurisdictions establish cap-and-trade systems, this somewhat fragmented near-term system could evolve into a broader bottom-up architecture that includes a wide set of direct linkages.

Whether such a decentralized architecture could achieve meaningful environmental results in a cost-effective manner depends on several

---

[132] See Jaffe, Ranson, and Stavins, *Linking Tradable Permit Systems* at 803 (cited in note 4).

[133] See Olmstead, S. M. and R. N. Stavins. (June 2010). *Three Key, Elements of Post-2012 International Climate Polity Architecture*. Belfer Center Discussion Paper 10-37 *17, Harvard University, online at http://belfercenter.ksg.harvard.edu/files/Stavins_Olmstead Montrea!Final-2.pdf (visited October 15, 2012).

[134] See UNFCCC, *Draft Decision-/ CP.15: Copenhagen Accord* (December 18, 2009), FCCC/CP/2009/L.7.

[135] See generally UNFCCC, *Establishment* of *an Ad Hoc Working Group on the Durban Platform for Enhanced Action* (cited in note 2).

factors. First, a sufficient number of large emitters would have to agree to participate in the system. Participation by industrialized countries would need to be self-motivated, and there are a number of potential incentives that might induce developing countries to participate. These include positive incentives (carrots), such as development assistance and the opportunity to sell allowances or offset credits, as well as negative incentives (sticks), such as carbon border adjustments or the imposition of graduation requirements as conditions for the opportunity to sell offset credits.

Second, participating nations would have to commit to substantial unilateral emissions reductions. In developed countries, these commitments would most likely be motivated by internal politics. In developing countries, commitments would most likely depend on participation incentives provided by developed countries. The emissions targets would either be decided unilaterally or negotiated during the process of establishing and renewing direct linkages. The set of voluntary commitments made thus far under the Copenhagen Accord and the Cancun Agreements are probably insufficient for achieving the politically endorsed international target of stabilizing greenhouse gas concentrations at 450 ppm CO_2-equivalent (related to limiting average global warming to 2°C).[136]

Third and finally, for such an international policy architecture to be cost-effective, it would require links among GHG trading systems in industrialized and developing countries. As discussed above, the near-term prospects for such a comprehensive set of links are mixed.

Conclusion

By replacing the UNFCCC's Berlin Mandate, the Durban Platform for Enhanced Action has opened an important window. National delegations from around the world now have a challenging task before them: to identify by 2015 (for implementation in 2020) a new international climate policy architecture that is consistent with the process, pathway, and principles laid out in the Durban Platform. This will require finding a way to include all key countries in a structure that brings about meaningful emissions reductions on an appropriate timetable at acceptable cost, while

[136] See Bosetti, V. *et al*. "Emissions pricing to stabilize global climate." *Nota di Lavoro*. **80**: 2, 12.

remaining within the overall framework and principles provided by the UNFCCC.

On both a positive and normative basis, there is considerable attraction to bottom-up, decentralized international policy architectures. Among these, the most promising may be linkage among tradable permit systems, whether in the form of a near-term, *de facto* architecture of organic linkages among regional, national, and sub-national cap-and-trade systems, or in the form of a long-term replacement for the centralized, top-down architecture that characterizes the Kyoto Protocol. The Durban Platform has improved the likelihood of establishing the types of developed-developing country linkages necessary to support these climate architectures.

Part V

The Paris Agreement

https://doi.org/10.1142/9789811292415_0021

Chapter 21

Linkage of Greenhouse Gas Emissions Trading Systems: Learning from Experience*

Matthew Ranson[†] **and Robert N. Stavins**[‡,§,‖,¶]

[†]*Abt Associates Inc., Cambridge, MA, USA*

[‡]*John F. Kennedy School of Government, Harvard University, Cambridge, MA, USA*

[§]*Resources for the Future, Washington, DC, USA*

[‖]*National Bureau of Economic Research, Cambridge, MA, USA*

[¶]*robert_stavins@harvard.edu*

Introduction

Recent efforts under the United Nations Framework Convention on Climate Change (UNFCCC) to develop a global response to the risks of climate change have focused on two negotiation tracks. One — extending the Kyoto Protocol with a second commitment period — faced major challenges and resulted in limited participation. Not only are a number of key industrialized countries on the side-lines (Canada, Japan, Russia, and the US), but the Protocol has failed to set emissions targets for the large,

*This chapter was originally published in *The Chicago Journal of International Law*, **13**(2), Winter 2013, 403–438.

rapidly growing emerging economies (principally China, India, Brazil, South Korea, South Africa, and Mexico).

A second track — negotiations based on the roadmap known as the Durban Platform for Enhanced Action — may eliminate the historical distinction in climate commitments between developed (Annex I) and developing (non-Annex I) countries. However, despite the Durban Platform's stated commitment to reach agreement on a new global climate regime by 2015, the history of international climate negotiations suggests that reaching a broad top-down international agreement to address climate change is likely to be extraordinarily difficult.

Given these challenges, the countries of the world have increasingly turned their attention in the UNFCCC negotiations to the possibility of a hybrid climate policy architecture for the 2015 agreement — one that would include top-down elements, for example, for monitoring, reporting, and verification, with a bottom-up pledge-and-review system, where each country would specify its own targets based upon domestic political feasibility. The most politically realistic mechanism for such a system to be cost-effective — and thus able to achieve more ambitious global emissions reductions — would be for it to facilitate decentralized linkages among regional, national, and sub-national climate policies (which in many jurisdictions have taken the form of emissions trading systems).

Such a system would require the ability of nations to form bilateral and multilateral agreements in which they would link their cap-and-trade systems by accepting each other's allowances or credits. In principle, the links could create cost savings and market liquidity for connected systems, while achieving the same aggregate reductions in GHG emissions. The linkage agreements could also provide mechanisms for countries to coordinate and harmonize their emissions caps, price controls, and other design features. Such decentralized linkage could augment and complement other elements of an international hybrid policy architecture.

One key question about this type of climate policy architecture is whether it can generate a sufficient quantity of GHG emissions reductions at reasonable cost (Heitzig, 2013). To help address this question, we draw on the past decade of experience with carbon markets to examine why systems choose to link, so that we can better assess the role that decentralized linkages may play in future international climate policy.

Two conclusions emerge about motivations for linkage. First, there exists a significant revealed preference for linking emissions trading systems. The last ten years have seen the organic growth of linkages between many of the world's cap-and-trade systems, both directly between systems, and indirectly via connections with credit systems such as the Clean Development Mechanism (CDM). This proliferation of linkages implies that for many nations the expected benefits of linkage outweigh expected costs.

Second, the decision to develop a link between two systems depends on a variety of economic, political, and strategic factors. Although it may seem obvious that the primary goal of linkage is to achieve the same level of emissions reductions at a lower cost, linkage is a multi-faceted policy decision used by political jurisdictions to achieve a variety of objectives. Many factors — ranging from geographic proximity to integrity of emissions reductions — influence decisions about linking. The evidence we present in this chapter is primarily qualitative, as the number of systems that have linked is not sufficient for reliable statistical analysis.

Because a global offset market is not emerging, achieving near-term cost savings through a system of indirect linkages is unlikely. Furthermore, delinking by New Jersey and Australia demonstrates that linkages can easily be undone, implying that linkages may not survive changes in domestic political support. Nonetheless, the many economic and political incentives for linking are likely to continue to produce direct connections among regional, national, and sub-national cap-and-trade systems. Although a bottom-up architecture may produce relatively modest global emissions reductions in the short term, it is likely to be more feasible politically than a stringent top-down agreement.

The remainder of this chapter is organized as follows. The second section presents evidence of how economic, political, and strategic factors have influenced decisions about linkage. The third section evaluates the potential role of linkage in global climate policy architecture. The final section concludes.

Economic, Political, and Strategic Determinants of Linkage

Many jurisdictions have revealed their preference for linking their domestic cap-and-trade policies with those of other jurisdictions. As of May 2014, there were international, regional, national, or sub-national cap-and-trade systems operating or scheduled for launch in 36 countries. These include the European Union Emissions Trading Scheme (EU ETS), the Regional Greenhouse Gas Initiative (RGGI) in the northeast US, the AB-32 system in California, eight regional pilots in China, and emissions trading systems in Kazakhstan, New Zealand, Quebec, Switzerland, South Korea, and Tokyo (World Bank, 2014).[1] Most have established or proposed at least one linkage with another cap-and-trade or credit system (Table 1). More discussion of these linkages is provided in the online supplementary material, as well as of other forms of non-traditional linkage.

The existence of these linkages implies that for the participating jurisdictions, the expected economic and political benefits of linkage outweigh expected costs. Of course, there are also many pairs of systems that, to date, have implicitly demonstrated a preference for *not* linking with each other. California and Quebec have not linked with the CDM, and the EU ETS has not linked with any of the North American systems. Some of these unrealized links will become critical in the future. This motivates an important question: why do systems choose to link or not to link?

Although it may seem obvious that the primary goal of linkage is to achieve the same level of emissions reductions at lower cost, linking is a multi-faceted policy decision that can be used by political jurisdictions to achieve a variety of objectives (Flachsland, Marschinski, & Edenhofer, 2009). We consider many factors — ranging from geographic proximity to integrity of emissions reductions — that may influence the decision to link.

Geographic Proximity

The single most significant predictor of systems linking may be geographic proximity (Table 1). The EU Member States are linked through the EU ETS; the northeastern US states are linked through RGGI; Quebec and California will link in 2014; and many aspects of New Zealand's cap-and-trade system were chosen for compatibility with Australia's (previously) planned system.

Analyses of negotiated trade agreements can provide some insight into this pattern, because one of the most robust findings from such analyses is that trade agreements are most likely between nations that are near each other (Tinbergen, 1962), a fact that is largely attributed to transportation costs and market information. Likewise, linkage could be facilitated if nearby jurisdictions also have similar environmental goals and economic conditions, a history of productive engagement on other issues, and familiarity with and connections between each other's regulatory and

[1]Because some aspects of the design of China's pilot cap-and-trade systems were still unclear at the time this article was written, we do not examine potential of linkages involving these systems.

Table 1. Linkages between emissions trading systems.

					Prices at enactment		Caps ($MtCO_2$)		
System 1	**System 2**	**Type of linkage**	**Enact. date**	**Effect. date**	**#1**	**#2**	**#1**	**#2**	**Notes and references**
Linkages among cap-and-trade systems									
27 EU nations	(via the EU ETS)	Multi	2003	2005	None	NA	Varied	2299	1, 12
Norway	EU ETS	One-way		2005					10
Norway	EU ETS	Multi	2007	2008	€0	€20	15	2080	2
Iceland	EU ETS	Multi	2007	2008	None	€20	0	2080[a]	2
Liechtenstein	EU ETS	Multi	2007	2008	None	€20	18	2080	2
Switzerland	EU ETS	Two-way[b]							3
Australia	EU ETS	One-way	2013[b]	2014	AU$25	€7–€8	TBD[c]		4, 11
Australia	EU ETS	Two-way[b]		2018	AU$25	€7–€8	TBD	1852	4
Australia	New Zealand	Two-way[b]					TBD		5
Australia	EU ETS, NZ	Delinking	2014	2014					24
California	Quebec	Two-way	2012/13	2014	$14	None	160	25	6, 14, 15
10 US states	(RGGI)	Multi	2005	2009	None	NA	Varied	168[d]	7
RGGI	Any CAT system	One-way	2005	2009	None	€9/€UA	168	2299[e]	8
RGGI	Any CAT system	Delinking	2013	2014	$3	€5/€UA	91	2299[e]	9
New Jersey	RGGI	Delinking	2011	2012	$2	$2	21	150	13

(*Continued*)

Table 1. (*Continued*)

System 1	System 2	Type of linkage	Enact. date	Effect. date	Prices at enactment		Caps ($MtCO_2$)		Notes and references
					#1	#2	#1	#2	
Linkages from cap-and-trade systems to credit systems									
EU ETS Phase 1	CDM	One-way	2004	2005	€9	$5	2299	NA[f]	1, 16, 17
EU ETS Phase 2	CDM	One-way	2004	2008	€9	$5	2299	NA[f]	1, 16, 17
EU ETS Phase 3	CDM	One-way	2004	2013	€9	$5	2299	NA[f,g]	1, 16, 22
EU ETS Phase 2	JI	One-way	2004	2008	€9	$6	2299	NA[f]	1, 16, 18
EU ETS Phase 3	Non-LDC CDM	Delinking	2012	2013	€6	E4	2084	NA	26
Switzerland	CDM	One-way	1999	2008	None	$4–$7	NA	NA	17, 19
New Zealand	CDM, JI, RMU	One-way	2008	2008	None	€11	NA	NA	17, 20, 21
Australia	CDM, JI	One-way	2011	2012/15	None	€6	TBD	NA	4

RGGI	Any credit system	One-way	2005	2009	None	\$5–8	110	NA[e]	8
RGGI	Any credit system	Delinking	2013	2014	None	\$5	165	NA[e]	9
California	Acre and Chiapas	One-way[b]						NA	25
Quebec	Acre and Chiapas	One-way[b]						NA	25
Tokyo ETS	CDM	One-way	2008	2010	\$142	\$18	13	NA[h]	23

Notes: NA, not applicable; TBD, to be determined. [a]Per EEA Joint Committee decision 146/2007, Iceland did not submit a National Allocation Plan for EU ETS Phase II, because it had no installations large enough to be covered by the cap-and-trade system. [b]Indicates a proposed linkage.[c]Participants in Australia's system may use EUAs for up to 50 percent of their compliance obligations. [d]The RGGI states signed an MOU in 2005, and then each passed authorizing legislation between 2006 and 2008. [e]The original Model Rule included language in section XX-10.3(b)(1) that allowed the use of allowances from foreign cap-and-trade systems or credit systems (including Kyoto flexibility mechanisms) if RGGI allowance prices exceeded a 'two-stage price trigger event' that began at \$10 in 2005 and increased by roughly 2 percent each year. The 2013 amendments to the Model Rule eliminated this linkage. [f]Credit price reflects pre-compliance offsets for which seller assumes risk.gUnder recent proposed rules, EU ETS participants will be entitled to use international credits during the 2012–2020 period up to the higher of two limits: (1) the international credit entitlement specified in the national allocation plan for Phase 2 or (2) 11 percent of the free allocation of EU allowances granted to them in that period.hUse of CDM credits is allowed only if domestic prices exceed a threshold, and if Tokyo-based credits are used as well.

Sources: 1, European Parliament (2004); 2, European Commission (2007b); 3, European Commission (2010); 4, Australian Government (2013); 5, Combet and Groser (2011); 6, CA ARB (2013a); 7, RGGI (2008); 8, RGGI (2013a); 9, RGGI (2013b), Mehling and Haites (2009); 10, Sopher and Mansell (2013); 11, European Commission (2012, 2013a); 12, European Commission (2007a); 13, NJ.com (2011); 14, CA ARB (2013b); 15, Que´bec MDDEFP (2013); 16, Sijm (2009); 17, UNDP (2009); 18, Allen Consulting (2005); 19, Sopher and Mansell (2013); 20, New Zealand Parliament (2008); 21, New Zealand Ministry of the Environment (2011); 22, European Commission (2013b); 23, EDF/IETA (2013); 24, ClimateWire (2013c); 25, EDF (2010); 26, European Commission (2011).

political systems. Linkages with neighbours may also be significantly more palatable to domestic audiences. Anecdotal evidence from California, where some legislators have expressed concerns about linking to 'far-flung jurisdictions' (ClimateWire, 2013a), is consistent with this.

Cost-Effectiveness

The most important economic motivation for linking may be the anticipated cost savings that come from the reallocation of abatement effort between systems with different marginal abatement costs. The system with the higher marginal cost benefits from purchasing relatively inexpensive allowances from the other system, allowing it to achieve its emission reduction goals at a lower cost. Conversely, the system with the lower marginal cost benefits from selling its allowances at higher prices, resulting in an inflow of revenue.

The net welfare gains from linking can be substantial (Carbone, Helm, & Rutherford, 2009). The best existing example may be the link between the EU ETS and the CDM, which has allowed regulated EU firms to purchase offsets from developing countries. Trotignon (2010) suggests that, between 2008 and 2009, EU ETS installations saved at least E280 million by purchasing Certified Emission Reductions (CERs) instead of making higher-cost domestic emissions reductions. Future projections also suggest large potential savings: for example, Gavard, Winchester, Jacoby, and Paltsev (2011) estimate that, by linking to a Chinese system with a business-as-usual cap, the costs of a 30 percent reduction in US CO_2 emissions by 2030 would be cut by more than half.

However, for some jurisdictions, other concerns — such as the environmental integrity of offsets — may be more important than cost savings. For example, the EU ETS has effectively delinked from the CDM for the post-2012 period. Furthermore, many potentially cost-saving bilateral linkages have not occurred at all, such as California–RGGI and EU–California. Finally, it is possible that the macro-economic welfare effect of linkage might be negative for some countries, for example, due to an interaction with a distortionary domestic tax system (Babiker, Reilly, & Viguier, 2004).

Distributional Impacts

Although the social welfare gains from linkage are important, the distribution of welfare impacts across regulated entities is also likely to matter

(Newell, Pizer, & Raimi, 2013). Not all regulated entities benefit from linkage, and whether individual firms are net losers or winners will depend on their marginal abatement costs, whether they are in the higher-cost or lower-cost linked system, and how allowances are initially allocated (via grandfathering or auctioning).

The relative political power of winners and losers could have strong impacts on governmental support for linking with another system. For example, the cost savings available from linkage may play well to regulated businesses in the higher-cost system, and high allowance prices may be popular with constituents that receive free allowances in the lower-cost system. On the other hand, large international revenue transfers may be a political liability in the system that makes payments. The interaction of allocation mechanisms and political incentives for linkage is a topic for future research. For example, while firms might oppose a cap-and-trade system with auctioned permits, after enactment such a system would provide regulated firms with financial incentives to support linkage to systems with lower allowance prices.

Market Liquidity and Price Stabilization

In principle, by increasing and diversifying the number of buyers and sellers in a carbon market, linkage can provide the dual benefits of increased liquidity and reduced price volatility. This is particularly important for smaller cap-and-trade systems with few participants. In fact, nearly all of the smallest cap-and-trade systems have taken steps to link with other systems. For example, Norway created a one-way link with the EU ETS in 2005, and then joined the EU ETS in 2008, New Zealand's ETS and the Japanese voluntary ETS have established one-way links to the CDM, and Switzerland is negotiating a two-way link with the EU ETS.

Linkage does appear to have increased the overall liquidity of allowance markets in these small cap-and-trade systems, but its contribution to price stability has been mixed (Mundaca & Richter, 2013). Although linkage may have reduced day-to-day fluctuations in prices, it has also increased the exposure of small systems to systematic risk. For example, due to New Zealand's decision to allow unrestricted use of Kyoto credits, New Zealand Unit (NZU) prices largely tracked CDM prices, which are in turn dependent on EU ETS prices. The collapse of European Union Allowance (EUA) prices in 2011 and 2012 propagated through this indirect linkage and led to a similar decline in NZU prices (Figure 1).

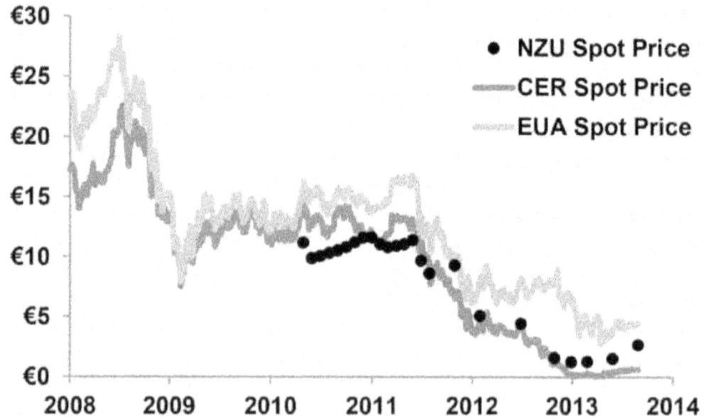

Figure 1. Spot prices for NZUs, CERs, and EUAs.

Note: All prices are shown in nominal euros.

Sources: SENDECO$_2$ (2013); Carbon CommTrade (2013).

Domestic Opposition to Cap-and-Trade

Supportive domestic political leadership is a necessary condition for the adoption of a cap-and-trade system, and, by extension, the decision to link (or de-link) with another jurisdiction. Consider two recent examples of elected politicians who have decided to eliminate their domestic cap-and-trade systems, thus effectively delinking from other emissions trading systems. First, in November 2011, Governor Chris Christie of New Jersey announced that he was issuing an executive order that would withdraw his state from RGGI (NJ.com, 2011). New Jersey's exit resulted in the retirement of 21 million short tons of CO_2 allowances (relative to a total RGGI cap of 150 million short tons).

Second, in July 2014, the newly elected Australian government, led by Prime Minister Tony Abbott, passed legislation to terminate Australia's plans to move to a cap-and-trade system (Taylor & Hoyle, 2014). This decision ended the previous government's negotiated deal for a one-way link with the EU ETS starting in 2014 and a two-way link starting in 2018.

International Political Strategy

Linkages are agreements between political jurisdictions, and, like other forms of international cooperation, they can involve strategic political behaviour. First, some nations may see linkage as a way to build support for international climate action by demonstrating leadership, coordinating policies, and developing mutual trust. The European Commission website states that:

> Linking the EU ETS with other cap-and-trade systems offers several potential benefits, including reducing the cost of cutting emissions, increasing market liquidity, making the carbon price more stable, leveling the international playing field and *supporting global cooperation on climate change*. (European Commission, 2013a; emphasis added)

Second, nations may be coerced into linkage as a condition for receiving other benefits. The eastern European Member States of the EU are a prime example. Many of these countries would have preferred not to join the EU ETS, but agreed to participate in multilateral linkage as a condition of receiving the 'club benefits' of EU membership (Ellerman & Buchner, 2007).

Finally, nations may use linkage as a 'carrot' to encourage the development of foreign emissions trading systems. In 2013, the EU ETS ceased accepting new offsets from CDM projects located outside of Least Developed Countries (LDCs), a decision that effectively excludes China and India (which together have produced 68 percent of CDM offsets to date) from selling CERs to the European market. This policy change is at least partially intended to encourage these two important emitters to develop their own cap-and-trade systems. The European Commission (2011) states that '[w]hile initially the use of international credits was allowed for cost-effective compliance, this has been complemented with the objective of actively using the leverage the EU possesses as the by far most important source of demand for international credits.'

Reduced Integrity of Emissions Reductions

Linkage can mean accepting some uncertainty about the quality of allowances or credits that are purchased from a linked system. This problem is particularly acute for links with credit systems, which suffer from imperfect additionality, the challenge of determining whether a claimed emissions reduction would have occurred anyway in the absence of the offset programme. As the world's largest credit system, the CDM has come under particular criticism about the limited additionality of its offsets. At the extreme, early CDM offsets for the destruction of hydrofluorocarbons may have had the perverse effect of creating incentives to build additional refrigerant-producing factories solely for the purpose of destroying their HFC-23 emissions (Carbon Trust, 2009). This problem had a clear effect on linkage: in 2013, the EU ETS ceased accepting CDM offsets based on HFC-23 destruction.

Even direct linkages with another cap-and-trade system can lead to problems with integrity of emissions reductions (Jaffe, Ranson, & Stavins, 2010). The issue is leakage: the incentive for firms in the lower-price system to move their emissions-generating economic activity to an unregulated jurisdiction, to avoid paying the higher post-linkage allowance price. Australia's previous government, for example, had expressed reluctance to link to sub-national systems due to concerns about leakage, because firms in sub-national systems may find it particularly easy to relocate to an unregulated jurisdiction within the same country (Bushnell, 2013).

Domestic Abatement Incentives

One of the primary effects of linkage is to reduce the price of allowances in the system that originally had a higher permit price. However, there are some reasons why a lower allowance price may be undesirable. Some jurisdictions may use cap-and-trade to establish domestic price incentives for investments in low-carbon infrastructure or technological innovation (Calel & Dechezlepretre, 2012). The lower post-linkage price will reduce these investment incentives. Similar issues may arise for cap-and-trade systems that are based on some notion of moral responsibility — the idea that domestic firms 'should' reduce their own emissions, instead of paying foreign firms to make equivalent emissions reductions.

In practice, widespread limits on the use of offsets from credit systems appear to be motivated by the desire to establish domestic abatement incentives. Most cap-and-trade systems place relatively strict limits on offset use (Table 2). Except for New Zealand, no system allows more than 20 percent of emissions to be covered with offsets, and few allow more than 10 percent. Although this doubtless reflects concerns about additionality, it is also motivated by the stated goal in many systems of achieving emissions reductions domestically.

Legal Compatibility

The legal frameworks that support most cap-and-trade systems are based on authorizing legislation that is implemented via regulations issued by an

Table 2. Limits on the use of offset credits.

System	Period	Limit as percent of cap[a]
EU ETS[b]	2013–2020	Varies
EU ETS: Austria	2008–2012	10
EU ETS: Belgium	2008–2012	8.4
EU ETS: Czech Republic	2008–2012	10
EU ETS: Estonia	2008–2012	0
EU ETS: Finland	2008–2012	10
EU ETS: France	2008–2012	13.5
EU ETS: Hungary	2008–2012	10
EU ETS: Germany	2008–2012	12
EU ETS: Greece	2008–2012	9
EU ETS: Ireland	2008–2012	10
EU ETS: Italy	2008–2012	14.99
EU ETS: Latvia	2008–2012	10
EU ETS: Lithuania	2008–2012	20
EU ETS: Luxembourg	2008–2012	10
EU ETS: Netherlands	2008–2012	10
EU ETS: Poland	2008–2012	10
EU ETS: Slovakia	2008–2012	7
EU ETS: Slovenia	2008–2012	15.76
EU ETS: Spain	2008–2012	20
EU ETS: Sweden	2008–2012	10
EU ETS: UK	2008–2012	8
Swiss ETS	2008–	8
New Zealand ETS	2008–	Unlimited
Australia's Clean Energy Act[c]	2012–	12.5
RGGI[d]	2009–	3.3
California's CAT system[e]	2013–	8
Quebec's CAT system[e]	2013–	8

Notes: [a]The limits presented in this table apply per regulated entity.
[b]Under new proposed rules, EU ETS participants will be entitled to use CDM and JI credits during the 2012–2020 period up to the higher of two limits:
(1) the international credit entitlement specified in the national allocation plan for Phase 2 or (2) 11 percent of the free allocation of EU allowances granted to them in that period.
[c]From 2012 to 2015, the government may impose a fee of AU$15 to AU$17 per credit. The 12.5 percent limit applies to Kyoto credits (ERUs and CERs).
[d]RGGI's limit rises to 5 percent if allowance prices exceed $7, and to 10 percent if allowance prices exceed approximately $10.
[e]Neither California nor Quebec recognize offsets from UNFCCC flexibility mechanisms, although California has recently completed an MOU with the goal of eventually allowing deforestation credits from the states of Acre, Brazil, and Chiapas, Mexico.
Sources: See text and European Commission (2007a, 2013b).

executive agency. For a link to be possible, the legislature must have the authority to link with a foreign jurisdiction, and the executive agency must have received authority to implement appropriate linking regulations.

Legal compatibility is particularly important for sub-national systems that may lack authority to negotiate treaties with foreign nations. The empirical pattern of linkage supports this hypothesis. There are many cases of linkages between sub-national states and provinces: the RGGI states are linked together; California and Quebec will link in 2014; and California is in the process of negotiating offset protocols with Acre, Brazil, and Chiapas, Mexico. However, we are not aware of any cases of a state or province establishing links with another nation or group of nations. As California Air Resources Board Chairwoman Mary Nichols has said, 'for a state to link with a sovereign nation presents some legal challenges that would be difficult to work through' (ClimateWire, 2013b).

Similarity of Emissions Targets and Prices

Countries with very different emissions-reduction ambitions may find it difficult to negotiate a link (Burtraw, Palmer, Munnings, Weber, & Woerman, 2013). Differences of ambition can lead to substantial differences in allowance prices, which can cause large revenue transfers that may be unpalatable to the general public. However, in theory, different ambitions need not be an important obstacle, because systems could implement an 'allowance exchange ratio' when they link (Burtraw *et al.*, 2013). For example, one system might allow its regulated entities to substitute 1.2 foreign allowances for one domestic allowance for the purposes of domestic compliance.

In practice, differences in ambition and prices appear to be significant barriers. For example, California has cited the collapse of EUA prices as a reason for not working to develop a link with the EU ETS (ClimateWire, 2013b). Similarly, Burtraw *et al.* (2013) argue that the absence of a link between RGGI and California is due in large part to the weakness of RGGI prices.

The understandable reluctance of many countries to engage in substantial revenue transfers leads to a climate policy irony: the linkages that could yield the greatest cost-effectiveness benefits — due to major differences in domestic allowance prices — may also be politically most difficult to implement. Conversely, the most politically feasible linkages are likely to have only modest cost-effectiveness benefits.

Loss of Control over Carbon Markets and Emissions Targets

Establishing a link with another system can mean sacrificing some control over domestic carbon prices. For example, after a two-way linkage occurs, prices will be determined by the equilibrium of aggregate supply and demand for allowances in the two systems. Because allowance demand is determined by the caps set by both jurisdictions, each faces the risk that the other may choose a cap that could create negative economic effects.

In practice, most nations have been price takers in linked systems. Figure 2 compiles information about all existing or proposed decisions by

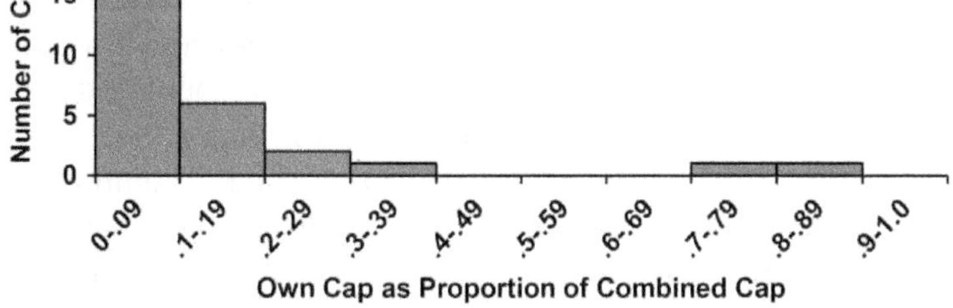

Figure 2. Histogram of ratio of emissions caps between linked systems.

Note: Each observation represents the existing or proposed decision by a nation or state to establish a linkage. For bilateral and multilateral linkages, each partner is included as a separate observation. The outcome variable is the ratio between the nation or state's domestic cap and the combined post-linkage cap in the joined system.

Source: see Table 1.

any nation or sub-national state to establish a link.[2] For each decision, the figure calculates the ratio between the jurisdiction's domestic cap and the combined post-linkage cap in the joined system. The figure shows that most jurisdictions enter into linkages in which their domestic cap accounts for less than 10 percent of the combined post-linkage cap, and in all but two cases, the ratio is less than 35 percent. The only exceptions are California's planned link with Quebec, and the EU ETS's planned (and now cancelled) link with Australia.

Not only does linkage require systems to give up some control over prices, it can also require them to relinquish some control over the ambition of their domestic emissions targets and to harmonize design features. For example, as part of the negotiations to link to the EU ETS, Australia had agreed to lower the maximum allowable domestic use of Kyoto units and to eliminate its planned price floor (Lancaster, 2012).

Despite the fact that linkage leads to loss of control over domestic carbon markets, many nations and sub-national jurisdictions have chosen to establish links, suggesting that control is not a determinative factor in countries' decisions.

Bottom-Up Architecture Based on Linkages

Could a bottom-up system of linkage become a fundamental part of a hybrid policy architecture to address climate change (Heitzig, 2013)? A two-part evolution of such a decentralized architecture is conceivable (Jaffe *et al.*, 2010). In the short term, indirect linkages through a common credit system such as the CDM might provide cost-effectiveness and market liquidity benefits. In the longer term, greater numbers of direct two-way and multilateral links might emerge. These links would encourage greater coordination of legislation, regulation, and institutions, while preserving national autonomy. The links, if successful, would help to develop mutual trust among nations, thus possibly paving the way for meaningful emissions reductions commitments from a broad set of participants.

[2]For the purposes of this analysis, we include each nation or state in a multilateral linkage as making a decision, but do not treat the system as a whole (e.g. RGGI or the EU ETS) as a decision maker. However, for bilateral linkages, we treat both partners as decisions makers (including, for example, the EU ETS decision to negotiate a link with Australia).

Although some jurisdictions have exhibited a preference for linking their cap-and-trade systems, experience suggests that decisions about linking are affected by many economic, political, and strategic considerations. Therefore, a key question about a hybrid climate policy architecture with direct linkages is whether it could succeed in generating a sufficient quantity of GHG emissions reductions at a reasonable cost. In the section "An Architecture of Linkages may Achieve Limited Results", where we evaluate the likely performance of linkage-based architecture on its own merits, the findings are not particularly encouraging, but when we compare such a bottom-up architecture with top-down alternatives in the section "An Architecture of Direct Linkages may Perform Better than the Alternatives", a more positive prognosis emerges.

An Architecture of Linkages may Achieve Limited Results

Based on recent experience, three challenges to the vision of a linkage-based policy architecture stand out. First, a robust global offset market can no longer be said to be emerging. From 2004 through 2012, the CDM provided indirect links between many of the world's cap-and-trade systems. Although CDM prices were largely determined by demand from the EU ETS, several other systems — including those in New Zealand, Japan, and Switzerland — relied on the CDM as a source of credits. Now, however, the CDM is losing its central role as a source of offsets for world carbon markets. Key factors for this decline include the EU ETS decision in 2013 to limit future CDM credits to projects from LDCs and the very low price of EUAs. Additionally, new cap-and-trade systems in California and Quebec have established their own protocols for certifying offsets and have shown little interest in accepting CERs. A second challenge to a linkage-based architecture is the reality that, once established, linkages are by no means permanent (Pizer & Yates, 2013). Although the trend over the past decade has been one of increasing connections among GHG trading systems, there have been several major exceptions, including New Jersey's withdrawal from RGGI in 2011, the EU ETS's decision to stop accepting credits from non-LDC countries in 2013, and Australia's cancellation of its planned cap-and-trade system, which ended the nation's plans to link with the EU ETS. These three examples of delinking demonstrate that, like any other agreement, linkages can be terminated. These examples may also imply that linkage would not provide incentives for nations to commit to emissions reductions targets that are opposed by domestic constituents. Finally, whether delinking might have longer-term climate policy consequences — for example, by establishing lasting political precedents in Australia and New Jersey — is not clear.

The third challenge is how to foster linkages when they are most needed. Linkage is easiest between systems with similar allowance prices, or at least similar abatement ambitions, conditional on their relative levels of economic development. On the other hand, there is less reason for linkage when conditions are homogeneous across systems. As of spring 2014, allowance prices in the EU ETS were near E5 per metric ton, allowance prices in California were slightly above the auction floor price of US$11.34 per metric ton, and RGGI allowance prices were approximately $4 per short ton.

An Architecture of Direct Linkages may Perform Better than the Alternatives

In principle, a top-down agreement among the nations of the world could produce a first-best solution to the problem of climate change. Although abatement costs, GHG emissions, and climate change vulnerability all differ across nations, the logic of Coase (1960) suggests that there exists some distribution of abatement responsibilities and side payments that could reduce global emissions while leaving each nation at least as well off as it would have been in the absence of global action. The problem, of course, is that the hurdles to negotiating a successful top-down agreement for this ultimate global commons problem are exceptionally great.

Under the 1997 Kyoto Protocol, industrialized (Annex I) countries agreed to take on GHG emissions targets for a first commitment period, running from 2008 to 2012. Although the Protocol constituted a major milestone, it was never on track to produce meaningful reductions in global GHG emissions. As a consequence of Canada's withdrawal from the treaty, the decisions by Japan and Russia not to take on emissions targets for the second commitment period, and the non-participation of the US, the Kyoto Protocol currently sets emissions restrictions for industrialized nations responsible for less than 15 percent of global GHG emissions. Additionally, nearly all of the countries that have accepted targets under this second commitment period belong to the EU — and thus have already agreed to similar EU ETS targets.

The Durban Platform for Enhanced Action, negotiated during the 2011 Conference of the Parties in Durban, South Africa, has opened up the possibility that the world's large emerging economies could take on quantitative emissions targets (Aldy & Stavins, 2012). However, despite this potential step forward, the Durban Platform only establishes a new negotiation process that has the goal of reaching an agreement by 2015 to bring all nations under the same legal regime by 2020. The history of climate negotiations — and of other international negotiations on topics such as trade — suggests that reaching such a broad agreement will be extraordinarily challenging.

Given the drawbacks of the Kyoto Protocol and the difficulty of establishing a new global agreement under the Durban Platform, even the medium-term prospects for practical implementation of a top-down architecture appear modest at best. So, although a top-down architecture might be a first-best approach if its enactment and implementation were politically realistic, it does not compare favourably against bottom-up and hybrid approaches when real-world feasibility is considered.

Nations have strong revealed preferences for linking, and the incentives underlying those preferences are likely to continue to produce additional direct connections among regional, national, and sub-national cap-and-trade systems. Although a bottom-up system of linkage on its own would be an imperfect and incomplete response, there is no reason it cannot play a significant role as part of a comprehensive hybrid policy architecture.

Conclusion

Developing an effective international policy architecture to address climate change has proven to be exceptionally challenging. The Kyoto Protocol has entered what is probably its final commitment period, and now covers only a small fraction of global GHG emissions. Under the Durban Platform for Enhanced Action, negotiators may now gravitate toward a hybrid system. This would combine top-down elements for a process of establishing targets (or at least procedures for assessing targets) with bottom-up elements of pledge-and-review tied closely to individual national policies and actions. Based on recent experience, the incentives for linking such national policies are likely to continue to produce direct connections among regional, national, and sub-national cap-and-trade systems. The growing network of decentralized, direct linkages among these systems may turn out to be a key part of a future hybrid climate policy architecture.

Acknowledgments

We are grateful for research assistance provided by John Agan, and helpful comments from Gilbert Metcalf, William Pizer, and participants at a presentation of the paper at the Nineteenth Conference of the Parties of the United Nations Framework Convention on Climate Change in Warsaw, Poland. The authors are responsible for any remaining errors.

References

Aldy, J. and R. N. Stavins. (2012). "Climate negotiations open a window: Key implications of the Durban Platform for Enhanced Action." Harvard Project on Climate Agreements. http://belfercenter.hks.harvard.edu/publication/22319.

Allen Consulting Group. (2005). "Report to New Zealand treasury: The cost of tradable emissions units under the Kyoto Protocol."

Australian Government. (2013). "Starting emissions trading on 1 July 2014: Policy summary." www.climatechange.gov.au/sites/climatechange/files/files/reducing-carbon/carbon-pricing-policy/cef-policy-summary-moving-ets.PDF.

Babiker, M., J. Reilly, and L. Viguier. (2004). "Is international emissions trading always beneficial?" *The Energy Journal*. **25**(2): 33–56.

Burtraw, D., K. L. Palmer, C. Munnings, P. Weber, and M. Woerman. (2013). *Linking by Degrees: Incremental Alignment of Cap-and-Trade Markets*. RFF Discussion Paper 13-04.

Bushnell, J. (2013). "A ton is never really a ton [Blog post]." *Energy Economics Exchange*, February 11, http://energyathaas.wordpress.com/2013/02/11/a-ton-is-never-really-a-ton-2.

Calel, R. and A. Dechezlepretre. (2012). *Environmental Policy and Directed Technological Change: Evidence from the European Carbon Market*. Working Paper No. 87, Centre for Climate Change Economics and Policy. http://personal.lse.ac.uk/calel/Calel%20and%20Dechezlepretre%20(2012).pdf.

CA ARB. (2013a). "Air Resources Board sets date for linking cap-and-trade program with Québec." Sacramento, CA: California Air Resources Board. www.arb.ca.gov/newsrel/newsrelease.php?id=430.

CA ARB. (2013b). "Quarterly auction 2, February 2013: Summary Results Report." Sacramento, CA: California Air Resources Board. www.arb.ca.gov/cc/capandtrade/auction/february_2013/updated_feb_results.pdf.

Carbon CommTrade. (2013). "Price history: Spot NZUs." https://www.commtrade.co.nz.

Carbone, J. C., C. Helm, and T. F. Rutherford. (2009). "The case for international emission trade in the absence of cooperative climate policy." *Journal of Environmental Economics and Management*. **58**(3): 266–280.

Carbon Trust. (2009). "Global carbon mechanisms: Emerging lessons and implications." www.carbontrust.com/resources/reports/advice/global-carbon-mechanisms.

ClimateWire. (2013a). "Legislature concerned about cap-and-trade links with other states, provinces." www.eenews.net/climatewire/2013/03/05/stories/1059977279.

ClimateWire. (2013b). "E.U. market troubles will prevent emissions trade linkage – Calif. air chief." www.eenews.net/climatewire/2013/04/19/stories/1059979761.

ClimateWire. (2013c). "New Australian government dismantling climate policies." www.eenews.net/climatewire/2013/09/12/stories/1059987111.

Coase, R. H. (1960). "The problem of social cost." *The Journal of Law and Economics*. **3**: 1–44.

Combet, G. and T. Groser. (2011). "Joint media release: Australia and New Zealand advance linking of their emissions trading schemes." www.climatechange.gov.au/sites/climatechange/files/media/March%20 2013/MR20111205B.pdf.

Ellerman, A. D. and B. K. Buchner. (2007). "The European Union Emissions Trading Scheme: Origins, allocation, and early results." *Review of Environmental Economics and Policy*. **1**(1): 66–87.

EDF. (2010). "Tropical forests protection pact hailed for protecting climate." New York, NY: Environmental Defense Fund. www.edf.org/news/tropical-forests-protection-pact-hailed-protecting-climate.

EDF/IETA. (2013). "Tokyo: The World's Carbon Markets: A case study guide to emissions trading. New York, NY: Environmental Defense Fund and International Emissions Trading Association."

European Commission. (2007a). Emissions trading: EU-wide cap for 2008–2012 set at 2.08 billion allowances after assessment of national plans for Bulgaria. http://europa.eu/rapid/press-release_IP-07-1614_en.htm.

European Commission. (2007b). "Emissions trading: Commission announces linkage EU ETS with Norway, Iceland and Liechtenstein." http://europa.eu/rapid/press-release_IP-07-1617_en.htm.

European Commission. (2010). "Opening negotiations with Switzerland on linking emissions trading systems." http://ec.europa.eu/clima/news/articles/news_2010110501_en.htm.

European Commission. (2011). "Questions and answers on use of international credits in the third trading phase of the EU ETS." http://ec.europa.eu/clima/policies/ets/linking/docs/q_a_20111114_en.pdf.

European Commission. (2012). "Press release: Australia and European Commission agree on pathway towards fully linking emissions trading systems." http://europa.eu/rapid/press-release_IP-12-916_en.htm.

European Commission. (2013a). "International carbon market." http://ec.europa.eu/clima/policies/ets/linking/index_en.htm.

European Commission. (2013b). "Climate Change Committee approves proposed regulation on international credit entitlements for 2013–2020." http://ec.europa.eu/clima/news/articles/news_2013071002_en.htm.

European Parliament. (2004). "Directive 2004/101/EC of the European Parliament and of the Council of 27 October 2004." *Official Journal of the European Union*, L 338/18. http://eur-lex.europa.eu/LexUriServ/LexUriServ.do?uri=CELEX:32004L0101:en:NOT.

Flachsland, C., R. Marschinski, and O. Edenhofer. (2009). "To link or not to link: Benefits and disadvantages of linking cap-and-trade systems." *Climate Policy*. **9**: 358–372.

Gavard, C., N. Winchester, H. Jacoby, and S. Paltsev. (2011). "What to expect from sectoral trading: A US–China example." *Climate Change Economics*. **2**(1): 9–26.

Heitzig, J. (2013). "Bottom up strategic linking of carbon markets: Which climate coalitions would farsighted players form?" Nota di Lavoro 48.2013.

Jaffe, J., M. Ranson, and R. N. Stavins. (2010). "Linking tradable permit systems: A key element of emerging international climate policy architecture." *Ecology Law Quarterly*. **36**: 789–808.

Lancaster, R. (2012). "Editorial." *Carbon Trading*. **1**(8): 1.

Mehling, M. and E. Haites. (2009). "Mechanisms for linking emissions trading schemes." *Climate Policy*. **9**: 169–184.

Mundaca, L. and J. L. Richter. (2013). "Challenges for New Zealand's carbon market." *Nature Climate Change*. **3**: 1006–1008.

Newell, R. G., W. A. Pizer, and D. Raimi. (2013). "Carbon markets 15 years after Kyoto: Lessons learned, new challenges." *Journal of Economic Perspectives*. **27**(1): 123–146.

New Zealand Ministry of the Environment. (2011). "Emissions trading scheme review 2011: Issues statement and call for written submission." Wellington: Emissions Trading Scheme Review Panel, Ministry for the Environment.

New Zealand Parliament. (2008). "Climate change response (emissions trading) amendment act 2008 (Public Act 2008 No. 85)." www.legislation.govt.nz/act/public/2008/0085/latest/DLM1130932.html.

NJ.com. (2011). "Gov. Christie announces N.J. pulling out of regional environmental initiative." www.nj.com/politics/index.ssf/2011/05/gov_christie_to_announce_nj_pu.html.

Pizer, W., and A. Yates. (2013). *Breaking Up May Not Be Hard to Do: Terminating Links Between Emission Trading Programs*. Working Paper.

Quebec MDDEFP. (2013). "The Québec cap and trade system for greenhouse gas emissions allowances: Regulatory information. Québec: Québec Ministère du Développement durable, de l'Environnement, de la Faune et des Parcs."

RGGI. (2008). "Regional greenhouse gas initiative model rule: 12/31/08 Final with Corrections." Part XX CO2 Budget Trading Program. New York, NY: Regional Greenhouse Gas Initiative.

RGGI. (2013a). "State statutes & regulations." New York, NY: Regional Greenhouse Gas Initiative. http://rggi.org/design/regulations.

RGGI. (2013b). "Summary of RGGI Model Rule changes, February 2013." New York, NY: Regional Greenhouse Gas Initiative.

SENDECO2. (2013). "CO2 Prices: 2008–2013. Lisboa: SENDECO2." www.sendeco2.com/uk/precio_co2.asp?ssidi=3.

Sijm, J. P. M. (2009). "Tradable carbon allowances: The experience of the EU and lessons learned. Petten: Energy Research Centre of the Netherlands." www.ecn.nl/docs/library/report/2009/e09078.pdf.

Sopher, P. and Mansell, A. (2013). "Norway — the world's carbon markets: A case study guide to emissions trading." Washington, DC: Environmental Defense Fund and International Emissions Trading Association. www.edf.org/sites/default/files/EDF_IETA_Norway_Case_Study_May_2013.pdf.

Taylor, R. and R. Hoyle. (2014). "Australia becomes first developed nation to repeal carbon tax." *Wall Street Journal*, July 17. http://online.wsj.com/articles/australia-repeals-carbon-tax-1405560964.

Tinbergen, J. (1962). *Shaping the World Economy: Suggestions for an International Economic Policy*. New York, NY: Twentieth Century Fund.

Trotignon, R. (2010). *Combining Cap-and-Trade with Offsets: Lessons from CER Use in the EU ETS in 2008 and 2009*. Working Paper 2011-03. Paris: Climate Economics Chair of Paris-Dauphine University.

UNDP. (2009). "The Clean Development Mechanism: An assessment of progress." New York, NY: United Nations Development Programme. http://assets.mediaglobal.org/documents/UNDP_Environment_and_Energy_Group_Report_The_Clean_Development_Mechanism.pdf.

World Bank. (2014). "State and trends of carbon pricing 2014." Washington, DC: World Bank. http://www-wds.worldbank.org/external/default/WDSContentServer/WDSP/IB/2014/05/27/000456286_20140527095323/Rendered/PDF/882840AR0Carbo040Box385232B00OUO090.pdf.

https://doi.org/10.1142/9789811292415_0022

Chapter 22

Facilitating Linkage of Climate Policies through the Paris Outcome*

Daniel M. Bodansky[†], Seth A. Hoedl[‡], Gilbert E. Metcalf[§,‖,††], and Robert N. Stavins[‖,¶,‡‡]

[†]*Sandra Day O'Connor College of Law, Arizona State University, Tempe, AZ, USA*

[‡]*Harvard Law School, Cambridge, MA, USA*

[§]*Department of Economics, Tufts University, Medford, MA, USA*

[‖]*John F. Kennedy School of Government, Harvard University, Cambridge, MA, USA*

[¶]*National Bureau of Economic Research, Cambridge, MA, USA*

[**]*Resources for the Future, Washington, DC, USA*

[††]*gmetcalf@tufts.edu*

[‡‡]*robert_stavins@harvard.edu*

Introduction

In the Durban Platform for Enhanced Action, adopted by the Conference of the Parties (COP) to the United Nations Framework Convention on

*This chapter was originally published in *Climate Policy*, 1–17, August 5, 2015.

Climate Change (UNFCCC) in 2011, the parties agreed to develop a 'protocol, another legal instrument or an agreed outcome with legal force under the Convention applicable to all Parties', for adoption at COP-21 in December 2015, in Paris (UNFCCC, 2012). It is likely that the Paris outcome will reflect a hybrid climate policy architecture — one that combines top-down elements, such as for monitoring, reporting, and verification (MRV), with bottom-up elements, including 'Intended Nationally Determined Contributions' (INDCs), detailing what a country intends to do to reduce emissions, based on domestic political feasibility and other factors (Bodansky & Diringer, 2014). This outcome will be embodied in a core agreement, which will be legally binding, as well as ancillary instruments such as annexes, national schedules, and/or COP decisions.

The ability to link regional, national, and sub-national climate policies will be essential to enhancing the cost-effectiveness of such a system — and thus the likelihood of achieving significant global emissions reductions. By 'linkage', we mean formal recognition by a GHG mitigation programme in one jurisdiction (a regional, national, or sub-national government) of emission reductions undertaken in another jurisdiction for the purposes of complying with the first jurisdiction's requirements.

This chapter analyses theoretical issues related to linkage among heterogeneous climate policy instruments and then applies this analysis to the Paris outcome with specific recommendations for how the outcome could facilitate the growth and operation of a robust system of international linkages of regional, national, and sub-national policies, and discusses how inappropriate or excessive rules could obstruct effective, bottom-up linkage.

Understanding Linkage

Separate and distinct policy instruments in different political jurisdictions may be linked together, essentially through mutual recognition and crediting for compliance. Linkage could occur between cap-and-trade and tax systems, between either of those systems and non-market regulatory systems, or among non-market regulatory systems.[1,2]

---

[1]Linkage is defined and examined in considerable detail in Jaffe, Ranson, and Stavins (2009), Metcalf and Weisbach (2012), and Ranson and Stavins (2013, 2015). We refer the reader to those articles for details on linkage design. Here, we briefly highlight some of the significant benefits and costs of linkage, again referring the reader to the articles above for a more extensive discussion of the issues.

[2]Linkage in the context of cap-and-trade systems generally involves allowance and financial transfers among private parties facilitated by the linkage rules. This might occur in

Advantages of Linkage

Linkage offers a variety of economic and political advantages. These advantages have been key motivating forces behind linkages that have already been established or are being planned. In particular, linkage facilitates cost-effectiveness, the achievement of the lowest-cost emissions reductions across the set of linked systems, and minimizes both the costs for individual countries (costs net of financial transfers) as well as the overall cost of meeting the collective cap.[3] It also reduces leakage to the extent that it contributes to price harmonization across carbon pricing systems. It can also reduce price volatility and market power (Bodansky, Hoedl, Metcalf, & Stavins, 2014), although it should be noted that the linking of markets also creates the potential for importing price volatility from other systems (Flachsland, Marschinski, & Edenhofer, 2009).

Linkage also allows a country to demonstrate global leadership, as some jurisdictions may see political benefits from supporting global action on climate change. For example, the European Commission has indicated that linking the European Union Emissions Trading System (EU ETS) with other cap-and-trade systems 'offers several potential benefits, including ... supporting global cooperation on climate change' (European Commission, 2014). The prospect of linkage may allow nations to exert greater diplomatic influence on unlinked, free-riding nations, encouraging them to take action on climate change. It can also contribute to a sense of 'momentum' that provides support for domestic climate policies. Also, linkage may provide regulatory stability, because it may be more difficult to introduce changes in an emission-reduction scheme when those changes require coordination with other countries with linked systems.[4]

It is possible that linkage and the set of harmonized rules and procedures that accompany it may provide cover for politically difficult decisions. Monitoring and verification procedures that are opposed by particular interest groups, for example, can be justified on the grounds that these procedures are needed to realize the benefits that accrue from linking with other jurisdictions.

---

more heterogeneous linked systems as discussed in Metcalf and Weisbach (2012), but also might entail systems in which jurisdictions trade emission reduction obligations and alter their tax or regulatory rules to reflect the adjusted INDCs.

[3] Although this is an economic merit of linkage, for political reasons price equalization may not be a near-term goal (Ranson & Stavins, 2015), as we discuss later.

[4] The flip side of regulatory stability is policy inflexibility; altering rules in linked systems requires coordination among all formally linked systems.

Linking heterogeneous systems can create political flexibility to pursue the domestic policy instrument that is most feasible politically, while retaining the option to link with other types of system. This may enable greater participation in linkage despite diverse political tastes (Metcalf & Weisbach, 2012). Finally, well-designed linkage systems may pave the way for other forms of cooperation among nations.

Challenges of Linkage

The advantages of linkage are real, but linkage also brings with it a number of challenges. Some of these challenges are economic, while others are political. First, linkage ties the environmental effectiveness of the entire linked system to the environmental integrity of individual members, making critical the role of MRV requirements (Ranson & Stavins, 2015). If one jurisdiction in a linked pair or large set of linked jurisdictions lacks the capacity or motivation to track emissions and emission allowances accurately (and/or the capacity or motivation to measure and verify offset credits), these loopholes will be exploited throughout the system, damaging the cost-effectiveness of the full set of linked policies.

Linkage itself can undermine environmental integrity. For example, linkage can result in double counting if transfers between countries are not properly accounted for and if, as a result, the same emissions reduction is counted towards compliance in more than one national system. Strategic behaviour could also produce adverse economic consequences in a set of linked systems in which a country with low ambition has incentives to loosen its domestic cap so that the resultant linked emissions price is more closely aligned with the country's private benefits from emissions abatement (Helm, 2003).[5]

While linkage has the potential to improve aggregate cost-effectiveness across linked jurisdictions, it can also have significant distributional implications between and within jurisdictions (Ranson & Stavins, 2015). Firms that were allowance buyers (firms with high abatement costs) in the jurisdiction with the higher pre-link allowance price will be better off as

[5]In a closely related game-theoretic analysis, Holtsmark and Sommervoll (2012) examine the incentives that nations face when they set their national emissions reduction targets under a bottom-up pledge-and-review system. They find that if countries anticipate that international emissions trading will be implemented, they have incentives to establish less ambitious reduction targets than if trading were not anticipated.

a result of the allowance price changes brought about by linking, as will allowance sellers (firms with low abatement costs) in the jurisdiction with the lower pre-link allowance price. Conversely, allowance sellers in the jurisdiction with the higher pre-link allowance price and allowance buyers in the jurisdiction with the lower pre-link allowance price will be hurt by the allowance price change that results from the link. For the jurisdiction that faces higher prices post-linkage, this means greater transfers from buyers to sellers (Newell, Pizer, & Raimi, 2013).[6]

In some cases, the desire to ensure a minimum level of domestic mitigation may be motivated by the expectation that domestic mitigation provides co-benefits unrelated to climate change, such as a reduction of localized air pollutants (Flachsland *et al.*, 2009). Linkage that reduces abatement in the local system may forfeit such politically important co-benefits. It is also possible, however, that the ability to link to other systems (and so enjoy the opportunity to achieve emission reductions at lower cost) may provide political support for greater ambition in mitigation goals.

Finally, linkage presents the political challenge of ceding some degree of national (or other jurisdictional) autonomy. Before two jurisdictions link, they may need to agree on how to reconcile design features they have separately established for their respective systems (Ranson & Stavins, 2013). As those design features may represent a compromise between competing stakeholder interests within a country, any changes could pose political hurdles.

Lessons Learned from Linkage to Date

Experience to date with explicit and implicit linkages of carbon policies across jurisdictions yields some potentially useful lessons (Ranson & Stavins, 2015). First, an increasing number of regions, nations, and sub-national jurisdictions have demonstrated their preference for linkage. Despite evident challenges, the current bottom-up trend of bilateral and multilateral linkages has demonstrated significant progress in the context of a potential future hybrid climate agreement. Second, linking carbon markets has proved 'powerful and effective', although the risk of linkage includes the reality that problems in one market can be transferred to other linked systems (World Bank, 2014).

---

[6] Within-jurisdiction distributional issues also abound, as discussed by Somanathan (2010) and Ranson and Stavins (2015).

Third, although there was demonstrable value to firms in Annex I countries from their use of Clean Development Mechanism (CDM) offsets for the purposes of cost mitigation, a functioning international market for such offsets does not appear likely to continue under the current political landscape, particularly given the changes in the EU ETS. Fourth, the International Transaction Log, part of the Kyoto Protocol process, played an important role by tracking traded units (Marcu, 2014). Fifth, linkages are not permanent, and are subject to national or sub-national political swings (as occurred in Australia), causing uncertainty for regulated firms (Ranson & Stavins, 2015).[7]

Finally, the benefits and attraction of linkage are likely to evolve over time. In the short run, the benefits may be more political (developing a sense of momentum and climate leadership) and administrative (learning by sharing, reducing duplicative administrative costs, and coordinating rules and procedures) than economic (this point is also stressed by Burtraw, Palmer, Munnings, Weber, & Woerman, 2013). Also in the short run, full price harmonization is unlikely, given restrictions on the magnitude of allowance flows observed in current linkage schemes (Ranson & Stavins, 2015). In the absence of full price harmonization, some efficiency-enhancing transactions will not take place.

In the long run, however, as carbon markets mature and nations adopt more ambitious mitigation targets, especially in light of the 2°C limit on warming that member states endorsed in the 2010 Cancun Agreements, it is reasonable to expect some loosening of constraints on linkage flows, contributing to enhanced price harmonization and increased cost effectiveness of carbon policy.

Linkage under a Future International Policy Architecture

Specific elements of a future international policy architecture under the Paris outcome could help facilitate the growth and operation of a robust system of international linkages between regional, national, and

[7] In most cases, however, systems were delinked before linkage came into effect. New Jersey's exit from the Regional Greenhouse Gas Initiative (RGGI) was a notable exception.

sub-national policies. On the other hand, other potential elements of the Paris outcome could impede effective, bottom-up linkage.

Elements that would Inhibit Effective Linkage

One design element that would have the effect of inhibiting international linkage would be overly prescriptive or restrictive rules on allowable trading across linked systems. A clear example would be a requirement (or even a preference) for domestic actions to achieve national commitments. Such a 'supplementarity principle' can render cross-border linkage difficult or impossible, and thereby drive up compliance costs, decrease international ambition, and reduce the feasibility of reaching an agreement.

For example, several provisions of the Kyoto Protocol suggest that internal emissions abatement should take precedence over compliance through the Protocol's flexibility mechanisms (International Emissions Trading, Joint Implementation, and the CDM),[8] but the precise meaning of this principle of supplementarity has been debated since the adoption of the Protocol. Also, limits on the use of foreign offsets for compliance are common in existing regional, national, and sub-national cap-and-trade systems.

A second (and related) issue is the confusion that can arise from competing and conflicting objectives and rules between the UNFCCC and regional or national trading systems. An example is the controversy over CDM credits issued for projects that target industrial gases such as HFC-23 and nitrous oxide (N_2O) from adipic acid production. Responding to concerns that access to CDM credits was creating perverse incentives to continue or even increase production of these gases, the EU ETS disallowed the use of CDM credits from industrial gas projects for the purposes of ETS compliance after 2012 (European Commission, 2011). The

[8]Article 6.1 of the Kyoto Protocol states that 'The acquisition of emission reduction units [through trading] shall be supplemental to domestic actions for the purposes of meeting commitments under Article 3.' Likewise, Article 17 states that 'Any such trading shall be supplemental to domestic actions for the purpose of meeting quantified emission limitation and reduction commitments under that article.' Article 12.3.b states that 'Parties included in Annex I may use the certified emission reductions accruing from such project activities [under the Clean Development Mechanism] to contribute to compliance with part of their quantified emission limitation and reduction commitments under Article 3 .. . ' (UNFCCC, 1998).

CDM Executive Board, however, continued to issue credits for these projects (albeit with greater restrictions on their use). The controversy sowed confusion and damaged perceptions of carbon trading in general (Marcu, 2014).

The potential for conflicting rules relates to a broader issue about how national or regional carbon mitigation systems become recognized as valid for the purposes of implementing the Paris outcome. Marcu (2014) notes two possible approaches (approval and transparency) by which reductions under domestic systems might become eligible for counting in the UNFCCC context. The first approach would require explicit COP approval of domestic systems, while the second would involve the development of model rules through COP negotiations. Domestic systems would then demonstrate how they conform to internationally agreed templates. The latter approach could be combined with a peer review process but would not require explicit COP approval.[9]

A third area of potential concern stems from a lack of clarity (or confusion) over objectives. For example, adding a 'sustainable development condition' to CDM projects can create confusion in markets (Marcu 2014). This in turn undermines trading across systems, an essential role of linkage.

Finally, rules that restrict which countries can link (for example, allowing linkage only among Annex I countries), or that make it difficult for countries to join the category of countries that can link, would inhibit effective linkage.

Elements that could Facilitate Effective Linkage

If linkage is to play a significant role in a hybrid international policy architecture, then several categories of design elements merit consideration for inclusion in the Paris outcome, either directly or by establishing a process for subsequent international negotiations. These elements include the following: the definition of compliance units; registries and tracking;

[9]Variations on these two approaches could build on the flexibility mechanisms described in Bodansky and Diringer (2014). These include offering alternatives under which different states may operate to comply with over-arching rules, offering default and opt-out clauses, offering opt-in procedures, providing contextual standards to provide flexibility where needed, and using guidelines that serve to set expectations (but not requirements) for behaviour and mechanism design.

monitoring, verification, and reporting of individual trades; interaction with cost-containment instruments; and oversight and monitoring of the market in aggregate.

Effective linkage requires common definitions of key terms, particularly with respect to the units that can be used for compliance purposes. This will be especially important for links between heterogeneous systems, such as between a carbon tax and a cap-and-trade system. A model rule for linkage could be particularly helpful in this area.[10]

Registries and tracking are necessary with linked systems, whether the links bring together a homogeneous or heterogeneous set of policies.[11] Indeed, a key role for the top-down part of a hybrid architecture that allows for international linkage of national policy instruments will be tracking, reporting, and recording allowance unit transactions. A centralized institution could maintain the accounts of parties that hold allowances, record transfers of allowances between account holders, and annually reconcile allowances and verified emissions. This is particularly important because of the likely omission of Assigned Amount Units from the post-2020 regime (Marcu, 2014). Some form of international compliance unit would contribute to more effective and efficient registry operation and would help avoid double-counting problems.

International compliance units would make the functioning of an international transaction log more straightforward and reduce the administrative burden of reconciling international registries with national registries (Marcu, 2014).[12] There is also a possible role for the UNFCCC to provide centralized registry services for countries that lack the capacity to develop national registries on their own (Marcu 2014). Finally, there may be economies of scale in regionalizing registries for certain developing

---

[10]In regard to market coverage, even a (homogeneous) set of national cap-and-trade systems will differ in many design elements, but not all of these elements will require coordination or harmonization. For example, systems may differ in their scope — i.e. in the sectors of their respective economies that are included under an emissions cap — but this difference need not create a barrier to linkage and trading.

[11]This could be particularly important to avoid double counting in overlapping jurisdictions.

[12]Prag *et al.* (2013) argue that mandating a standard type of international compliance unit type may not improve accountability and could add complexity as domestic mitigation schemes evolve over time.

countries under the auspices of the UNFCCC or some other multilateral institution (for example, the World Bank or a regional development bank).

More broadly, any system, with or without linkage, will require monitoring, verification, and reporting of emissions. Likewise, compliance and enforcement mechanisms are of generic need in any effective policy architecture.

The interaction of linked systems with cost-containment elements (banking, borrowing, offsets, and price-stabilization mechanisms), in the case of cap-and-trade systems, raises particular issues in the context of linkage, because in some cases these mechanisms automatically propagate from one linked system to another.

Common rules for approving and measuring offsets may be important, and — more broadly — a tiered system of offset categories could be helpful, with jurisdictions choosing their own 'exchange rates' for each category.

Finally, market oversight and monitoring, together with various safeguards against market manipulation such as by large holders of allowances who may be able to exercise market power, may increase confidence in the system. However, national and international institutions may already exist, or need only relatively minor additional capacity, to provide these functions.

From the Conceptual to the Concrete: International Law and Linkage

Possible Functions of the UNFCCC Regime with Respect to Linkage

The Paris outcome could play at least four different roles with respect to linkage of heterogeneous policy instruments. First, it could discourage linkage, either by not allowing countries to count international transfers toward their mitigation contributions, or by limiting the number or types of transferred units that can be counted for compliance purposes. Second, it could be silent on the topic of linkage, creating legal and regulatory uncertainty about whether international transfers are allowed. Third, it could expressly authorize linkage but not provide any further details about how linkage should occur, leaving it up to future UNFCCC negotiating sessions to work out the details or to national governments to develop bilateral or multilateral linkage arrangements. Finally, the Paris outcome could establish institutional arrangements and rules that facilitate and promote linkage.

In pursuing this last role — namely, facilitating and promoting linkage — the UNFCCC regime could serve three related functions. First, it could provide an international infrastructure for linkage — for example, an international system for MRV, an international transaction log to register transfers between national systems and prevent double counting, and an international compliance mechanism. Second, it could play a regulatory function, for example by establishing minimum standards to ensure that linkage arrangements do not undermine the environmental integrity of international and domestic climate change efforts or by requiring international certification for linkage arrangements that will be used for international compliance. Third, the UNFCCC could also play a coordinating function, providing harmonized or model rules for national trading systems and/or international linkages in order to reduce the transaction costs of linkage.

Key Variables

Rules relating to linkage could be formulated in many different ways in the Paris outcome. They could be mandatory or optional; uniform or harmonized; and formalized in a legally binding, hard-law instrument, such as a treaty, or in a non-binding instrument, such as a COP decision, model rule, or guidance document.

International trade and finance instruments provide illustrations of these different options, as well as insights into how GHG linkage could be governed. Presently, a wide range of different types of agreements and organizations govern international trade and finance. An analysis of these approaches shows how different governance functions relating to linkage can be legally implemented, demonstrates that different governance approaches are preferred for different objectives, and suggests that some types of legal instrument are better suited to implementing a particular governance function.

Mandatory vs. Optional

Rules for multilateral linkage in the Paris outcome could be mandatory or optional. International instruments relating to finance and trade provide illustrations of these options. The General Agreement on Tariffs and Trade

(GATT), for example, sets mandatory rules limiting barriers to trade such as quotas. By contrast, the Convention on the International Sale of Goods (CISG) sets default rules, which parties are free to depart from in negotiating sales contracts. The Organisation for Economic Co-operation and Development (OECD) Model Tax Convention (OECDMTC) is even less directive than the CISG, in that it merely serves as a template that nations can choose to use as a starting point for bilateral negotiations.

In general, mandatory rules are appropriate to address 'cooperation' problems, where each nation has an incentive to cooperate only if it has an assurance that other nations will reciprocate. In contrast, optional rules — such as the CISG or OECDMTC rules — are useful in addressing 'coordination' problems, where harmonized rules help to lower transaction costs.

The Paris outcome could include a mixture of mandatory and optional elements. For example, it could commit parties undertaking linkage to a system of international tracking and review, but leave issues related to market coverage, cost containment, and treatment of new emitters and emitter closures to be addressed through informal coordination among national regulators or through the development of a model rule or guidelines by the COP, the Subsidiary Body for Implementation (SBI), or a non-UNFCCC institution.

Uniform vs. Harmonized

Multilateral linkage rules could provide for greater or less uniformity among national policies or linkage arrangements. Some international instruments specify highly detailed rules, which produce uniform results. The Kyoto Protocol and Marrakesh Accords, for example, prescribe precise rules to track and account for transfers of compliance units between parties. Other instruments prescribe more general standards, which harmonize national approaches (i.e. ensure some level of similarity), but give parties flexibility to take into account their particular circumstances. The Intergovernmental Panel on Climate Change (IPCC) inventory guidelines, for example, provide methodologies for estimating GHG emissions, but allow nations to choose among different tiers so that officials can use methods appropriate for their resources and can focus on those emissions that are most significant to their national totals (IPCC, 2006).

Uniformity and harmonization each have their advantages. Uniformity reduces transaction costs and creates greater policy certainty, while harmonization allows nations to take into account their particular circumstances and values, and therefore tends to be easier to achieve. Moreover, harmonization leaves some room for nations to experiment and may thus promote more dynamic systems that have a greater capacity to evolve over time.

From the perspective of market participants, international carbon trading would be easiest if every nation adopted the same linkage rules, so that trade between any two countries occurred in exactly the same way. However, this level of uniformity is unlikely to be achieved in the near term (if ever), and is unnecessary for linkage to be widely adopted. While some elements of linkage may require uniform rules, most can be addressed by harmonized rules — in other words, rules that are similar but not identical. For example, uniform rules may be needed to define the units of trade and to track units to avoid double counting internationally (Tuerk, Michael, Christian, & Wolfgang, 2009). However, procedures for MRV and crediting may require only broad adherence to minimum standards, to ensure that emission reductions actually occur, while leaving countries free to adopt more stringent rules that limit the use of emissions credits.

Importantly, some issues relevant to linkage can be addressed through local, non-harmonized rules. For example, national cap-and-trade systems could adopt different allocation methods and yet still be effectively linked. Insisting on uniform rules for all elements of linkage in the Paris outcome would thus be unnecessary and counter-productive. It would not yield more linkage activity, and it would delay the adoption of international legal instruments to facilitate linkage. A mixture of more and less uniform rules, providing for a spectrum of harmonization, is best for facilitating linkage.

Hard vs. Soft

Multilateral linkage rules could be contained in international instruments that are either 'hard' or 'soft' (Shelton, 2003). Treaties such as the UNFCCC, the Kyoto Protocol, the GATT, and the CISG represent hard law, and are legally binding as a matter of international law. By contrast, political agreements, guidelines, model rules, recommendations, and standards serve a prescriptive function but are not legal instruments — hence they represent soft law. It appears likely that the Paris outcome will include both hard and soft law elements, including a core agreement that is legally binding, as well as schedules and COP decisions that may have a 'softer' character.

Because hard law instruments provide a stronger signal of commitment than soft law instruments and are potentially applicable directly in domestic courts, they are useful for addressing issues where reciprocity or domestic enforcement is important (Tuerk *et al.*, 2009). Hard law instruments provide greater certainty, but are generally more difficult to negotiate and revise. For example, the World Trade Organisation (WTO) Uruguay Round agreements took eight years to negotiate, and the Doha Round of revisions to the WTO is still under way after thirteen years.

By contrast, soft law instruments are typically easier to adopt and amend, thus making them useful for addressing issues in their early phases, when there may not be sufficient political will to adopt a treaty or when it may be necessary to revise the rules on a regular basis in response to new information and circumstances. The Basel Capital Accords, for example, were quickly revised in response to the 2008 financial crisis, with Basel III being adopted in 2010.

A number of soft law standards have already been adopted to harmonize national climate mitigation systems, outside of the UNFCCC. For example, the International Organization for Standardization (ISO) has promulgated standards for monitoring and reporting GHG emissions and emissions reductions at the organization and project level (ISO, 2009a, 2009b, 2013a). ISO standards also exist for validating or verifying GHG reduction claims (ISO, 2009c, 2011, 2013b).

A mixture of hard and soft law instruments might be best suited to facilitate linkage. Key elements might be contained in a hard law instrument that is comparatively difficult to amend. A provision in a hard law instrument that mitigation-unit transfers can count towards a party's emission-reduction contribution would facilitate widescale linkage. A hard law instrument might also include model rules defining the units to be used for linkage, a requirement that parties allow international tracking of units in order to engage in linkage, and an articulation of general principles related to environmental integrity, such as a prohibition on double counting.

Other elements of linkage, however, could potentially be addressed in soft law instruments or through informal coordination among national regulators. Either of these approaches would allow for greater flexibility to make changes in the future. For example, minimum standards for national and international MRV, registries, and crediting mechanisms might be set forth in soft law instruments. Although soft law instruments are not legally binding, compliance with minimal standards could be assured by making compliance a condition of linkage by the linking jurisdictions, just as national governments have required compliance with the Financial Action Task Force (FATF) and Basel Committee standards as a condition for granting access to their domestic financial markets.

Relationships among Variables

Mandatoriness, uniformity, and legal form are independent variables; they need not co-vary. The capital adequacy requirements in the Basel Accords are phrased in mandatory rather than optional terms, even though the various Basel Accords are soft law instruments. Similarly, ISO standards may be very precise, even though they are not legally binding. Conversely, the CISG is a legal agreement, and hence qualifies as hard law, even though it sets forth non-mandatory, default rules from which parties may deviate.

Nevertheless, mandatoriness, uniformity, and legal form are related in that they all tend to increase the capacity of a rule to constrain behaviour. Thus, rules that address systemic risks or collective action problems are ideally formulated in precise, mandatory, and legally binding terms, all else being equal. By contrast, rules intended to address coordination problems may be optional and soft.

Elements of a 2015 Paris Outcome

The broad contours of the Paris outcome are beginning to come into focus and it is possible to make some preliminary observations about how linkage issues might be addressed. The Paris outcome is likely to include, at its core, a legal instrument (the core agreement) that establishes parties' basic commitments as well as the regime's institutional arrangements. Given the difficulties of negotiating a legal document in the relatively little time remaining before the Paris COP, as well as the difficulty, for some countries, of ratifying an elaborate agreement, the core agreement is likely to be comparatively brief, addressing only essential issues and doing so in a minimalist manner. More detailed rules addressing issues such as linkage are likely to be put forward in COP decisions. These could be adopted concurrently with the core agreement, as part of the Paris outcome, or, more likely, the core agreement could authorize the COP to adopt rules on linkage at subsequent sessions.

If the Paris outcome leaves the development of rules on linkage to future COP decisions, a key question will be whether these rules must be adopted before linkage can occur. If so, opponents of linkage would have tremendous leverage, because COP decisions require consensus. Alternatively, the Paris outcome could allow parties to move forward with linkage while simply authorizing the COP to adopt additional rules regarding linkage at a future date.

Authorization of Linkage

The Paris outcome may not need to authorize linkage between parties, because linkage is already authorized by Article 4.2(a) of the UNFCCC (1992). Nevertheless, an explicit statement that parties may transfer portions of their INDCs to other parties and that parties can use transferred units from other jurisdictions to achieve their INDCs would be helpful in providing certainty both to governments and private market participants. In addition, if it were deemed desirable to allow linkage between parties and non-parties to the core agreement, the core agreement should explicitly authorize such linkage.[13] Similarly, the core agreement might authorize the use of CDM credits by parties in achieving their INDCs, thereby providing a common crediting platform.

Minimum Standards to Ensure Environmental Integrity

Rules aimed at ensuring environmental integrity could, in theory, be contained in the core agreement itself or in subsequent COP decisions. However, it is unlikely that detailed rules for linkage can be developed in time for inclusion in the core agreement. Nor would including such detailed rules in the core agreement be desirable. Given the difficulties of amending a legally binding instrument, including linkage rules in the core agreement would make it difficult for these rules to evolve in light of experience.

---

[13] Although allowing linkages with non-parties would enhance cost-effectiveness, it would diminish the incentive of non-parties to join the core agreement.

For this reason, minimum standards to ensure environmental integrity should be elaborated in COP decisions or by another means, instead of the core agreement — this would include, for example, establishing the requirements for national and international MRV, registries, and crediting mechanisms (Hood, Briner, & Rocha, 2014; Tuerk *et al.*, 2009). In this case, the function of the core agreement with respect to linkage might be confined to articulating general principles related to environmental integrity, while also authorizing the COP, or another organization, to develop more detailed rules. Minimum standards would not require uniformity among national systems or linkage agreements. MRV and crediting procedures only need to be credible, not identical, in order for linkage to occur and be sustained (Tuerk *et al.*, 2009). Parties could have some flexibility in designing their national systems for MRV and crediting, as long as their systems satisfied the minimum requirements of the core agreement.

As noted earlier, most minimum standards for trade and financial linkages have been developed through soft law instruments, because these instruments are typically easier to negotiate and adopt and can also be revised more easily, allowing them to evolve over time in response to changing needs and circumstances (Brummer, 2011). Rules for multilateral linkage could also be developed outside the UNFCCC process by institutions that bring together national regulators, market participants, and private experts. The ISO is one possibility (Metcalf & Weisbach, 2012), as is the World Bank's Partnership for Market Readiness, but a new, informal institution addressing mitigation linkage is another alternative.

Whatever minimum standards are adopted for multilateral linkage, oversight of compliance would be important to ensure the integrity both of the core agreement (to the extent transfers are permitted for international compliance purposes) and of the linked national systems (to the extent transfers count towards domestic compliance). Oversight functions could be performed by a UNFCCC institution such as the expert review groups that currently review Annex I inventories, by national authorities in linked systems, or by an outside body.

Default/Model Rules

Many elements of GHG linkage could be addressed through default or model rules, from which states are free to deviate at their discretion. For example, a model rule might define key terms, including the compliance units (for example, metric tons of CO_2 equivalent). Rules that may benefit from this approach are typically concerned with the details of linking two regulatory systems. For example, two nations interested in linking their GHG cap-and-trade systems would have to consider rules regarding market coverage, cost containment, banking and borrowing, compliance periods, allocation methods, and the treatment of new emitters and emitter closures (Metcalf & Weisbach 2012; Tuerk *et al.*, 2009). Additional rules would be desirable for linking heterogeneous systems. For example, efforts to link a tax system and a cap-and-trade system must consider the treatment of emission tax payment credits (Metcalf & Weisbach, 2012).

Developing uniform rules to address all of these issues is unrealistic. Current and planned regulatory systems for GHG mitigation vary significantly in size, design, characteristics, and scope. They are tailored to achieve domestic policy objectives and reflect domestic circumstances and the domestic evolution of climate policy (Tuerk *et al.*, 2009). Thus, rules for linking disparate systems would probably need to be too different to support a uniform or even minimum-standard approach.

Despite the need for local flexibility, a degree of harmonization could be achieved through default rules that facilitate linkage by providing a common framework for jurisdictions to use when developing their own bilateral or plurilateral linkage agreements. In other words, jurisdictions would not need to develop bilateral agreements from scratch; they could choose to adopt some or all of the default rules and thereby shorten the time needed to develop linkage agreements. In addition, the existence of default rules may encourage efforts to harmonize disparate systems over time. As nations reform and update their linkage agreements, they may choose to match the default rules more closely. Over the long term, such harmonization would reduce transaction costs for market participants by reducing the number of different rules that must be learned.[14]

---

[14]The Convention on Contracts for the International Sale of Goods (CISG) and the OECD Model Tax Convention (OECDMTC) illustrate the role of default rules in lowering transaction costs. The CISG provides a set of substantive rules that parties can use to prepare contracts; these have become a *lingua franca* of international commerce (Kro¨ll *et al.*, 2011) and are enforceable in domestic courts. The OECDMTC serves as a basis for over 225 bilateral tax treaties (Miller & Oats, 2014). Although the OECDMTC is not binding on any nation, the terms of the convention are so commonly adopted as part of bilateral treaties that they represent, in effect, default rules for bilateral linkages between tax systems.

Default rules for GHG linkage could be developed by the COP or by an outside institution, and could be adopted via a hard law multilateral convention or a soft law approach. The hard law approach would deliver maximal certainty and probably has the greatest chance of eventually creating *de facto* uniform rules. However, a hard law approach also has several disadvantages. Negotiations may be difficult if not impossible given the disparities between existing and planned systems. Furthermore, because linked carbon markets are a relatively recent phenomenon, rules that appear optimal today may not be optimal in the future. A model law approach would provide flexibility and allow default rules to evolve through an iterative process, just as model tax treaties have evolved over time.[15] Once linked carbon markets are mature — perhaps decades in the future — a multilateral convention might be appropriate to encourage the default rules to evolve into uniform rules that would reduce transaction costs.

Conclusion

The upcoming Paris Conference of the Parties (COP) is a critical next step in the ongoing international process to reduce global GHG emissions. Whether the Paris outcome will be sufficiently ambitious to put the world on a path towards limiting global average warming to 2°C, as agreed in Cancun, remains to be seen. In general, greater ambition is more easily realized when costs are low. Market-based mechanisms are an important element in the portfolio of potential actions that can lead to cost-effective solutions. Linkage — between and among market and non-market systems for reducing GHG emissions — is another key element. This article's contribution is to catalogue and assess a variety of ways in which the Paris outcome, and more generally the ongoing negotiations, can facilitate and advance linked systems.

The minimum requirement for the Paris agreement is to do no harm, which silence would accomplish, but if linkage is to play a significant role in a hybrid international policy architecture, then several categories of design elements merit serious consideration for inclusion in the Paris

[15] In the US context, the Clean Air Task Force has proposed that the US Environmental Protection Agency issue a model rule for interstate emissions trading, under its proposed power plant rule under section 111(d) of the Clean Air Act (Clean Air Task Force, 2014).

outcome, either directly or by establishing a process for subsequent international negotiations. In general, effective linkage requires common definitions of key terms, including particularly the units to be used for compliance purposes. This will be particularly important for links between heterogeneous systems, and it is an area where a model rule could be particularly helpful.

Second, linkage requires registries and tracking mechanisms, whether the systems being linked are homogeneous or heterogeneous. Indeed, a key role for the top-down part of a hybrid architecture that allows for international linkage of national policy instruments will be the tracking, reporting, and recording of allowance unit transactions. International compliance units would make the functioning of an international transaction log more straightforward and reduce the administrative burden of reconciling international registries with national registries. Minimum standards for approving and measuring offsets may be important. Furthermore, market oversight and monitoring may increase confidence in the system, although in some cases, national and international institutions that can provide oversight already exist and may need only relatively minor additional capacity to assume these functions.

Including detailed linkage rules in the core agreement is not desirable as this could make it difficult for rules to evolve in light of experience. Instead, minimum standards to ensure environmental integrity should be elaborated in COP decisions, or by other means; for example, the COP could establish minimum requirements for national monitoring, reporting, and verification (MRV), registries, and crediting mechanisms. In terms of linkage, the function of the core agreement might be confined to articulating general principles relating to environmental integrity, while also authorizing the COP or another organization to develop more detailed rules. Whatever minimum standards are adopted, oversight of compliance will be important to ensure the integrity both of the Paris outcome and of linked national systems.

Many elements of GHG linkage can be addressed through default or model rules from which nations are free to deviate at their discretion. Rules that may benefit from this approach are typically concerned with the details of linking two regulatory systems. For example, nations interested in linking their cap-and-trade systems would have to consider rules for market coverage, cost containment, banking and borrowing, compliance periods, allocation methods, and the treatment of new emitters and emitter closures. Additional rules may be needed for linking of heterogeneous systems.

Developing uniform rules to address all of these issues is unrealistic. Instead, a degree of harmonization could be achieved through default rules that facilitate linkage by providing a common framework for nations to use when developing their own linkage agreements. Although there is no need for the core agreement itself to elaborate harmonized linkage rules, it might authorize the COP to develop default linkage rules that nations can use in negotiating bilateral linkage agreements.

Ultimately, the most valuable outcome of Paris regarding linkage might simply be the inclusion in the core agreement of an explicit statement that parties may transfer portions of their INDCs to other parties and that these transferred units may be used by the transferees to implement their INDCs. From a legal perspective, such a statement would help provide certainty both to governments and private market participants. Such a minimalist approach will allow diverse forms of linkage to arise, among what will inevitably be highly heterogeneous INDCs, thereby advancing the dual objectives of cost-effectiveness and environmental integrity in the international climate policy regime.

Acknowledgments

The authors gratefully acknowledge research assistance from John Agan, valuable comments on a previous version of the article from Dallas Burtraw, Mariana Conte Grand, Denny Ellerman, Christian Flachsland, Andrei Marcu, Matthew Ranson, Eswaran Somanathan, Robert Stowe, David Weisbach, and Jonathan Wiener, and financial support from the International Emissions Trading Association and six of its members (Chevron, GDF-Suez, Global CCS Institute, Rio Tinto, Shell, and TransCanada). The authors, however, are fully responsible for any errors and all opinions expressed in this chapter.

References

Bodansky, D. and E. Diringer. (2014). “Building flexibility and ambition into a 2015 climate agreement.” Arlington, VA: Center for Climate and Energy Solutions.

Bodansky, D., S. Hoedl, G. E. Metcalf, and R. N. Stavins. (2014). *Facilitating Linkage of Heterogeneous Regional, National, and Sub-National Climate Policies Through a Future International Agreement*. Discussion Paper. Cambridge, MA: Harvard Project on Climate Agreements, Belfer Center for Science and International Affairs, Harvard Kennedy School. http://belfercenter.ksg.harvard.edu/files/harvard-ieta-linkage-paper-nov-2014.pdf.

Brummer, C. (2011). *Soft Law and the Global Financial System: Rule Making in the 21st Century.* Cambridge, UK: Cambridge University Press.

Burtraw, D., K. L. Palmer, C. Munnings, P. Weber, and M. Woerman. (2013). *Linking by Degrees: Incremental Alignment of Cap-and-Trade Markets.* Discussion Paper 13-04. Washington, DC: Resources for the Future.

Clean Air Task Force. (2014). "Power switch: An effective, affordable approach to reducing carbon pollution from existing fossil-fueled power plants." Boston, MA.

European Commission. (2011). "Commission regulation (EU) no. 550/2011 of 7 June 2011." http://eur-lex.europa.eu/LexUriServ/LexUriServ.do?uri=OJ:L:2011:149:0001:0003:EN:PDF.

European Commission. (2014). "International carbon market." http://ec.europa.eu/clima/policies/ets/linking/index_en.htm.

Flachsland, C., R. Marschinski, and O. Edenhofer. (2009). "To link or not to link: Benefits and disadvantages of linking cap-and-trade systems." *Climate Policy*. **9**: 358–372.

Helm, C. (2003). "International emissions trading with endogenous allowance choices." *Journal of Public Economics*. **87**: 2737–2747.

Holtsmark, B. and D. E. Sommervoll. (2012). "International emissions trading: Good or bad?" *Economics Letters*. **117**: 362–364.

Hood, C., G. Briner, and M. Rocha. (2014). *GHG or not GHG: Accounting for Diverse Mitigation Contributions in the Post-2020 Climate Framework.* Climate Change Expert Group Paper No. 2014(2). Paris: OECD.

IPCC. (2006). 2006 IPCC Guidelines for National Greenhouse Gas Inventories. Hayama: Intergovernmental Panel on Climate Change. www.ipcc-nggip.iges.or.jp/public/2006gl.

ISO. (2009a). "ISO 14064-1:2006 Greenhouse gases — Part 1: Specification with guidance at the organization level for quantification and reporting of greenhouse gas emissions and removals." Geneva: International Organization for Standardization.

ISO. (2009b). "ISO 14064-2:2006 Greenhouse gases — Part 2: Specification with guidance at the project level for quantification, monitoring and reporting of greenhouse gas emission reductions or removal enhancements." Geneva: International Organization for Standardization.

ISO. (2009c). "ISO 14064-3:2006 Greenhouse gases — Part 3: Specification with guidance for the validation and verification of greenhouse gas assertions." Geneva: International Organization for Standardization.

ISO. (2011). "ISO 14066:2011 Greenhouse gases — Competence requirements for greenhouse gas validation teams and verification teams." Geneva: International Organization for Standardization. www.iso.org/iso/ catalogue_detail?csnumber=43277.

ISO. (2013a). "ISO/TR 14069:2013 Greenhouse gases — Quantification and reporting of greenhouse gas emissions for organizations — Guidance for the application of ISO 14064-1." Geneva: International Organization for Standardization. www.iso.org/iso/catalogue_detail.htm?csnumber=43280.

ISO. (2013b). "ISO 14065:2013 Greenhouse gases — Requirements for greenhouse gas validation and verification bodies for use in accreditation or other forms of recognition." Geneva: International Organization for Standardization. www.iso.org/iso/catalogue_detail?csnumber=60168.

Jaffe, J., M. Ranson, and R. N. Stavins. (2009). "Linking tradable permit systems: A key element of emerging international climate policy architecture." *Ecology Law Quarterly*. **36**: 789–808.

Kröll, S., L. Mistelis, and P. P. Viscasillas. (2011). Introduction to the CISG. In S. Kröll, L. Mistelis, and P. P. Viscasillas (Eds.), *The United Nations Convention on Contracts for the International Sale of Goods: Article by Article Commentary*, pp. 19–20. Munich: CH Beck/Hart Publishing.

Marcu, A. (2014). *The Role of Market Mechanisms in a Post-2020 Climate Change Agreement*. Special Report 87. Brussels: Centre for European Policy Studies. www.ceps.eu/book/role-market-mechanisms-post-2020-climate-change-agreement.

Metcalf, G. and D. Weisbach. (2012). "Linking policies when tastes differ: Global climate policy in a heterogeneous world." *Review of Environmental Economics and Policy*. **6**(1): 110–129.

Miller, A. and L. Oats. (2014). *Principles of International Taxation*, 4th ed. Haywards Heath: Bloomsbury Professional.

Newell, R., W. Pizer, and D. Raimi. (2013). "Carbon markets 15 years after Kyoto: Lessons learned, new challenges." *Journal of Economic Perspectives*. **27**: 123–146.

Prag, A., C. Hood, and P. M. Barata. (2013). *Made to Measure: Options for Emissions Accounting Under the UNFCCC*. Climate Change Expert Group Paper No. 2013(1). Paris: OECD.

Ranson, M. and R. N. Stavins. (2013). "Post-Durban climate policy architecture based on linkage of cap-and-trade systems." *The Chicago Journal of International Law*. **13**: 403–438.

Ranson, M. and R. N. Stavins. (2015). Linkage of greenhouse gas emissions trading systems: Learning from experience. *Climate Policy*. **16**, 284–300.

Shelton, D. (2003). *Commitment and Compliance: The Role of Non-Binding Norms in the International Legal System*. Oxford, UK: Oxford University Press.

Somanathan, E. (2010). "What do we expect from an international climate agreement? A perspective from a low-income country." In J. E. Aldy and R. N. Stavins (eds.), *Post-Kyoto International Climate Policy: Implementing Architectures for Agreement*, pp. 599–617. Cambridge, UK: Cambridge University Press.

Tuerk, A., M. Michael, F. Christian, and S. Wolfgang. (2009). "Linking carbon markets: Concepts, case studies, and pathways." *Climate Policy*. **9**: 341–357.

UNFCCC. (1992). "Text of the convention." http://unfccc.int/essential_background/convention/items/6036.php.

UNFCCC. (1998). "Kyoto Protocol to the United Nations Framework Convention on Climate Change." http://unfccc.int/resource/docs/convkp/kpeng.pdf.

UNFCCC. (2012). "Report of the Conference of the Parties on its seventeenth session, held in Durban from 28 November to 11 December 2011. FCCC/CP/2011/9/Add.1, Decision 1/CP.17." http://unfccc.int/resource/docs/2011/cop17/eng/09a01.pdf.

World Bank. (2014). "State and trends of carbon pricing 2014." Washington, DC: World Bank. http://documents.worldbank.org/curated/en/2014/05/19572833/state-trends-carbon-pricing-2014.

https://doi.org/10.1142/9789811292415_0023

Chapter 23

Linking Climate Policies to Advance Global Mitigation: Joining Jurisdictions Can Increase Efficiency of Mitigation[*]

Michael A. Mehling[†,‖], Gilbert E. Metcalf[‡,§,‖,††], and Robert N. Stavins[§,‖,¶,,‡‡]**

[†]*Massachusetts Institute of Technology, Cambridge, MA, USA*

[‡]*University of Strathclyde, Glasgow, UK*

[§]*Tufts University, Medford, MA, USA*

[‖]*John F. Kennedy School of Government, Harvard University, Cambridge, MA, USA*

[¶]*Resources for the Future, Washington, DC, USA*

[**]*National Bureau of Economic Research, Cambridge, MA, USA*

[††]*gmetcalf@tufts.edu*

[‡‡]*robert_stavins@harvard.edu*

The November 2017 negotiations in Bonn, Germany, under the auspices of the United Nations Framework Convention on Climate Change (UNFCCC) validated that the Paris Agreement has met one of two necessary conditions

[*]This chapter was originally published in *Science*, **359**(6379), 997–998, March 2, 2018.

for success. By achieving broad participation, including 195 countries, accounting for 99 percent of global greenhouse gas (GHG) emissions (UNFCCC, 2018), the agreement dramatically improves on the 14 percent of global emissions associated with countries acting under the Kyoto Protocol (UNFCCC, 2017), the international agreement it will replace in 2020. But the second necessary condition, adequate collective ambition of the nationally determined contributions (NDCs) that countries have individually pledged, has not been met. One promising approach to incentivize countries to increase ambition over time is to link different climate policies, such that emission reductions in one jurisdiction can be counted toward mitigation commitments of another jurisdiction. Drawing on our research and our experiences in Bonn, we explore options and challenges for facilitating such linkages in light of the considerable heterogeneity that is likely to characterize regional, national, and subnational policy efforts.

Linkage is important, in part, because it can reduce the costs of achieving a given emissions-reduction objective (Mehling *et al.*, 2017). Lower costs, in turn, may contribute politically to embracing more ambitious objectives. In a world where the marginal cost of abatement (that is, the cost to reduce an additional ton of emissions) varies widely, linkage improves overall cost-effectiveness by allowing jurisdictions to finance reductions in other jurisdictions with relatively lower costs while allowing the former jurisdictions to count the emission reductions toward targets set in their NDCs (see the figure). For example, the baseline efficiency of energy use in low-income countries is very low, relative to high-income countries. Linking can leverage such differences to reduce overall mitigation cost. In effect, linkage drives participating jurisdictions toward a common cost of carbon, equalizing the marginal cost of abatement and producing a more efficient distribution of abatement activities. These benefits could potentially reduce the cost of achieving the emissions reductions specified in the initial NDCs under the Paris Agreement 32 percent by 2030 and 54 percent by 2050 (World Bank, Ecofys, and Vivid Economics, 2016).

In addition to lowering costs, linkage can improve the functioning of individual markets, reducing market power by including more firms and reducing price volatility by enlarging the market. Beyond such direct economic benefits, political benefits exist. As jurisdictions band together, linking can signal political momentum that contributes to more policies where they do not yet exist and more ambitious policies where they are already in place. Also, administrative economies of scale can be achieved through knowledge sharing in policy design and operation and through shared administrative costs. Finally, and importantly, linkage can allow for the key UNFCCC equity principle of "common-but-differentiated responsibilities and respective capabilities" to be pursued without sacrificing cost-effectiveness.

There are also legitimate concerns with linkage, including distributional impacts within and across jurisdictions, even though aggregate abatement costs are reduced. Because linking is inherently voluntary, however, linking will generally not occur unless both parties to a link anticipate that overall benefits of the link, including revenue from selling emission reductions, will outweigh costs. Likewise, individual exchanges made between compliance entities are voluntary.

Transferring pollution obligations can raise concerns about environmental justice. Although GHGs are a global pollutant, changes in GHG emissions can affect emissions of correlated local pollutants (for example, particulate matter). This is a reasonable concern, but linkage could help reduce correlated local pollution in developing countries, because jurisdictions that take on increased mitigation efforts as a result of linkage, many of which will be low-income developing countries, will see local pollution decrease along with lower GHG emissions.

A more serious concern of linkage stems from the automatic propagation of some design elements from one system to another, in particular, cost-containment mechanisms in cap-and-trade systems — banking, borrowing, and price collars. This means that there is decreased autonomy, as rules in one system can affect prices in another. All of this refers to what we think of as "hard linkage," a formal recognition by a mitigation program in one jurisdiction of emission reductions undertaken in another jurisdiction for purposes of complying with the first jurisdiction's mitigation program. Examples of hard linkage are the links between cap-and-trade systems in the state of California, USA, and Québec, Canada, and, more recently, the European Union (EU) and Switzerland.

But another possibility is "soft linkage," by which we mean an agreement — explicit or implicit — to harmonize carbon prices either at a specific level or within overlapping bands. With soft linkage, there is no recognition of emission reductions in one system by the other system for purposes of compliance. Still, by aligning carbon prices, such harmonization improves overall economic efficiency.

Linkage in the Paris Agreement

Article 6.2 of the Paris Agreement provides a foundation for linkage by recognizing that parties to the agreement may "choose to pursue voluntary cooperation in the implementation of their" NDCs through "the use of internationally transferred mitigation outcomes" (ITMOs) (UNFCCC, 2015). In contrast to the Kyoto Protocol (which also includes provisions for international cooperation), the voluntary and flexible architecture of the Paris Agreement allows for wide variation, not only in the types of climate policies countries choose to implement but also in the form and stringency of the abatement targets they adopt.

To be clear, there are three conceptually — and operationally — distinct aspects of international policy linkage: (i) (the focus of our analysis) provisions in Article 6.2 of the Paris Agreement and related guidance that can facilitate international linkage, by providing, for example, for ITMOs to be used as an accounting mechanism when "compliance" with NDCs is measured; (ii) agreements between two or more jurisdictions to recognize emission reductions generated in the other jurisdictions; and (iii) two or more compliance entities, one in each of the linked jurisdictions, engage in an exchange, for example, permitting allowances to move between cap-and-trade systems.

Linkage is relatively straightforward when policies involved are similar. But there are several potential sources of heterogeneity: type of policy instrument (e.g., taxes, cap-and-trade, performance or technology standards); level of government jurisdiction involved (e.g., regional, national, subnational); status under the Paris Agreement (that is, whether or not the jurisdiction is a party to the agreement or within a party); nature of the policy target (e.g., absolute mass-based emissions, emissions intensity, change relative to business-as-usual); and operational details of the country's NDC (e.g., type of mitigation target, choice of target and reference years, sectors and GHGs covered). Most forms of heterogeneity, however, do not present insurmountable obstacles to linkage.

In principle, the most straight-forward case of international climate policy linkage would be a pair of national cap-and-trade systems in parties to the agreement, with each using an absolute (mass-based) target in its NDC (for example, cap-and-trade systems in New Zealand and Switzerland). A less obvious case would be a pair of subnational policies — one a carbon tax and one a cap-and-trade system (for example, carbon tax in British Columbia, Canada, and cap-and-trade in Tokyo, Japan). Both policies can be designed to facilitate heterogeneous linkage (Metcalf and Weisbach, 2012). Another case of heterogeneous linkage might be between the EU emissions trading system and California's cap-and-trade program. All of these would be conceptually feasible and merit consideration, although each raises issues that require attention and call for specific accounting guidance, if linkage is to include the use of ITMOs under the Paris Agreement.

A Path Forward

Parties to the Paris Agreement are working to elaborate guidance on Article 6.2 but have expressed widely differing views on what issues to include (Obergassel and Asche, 2017). In Bonn, parties signaled agreement on the need to offer at least minimal guidance on how to account for transfers of ITMOs. Beyond that, however, positions diverge on whether to address broader questions that bear on linkage under Article 6.2. Particular divisions center around issues of environmental integrity, governance, and sustainable development.

Our analysis, based on case studies of various types of heterogeneous linked systems, reveals common themes (Mehling *et al.*, 2017). What emerges is the importance of guidance on Article 6.2 that sets out a robust accounting framework to prevent double counting of GHG reductions, to ensure that the timing (vintage) of claimed reductions and respective ITMO transfers is correctly accounted for, and to ensure that participating countries make appropriate adjustments for emissions or reductions covered by their NDCs when using ITMOs. Suggested approaches for ITMO accounting under Article 6.2 (Mehling *et al.*, 2017) include, in particular, how to make adjustments to national emission budgets to account for ITMOs and how to account for heterogeneous base years, different vintages of targets and outcomes, and transfers between parties and non-parties to the agreement. These issues were identified, if not yet resolved, during the negotiations on Article 6.2 in Bonn. As negotiators proceed to address them, they can draw on a wealth of experience and existing research (Jaffe *et al.*, 2009; Ranson and Stavins, 2016; Bodansky *et al.*, 2016; Mehling, 2016). Future study should expand on the specific conditions of accounting and ITMO transfers under the evolving architecture of the Paris Agreement.

An important insight from our analysis, however, is that parties should exercise caution when developing guidance that goes beyond accounting issues. Onerous conditions related to the ambition or integrity of domestic action, for instance, could deter linkage. This does not mean that such concerns should be neglected; rather, they are best addressed under separate corresponding negotiating tracks — such as the Talanoa

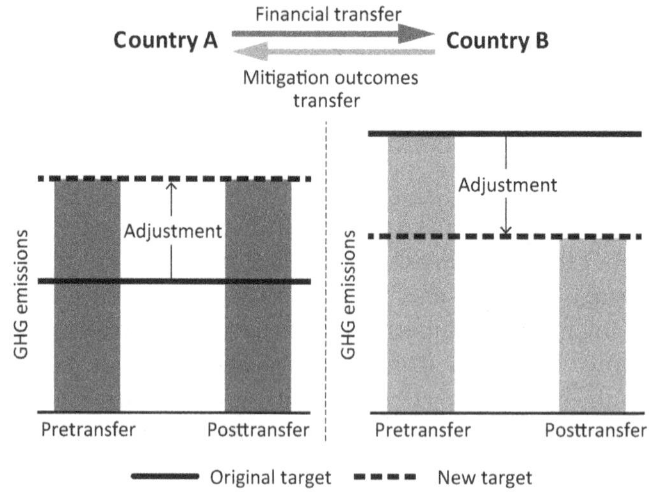

Notes: Transferring mitigation outcomes.

Rather than reduce its greenhouse gas (GHG) emissions to meet its original target, country A cooperates with country B, which can reduce emissions at lower cost. Incentivized to reduce emissions, country B sells part of its mitigation outcome to country A. Both targets are adjusted to reflect the transfer, and country A meets its adjusted target at lower cost than if it had reduced its own emissions.

dialogue, to take stock of collective efforts of parties — or the enhanced transparency framework under Article 13 of the Paris Agreement.

Clear and consistent guidance for accounting of emissions transfers under Article 6.2 can contribute to greater certainty and predictability for parties engaged in voluntary cooperation, facilitating expanded use of linkage. Too much guidance, however, particularly if it includes restrictive quality or ambition requirements, might impede linkage and dampen incentives for cooperation. Such a combination of common accounting rules and an absence of restrictive criteria and conditions may accelerate linkage and allow for broader and more ambitious policy cooperation, which can increase the potential for parties to scale up the ambition of their NDCs. That may ultimately foster stronger engagement between parties (and non-parties), as well as with regional and subnational jurisdictions.

The parties to the Paris Agreement will continue negotiations in May, toward a goal of agreeing to a finalized rule book for Article 6 at the annual UNFCCC summit in Katowice, Poland, in December 2018. Decisions that the negotiators reach this year could greatly advance, or impede, international climate policy linkage and thereby play a key role in determining the fate of the Paris Agreement.

Acknowledgments

The authors acknowledge comments from S. Biniaz, D. Bodansky, C. Haug, C. Hood, and A. Marcu and financial support from the Enel Foundation.

References

Bodansky, D. M., S. A. Hoedl, G. E. Metcalf, and R. N. Stavins. (2016). "Facilitating linkage of climate policies through the Paris outcome." *Climate Policy*. **16**: 956–972.

Jaffe, J., M. Ranson, and R. N. Stavins. (2009). "Linking tradable permit systems: A key element of emerging international climate policy architecture." *Ecology Law Quarterly*. **36**: 789–808.

Mehling, M. A. (2016). "Legal frameworks for linking national emissions trading systems." In C. P. Carlarne, K. R. Gray, and R. G. Tarasofsky (eds.), *The Oxford Handbook of International Climate Change Law*, pp. 261–288. Oxford, UK: Oxford University Press.

Mehling, M. A., G. E. Metcalf, and R. N. Stavins. (2017). *Linking Heterogeneous Climate Policies (Consistent with the Paris Agreement.* Discussion Paper ES 17-6. Cambridge, MA: Harvard Project on Climate Agreements.

Metcalf, G. E. and D. Weisbach. (2012). "Linking policies when tastes differ: Global climate policy in a heterogeneous world." *Review of Environmental Economics and Policy*. **6**: 110–129.

Obergassel, W. and F. Asche. (2017). *Shaping the Paris Mechanisms Part III: An Update on Submissions on Article 6 of the Paris Agreement.* JIKO Policy Paper 05/2017. Wuppertal: Wuppertal Institute for Climate, Environment, and Energy.

Ranson, M. and R. N. Stavins. (2016). "Linking climate policies: A survey of the literature." *Climate Policy*. **16**: 284–300.

UNFCCC. (2015). "Paris Agreement, Article 6." In *Conference of the Parties, Twenty-First Session*, pp. 7–8. Paris, France: United Nations.

UNFCCC. (2017). "Kyoto Protocol." http://unfccc.int/kyoto_protocol/items/2830.php.

UNFCCC. (2018). "Paris Agreement — Status of Ratification." http://unfccc.int/paris_agreement/items/9444.php

World Bank, Ecofys, & Vivid Economics. (2016). *State and Trends of Carbon Pricing 2016.* Washington, DC: World Bank.

https://doi.org/10.1142/9789811292415_0024

Chapter 24

Linking Heterogeneous Climate Policies (Consistent with the Paris Agreement)[*]

Michael A. Mehling[†], Gilbert E. Metcalf[‡,], and Robert N. Stavins[§,‖,¶,††]**

[†]*Center for Energy and Environmental Policy Research, Massachusetts Institute of Technology, University of Strathclyde School of Law, Cambridge, MA, USA*

[‡]*Tufts University, Medford, MA, USA.*

[§]*John F. Kennedy School of Government, Harvard University, Cambridge, MA, USA*

[‖]*Resources for the Future, Washington, DC, USA*

[¶]*National Bureau of Economic Research, Cambridge, MA, USA*

[**]*gmetcalf@tufts.edu*

[††]*robert_stavins@harvard.edu*

The Paris Agreement to the United Nations Framework Convention on Climate Change has achieved one of two key necessary conditions for ultimate success — a broad base of participation among the countries of the world. But another key necessary condition has yet to be achieved — adequate collective ambition of the individual nationally determined

[*]This chapter was originally published in *Environmental Law*, **8**(4), 647–698, 2019.

contributions. How can the climate negotiators provide a structure that will include incentives to increase ambition over time? An important part of the answer can be international linkage of regional, national, and subnational policies, that is, formal recognition of emission reductions undertaken in another jurisdiction for the purpose of meeting a Party's own mitigation objectives. A central challenge is how to facilitate such linkage in the context of the very great heterogeneity that characterizes climate policies along five dimensions: type of policy instrument, level of government jurisdiction, status of that jurisdiction under the Paris Agreement, nature of the policy instrument's target, and the nature along several dimensions of each Party's Nationally Determined Contribution. We consider such heterogeneity among policies, and identify which linkages of various combinations of characteristics are feasible; of these, which are most promising; and what accounting mechanisms would make the operation of respective linkages consistent with the Paris Agreement.

Introduction

The Paris Agreement, adopted by the Twenty-First Conference of the Parties of the United Nations Framework Convention on Climate Change (UNFCCC),[1] features a hybrid policy architecture, which combines top-down elements for monitoring, reporting, and verification,[2] with bottom-up elements, including Nationally Determined Contributions (NDCs) that specify what each country intends to do to reduce its emissions, taking into account domestic political feasibility and other relevant factors.[3] With this architecture, the Agreement represented a dramatic departure from almost two decades of negotiations prior to the Fifteenth Session of the Conference of the Parties in Copenhagen in 2009,[4] and thereby appeared to achieve a key necessary condition for ultimate success, namely adequate scope of participation, with participating nations

[1] U.N. Framework Convention on Climate Change, *Adoption of the Paris Agreement*, 2–3, U.N. Doc. FCCC/CP/2015/10/Rev.1 (December 12, 2015) [hereinafter Paris Agreement].

[2] *Id.* at 6, 24.

[3] *Id.* at 24.

[4] See *generally* U.N. Framework Convention on Climate Change, *Report of the Conference of the Parties on Its Fifteenth Session, held in Copenhagen from 7 to 9 December 2009*, 5–7, U.N. Doc. FCCC/CP/2009/11/Add.1 (March 30, 2010) (text of the Copenhagen Accord).

accounting for approximately 97 percent of global greenhouse gas (GHG) emissions,[5] in contrast with the Kyoto Protocol (current, second commitment period), which accounts for 14 percent of global emissions from participating nations with quantified targets.[6]

The other key necessary condition for ultimate success of this new approach is adequate, collective ambition of the individual NDCs, including net emissions reductions that would put the world on a path toward achieving the global goal of limiting temperature increases to well below 2°C.[7] A central question is how to provide a structure, incentives, or both that will facilitate increases in ambition over time. International linkage of regional, national, and sub-national policies can be an important part of the answer.

By linkage, we mean a formal recognition by a GHG mitigation program in one jurisdiction (a regional, national, or sub-national government) of emission reductions undertaken in another jurisdiction for purposes of complying with the first jurisdiction's mitigation policy.[8] Linkage can be very straightforward, as with the bilateral recognition of allowances under two cap-and-trade regimes,[9] but linkage can also take place among a heterogeneous set of policy instruments, such as between systems of performance standards, carbon taxes, and cap-and-trade.[10]

Leading up to the Paris Agreement, linkage was a core focus of one key track of international climate negotiations, namely the Framework for

---

[5] Stavins, R. N. (November 2017). "Linking heterogeneous climate policies (and activities at COP-23 in Bonn." *Huffington Post*. https://perma.cc/WMT7-433H. If the United States proceeds to withdraw from the Paris Agreement, as it has announced it will do, the share of global GHG emissions associated with nations participating in the Agreement will fall from 97 percent to 82 percent. *Id.*

[6] *Id.*

[7] Paris Agreement, *supra* note 1.

[8] Our use of the term linkage should not be confused with the concept of linkage in the international relations literature, where it refers to negotiated agreements between countries in which multiple issues are negotiated and "linked" for purposes of coming to agreement on the overall package. *See* Haas, E. (1980). "Why collaborate? Issue-linkage and international regimes." *World Politics*. **32**: 357, 373.

[9] Ranson, M. and Stavins, R. N. (2013). *Linkage of Greenhouse Gas Emissions Trading Systems: Learning from Experience 3–5*. Harvard Kennedy School Faculty Research Working Paper Series, Discussion Paper ES 2013-2. https://perma.cc/8WX8-AB65.

[10] *Id.*

Various Approaches (FVA), which originated at Thirteenth Session of the Conference of the Parties in Bali, Indonesia in 2007.[11] One challenge for negotiators in Paris was to ensure that the Agreement they reached would facilitate the growth and operation of international linkages, and, at a minimum, not put in place inappropriate or excessive rules that would obstruct effective, bottom-up linkage.[12] This was achieved with Article 6 of the Paris Agreement,[13] which recognizes that some Parties[14] to the Agreement "choose to pursue voluntary cooperation in the implementation of their nationally determined contributions" through "the use of internationally transferred mitigation outcomes."[15]

A challenge now for jurisdictions around the world considering international linkages, as well as for those preparing guidance for the implementation of the Paris Agreement, is the substantial degree of heterogeneity that characterizes climate policies along three dimensions: different types of policy instruments, different levels of political jurisdictions implementing those policies, and different types of targets. Our purpose is to consider such heterogeneity among policies, and identify which linkages of various combinations of characteristics are feasible; of

[11] See U.N. Framework Convention on Climate Change. (March 14, 2008). *Report of the Conference of the Parties on Its Thirteenth Session, Held in Bali from 3 to 15 December 2007*, 3–4, U.N. Doc. FCCC/CP/2007/6/Add.1. https://perma.cc/GLB4-WYGP (text of the Bali Action Plan).

[12] See Bodansky, D. M. *et al.* (2016). "Facilitating linkage of climate policies through the Paris outcome." *Climate Policy*. **16**: 956, 957.

[13] Full text of Article 6 is available at Appendix 1.

[14] Parties to the Agreement are individual countries plus the European Union. See *7. d) Paris Agreement*, U.N. Treaties Collection, https://perma.cc/SS88-VP5W (listing Parties to the Paris Agreement as of Oct. 9, 2018).

[15] Neither Article 6 of the Paris Agreement nor the text of the accompanying decision offers a definition of an Internationally Transferred Mitigation Outcome (ITMO), but the International Emissions Trading Association has proposed the following:

> An internationally transferred mitigation outcome (ITMO) is the subtraction of a given absolute quantity of greenhouse gas emissions measured in tonnes of carbon dioxide equivalent from the quantitatively defined nationally determined contribution of a given Party . . . and the addition of an equivalent amount to the quantitatively defined nationally determined contribution . . . of another Party. INT'L EMISSIONS TRADING ASS'N, ARTICLE 6 OF THE PARIS AGREEMENT IMPLEMENTATION GUIDANCE: AN IETA 'STRAW PROPOSAL' 3 (2017), https://perma.cc/UK56-NRUA.

these, which are most promising and what accounting mechanisms (under Article 6) would make the operation of respective linkages consistent with the Paris Agreement. After a failed attempt in December 2018 in Katowice, Poland, to reach consensus on operational details for Article 6, Parties to the Agreement are scheduled to adopt such guidance at the Second Session of the Conference of the Parties serving as the Meeting of the Parties to the Paris Agreement (CMA) in Santiago, Chile, in November 2019.[16]

To be clear, there are thus three conceptually — and operationally — distinct aspects of international policy linkage: (1) provisions in Article 6 of the Paris Agreement and related guidance that can facilitate international linkage, by providing — for example — for Internationally Transferred Mitigation Outcome (ITMOs) to be used as an accounting mechanism when "compliance" with NDCs is measured; (2) agreements between two jurisdictions (Parties to the Paris Agreement or possibly sub-national jurisdictions) to recognize emission reductions generated in the other jurisdiction; and (3) two or more compliance entities, with at least one in each of the linked jurisdictions, engage in an exchange, such as with allowances moving between two cap-and-trade systems.

The chapter is organized as follows. In the second section we briefly review the arguments for linkage. In the third section we examine the various options that exist under the major types of policy heterogeneity, relating these to the current status of climate policies around the world and to the actual NDCs submitted under the Paris Agreement. In the fourth section we identify five key cases of potential climate policy linkages, and examine each of these from a physical, economic, and legal perspective. Then, in the final section we conclude by drawing on our analysis to identify common threads, lessons, policy implications, and pending questions still to be answered.

Why is Linking Important?

The major economic argument for linkage is cost effectiveness, meaning the ability to achieve a given level of emission reductions at the lowest cost to society. Since a major impediment to ambitious climate policy is

[16]U.N. Framework Convention on Climate Change, *Matters Relating to Article 6 of the Paris Agreement and Paragraphs 36–40 of Decision 1/CP.21*, https://perma.cc/M79H-HT37 (sets out mandate for continued negotiations).

concern about the economic cost of mitigation, any policy that can lower the cost of mitigation should lower political resistance to ambitious policy.[17] We explain and demonstrate in Appendix 2 how equalizing the marginal cost of abatement across firms is a necessary condition for a globally cost effective policy.

Linkage provides a mechanism to facilitate a shift of abatement activities from one country to another by allowing firms in the first country to count emission reduction efforts they facilitate in the second country towards meeting their own obligations (in the first country).[18] How this mechanism operates depends on the type of climate policy in effect in each of the linking countries, as we discuss below.[19]

Thus, a major argument for linkage is the aggregate cost savings that linkage can bring about through convergence toward a common price of carbon — whether explicit with carbon-pricing instruments or implicit with other policy instruments — in the two linked jurisdictions. It has been estimated that international linkage could reduce the cost of achieving the emissions reductions specified in the initial set of NDCs under the Paris Agreement by 32 percent by 2030 and by 54 percent by 2050.[20] Another potential merit of linkage is improvement in the functioning of the individual markets through reduced market power and reduced total price volatility, although the link also potentially transmits price volatility from one jurisdiction to another.[21] Importantly, under the Paris Agreement's structure

---

[17] See World Bank & Ecofys, State and Trends of Carbon Pricing 2016, 24 (2016). Global cost is certainly not the only impediment to climate policy. Countries care about how that global cost is allocated among countries, and have concerns about how policy may affect future development opportunities. However, those concerns may be more easily addressed as global costs are decreased through the use of cost-effective policies. That said, cost-effectiveness in achieving any short-run climate policy goal may not ensure the longer-term energy-sector transformation needed to move to a zero-carbon economy. So, while equalizing marginal abatement costs is a necessary condition for global cost effectiveness, it is not sufficient for achieving all long-term goals.

[18] See Bodansky *et al.*, *supra* note 12, at 957–958.

[19] Note that in the case illustrated in Appendix 2, allowance price (in cap-and-trade systems) in Country A fall from P_A to P, and increase in country B from P_B to P.

[20] See State and Trends of Carbon Pricing 2016, *supra* note 17, at 83, 86.

[21] Flachsland, C. *et al.* (2009). "To link or not to link: Benefits and disadvantages of linking cap-and-trade systems." *Climate Policy*. **9**: 358, 361. Ranson, M. and R. N. Stavins. (2013). "Post-Durban climate policy architecture based on linkage of cap-and-trade systems." *Chicago Journal of International Law*. **13**: 403, 409.

of voluntary statements of targets by each Party through its NDC, linkage holds promise of providing a means to achieve cost-effectiveness without sacrificing the UNFCCC's principle of common but differentiated responsibilities and respective capabilities.[22]

Linkage also raises legitimate concerns, however, including the distributional impacts that will be felt in each jurisdiction, due to the presence of both winners and losers among individual firms and ultimately among different consumer groups to the extent changes in allowance prices are passed through to final consumers. For example, when allowance prices change (converge) in two linked cap-and-trade systems, firms that are allowance buyers benefit if they are in the system where prices fall, whereas firms that are allowance sellers benefit if they are in the system where prices increase.[23] In addition, as we discuss below, linkage can bring about the automatic propagation of some design elements (in particular with cap-and-trade systems, cost-containment mechanisms, such as banking provisions) from one jurisdiction to another.[24] More generally, linkage can translate into a loss of sovereignty and thus reduced autonomy for the linking jurisdictions.[25] A broader concern is that, from a game-theoretic perspective, the possibility of linkage can induce parties to put in place less ambitious national targets so as to create cheap surplus units that their firms could sell into the linked market.[26]

The economic argument for linkage suggests that we would expect to observe linkages between political jurisdictions with widely divergent marginal costs of abatement (or, equivalently, shadow prices of carbon[27]).

---

[22] Bodansky *et al.*, *supra* note 12, at 957.

[23] Jaffe, J. *et al.* (2009). "Linking tradable permit systems: A key element of emerging international climate policy architecture." *Ecology Law Quarterly*. **36**: 789, 797.

[24] Ranson, M. and R. N. Stavins, *Linkage of Greenhouse Gas Emissions Trading Systems: Learning from Experience*, *supra* note 9, at 1–2.

[25] *Id.* at 16.

[26] See, e.g., Helm, C. (2003). "International emissions trading with endogenous allowance choices." *Journal of Public Economics*. **87**: 2737, 2738. See generally Green, J. F. (2017). "Don't link carbon markets." *Nature*. 543: 484. (containing a broad critique of linking).

[27] "Shadow price" refers to the cost to an economy of reducing emissions by one ton through regulation. Regulatory actions to reduce emissions (for example, fuel economy or carbon intensity standards) impose a cost per ton of emissions reductions. Because this cost is not explicitly observed (as a tax rate or allowance price), it is referred to as a shadow price.

To date, linkage agreements, whether enacted or under discussion, have been between jurisdictions with relatively similar carbon prices (for example, California and Québec) undercutting the major economic argument for linkage.[28] These linkages may be driven by political and administrative benefits more than economic benefits. The political benefits from linking policies may stem from such linkage providing a sense of momentum to which political supporters of climate policy can point and so build support.[29] And once a link has been established, it may create path dependency that favors continued climate action, given barriers to termination of a link.[30] Since greenhouse gas emissions are a global pollutant, no politician wants to appear to be acting unilaterally to control emissions. Linking with other jurisdictions is a tangible signal of a multilateral approach to the climate problem.

There are also administrative economies of scale through linkage. Jurisdictions can share best practices in designing and operating emission control policies and so learn from each other. They can also share administrative and oversight costs and so avoid costly duplication of control efforts. This can be especially important for smaller jurisdictions which can piggy-back on the existing administrative structure of programs in larger jurisdictions with which they link.

Since the primary economic argument for linkage is equalization of carbon prices across political jurisdictions, it is worth noting that agreements could also be made to harmonize carbon prices. We distinguish between *hard linkage*, defined above as a formal recognition by a GHG mitigation program in one jurisdiction (a regional, national, or sub-national government) of emission reductions undertaken in another jurisdiction for purposes of complying with the first jurisdiction's mitigation program,[31] and *soft linkage*. Soft linkage is an agreement (explicit or implicit) to harmonize carbon prices either at a given price or within some band.[32]

---

[28] See Green, *supra* note 26, at 484.

[29] See Bodansky *et al.*, *supra* note 12, at 957–958.

[30] Pizer, W. and Yates, A. (2015), "Terminating links between emission trading programs." *Journal of Environmental Economics and Management*. **71**: 142, 145.

[31] See Bodansky *et al.*, *supra* note 12, at 964.

[32] On the rationale for such a price band, see Carbon Disclosure Project N. Am., Carbon Pricing Corridors: The Market View (2017), https://perma.cc/GF5R-FV7L.

Soft linkage could be accomplished in a number of ways, including a carbon club[33] or an agreement among countries to set a common price band for unlinked cap and trade programs. A price band is achieved by setting a *price collar*, or a combination of a price ceiling, typically implemented through a safety valve price at which the government agrees to sell allowances to all comers, and a price floor, which can be established through a reserve price on the auctioning of new allowances.[34] Countries might also agree on overlapping price bands where certain sets of countries are allowed a lower price band than others.

Such soft linkage can preserve the economic benefits of price harmonization while not requiring the formal administrative structure nor oversight of trading to avoid double-counting of emission reductions for reporting of Internationally Transferred Mitigation Outcomes (ITMOs). It can also provide the political benefits of coordination and momentum building across political jurisdictions that may be important as the Paris Agreement is initially implemented and efforts to raise ambition proceed.

That said, our major focus in this Article is on ways in which linkage design involving cross-border transfers can be used to help countries implement and achieve their NDCs under the Paris Agreement. Therefore, we focus — for the most part — on hard linkage systems, with just one of the five cases we later explore being an example of soft linkage.

Forms of Heterogeneity that Can Affect Linkage of Climate Policies

Policies have many attributes in their design, but for purposes of our analysis, it is helpful initially to separate these attributes into three categories: policy instrument, political jurisdiction, and target. We further divide our consideration of political jurisdiction into two types of heterogeneity: level of government engaged in the policy and prospective linkage (regional, national, or sub-national), and status under the Paris Agreement (Party or non-Party). Also, our consideration of the type of target is divided into two

[33] Nordhaus, M. (2015). "Climate clubs: Overcoming free-riding in international climate policy." *American Economic Review*. **105**: 1339, 1340.

[34] See Carbon Disclosure Project N. AM., *supra* note 32, at 14.

distinct issues: the type of policy-instrument target, and the type of NDC target. We examine options within each of these five categories in turn.

Heterogeneity of Policy Instruments

Four major types of policy instruments have been implemented, planned, or at least proposed to reduce GHG emissions: trading systems (cap-and-trade systems, as well as emission-reduction-credit systems), taxes, performance standards, and technology standards.[35] Of the major types of policy instruments, all but technology standards may be linked, essentially through mutual recognition and crediting for compliance. Linkage can occur between cap-and-trade and tax systems, between either of those systems and non-market regulatory (performance-standard) systems, or among non-market regulatory systems.[36]

As of 2018, around 15 percent of global GHG emissions were covered by carbon-pricing regimes — emissions trading and carbon taxes — with the number of implemented systems having increased from two in 1990 to about forty-five in 2017.[37] Actual carbon prices are — for the most part — higher in tax systems than in trading systems, but the emissions coverage of trading systems is much greater.[38] These implemented and planned systems are largely found in the member countries of the Organisation for

---

[35] See generally Bodansky *et al.*, *supra* note 12.

[36] Haug, C. *et al.* (2015). "Toward a global price on carbon: Pathways for linking carbon pricing instruments." *Perma cc*, 4, https://perma.cc/6YS9-BDJ5; Hahn, R. W. and Stavins, R. N. (1999). "What has the Kyoto Protocol wrought? The real architecture of international tradeable permit markets." *SSRN*, 8; Metcalf, G. E. and Weisbach, D. (2012). "Linking policies when tastes differ: Global climate policy in a heterogeneous world." *Review of Environmental Economics and Policy*. **6**: 110, 118–119.

[37] World Bank & Ecofys, State and Trends of Carbon Pricing 2017 13 (2017), https://perma.cc/GQ4Y-W433.

[38] In implemented carbon-pricing systems, carbon prices (either market-determined allowance prices in cap-and-trade systems or tax rates in carbon tax systems) vary greatly — from less than \$1 to more than \$140 per ton of CO_2 equivalent. See *Id.* at 14. For a discussion of the role of market mechanisms under the Paris Agreement, see Wang-Helmreich, H. *et al.* (2017). *Potentials and Limitations of Different Requirements (Offsetting) in Bilateral and Global Carbon Pricing Systems*. Report, On behalf of the German Environment Agency, https://perma.cc/Y3YD-E3BA.

Economic Co-operation and Development (OECD), plus a few others.[39] When China's national CO_2 emissions trading system, which is being phased in by 2020, reaches its full scale covering half of the country's emissions, the share of global emissions subject to carbon pricing will increase from 15 percent to between 20 percent and 25 percent.[40]

In the context of the Paris Agreement, some two-thirds of Parties, accounting for 58 percent of global GHG emissions, stated in their initial NDCs under the Agreement that they are considering the use of carbon pricing to achieve their NDC targets.[41] In this case, the geographic distribution is much broader than for implemented or even planned carbon-pricing systems, and includes many developing countries.

Links Between Cap-and-Trade Systems

Cap-and-trade programs provide the most straightforward opportunity for linkage, by allowing firms (emission sources) in one jurisdiction to comply either with local allowances or equivalent allowances from another, linked system.[42] These and other linkages involving transfers across jurisdictions (hard linking, as defined above) can be direct or indirect. In the case of cap-and-trade systems, direct linkage occurs between two systems when one participating jurisdiction agrees to accept allowances from the other jurisdiction for purposes of compliance with the local cap.[43] Indirect linkage occurs when two systems do not accept allowances from each other, but both accept allowances from a common third party.[44] Direct linkage can occur on a one-for-one basis, where an allowance from one jurisdiction is accepted in place of an allowance for the same amount of

---

[39] See *Few Countries are Pricing Carbon High Enough to Meet Climate Targets*, OECD (September 18, 2018), https://perma.cc/B82Y-SCDK.

[40] State and Trends of Carbon Pricing 2017, *supra* note 37, at 11.

[41] State and Trends of Carbon Pricing 2017, *supra* note 37, at 22.

[42] Jaffe, J. and Stavins, R. N. (2008). *Linkage of Tradable Permit Systems in International Climate Policy Architecture*. HKS Working Paper No. RWP08-035, Faculty Research Working Paper Series, Harvard Kennedy School. https://perma.cc/Y4UK-TVVY.

[43] *Id.* at 8.

[44] Ranson & Stavins, *Post-Durban Climate Policy Architecture Based on Linkage of Cap-and-Trade Systems*, *supra* note 21, at 408.

emissions in another jurisdiction,[45] or a trading ratio (exchange rate) can apply to allowance transfers between the two systems.[46]

The political challenges of implementing a set of exchange rates could be considerable, in part because such exchange rates might be seen as representing a value judgment regarding the environmental integrity of emissions reductions claimed by a Party's domestic policy instrument. Furthermore, while exchange rates can facilitate linking programs with different levels of ambition (and carbon prices), they blunt, if not eliminate, the economic benefits of linkage by preventing the equalization of carbon prices across jurisdictions.[47] The political and administrative benefits remain, however, and the use of exchange rates could be designed with a phase-out so that allowances trade at parity after some designated period of time.

Direct linkage can be bilateral (two-way), where both systems accept allowances or credits from the other system for compliance, or unilateral (one-way), where only one of two systems allows credits from the other for compliance.[48] Even with the straightforward case of a linkage between two

---

[45] *Id.* at 407; see also Ranson & Stavins, *Linkage of Greenhouse Gas Emissions Trading Systems: Learning from Experience*, *supra* note 9, at 3.

[46] If systems wish to preserve different levels of ambition, they can put in place a number of mechanisms to do so. First, they can recognize allowances from the other jurisdiction with an exchange rate. For example, a country with a more aggressive cap might agree to accept allowances from a country with a less aggressive cap but apply an exchange rate so that, for example, three tons of emission allowances from the other country would be required for one ton of compliance domestically. See Burtraw, D. *et al.* (2013). *Linking by Degrees: Incremental Alignment of Cap-and-Trade Markets*. Discussion Paper RFF DP 13-04, Resources for the Future. https://perma.cc/6MY2-PB3V. Second, a country can place a limit on the use of allowances from other systems. Third, a country could require a payment to "top up" each foreign allowance approved for compliance purposes. For example, if an allowance from a system with a less ambitious cap (and an allowance price of $10) were used for compliance in a system with a more ambitious cap (and an allowance price of $25), the complying entity in the second system could be required to surrender the foreign allowance together with a payment of $15 to account for the difference. Note that the fee in this type of top-up approach could be set below the difference in allowance value (i.e., at less than $15 in the example given) to preserve some positive incentive for trading. See Bodansky *et al.*, *supra* note 12, at 957–58.

[47] See generally Schneider, L. *et al.* (2017). "Restricted linking of emissions trading systems: Options, benefits, and challenges." *International Environmental Agreements*. **17**: 883.

[48] Ranson & Stavins, *Post-Durban Climate Policy Architecture Based on Linkage of Cap-and-Trade Systems*, *supra* note 21, at 407.

cap-and-trade systems, a number of issues can arise.[49] We discuss these issues later in our analysis of key cases of potential climate policy linkages.

Links Between Heterogeneous Policy Instruments

By the time the Paris Agreement was adopted in December 2015, twenty regional, national, or sub-national CO2 cap-and-trade systems were either operating or scheduled to launch in forty countries.[50] These include the European Union Emissions Trading System (EU ETS), the Regional Greenhouse Gas Initiative (RGGI) in the northeast United States, seven regional pilots in China,[51] and emissions trading systems in California, Kazakhstan, New Zealand, Québec, Switzerland, and Tokyo.[52] Of these, most had established or proposed at least one international linkage with another cap-and-trade or credit system.[53]

Not all countries will employ cap-and-trade instruments as their means of reducing GHG emissions under the Paris Agreement, however. Other instruments include carbon taxes or fees, emission reduction credit (ERC) or offset systems, such as the Kyoto Protocol's Clean Development Mechanism (CDM),[54] and traditional regulatory approaches, including performance standards and technology standards.[55] In this context, we think of linkage as a means of narrowing or eliminating differences in the actual or shadow price of carbon (the marginal cost of abatement) through

---

[49] Jaffe *et al.*, *supra* note 23, at 799; Ranson & Stavins, *Post-Durban Climate Policy Architecture Based on Linkage of Cap-and-Trade Systems*, *supra* note 21, at 408–409; Burtraw *et al.*, *supra* note 46, at 21–22.

[50] World Bank and Ecofys (2014). *State and Trends of Carbon Pricing 2014*. Washington, DC: World Bank Group. https://perma.cc/RPA3-CJLN.

[51] An eighth pilot system was launched in 2016 by the government of Fujian Province (but not mandated by China's National Development and Reform Commission). International Carbon Action Partnership (ICAP). (2018). *Emissions Trading Worldwide: ICAP Status Report 2018*. Report 24–25, 72. https://perma.cc/T4U9-ASMR.

[52] *Id.* at 24–25; World Bank and Ecofys (2014). *State and Trends of Carbon Pricing 2014*. Washington, DC: World Bank Group. *supra* note 50, at 14–16.

[53] International Carbon Action Partnership (ICAP), *supra* note 51, at 29.

[54] *The Clean Development Mechanism*, U.N. Framework Convention on Climate Change, https://perma.cc/BX55-KLAX (last visited December 20, 2018).

[55] See Bodansky *et al.*, *supra* note 12, at 13.

policies that allow carbon regimes in different political jurisdictions to interact in various ways.

Consider linkage between a cap-and-trade system and a carbon tax system. Firms under a cap-and-trade program could sell allowances to firms required to pay the carbon tax, allowing the purchasing firm to lower its tax obligation by the amount of allowances it submits for retirement. Operationally, firms could be allowed to exempt from their carbon tax base any emissions for which they have allowances that they surrender in the taxing jurisdiction. The national accounting for UNFCCC reporting purposes need be no different than the accounting for allowance transfers between two linked cap-and-trade programs. There would be an appropriate adjustment in the two Parties' national inventories for the aggregate amount of allowances used in the tax system.

For two-way linked systems, firms might be allowed to pay taxes at a higher level than they owe based on their emissions and in return receive certified Emission Tax Payment Credits (ETPCs)[56] from their government that they could sell to firms that are operating under a cap-and-trade program. Within the cap-and-trade program, firms could use ETPCs just as they would the equivalent quantity of allowances for purposes of compliance. Since the use of ETPCs relaxes the cap in the cap-and-trade system in return for a payment to the other system, symmetry with the treatment of allowance trading (or allowance use in a linked cap-and-trade with tax system) would suggest that national inventories would be adjusted such that the mitigation obligation in the cap-and-trade system is relaxed by the amount of ETPCs used while the mitigation obligation in the carbon tax system is tightened similarly. The two systems might agree, however, to a different arrangement. They might agree not to adjust their national inventories at all or make a partial adjustment conditional on the sum of the inventories remaining unchanged. Whatever arrangement is agreed upon would be communicated to the appropriate UNFCCC body as part of national reporting by each Party.

Likewise, either a carbon tax or a cap-and-trade system could be linked with policies that provide subsidies for emissions reductions, which could be traded like ERCs to be used in place of allowances to comply with a cap-and-trade program or as ETPCs for compliance with a carbon tax.[57]

---

[56] See Metcalf & Weisbach, *supra* note 36, at 122.

[57] See *Id.* at 110, 112–114. For example, Mexico's carbon tax in principle allows the use of offset credits from projects under the Kyoto Protocol's Clean Development Mechanism (CDM) in lieu of tax payments, although the rules to render this link operational have yet

In principle, market-based mechanisms[58] (mainly taxes and cap and trade) could be linked with a performance-based regulatory system. If the regulation is in the form of a quantity standard (for example, tons of carbon-dioxide-equivalent reduction), firms could buy allowances or ETPCs from another market to meet the required quantity of reduction, or achieve reductions in excess of the regulatory minimum and then sell additional reductions as ERCs. As we discuss later in our examination of heterogeneity in types of NDC targets, intensity standards may be translated into quantity standards at the source or firm level (per total output, total sales, or whatever denominator the regulation prescribes), thus allowing for linkage.[59] Technology standards present a considerably greater challenge, because it is difficult to verify the additionality of emissions reductions from meeting or exceeding a technology standard.[60] Even a one-way link, which might allow firms facing the technology mandate to purchase offsets or allowances from another system, would be challenging to implement.[61] In principle, credits could be used to attribute reductions to companies that outperform expected emissions reductions from a technology standard; these credits could then be sold to foreign markets.[62] However, the degree of uncertainty of emissions impacts of technology standards argues against linking such systems.

In addition to heterogeneity regarding the type of instrument, climate policies can also differ in terms of the legal nature of instruments. Differences can be with regard to the degree of formality of instruments and the position of implementing rules in the hierarchy of norms, as well

---

to be elaborated. See *ICAP Newsletter: Global Trends in Emissions Trading*, Int'l Carbon Action P'ship (June 12, 2014), https://perma.cc/VNX8-C592 (noting Mexico's announcement of a cap-and-trade system for carbon emissions); *see also* Wang-Helmreich *et al.*, *supra* note 38, at 13.

[58] We define market-based mechanisms as policy instruments that alter the price of emitting activities relative to non-emitting activities. Examples include taxes and cap-and-trade systems that explicitly price emissions, as well as subsidies for clean technologies (feed-in tariffs and renewable portfolio standards) that alter the price of non-emitting energy sources relative to emitting sources. Market-based approaches do not prohibit emissions by individual firms; rather they put a common price on emissions at the margin. The result — in a well-designed system — can be cost-effective (cost-minimizing) achievement of the environmental target.

[59] Metcalf & Weisbach, *supra* note 36, at 118.

[60] *Id.* at 126–127.

[61] *Id.* at 126.

[62] *Id.* at 117–118.

as in the degree of normativity, that is, whether an instrument is legally binding or not.

Regarding the degree of formality, differences can relate to whether a climate policy instrument has been adopted at a relatively higher level in the normative hierarchy, such as a formal statute adopted by a national legislature, or at a lower level, such as an executive order or administrative decree.[63] A higher degree of formality will typically mean that the instrument is more resilient to political and judicial challenge, and that it takes precedence over lower level rules in the event of conflict.[64] This tends to afford the policy greater certainty and predictability, which may influence a linking partner when deciding whether or not to link.

As for the degree of normativity, legally binding force means that adherence is not optional as a matter of law, with violations carrying the threat of punitive sanctions enforced by public authorities.[65] While most climate policy instruments are mandatory, several countries (for example, South Korea, Switzerland, and the United Kingdom) have relied on voluntary instruments before transitioning to mandatory policies.[66]

Generally speaking, differences in the degree of formality and normativity need not be obstacles to linking, although informal or voluntary instruments will tend to offer a lower assurance of compliance and reduced accountability of participating entities. Taken together, these

---

[63] *Compare* Clean Air Act, 42 U.S.C. §§7401–7671q (2012) (statute passed by U.S. legislature) *with* Determining Conformity of Federal Actions to State or Federal Implementation Plans, 40 C.F.R. § 93 (2017) (regulation establishing standards for implementing Clean Air Act).

[64] See, e.g., Chevron, U.S.A., Inc. v. Nat. Res. Def. Council, Inc., 467 U.S. 837, 842–843 (1984) (stating administrative regulations cannot conflict with clear statutory intent). While specific circumstances will differ from jurisdiction to jurisdiction, a higher degree of formality also tends to entail a more onerous adoption procedure, such as passage by various committees and approval by one or more legislative chambers with a specified majority vote.

[65] Because of these potential consequences, the heightened normativity of legally binding rules is typically premised on observance of strict, formal requirements, such as a suitable legal basis and specific adoption procedures, with mandatory content worded in clear and determinate language.

[66] See, e.g., *UK Government Announces New Mandatory Streamlined Energy and Carbon Reporting (SECR) Framework for All Large UK Businesses*, Econometrica, https://perma.cc/3JKE-GP9X (last visited December 20, 2018).

uncertainties diminish the predictability of policy outcomes, and can affect the confidence and trust instilled in potential linking partners.

Experience with Linkage of Climate Policy Instruments

As of now, climate policy linkages have largely — but not exclusively — been between trading systems.[67] The first panel in Table 1 lists former, existing, and planned direct linkages between mandatory cap-and-trade systems.[68] There have been two cases of planned one-way linkages, both now abandoned. One was Australia's plan to accept EU ETS allowances beginning in July 2015.[69] Due to political changes in the country, however, Australia rescinded its existing carbon tax and planned cap-and-trade system in July 2014, which terminated the announced linkage.[70] The other example of one-way linkage was the language in RGGI's 2006 amendment to its Memorandum of Understanding that made it possible, subject to further approval, for participants to use allowances from foreign cap-and-trade systems when and if RGGI allowance prices exceeded a specified trigger price (the trigger price started at $10 per ton of CO_2 in 2005, and increased by roughly 2 percent each year).[71] Because RGGI prices remained well below the trigger price, this one-way linkage option was never exercised.[72] The 2013 updates to the RGGI Model Rule ended this conditional linkage.[73]

---

[67] See *infra* Table 1.

[68] The two-way linkages described in Table 1 can be bilateral or multilateral. We distinguish them in the table by denoting the former as "Two-way" and the latter as "Multilateral." The multilateral linkages are all two-way.

[69] Australia to Link with EU ETS in 2015, *Sydney Morning Herald* (August 28, 2012), https://perma.cc/W5X3-MHZ8.

[70] Brad Plumer, *Australia is Repealing Its Controversial Carbon Tax*, Vox (July 17, 2014), https://perma.cc/3JVW-J389.

[71] See *Memorandum of Understanding*, Regional Greenhouse Gas Initiative (Dec. 20, 2005), https://perma.cc/UX5Q-K28Y; *Amendment to Memorandum of Understanding*, Regional Greenhouse Gas Initiative (Aug. 8, 2006), https://perma.cc/XRX5-N7D5.

[72] See William Shobe, Reserve Price Analysis Task: Performed for RGGI Inc. on Behalf of the Participating States 12 (2010), https://perma.cc/KMP7-XUG6.

[73] Reg'l Greenhouse Gas Initiative, Summary of RGGI Model Rule Changes 3 (2013), https://perma.cc/3S2V-EFUT.

Table 1. Existing regional, national, and sub-national climate policy linkages.[a]

System 1	System 2	Type of linkage	Enact. date	Effect. date	Prices at enactment #1	Prices at enactment #2	Caps ($mtCO_2$) #1	Caps ($mtCO_2$) #2	Notes
Linkages among cap-and-trade systems									
28 EU nations	(via the EU ETS)	Multi	2003	2005	None	na	varied	2,299	
Norway	EU ETS	One-way		2005					
Norway	EU ETS	Multi	2007	2008	€0	€20	15	2,080	
Iceland	EU ETS	Multi	2007	2008	None	€20	0	2,080	G
Liechtenstein	EU ETS	Multi	2007	2008	None	€20	18	2,080	
Switzerland	EU ETS	Two-way	*						
Australia	EU ETS	One-way	2013*	2014	AUD$25	€7-€8	TBD		C
Australia	EU ETS	Two-way	*	2018	AUD$25	€7-€8	TBD	1,852	
Australia	New Zealand	Two-way	*				TBD		
Australia	EU ETS, NZ	Delinking	2014	2014					
California	Quebec	Multi	2012/13	2014	$14	none	160	25	I
California	Ontario	Multi	2017	2018	$15	$15	442	166	I
9 U.S. states	(RGGI)	Multi	2005	2009	None	na	varied	168	A
RGGI	Any CAT system	One-way	2005	2009	None	€9/EUA	168	2,299	B
RGGI	Any CAT system	Delinking	2013	2014	$3	€5/EUA	91	2,299	B
New Jersey	RGGI	Delinking	2011	2012	$2	$2	21	150	
Linkages from cap-and-trade systems to credit systems									
EUETS Phase 1	CDM	One-way	2004	2005	€9	$5	2,299	na	D
EUETS Phase 2	CDM	One-way	2004	2008	€9	$5	2,299	na	D
EUETS Phase 3	CDM	One-way	2004	2013	€9	$5	2,299	na	D,E
EUETS Phase 2	JI	One-way	2004	2008	€9	$6	2,299	na	D
EUETS Phase 3	Non-LDC CDM	Delinking	2012	2013	€6	€4	2,084	na	
Switzerland	CDM	One-way	1999	2008	None	$4-$7	na	na	
New Zealand	CDM, JI, RMU	One-way	2008	2008	None	€11	na	na	

Australia	CDM, JI	One-way	2011	2012/15	None	€6	TBD	na	
RGGI	Any credit system	One-way	2005	2009	None	$5-8	110	na	B
RGGI	Any credit system	Delinking	2013	2014	None	$5	165	na	B
California	Acre and Chiapas	One-way	*					na	
Quebec	Acre and Chiapas	One-way	*					na	
Tokyo ETS	CDM	One-way	2008	2010	$142	$18	13	na	F
Linkage from carbon tax to credit systems									
Mexico	CDM	One-Way	2013	2014	None	€.4	na	na	H
South Africa	CDM, VCS	One-Way	2013	Delayed					

Notes:

[a]Ranson & Stavins, *Linkage of Greenhouse Gas Emissions Trading Systems: Learning from Experience*, *supra* note 9, at 22. This table was updated by the Authors of this Article.

*indicates a proposed linkage.

A — The RGGI states signed a MOU in 2005, and then each passed authorizing legislation between 2006 and 2008.

B — The original Model Rule included language (Section XX-10.3(b)(1)) allowing the use of allowances from foreign cap-and-trade or credit systems (including Kyoto flexibility mechanisms) if RGGI allowance prices exceeded a "two-stage price trigger event" that began at $10 in 2005 and increased by roughly 2 percent each year. The 2013 amendments to the Model Rule eliminated this linkage.

C — Participants in Australia's system were going to be able to use EUAs for up to 50 percent of their compliance obligations.

D — Credit price reflects pre-compliance offsets for which seller assumes risk.

E — EU ETS participants are entitled to use international credits during the 2012–2020 period up to the higher of two limits: (a) the international credit entitlement specified in the national allocation plan for Phase 2; or (b) 11 percent of the free allocation of EU allowances granted to them in that period.

F — Use of CDM credits is allowed only if domestic prices exceed a threshold, and if Tokyo-based credits are used as well.

G — Per EEA Joint Committee decision 146/2007, Iceland did not submit a National Allocation Plan for EU ETS Phase II, since it had no installations large enough to be covered by the cap-and-trade system.

H — Mexico allows companies to pay with CDM credits in lieu of tax payments equal to the credit market value at the time of paying the tax; however, only CDM projects developed in Mexico can be used in this way. The price shown in the table if from RGGI.

I — Information on the cap at the time of linkage. California's cap expanded significantly in 2015 with the upstream inclusion of heating and transportation fuel emissions. Ontario has withdrawn from the link following a change in the province's leadership in June 2018.

Importantly, Table 1 includes the prominent 2014 linkage between California's and Québec's cap-and-trade systems, under which their respective systems are not only linked, but also tightly harmonized, and hold joint allowance auctions.[74] Although Australia formerly had plans for a two-way linkage with the EU ETS beginning in 2018, the repeal of Australia's cap-and-trade system ended this link as well.[75] While these are not always characterized as linkages, we include in Table 1 what we consider two examples of multilateral linkage: among the EU ETS nations and among the RGGI states. While these are not technically linkages between independent cap-and-trade systems, they involve national or subnational jurisdictions participating in an integrated, cross-border carbon market. Because of the similarities to linkage, it can be useful to think of such systems as sets of linked cap-and-trade programs.[76]

---

[74]Ontario joined the link in 2017. See Agreement on the Harmonization and Integration of Cap-and-Trade Programs for Reducing Greenhouse Gas Emissions, Calif.-Ont.-Qué., September 22, 2017, https://perma.cc/PF7P-ZCVN. Linkage between these jurisdictions occurred under the auspices of the Western Climate Initiative (WCI). *Id.* Following a change in leadership after elections in June 2018, however, Ontario's continued participation is currently in doubt. See Paola Loriggio, Ontario Introduces Legislation to Scrap Cap-and-Trade Program, *CTV NEWS* (July 25, 2018), https://perma.cc/AA32-3UCA.

[75]See New Australian Government Dismantling Climate Policies, E&E News (Sept. 12, 2013), https://perma.cc/2H8Q-UUNJ. Less defined, but a potential precursor of a bilateral linkage, is a Memorandum of Understanding (MOU) signed in 2014 by the Governor of California and the government of Mexico to coordinate climate policy efforts, including the possible development and implementation of "carbon pricing systems and other market-based instruments," Debra Kahn, Gov. Brown Signs Pact to Work with Mexico on Carbon Pricing and Other Climate, Environmental Programs, *E&E NEWS* (July 29, 2014), https://perma.cc/EUS9-CKMF. Also, in 2013, California, Oregon, Washington, and British Columbia established the Pacific Coast Collaborative to coordinate climate policies. See About, Pac. Coast Collaborative, https://perma.cc/9FTS-5TDP (last visited, December 20, 2018). In addition, a relevant MOU exists between the governments of Québec and Mexico. See News Release, Office of the Premier, Ont., Ontario Working with Québec and Mexico to Advance Carbon Markets (August 31, 2016), https://perma.cc/34CC-356D (announcing signing of the Joint Declaration Between the Ministry of Environment and Natural Resources of the United Mexican States, the Government of Ontario, and the Gouvernement du Québec).

[76]See generally Ellerman, A. D. and Buchner, B. K. (2007). "The European Union Emissions Trading Scheme: Origins, allocation, and early results." *Review of Environmental Economics and Policy*. **1**: 66.

The second panel in Table 1 lists (one-way) linkages in which cap-and-trade systems accept offsets from ERC systems. By far the most important credit system, in terms of the volume of credits created, is the Kyoto Protocol's CDM.[77] Several cap-and-trade systems, including those of the European Union, Switzerland, and New Zealand, have established such one-way linkages.[78] Of these, the European Union has been the dominant purchaser of CDM credits: as of 2011, over 80 percent of issued CDM Certified Emissions Reductions (CERs) were used by EU ETS compliance entities or were being held in EU carbon registry accounts.[79]

The third panel in Table 1 lists examples of a link between heterogeneous policy instruments, namely a carbon tax that allows the use of offsets generated within the same or a different jurisdiction. Under Mexico's carbon tax on fossil fuels,[80] firms will be able to use offset credits from domestic CDM projects developed in Mexico to meet all or part of their tax liability.[81] South Africa has planned to allow use of offsets in lieu of tax payments when its carbon tax goes into effect,[82] and Chile is considering a similar option for its carbon tax.[83]

In addition to the system-level linkages shown in Table 1, some nations have participated in a different form of cross-border transfers via the trading of Assigned Amount Units (AAUs) under the Kyoto Protocol's

---

[77] Igor Shishlov & Valentin Bellassen, 10 Lessons from 10 Years of the CDM 1 (2012), https://perma.cc/D7RR-T4XZ.

[78] See *infra* Table 1.

[79] See Shishlov & Bellassen, *supra* note 77, at 16. Other proposals for offset programs exist. California has negotiated a Memoranda of Understanding with the provinces of Acre, in Brazil, and Chiapas, in Mexico, to work together to develop a framework to allow the use of offsets from those states in California's cap-and-trade system under AB 32. The REDD Offset Working Grp., California, Acre and Chiapas: Partnering to Reduce Emissions from Tropical Deforestation 2 (Evan Johnson ed.), https://perma.cc/427A-WDKW.

[80] The tax was initially set at \$3.50 per ton of carbon dioxide equivalent (tCO2e). See *ICAP Newsletter: Global Trends in Emissions Trading*, *supra* note 57.

[81] World Bank and Ecofys (2014). *State and Trends of Carbon Pricing 2014*. Washington, DC: World Bank Group. *supra* note 50, at 81.

[82] Brendon Bosworth, Offsets to Cushion South African Carbon Tax, *Inter Press Service News Agency* (May 28, 2014), https://perma.cc/YTZ9-GFKJ.

[83] Wang-Helmreich *et al.*, *supra* note 38, at 16.

Article 17.[84] The Protocol assigns each Annex I Party a quantity of AAUs equal to its GHG emissions target for a given commitment period, measured in metric tons of CO_2-equivalent.[85] The Protocol then requires each Annex I Party, at the end of a commitment period, to surrender enough AAUs to cover its actual emissions over the period.[86] If a country's emissions exceed its AAUs, it is allowed to make up the difference by purchasing AAUs from another country under Article 17 of the Kyoto Protocol or by obtaining emissions credits under one of the Protocol's project-based mechanisms — Joint Implementation and the CDM.[87] While both AAU trading and linkage involve cross-border transfers, the former occurs within a single governance framework created by the Kyoto Protocol, with countries as market participants, while the latter occurs between different national or subnational policies, and can involve a variety of actors as market participants.

In principle, AAU trading between nations creates implicit linkages between their domestic carbon abatement policies. In practice, however, the market for AAUs has involved a very limited number of participants.[88] This should not be surprising, given that governments are not simple cost-minimizing entities and lack necessary information about abatement costs.[89] There have also been a few instances of partial and unconventional

[84]*Emissions Trading*, U.N. Framework Convention on Climate Change (2018), https://unfccc.int/process/the-kyoto-protocol/mechanisms/emissions-trading.

[85]Temple, J. F. (2002). "The Kyoto Protocol: Will it sneak Up on the U.S.?" *Brooklyn Journal of International Law*. **28**: 213, 224.

[86]See *Emissions Trading*, *supra* note 84.

[87]*Id.*; see also Kyoto Protocol to the United Nations Framework Convention on Climate Change, December 10, 1997, U.N. Doc FCCC/CP/1997/7/Add.1, 37 I.L.M. 22 (1998) [hereinafter Kyoto Protocol].

[88]Ranson & Stavins, *Linkage of Greenhouse Gas Emissions Trading Systems: Learning from Experience*, *supra* note 9, at 5.

[89]See *Id.* at 1, 3 (stating that the proposed linkage system would allow countries' trading systems to be more cost-effective and aware of abatement costs, whereas this is not the case currently); see also HAHN & STAVINS, *supra* note 36. Most AAUs have been purchased by Japanese firms, the government of Spain, or the World Bank. Ranson & Stavins, *Linkage of Greenhouse Gas Emissions Trading Systems: Learning from Experience*, *supra* note 9, at 23. Other buyers have included Austria, Belgium, Ireland, Japan, Luxembourg,

linkage, including some cases of what Burtraw *et al.* refer to as "linking by degrees."[90] Such linkages have occurred when jurisdictions have taken actions that fell short of establishing a formal link but nonetheless brought their systems into closer alignment.[91]

As noted above, linkages among carbon tax systems can be direct or indirect. Carbon taxes are currently in place or planned in Argentina, British Columbia, Chile, Colombia, Denmark, Finland, France, Iceland, Ireland, Japan, Mexico, Norway, Portugal, South Africa, Spain, Sweden, Switzerland, and the United Kingdom.[92] Some of these taxes have been expressly introduced with the intention of complementing the carbon price established by a cap-and-trade system by, for example, extending a carbon price to sectors not covered by an existing cap-and-trade system.[93]

---

the Netherlands, Portugal, and one U.S. firm. *Id.* Virtually all transactions occurred between 2008 and 2012, and involved sales by economies in transition — specifically, central and eastern European countries. *Id.* The sole exception was a very small sale of AAUs by New Zealand in 2010. See *Id.*

[90] Burtraw *et al.*, *supra* note 46, at 1, 4.

[91] Examples include Australia and California signing a memorandum of understanding in 2013 on sharing information and experience with cap-and-trade systems and with linkage. Memorandum of Understanding, Austl.-Cal., Jul. 30, 2013, at 4, https://perma.cc/8YBS-4R33. Similarly, California and RGGI have engaged in information sharing and have adapted some design elements from each other, while the state of Washington and the United Kingdom have engaged in a partnership to collaborate on carbon-market design, as well as other issues. Burtraw *et al.*, *supra* note 46, at 44; see State of Wash. & U.K. Dep't of Energy and Climate Change, Report on the Collaboration Between Washington State and the UK Government on Climate Change 1–2 (2014). Other examples include bilateral arrangements between the EU and China, the European Bank for Reconstruction and Development (EBRD) and Kazakhstan, Germany and Mexico, and many others which have provided capacity building, analytical and technical support, and financial assistance to accelerate the deployment of carbon trading policies in emerging and transition economies. See Biedenkopf, K. *et al.* (2017). "A global turn to greenhouse gas emissions trading? Experiments, actors, and diffusion." *Global Environmental Politics*. **17**: 1–11. 3 (discussing a survey of studies that have been published on the proliferation of greenhouse gas emissions trading systems worldwide).

[92] World Bank and Ecofys (2018). *State and Trends of Carbon Pricing 2018*. Washington, DC: World Bank Group. https://perma.cc/93UN-3FS3.

[93] *Id.* at 19.

Lessons Learned from Experience with Linkage of Climate Policy Instruments

Experience to date with explicit and implicit linkages of carbon policies across jurisdictions yields some potentially useful lessons.[94] First, a number of regions, nations, and sub-national jurisdictions have demonstrated their preference for linkage, despite the challenges.[95] Second, linking carbon markets has proved, in the words of a World Bank Report, "powerful and effective," although the risks of linking include that problems in one market can be transferred via linkage to other systems.[96] Specifically, the World Bank Report cites the link between the New Zealand cap and trade system and the CDM market as critical for keeping costs in the New Zealand system down.[97] Similarly, the report notes that CER prices were "heavily dependent" on the EU ETS price, and this helped to get the CDM market up and running.[98] Third, although there was value to firms in Annex I countries (with emissions reduction commitments) under the Kyoto Protocol from their use of CDM offsets for purposes of cost mitigation, a functioning international market for such offsets does not appear likely to continue, particularly given restrictions on the use of such offsets in the EU ETS.[99] Fourth, the International Transaction Log, part of the Kyoto Protocol process, played a valuable role by tracking traded units and preventing double counting.[100]

---

[94] See, e.g., Tuerk, A. *et al.* (2009). "Linking carbon markets: Concepts, case studies and pathways." *Climate Policy*. **9**: 341, 344. Ranson & Stavins, *Linkage of Greenhouse Gas Emissions Trading Systems: Learning from Experience*, *supra* note 9, at 3; Newell, R. G. *et al.* (2013). "Carbon markets 15 years after Kyoto: Lessons learned, new challenges." *Journal of Economic Perspectives*. **27**: 123, 140. Bodansky *et al.*, *supra* note 12, at 957.

[95] Ranson & Stavins, *Linkage of Greenhouse Gas Emissions Trading Systems: Learning from Experience*, *supra* note 9, at 3.

[96] World Bank and Ecofys (2014). *State and Trends of Carbon Pricing 2014*. Washington, DC: World Bank Group, *supra* note 50, at 34.

[97] *Id.*

[98] *Id.*

[99] See Decision 2015/1814, of the European Parliament and of the Council of 6 October 2015 Concerning the Establishment and Operation of a Market Stability Reserve for the Union Greenhouse Gas Emission Trading Scheme and Amending Directive 2003/87/EC, 2015 O.J. (L. 264).

[100] Marcu, A. and Centre for European Policy Studies. (2014). *The Role of Market Mechanisms in a Post-2020 Climate Change Agreement*. Report No. 87. https://perma.cc/HSY7-SXJJ.

Fifth, linkages are not permanent, as both the linkages themselves and the policies to be linked can be vulnerable to national or sub-national political swings (as occurred in Australia, Canada, and the United States).[101] This causes uncertainty for regulated firms.[102] Sixth and finally, the benefits and attraction of linkage are likely to evolve over time. In the short run, the benefits may be more political and administrative than economic.[103] Perfect price (or shadow price) convergence is unlikely in the short run under many linkages, given restrictions on the magnitude of allowance flows observed in most linkage schemes.[104] In the long run, however, as markets mature and countries adopt more ambitious mitigation targets, it may be reasonable to expect some loosening of constraints on linkage flows, contributing to enhanced price harmonization and greater cost-effectiveness of carbon policy.[105]

Heterogeneity of Jurisdictions

Two types of jurisdictional heterogeneity are relevant for international linkage in the context of the Paris Agreement: level of government jurisdiction, and status of that jurisdiction as a Party (or located geographically

[101] Ranson & Stavins, *Linkage of Greenhouse Gas Emissions Trading Systems: Learning from Experience*, *supra* note 9, at 11, 13; Pizer & Yates, *supra* note 30, at 5.

[102] Ranson & Stavins, *Linkage of Greenhouse Gas Emissions Trading Systems: Learning from Experience*, *supra* note 9, at 11, 13.

[103] Burtraw *et al.*, *supra* note 46, at 2–3.

[104] See *infra* Table 1.

[105] We conjecture that linkage may lead indirectly to price harmonization. Here is an example for two countries with cap-and-trade systems. Country A has a cap-and-trade system in place with a current allowance price in the $15 per ton range. Now assume country B decides to set up a cap-and-trade system and, for political and administrative reasons, decides it would like to link to country A's system. Country B might decide, as part of it design process, to set a cap so that its expected allowance price is close to that of country A. In effect, country A serves as a carbon-pricing leader and country B follows that lead as it negotiates a linked system. Once the countries link their systems, it may appear that there was no economic benefit from linking, given their similar carbon prices. But if our conjecture is correct, then linkage opportunities in such situations do in fact provide economic as well as political and administrative benefits. The alignment of prices occurred in this instance through program design rather than through trading in sufficiently deep markets. Whether or not this conjecture is empirically valid is left as a future research topic.

within a Party in the case of sub-national jurisdictions) or non-Party of the Paris Agreement.

Level of Jurisdiction

It is broadly recognized that the fact that GHGs mix in the atmosphere renders climate change a global commons problem.[106] This, in turn, suggests that global cooperation will be necessary to address the problem successfully and the highest levels of effective governance need to be engaged in executing effective policies. On this basis, the countries of the world are the appropriate actors for engaging in such cooperation. International relations are primarily conducted between countries, and they can work through international arrangements such as the UNFCCC and the Paris Agreement, and through regional economic integration organizations such as the European Union, to address climate change. For international climate policy linkage, relevant levels of jurisdictions therefore include — at a minimum — countries and regional organizations (the European Union).

In addition, a number of sub-national jurisdictions — in particular, state and provincial governments — have put in place, are planning, or are contemplating the launch of meaningful climate change policies, including cap-and-trade systems, carbon taxes, and various kinds of conventional standards.[107] In some cases, these may function as substitutes for or supplements to national policies (for example, in the United States),[108] and in other cases, these sub-national policies will function as part of

---

[106] See, e.g., Engel, K. H. and Saleska, S. R. (2005). "Subglobal regulation of the global commons: The case of climate change." *Ecology Law Quarterly*. **32**: 183, 186. (discussing government actions "to address the global commons problem of climate change").

[107] See, e.g., Michael J. Coren, *California's 2018 Legislative Blitzkrieg Delivered its Most Ambitious Climate Policies Ever*, QUARTZ (Oct. 2, 2018), https://perma.cc/6KZE-SQSB (discussing climate change focused laws passed by California in 2018); see also David Roberts, *A Green New Deal is on the Ballot in Washington State this Year*, Vox (Sept. 28, 2018), https://perma.cc/L89D-GNE8 (stating that Washington State has an upcoming ballot initiative regarding a tax on carbon emissions).

[108] See, e.g., Roberts, *supra* note 107 (claiming that with "President Donald Trump's administration dismantling federal climate policy as fast as it can, all eyes have turned to the states").

integrated national systems (as in Canada).[109] Furthermore, in some countries, including Japan and the United States, cities may come to play significant policy roles.[110] Hence, a third important jurisdictional level for potential linkage — in addition to the international and regional — is the sub-national. This could, under the right conditions, become a particularly important level for future linkage in light of the U.S. administration's announcement that it will withdraw from the Paris Agreement.[111]

It is demonstrably true that effective sub-national climate policy linkages are feasible in the physical and economic senses, as such linkages have existed and operated for some time, both within a single country in the case of the RGGI states,[112] and internationally in the case of California and Quebec.[113] Taking the California-Quebec link as an example, if there were no international climate agreement in force, then the only major issue would be whether double-counting is avoided both at the sub-national and the national level, as each jurisdiction quantifies its emissions inventory and accounts for progress towards mitigation goals. At the sub-national level, the California-Quebec link ensures proper accounting through close coordination of the systems.[114]

An international climate agreement is very much in place, however, and this gives rise to important questions of international law.[115] Because sub-national entities are not currently allowed to join the UNFCCC and the Paris Agreement as formal Parties,[116] their emissions have to be

---

[109] See generally Mascher, S. (2018). "Striving for equivalency across the Alberta, British Columbia, Ontario and Quebec carbon pricing systems: The Pan-Canadian carbon pricing benchmark." *Climate Policy*. **18**: 1012.

[110] See, e.g., *Paris Climate Agreement*, Climate Mayors, https://perma.cc/ZDB6-TDDF (last visited December 20, 2018) (statement of 407 U.S. mayors committing to "adopt, honor, and uphold Paris Climate Agreement goals").

[111] See Michael D. Shear, *Trump Will Withdraw U.S. from Paris Climate Agreement*, *New York Times* (June 1, 2017), https://perma.cc/N25E-J24T.

[112] Schmalensee, R. L. and Stavins, R. N. (2017). "Lessons learned from three decades of experience with cap and trade." *Review of Environmental Economics and Policy*. **59**: 66.

[113] See *infra* Table 1.

[114] Benjamin Görlach *et al*., Designing Institutions, Structures and Mechanisms to Facilitate the Linking of Emissions Trading Schemes 70–74 (2015).

[115] See Paris Agreement, *supra* note 1.

[116] See *Id.*, at art. 20 (limiting accession to the Paris Agreement to "States and regional economic integration organizations"). Sovereign countries and certain international organizations (such as the EU) have traditionally been the main subjects of international

accounted for and reported at the national level. Ensuring consistency between the sub-national and national level is therefore up to the country of which the sub-national entity forms part. To the extent that Parties to the Agreement seek to use ITMOs, including any ITMOs transferred between their sub-national jurisdictions, towards their NDCs, such accounting would need to be consistent with the Agreement, including any guidance on accounting adopted by the Parties.

Additionally, Article 6.3 of the Agreement states that use of ITMOs towards NDC achievement shall be "authorized by participating Parties."[117] While this wording does not, for instance, preclude trading across the link between California and Quebec, it does require both Canada and the United States — as the participating Parties — to authorize the use of transferred allowances toward national NDC achievement.[118] If the United States withdraws from the Paris Agreement, as it has announced, Canada may be precluded from counting Californian allowances when it measures progress towards its NDC goals.[119]

Also, legal and procedural constraints imposed by national law can limit the types of arrangements available to sub-national jurisdictions when these establish a link. The U.S. Constitution, for example, expressly reserves the ability to adopt binding international treaties to the Federal Government,[120] which means that the arrangement California entered with

---

law. See Besson, S. (2011). "Sovereignty, international law and democracy." *European Journal of International Law*. **22**: 373, 376. Although, there are examples of treaties with and between sub-national jurisdictions. See Hollis, D. B. (2005). "Why state consent still matters: Non-state actors, treaties, and the changing sources of international law." *Berkeley Journal of International Law*. **23**: 137, 146.

[117] Paris Agreement, *supra* note 1.

[118] See *Id.* at 24.

[119] See discussion *infra* Part III.B.2.

[120] Under Article II of the Constitution, only the President "shall have Power, by and with the advice and consent of the Senate, to make treaties, provided two-thirds of the Senators present concur." U.S. CONST. art. II, §2, cl. 2. In Article I, the Constitution goes on to expressly prohibit any state from entering into a "treaty, alliance, or confederation" or from entering "without the Consent of Congress . . . into any Agreement or Compact . . . with a foreign Power." U.S. CONST. art. I, §10. For further discussion and secondary sources, see Mehling, M. A. (2009). "Linking of emission trading schemes." In D. Freestone and C. Streck (eds.), *Legal Aspects of Carbon Trading: Kyoto, Copenhagen, and Beyond*, Volume 108, 129–130.

Ontario and Quebec in 2017, despite being designated an "agreement,"[121] lacks the binding legal force of an international treaty. While the agreement has been implemented in each jurisdiction through sub-national rules and its provisions therefore have acquired legal force, California, Ontario and Quebec retain the right to unilaterally amend their laws and regulations, including termination of the link,[122] as evidenced by the withdrawal from the link by Ontario in 2018. A binding international treaty, by contrast, could only be amended or terminated subject to the conditions set out in the treaty itself, and would offer additional recourse to each Party in the event of a breach of obligations.

In addition, national law can impose substantive restrictions on linkages at the sub-national level. To draw again on the United States for an example, scholarly debate has discussed whether U.S. federal law limits the ability of states to introduce and link sub-national climate policies through the dormant Commerce Clause, a provision in the Constitution which prevents states from interfering with interstate commerce.[123]

Status Under the Paris Agreement

Two considerations arise for potential international linkages with regard to the status of the affected jurisdictions under the Paris Agreement. First, there is the question of whether a specific regional economic integration

---

[121] Agreement on the Harmonization and Integration of Cap-and-Trade Programs for Reducing Greenhouse Gas Emissions, *supra* note 74, at art. 1.

[122] Parties acknowledge this in the preamble when they state that "the present Agreement does not, will not and cannot be interpreted to restrict, limit or otherwise prevail over relevant national obligations of each Party, if applicable, and each Party's sovereign right and authority to adopt, maintain, modify, repeal or revoke any of their respective program regulations or enabling legislation." *See Id.* In it, they have nonetheless committed to observe certain procedures enacted on a reciprocal basis in sub-national legislation. See generally Mehling, M. A. (2016). "Legal frameworks for linking national emissions trading systems." In K. R. Gray *et al.* (eds.), *The Oxford Handbook of International Climate Change Law*, p. 261.

[123] See, e.g., Ferrey, S. (2014). "Carbon outlasts the law: States walk the constitutional line." *Boston College Environmental Affairs Law Review*. **41**: 309–311. Shanske, D. (2014). "State-level carbon taxes and the dormant commerce clause: Can formulary apportionment save the world?" *Chapman Law Review*. **18**: 191, 193. Welton, S. H. (2012). "State dynamism, federal constraints: Possible constitutional hurdles to cross-border cap-and-trade." *National Resources & Environment*. **27**: 36, 39–40.

organization (such as the European Union) or country is a Party to the Agreement. This question is of interest primarily because of the U.S. Administration's announcement that it will withdraw from the Paris Agreement.[124]

Second, as described above, sub-national jurisdictions may play important climate policy roles in the future. Given the broad membership of the Paris Agreement, such sub-national jurisdictions will more often than not be located within a Party to the Agreement, as is currently the case with Canadian provinces. If Canada wants to use any ITMOs transferred at the sub-national level (for example, through climate policy links between Canadian provinces and a foreign jurisdiction) towards achievement of its NDC, the required authorization and accounting will have to occur at the national level.[125] But in some cases, one or both of the sub-national jurisdictions might be located within a non-Party to the Agreement, as would be the case for California if the United States withdraws from the Agreement.

As already discussed in Part II.B.1, whether and how non-Parties (or sub-national jurisdictions located within non-Parties) can participate in ITMO transfers under Article 6 of the Agreement is still subject to debate. While the wording of Article 6.3 clearly states that only the *use* of ITMOs to achieve NDCs requires authorization by participating Parties — suggesting, *e contrario*, that mere transfers are not conditional on Party status or approval[126] — it is less clear whether that also means that both sides of a transfer must be Parties (or located within Parties). Should the United States withdraw from the Paris Agreement as announced, this question will be of significant relevance for the link between California and Québec.

The ability to continue trading allowances across the link between these sub-national jurisdictions is not in question. Rather, the question is whether Canada — a Party to the Agreement — could then still claim allowances transferred from California — which would be located within a non-Party, the United States — towards achievement of the Canadian

---

[124] See Shear, *supra* note 111.

[125] See *supra* Part III.B.1.

[126] This is also reflected in the wording of Article 6.1, which carefully avoids stating that voluntary cooperation as such requires any form of authorization, a concern of Parties already engaged (or planning to engage) in linking and other forms of bilateral or regional climate cooperation. See generally Howard, A. (2017). "Voluntary cooperation (Article 6)." In Daniel Klein *et al.* (eds.), *The Paris Agreement on Climate Change: Analysis and Commentary*, pp. 178–195.

NDC. The wording of Article 6 provides no definitive answer to that question: although it mentions "Parties" throughout as the participants in cooperative approaches, including ITMO transfers, it does not expressly rule out involvement of non-Parties.[127] Under international law, which is by default a permissive system,[128] this could support an interpretation that Article 6 does not, in itself, prevent a Party like Canada from obtaining ITMOs from a non-Party and using these towards its NDC.

Even Article 6.3 and its requirement that "participating Parties" authorize such use would not necessarily rule out the foregoing interpretation, given that Canada would be the only "participating Party" to the transaction and its authorization could thus satisfy a permissive reading of Article 6.3.[129] Indeed, if the authorization requirement in Article 6.3 primarily aims to protect Parties from uncoordinated transfers (for example, by a sub-national jurisdiction) that could jeopardize achievement of their NDCs, this permissive interpretation would also be supported by the *ratio legis*, or intent of the law: as a non-Party, the United States would not be held to achievement of an NDC, and thus would not require the protection afforded by an authorization requirement under Article 6.3.[130]

Still, because non-Parties would not be subject to the progressive ambition requirement and enhanced transparency framework of the Paris Agreement, among other treaty elements, such a permissive interpretation might meet with resistance by Parties concerned about transparency and the integrity of ITMOs. For now, the wording of Article 6.2 allows different interpretations, and it is unclear whether the subsequent guidance on operational details agreed on by Parties will bring further clarification: this question goes beyond matters purely related to accounting, and may thus exceed the limited mandate to elaborate such guidance.[131] Given the practical importance of this question in the event of a U.S. withdrawal, however, some form of clarification by Parties — whether through the guidance on Article 6.2, or an authoritative interpretation adopted at a

---

[127] See Paris Agreement *supra* note 1.

[128] See Case of the S.S. Lotus (France v. Turkey), Judgment, 1927 P.C.I.J. (ser. A) No. 10, at 45–47 (Sept. 7).

[129] See Paris Agreement *supra* note 1.

[130] We thank Susan Biniaz for bringing this point to our attention.

[131] See U.N. Framework Convention on Climate Change, *Report of the Conference of the Parties on its Twenty-First Session, Addendum*, 6–7, FCCC/CP/2015/10/Add.1 (Jan. 29, 2016), https://perma.cc/PX8K-XQLL.

session of the CMA[132] — would be helpful to provide legal certainty to market participants. Draft text for guidance on Article 6.2 discussed during negotiations in 2018 suggests an intention to limit participation to Parties to the Paris Agreement.[133] But even if such a restrictive interpretation prevails, under which ITMOs transferred from a non-Party cannot be used towards NDC achievement, restricted linking — for example, through a gateway solution[134] — might still allow for limited transfers and accounting toward NDCs.

Heterogeneity of Targets

There are two senses in which heterogeneity of targets may affect linkage. One is with regard to a given pair of linked policy instruments themselves; the other is with regard to the respective targets adopted by a pair of Parties to an international agreement, in particular, the Paris Climate Agreement.

Like policy instruments,[135] targets under an international agreement or a domestic instrument can differ in their degree of formality and normativity. They can be enacted in a more or less formal manner and can be legally binding or merely aspirational in nature. Many Parties to the Paris Agreement have, for example, elaborated their NDCs and the mid- and long-term targets contained therein as programmatic or strategy

---

[132] See *Conference of the Parties Serving as Meeting to the Parties to the Paris Agreement (CMA)*, U.N. Framework Convention on Climate Change, https://perma.cc/XJ57-G5AY (last visited December 20, 2018).

[133] See U.N. Framework Convention on Climate Change, Draft CMA Decision on Guidance on Cooperative Approaches Referred to in Article 6, Paragraph 2, of the Paris Agreement 4 (2018), https://perma.cc/GDC6-EXMM.

[134] This refers to the approach considered historically for possible linkage between the EU ETS and a U.S. cap-and-trade system when the EU was an Annex B Party of the Kyoto Protocol and the United States was not. It would have facilitated bidirectional transfers between both jurisdictions by stripping the Assigned Amount Unit (AAU) — the main accounting unit under the Kyoto Protocol — from EU allowances whenever the latter were transferred to the U.S., and would have restored such stripped AAUs to any units transferred from the U.S. to the EU, thereby ensuring consistency with the EU's accounting under the Kyoto Protocol. See Roßnagel, A. (2008). "Evaluating links between emissions trading schemes: An analytical framework." *Carbon & Climate Law Review*. **2**: 394, 401, 403–404. Sterk W. *et al.* (2006). *Ready to Link Up? Implications of Design Differences for Linking Domestic Emissions Trading Schemes*. Working Paper No. I/06, Wuppertal Institute for Climate, Environment & Energy JET-SET. https://perma.cc/HE5C-9VB4.

[135] See *supra* Part III.A.

documents, denying them the status and political resilience of formal legislation.[136] Even where targets have been set out in binding executive orders or decisions, they afford only limited accountability, as the same or any future administration can choose to amend or annul the targets at any time;[137] by contrast, formal legislation provides greater assurance that successive administrations will be bound to the targets enshrined therein unless and until the legislature chooses to formally enact changes. As with policy instruments, differences in the legal nature of targets do not have to preclude linking, although they can factor into the broader assessment of the risks and benefits arising from a link.

Policy Instrument Targets

In terms of the respective targets of a linked pair of policy instruments, relevant policies will tend to be expressed in the form of a GHG metric, such as metric tons of CO_2-equivalent. Of these, a majority may use absolute targets, whether a mass-based aggregate cap in a cap-and-trade system, a specific tax rate in a carbon tax system, or mass-based individual limits in a regulatory system using a performance standard.[138]

It is also possible that an aggregate or individual limit in a performance standard could be defined as a rate-based target (for example, tons of CO_2 emissions per kilowatt hour of electricity output).[139] In this case, it is straightforward to translate the rate-based target into mass-based units for purposes of trading (and linking) in a cap-and-trade system, and to translate it into mass-based units for purposes of linking in a performance standard system. If future vintages of emissions are involved in trading,

---

[136] See generally Bodansky, D. M. (2016). "The legal character of the Paris Agreement." *Review of European Community & International Environmental Law*. **25**: 142. Rajamani, L. and J. Brunnée (2017). "The legality of downgrading nationally determined contributions under the Paris Agreement: Lessons from the US disengagement." *Journal of Environmental Law*. **29**: 537.

[137] Bodansky, D. M. (2016). "The Paris Climate Change Agreement: A new hope?" *American Journal of International Law*. **110**: 288, 301.

[138] See Di Leva, C. E. and Shi, X. (2016). "The Paris Agreement and the international trade regime: Considerations for harmonization." *Sustainable Development Law & Policy*. **17**: 20–21.

[139] See Enion, R. M. (2012). "Using section 111 of the clean air act for cap-and-trade of greenhouse gas emissions: Obstacles and solutions." *UCLA Journal of Environmental Law and Policy*. **30**: 5. (discussing rate-based standards under the Clean Air Act).

such as through banking provisions, then anticipated output (*ex ante* projections) could presumably constitute the denominator, which itself could evolve over time.

If a regional, national, or sub-national policy were to use relative mass-based targets (for example, aggregate tons of emissions compared with anticipated Business-as-Usual (BAU) emissions), then it would be necessary to translate the aggregate relative target into simple mass terms for exchanges to take place, using *ex ante* quantitative estimates of BAU emissions.

Some targets may not be amenable to linking. China, for example, set a target of increasing its share of non-fossil fuels in primary energy consumption to "around 20 percent" by 2030.[140] One might imagine making some assumption about the fuels that are displaced and their carbon content to convert this target into an emissions target, but even then, it is not clear that China would want to link this particular target if the goal is to incentivize the growth of non-fossil fuel energy sectors in the country.

NDC Targets Under the Paris Agreement

A key characteristic of the Paris Agreement's structure that led directly to the remarkably broad scope of achieved participation is the bottom-up structure of NDCs, and the fact that individual contributions are left to the discretion of respective Parties.[141] This means that the specified contributions are not legally binding under international law, as clarified by Article 4.2 where it states that each Party shall prepare, communicate and maintain successive NDCs that it "intends to achieve."[142] Accordingly, substantial flexibility was granted regarding both the form and content of such contributions.[143] Consequently, the NDCs are exceptionally

[140] China to Boost Non-Fossil Fuel Use to 20 Percent by 2030: State Planner, *Reuters*, Apr. 25, 2017, https://perma.cc/J4FH-XXQT.

[141] Bodansky, *The Paris Climate Change Agreement: A New Hope? supra* note 137, at 301.

[142] U.N. Framework Convention on Climate Change, *Report of the Conference of the Parties on its Twenty-First Session* U.N. Doc. FCCC/CP/2015/10Add.1, at 23 (December 13, 2015).

[143] The Decision by the Conference of the Parties to invite the submission of INDCs twice underscored that this invitation was "without prejudice to the legal nature of the contributions." *See* U.N. Framework Convention on Climate Change, *Report of the Conference of the Parties on its Nineteenth Session*, ¶2(b), FCCC/CP/2013/10/Add.1 (January 31, 2014); likewise, the subsequent Decision detailing the type of information that could be included in the INDCs indicated that such inclusion was voluntary. *See* U.N. Framework Convention

heterogeneous, including in regard to the ambition and the nature of quantitative targets. This is important for potential international linkages that would be tracked through ITMOs (to avoid double-counting of emissions reductions or other actions by Parties).

By the time the Paris Agreement came into force on November 4, 2016, 163 Intended Nationally Determined Contributions (INDCs) had been submitted to the UNFCCC Secretariat by Parties to the Convention.[144] Among the features of these INDCs and NDCs[145] that are relevant for potential international linkages are target type, reference year, target year, sectoral and geographic scope of coverage, GHGs covered, target conditionality, methodologies including for estimating global warming potential (GWP) of GHGs, and intended use of market mechanisms.[146]

Target Type

Whereas under the Kyoto Protocol, all countries with emissions reduction responsibilities (largely the industrialized countries listed in Annex I of the Protocol) had quantified reduction objectives expressed relative to historic emission levels,[147] under the Paris Agreement such mass-based absolute emission limits are only one of a number of types of targets employed.[148] Of 163 submitted NDCs, 43 are in the form of absolute GHG targets.[149] These account for 41 percent of global emissions.[150]

---

on Climate Change, *Report of the Conference of the Parties on its Twentieth Session*, ¶14, FCCC/CP/2014/10/Add.1 (Feb. 2, 2015).

[144] Asian Development Bank, United Nations Climate Change Conference Marrakech, Morocco, November 7–8, 2016 1–2 (2017), https://perma.cc/82LD-Z98V.

[145] As Parties ratify the Agreement, their INDCs become NDCs. Mengpin Ge & Kelly Levin, *INSIDER: What's Changing As Countries Turn INDCs into NDCs? 5 Early Insights*, World Resources Inst. (April 18, 2018), https://perma.cc/GC94-AL3B. Hereafter, for convenience, we refer both to INDCs and NDCs as NDCs, except where the context requires differentiation for clarity.

[146] See *infra* Table 2.

[147] *Kyoto Protocol*, Climate Change Connection, https://perma.cc/KN35-EAW2 (last updated September 26, 2016) ("[E]ach industrialized country set a binding greenhouse gas emission target to reduce emissions below 1990 levels by 2012.").

[148] See Jakob Graichen *et al.*, Categorization of INDCs in the Light of Art. 6 of the Paris Agreement 7 (2016), https://perma.cc/EAE9-5T9J. Table 2 provides an overview of key features of all submitted (I)NDCs.

[149] *Id.*

[150] *Id.*

Table 2. Key relevant features of submitted INDCs and NDCs.[a]

Feature	Option employed	Number of INDCs/NDCs	Share of global emissions
GHG Target Type	Absolute GHG (mass-based)	43	41%
	GHG Relative to BAU	74	16%
	GHG Intensity (per unit of GDP)	10	33%
	Other & No GHG Emissions Target	36	6%
Non-GHG Target Type	Renewable Energy (only)	63	13%
	Energy Efficiency (only)	1	0%
	Forestry (only)	10	2%
	Multiple Non-GHG Targets	63	13%
	No Non-GHG Target	72	49%
Conditionality	Unconditional (only)	34	68%
	Conditional (only)	49	12%
	Combination	80	16%
Base Year	Historic Year or Fixed Level	53	74%
	Projected BAU Emissions	79	16%
	Not Specified	31	6%
Target Year	Single Year (2030)	106	70%
	Single Year (other year)	11	20%
	Multiple Years (2030 and at least one other year)	11	1%
	Not Specified	35	6%
Sectoral Coverage	All Sectors	71	86%
	Energy plus 1-3 Other Sectors	66	7%
	Energy (only)	20	1%
	Some Energy Sub-Sectors (only)	6	2%
GHG Coverage	All GHGs (using Kyoto Protocol definitions)	39	57%
	CO_2 plus some others	85	8%
	CO_2 (only)	16	25%
	Not Specified	23	6%

Table 2. (*Continued*)

Feature	Option employed	Number of INDCs/NDCs	Share of global emissions
Global Warming Potentials	IPCC AR2	45	5%
	IPCC AR4	33	45%
	IPCC AR5	3	4%
	Not Specified	82	42%

Note: [a]Graichen *et al.*, *supra* note 148 (as of October 12, 2016).

GHG intensity targets — emissions per unit of economic activity — characterize another ten NDCs, accounting for 33 percent of global emissions, and GHG targets relative to BAU emissions are found in seventy-four NDCs, which account for just 16 percent of global emissions.[151] Thus, 90 percent of global emissions are covered by a total of 127 NDCs employing absolute, intensity, or relative targets.[152] The remainder use a variety of other types of quantitative targets, including GHG emissions peaking in a specific year, degree of penetration of renewable energy sources, and improvements in energy efficiency.[153] With the exception of Turkey, all Annex I countries (plus twenty-nine non-Annex I countries) use absolute GHG targets in their NDCs.[154]

Linkage is most straightforward when both systems employ absolute (mass-based) targets. Linkage is also possible with jurisdictions expressing their aggregate targets as relative to BAU or in terms of carbon intensity of the economy, since exchanges can still be in mass terms, and the impacts on aggregate targets (such as through the ITMOs of Article 6) can be calculated by employing *ex ante* quantitative estimates of BAU emissions, which are often contained in the NDCs themselves, or by converting the intensity target to an absolute target once the relevant level of economic activity (such as Gross Domestic Product, "GDP") is known after the target year.[155]

---

[151] *Id.*

[152] *Id.*

[153] *Id.* at 9.

[154] *Id.*

[155] For an example of a methodology to convert rate-based targets to mass-based targets, see U.S. Entvl. Prot. Agency, Translation of the Clean Power Plan Emission Rate-Based CO_2 Goals to Mass-Based Equivalents (2014), https://perma.cc/Q54V-SFX5.

Also, it should be noted that fully unconditional targets are employed by thirty-four NDCs, accounting for 68 percent of global emissions; conditional targets are used by forty-nine NDCs, accounting for 12 percent of emissions; and a mix of unconditional and conditional targets are found in eighty NDCs, accounting for 16 percent of global emissions.[156] The conditional targets are most often specified as contingent upon international support being provided in the form of financial support or technology transfer.

Reference and Target Years

Of 163 submitted NDCs, 79 use (projected) BAU emissions as their base.[157] Note that some countries may use a dynamic BAU baseline, whereby they update their BAU projections over time, whereas others may stick with their original BAU estimate.[158] With regard to dynamic baselines or with BAU baselines that are determined after the fact (for example, a BAU constructed in 2030), the effective ambition of the NDC targets may be driven by the uncertainty surrounding the BAU estimates, possibly making it difficult for sources in such countries to know whether they should be "buyers" or "sellers" under any international linkage.

On the other hand, fifty-three submissions have employed an historic base year or a fixed level of emissions, accounting for 74 percent of global emissions.[159] This is extremely valuable for firms or monitors wishing to understand the stringency or precise level of the target and resulting shadow price of emissions. The specific base years or the specific emissions levels specified may differ among countries, but this need not impose any accounting problems for ITMOs in reconciling activities carried out between firms under linkage arrangements.

The vast majority of NDCs (117) have used 2030 as their target year.[160] These NDCs account for over 70 percent of global emissions.[161] A dozen other countries have identified some other year (2020, 2025, 2035, or 2050) as the time at which they will achieve their specified target.[162] If

[156] Graichen *et al.*, *supra* note 148, at 7.

[157] *Id.*

[158] *Id.* at 9.

[159] *Id.* at 7.

[160] *Id.* at 7, 9.

[161] *Id.* at 7.

[162] *Id.* at 9.

a time-path of annual targets is not offered by an NDC, which is usually the case, then a simple linear (or some other) interpolation could be used for the purpose of accounting for necessary ITMO transfers.[163] Linkage between systems with different target years should not present a problem, but accounting rules will need to be clear on transfer of ITMOs between such linked systems.[164]

Sectoral and Geographic Coverage

Some seventy-one NDCs, which account for 86 percent of global emissions, are economy-wide in their coverage.[165] The other ninety-two NDCs include the energy sector, frequently in combination with some limited set of other sectors.[166] Nearly all NDCs cover the entire territory of respective countries.

Linkages between climate policies in different jurisdictions need not be affected by differences in sectoral or geographic coverage. However, accounting for executed international transfers through ITMOs can be challenging when limited sectors or geographic areas within countries are covered by their respective policies. The challenge — indeed, the problem — arises when there is significant emissions leakage from regulated to unregulated sectors or from regulated to unregulated geographic areas. Then, what appears to be an emission reduction from a particular country may be less than it appears to be, because of a consequent emissions increase in the unregulated sector/area.

GHG Coverage

The Paris Agreement addresses reductions in all GHGs not controlled by the Montreal Protocol, including carbon dioxide (CO_2), methane (CH_4),

---

[163] Because guidance on Article 6.2 might not address how to account for ITMO transfers in non-target years, it will be up to Parties to voluntarily agree to a methodology consistent with whatever accounting rules the Parties do adopt. If two or more Parties want to facilitate linkage and count transferred ITMOs towards NDC achievement, they should also be incentivized to agree to such rules.

[164] See Org. for Econ. Co-operation & Dev., *Workshop Summary: Workshop on "Corresponding Adjustment" As Part of Article 6 Accounting* 5 (2017), https://perma.cc/M95V-BQ9H [hereinafter OECD WORKSHOP SUMMARY].

[165] Graichen *et al.*, *supra* note 148, at 7.

[166] *Id.* at 9.

nitrous oxide (N_2O), hydrofluorocarbons (HFCs), perfluorocarbons (PFCs), sulphur hexafluoride (SF), and nitrogen trifluoride (NF).[167] It is up to each Party, however, to determine which GHGs to include in its NDC.[168] Presumably, all NDCs include CO_2 emissions, although 23 of the 163 submitted (accounting for 6 percent of global emissions) do not specify the gases covered.[169] Forty NDCs explicitly cover all GHGs, accounting for 57 percent of global emissions, using one of two Kyoto Protocol lists.[170] Another eighty-five specify CO_2 plus some other GHGs, and sixteen specify coverage of CO_2 only.[171]

As with limited sectoral and geographic scope,[172] there is not necessarily an issue here for linkage *per se*, but proper accounting for executed international transfers through ITMOs could be problematic if there is significant leakage from regulated to unregulated GHGs. However, leakage across GHGs would seem to be much less likely than sectoral or geographic leakage.

Global Warming Potential Values

When NDCs include more than a single GHG (CO_2), then calculations are required to convert emissions and emissions reductions of various other GHGs to a common unit, CO_2 equivalent. Such calculations involve not only information regarding the impacts of specific GHGs on radiative forcing, but also an assumed time period for the calculation, since the

---

[167] *Id.* at 10.

[168] *Id.* at 8.

[169] *Id.*

[170] *Id.* at 10. In the Kyoto Protocol's first commitment period, the first six GHGs were included. *Kyoto Protocol — Targets for the First Commitment Period*, U.N. Framework Convention Climate Change, https://perma.cc/78CV-8NVK (last visited Dec. 20, 2018). In the second commitment period, all seven are covered. *Kyoto 2nd Commitment Period (2013–2020)*, Eur. Commission, https://perma.cc/2R69-PJ6G (last visited Dec. 20, 2018). Under the UNFCCC, GHGs covered by the Vienna Convention for the Protection of the Ozone Layer and its Montreal Protocol are excluded.

[171] See Graichen *et al.*, *supra* note 148, at 8; see also *infra* Table 2.

[172] See *supra* notes 165–166 and accompanying text.

GHGs display dramatically different lag times in the atmosphere.[173] The results of such estimates are the GWP of each GHG, which also depends upon existing concentrations of these gases in the atmosphere.

The Intergovernmental Panel on Climate Change (IPCC) has periodically updated the estimated GWP of each of the GHGs. More than half of country submissions (eighty-two NDCs accounting for 42 percent of global emissions) do not specify what GWP values are used, whereas thirty-three NDCs (covering 45 percent of global emissions) rely on GWPs from the Fourth Assessment Report of the IPCC, forty-five NDCs (covering 5 percent of emissions) rely on Second Assessment Report of the IPCC estimates, and just three NDCs (covering about 4 percent of global emissions) state their reliance on the most recent Fifth Assessment Report of the IPCC values.[174] In principle, the use of different assumed GWPs by different NDCs can render more difficult the accounting exercise to be carried out for ITMOs.

Heterogeneity of NDCs of Key Countries

Given that the twenty largest economies (G20) — counting the European Union as one — account for approximately 80 percent of global GHG emissions,[175] it is reasonable to focus on that subset of the 195 Parties to the Paris Agreement when thinking about the challenges posed by heterogeneity across NDCs. Doing so reveals a much less challenging picture than emerges when reviewing the full set of 163 NDCs. Among the G20 countries, all but one (Saudi Arabia) employ absolute, relative, or intensity targets; nearly all cover all sectors of their respective economies, as well as all GHGs; and only India and Saudi Arabia utilize pure conditionality in their NDCs.[176]

---

[173] Rogelj, J. *et al.* (2017). "Understanding the origin of Paris Agreement emission uncertainties." *Nature Communications*. **8**: 15748. https://perma.cc/9QHY-PHLZ.

[174] Graichen *et al.*, *supra* note 148, at 8; see also *infra* Table 2.

[175] See Graichen *et al.*, *supra* note 148, at 12; see also *infra* Table 3.

[176] Graichen *et al.*, *supra* note 148, at 12–13. Some countries have multiple targets. As noted above, China's NDC includes a non-fossil fuel penetration target. *Id.* But it is still the case that it has a GHG target that presumably would be the focus of any linking activity.

Table 3. Selected key features of G20 INDCs and NDCs.[a]

Party	Share of global emissions	GHG target	Non-GHG targets	Sectoral coverage	GHG coverage	Conditionality
Argentina	1%	Relative to BAU		All Sectors	All GHGs	Combination
Australia	1%	Absolute GHG	Renewable Energy	All Sectors	All GHGs	Unconditional
Brazil	2%	Absolute GHG	Renewable Energy	All Sectors	All GHGs	Unconditional
Canada	2%	Absolute GHG		All Sectors	All GHGs	Unconditional
China	25%	GHG Intensity	Multiple Non-GHG	All Sectors	CO_2	Unconditional
European Union	11%	Absolute GHG		All Sectors	All GHGs	Unconditional
India	7%	GHG Intensity	Multiple Non-GHG	All Sectors	All GHGs	Conditional
Indonesia	2%	Relative to BAU	Renewable Energy	All Sectors	CO2, etc.	Combination
Japan	3%	Absolute GHG	Renewable Energy	All Sectors	All GHGs	Unconditional
South Korea	1%	Relative to BAU		(No LUCF)	All GHGs	Unconditional
Mexico	1%	Relative to BAU		All Sectors	All GHGs	Combination
Russian Federation	5%	Absolute GHG		All Sectors	All GHGs	Unconditional
Saudi Arabia	1%		Actions Only	Energy Sub-Sec	Not Specified	Conditional
South Africa	1%	GHG Peaks		All Sectors	All GHGs	Combination
Turkey	1%	Relative to BAU	Renewable Energy	All Sectors	All GHGs	Combination
United States	15%	Absolute GHG		All Sectors	All GHGs	Unconditional

Note: [a]*Id.* at 13.

Illustrative Cases of Potential Climate Policy Linkages

Here we examine the feasibility of some illustrative cases of potential international linkage of climate policies in ways that would be consistent with the Paris Agreement, taking into account the three categories and two sub-categories of heterogeneity elaborated in Part III: policy instrument, jurisdiction (distinguishing level of jurisdiction and status (Party or non-Party) under the Paris Agreement), and target (distinguishing policy target and NDC target).[177]

As discussed above, the major options for policy instruments are carbon tax, cap-and-trade, performance standard, and technology standard. Jurisdictions are regional (the European Union), national, or sub-national (mainly states and provinces). Status (in relation to the Paris Agreement) is either Party or non-Party. Policy targets (of a given carbon tax or cap-and-trade system, for example) include absolute mass-based, relative (to BAU) mass-based, and carbon intensity; and NDC targets include absolute GHG, relative GHG, GHG intensity, and non-GHG targets.

We consider five illustrative cases of potential linkages, some of which map approximately to existing examples, but most of which are included to span some of the potentially important possibilities[178]:

(1) linkage between two mass-based cap-and-trade systems, both at the national level, with both countries Parties to the Paris Agreement using absolute GHG targets in their respective NDCs;
(2) linkage between a mass-based carbon tax and a mass-based cap-and-trade system, both at the sub-national level, and both jurisdictions located within countries that are Paris Agreement Parties with absolute GHG NDC targets;
(3) linkage between two mass-based cap-and-trade systems, one regional and one sub-national, with the regional system a Party of the Paris

[177] See *infra* Table 4.

[178] Given the greater relevance for linking, all cases involve policy instruments (and targets) that are based on some form of GHG metric (such as metric tons of CO_2 equivalent), although, as noted above, policies based on other metrics — such as a specific volume or share of renewable energy — could also feature in a link (potentially requiring conversion into a fungible metric when metrics are not identical). Also, accounting for transfers in emissions inventories will necessitate translation into a GHG metric.

Table 4. Five cases of potential linkages for five categories of heterogeneity.

	Categories of heterogeneity				
		Jurisdiction/Scope		Target	
Case	**Policy instrument**	**Level of jurisdiction**	**Status under Paris agreement**	**Policy instrument**	**NDC**
1	Cap-and-Trade + Cap-and-Trade	National + National	Party + Party	Mass-Based + Mass-Based	Absolute GHG + Absolute GHG
2	Carbon Tax + Cap-and-Trade	Sub-National + Sub-National	In a Party + in a Party	Mass-Based + Mass-Based	Absolute GHG + Absolute GHG
3	Cap-and-Trade + Cap-and-Trade	Regional + Sub-National	Party + in a Non-Party	Mass-Based + Mass-Based	Absolute GHG + N/A
4	Performance Standard + Cap-and-Trade	National + National	Party + Party	Rate-Based + Mass-Based	Absolute GHG + Relative GHG
5	Carbon Tax + Carbon Tax	National + National	Non-Party + Non-Party	Mass-Based + Mass-Based	N/A

Agreement and the sub-national system in a non-Party country, with an absolute GHG NDC target in the former;

(4) linkage between a rate-based performance standard with a mass-based cap-and-trade system, both at the national level, both Parties of the Paris Agreement, with an absolute GHG NDC target and a relative GHG NDC target, respectively; and

(5) linkage between two mass-based carbon taxes, both at the national level in non-Party countries (without NDCs).

Case 1: Two National Mass-Based Cap-and-Trade Systems, Paris Agreement Parties, Absolute NDC Targets

This is the most straightforward case for international climate policy linkage, and one reason we include it is to provide a convenient base case for comparison. With two countries, both of which are Parties to the Paris Agreement and employ absolute mass-based GHG targets in their NDCs,[179] the prerequisites for straightforward linkage are met. Furthermore, the fact that the pair of countries both use national mass-based cap-and-trade systems makes this hypothetical case ideally suited for linkage. An illustration of this case would be — in principle — linkage between New Zealand and Switzerland.

Even in this simplest case, however, concerns might be expressed about the effects of such a link.[180] Fortunately, the vast majority of these concerns are actually not impediments to linkage.[181] Most are not concerns about linkage *per se*, but broader concerns about design alignment (for its own sake). Also, note that a number of these concerns are not specific to cap-and-trade systems; they may arise with other policy instruments as well.

First of all, concerns are often expressed regarding differences in allowance prices between two systems that are candidates for linking.[182] Of course, if there is no difference in the allowance price between two jurisdictions, then there is little to be gained on cost-effectiveness grounds through linkage, since the identical allowance prices indicate that marginal abatement costs are already equated, and hence overall reductions will be achieved cost-effectively. As the difference between allowance prices increases, the potential economic benefits of linkage increase, with greater gains in cost-effectiveness.

However, as allowance prices converge, lower or higher prices in the two linked systems can impair other policy objectives, such as price-induced technological change. Furthermore, an allowance price increase in a system prone to emissions leakage can increase global emissions. More broadly, allowance price changes can induce increases or decreases in co-benefits as emissions reductions are re-allocated. In any event, while

[179] Examples of national Paris Agreement Parties with absolute, mass-based NDC targets include: Australia, Brazil, Canada, Japan, Russia, and — for the time being — the United States. See *infra* Table 3.

[180] See Green, *supra* note 26, at 484–485.

[181] See Jaffe, J. and R. N. Stavins. (2008). *Linking a U.S. Cap-and-Trade System for Greenhouse Gas Emissions: Opportunities, Implications, and Challenges*. Working Papers 08-01, AEIBrookings Joint Ctr. for Regulatory Studies. https://perma.cc/PX5C-YAMJ; Jaffe *et al.*, *supra* note 23, at 800.

[182] See Jaffe *et al.*, *supra* note 23, at 800–801.

price convergence will produce aggregate net benefits (cost savings), there are distributional implications since there will be both winners and losers among compliance entities in both systems, as we examined in Part II, above. Likewise, international capital flows can be induced by linkage. Because exchanges under a linkage arrangement are voluntary, these capital flows necessarily are beneficial to the entities involved in the trading. However, there may be political objections to potentially large capital flows.[183]

A second area of frequently expressed concern relates to the scope of sectoral coverage. However, linked systems need not cover the same sectors, although a single-sector system, for example, is automatically linked with all sectors covered by the other system. Still, the scope of coverage can affect differences in allowance prices (taking us back to the first concern, above). An example is a cap-and-trade system that covers one sector with high marginal abatement costs linked with a cap-and-trade system in another country that covers several sectors — including the sector covered in the first country's system. If the additional sectors included in the second country's system have greater scope for emissions reduction at low cost, then linking the first country's system with the second country's system gives firms in the former country access to low cost allowances that can be used in place of high cost abatement options in their own country.

Third, differences in the point of regulation — ranging from a fully upstream system (that regulates the carbon content of the three fossil fuels as they enter the economy) to a fully downstream system (that regulates CO_2 emissions) — give rise to legitimate concerns about possible double-counting of emissions when fuel in an upstream system is used in a downstream system. However, this issue arises whether or not the systems are linked. Assume country A measures emissions upstream. Fuel extracted and exported to country B, which measures emissions on combustion, would be counted both by country A and B. This is a more fundamental issue about NDC coverage. Presumably NDCs are focused on emissions related to domestic consumption in which case the solution is simple: any

[183] If differences in allowance prices and resulting capital flows between systems are perceived to result largely from differences in the stringency of their caps, there is more likely to be political resistance to the capital flows. Jaffe & Stavins, *Linking a U.S. Cap-and-Trade System*, *supra* note 181, at 24.

upstream system should exclude exported fossil fuel from allowance requirements (or, more generally, from coverage under the NDC).

Fourth, concerns can arise (although not in our Case 1) over differences in the nature of the caps of two systems, such as between an absolute cap and an intensity cap (per unit of GDP or other output measure). If a link increases economic activity or output, then total emissions can increase. But it is also possible that a link cuts economic activity/output, and thereby decreases total emissions. Fifth, concerns may arise among some firms over differences in the point (in the economy) of the allocation of allowances (again, upstream versus downstream, for example). These differences need not be any barrier to linkage, although this will affect the distributional implications of the policies in both jurisdictions.

Sixth, concerns may arise over potential differences in the nature of the allocation in the two jurisdictions, for example, auctioning versus free distribution. Under typical conditions, the method of allocation has no effect on the allowance price (opportunity cost) in the two systems, but will have distributional implications within both jurisdictions. When an output-based updating allocation is used within one of the systems to address competitiveness concerns, however, the result can be that total costs will increase.

Seventh, an important concern is the possibility of significant differences between the two jurisdictions' systems in terms of monitoring, reporting, and enforcement provisions. Lax enforcement in one country can propagate through linkage and trading to increase emissions in both systems. Eighth and finally, different cost-containment provisions may be found in two systems that are candidates for linking: offsets, banking, and price floor/ceiling. The concern is that once linkage occurs and trading commences, there is automatic propagation of these cost-containment elements from one system to the other.

None of these potential concerns are impediments in and of themselves to the prospects for international policy linkage, but they are issues to keep in mind. By allowing Parties to operationalize linkages through the transfer of ITMOs, the Paris Agreement's Article 6.2 and subsequent guidance on its implementation can provide a credible accounting framework for the national aggregation of the firm-firm (source-source) international trading that would occur under this country-country linkage.[184]

[184] *See* Paris Agreement *supra* note 1. ("Parties shall . . . apply robust accounting to ensure . . . the avoidance of double counting.").

Case 2: Two Sub-National Systems (Carbon Tax and Cap-and-Trade), Both in Paris Agreement Parties with Absolute NDC Targets

This second case differs from the first case in two ways. First, both of the linkage candidates are sub-national policies, and, second, here one of the two is a carbon tax, while the other is a cap-and-trade system. Both jurisdictions are located within Parties to the Paris Agreement (which both employ absolute NDC targets). This situation would correspond, for example, to a linkage arrangement between the city of Tokyo (which has a cap-and-trade system) and the Canadian province of British Columbia (which has a carbon tax).[185]

This second linkage case is feasible, although not as simple as Case 1.[186] As explained above, the policy-instrument heterogeneity could be addressed through the use of Emission Tax Payment Credits (ETPCs).[187] In the carbon-tax jurisdiction, firms could pay taxes at a higher level than they owe based on their emissions, and then sell certified ETPCs to firms operating in the cap-and-trade jurisdiction. Within the cap-and-trade program, firms could use ETPCs as they would the equivalent quantity of allowances for purposes of compliance. Firms in the cap-and-trade jurisdiction could sell allowances to firms required to pay a carbon tax in the other jurisdiction, allowing the purchasing firm to reduce its tax obligation by the amount of allowances it submits for retirement.[188] The trading would be on a mass-based equivalence, that is, the tax liability for one ton of GHG emissions would be offset by surrendering one ton of allowances.

Note that Case 1 partly converges to this case where one of the cap-and-trade systems in Case 1 has a very narrow price collar. The previous issues of design heterogeneity apply here, plus some special considerations. Unrestricted linkage will turn the cap-and-trade system into an

---

[185] See World Bank & Ecofys, State and Trends of Carbon Pricing 2014, *supra* note 50, at 63, 79.

[186] Many of the concerns considered in Case 1 also apply in this second case and in the subsequent cases, but for purposes of brevity we do not repeat our analysis from the discussion of Case 1.

[187] See discussion *supra* Part III.A.2.

[188] Metcalf & Weisbach, *supra* note 36, at 122.

implicit carbon tax system, which introduces two concerns. First, the absolute limit (cap) on emissions in the cap-and-trade jurisdiction is broken as a result of the link with the tax jurisdiction. Second, the tax revenues in the taxing jurisdiction can be reduced as a result of the link.

As outlined earlier, because the two participants to the link in this case are sub-national jurisdictions, they cannot currently be Parties to the Paris Agreement.[189] That said, they are both located within Parties with absolute GHG targets in their respective NDCs. In order to ensure consistency with Article 6.3 of the Paris Agreement, the use of ITMOs to achieve an NDC needs to be authorized by the participating Parties.[190] Each Party will also need to account for the transfers by way of a *national aggregation* of the firm-firm international exchanges under the link. For the carbon tax and any ETPCs issued under it, such accounting will involve a calculation of the emission reductions achieved through overpayment of the tax liability. As for the cap-and-trade system, units are already commonly denominated in absolute amounts of GHG emissions, making this task easier. Ensuring that the accounting principles in the Paris Agreement and any subsequent guidance are observed will be up to the national reporting systems of the two Parties, as well as any registry systems used to track unit holdings, transfers, and cancellations.

Case 3: Two Cap-and-Trade Systems, One a Regional Party of the Paris Agreement (with an Absolute NDC Target) and One a Sub-National System in a Non-Party

This third case of potential linkage represents greater diversity than the first two cases. Here, one of the policies being linked is a mass-based cap-and-trade system in a regional economic integration organization that is a Party of the Paris Agreement and that has an absolute GHG NDC target. This corresponds to the European Union Emissions Trading System (EU ETS). The other policy is also a mass-based cap-and-trade system but is being used by a sub-national jurisdiction that is located in a country that is not a Party to the Paris Agreement. This would correspond to California's

[189] See discussion *supra* Part III.B.1.

[190] See Paris Agreement *supra* note 1.

economy-wide cap-and-trade system when and if the United States completes its withdrawal from the Paris Agreement in November 2020.[191]

The fact that one cap-and-trade system is multinational and the other cap-and-trade system is sub-national presents no fundamental problems from a physical or economic perspective. Likewise, as previously discussed, the fact that their scopes and sectoral coverage differ is not an impediment to effective linkage. It bears noting that both jurisdictions mentioned as examples for this case, the European Union and California, have substantive linking conditions spelled out in the legislation setting up their cap-and-trade systems.[192] For the European Union, linking its cap-and-trade system to jurisdictions other than those with quantitative targets under the Kyoto Protocol is only possible if these have "compatible mandatory greenhouse gas emissions trading systems with absolute emissions caps."[193] Likewise, California requires that any linking partner have "adopted program requirements for greenhouse gas reductions . . . that are equivalent to or stricter than those required" in California.[194] Depending on how the terms "compatible" and "stricter" are interpreted, both conditions could, in principle, be met if the European Union and California chose to link.

A more significant challenge arising from this case relates to the divergent status of the two jurisdictions under the Paris Agreement. As discussed earlier, the wording of Article 6 does not provide certainty on whether and how ITMOs transferred from the non-Party might be used by the Party towards achievement of its NDC.[195] Pending further clarification of the sparse wording of Article 6 through subsequent guidance on its

---

[191] See Jason Ye, Ctr. for Climate & Energy Sols., Summary of California's Extension of Its Cap-and-Trade Program 1 (2017), https://perma.cc/DD5R-TES5 (stating the program is extended to 2030 and covers nearly 85 percent of the state's total GHG emissions).

[192] See Directive 2003/87/EC, of the European Parliament and of the Council of 13 October 2003 Establishing a Scheme for Greenhouse Gas Emission Allowance Trading Within the Community and Amending Council Directive 96/61/EC, 2003 O.J. (L 275) 32, 39; Cal. Gov't Code §12894.5 (West 2018).

[193] Directive 2009/29/EC, of the European Parliament and of the Council of 23 April 2009 amending Directive 2003/87/EC so as to Improve and Extend the Greenhouse Gas Emission Allowance Trading Scheme of the Community, art. 25(1a), 2009 O.J. (L 140) 63, 81.

[194] Cal. Gov't Code §12894.5.

[195] See *supra* notes 126–128 and accompanying text.

implementation, the European Union could encounter difficulties if it sought credit towards achievement of its NDC for emissions reductions transferred from California, should the United States follow through with its announced withdrawal from the Paris Agreement. Different possible interpretations of Articles 6.2 and 6.3 will result in different answers to this question, and Part III.B.2 already examined the alternative interpretations, as well as some of the main arguments supporting each option. Unconstrained by the need to adhere to international accounting rules, meanwhile, California would have greater latitude in how it treats any such transactions, and could unilaterally decide whether and how to recognize EU allowances for domestic compliance and accounting purposes.

Case 4: National Performance Standard with Absolute GHG NDC Target and Mass-Based National Cap-and-Trade with Relative GHG Target, Both Parties to the Paris Agreement

This departs from the three previous cases in several ways and corresponds to a potential linkage between Japan's various national performance standards for appliances, vehicles and building (all under an absolute GHG NDC target) and South Korea's national mass-based cap-and-trade system (under a GHG NDC target that is relative to BAU emissions).[196]

First, this case features the combination of a performance standard in one country with a cap-and-trade system in another. As discussed above, this need not be an impediment to linkage. If the performance standard is a mass-based quantity standard, firms can buy allowances from the cap-and-trade system (or ETPCs from a carbon tax system) to meet required reductions (or firms can achieve reductions in excess of the regulatory minimum and sell additional reductions as ERCs). If the performance-standard system is an emissions rate-based standard, actions under the system can still be translated into mass-based outcomes, which can then form the basis of any trades. Specifically, rate-based (intensity) standards can be translated into quantity standards at the source or firm level (per total output, total sales, or whatever denominator the regulation prescribes), which ultimately allows for linkage.

[196]Graichen *et al.*, *supra* note 148, at 8, 9.

Another aspect of this case that differs from the previous cases is the heterogeneity in the types of NDC targets, with the performance-standard country using an absolute GHG target and the cap-and-trade country using a relative (to BAU) GHG target. Linkage is possible with jurisdictions expressing their aggregate targets as relative to BAU, because exchanges can be in mass terms, and the impacts on aggregate targets (through the ITMOs of Article 6) can be calculated by employing *ex ante* quantitative estimates of BAU emissions. Most NDCs that specify a target relative to BAU also set out a BAU projection for the target year, allowing direct conversion of the national target into absolute mass-based terms.[197] The same issues arise here as discussed above around the degree to which the BAU target is fixed or subject to revision.

Case 5: Two National Mass-Based Carbon Tax Instruments in Non-Parties of the Paris Agreement

This final case corresponds to what some analysts have proposed as an alternative approach to international climate policy cooperation, which they consider superior to the approaches taken by the UNFCCC and the Paris Agreement.[198] It also may correspond to what some policy makers consider a reasonable fallback position if the Paris Agreement coalition were to collapse.[199] Here we have a pair of national mass-based carbon tax systems, where neither country is a Party to the Paris Agreement.

In the most direct manifestation of this, a pair or — as proposed by Nordhaus[200] — a set of countries would each put in place a domestic carbon tax. Each participating country would keep for itself the revenue generated, and simultaneously institute significant border adjustments against imports from non-participants, in order to provide incentives for countries to participate in this "club" and thereby overcome the free-rider problem of climate change protection. A parallel approach featuring domestic cap-and-trade systems rather than carbon taxes could be similar, depending upon its design.[201] This is an example of soft linkage as described earlier.

---

[197] See *Id.* at 8, 9, 13.

[198] See Nordhaus, *supra* note 33, at 1368.

[199] See *Id.*

[200] *Id.* at 1341.

[201] Keohane, N. *et al.* (2017). "Toward a club of carbon markets." *Climatic Change*. **144**: 81, 82.

Whether such systems would be likely to achieve the same, lesser, or greater degrees of aggregate emissions reductions as will cooperation under the Paris Agreement is an open question, well outside the scope of our analysis. But, within the scope of our investigation, it is clear that the international linkage elements of such an approach would be feasible, as with our simplest example, the benchmark of Case 1. No linkage beyond an agreement on a carbon price would be needed, although past experience has shown that international cooperation on tax harmonization is challenging.

Common Threads, Policy Implications, and Pending Questions

Most features of heterogeneity — including those associated with heterogeneous policy instruments, heterogeneous jurisdictions, and heterogeneous targets — do not present insurmountable obstacles to linkage.[202] However, some of these characteristics present challenges and indicate the need for specific accounting guidance if linkage is to include the use of transferred ITMOs towards achievement of NDCs, as provided for in Articles 6.2 and 6.3 of the Paris Agreement. With their sparse wording and remaining ambiguities, these PA provisions reflect a compromise that intentionally does not address important questions of implementation. Parties have therefore included a mandate in Article 6.2, charging the CMA with adoption of relevant guidance; this guidance will, in turn, be informed by a recommendation developed by the Subsidiary Body for Scientific and Technological Advice (SBSTA) under the decision accompanying the Paris Agreement.[203]

The following subparts of this Article consider issues that could arise in such guidance, the extent to which these issues are included in the mandate to elaborate guidance, and the implications of both questions for linkage.[204]

---

[202] Metcalf & Weisbach, *supra* note 36, at 22.

[203] See *Adoption of the Paris Agreement*, *supra* note 131, Article 6.2 , at 24.

[204] See also Int'l Emissions Trading Ass'n, A Vision for the Market Provisions of the Paris Agreement (May 2016), https://perma.cc/VUZ3-6JPS (examining the use of carbon pricing to encourage international links to advance the goals of the Paris Agreement).

Pursuant to Article 6.2, the mandate to adopt guidance clearly extends to robust accounting, including avoidance of double counting, when using transferred ITMOs towards NDC achievement.[205] It is less clear, however, whether such guidance can also stipulate material provisions that go beyond accounting issues, for instance on matters of environmental integrity and governance.[206] Part V.C concludes with thoughts on the outlook for heterogeneous linkage that will be consistent with the Paris Agreement.

Accounting Treatment of ITMO Transfers and Use

Robust accounting methods will be needed to prevent double-counting of emission reductions and to ensure that the timing (vintage) of emissions reductions and of respective ITMO transfers are correctly accounted for. The targets set out in NDCs display substantial heterogeneity with regard to target type, reference and target years, sectoral and gas coverage, and GWP assumptions. Accounting for emissions and ITMO transfers under the Paris Agreement will therefore present much greater challenges than under the Kyoto Protocol, where all commitments consisted of absolute emission budgets with the same target years and generally the same reference year.[207] Acknowledging this challenge, Parties included a clear mandate in Article 6.2 to adopt guidance on robust accounting and avoidance of double-counting for cooperative approaches that involve the use of ITMOs towards NDC achievement.[208]

A starting point for guidance on accounting is the fact that, absent some form of accounting framework, ITMOs create the potential for double-counting and thus for greater GHG emissions than would occur in the absence of ITMO transfers.[209] Avoiding double-counting of emission reductions, whether through double issuance, double claiming, or double use, can therefore be expected to feature centrally in the guidance on Article 6.2. A related operational question concerns how Parties make adjustments for emissions or reductions covered by their NDCs when

---

205 *Adoption of the Paris Agreement*, *supra* note 131, Article 6.2, at 24.

206 *Id.*

207 *Confrontation or Convergence? Surveying Submissions on Article 6 of the Paris Agreement*, Carbon Mechanisms Rev., Nov.–Dec. 2016, at 4, 7, https://perma.cc/9QXG-UU2U.

208 *Adoption of the Paris Agreement*, *supra* note 131, Article 6.2, at 24.

209 See Lambert Schneider *et al.*, Environmental Integrity Under Article 6 of the Paris Agreement 43–44 (2017), https://perma.cc/S75X-NKUM.

using ITMOs, the so-called "corresponding adjustments" referenced in the decision that accompanied the Paris Agreement.[210] Some alternative approaches have been identified to effect this adjustment: an adjustment based on an emissions budget, in which ITMOs are added or subtracted to reach an adjusted emissions level, or an adjustment based on the NDC target level, in which ITMOs are added or subtracted to reach an adjusted target level.[211] While neither approach is necessarily superior, uniformity across approaches will be important to avoid inconsistencies.

Additional issues that may arise when accounting for ITMO transfers under Article 6 include how to quantify ITMOs (whether through carbon taxes, cap-and-trade instruments, performance standards, or other domestic policy instruments), how to account for differences in assumed GWP, and heterogeneous base years as well as different vintages of targets and outcomes.[212] Guidance on Article 6.2 could give attention to these issues, and also address the accounting implications of different types of targets, such as absolute and relative GHG targets,[213] as well as the metrics used to account for ITMOs — will there be a single common metric, such as

[210]See *Adoption of the Paris Agreement*, *supra* note 131, at ¶36.

[211]See OECD Workshop Summary, *supra* note 164, at 11. Additionally, negotiators have discussed corresponding adjustment on a buffer-registry or an emission reduction basis. See U.N. Framework Convention on Climate Change, *supra* note 133, at 5.

[212]See Lambert Schneider *et al.*, Robust Accounting of International Transfers Under Article 6 of the Paris Agreement: Preliminary Findings 13–14, 19, 24–27 (2016), https://perma.cc/59TQ-3SJV. *See generally* Howard, *supra* note 126. Heterogeneous historic base years in NDCs do not impose accounting problems for ITMOs in reconciling activities carried out between firms under linkage arrangements, but differences in target years will need to be recognized and reconciled through a linear (or other) normalization for calculating appropriate accounting of ITMO transfers (if full time-paths of targets are not offered by the respective NDCs). See OECD Workshop Summary, *supra* note 164, at 27–31.

[213]Absolute (mass-based) targets may require the least scrutiny, but exchanges between jurisdictions expressing their aggregate targets as relative to BAU or in terms of carbon intensity of the economy are also feasible. This is because the exchanges themselves can still be in mass terms, and hence the impacts on aggregate targets (through ITMOs) can be calculated by employing *ex ante* quantitative estimates of BAU emissions, or by converting the intensity target to an absolute target once the relevant level of GDP is known. See Nicolas Kreibich and Wolfgang Obergassel, Carbon Markets After Paris: How to Account for the Transfer of Mitigation Results? 10–11 (2016), https://perma.cc/7HWX-VEX9.

tons of CO_2 equivalent, or will there be multiple metrics, including, for example, other measures such as installed capacity of renewable power?[214]

Broader questions related to NDCs and ITMOs that nonetheless have a bearing on accounting under Article 6.2 include the nature of NDC targets, and whether these are to be treated as strict numerical targets that need to be precisely achieved; the nature and scope of ITMOs, which are hardly defined, let alone fully described in the Agreement and accompanying decisions; tracking of the transfer and use of ITMOs via a registry; and finally, given different potential interpretations of Articles 6.2 and 6.3, whether transfers to or from non-Parties (or sub-national jurisdictions therein) are possible, and how they should be accounted for.

Uniform guidance on these issues could arguably help ensure consistency across ITMO transfers, and afford greater certainty and predictability to Parties engaged in voluntary cooperation. As a result, guidance on these issues could potentially facilitate and promote expanded use of linkage between Parties to the Paris Agreement. Whether some or all of these issues can be addressed in the guidance on Article 6.2 is doubtful, however. It is important to recognize that the mandate for guidance on Article 6.2 does not expressly mention these issues,[215] and any attempt to address them with centralized standards will therefore likely invite opposition and criticism from some Parties that the CMA is exceeding its mandate and violating the decentralized spirit of the Paris Agreement. Indeed, some of the issues mentioned above, such as a registry infrastructure to track ITMO transfers, can also be dealt with at the domestic level, and it is therefore a legitimate question whether these issues necessarily have to be included in Article 6.2 guidance, or can equally and perhaps more efficiently be addressed by individual Parties.

That said, to satisfy the mandate in Article 6.2, the CMA must adopt guidance that helps ensure robust accounting of ITMO use towards NDC achievement, and avoidance of double counting. As the CMA and SBSTA

---

[214] This relates to a broader question of whether ITMOs will be, in effect, a single unit of compliance, or whether there will be various types. Among Parties that have expressed a preference on this issue, a majority seems to favor expressing ITMOs in tons of CO_2 equivalent. *Confrontation or Convergence? Surveying Submissions on Article 6 of the Paris Agreement*, *supra* note 207, at 5. Still, that leaves room for different types of transferable units, which might be allowances, credits (which would include offset credits, but also could include ERCs and ETPCs), or target/inventory adjustments.

[215] See Paris Agreement, *supra* note 1.

consider what this mandate entails, they may also decide to address some of the other issues mentioned above. Although it failed to secure consensus in the CMA, the draft decision submitted by SBSTA during the climate summit in Katowice, Poland, in December 2018 already indicated an intent to address issues such as ITMOs, NDCs and infrastructure.[216]

Potential Further Issues for Attention

Beyond issues related to accounting and avoidance of double counting, Parties have also suggested a number of further issues for inclusion or clarification in guidance on Article 6.2. Some Parties, for example, have argued in favor of ensuring that a transferred ITMO corresponds to actual emission reductions.[217] Other issues identified (but not agreed) by individual Parties for potential inclusion in guidance on Article 6.2 include[218]: principles; definitions; special circumstances of the least developed countries and small island developing States; governance; participation responsibilities; tracking of ITMOs; reporting; review; infrastructure; safeguards and limits; overall mitigation in global emissions; a mandatory share of proceeds from ITMO transactions that would be earmarked for adaptation; and addressing negative social and economic impacts.[219] As noted, however, these issues go beyond the mandate of the CMA under Article 6.2, and may therefore not find their reflection in the final guidance scheduled for adoption by Parties at COP24 or thereafter.

Many of these issues relate to the environmental implications of ITMO use, and how to safeguard or strengthen environmental integrity and ambition. Four specific areas of potential concern can be identified. First, in situations where a country that is proposing a transfer has an NDC

---

[216] See Framework Convention on Climate Change, *supra* note 133.

[217] See, e.g., *Views of Brazil on the Guidance Referred to in Article 6, Paragraph 2, of the Paris Agreement*, U.N. Framework Convention Climate Change, https://perma.cc/M9CG-B776 (last visited December 20, 2018).

[218] See Andrei Marcu, Article 6 of the Paris Agreement: Reflections on Party Submissions Before Marrakech 6–11 (2017), https://perma.cc/V9LE-KBS3; *Confrontation or Convergence? Surveying Submissions on Article 6 of the Paris Agreement*, *supra* note 207, at 7– 8.

[219] See U.N. Framework Convention on Climate Change, *supra* note 133. It bears noting, however, that this draft decision failed to secure consensus during the 2018 session of the CMA, with a new version expected to emerge from negotiations in 2019.

target that is less stringent than its BAU emissions, and hence has a so-called "hot air" target, ITMOs could undermine the integrity of the transferee's NDC.[220] Second, situations where ITMO transfers involve NDCs with limited sectoral or geographic coverage create the potential for leakage, and therefore should receive special attention if and only if significant leakage from regulated to unregulated sectors or geographic areas is anticipated. Third, the same holds true for GHG coverage, but it is less likely that there would be significant anticipated leakage from regulated to unregulated GHGs. And fourth, if ITMO transfers are possible from non-Parties or from sectors and activities that are not covered by an NDC, the ability to engage in such transactions — particularly if the transferred ITMOs can be used towards NDC achievement — could foster an incentive to refrain from becoming a Party or from including such activities and sectors in the scope of the NDC. That, in turn, would work against the goal of moving towards progressively more ambitious NDCs with greater sectoral and geographic coverage.

While some Parties have sought inclusion of integrity and ambition criteria in the guidance on Article 6.2, and can point to the references in Article 6 to environmental integrity, transparency, governance, and sustainable development, the current mandate in the Paris Agreement and the accompanying decision does not give reason to expect they will succeed. Parties do have the option of adopting, by consensus, an authoritative interpretation of Article 6.2 that supports a more expansive mandate, but such a consensus — if it exists — would arguably have already found its reflection in the Paris Agreement itself. Given that Parties instead rejected any form of centralized governance architecture,[221] it is unclear that guidance

[220]Whereas the full set of NDC targets under the Paris Agreement would bring about a significant decrease in global emissions in 2030 relative to BAU, one analysis estimates that more than 65 percent of those emissions reductions could be negated if all "hot air" from NDCs that are less stringent than BAU were transferred internationally to other participating countries. Schneider *et al.*, Environmental Integrity Under Article 6 of the Paris Agreement, *supra* note 209, at 4.

[221]See Marcu, Article 6 of the Paris Agreement, *supra* note 218, at 9 (acknowledging ambiguities regarding centralized versus decentralized government framework); *Confrontation or Convergence? Surveying Submissions on Article 6 of the Paris Agreement*, *supra* note 207, at 6 (acknowledging uncertainty behind governance framework).

can extend far beyond key accounting issues, despite early attempts to do so during the Katowice talks in 2018.[222] In the end, the limited mandate afforded to the CMA will likely mean that jurisdictions retain ample flexibility regarding whether and how to engage in voluntary cooperation.[223]

The Outlook for Heterogeneous Linkage Consistent with the Paris Agreement

As they negotiate the work program on implementation of the Paris Agreement, Parties have an opportunity to define clear and consistent guidance for accounting of emissions transfers under Article 6. During the Twenty-Third Conference of the Parties in Bonn in November 2017, Parties signaled agreement on the need to offer at least minimal guidance on how to account for transfers of ITMOs, but expressed widely differing views on broader principles and technical details.[224] Negotiations in Bonn merely resulted in a decision to narrow down areas of convergence and elaborate "draft elements of guidance" during the course of the following year,[225] and while a final decision was expected for the Twenty-Fourth Conference of the Parties in Katowice, Poland, in December 2018, Parties failed to reach consensus and decided to postpone adoption of operational details on Article 6. As such, these have become the only major agenda item in the Paris Agreement Work Program — informally known as the "Paris Rulebook" — to be deferred to 2019, with a decision now expected during the 2nd Session of the CMA in Santiago, Chile, in November 2019.

---

[222] At one point counting nearly thirty pages in length, the latest draft text on guidance for Article 6.2 was eventually narrowed down to a mere eight pages in Katowice. See U.N. Framework Convention on Climate Change, The Katowice Texts: Proposal by the President 31–38 (2018), https://perma.cc/7AWG-LB9J.

[223] See Andrei Marcu, Int'l Ctr. for Trade and Sustainable Dev., Issues for Discussion to Operationalise Article 6 of the Paris Agreement 7 (2017) (recognizing ambiguity regarding enforcement of voluntary cooperation).

[224] See Obergassel, W. and F. Asche. (2017). *Shaping the Paris Mechanisms Part III: An Update on Submissions on Article 6 of the Paris Agreement* 14–16. JIKO, Policy Paper No. 05/2017. (showing different preferences of various Parties relating to ITMO guidance).

[225] U.N. Framework Convention on Climate Change, *Guidance on Cooperative Approaches Referred to in Article 6, Paragraph 2, of the Paris Agreement*, FCCC/SBSTA/2017/L.26 (November 14, 2017).

Any issues that elude a consensus decision will be omitted from guidance and left to the discretion of individual Parties.

If they can set aside political differences and agree on a robust accounting framework for ITMO transfers and use, Parties will create an enabling context for strengthened linkage of climate policies across jurisdictions. Just as the CDM created an offset crediting framework that was subsequently recognized in a number of domestic cap-and-trade systems, resulting in several indirect links, a minimum set of harmonized accounting rules adopted in guidance on Article 6.2 of the Paris Agreement could form the basis of a common accounting framework for emission transfers. That, in turn, could help ensure the fungibility of units and promote the transparency and credibility of domestic policy efforts, making it easier for jurisdictions to enter into linking arrangements.[226]

If guidance extends beyond a shared core of accounting rules, the opposite could become true: restrictive quality or ambition requirements might inadvertently impede linkage, or render it more difficult. That does not mean that integrity and ambition should be neglected — indeed, experience with the CDM has shown that concerns about integrity shortcomings ultimately undermined the market for CDM offset credits. But questions of ambition are more appropriately addressed under the corresponding negotiating tracks, such as the "Talanoa Dialogue" to take stock of the collective efforts of Parties, or the enhanced transparency framework under Article 13 of the Paris Agreement.[227] True to the spirit of the Paris Agreement, less may be more in this case, and definition of environmental and other standards may be best left to the regional, national and sub-national jurisdictions who choose to link.

If the combination of common accounting rules and an absence of excessively restrictive criteria and conditions can accelerate linkage and allow for broader and deeper climate policy cooperation, it could also increase the latitude of Parties to scale up the ambition of their NDCs. And that may ultimately foster stronger engagement between Parties and non-Parties, as well as with regional and sub-national jurisdictions.

[226] See generally Howard, *supra* note 126.

[227] See Mehling, M. A. *et al.* (2018). "Linking climate policies to advance global mitigation." *Science*. **359**: 997, 998. (arguing against inclusion of questions related to ambition in the scope of guidance on Article 6.2).

Appendices

Appendix 1: Paris Agreement Article 6[228]

(1) Parties recognize that some Parties choose to pursue voluntary cooperation in the implementation of their nationally determined contributions to allow for higher ambition in their mitigation and adaptation actions and to promote sustainable development and environmental integrity.
(2) Parties shall, where engaging on a voluntary basis in cooperative approaches that involve the use of internationally transferred mitigation outcomes towards nationally determined contributions, promote sustainable development and ensure environmental integrity and transparency, including in governance, and shall apply robust accounting to ensure, inter alia, the avoidance of double counting, consistent with guidance adopted by the Conference of the Parties serving as the meeting of the Parties to this Agreement.
(3) The use of internationally transferred mitigation outcomes to achieve nationally determined contributions under this Agreement shall be voluntary and authorized by participating Parties.
(4) A mechanism to contribute to the mitigation of greenhouse gas emissions and support sustainable development is hereby established under the authority and guidance of the Conference of the Parties serving as the meeting of the Parties to this Agreement for use by Parties on a voluntary basis. It shall be supervised by a body designated by the Conference of the Parties serving as the meeting of the Parties to this Agreement, and shall aim:

    (a) To promote the mitigation of greenhouse gas emissions while fostering sustainable development;
    (b) To incentivize and facilitate participation in the mitigation of greenhouse gas emissions by public and private entities authorized by a Party;
    (c) To contribute to the reduction of emission levels in the host Party, which will benefit from mitigation activities resulting in emission reductions that can also be used by another Party to fulfil its nationally determined contribution; and
    (d) To deliver an overall mitigation in global emissions.

[228] Paris Agreement, *supra* note 1, art. 6.

(5) Emission reductions resulting from the mechanism referred to in paragraph 4 of this Article shall not be used to demonstrate achievement of the host Party's nationally determined contribution if used by another Party to demonstrate achievement of its nationally determined contribution.
(6) The Conference of the Parties serving as the meeting of the Parties to this Agreement shall ensure that a share of the proceeds from activities under the mechanism referred to in paragraph 4 of this Article is used to cover administrative expenses as well as to assist developing country Parties that are particularly vulnerable to the adverse effects of climate change to meet the costs of adaptation.
(7) The Conference of the Parties serving as the meeting of the Parties to this Agreement shall adopt rules, modalities and procedures for the mechanism referred to in paragraph 4 of this Article at its first session.
(8) Parties recognize the importance of integrated, holistic and balanced non-market approaches being available to Parties to assist in the implementation of their nationally determined contributions, in the context of sustainable development and poverty eradication, in a coordinated and effective manner, including through, inter alia, mitigation, adaptation, finance, technology transfer and capacity-building, as appropriate. These approaches shall aim to:

    (a) Promote mitigation and adaptation ambition;
    (b) Enhance public and private sector participation in the implementation of nationally determined contributions; and
    (c) Enable opportunities for coordination across instruments and relevant institutional arrangements.

(9) A framework for non-market approaches to sustainable development is hereby defined to promote the non-market approaches referred to in paragraph 8 of this Article.

Appendix 2: Achieving Global Cost Effectiveness

A necessary condition for globally cost effective policy is that the marginal cost of abatement be equalized across sources of emissions. The figure below, adapted from Metcalf and Weisbach (2010), illustrates the gains from satisfying this condition. The box has width equal to Q^{Total}, the total amount of emissions to be reduced. We measure emissions reductions by country A starting at the lower left corner of the box, with increasing

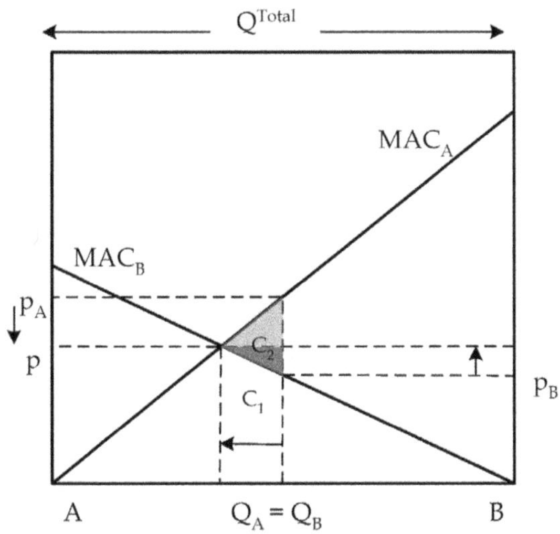

abatement occurring as we move to the right. The upward sloping line denoted MAC_A is the marginal abatement cost function for country A. It is upward sloping to reflect the fact that reducing emissions is increasingly costly as abatement rises. Emission reductions by country B are measured from the bottom right corner, with increasing abatement as we move to the left. Country B's marginal abatement cost curve starts at the lower right corner of the box and increases as we move to the left, but is less steep that that of country A. Thus, Country A is the high-cost controller in this example.

The figure illustrates a policy agreement where each country agrees to reduce emissions by the same amount. The marginal abatement cost for country A is higher than the marginal abatement cost for country B at the point where Q_A equals Q_B. If abatement activity were to shift one unit of emissions from country B to country A (shift one unit of emissions abatement from country A to B), the savings in aggregate abatement costs would equal the vertical distance between the two marginal abatement cost curves. If abatement responsibilities were shifted from country A to country B until the marginal abatement costs were equalized across the two countries, we would achieve reductions in aggregate abatement costs equal to the area of the shaded triangle in the figure, labeled C_2. Once marginal abatement costs are equalized, no opportunities exist for further reductions in abatement costs by reallocating abatement activity between the two countries.

Acknowledgements

The authors gratefully acknowledge valuable comments on a previous version of the Article by Susan Biniaz, Daniel Bodansky, Constanze Haug, Christina Hood, and Andrei Marcu; and financial support from the Enel Foundation. The authors, however, are fully responsible for any errors and all opinions expressed in this chapter.

https://doi.org/10.1142/9789811292415_0025

Chapter 25

Double Counting and the Paris Agreement Rulebook: Poor Emissions Accounting Could Undermine Carbon Markets*

Lambert Schneider[†,*], Maosheng Duan[‡,†††], Robert N. Stavins[§,¶,||,‡‡‡], Kelley Kizzier[**], Derik Broekhoff[††], Frank Jotzo[‡‡], Harald Winkler[§§], Michael Lazarus[††], Andrew Howard[¶¶], and Christina Hood[|||]**

[†]*Oeko-Institute, Berlin, Germany*

[‡]*Institute of Energy, Environment and Economy, Tsinghua University, Beijing, China*

[§]*John F. Kennedy School of Government, Harvard University, Cambridge, MA, USA*

[¶]*Resources for the Future, Washington, DC, USA*

[||]*National Bureau of Economic Research, Cambridge, MA, USA*

[**]*Environmental Defense Fund, New Orleans, LA, USA*

[††]*Stockholm Environment Institute, Seattle, WA, USA*

[‡‡]*Crawford School of Public Policy, Australian National University, Canberra, Australia*

---

*This chapter was originally published in *Science*, **366**(6462), 180–183, 2019.

[§§]*Energy Research Centre, University of Cape Town, South Africa*

[¶¶]*Koru Climate, Bonn, Germany*

[||]*Compass Climate, Paekakariki, New Zealand*

[***]*l.schneider@oeko.de*

[†††]*duanmsh@mail.tsinghua.edu.cn*

[‡‡‡]*robert_stavins@harvard.edu*

The 24th International Climate Conference in Katowice, Poland, in December 2018 was a major achievement in the multilateral response to climate change. More than 190 countries managed to agree on nearly all elements of a comprehensive rulebook that puts flesh on the bones of the 2015 Paris Agreement. The rules require, for the first time, that all countries provide detailed information on their climate change mitigation targets and regularly report on their progress in implementing and achieving them. However, one important chapter is still missing: rules for international carbon markets discussed under Article 6 of the Paris Agreement. Competing views on how to avoid "double counting" — counting the same emission reduction more than once to achieve climate mitigation targets — were a major roadblock to reaching consensus. Completing the missing chapter on Article 6 will be one of the key tasks when countries reconvene at the 25th International Climate Conference in Santiago, Chile, in December of this year. We highlight why resolving double counting is critical for achieving the goals of the Paris Agreement and identify essential ingredients for a robust outcome that ensures environmental effectiveness and facilitates cost-effective mitigation.

Carbon markets can involve three distinct yet closely related levels of actions. First, national or regional jurisdictions can establish policies, such as emissions trading systems, that enable firms to trade emission permits, or credits for having reduced emissions relative to a baseline. Second, jurisdictions can link their policy instruments, which allows these permits or credits to be traded across international borders (Mehling *et al.*, 2018). Third, and our focus, Article 6 of the Paris Agreement establishes a framework that allows countries to count these international transfers when demonstrating achievement of their targets under the Paris Agreement.

Carbon markets provide flexibility in where and when greenhouse gas (GHG) emissions are reduced and thereby can lower the aggregate cost of achieving climate mitigation targets. This could help governments adopt more ambitious targets (Mehling *et al.*, 2018; Bodansky *et al.*, 2016; Flachsland *et al.*, 2009). Efficiency gains associated with carbon markets could thus help achieve the deep emissions cuts that are necessary to reach the goal of the Paris Agreement of holding the increase in the global average temperature to well below 2°C above pre-industrial levels and pursuing efforts to limit it 1.5°C. If not robustly designed and implemented, however, carbon markets could lead to greater emissions and higher costs and thus undermine the agreement (Schneider and La Hoz Theuer, 2019).

Avoiding Double Counting

Double counting of emission reductions is one of the main ways in which the integrity of carbon markets could be undermined. If it is not prevented, actual GHG emissions could end up being greater than the aggregated achievement that the countries (or private sector entities) participating in the carbon market report (Hood *et al.*, 2014; Schneider *et al.*, 2017). Avoiding double counting is thus fundamental for the integrity and healthy functioning of any carbon market and critical for the credibility of the Paris regime.

In the context of the Paris Agreement, a robust system to account for international transfers of emission reductions is the main ingredient needed to avoid double counting. The basic principle is simple: The international transfer of emission reductions should not lead to higher total emissions than if the participating countries or entities had met their targets individually (Hood *et al.*, 2014; Schneider *et al.*, 2017). Article 6.2 of the Paris Agreement establishes such an accounting framework. It avoids double counting through a form of double-entry bookkeeping, referred to as "corresponding adjustments." As with bank transfers, an entry in one account requires a corresponding, opposite entry to another account. Under the Paris Agreement, the relevant currency is emission reductions: The country selling emission reductions makes an addition to its emission level, and the country acquiring the emission reductions makes a subtraction. Both countries prepare an emissions balance in which the country's target level is compared with its emissions, adjusted for any international transfers of emission reductions (Winkler *et al.*, 2018).

To implement this approach, negotiators are considering various further ingredients — in particular, requirements for countries to clarify their targets in terms of GHG emissions; to track international transactions of emission reductions through electronic registry systems; and to regularly report on their emissions and carbon market transactions, subject to a technical review.

Addressing double counting is critical because nearly half of the Parties to the Paris Agreement have signaled their intent to use carbon markets, many of them as sellers of emission reductions (World Bank & Ecofys, 2018). The European Union and Switzerland, for example, agreed to link their emissions trading systems and to count the resulting transfers of emission reductions toward their targets under the Paris Agreement. A similar arrangement might be made if the United Kingdom leaves the European Union. Several countries have announced their intent to achieve net-zero emissions between 2030 and 2050, including through the purchase of emission reductions from other countries. Some countries, such as Japan and Switzerland, have already started purchasing emission reductions.

The largest demand for emission reductions may not come from a country but from airlines. Because of the difficulty of attributing emissions from international aviation to a particular country, the Kyoto Protocol mandated the International Civil Aviation Organization (ICAO) to address these emissions. In 2016, ICAO adopted a new global scheme that requires airlines to offset any increase in carbon emissions from international flights above 2020 levels. Over the scheme's operational period from 2021 to 2035, airlines could demand as much as 1.6 billion to 3.7 billion emission reduction credits (Warnecke *et al.*, 2019), compared with about 2 billion credits purchased by countries to meet their Kyoto commitments in the period from 2008 to 2020.

Next to using carbon markets for compliance purposes, organizations and individuals increasingly purchase emission reductions to voluntarily offset their emissions. There is considerable debate whether double counting needs to be avoided for such purchases or whether these emission reductions can be used by both countries to achieve the Paris targets and the organizations or individuals to offset their emissions (International Carbon Reduction & Offsetting Alliance, 2017).

If these transactions are to be credible, they must be underpinned by international accounting rules that prevent double counting. But why are such rules so highly controversial in international negotiations? Resolving double counting is politically challenging because countries have different interests and hence different interpretations of what the requirements of the Paris Agreement mean. It is also technically challenging because countries communicated rather diverse mitigation pledges under the Paris Agreement, which makes accounting complex.

Political Obstacles

The Paris Agreement is explicit that double counting shall be avoided. Still, countries wrangle not only over how double counting should be avoided but also what constitutes double counting and whether it should be avoided under all circumstances (Obergassel and Asche, 2017).

Some countries have proposed that seller countries should not have to apply corresponding adjustments if the emission reductions are generated under the new, internationally governed crediting mechanism established by Article 6.4 of the Paris Agreement. This new mechanism is commonly viewed as a successor to the Clean Development Mechanism (CDM), which allows developed countries, who have mitigation commitments under the Kyoto Protocol, to acquire emission reduction credits generated from projects in developing countries, who do not have such commitments under Kyoto. The CDM and the new Paris mechanism both require that certified emission reductions must be "additional" (that they would not have occurred without the carbon market incentives). Brazil, supported by a few others, has argued that the requirement of additionality obviates the need for corresponding adjustments by seller countries because it ensures that the emission reductions go beyond the climate action that the country would pursue to achieve its Paris mitigation target. This position would implement accounting similar to the Kyoto Protocol, in which only developed countries have climate mitigation targets, so there would be no need for developing countries to account for transfers of emission reductions. However, it could result in double counting in the new context of the Paris Agreement, under which all countries have pledged climate mitigation contributions. Most countries therefore support that corresponding adjustments be applied by both selling and acquiring countries under the new Paris mechanism. Disagreement over this matter was central to the failure to reach consensus on carbon market rules in Katowice (Marcu and Rambharos, 2019).

Countries are also wrestling with avoiding double counting across different United Nations regimes. Under ICAO, countries have formally agreed that double counting between countries' mitigation targets and

ICAO's aviation scheme should be avoided (International Civil Aviation Organization, 2016). Yet under the Paris Agreement, some countries, most vocally Saudi Arabia, have taken the position that international rules under Article 6 should not address such double counting, arguing that Article 6 only refers to transfers of emission reductions to achieve Paris targets but not transfers to airlines, and that ICAO and the Paris Agreement are independent treaties. Without a requirement for countries to apply corresponding adjustments for emissions reductions sold to the aviation industry, however, there is a risk that these reductions are double counted: once by the selling countries to achieve their Paris targets and once by airlines to achieve their obligations under ICAO. Failure to resolve this matter could undermine the integrity of ICAO's scheme and cause some countries to abandon it.

Another controversy relates to how much international oversight is needed to ensure robust accounting (Obergassel and Asche, 2017; Marcu and Rambharos, 2019). To preserve integrity and avoid the risk of a race to the bottom, some countries, including Senegal and South Africa, argued for more international oversight — not only for the mechanism established by Article 6.4 but for any carbon market cooperation among countries. This could, for example, include more detailed rules rather than principles, or participation requirements that countries must satisfy to engage in transfers. Other countries — including Australia, Canada, Japan, and the United States — had opposed strong international oversight for bilateral carbon market approaches, arguing for more national sovereignty and flexibility in implementing bilateral carbon market cooperation. Countries are now moving toward an approach in which they report on how they ensure accounting in accordance with the Paris rulebook and their reports are subject to a technical review.

Diverse Climate Pledges

Climate pledges made by countries under the Paris Agreement are diverse. Many countries have formulated their pledges as some form of GHG emissions targets, whereas others have used different metrics, such as targets for the penetration of renewable sources. Some pledges do not cover all sectors of the economy or all GHGs; some are conditional on the provision of support from other countries; and some have no quantitative targets whatsoever, only qualitative descriptions of actions or strategies. Countries have also chosen different time periods for their targets; many have pledged targets for a single year — most 2030, some 2025 — whereas

Without agreed-upon rules, there is a risk that emission reductions are double counted — once by the selling countries to achieve their Paris targets and once by airlines to achieve their obligations under the ICAO. Failure to resolve this matter could undermine the integrity of ICAO's scheme and cause some countries to abandon it.

some have chosen a multiyear period, such as 2021 to 2030. And some pledges are simply unclear; for example, they lack a clearly defined scope of the target or express a target as a deviation from business as usual without having determined their business-as-usual emissions (Graichen *et al.*, 2016). All of these factors make accounting complex. One important matter is how best to account for transfers in the context of different target time frames (Hood *et al.*, 2014; Schneider *et al.*, 2017; Obergassel and Asche, 2017; Marcu and Rambharos, 2019). For example, South Korea has proposed that countries should be allowed to count emission reductions achieved in another country over many years (for example, from 2021 to 2030) to achieve a target for a single year only (for example, 2030). This could undermine environmental integrity in various ways — for example, if the seller country would only account for transfers that occurred in its target year (for example, 2030) (Hood *et al.*, 2014; Schneider *et al.*, 2017). But how to account for transfers of emission reductions generated in pre-target years is an open question. Adopting multiyear targets or trajectories, although potentially politically difficult, would be much more tractable for carbon market accounting. It would ensure continuous accounting over time and provide for integrity and transparency.

There is also debate whether, and under which conditions, countries should be allowed to sell emission reductions from GHGs or economic sectors that they have not included in their targets under the Paris Agreement (for example, a country reducing and selling CH_4 emissions, whereas its Paris target only includes CO_2) (Spalding-Fecher, 2017). In this case, the transfer of these emission reductions would not lead to double counting, and corresponding adjustments would thus not be necessary on the part of seller countries. However, allowing such transfers without adjustments by seller countries could create a disincentive for them to include more sectors and GHGs in their future targets because doing so would compel them to make adjustments any time they wish to sell such emission reductions.

To address this concern, some countries have proposed that international rules require that seller countries apply corresponding adjustments for all transfers, regardless of whether the emission reductions occur within or outside the scope of their Paris targets. This would create incentives for seller countries to expand the scope of their targets and make accounting simpler because it would avoid the need to determine whether emission reductions occur inside or outside the scope of their targets. However, such an approach could make it more difficult to use international carbon markets for reducing emissions that occur outside the scope of Paris targets. To resolve these issues, one option considered in the negotiations is a grace period for the application of corresponding adjustments.

To Succeed in Santiago

Common international accounting rules for cooperation through carbon markets are essential, for two reasons. First, the credibility and integrity of the international climate regime could be undermined if countries would pursue their own, less robust accounting approaches. Second, countries or firms might refrain from using carbon markets if they do not have clarity regarding whether they can claim the emission reductions they acquire. Success in Santiago is therefore critical. We propose several principles to guide the negotiations.

First, a single set of common international accounting rules should apply under the Paris Agreement, irrespective of which carbon market mechanism is used to generate emission reductions and irrespective of whether these reductions are used by countries to achieve their Paris targets or by other entities, such as airlines to achieve their mitigation obligations under ICAO. This is important for avoiding double counting and for creating a level playing field for international carbon markets.

Second, ensuring robust accounting, regardless of how mitigation targets are expressed, is essential. This is most easily achieved by accounting in common GHG emission metrics and over continuous multiyear periods, with corresponding adjustments applied to all relevant years, rather than only to single target years. For some countries, this could require clarifying what their current mitigation pledges mean in terms of GHG emission levels over time.

Third, the Paris Agreement foresees that over time, all countries will move toward economy-wide targets. Robust accounting would be greatly facilitated if all countries adopted targets that are economy-wide, cover all GHGs, apply to common multiyear time periods, and are expressed as GHG emissions.

Next to resolving double counting, negotiators will need to address other controversial matters to reach agreement in Santiago, including whether a proportion of carbon market transactions revenue levied to pay for climate change resilience should only apply to the mechanism under Article 6.4 or to all international transfers under the Paris Agreement; whether tradable emission units left over from the CDM or from overcompliance with the Kyoto Protocol targets may be used to achieve Paris targets after 2020; and how other environmental integrity risks, such as transfers that are not backed by actual emission reductions, should be addressed.

To build a solid basis for international cooperation that can cost-effectively combat climate change, the Paris Agreement needs international carbon market rules that ensure environmental integrity and avoid double counting. Otherwise, international carbon markets might instead seriously undermine this carefully constructed climate agreement.

Acknowledgments

Maosheng Duan acknowledges funding from National Natural Science Foundation of China (project 71690243) and Ministry of Science and Technology of China (project 2017YFA0605304).

References

Bodansky, D. M., S. A. Hoedl, G. E. Metcalf, and & R. N. Stavins. (2016). "Facilitating linkage of climate policies through the Paris outcome." *Climate Policy*. **16**: 956–972.

Flachsland, C., R. Marschinski, and O. Edenhofer. (2009). "To link or not to link: Benefits and disadvantages of linking cap-and-trade systems." *Climate Policy*. **9**: 358–372.

Graichen, J., M. Cames, and L. Schneider. (2016). *Categorization of INDCs in the Light of Art. 6 of the Paris Agreement.* Discussion Paper. Dessau-Roßlau: German Environment Agency.

Hood, C., G. Briner, and M. Rocha. (2014). *GHG or not GHG: Accounting for Diverse Mitigation Contributions in the Post-2020 Climate Framework.* Paris: OECD/IEA.

International Carbon Reduction & Offsetting Alliance. (2017). *Guidance Report: Pathways to Increased Voluntary Action by Non-State Actors.* London: ICROA.

International Civil Aviation Organization. (2016). *Assembly Resolution A39-22/2: Consolidated Statement of Continuing ICAO Policies and Practices Related to Environmental Protection — Global Market-Based Measure (MBM) Scheme*. Montreal: ICAO.

Marcu, A. and M. Rambharos. (2019). *Rulebook for Article 6 in the Paris Agreement: Takeaway from the COP 24 Outcome*. Brussels: European Roundtable on Climate Change and Sustainable Transition.

Mehling, M. A., G. E. Metcalf, and R. N. Stavins. (2018). "International cooperation to address climate change challenges." *Science*. **359**: 997–998.

Obergassel, W. and F. Asche. (2017). *Shaping the Paris Mechanisms Part III: An Update on Submissions on Article 6 of the Paris Agreement.* Wuppertal: Wuppertal Institut.

Schneider, L. and S. La Hoz Theuer. (2019). "Environmental integrity of international carbon market mechanisms under the Paris Agreement." *Climate Policy*. **19**: 386–401.

Schneider, L., J. Füssler, S. La Hoz Theuer, A. Kohli, J. Graichen, S. Healy, and D. Broekhoff. (2017). *Robust Accounting of International Transfers Under Article 6 of the Paris Agreement.* (Discussion Paper). Dessau-Roßlau: German Environment Agency.

Spalding-Fecher, R. (2017). *Article 6.4 Crediting Outside of NDC Commitments Under the Paris Agreement: Issues and Options.* Oslo: Carbon Limits.

Warnecke, C., L. Schneider, T. Day, S. La Hoz Theuer, and H. Fearnehough. (2019). "Robust eligibility restrictions for offset credits are needed for CORSIA to truly compensate for the growth in aviation's carbon emissions." *Nature Climate Change*. **9**: 218–220.

Winkler, H., R. Spalding-Fecher, D. Broekhoff, and L. Schneider. (2018). *The Balance Sheet Summary: An Essential Tool for Transparency and Robust Accounting in Mitigation and Markets*. Policy Brief. Cape Town: Energy Research Centre, University of Cape Town.

World Bank & Ecofys. (2018). *State and Trends of Carbon Pricing 2018.* Washington, DC: World Bank.

Part VI

Wine Production and Consumption

https://doi.org/10.1142/9789811292415_0026

Chapter 26

The Value of Terroir: Hedonic Estimation of Vineyard Sale Prices*

Robin Cross[†,], Andrew J. Plantinga[‡,††], and Robert N. Stavins[§,¶,‖,‡‡]**

[†]*Department of Agricultural and Resource Economics, Oregon State University, Corvallis, OR, USA*

[‡]*Bren School of Environmental Science and Management, University of California, Santa Barbara, CA*

[§]*John F. Kennedy School of Government, Harvard University, Cambridge, MA, USA*

[¶]*Resources for the Future, Washington, DC, USA*

[‖]*National Bureau of Economic Research, Cambridge, MA, USA*

[**]*robin.cross@oregonstate.edu*

[††]*plantinga@bren.ucsb.edu*

[‡‡]*robert_stavins@harvard.edu*

*This chapter was originally published in *Journal of Wine Economics*, **6**(1), 1–14, 2011.

Wine producers and enthusiasts use the term "terroir," from the French *terre* (meaning land), to refer to the special characteristics of a place that impart unique qualities to the wine produced. The Appellation d'Origine Contrôlée (AOC) system in France, and similar systems adopted in other major wine-producing countries, are based upon the geographic location of grape production, and are therefore predicated on this notion of terroir. Under a parallel U.S. system, production regions are designated as American Viticultural Areas (AVAs), with finer geographical designations known as sub-AVAs. Such designations allow wineries to identify the geographical origin of the grapes used in producing their wines, and — equally important — seek to prevent producers outside the AVA from making false claims about the nature and origin of their wines.

What is the value of terroir in the American context? Does the "reality of terroir" — the location-specific geology and geography (including climate) — predominate in determining the quality of wine? Does the "concept of terroir" — the location within an officially named appellation — impart additional value to grapes and wine? More to the point, does location within such an appellation impart additional value to vineyards?

The central question we address is whether measurable site attributes — such as slope, aspect, elevation, and soil type — or appellation designations are more important determinants of vineyard prices.[1] We do this by conducting a hedonic price analysis to investigate sales of vineyards in Oregon's Willamette Valley, one of the most important wine-producing regions in the United States.[2]

How should site attributes and sub-AVA designations influence vineyard prices? If site attributes significantly affect wine quality and if consumers are able to discriminate such quality, then vineyard prices would depend on site attributes alone,[3] and AVA designations would be redundant. Alternatively, consumers might not be able to discriminate among wines perfectly and might use AVA designations as signals of average

---

[1]The notion of terroir sometimes extends beyond natural endowments to encompass the history and culture of a place, but we use a narrower and more common definition of terroir focused on physical attributes of the location (Gergaud and Ginsburgh, 2010).

[2]The Willamette Valley is designated as an AVA. Within the valley, there are six sub-AVAs: Chehalem Mountains, Yamhill-Carlton District, Ribbon Ridge, Dundee Hills, McMinnville, and Eola-Amity Hills.

[3]Wine quality is affected not only by site attributes, but also by the quality of growing stock, as well as vineyard management, and the skills and resources of the winemaker.

quality of wines from respective areas, and/or might derive utility directly from drinking wines which they know to be of particular pedigree. In this intermediate case, site attributes and AVA designations would influence vineyard prices, with the variables for site attributes measuring how producers value intra-AVA differences in vineyard characteristics. Presumably, producers attach premiums to site attributes that enhance wine quality, provided that consumers can perceive and are willing to pay for such quality differences.

What if, at the extreme, variation in vineyard prices is explained completely by AVA designations (that is, site attributes are irrelevant)? This would indicate that terroir matters economically — as a concept, though not as a fundamental reality. Producers might recognize the value of the AVA designation because they know that consumers will pay more for the experience of drinking wine from designated areas.[4] But the fact that site attributes are unimportant suggests that consumers cannot discern quality differences. Any appreciation they might express for an area's terroir would essentially be founded on reputation, not reality.

In the next section of the chapter, we discuss some related research from the wine economics literature. Then, in the second section, we describe the data we employ, as well as our estimation strategy. In the third section, we present our results plus some robustness checks. The last section concludes.

Previous Literature

Our analysis is related to and builds upon previous work by others. In one recent study, Gergaud and Ginsburgh (2008) find that site attributes of vineyards in the Haut-Médoc appellation in Bordeaux have no effect on wine prices or ratings, after controlling for producer differences in wine-making technology. Our study builds on this work by examining — in addition to site characteristics — the value assigned to appellation designations. Further, we are able to measure site characteristics more precisely than Gergaud and Ginsburgh by using GIS-based information to develop highly detailed physiographic profiles of each parcel.

[4]Alternatively, buyers might be less informed than sellers about how vineyard attributes affect wine quality, and, therefore, use the AVA designation as a signal of quality. Or producers may bid up the value of vineyards located in designated appellations because there is prestige associated with owning vineyards in such areas.

In another recent study, Ashenfelter and Storchmann (2010) investigate the effects of climate on vineyards in the Mosel Valley. As in our study, the authors have fine-scale data on vineyard characteristics. They find that site characteristics — including slope, orientation, soil types, soil depth, and altitude — as well as solar radiation are significant determinants of vineyard quality. We do not include climate variables in our analysis, because of trivial variation in rainfall, humidity, and wind across the relevant portion of the Willamette Valley, but our site attribute variables proxy for the amount of solar radiation received by vineyards.

An important similarity and difference with our study concerns respective dependent variables. Gergaud and Ginsburgh (2008) and Ashenfelter and Storchmann (2010) employ measures that are based on wine prices or ratings. Our dependent variable, vineyard sale prices, is preferable in the context of our investigation into the value of terroir, because it avoids potentially confounding influences on our results of non-vineyards inputs into wine production (such as labor and wine-making techniques). Provided that these inputs are variable and reproducible, profit-maximization implies that the optimal levels of these inputs are implicit functions of fixed and non-reproducible vineyard attributes and input and output prices that are constant across the vineyards in our sample. As such, we can estimate the implicit prices of vineyard attributes using a simple hedonic equation for vineyard sales.

As we suggest above, if consumers have limited information about specific vineyards or are unable to judge differences in quality among wines, then they might use appellation designations as signals of quality of wines from respective areas. In fact, the results of many blind taste tests indicate that wine consumers have very limited ability to distinguish intrinsic qualities of wine (sweetness, acidity, tannins, etc.), and instead judge quality by relying on extrinsic signals, such as price, origin, and wine-maker reputation.

For example, Veale and Quester (2008) found that tasters' perceptions of quality were strongly correlated with price and country of origin, but not with intrinsic qualities related to taste. Similarly, Goldstein *et al.* (2008) found that when price information is withheld, non-expert tasters show no preference for more expensive wines and even show a slight preference for less expensive wines.[5]

[5]Tasters with some wine training demonstrated a non-negative relationship between price and enjoyment. However, Hodgson (2009a, 2009b) has found that even wine judges have

Data and Estimation Strategy

Dependent Variable for Hedonic Estimation: Vineyard Value

In order to investigate the relationship between vineyard sales prices, site attributes, and appellation designation, we employ a new data set on vineyard sales provided by Northwest Farm Credit Services, a lending institution specializing in agriculture. The database includes the universe of 104 sales between 1995 and 2007 of properties in the Willamette Valley that included vineyards and vinelands.[6] In addition to total sale price, size, and location of property, sales records include an appraiser's estimate of the value of non-vineyard assets, such as dwellings and other buildings, winery equipment, and non-vineyard land. We subtract the estimated values of these non-vineyard assets from the total sale price to obtain the value of vineyards in each sale.

A remaining complication is that vineyards differ in terms of grape varietals planted, whether rootstocks are resistant to phylloxera, and type of trellis system in place. This heterogeneity accounts for some portion of the difference in sale prices. Because terroir relates exclusively to non-transferable attributes of vineyards, such as soils, elevation, slope, and climate, we also subtract from the vineyard value the appraiser's estimate of the value of all vineyard enhancements. This leaves us with the estimated price of bare land for vineyards. After converting these values to 2007 dollars using the Consumer Price Index, and dividing by the area of vineyards, we obtain the real per-acre vineyard value for each property, denoted *vinevalue*. The log of this variable is the dependent variable in our hedonic model.

Vineyard Attributes

The sales records from Northwest Farm Credit Services provide information about average characteristics of vineyards included in each sale. We

---

difficulty consistently evaluating wines. Using data on over 4,000 wines entered in 13 competitions, Hodgson (2009a) found that the probability of winning a Gold medal in one competition was statistically independent of winning a Gold medal in another competition. Further, Hodgson (2009b) found that judges at the 2009 California State Fair commercial wine competition were inconsistent in their evaluations.

[6]Vinelands are areas that can be developed for vineyards. We use the term "vineyards" to refer collectively to vineyards and vinelands.

develop more precise measures, using GIS-based information on slope, aspect, elevation, and soils. The location of each parcel is determined from tax lot boundaries and matched to GIS maps of physiographic variables.[7]

Parcels are divided into 10-meter pixels and each pixel is classified according to 14 slope, 16 aspect, 86 elevation, and 8 soil group categories. For example, slope categories are 2–4°, 4–6°, and so forth. Elevation categories are 150–159 feet, 160–169 feet, and so on. Because the number of categories exceeds the number of observed sales, we combine them following conventional wisdom about which vineyard attributes are most favorable or unfavorable.[8] We then compute the percentages of each parcel in each of these aggregated categories, and use these as independent variables in our hedonic regressions. The definitions of all variables are found in Table 1.

As discussed above, the elevation, slope, and aspect variables determine the amount of solar radiation received at each site and, thus, are proxies for one important component of climate. We did not include additional controls for rainfall, humidity, and wind because these factors exhibit little variation within the Willamette Valley.

We conducted sensitivity analyses on the site attribute variables. Because there are other reasonable ways to specify the categories discussed above, we explored alternative definitions, and found that our results were not sensitive to these changes. Another issue with the site attribute variables is that they are defined for the entire property, not only

---

[7]The tax lot information was obtained from county tax assessors' offices. Contour information was derived from USGS National Elevation Dataset data at 10 and 30 meter scales (http://seamless.usgs.gov/ned1.php). Soil information came from the USDA/NRCS Soil Data Mart (http://soildatamart.nrcs.usda.gov/).

[8]We define three elevation variables: best (250–450 feet), possible (200–250 feet, 450–650 feet), and too low or too high (<200 feet, >650 feet), denoted *bestelev*, *posselev*, and *lowhighelev*, respectively. Vineyards that are too high or too low face greater risk of frost and low temperatures that inhibit ripening. South-facing slopes are regarded as preferable. We define the aspect variables as south (*south*), southeast or southwest (*southew*), east or west (*eastwest*), and north (*north*). Jory-Nekiah and Willakenzie-Hazelair are considered the best soils for producing pinot noir, and so we define *bestsoil* as the share of the parcel with either of these soils. The two other soil variables are *goodsoil* (Amity-Dayton, Bellpine, Laurelwood, or Yamhill soils) and *poorsoil* (Willamette-Woodburn and other soils). Finally, vineyards that are too flat (<2 degrees) tend to be poorly drained and those that are too steep (>12 degrees) are difficult to harvest. We define *bestslope* as the percentage of the parcel with slopes between 2 and 12 degrees and *flatsteep* as the residual.

Table 1. Variable definitions.

Variable	Definition
vinevalue	real per-acre vineyard value
vineacres	area of the parcel in vineyards, in acres
bestelev	share of the parcel with best elevation (250–450 feet)
posselev	share of the parcel with possible elevation (200–250 feet, 450–650 feet)
lowhighelev	share of the parcel with low (<200 feet) or high (>650 feet) elevation
south	share of the parcel with south aspect
southew	share of the parcel with southeast or southwest aspect
eastwest	share of the parcel with east or west aspect
north	share of the parcel with north aspect
bestsoil	share of the parcel with best soils (Jory-Nekiah, Willakenzie-Hazelair)
goodsoil	share of the parcel with good soils (Amity-Dayton, Bellpine, Laurelwood, Yamhill)
poorsoil	share of the parcel with poor soils (Willamette-Woodburn, others)
bestslope	share of the parcel with the best slope (2–12 degrees)
flatsteep	share of the parcel that is flat (<2 degrees) or steep (>12 degrees)
percentvine	share of the parcel that is in vineyards
eola	indicator variable equal to 1 if the parcel is in Eola-Amity Hills sub-AVA; 0 otherwise
mcminnville	indicator variable equal to 1 if the parcel is in McMinnville sub-AVA; 0 otherwise
yamhill	indicator variable equal to 1 if the parcel is in Yamhill-Carlton sub-AVA; 0 otherwise
dundee	indicator variable equal to 1 if the parcel is in Dundee Hills sub-AVA; 0 otherwise
chehalem	indicator variable equal to 1 if the parcel is in Chehalem Hills sub-AVA; 0 otherwise
nosub	indicator variable equal to 1 if the parcel is not in a sub-AVA; 0 otherwise
saledate	indicator variable equal to 1 if sale occurred after the official designation of the sub-AVA; 0 otherwise
distancesub	distance to nearest sub-appellation, in feet; 0 for parcels in a sub-AVA

the vineyard portion of the parcel. Unfortunately, we cannot refine these measures, because we do not know exactly where vineyards are located within parcels. Instead, we conduct two robustness tests, discussed below, to explore whether our results are affected by this measurement error. For this purpose, we construct a variable, denoted *percentvine*, measuring the percentage of the parcel in vineyards.

In addition to the site attribute variables, we construct a variable for the area of the vineyards (*vineacres*) and indicator variables for the location of a parcel within a sub-AVA (*eola* for Eola-Amity Hills, *mcminnville* for McMinnville, *yamhill* for Yamhill-Carlton, *dundee* for Dundee Hills, *chehalem* for Chehalem Hills, and *nosub* if the parcel is outside these sub-AVAs).[9] Parcels outside of sub-AVAs are demarcated as being in the Willamette Valley AVA. It is important to acknowledge that, although the Willamette Valley AVA was established in 1984, the sub-AVA designations were not officially adopted until 2005 and 2006. Prior to this time, the areas that would later be designated as sub-AVAs were well recognized by wine producers, and it was common practice to label the origin of wines using the same geographical terms.[10] We construct a variable, *saledate*, equal to 1 if the sale occurred after the respective sub-AVA designation became official and 0 otherwise, and use it to test for changes in the effects of the sub-AVA designation.

Finally, for use in robustness tests, we computed the straight-line distance from each parcel to the nearest sub-AVA. This variable, denoted *distancesub*, equals 0 if the parcel is within a sub-AVA.

Summary statistics for all variables are presented in Table 2. The average unlogged price for vineyards (*vinevalue*) is about $10,000 per acre, with prices ranging from $2,500 to $42,000 per acre. Given that our sample includes only parcels with vineyards, we must have within- sample variation in site attributes if we hope to measure effects of terroir. The statistics in Table 2 reveal that 31.3, 47.0, 34.5, and 87.3 percent of the land within our sample of parcels, respectively, faces directly south, and has the best elevation, soils, and slopes. At the other extreme, 16.8, 15.8, 35.0, and 12.7 percent of the land, respectively, is in the least desirable categories for aspect, elevation, soils, and slope. With the possible

[9] We have no observations of sales within the Ribbon Ridge sub-AVA.

[10] For example, in 2004, Archery Summit labeled their Red Hills Estate wine "Dundee Hills Pinot Noir."

Table 2. Summary statistics.

Variable	Mean	Standard error	Minimum	Maximum
vinevalue	10149	5917	2500	42000
vineacres	43.48	46.53	7	400
bestelev	0.470	0.392	0	1
posselev	0.372	0.330	0	1
lowhighelev	0.158	0.312	0	1
south	0.313	0.226	0	0.994
southew	0.338	0.161	0.006	0.995
eastwest	0.181	0.123	0	0.560
north	0.168	0.176	0	0.707
bestsoil	0.345	0.418	0	1
goodsoil	0.305	0.377	0	1
poorsoil	0.350	0.374	0	1
bestslope	0.873	0.141	0	1
flatsteep	0.127	0.141	0	1
percentvine	0.681	0.214	0.162	1
eola	0.125	0.332	0	1
mcminnville	0.029	0.168	0	1
yamhill	0.163	0.372	0	1
dundee	0.231	0.423	0	1
chehalem	0.144	0.353	0	1
nosub	0.308	0.464	0	1
saledate	0.171	0.379	0	1
distancesub	36430	86750	0	355833
Number of observations = 104				

exception of the slope variable, these statistics suggest that our sample reflects a significant range of physiographic conditions.

Results and Robustness Tests

For our basic model, we regress the log of *vinevalue* on *vineacres*, the square of *vineacres* (*sqvineacres*), site attributes, sub-AVA designations,

Table 3. Estimation results: Basic model.

Variable	Estimate	Standard error	p-value
constant	8.582	0.3328	0.000
vineacres	−0.005	0.0021	0.013
sqvineacres	0.000014	0.000006	0.016
bestelev	0.157	0.1539	0.311
posselev	0.130	0.1641	0.430
south	0.202	0.2684	0.453
southew	−0.088	0.2673	0.743
eastwest	0.270	0.4710	0.567
bestsoil	−0.030	0.1565	0.850
goodsoil	0.048	0.1369	0.725
bestslope	0.075	0.2856	0.792
eola	0.438	0.1382	0.002
mcminnville	0.154	0.2303	0.504
yamhill	0.529	0.1350	0.000
dundee	0.852	0.1425	0.000
chehalem	0.482	0.1246	0.000

Dependent variable = log of vinevalue
Number of observations = 104
Adj. R-squared = 0.422

and a constant term. The omitted variables are *lowhighelev*, *north*, *poorsoil*, *flatsteep*, and *nosub*. Because these are the least desirable categories, we expect the coefficients on the included site attribute and sub-AVA variables to be positive.

The results, in Table 3, reveal that most of the estimated coefficients on the site attribute variables are positive, but none are significantly different from zero. The smallest p-value is 0.311, and none of the estimates are even marginally significant.[11] In contrast, four of the five estimated coefficients for sub-AVA are significantly different from zero at better than the 1 percent level. Parcels within the Eola-Amity Hills, Yamhill-Carlton, Dundee Hills, and Chehalem Hills sub-AVA sell for significantly

[11] The results do not change appreciably if we use robust standard error estimates.

more than parcels without a sub-AVA designation. In 2007 dollars, the premiums associated with location within these sub-AVAs were, respectively, \$2,933, \$3,721, \$7,163, and \$3,306 per acre.

Pairwise *F*-tests indicate that the coefficient on *dundee* is different from those on *eola*, *yamhill*, and *chehalem*, but that the coefficients on *eola*, *yamhill*, and *chehalem* are statistically indistinguishable from one another. The coefficients on parcel size indicate that the per-acre price falls as the parcel size increases, but at a diminishing rate. Finally, the adjusted R^2 is 0.422, reasonably high for cross-section data.

As mentioned above, the sub-AVA designations did not become official until 2005 and 2006. For the Eola-Amity Hills, Yamhill-Carlton, and Dundee Hills sub-AVAs, our sample includes sales that occurred before and after the official designation. To test for a corresponding shift in the sub-AVA premium in these cases, we interact *eola*, *yamhill*, and *dundee* with *saledate* and add these variables to the basic model. We find that the coefficient estimates are positive and significant in all cases, indicating a rise in the premiums following the official adoption of the sub-AVAs.[12]

Why are the impacts of site attributes on sales price insignificant? As mentioned above, the site attribute variables are measured over the entire parcel, not just the vineyard portion, which may decrease the precision of these variables and explain why the estimated coefficients are not significantly different from zero. To explore this possibility, we restrict the sample to parcels that are at least 50 percent vineyards (*percentvine* $\geq$ 0.50). For the entire sample, an average of 68 percent of the parcel area is vineyards, with a minimum of 16 and a maximum of 100 percent (Table 2). With a 50 percent cut-off, we still have 83 observations with which to estimate the model. The results (not reported, but available upon request) show little change from the basic model. None of the coefficient estimates for site attributes are significantly different from zero, and the estimates for sub-AVAs have similar magnitude and significance level. Qualitatively, the findings remain the same for cut-off values of 68 percent and 75 percent. We also re-estimate the basic model with *percentvine* entered as an independent variable in the basic model. The associated coefficient is not significantly different from zero.

[12]The Eola-Amity Hills premium increases from \$590 to \$5,621 per acre, the Yamhill-Carlton premium increases from \$2,186 to \$7,064 per acre, and the Dundee Hills premium increases from \$4,440 to \$15,474 per acre. The full set of results is available from the corresponding author upon request.

Another possible explanation for the insignificance of the site attribute variables is that their effects could be masked by the sub-AVA designations. The sub-AVA designations are supposed to be based on the area's terroir. In this case, the sub-AVA variables would measure the average effect of the site attributes of parcels within the sub-AVA, and dropping the sub-AVA variables would increase the explanatory power of the site attributes. We find this result in the case of the *bestsoil* variable, which has a positive and significant (5 percent level) coefficient when we omit the sub-AVA variables (Table 4).

Further investigation reveals that the *bestsoil* variable is highly correlated with the indicator variable for the Dundee Hills sub-AVA (*dundee*) but not with the other sub-AVA variables.[13] Thus, the model in Table 4 does not identify whether higher vineyard prices are the result of soils or location within the Dundee Hills sub-AVA. We split the sample into two groups — parcels inside and outside the Dundee Hills sub-AVA — and estimate separate models with only the site attribute variables. In both cases, the coefficient on the *bestsoil* variable is insignificant, suggesting that it is the Dundee Hills location, and not better soils, that raises vineyard prices.[14]

A further check is to see if there is variation in the site attributes within sub-AVAs. If not, then the effects of the site attributes will be captured by the sub-AVA variables. Table 5 reports the standard deviation of the site attributes for the whole sample and for parcels within each sub-AVA. The statistics indicate similar variation in site attributes within and across sub-AVAs.

Finally, if the terroir of a sub-AVA has important influences on wine quality, then parcels that are outside, but close to, sub-AVAs should be valued more than parcels that are farther away. We re-estimate the basic model with the variable *distancesub* included. This corresponding p-value is 0.45.[15]

---

[13] The simple correlation coefficient for *bestsoil* and *dundee* is 0.69.

[14] There are 24 parcels inside the Dundee Hills sub-AVA and 80 parcels outside. With these sub-samples, the p-values for the *bestsoil* variable are, respectively, 0.81 and 0.90. Although the mean of *bestsoil* is higher for parcels inside the Dundee Hills sub-AVA (0.87 compared to 0.19), there is considerable variation in the *bestsoil* variable within the sub-samples. In both cases, *bestsoil* has a standard deviation of about 0.30 and minimum and maximum values of 0 and 1, respectively.

[15] A similar result is obtained when we drop two observations for parcels that are outside but closest to the McMinnville sub-AVA. There is no premium associated with being inside this sub-AVA. Full results are available from the corresponding author upon request.

Table 4. Estimation results: No sub-AVA variables.

Variable	Estimate	Standard error	*p*-value
constant	8.822	0.3842	0.000
vineacres	−0.008	0.0024	0.001
sqvineacres	0.000018	0.000007	0.009
bestelev	0.255	0.1766	0.152
posselev	−0.009	0.1933	0.961
south	0.102	0.3101	0.743
southew	−0.189	0.3104	0.544
eastwest	0.337	0.5298	0.526
bestsoil	0.494	0.1443	0.001
goodsoil	0.242	0.1422	0.093
bestslope	0.192	0.3370	0.571

Dependent variable = log of vinevalue
Number of observations = 104
Adj. R-squared = 0.165

Table 5. Standard deviation of site attributes by sub-AVA.

Variable	All	Eola	Mcminnville	Yamhill	Dundee	Chehalem	Nosub
bestelev	0.392	0.287	0.405	0.249	0.370	0.416	0.390
posselev	0.330	0.267	0.306	0.159	0.360	0.330	0.374
lowhighelev	0.312	0.031	0.166	0.166	0.424	0.259	0.305
south	0.226	0.138	0.249	0.209	0.335	0.169	0.185
southew	0.161	0.095	0.078	0.172	0.221	0.093	0.154
eastwest	0.123	0.104	0.102	0.084	0.144	0.141	0.113
north	0.176	0.190	0.097	0.224	0.145	0.143	0.170
bestsoil	0.418	0.305	0.007	0.213	0.292	0.311	0.313
goodsoil	0.377	0.162	0.425	0.314	0.133	0.433	0.344
poorsoil	0.374	0.326	0.432	0.215	0.218	0.461	0.372
bestslope	0.141	0.077	0.019	0.131	0.115	0.109	0.188
flatsteep	0.141	0.077	0.019	0.131	0.115	0.109	0.188

Number of observations = 104

Table 6. External evidence on sub-AVA rankings.

Our results		**Wine Spectator**		**Robert Parker**	
sub-AVA	**Vineyard premium**	**sub-AVA**	**Avg. bottle price**	**sub-AVA**	**Avg. bottle price**
Willamette Valley	$0	McMinnville	$40.40	McMinnville	$42.60
McMinnville	$0	Willamette Valley	$46.30	Willamette Valley	$47.40
Eola-Amity Hills	$2,933	Yamhill-Carlton	$48.50	Yamhill-Carlton	$48.20
Chehalem Mountains	$3,306	Eola-Amity Hills	$51.30	Eola-Amity Hills	$49.90
Yamhill-Carlton	$3,721	Chehalem Mountains	$52.00	Dundee Hills	$54.20
Dundee Hills	$7,163	Dundee Hills	$58.70	Chehalem Mountains	$54.60

Note: The vineyard premium is the increment in sale price (in 2007 dollars per acre) resulting from location inside a sub-AVA.

Our results indicate that the significant premiums associated with sub-AVA designations are unrelated to observable site attributes. An alternative explanation is that bottle prices for wines from sub-AVAs command higher prices (for reputational reasons), which bids up the prices of sub-AVA vineyards. To examine this possibility, we summarized data on 2006 Pinot Noir bottle prices for the Willamette Valley AVA and for each sub-AVA. From the *Wine Spectator* database, we obtained 243 observations, and from the *Wine Advocate* (Robert Parker) database 310 observations. In Table 6, we report the vineyard premiums (in 2007 dollars), based on the results from Table 3, plus the average bottle prices (in 2007 dollars) from our two wine data sources. The rankings of vineyard premiums are broadly consistent with bottle rankings. McMinnville and Willamette Valley are at the bottom in all rankings and Dundee Hills is at or second from the top. Of course, the bottle prices are also affected by the skills and reputations of wine-makers, and so these results are, at most, suggestive of correlation between vineyard and bottle prices.[16]

[16]Because there is considerable variation in bottle prices within sub-AVAs, we cannot reject the null hypothesis that average bottle prices are the same across sub-AVAs.

Conclusions

We have estimated a hedonic model of vineyard prices in Oregon to examine whether they vary systematically with designated appellation, after controlling for site attributes. Despite using precise measures of site attributes, we do not find evidence of a significant effect of these variables on vineyard prices, and a series of robustness tests does not alter this finding. But, we do find that vineyard prices are strongly determined by whether or not parcels are inside specific sub-AVAs. The delineation of sub-AVAs is intended to capture the unique characteristics of a geographical area as they relate to grape production.[17] That is, sub-AVAs are supposed to reflect the area's terroir. Our finding that the physical characteristics of vineyards are not priced implicitly in the land market raises questions about whether sub-AVA designations have a meaningful connection — in reality — with terroir.

Nevertheless, our results make clear that the concept of terroir matters economically. Buyers and sellers of vineyard parcels in the Willamette Valley of Oregon attach a significant premium to the sub-AVA designations, ranging from about $3,000 per acre for Eola-Amity Hills, Chehalem Mountains, and Yamhill-Carlton, to over $7,000 per acre for Dundee Hills. One possibility is that buyers are less informed than sellers about how the attributes of a vineyard will affect wine quality and, therefore, rely on sub-AVA designations as quality signals. Either way, consumers are evidently willing to pay more for the experience of drinking wines from these areas. While they may not discriminate among wines in terms of their intrinsic qualities, consumers are responding to extrinsic qualities of wines, such as price and area of origin.

Acknowledgments

The authors are grateful to Charles Mason, Larry Lev, and session participants at the 2009 American Association of Wine Economics and 2011 Allied Social Science Association meetings for helpful comments on a previous version of this paper (Cross, Plantinga, and Stavins, 2011), but all remaining errors are their own.

[17]The Bureau of Alcohol, Tobacco, and Firearms, which designates AVAs in the United States, defines a viticultural area as, "a delimited, grape-growing region distinguishable by geographical features."

References

Ashenfelter, O. and K. Storchmann. (2010). "Using hedonic models of solar radiation and weather to assess the economic effect of climate change: The case of Mosel Valley vineyards." *Review of Economics and Statistics*. **92**(2): 333–349.

Cross, R., A. J. Plantinga, and R. N. Stavins. (2011). "What is the value of terroir?" *American Economic Review Papers and Proceedings*, forthcoming.

Gergaud, O. and V. Ginsburgh. (2010). "Natural endowments, production technologies and the quality of wines in Bordeaux: Does terroir matter?" *The Economic Journal*. **118**: F142–F157.

Goldstein, R., J. Almenberg, A. Dreber, J. W. Emerson, A. Herschkowitsch, and J. Katz. (2008). "Do more expensive wines taste better? Evidence from a large sample of blind tastings." *Journal of Wine Economics*. **3**(1): 1–9.

Hodgson, R. T. (2009a). "An analysis of the concordance among 13 U.S. wine competitions." *Journal of Wine Economics*. **4**(1): 1–9.

Hodgson, R. T. (2009b). "How expert are "expert" wine judges?" *Journal of Wine Economics*. **4**(2): 233–241.

Veale, R. and P. Quester. (2008). "Consumer sensory evaluations of wine quality: The respective influence of price and country of origin." *Journal of Wine Economics*. **3**(1): 10–29.

https://doi.org/10.1142/9789811292415_0027

Chapter 27

Terroir in the New World: Hedonic Estimation of Vineyard Sale Prices in California*

Robin Cross[†,], Andrew J. Plantinga[‡,††], and Robert N. Stavins[§,¶,‖,‡‡]**

[†]*Department of Agricultural and Resource Economics, Oregon State University, Corvallis, OR, USA*

[‡]*Bren School of Environmental Science and Management, University of California, Santa Barbara, CA*

[§]*John F. Kennedy School of Government, Harvard University, Cambridge, MA, USA*

[¶]*Resources for the Future, Washington, DC, USA*

[‖]*National Bureau of Economic Research, Cambridge, MA, USA*

[**]*robin.cross@oregonstate.edu*

[††]*plantinga@bren.ucsb.edu*

[‡‡]*robert_stavins@harvard.edu*

*This chapter was originally published in *Journal of Wine Economics*, **12**(3), 282–301, 2017. doi:10.1017/jwe.2017.27.

Introduction

An important concept underlying wine production and appreciation in the Old World (France, Germany, Italy, and Spain) is *terroir*, which refers to the characteristics of a location that impart special qualities to the wine produced (Gergaud and Ginsburgh, 2010). In France, the Appellation d'Origine Contrôlée (AOC) system — and similar systems adopted in other major wine-producing countries — is based on the geographic location of grape production and is thereby predicated on this notion of *terroir*. A considerably more recent U.S. system of American Viticultural Areas (AVAs) likewise reflects the location of grape production. Finer geographical designations are known as Sub-AVAs.

These AVA and Sub-AVA designations allow wineries to identify the origin of the grapes used in producing their wines, but what is the real value of *terroir* in this American context? Does the "reality of *terroir*" — the location-specific geology and geography (including climate) — predominate in determining the quality of wine, as is assumed to be the case in Europe? And/or does the "concept of *terroir*" — the location within an officially named appellation — impart reputational value to grapes and the wine they yield? Does the location within an appellation impart additional value to vineyards?

To address these questions, and thereby the fundamental question of the role of *terroir* in New-World wine production, we examine whether observable site attributes — slope, aspect, elevation, and climate — or appellation designations are more important determinants of vineyard prices in the most important wine-producing region in the United States: Napa and Sonoma Counties in California. We carry out this examination with a hedonic price analysis of vineyard sales.[1] By focusing on vineyard sale prices rather than wine (bottle) prices, we can directly examine the price effects of *terroir* and avoid confounding influences of nonvineyard inputs into wine production, including the skills and techniques of the winemaker.

It is conceivable that site attributes, AVA designations, or both influence vineyard prices. At one extreme, if site attributes affect wine quality

[1] We previously carried out an analysis of vineyard sales in the Willamette Valley of Oregon (Cross, Plantinga, and Stavins, 2011a, 2011b). In addition to the different geographic application, our analysis here differs from and improves significantly upon our previous work in ways we describe later.

and consumers are able to discriminate such quality, then vineyard prices would depend on site attributes alone,[2] because AVA designations would simply be redundant.

At the other extreme, site attributes might be irrelevant, with vineyard prices being fully explained by AVA designations. In this case, the implication is that *terroir* matters economically as a concept but perhaps not as a fundamental biophysical reality. There might be three possible explanations for this. First, if producers believe that consumers will pay more for wines from more-prestigious designations, then they might be more willing to pay for vineyard properties in those areas.[3] In this case, any appreciation that consumers might express for an area's *terroir* would be founded on reputation rather than reality.[4] Second, if buyers are less informed than sellers about vineyard attributes and how they affect wine quality, then buyers might use AVA designations as signals of quality. Third, producers might bid up the value of vineyards located in designated appellations because of the personal prestige associated with owning these properties.

An intermediate case lies between these two extremes of, on the one hand, the bio-physically dominant reality of *terroir* (and the consequent redundancy of AVA designations) and, on the other hand, *terroir*'s mattering not as a fundamental reality but only as a concept economically (and the consequent insignificance of site attributes in explaining vineyard prices). In the intermediate case, consumers might be able to discriminate imperfectly among wines and might therefore use AVA designations as signals of the average quality of wines from respective areas, or they might derive utility directly from drinking wines that they know to be of particular pedigrees. In this intermediate case, site attributes and AVA designations would influence vineyard prices, with estimated coefficients for site attributes measuring how producers valued intra-AVA differences in vineyard characteristics. In other words, producers would attach premiums to

[2]Of course, wine quality is affected not only by location attributes but also by the quality of growing stock, vineyard management, and the skills and resources of the winemaker.

[3]Blind taste tests indicate that consumers have very limited ability to distinguish intrinsic qualities of wine (for example, sweetness, acidity, and tannins) and instead judge quality by relying on extrinsic signals, such as price, origin, and winemaker reputation (Veale and Quester, 2008; Goldstein *et al.*, 2008).

[4]This assumes that unobserved factors do not affect quality and are not correlated with AVA designations. We examine this possibility below.

site attributes that enhanced wine quality if consumers could perceive and were willing to pay for quality differences.

By executing a hedonic analysis of the factors affecting vineyard sales prices in Napa and Sonoma Sub-AVAs,[5] we distinguish among these three cases and thereby assess the value of *terroir* in the California context. In our previous analysis of vineyard sales in Oregon's Willamette Valley, we found that AVA designations but not site attributes were significant, meaning that *terroir* mattered economically but not biophysically. In the case of California's premier wine-production regions, we find a more nuanced result in which AVA designations *and* location attributes significantly affect vineyard sale prices, supporting the intermediate case in which *terroir* is validated as a conceptual and as a fundamental reality.

In the second section, we briefly review previous, related literature and highlight the differences between this analysis and our previous work in Oregon. In the third section, we describe our analytical approach, including our treatment of potential sample-selection bias. In the fourth section, we describe our empirical results. Finally, we conclude in the last section.

Previous Literature

The analysis we document in this chapter builds on our previous work and that of others,[6] including Gergaud and Ginsburgh (2010). We build on their work by examining the effects of appellation designations in addition to the effects of site characteristics. By using GIS-based information to develop detailed physiographic profiles of parcels, we are able to measure site characteristics more precisely than have most previous researchers. Earlier studies using fine-scale data include Ashenfelter and Storchmann's (2010) investigation of the effects of climate on vineyards in the Mosel Valley and the analysis by Gergaud, Plantinga, and Ringeval-Deluze (2017) of the price effects of obsolete vineyard ratings in the Champagne region.

Our analysis also differs from most previous work by employing vineyard sale prices as the dependent variable instead of wine (bottle) prices or ratings (Ashenfelter and Storchmann, 2010; Castriota and Delmastro, 2015; Costanigro, McCluskey, and Goemans, 2015; Gergaud

[5]For reasons discussed below, our analysis focuses on the effects of Sub-AVAs.

[6]For a more complete review of the literature, see Cross, Plantinga, and Stavins (2011a).

and Ginsburgh, 2010). In our investigation into the value of *terroir*, this difference avoids the potentially confounding influences of nonvineyard inputs into wine production (such as winemaking techniques) and reputational effects of producers and regions. Costanigro, McCluskey, and Goemans (2015) find evidence of reputation premia attached to wine bottle prices after controlling for quality scores from blind tastings by experts.

Although the overall purpose of our analysis — assessing the value of *terroir* in a New-World context — is similar to our previous work (Cross, Plantinga, and Stavins, 2011a, 2011b), this study departs from and significantly improves on that work in several ways. First, our current measurement of vineyard attributes is much more precise. In our previous work, we measured those attributes as average values across entire parcels, but here we geographically locate each vineyard within the sold property and measure its specific local attributes. Second, we control for the effects of varietals on vineyard prices. For our previous study of the Willamette Valley of Oregon, we lacked information on varietals, although we knew that Pinot Noir accounted for about three-quarters of vineyard acreage in that region. Third, we now examine the effects of climate, as meaningful climatic variations exist within the geographic Napa-Sonoma region. Fourth, because we have information about vineyard sales outside any AVA or Sub-AVA, we can estimate the contribution of Sub-AVAs to vineyard prices. Fifth, as we explain below, we suspect that the sample of sold parcels may not be representative of the population of vineyard parcels in the Napa-Sonoma region. We therefore locate and measure attributes of the universe of vineyards — sold or not — in Napa and Sonoma Counties and adjust the results for potential sample-selection bias.

Analytical Approach

We investigate the relationship between vineyard sales prices, site attributes, and appellation designations with extensive data on vineyard sales in Napa and Sonoma Counties for the years 1991 through 2007. With a hedonic model of vineyard sales prices, we can identify the degree to which sales prices were associated with site attributes and appellation designations and thereby can assess the degree to which *terroir* functions as a concept, a reality, or both.

The hedonic price model is a reduced-form equilibrium model and thus captures demand and supply factors. In our application, we expect prices to be determined primarily by the demand for grapes and for the wine produced from those grapes. Given that we analyze properties with existing vineyards, any fixed costs of vineyard establishment are sunk and will not be reflected in market prices. Grape production also involves variable costs for vineyard management and harvest. However, with the possible exception of steeply sloped parcels, we would expect little variation in variable costs among vineyards in our sample.

In a competitive market, the price of a vineyard equals the present discounted value of the anticipated stream of rents generated by the land. These rents may vary in the future with changes in climate, technology, and other factors that make a given vineyard parcel more or less productive. Although we do not explicitly model the future rent stream, the site attributes in our model capture, to some degree, expectations of future rent changes. For example, if higher elevations are expected to become better suited for grape production under future climate changes, this trait should raise the current value of higher-elevation sites and be reflected in the estimated elevation parameters. In fact, a recent study by Severen, Costello, and Deschenes (2016) finds evidence that climate-change forecasts are being reflected in current farmland prices.

Dependent Variable for Hedonic Estimation: Vineyard Value

The dependent variable in our hedonic model is the natural log of real vineyard price per acre, denoted as *lnP*. Many sales include nonvineyard assets, such as buildings and additional, nonvineyard land. So, to obtain the price of vineyards, we subtract from total sales price the appraiser-based estimate of the value of nonvineyard assets (buildings, building sites, plantable and residual land, and winery permits). Then, by dividing the vineyard price by the vineyard area and expressing the result in constant (2007) dollars using the Consumer Price Index, we construct our dependent variable.

Independent Variables for Hedonic Estimation

Key independent variables include measures of vineyard area; indicator variables for AVAs and Sub-AVAs; shares of vineyards planted in various varietals; shares of vineyards in different aspect, elevation, and slope categories; and variables for local climate (Table 1). Soil characteristics are

Table 1. Variable definitions and summary statistics.

Variable name	Definition	Obs	Mean	Std dev	Min	Max	Sum
Vineyard price							
P	Vineyard price per acre in constant 2007 dollars	188	122,046	89,111			
Vineyard area							
A	Vineyard area in acres	188	33.1	39.0			
A^2	Vineyard area squared	188	2,611.6	9,332.9			
AVA indicator variables							
AVA_0	Northern Sonoma AVA	188	0.239	0.428	0	1	45
AVA_1	Napa Valley AVA	188	0.521	0.501	0	1	98
AVA_2	Russian River AVA	188	0.032	0.176	0	1	6
AVA_3	Sonoma Coast AVA	188	0.138	0.346	0	1	26
AVA_4	Sonoma Valley AVA	188	0.064	0.245	0	1	12
AVA_5	Alexander Valley sub-AVA	188	0.128	0.335	0	1	24
AVA_6	Atlas Peak sub-AVA	188	0.011	0.103	0	1	2
AVA_7	Bennett Valley sub-AVA	188	0.016	0.126	0	1	3
AVA_8	Calistoga sub-AVA	188	0.043	0.202	0	1	8
AVA_9	Chalk Hill sub-AVA	188	0.021	0.145	0	1	4
AVA_{10}	Coombsville sub-AVA	188	0.011	0.103	0	1	2
AVA_{11}	Diamond Mountain sub-AVA	188	0.005	0.073	0	1	1
AVA_{12}	Dry Creek sub-AVA	188	0.090	0.288	0	1	17
AVA_{13}	Fort Ross sub-AVA	188	0.005	0.073	0	1	1
AVA_{14}	Green Valley sub-AVA	188	0.011	0.103	0	1	2
AVA_{15}	Howell Mountain sub-AVA	188	0.011	0.103	0	1	2
AVA_{16}	Knights Valley sub-AVA	188	0.016	0.126	0	1	3

(*Continued*)

Table 1. (*Continued*)

Variable name	Definition	Obs	Mean	Std dev	Min	Max	Sum
AVA_{17}	Los Carneros sub-AVA	188	0.101	0.302	0	1	19
AVA_{18}	Mount Veeder sub-AVA	188	0.027	0.161	0	1	5
AVA_{19}	Oak Knoll sub-AVA	188	0.101	0.302	0	1	19
AVA_{20}	Oakville sub-AVA	188	0.037	0.190	0	1	7
AVA_{21}	Rutherford sub-AVA	188	0.053	0.225	0	1	10
AVA_{22}	Spring Mountain sub-AVA	188	0.021	0.145	0	1	4
AVA_{23}	St. Helena sub-AVA	188	0.048	0.214	0	1	9
AVA_{24}	Yountville sub-AVA	188	0.011	0.103	0	1	2
AVA_{25}	Bennett Valley & Sonoma Mountain sub-AVAs	188	0.011	0.103	0	1	2
AVA_{26}	Dry Creek & Rockpile sub-AVAs	188	0.005	0.073	0	1	1
Varietals							
V_0	Share of vineyard planted in other varietals	188	0.032	0.176	0	1	
V_1	Share of vineyard planted in cabernet sauvignon	188	0.324	0.410	0	1	
V_2	Share of vineyard planted in chardonnay	188	0.292	0.376	0	1	
V_3	Share of vineyard planted in cabernet franc	188	0.009	0.038	0	0.333	
V_4	Share of vineyard planted in merlot	188	0.146	0.270	0	1	
V_5	Share of vineyard planted in pinot noir	188	0.068	0.186	0	1	
V_6	Share of vineyard planted in sauvignon blanc	188	0.034	0.119	0	1	

Table 1. (*Continued*)

Variable name	Definition	Obs	Mean	Std dev	Min	Max	Sum
V_7	Share of vineyard planted in syrah	188	0.028	0.124	0	1	
V_8	Share of vineyard planted in zinfandel	188	0.068	0.213	0	1	
Vineyard aspect							
Asp_0	Share of vineyard with west aspect	188	0.066	0.100	0	0.520	
Asp_1	Share of vineyard with east aspect	188	0.113	0.135	0	0.686	
Asp_2	Share of vineyard that is flat (no aspect)	188	0.015	0.089	0	1	
Asp_3	Share of vineyard with north aspect	188	0.103	0.151	0	0.753	
Asp_4	Share of vineyard with northeast aspect	188	0.176	0.222	0	0.868	
Asp_5	Share of vineyard with northwest aspect	188	0.049	0.077	0	0.432	
Asp_6	Share of vineyard with south aspect	188	0.182	0.193	0	0.915	
Asp_7	Share of vineyard with southeast aspect	188	0.141	0.171	0	0.909	
Asp_8	Share of vineyard with southwest aspect	188	0.155	0.197	0	0.896	
Vineyard elevation							
E_0	Share of vineyard 600 to 700 feet	188	0.013	0.098	0	0.781	
E_1	Share of vineyard 0 to 100 feet	188	0.708	0.441	0	1	
E_2	Share of vineyard 100 to 200 feet	188	0.132	0.308	0	1	
E_3	Share of vineyard 200 to 300 feet	188	0.060	0.202	0	1	

(*Continued*)

Table 1. (*Continued*)

Variable name	Definition	Obs	Mean	Std dev	Min	Max	Sum
E_4	Share of vineyard 300 to 400 feet	188	0.039	0.168	0	1	
E_5	Share of vineyard 400 to 500 feet	188	0.029	0.149	0	1	
E_6	Share of vineyard 500 to 600 feet	188	0.020	0.116	0	1	
Vineyard slope							
S_0	Share of vineyard 0 to 1 degree slope	188	0.406	0.406	0	1	
S_1	Share of vineyard 1 to 2 degree slope	188	0.142	0.165	0	0.907	
S_2	Share of vineyard 2 to 5 degree slope	188	0.166	0.197	0	0.691	
S_3	Share of vineyard 5 to 20 degree slope	188	0.257	0.326	0	0.957	
S_4	Share of vineyard 20 to 30 degree slope	188	0.027	0.075	0	0.489	
S_5	Share of vineyard over 30 degree slope	188	0.002	0.009	0	0.070	
Climate variables							
T_1	Average temperature difference in July in °F	188	19.3	1.2	16.2	20.8	
T_2	Average temperature difference in August in °F	188	18.9	1.1	15.7	20.3	
T_3	Average temperature difference in September in °F	188	18.2	0.7	15.5	19.5	
R_1	Average growing season precipitation in cm	188	475.1	88.9	315.3	713.8	

Table 1. (*Continued*)

Variable name	Definition	Obs	Mean	Std dev	Min	Max	Sum
R_2	Average summer precipitation in cm	188	22.7	3.3	15.4	32.5	
Selection equation variables							
sale_count	Number of sales within 2 km	188	7.7	7.1	0.0	30.0	
vineyard_share	Share of the parcel in vineyards	188	0.628	0.264	0.040	1.019	

another potential determinant of vineyard prices. Based on an analysis described below, we control for soils using AVA dummy variables. We include vineyard area (A) and the square of this variable (A^2), because in our previous work in the Willamette Valley of Oregon, we found that the per-acre price declines as the parcel size increases, consistent with volume discounts offered by sellers.

Indicator variables are included for 20 Sub-AVAs in which we observe vineyard sales. Three Sub-AVAs in Napa County (Chiles Valley, Stags Leap, and Wild Horse Valley) and three in Sonoma County (Carneros, Moon Mountain, Pine Mountain) are excluded due to lack of sales observations. A few properties are located in more than one Sub-AVA, and so we create separate categorical variables for these sales.[7] It is possible for vineyards to be within an AVA (Napa Valley, Russian River Valley, Sonoma Coast, or Sonoma Valley) but not within a Sub-AVA. When we include AVA dummies to control for soil characteristics, we cannot separately identify the effects of AVA designation. In total, we include 22 mutually exclusive indicator variables for Sub-AVAs. We compute the share of the vineyard planted in each of nine varietals: Cabernet Sauvignon, Chardonnay, Cabernet Franc, Merlot, Pinot Noir, Sauvignon Blanc, Syrah, Zinfandel, and other. If all vineyards are planted in the optimal varietal, conditional on site attributes, we do not expect the selected

[7]These variables are labeled "bennettsonomamtn" and "drycreekrockpile" in the tables found below.

varietal to influence vineyard price. But if significant costs are associated with changing varietals, we may find price premiums associated with prized varietals, such as Cabernet Sauvignon. To estimate the price model, we omit the "other varietal" category.

We include variables for aspect, elevation, and slope of each vineyard, which are the key attributes — along with climate (see below) — that are often mentioned as indicators of *terroir*. We compute the share of the vineyard in each of nine aspect cate-gories (south, southeast, southwest, etc.), including a category for "flat ground" and omitting the "west" category when the model is estimated. Elevation variables measure the share of the vineyard in each of seven categories (0 to 100 feet, 100 to 200 feet, etc.), with "600 to 700 feet" being the omitted category. Finally, we include variables for the share of each vineyard in six slope categories (1 to 2°, 2 to 5°, etc.), omitting the "0 to 1°" category.

We construct climate variables of temperature and precipitation using historical (1980 to 1989) weather data.[8] We compute the average difference between the daily high temperatures and daily low temperatures during the maturation and harvest period (July, August, and September).[9] Warm temperatures contribute to grape maturation, and daily temperature fluctuations are associated with acid and sugar development and flavor complexity (Robinson, 2006). We measure average precipitation over the entire growing season (February through September) as well as during the maturation and harvest period. Soil moisture levels as well as precipitation at bud break, fruit set, and harvest play important roles in vine health and fruit quality (Matthews and Anderson, 1989).

Soil characteristics are a potentially important indicator of *terroir*. Gergaud *et al.* (2017) find that vineyard prices in the Champagne region of France are significantly affected by the parcels' limestone content. In contrast with our earlier work on the Willamette Valley of Oregon (Cross *et al.*, 2011a), in which vineyards are found primarily on three or four soil

---

[8] We are assuming that climate change did not occur during the period of analysis (1991–2007) in a way that affected vineyard prices. It would be desirable to test this assumption by comparing earlier climate data to later climate data, but the fine-scale climate data we use from PRISM (see the Data Appendix) are not useful for this purpose.

[9] Schlenker and Roberts (2009) find that extreme temperature events have significant effects on crop yields.

In an alternate specification, we include the levels of monthly average minimum and maximum tempera- tures rather than the differences. Our results are qualitatively the same.

types, vineyards in Napa and Sonoma Counties are found on sites with a much larger number of soil types. For the most disaggregated classification, 307 soil types are represented in our dataset (Natural Resource Conservation Service, 2016), making it infeasible to include variables for soil types in the hedonic price model.

A major concern with omitting soil variables from the hedonic model is that they may be correlated with the AVA and Sub-AVA designations, which could bias our parameter estimates.[10] However, because we observe the locations and characteristics of all (sold and unsold) vineyards in Napa and Sonoma Counties, we can use the entire dataset to investigate whether soils are a significant determinant of AVA and Sub-AVA designations. To this end, we estimate a series of index function models (one for each AVA or Sub-AVA) in which an unobserved index y_j^* determines whether a given vineyard is included in the *j*th AVA or Sub-AVA. For each vineyard, we observe the binary outcome y_j, where y_j takes a value of 1 if the vineyard is part of the *j*th AVA or Sub-AVA, and is 0 otherwise. The outcome variable is assumed to be related to the index as follows: $y_j = 1$ if $y_j^* > 0$ and $y_j = 0$ if $y_j^* \leq 0$. Further, the index is expressed in terms of observable vineyard characteristics X and an unobserved disturbance term ε according to $y_j^* = X'\beta_j + \varepsilon$, where β_j is a vector of parameters for the *j*th AVA or Sub-AVA.

We estimate the β parameters using the linear probability model $y_j = X'\beta_j + \varepsilon$. With this model, we can more easily address spatial correlation in the errors than with a probit or logit specification. Because the AVAs and Sub-AVAs are geographically distinct areas, we might expect the errors to be correlated within AVAs or Sub-AVAs. We compute cluster-robust standard errors, where the clusters are defined as AVAs for the AVA models and Sub-AVAs for the Sub-AVA models. In all models, the independent variables include the varietal, aspect, elevation, and slope shares and the climate measures, as described above. We also include a set of variables for soil characteristics. We have four alternative sets of soil variables, which vary by degree of specificity: Each set includes 6, 24, 78, or 307 variables. We estimate a separate set of AVA and Sub-AVA models for each set of soil variables.

---

[10]New AVA determinations are made by the Federal Alcohol and Tobacco Tax and Trade Bureau according to geographic features — primarily soil, elevation, geology, and climate, although other distinguishing features can be considered (Alcohol and Tobacco Tax and Trade Bureau, 2012).

We find that soil characteristics are significant determinants of AVA designations, but not of Sub-AVA designations. Depending on which soil variables we use, between 2 and 21 percent of the estimated parameters on the soil variables are significantly different from zero in the AVA model sets. In contrast, at most 1 percent of the coefficient estimates for the soil variables are significant in Sub-AVA model sets. For the Sub-AVA models, the probability of Type II error is sufficiently low so that we can ignore the effects of soil at the Sub-AVA scale. However, the results for the AVA models suggest that we need AVA-level controls for soil. The most general approach is to include dummy variables for each of the AVAs, which is the approach we use. The dummy variable for the Northern Sonoma AVA is omitted for estimation.

Correcting Possible Sample-Selection Bias

In terms of land area, the vineyards sold between 1991 and 2007 represent only about 7 percent of all vineyard acreage in Napa and Sonoma, which suggests that our sample of sold vineyards may not be representative of the complete universe of vineyards. If a systematic basis determines which vineyards sell, failure to account for such selection in our sample would be a specification error that could produce inconsistent estimates (Heckman, 1979). To avoid this problem, we estimate the hedonic price model using Heckman's two-step estimation procedure. In the first step, we estimate a probit model in which the dependent variable is a binary indicator of whether a parcel sold, drawing on data for the universe of vineyards within Napa and Sonoma Counties. With these estimation results, we construct the inverse Mill's ratio, which is the ratio of the probability density function to the cumulative distribution function of the standard normal distribution (the probit model assumes that the error term follows a standard normal distribution). With Heckman's procedure, this ratio is included as a variable in the hedonic price equation estimated in the second step.

Heckman's two-step estimator can be unreliable in the absence of exclusion restrictions (Vella, 1998). For our application, we identify two variables that can potentially explain whether a vineyard sells but that we expect to be uncorrelated with vineyard price. The first is the number of sold vineyards within a 2-kilometer buffer around a vineyard, excluding the vineyard itself (*sale_count*). If certain attributes of properties make them more likely to sell, and these attributes are spatially correlated, then the probability that a vineyard sells will increase in the count of nearby sales.[11]

The other excluded variable is the share of the total parcel planted in vineyards (*vineyard_share*). Potential buyers can learn more about the value of nonvineyard land for grape production as the share of the parcel in vineyards increases. If buyers are seeking to expand the planted area, parcels with a larger vineyard share are more sought after and potentially more likely to sell. Better information about vineyard quality should raise the value of nonvineyard land but not affect the price of established vineyards.

These two variables are included in the first-stage probit model with those exogenous variables from the hedonic model that we can measure for unsold parcels. In addition, we include a set of year dummies in the hedonic model. Our data include sales in 1991 and the years 1993 to 2007. The dummy variable for 1991 is omitted for estimation.

Second-Stage Estimation of the Hedonic Price Function

After estimating the first-stage probit model and deriving from it the inverse Mills ratio, we specify the following hedonic price function and estimate its parameters:

$$\begin{aligned}\ln P_i &= \alpha + \beta_1(A_i) + \beta_2(A_i^2) + \sum_{j=1}^{26}\gamma_j(AVA_{ij}) + \sum_{k=1}^{8}\delta_k(V_{ik}) + \sum_{l=1}^{8}\zeta_l(Asp_{il}) \\ &\quad + \sum_{n=1}^{6}\theta_n(E_{in}) + \sum_{q=1}^{5}\kappa_q(S_{iq}) + \sum_{r=1}^{3}\mu_r(T_{ir}) + \sum_{s=1}^{2}\lambda_s(R_{is}) + \sum_{t=1}^{15}\pi_t(Y_t) \\ &\quad + \rho(M_i) + \varepsilon_i, \qquad (1)\end{aligned}$$

where: P_i = real vineyard sales price per acre for sale i (i = 1 to 188, as explained in text); α = intercept; A_i = size of vineyard (acres); AVA_{ij} = AVA dummy variable or Sub-AVA designation j (where j = 1 to 26); V_{ik} = share of vineyard planted to varietal k (k = 1 to 8); Asp_{il} = share of vineyard located in aspect category l (l = 1 to 8); E_{in} = share of vineyard located in

[11]This assumes that we have correctly specified the set of independent variables. Conditional on these, the count of nearby sales varies only with factors that explain the likelihood of a sale.

elevation category n (n = 1 to 6); S_{iq} = share of vineyard located in slope category q (q = 1 to 5); T_{ir} = difference between average high and average low temperature in month r (July through September); R_{is} = average precipitation over February through September (s = 1) and July through September (s = 2); Y_t = dummy variable for sale in year t (1993 through 2007); M_i = inverse Mills ratio from first-stage regression; and ε_i = error term.

Estimation of the Contribution of Sub-AVAs to Vineyard Prices

We use the estimated parameters from the above hedonic price model to calculate fitted values of the dependent variable to estimate the contribution that each Sub-AVA makes to vineyard sales prices. To do this, let

$\ln\widehat{P}_i$ = fitted value for vineyard i; and $\ln\widehat{P}_i^{\text{noAVA}}$ = fitted value for vineyard i, excluding Sub-AVA parameter.

Then,

$$C_i^1 = \ln\widehat{P}_i - \ln\widehat{P}_i^{\text{noAVA}} \approx \left(\widehat{P}_i - \widehat{P}_i^{\text{noAVA}}\right)\Big/\widehat{P}_i, \tag{2}$$

which is the Sub-AVA's percentage contribution to price.

This approximation becomes less reliable as the difference between $\widehat{P}_i$ and $\widehat{P}_i^{\text{noAVA}}$ increases. Therefore, we also compute

$$C_i^2 = \ln\widehat{P}_i - \ln\widehat{P}_i^{\text{AVA}} \tag{3}$$

where $\ln\widehat{P}_i^{\text{AVA}}$ = fitted value for vineyard i with only the Sub-AVA parameter included.

Then, C_i^2 approximates the percentage contribution of all non-AVA factors to price. By scaling C_i^1 and C_i^2 so that they sum to unity, the scaled version of C_i^1 can be used as our estimate of the Sub-AVA contribution to the sale price of vineyard i. The average of these values for all vineyards within each Sub-AVA yields our estimate of the contribution of the Sub-AVA to vineyard sales prices.

Sample Statistics and Econometric Results

Before turning to the results of our analysis, we examine summary statistics from the dataset we developed (Table 1). During the 17-year sample period (1991 to 2007), a total of 448 sales of vineyards were documented in Napa and Sonoma Counties. Of these, we verified the exact location of 359 sales, and for 188 sales, we subtracted improvements from vineyard prices, identified acreages of grape varietals, and associated Assessor Parcel Numbers (see Data Appendix). This revised dataset became the sample for our analysis.

Within this sample, the sale price averaged about $122,000 per vineyard-acre (in 2007 dollars), with a broad range of prices, as indicated by a standard deviation of nearly $90,000 (Table 1). Sale parcels contained on average about 33 acres of planted vineyards, representing about 63 percent of parcel areas. The largest share of vineyard area of sold parcels (12.7 percent) was in the Alexander Valley Sub-AVA, and the most common varietal was Cabernet Sauvignon (32 percent of all varietals by land area). Dominant geographic features included direct southern exposure at 18 percent of vineyard acreage sold, lower elevations (0 to 50 feet) at 71 percent, and level slopes (0 to 1 degree) at 41 percent. Price and acreage minima and maxima are excluded from Table 1 to preserve confidentiality.

First-Stage Econometric Results

Sold parcels may not be representative of the population of vineyard parcels as a whole in the Napa-Sonoma region. Combined with the selection of our sample for analysis (42 percent of observed sales), this suggests the distinct possibility of sample selection bias' being introduced into the analysis. For this reason, we use Heckman's two-step estimation procedure. The first-stage probit model includes as the dependent variable an indicator of whether a parcel sold, drawing on data for the universe of vineyards within Napa and Sonoma Counties. The estimated coefficients on the two identifying variables are found to be significantly different from zero with the expected signs. The results indicate that marginal changes in the number of sales within 2 kilometers and the vineyard share of the parcel increase the probability that a vineyard is sold by 0.002 and 0.06, respectively.

From the first stage, we construct the inverse Mill's ratio and include it as a variable in the hedonic price equation. As evidence of sample selection, note the significance of the coefficient on the inverse Mill's ratio (Melino, 1982) in the second-stage hedonic regression — the z-value is 0.031 (Table 2). When the inverse Mill's ratio is omitted from the second-stage model, many of the coefficient estimates are smaller in absolute value and less precisely estimated. The key estimation results of both stages are reproduced in Table 2.

Table 2. Two-stage Heckman estimation results.

Variable name	Coefficient	$P(>\|z\|)$
Vineyard area		
A	−0.006	0.006
A^2	0.00002	0.028
AVA indicator variables		
AVA_1	1.027	0.044
AVA_2	0.796	0.145
AVA_3	1.155	0.028
AVA_4	1.552	0.004
AVA_5	0.969	0.044
AVA_6	−0.602	0.134
AVA_7	−0.534	0.196
AVA_8	−0.041	0.884
AVA_9	0.055	0.831
AVA_{10}	−0.088	0.801
AVA_{11}	−0.489	0.420
AVA_{12}	1.132	0.023
AVA_{13}	−0.931	0.228
AVA_{14}	0.868	0.017
AVA_{15}	0.176	0.676
AVA_{16}	1.417	0.008
AVA_{17}	0.352	0.140
AVA_{18}	0.004	0.990
AVA_{19}	0.338	0.145
AVA_{20}	0.780	0.011
AVA_{21}	1.263	<0.000
AVA_{22}	0.579	0.261
AVA_{23}	0.908	0.002
AVA_{24}	1.125	0.003
AVA_{25}	−0.325	0.467
AVA_{26}	1.716	0.019

Table 2. *(Continued)*

Variable name	**Coefficient**	***P*(>|*z*|)**
Varietals		
V_1	0.899	<0.000
V_2	0.123	0.587
V_3	0.299	0.789
V_4	0.498	0.033
V_5	0.383	0.197
V_6	0.712	0.034
V_7	0.422	0.262
V_8	0.124	0.620
Vineyard aspect		
Asp_1	−0.075	0.885
Asp_2	−1.036	0.082
Asp_3	−0.425	0.409
Asp_4	−0.509	0.299
Asp_5	−0.551	0.557
Asp_6	0.161	0.721
Asp_7	−0.738	0.135
Asp_8	−1.032	0.061
Vineyard elevation		
E_1	−1.203	0.163
E_2	−1.101	0.205
E_3	−1.796	0.042
E_4	−0.807	0.367
E_5	−0.759	0.394
E_6	−1.037	0.309
Vineyard slope		
S_1	−0.476	0.081
S_2	−0.044	0.853
S_3	−0.203	0.357
S_4	2.837	0.001
S_5	−15.542	0.024

(Continued)

Table 2. *(Continued)*

Variable name	Coefficient	$P(>\|z\|)$
Climate variables		
T_1	0.140	0.705
T_2	−0.308	0.406
T_3	0.094	0.646
R_1	−0.003	0.165
R_2	0.098	0.042
Constant	13.3	<0.000
Inverse Mill's ratio	0.286	0.031
Observations	188	
Dependent variable = ln*P*		
Identifying variables in the selection equation		
sale_count	0.044	<0.000
vineyard_share	1.210	<0.000

Results from the Hedonic Price Equation

Beginning with the site characteristics, the results indicate that some factors that would be assumed to contribute to *terroir* are significant, while others are not. In terms of effect of slope, there is a positive price premium for vineyards with a 20 to 30 degree slope (relative to flat ground), but a large negative effect for anything steeper. Although none of the aspect variables is significant, all the elevation variables are negative, with one category (200 to 300 feet) significant at the 5-percent level. Summer average precipitation has a positive and significant effect on vineyard prices, while none of the other climate variables is significant.[12]

Turning to the viticultural area designations, most of the coefficients on the Sub-AVA indicator variables are positive, and nine are significantly different from zero (at the 5-percent confidence level), indicating price premiums for being inside many designated appellations. In seven cases,

[12]In terms of control variables, per-acre vineyard prices are found to decline with parcel size, but at an increasing rate (that is, the effect becomes smaller in absolute value). At the mean of the data, the effect of parcel size is negative. Higher prices for vineyards are associated with those planted in Cabernet Sauvignon, Merlot, and Sauvignon Blanc, with the largest premium for Cabernet Sauvignon.

Table 3. Estimated contribution of sub-AVAs to vineyard prices.

Sub-AVA	**Share of vineyard price**
Alexander	0.093
Atlaspeak	0.000
Bennett	0.000
Calistoga	0.000
Chalkhill	0.005
Coombsville	0.000
Diamond	0.000
Drycreek	0.106
Ftross	0.000
Greenvalley	0.075
Howell	0.015
Knights	0.131
Loscarneros	0.033
Mtveeder	0.000
Oakknoll	0.031
Oakville	0.070
Rutherford	0.107
Springmtn	0.051
Sthelena	0.079
Yountville	0.098
Bennettsonomamtn	0.000
Drycreekrockpile	0.155

the estimated coefficients are negative, but none is significantly different from zero. The largest premiums are for the Knights Valley, Rutherford, and Dry Creek Sub-AVAs. Using the estimated parameters from the hedonic price model, calculated fitted values of the dependent variable provide estimates of the contribution that each Sub-AVA makes to vineyard sales prices (Table 3). These contributions to vineyard prices range from about 0 percent to nearly 16 percent.[13]

[13]The contribution is negative when the coefficient on the Sub-AVA indicator is negative. In these cases, the predicted contribution is set to zero.

Implications of the Results

In trying to sort out the meaning of *terroir* in the New-World context, the question we pose is essentially whether site attributes, AVA designations, or both influence vineyard prices. If site attributes affect wine quality (and if consumers are able to discriminate such quality), then vineyard prices depend on site attributes alone, because AVA designations are redundant. At the other extreme, if site attributes are irrelevant, with vineyard prices being fully explained by AVA designations, then *terroir* matters economically as a concept but not as a fundamental biophysical reality.

Our results support the intermediate case in which geographically based designations and some location-specific biophysical attributes are associated with the sales prices of vineyards. That said, the balance of the evidence supports the key role played by Sub-AVA designations, thereby supporting the notion that in Napa and Sonoma Counties, *terroir* matters economically as a concept but less so as a fundamental biophysical reality.

Conclusion

We have estimated a hedonic model of vineyard prices in one of the premier wine production areas of the New World — northern California's Napa and Sonoma Counties — to examine critically the notion of *terroir*, which plays such an important role in the production and appreciation of Old-World wines from the best locations in Europe. We examine whether Napa and Sonoma vineyard prices vary systematically with designated appellation, after controlling for site attributes.

Using precise measures of site attributes, we find mixed results — namely, that some site attributes have significant effects on vineyard sales prices, but others do not. The fact that some physical characteristics of vineyards are priced implicitly in the land market but others are not raises questions about whether Sub-AVA designations have a meaningful connection in reality with *terroir*. In our earlier study in Oregon, we reach a starker conclusion, finding that only AVA designations explain variation in vineyard prices.

We find more consistent results regarding designated appellations, with vineyard prices strongly affected by whether parcels are inside specific Sub-AVAs. This result indicates that *terroir* matters economically, with buyers and sellers of vineyard parcels in Napa and Sonoma Counties attaching significant premiums to specific designations. This is likely because consumers are willing to pay more for the experience of drinking wines from these areas. As studies using very different methodologies have found, although consumers may not discriminate much among wines in terms of their intrinsic qualities, they do respond to extrinsic attributes of wines, including prices and areas of origin.

In summary, site attributes and AVA designations influence vineyard prices, with estimated coefficients for site attributes measuring how producers value intra-AVA differences in vineyard characteristics. Producers attach premiums to site attributes that enhance wine quality if consumers can perceive and are willing to pay for such quality differences.

Data Appendix

Vineyard Sale Price

A detailed database of vineyard sales was obtained from an appraisal firm specializing in vineyards and wineries (Correia-Xavier, Inc., 2008). The database includes all vineyard sales in Napa and Sonoma Counties between 1991 and 2007. Appraised values are broken out for non-ineyard-related improvements, including residential and agricultural buildings, building site values, and winery permits. Vineyard sales values are obtained by removing any nonvineyard values from total sales prices and deflating to constant 2007 dollars using the Consumer Price Index.

Vineyard Boundaries

Improving on previous studies, we measure site attributes, such as climate, slope, aspect, and elevation, for the planted vineyards within each property instead of across the property as a whole. To obtain vineyard boundaries within sale parcels, we construct a digitized map of the sale parcel boundaries from historical Geographic Information System (GIS) records available at the Napa and Sonoma County Assessors' Offices. Sales are matched to their digitized records using their Assessor Parcel Numbers (APNs) at the time of sale. The parcel map is then overlaid with digitized aerial photographs from county archives taken at or near the date of sale.[14]

[14]Napa County aerial imagery is available for 1993, 2002, and 2003 to 2006 at the 1-meter to 1-foot resolution and 2007 at the 1-foot to 6-inch resolution. Sonoma County images are available for 1993, 2000, and 2004 to 2006. The 2000 Sonoma image provides 1-foot resolution, while all others are at 1-meter resolution.

Vineyard boundaries are identified visually from the aerial images using GIS software (ArcGIS Version 10). Significant roads, driveways, trees, and outbuildings are excluded from vineyard areas.

We also generate a map of vineyard boundaries for all Napa and Sonoma Counties parcels, both sold and unsold. We obtain this census of vineyards by over-laying each county's APN layer with an aerial image, identifying vineyards visually, and delineating in ArcGIS. For this step, the aerial photo layers from 2000 and 2007 provide the best resolution for Sonoma and Napa Counties, respectively. For matching, APN boundary layers from 2000 and 2010 are used for Sonoma and Napa, respectively. A total of 10,323 vineyards is identified.[15]

Vineyard Attributes

Another improvement over previous studies is the measurement of climatic variation across vineyards. Precipitation is measured for the effective growing season (February through September) as well as for the maturation and harvest period (July through September). Daily temperature fluctuation is measured for each month of the maturation and harvest period (July, August, and September). Daily climate observations are obtained from the PRISM Climate Group's 1980–present spatial climate database. Daily averages are calculated over the 10-year period of 1980 to 1989 to prevent overlap with the earliest vineyard sale database record.

Geographic attributes, including slope, aspect, and elevation, are obtained by dividing vineyards into 10-meter pixels and matching each pixel to its corresponding pixel in the National Elevation Dataset (U.S. Geological Survey, 2011). Each vineyard attribute, along with the two parcel-level sample-selection controls, including sales within a 2-kilometer buffer and the proportion of a parcel in vineyards, is calculated within the ArcGIS software environment.

The shares of vineyards located in specific AVAs and Sub-AVAs are determined by overlaying the vineyard boundary maps with digitized Sub-AVA maps for Napa and Sonoma Counties in ArcGIS. Public copies of the digitized AVA maps are made available by the two counties.

[15]In the case of a tax lot (APN) boundary change between 2007 and 2010, the delay between Napa's aerial photo date and APN layer date could result in a particular vineyard's belonging in one APN in 2007 but showing up in a different parcel in 2010. This seems unlikely, however, because APN reshaping is infrequent. Such a change is not expected to have a meaningful impact on the results.

Acknowledgements

The authors are grateful to data scientists at Watershed Sciences who donated their time for aerial image matching and meticulous vineyard-boundary digitization. Thanks are also due to Orley Ashenfelter, Victor Ginsburgh, Karl Storchmann, and two anonymous reviewers for their very helpful comments. All remaining errors are the responsibility of the authors.

References

Alcohol and Tobacco Tax and Trade Bureau. (2012). *American Vinicultural Area (AVA) Manual for Petitioners*. TTB P 5120.4. Washington, DC: Author.

Ashenfelter, O. and K. Storchmann. (2010). "Using hedonic models of solar radiation and weather to assess the economic effect of climate change: The case of Mosel Valley vineyards." *Review of Economics and Statistics*. **92**(2): 333–349.

Environmental Systems Research Institute. (2012). "ArcGIS (Version 10) [Computer Software]." Redlands, CA: Author. Retrieved from http://www.esri.com.

Castriota, S. and M. Delmastro. (2015). "The economics of collective reputation: Evidence from the wine industry." *American Journal of Agricultural Economics*. **97**(2): 469–489.

Correia-Xavier, Inc. (2008). "Winery and vineland sales." Retrieved on February 6, 2008, from http://www.c-x.com.

Costanigro, M., J. J. McCluskey, and C. Goemans. (2015). "The economics of nested names: Name specificity, reputations, and price premia." *American Journal of Agricultural Economics*. **92**(5): 1339–1350.

Cross, R., A. J. Plantinga, and R. N. Stavins. (2011a). "The value of terroir: Hedonic estimation of vineyard sale prices." *Journal of Wine Economics*. **6**(1): 1–14.

Cross, R., A. J. Plantinga, and R. N. Stavins. (2011b). "What is the value of terroir?" *American Economic Review Papers and Proceedings*. **101**(3): 152–156.

Gergaud, O. and V. Ginsburgh. (2010). "Natural endowments, production technologies and the quality of wines in Bordeaux: Does terroir matter?" *Economic Journal*. **118**: F142–F157.

Gergaud, O., A. J. Plantinga, and A. Ringeval-Deluze. (2017). "Anchored in the past: Persistent price effects of obsolete vineyard ratings in France." *Journal of Economic Behavior and Organization*. **133**: 39–51.

Goldstein, R., J. Almenberg, A. Dreber, J. W. Emerson, A. Herschkowitsch, and J. Katz. (2008). "Do more expensive wines taste better? Evidence from a large sample of blind tastings." *Journal of Wine Economics*. **3**(1): 1–9.

Heckman, J. J. (1979). "Sample selection bias as a specification error." *Econometrica*. **47**(1): 153–161.

Matthews, M. and M. Anderson. (1989). "Reproductive development in grape (Vitis vinifera L.): Responses to seasonal water deficits." *American Journal of Enology and Viticulture*. **40**(1): 52–60.

Melino, A. (1982). "Testing for selection bias." *Review of Economic Studies*. **49**(1): 151–153.

Natural Resource Conservation Service. (2016). "Web soil survey." United States Department of Agriculture. Retrieved on April 28, 2016, from https://websoilsurvey.sc.egov.usda.gov/.

PRISM Climate Group. (n.d.). "Spatial climate datasets for the contiguous United States." Retrieved from http://prism.oregonstate.edu.

Robinson, J. (2006). *The Oxford Companion to Wine*, 3rd ed. Oxford, UK: Oxford University Press.

Schlenker, W. and M. J. Roberts. (2009). "Nonlinear temperature effects indicate severe damages to U.S. crop yields under climate change." *Proceedings of the National Academy of Sciences*. **106**(37): 15594–15598.

Severen, C., Costello, C., & Deschenes, O. (2016). *A Forward Looking Ricardian Approach: Do Land Markets Capitalize Climate Change Forecasts? Technical Report*. Cambridge, MA: National Bureau of Economic Research.

U.S. Geological Survey. (2011). "The national elevation dataset." Retrieved from http://nationalmap.gov/3dep_prodserv.html.

Veale, R. and P. Quester. (2008). "Consumer sensory evaluations of wine quality: The respective influence of price and country of origin." *Journal of Wine Economics*. **3**(1): 10–29.

Vella, F. (1998). "Estimating models with sample selection bias: A survey." *Journal of Human Resources*. **33**(1): 127–169.

https://doi.org/10.1142/9789811292415_0028

Chapter 28

Film Review: Jason Wise, Somm*

Robert N. Stavins

John F. Kennedy School of Government, Harvard University, Cambridge, MA, USA

Resources for the Future, Washington, DC, USA

National Bureau of Economic Research, Cambridge, MA, USA

robert_stavins@harvard.edu

JASON WISE (Director), Somm, written by Jason Wise. First Run Features, 2013, 94 minutes.

There is no point in hiding the headline: Somm, a new film written and directed by Jason Wise, is the best movie about the world of wine since Sideways. One was a work of fiction, and the other is a documentary, but both beautifully capture the passion that characterizes so many wine people — whether amateurs who love drinking wine (Miles and Maya in Sideways), or professionals who love producing and serving it (the sommeliers, chefs, and wine makers who populate Somm). Both films made me laugh; and both films made me cry. With Somm, the production values are so high, the cinematography so beautiful, and the music so evocative that you will forget at times that this is a documentary.

---

*This chapter was originally published in *Journal of Wine Economics*, **8**, 238–241, 2013. doi:10.1017/jwe.2013.30.

Somm is slang for sommelier, the wine professional typically found in fine restaurants. The sommelier — or wine director — is responsible for all aspects of wine service, with particular expertise in wine and food pairing. But some of the most important responsibilities of the best sommeliers are not in the front of the house, but behind the scenes: wine list development, wine procurement, storage, and cellar rotation, as well as staff training. In the film's introduction, Chef Michael Mina describes sommeliers as "the new rock-stars of the industry."

The storyline follows a group of four thirty-something men, three of whom live with their respective wives and girlfriends in San Francisco, and are working as sommeliers in various establishments: Brian McClintic, an affable former baseball player and screenwriter; DLynn Proctor, an intense and self-confident professional; Dustin Wilson, a young man who exudes modesty and warmth, and moved from Montagna at The Little Nell in Aspen to RN74 in San Francisco, with its Burgundy rich wine list; and Ian Cauble, whose life has been dedicated to wine since college, is remarkably knowledgeable about wine, and has an incredible nose and palate for tasting.

As the film opens, each has already been celebrated as one of the best young, up-and-coming sommeliers in the country, and each has gone through significant wine education, having achieved the first three levels of their professional association's certification: Level I (Introductory), Level II (Certified Sommelier), and Level III (Advanced Sommelier). Each now aspires to join the Court of Master Sommeliers, the absolute pinnacle of the profession, a level achieved by only 200 people globally over half a century.

Becoming a Master Sommelier requires passing a three-day exam that is offered only once per year and covers three components: theory, service, and blind tasting. On average, candidates sit for the exam two to three times, and some take it as many as six times. One has three years to pass all three parts. If that is not accomplished, one has to start from scratch. (As Jancis Robinson wrote in her autobiography, Tasting Pleasures: Confessions of a Wine Lover, which I reviewed in this journal in 2007, she was the first person outside of the wine trade to pass the exam.)

Every Master Sommelier interviewed in the film says that the exam was the hardest thing they have ever done in their life. Ian is clearly regarded by the other three (and by the film's writer/director) as the one most likely to succeed at this most challenging of tests. The three sommeliers signify their respect by calling him, "Dad."

The film follows their days, weeks, and months — indeed years — of preparation for the Master Sommelier exam, and finally follows them from San Francisco to Dallas where the exam is to be given. Ian candidly acknowledges that "every moment of my life has been how am I going to prepare for this exam." Separately, his girlfriend confirms that "the most important thing in his life is wine, then family, and then me."

Mixed with the main thread of the foursome preparing for the exam are interviews with other sommeliers and vintners about a variety of topics, ranging from the history of wine production in Europe to techniques of viticulture and oenology. Talking heads quickly fade, their words illustrated by scenes that will warm any wine-lover's heart, ranging from the gate at Romanee Conti to a hillside castle in Rheingau, Germany, where the cellar master lovingly pulls out a bottle of 1735 Schloss Johannisberg Riesling.

The film begins with three weeks remaining before the exam, for which the four men have been preparing for well over a year. One of the many characters featured along the way is Fred Dame, the first American to pass the exam, who did so in 1964 in the United Kingdom, and subsequently brought the exam and the system to the United States. We watch as he, along with other Master Sommeliers, help the four young men prepare.

The best I could come up with when trying to relate my life experiences to this was to think back to graduate school, thirty years ago, when I was working with my study group at the end of our first year of the Harvard Ph.D. program in economics, studying together to prepare for the "general examinations" that are the culmination of the first year. But, as intense and stressful as that was, it was nothing like this.

Likewise, the four men's obsessive use of flash cards — day and night — to memorize the most obscure wine facts in preparation for the theory component of the exam reminded me of my experience decades ago teaching myself a tribal language when living in West Africa, but each of these guys has prepared thousands of cards; indeed, Dustin mentions that he has over four thousand!

It is the scenes of the foursome preparing for the blind-tasting component of the exam that will probably be most gripping for the readers of this journal. In the exam, one is presented with six wines — three whites and three reds — and a total of 25 minutes to describe for each: the wine's structure, body, alcohol, climate, varietal(s), precise geographic location, and vintage.

Why does blind tasting matter? Various people in the film argue that such blind ("deductive") tasting increases and improves one's perception. One travels along a road, then it forks, choose a path, then it forks again, choose a path, and eventually the taster arrives at the wine. Ian swirls and sniffs a glass, and then in rapid succession rattles off: "This wine is from the old world. This wine is from France. This wine is from the Rhone Valley. This wine is from the northern Rhone. This wine is St. Joseph. This wine is from 2008." Along the way, the scents discussed range from comparing fresh violet (a young Nebiolo) with dried violet (an old Nebiolo), to the much more esoteric, such as a freshly opened can of tennis balls versus a new garden hose!

Why all this exhaustive preparation for the exam? The answer comes from an analogy provided by one Master Sommelier. "Who will be a great maker of samurai swords? It will be someone who had a great teacher, who had a great teacher, who had a great teacher." So, it is with the best sommeliers. It is not a natural talent, but a learned skill. But anyone who is familiar with academic studies of tasting results, and is skeptical of the ability of professionals, let alone others, to consistently identify wines and rank their quality, will find support for their skepticism in several dramatic and key scenes in Somm.

Two-thirds of the way through the 93 minutes of Somm, Brian, DLynn, Dustin, and Ian each makes his way to the exam locale in Dallas, Texas. Fifty people will sit for the exam. We learn later that six will pass.

Watching them holed up in their respective hotel rooms, continuing to cram days before the exams are to begin brought forth memories of another film, forty years ago — the young 1Ls (first-year students) of Harvard Law School cramming in a Cambridge hotel room for their final exams in The Paper Chase, the 1973 film based on John Jay Osborn Jr.'s novel.

Finally, with 20 minutes left in Somm, the exams begin for Brian, DLynn, Dustin, and Ian. The tension matches that found in the best suspense film. With 5 minutes left, each of the four learns the results, and we — as viewers — are present in the room with each as they learn their fate.

* * *

My wife and I arrived for a dinner in Manhattan we had been looking forward to for months. We had canceled our reservation at *per se*, so that we could experience Eleven Madison Park, the Three Michelin Star and New York Times Four Star restaurant that has been ranked as one of the five best restaurants anywhere in the world.

Maitre D'Zach Fischer guided us through the sixteen-course tasting menu prepared brilliantly by Chef Daniel Humm. The menu and execution were sublime, the paired wines were fascinating even for a jaded collector, and the service was absolutely impeccable. Each and every course involved elaborate theater of presentation, was beautiful to behold, and was flavorful beyond words.

The wines? Each was brought to us and lovingly described by Eleven Madison Park's wine director, Dustin Wilson, one of the four young men from Somm. His lapel clearly featured the small Sommelier pin, the color of which signifies the respective level of achievement: Certified Sommelier, purple; Advanced Sommelier, green; and Court of the Master Sommeliers, red. Dustin's pin is small, but its color is vivid. To discover the hue, please see the movie, or have dinner at Eleven Madison Park. Neither will soon be forgotten.

https://doi.org/10.1142/9789811292415_0029

Chapter 29

Film Review*: David Roach and Warwick Ross, Red Obsession

Robert N. Stavins

John F. Kennedy School of Government, Harvard University, Cambridge, MA, USA

Resources for the Future, Washington, DC, USA

National Bureau of Economic Research, Cambridge, MA, USA

robert_stavins@harvard.edu

DAVID ROACH and WARWICK ROSS (Directors): *Red Obsession*. Written by David Roach and Warwick Ross. Lion Rock Films, 2013, 75 minutes.

What begins as a documentary about the production of premium red wine in Bordeaux evolves into a treatise on the global economics of the industry. For readers of this journal, the lovingly photographed history of wine production in *Red Obsession* will be entertaining, if not enlightening; but the assessment of the global economics of wine production and consumption will be trivial and quite possibly annoying. So, even if not a feast for the mind, the film is a treat for the senses, with credit going to cinematographers Steve Arnold and Lee Pulbrook and composer Burkhard von Dallwitz.

*This chapter was originally published in *Journal of Wine Economics*, **8**(3), 355–360, 2013. doi:10.1017/jwe.2013.037.

The first half of the film is filled with lovely panoramas of the five Premiers Crus estates of Bordeaux — Haut-Brion, Lafite-Rothschild, Latour, Margaux, and Mouton Rothschild — plus interviews with some of the towering figures of contemporary Bordeaux. The scenes will be familiar to oenophiles but welcome for their beauty. Likewise, the interviews provide little new information for wine aficionados, but it's a treat nonetheless to hear directly from winemakers such as Christian Moueix (who oversees production at Château Pétrus, among other estates) and proprietors such as Corinne Mentzelopoulos (now the sole shareholder of Château Margaux). Soon, natural scenes of vineyards are interspersed with scenes of the key commerce that occurs during "en primeur" week in Bordeaux.

One can only be impressed that the writers/directors David Roach and Warwick Ross were able to gain access to the region's key players. Apparently, Roach and Ross had to spend six months just convincing some of them to talk, after they felt they had been burned by the 2004 documentary *Mondovino*, which portrayed the Bordeaux elite as villains.

Without explanation for the general audiences for whom the film is intended, the film focuses almost exclusively on a single, very special segment of the world of red wine: the Premiers Crus of Bordeaux. These same audiences may be pleased that the film is narrated by actor Russell Crowe, despite the fact that somewhat ironically he recently portrayed a London financial trader who is aggressively disdainful of French wine culture in the (very loose) film adaptation of Peter Mayle's novel *A Good Year*.

Halfway through the film, we learn that traditional Bordeaux markets in the United States and the United Kingdom are weakening, and that a robust new market for premium Bordeaux is developing in China. Much of the second half of the film is essentially an examination of contemporary Chinese character, ambition, and taste. The focus is on the richest of the rich. With an estimated 600 (US dollar) billionaires in the new, post-Mao China (and presumably many thousands of millionaires), a market has exploded for the greatest wines of Bordeaux. One wealthy Chinese industrialist, who has made his fortune manufacturing sex toys, has a collection worth $60 million, with bottles of Lafite-Rothschild scattered throughout his house.

Interviews with wine critics, journalists, and winemakers reveal the way the industry works, how demand exceeds supply, how the weather determines yield and quality, and how the prices of the likes of Margaux and Lafite-Rothschild are set. Of course, all of this is a textbook example of what all budding economics students learn in their first year — the laws of supply and demand. Supply of the first growths of Bordeaux is limited. Even with a season of ideal rainfall and perfect temperatures, there is only so much wine that can be produced. Higher prices may cause Louis Vuitton to make more purses and Maserati more GranTurismi, but Latour will not expand its output. Supply of these brands is infinitely inelastic.

As for demand for the best of Bordeaux, it is rapidly increasing. As China's economy has grown at breathtaking rates in recent years, so too has demand for luxury goods. China is now the world's largest importer of fine wine from Bordeaux. Robust and rising demand, combined with inelastic supply: an obvious recipe for price escalation. If only the film had explained that clearly and simply.

However, the film does provide a hint — although no more than a hint — of why the prices of the first growths have increased so dramatically relative to the prices of other classified Bordeaux. This comes from the film's extended discussion of Chinese character, ambition, and taste. One observer after another comments on the Chinese fascination with labels and brands. Combine this with the emergence of China's billionaire and millionaire *nouveaux riches*, and the result is dramatically increased demand for the top tier of luxury-good brands, in particular, for collectibles — whether paintings by French Impressionists or classic wines by Lafite Rothschild.

The film reminds us that a Chinese proverb says, "Remember to dig the well before you are thirsty." So, in addition to being important and growing Bordeaux consumers, Chinese entrepreneurs are now trying to become meaningful competitors, as they seriously invest in their own wine-making efforts, with wineries that may not produce the best wines but are built to resemble the great châteaux of Bordeaux.

https://doi.org/10.1142/9789811292415_0030

Chapter 30

Film Review[*]: David Kennard, A Year in Burgundy

Robert N. Stavins

John F. Kennedy School of Government, Harvard University, Cambridge, MA, USA

Resources for the Future, Washington, DC, USA

National Bureau of Economic Research, Cambridge, MA, USA

robert_stavins@harvard.edu

DAVID KENNARD (Director): *A Year in Burgundy*. Written by David Kennard. InCA Productions, 2013, 91 minutes.

Imagine driving through a lovely, bucolic setting on the road from Mâcon to Dijon through picturesque vineyards north of Chalon-sur-Sâone. You lean back to enjoy the view, thinking about the superb wines produced from these tiny, garden-sized properties by dedicated vignerons. And then your focus, your reflections, and indeed your pleasure are shattered by unnecessary chatter — the annoying verbal commentary delivered by your guide. That mixed bag captures the beauty, the interest, and the limitation of this new film from producer, director, and writer David Kennard, who, it should be said, has built a remarkably diverse portfolio of

[*]This chapter was originally published in *Journal of Wine Economics*, **9**(1), 100–107, 2014. doi:10.1017/jwe.2014.5. © American Association of Wine Economists.

documentaries over his 30-year career, ranging from natural science (Carl Sagan's acclaimed PBS series *Cosmos* and the superb BBC series *Connections* with James Burke) to the performing arts (*Keeping Score*, with Michael Tilson Thomas).

As academics, we are trained to lay out for the reader our theory, the facts, our analysis, and our conclusions in clear, concise language. But in creative writing, the best authors describe situations and the words and thoughts of characters, but never tell the reader what conclusions to draw or what emotions to feel. The same difference is found in dramatic films, with second-rate Hollywood movies making everything absolutely explicit, virtually telling the audience what to think and feel, while the best films provide no more than building blocks upon which members of the audience can develop their own thoughts and feelings. With documentary films, this distinction can also be key. Some of the best documentaries provide no more than pictorial, musical, and verbal inspiration, leaving the audience to come to its own conclusions (see my recent review of *Somm* in *Journal of Wine Economics*, 8(2), pp. 238–241).

In *A Year in Burgundy*, the narrator speaks too often and tells us too much. For example, it would have been effective to allow the film's scenes, interviews, and conversations to inspire in the viewer the recognition that the best winemakers of Burgundy are true artisans, perhaps even artists. Instead, the narrator states flatly, as in a lecture, that "the greatest winemakers are artists." And this is in the first minute of the movie!

The film focuses on Martine Saunier, a French-born, California-based wine importer. We follow her over the course of a challenging year (2011) in Burgundy as she meets with five client producers in their vineyards and wineries in Burgundy. When we first observe her, she is celebrated by the narrator in glowing terms, which struck me as perhaps a bit excessive for a wine importer and distributor. But I came to find the characterization particularly annoying by the end of the film, when I learned that she (together with David Kennnard) was the film's senior producer.

Saunier's first job after college was in marketing, and it shows. Is it unfair of me to note that we are not told in the film that Madame Saunier sold her wine-importing business, Martine's Wines, in 2012 or that the lovely family home that has "been in her family for centuries," where we first see her climbing into her Citroën Deux Chevaux to visit her growers, has in fact been converted to a B&B by her brother?

With Martine, we visit (from south to north): Dominique Cornin in the Mâconnais of southern Burgundy; Michel Gay and Domaine

Morey-Coffinet in Côte de Beaune; and Bruno Clavelier, Christophe Perrot-Minot, and Domaine Leroy, who have vineyards in the Côte de Nuits.

The film begins in the spring, when Martine visits Domaine Morey-Coffinet with its proprietor Michel Morey, who runs the business with his son, Thibault. Michel explains, "I think no one has a particular gift at the start. As little children, we grow up surrounded by vines and wine cellars, by fathers and grandfathers who talk about wine, and the aromas and the tannins. I think that even as a little child, even if you don't taste it, you start to get a feeling for wine quite quickly. By the age of five or six, Thibault could identify different wines by their smell." Thibault responds, "When I was young, it was my passion. I only went to school because I had to. When I came home, I joined my parents in the vineyards and the cellars." No narration is necessary to frame or explain the message.

As summer arrives, we travel to the best region for Pinot noir — the Côte de Nuits, north of Beaune — visiting vineyards in the hills just above Vosne-Romanée and learning about the rocky soils and unique microclimate of a small closed valley. Gradually, the incredible diversity of the terroir of Burgundy begins to emerge: 400 different wines produced in the single village of Chassagne Montrachet.

But most rewarding is the time that we spend with Madame Lalou Bize-Leroy, owner and proprietor of Domaine Leroy. At the time, she was 79 years old (or "young" in her case, as the cliché goes). She is youthful and enthusiastic, and her backstory is an interesting one, though unfortunately left out of the film. Born in 1932 as Marcelle Leroy, she established herself as a businesswoman in the Burgundy wine business in the 1950s, when she took over the négociant business of her father, Henri Leroy. Beginning in 1974, she was co-managing director of Domaine de la Romanée-Conti (DRC). Along with Aubert de Villaine, she was credited with helping to build DRC, but a series of disagreements, including apparently her displeasure at de Villaine's involvement in the "Judgment of Paris" wine tasting, led to her ouster in 1992.

After leaving DRC, Madame Lalou focused on her family's properties, and built the holdings, excellence, and reputation of Domaine Leroy. Like the others in the film, she is a hands-on producer, carefully supervising each and every stage of growth, harvest, and production. Listening to her speak in the film — gently yet passionately — about the lives of her vines and her absolute dedication to biodynamic farming methods, I was reminded of listening several years ago to another master grower and vigneron, thousands of miles away: Christophe Baron, the exceptionally talented Frenchman who has been producing his magnificent Cayuse wines in Walla Walla, Washington, since 1997.

About halfway through the film, it is fall, at the time of harvest. The narrator states that the harvest is difficult because of the possibility of impending rain; however, the light music accompanying this commentary does not convey tension but, rather, a carefree mood, as student pickers move through the vineyards. When the narrator announces, "There's tension in the air," it has precisely the opposite effect, because we as viewers have not felt the tension. What a contrast with *Somm*, in which the viewer clearly sensed the stress felt by that documentary's main characters: four young men preparing for an exam to join the Court of Master Sommeliers.

Ironically, among the most beautiful scenes in the film — in terms of pure aesthetics — are the landscapes following harvest, after the grapes are gone and the leaves of the vines begin to die, going from subtle shades of yellow to bright red. These scenes, with vineyards in the foreground, the village behind, and a hillside behind, look like a painter's intoxicant. If we squint just a bit, it is not difficult to imagine a landscape by Claude Monet before our eyes.

As winter arrives, we move from the open and public process of harvest to the closed and very private, even confidential process of winemaking. Every vigneron has his or her own methods, including a wide range of approaches just for punching down the grapes inside the vats to maximize extraction. Down in the cellars, the wines are now in barrels, sometimes topped up once per week to avoid exposure to air due to ongoing evaporation. Then comes *battonage,* the gentle stirring of the wine in barrels to mix the sediment with the liquid, a couple of times a week if the wine is too acidic.

Then, as scenes of automated bottling fill the screen, a winemaker laments, "Burgundy wines ought to be all different, but science now allows us to make wines that are all the same. That's a pity — they all used to have their own character, like human beings. Progress is pushing all of us to make the same kind of wine." This comment, which may be accurate, does not square with what we have otherwise seen and heard in the film, leaving me to wonder, has Burgundy too been "Parkerized"?

Suddenly, the scene moves 4,000 miles westward, to Blackberry Farm, an intimate luxury hotel and resort located on a pastoral 4,200-acre estate in the Great Smoky Mountains of Tennessee. An affluent group of friends meets in the wine cellar to enjoy glasses of Burgundy, including some of the same wines that we have followed during the year, albeit samples from earlier vintages. It turns out, of course, that the evening is hosted by Martine Saunier. She introduces Thibault Morey — strange to see him well-dressed and thousands of miles away from his father's Burgundy property. Then, it's upstairs for dinner, presumably with one of Martine's wines paired with each course.

At the conclusion, we are transported back to Burgundy, and amid the barren scene of old vines, cloudy skies, and cold weather, the families begin to prune their vines. They burn the dead wood in the field in the midst of the rows, just as they have been doing for hundreds of years. And, as the narrator inevitably reminds us, "there are lots of things they do in Burgundy that they have been doing for hundreds of years." In a few months, the first signs of spring will arrive, and then it will be another year in Burgundy.

A Year in Burgundy is the first in a series of documentaries on fine wine forthcoming from director David Kennard. He has just completed *A Year in Champagne*. I will certainly watch his new film, because I expect it to be beautiful and informative, but I hope there will be less narration, and more reliance on the film's characters and scenes, and thereby more trust in its audience. Less can, indeed, be more.

https://doi.org/10.1142/9789811292415_0031

Chapter 31

Film Review: Rudi Goldman: Burgundy: People with a Passion for Wine*

Robert N. Stavins

John F. Kennedy School of Government, Harvard University, Cambridge, MA, USA

Resources for the Future, Washington, DC, USA

National Bureau of Economic Research, Cambridge, MA, USA

robert_stavins@harvard.edu

RUDI GOLDMAN (Director/Producer): *Burgundy: People with a Passion for Wine*. Media in English/Rudi Goldman Productions, Amsterdam, 2017, 60 min, DVD NTSC Format, all Regions, $19.95.

The best documentaries — on any subject — are informative, entertaining, and even touching. Think of Ken Burns's PBS series, *The Civil War*, or — in the realm of oenonomy — Jason Wise's *Somm* (reviewed, volume 8, 2013, pp. 238–241). Rudi Goldman's new film, *Burgundy: People with a Passion for Wine*, meets at least the first two requirements, which are necessary, if not sufficient conditions for documentary film excellence.

*This chapter was originally published in *Journal of Wine Economics*, **13**(2018): 105–108. doi:10.1017/jwe.2018.5.

Goldman's film surpasses another recent documentary about the Burgundy wine scene, David Kennard's *A Year in Burgundy* (reviewed, volume 9, 2014, pp. 100–103). Both offer high-quality cinematography, beautiful to view from a Blu-ray disc on a large-format, high-definition display. But whereas Kennard employed a ponderous narrator to tell his viewers what to think, Wise and now Goldman trust their respective audiences to come to their own conclusions, stimulated by the pictorial, musical, and verbal inspiration the films provide.

One reason we do not miss the presence of a narrator in *Burgundy* is that several of the film's dozen talking heads — all winemakers *and* wine lovers — are both articulate and insightful. It is fortuitous that we can benefit repeatedly from the thoughts of an American, Alex Gambal, who left the world of real estate decades ago to explore Burgundy, and after attending the adult viticultural school in Beaune, launched Maison Alex Gambal in 1997. His Pinot Noir grapes range from those sourced from Grand Cru vineyards in Charmes-Chambertin and Batard-Montrachet, to Premier Cru, and more modest Communal and Regional bottlings.

In a striking segment that will be of particular interest to readers of this *Journal*, Gambal describes what he calls "the irony" of Burgundy. Only two cépages may be grown and vinified in the region — Pinot Noir and Chardonnay; and the Appellation d'Origine Contrôlée (AOC) rules on planting, growing, harvesting, vinification, and bottling are exceptionally severe. Yet, these constraints, this discipline leads to the production of celebrated products — the Grand Cru and Premier Cru wines of Burgundy.

We are reminded of the discipline that is provided by a musical form, such as a Baroque trio sonata (or — for that matter — by an academic discipline, which may limit scope and acceptable methodology, and thereby lead to rigor and insight). Gambal laments those who operate within the discipline of Burgundy, possess a superb instrument (their particular terroir), but due to their lack of skill or temperament, fail to produce a product that measures up. They possess a Stradivarius, but play it like a fiddle.

Of course, this raises the ongoing issue of the relative importance of terroir versus the skill and dedication of the winemaker in the winery. To some degree, Gambal's critique flies in the face of conventional wisdom. For many years, it has been accepted that terroir is the greater determinant of quality in old world wines (hence, the convention of naming wines by their location), while there has been considerable doubt about this in the case of new world wines (hence, the convention of naming wines by varietal).[1]

[1] An econometric analysis of this debate can be found in this *Journal* (Cross, Plantinga, and Stavins, 2011, 2017).

A somewhat different — and distinctly French — take on the Burgundian irony is offered by Jacques Lardière, retired head winemaker of Maison Louis Jadot in Beaune. Reflecting on how the combination of excellent terroir married with the constraints of the AOC system can produce such a sublime product, he concludes with a mischievous smile, "C'est magique."

The person with the second-most air time in *Burgundy* is not only interesting, but charming — Véronique Drouhin-Boss, the fourth-generation winemaker of Maison Joseph Drouhin in Beaune (as well as Domaine Drouhin in the Dundee Hills of Oregon). She takes us into the 11th century cellar, where she played as a small child, and opens a series of bottles, beginning with a Chardonnay — the Maison's Clos des Mouches, from a vineyard purchased by her grandfather. Tasting this Premier Cru, she is captured by the nose of the young wine, and reflects with us on how the nose will evolve as the wine matures. Later, we return to her cellar to taste the superb 2009 vintage of Joseph Drouhin Chambolle-Musigny and Gevrey-Chambertin.

That Burgundy produces excellent vintages perhaps no more than once per decade is a consequence of its climate. The weather is a significant challenge, with its short growing season at 47 degrees latitude (albeit with many sunny days). The consequence and drama of the stochastic relationship between climate and weather is brought home through our experience of a hail storm, which lasts only four minutes, yet results in the loss of 50 percent of the year's crop!

In this world, dedicated small-scale vignerons (owner-grower-winemakers) continue to operate. Sixty-year old Bernadette Ecobichon, sitting in her modest home in Meursault, aspires to maintain her family's long tradition of excellence. In Puligny-Montrachet, each sub-area is incredibly small, ranging from one hectare to 10 hectares (and totaling no more than 25 hectares). From this terroir come wines that age gracefully for 30 years or more, such as in Chassagne-Montrachet, where Philippe Duvernay, the winemaker and co-owner of Domaine Coffinet-Duvernay, uses his pipette to extract and taste a sample of the young wine, aging slowly in oak barrels.

Those barrels are also a key part of the creation of the wines of Burgundy, and we are privileged to visit one of the most renowned of all cooperage — Tonnellerie François Frères in Saint-Romain, where we go through the process from sawmill to final toast, guided by Romain Schneider (who insists, of course, on the complete superiority of French to American oak!).

Like most wines, those of Burgundy are best enjoyed when dining, and fortunately there is abundant opportunity for good pairings throughout the film. We stop at Le Charlemagne, where Laurent Peugeot, the chef/owner of a Michelin-starred restaurant in Pernand-Vergelesses, emphasizes that just as every small part of Burgundy differs in regard to wine, so too with regard to cuisine. At Château de Santenay, we join a dinner for winemakers, where Jérôme Brochot, Michelin-starred chef/owner in Montceau-les-Mines, explains his thought process for pairing wines with a meal. And Olivier Leflaive, the winemaker and owner of Maison d'Olivier Leflaive, sits at a table in his restaurant in Puligny-Montrachet, and explains the importance of balance, which for him means that "the best wedding between the wine and the food" must be executed with "finesse and elegance."

What is a French wine documentary without some visits to the banquets that are such a large part of the wine scene in that country? We visit the Palais des Congrès de Beaune for the Great Burgundy Wine Festival, a three-day event of tasting during wine auction weekend. Three thousand different wines are tasted!

A visit to the Hospices de Beaune provides an opportunity for retired winemaker Roland Masse to taste the 2013 vintage in barrels and predict how it will taste in two to ten years. This leads to the November 2012 auction, the 152nd such annual auction for charity for the local hospital. It is important each year, because it is the first presentation of the harvest.

Finally, at Château de Meursault, we join La Paulée de Meursault, a dinner with abundant wine for winemakers and invited lovers of Burgundy from around the world. The wines are poured by the winemakers themselves for the 800 assembled guests. Here we see many of the winemakers we met earlier in the film, now sitting for dinner or standing to pour their wines. Remarkably, one invited guest, Anthony Hanson, British Master of Wine and senior consultant to Christie's, proceeds to swirl, sniff, … and then pour his entire glass into a spit bucket *without* so much as putting the wine to his lips. The winemaker is crushed, but so it is in the real world.

Overall, the film's testimony to the people who have a very special passion for the wines of Burgundy reminds me of a high-point in Alexander Payne's feature film, *Sideways* (reviewed, volume 1, May 2006, pp. 91–93), when Maya (Virginia Madsen) asks Miles (Paul Giamatti) why he is so enamored with Pinot Noir. He responds with a memorable statement that might have been uttered by any of the real-life characters in *Burgundy*:

> It's a hard grape to grow. ... It's thin-skinned, temperamental, ripens early. It's not a survivor like Cabernet that can grow anywhere and thrive even when neglected. Pinot needs constant care and attention and in fact can only grow in specific little tucked-away corners of the world. And only the most patient and nurturing growers can do it really, can tap into Pinot's most fragile, delicate qualities. Only when someone has taken the time to truly understand its potential can Pinot be coaxed into its fullest expression. And when that happens, its flavors are the most haunting and brilliant and subtle and thrilling and ancient on the planet.

Near the end of *Burgundy*, New York sommelier Michael Madrigale (recently of the Boulud restaurant empire), is one of the guests at La Paulée de Meursault. Clearly in love with the wines, the cuisine, and the passion that permeates the luncheon, he turns to the camera and confesses that each year "there's something magnetic about Burgundy that brings you here." Enough said, except for some personal advice, based on my own experience with the film. Make sure you have a good bottle of Burgundy available in your cellar — perhaps a Premier Cru, if not a Grand Cru — that you can open and enjoy, as I did, with the film or shortly thereafter. You will not regret it.

References

Cross, R., A. J. Plantinga, and R. N. Stavins. (2011). "The value of terroir: Hedonic estimation of vineyard sale prices." *Journal of Wine Economics*. **6**(1): 1–14.

Cross, R., A. J. Plantinga, and R. N. Stavins. (2017). "Terroir in the New World: Hedonic estimation of vineyard sale prices in California." *Journal of Wine Economics*. **6**(1): 267–281.

https://doi.org/10.1142/9789811292415_0032

Chapter 32

Book Review: Gert Crum and Jan Bartelsman: Le Domaine de la Romanée-Conti*

Robert N. Stavins

John F. Kennedy School of Government, Harvard University, Cambridge, MA, USA

Resources for the Future, Washington, DC, USA

National Bureau of Economic Research, Cambridge, MA, USA

robert_stavins@harvard.edu

When I first opened the package containing this massive volume about the fabled Domaine de la Romané-Conti (known by oeneophiles around the world as DRC), my first thought was the episode of *Seinfeld*, first aired in 1994, in which Kramer promotes on *Live with Regis and Kathie Lee* a new book he has written — a coffee table book about coffee tables. The book has folding legs on its back cover, so that the book itself becomes a coffee table. Kramer's book was small compared with this new offering by Gert Crum, with stunning photography by Jan Bartelsman. At considerably more than a foot high and nearly a foot wide, and weighing in at close to

*This chapter was originally published in *Journal of Wine Economics*, **14**(2019), 224-227. doi:10.1017/jwe.2019.22.
Brewed at the Benedictine Brewery of Mount Angel Abbey in Oregon.

10 pounds (and priced quite modestly at 100 Euros), this book could well function as a respectable coffee table in many a Manhattan apartment!

This luxurious version with updated text and new photography is the latest revision of Crum's award-winning 2005 treatise. This is not a reference book *per se*, if for no other reason than its dimensions and heft preclude one keeping it anywhere other than on a large living room coffee table. Rather, it is a compendium of well-written essays plus stunning photographs that together tell the story of this most remarkable domaine, beginning nearly 800 years ago when the Abbey of Saint Vivant acquired four and a half acres of vineyards in Vosne, known as Cru de Clos. Apparently the monks were too immersed in prayer to have time to cultivate the vineyards, so they leased the property to others. In the 17th century, the de Croonembourg family obtained the land through marriage, and named it La Romanée, but for reasons that have never been documented.

In 1760, André de Croonembourg sold the domaine to Louis François I de Bourbon, the Prince of Conti. Two years later, the Prince added his own name to the vineyard; henceforth Romanée-Conti. This may have revealed some degree of narcissism, but the Prince was clearly a devout hedonist and lover of the grape, as he refused to sell any of the wine produced, keeping it all for his household consumption!

Over the subsequent hundred years, the Romanée-Conti vineyard was sold from one family to another until Jacques-Marie Duvault-Blochet expanded the domaine with new holdings in Échezeaux, Grands Échezeaux, and Richebourg. It was only "very recently" — in 1933 — that La Tâche was added to the Domaine. Since 1942, two families have co-owned DRC — the de Villaine family and the Leroy/Roch family.

Madame Lalou Bize-Leroy, now 87 years old, is well known as the owner and proprietor of Domaine Leroy. (I wrote about her in a previous review in this journal (Stavins, 2014)). In 1974, she became co-managing director of DRC with Aubert de Villaine. Together they helped build DRC's reputation to its current heights, but a series of disagreements, including her displeasure at de Villaine's involvement in the "Judgment of Paris" wine tasting, led to her being ousted in 1992. At the Paris competition, de Villaine had favored the French Cabernets over those from California, but had committed the sin of judging the California Chardonnays to be the approximate equal of those from the motherland (Ashenfelter and Quandt, 1999). To this day, Aubert de Villaine, now 80 years of age, remains co-owner and co-director of DRC with Henry-Frédéric Roch.

Today, DRC produces seven red wines from Pinot Noir grapes in seven vineyards (of seven distinct Grand Cru appellations): Romanée-Conti (4.5 acres producing about 450 cases per year); La Tâche (15 acres); Richebourg (8.7 acres); Romanée-Saint-Vivant (13 acres); Grands Échezeaux (8.7 acres); Échezeaux (11.5 acres); and, since 2008, Corton (7 acres). In addition, the DRC produces from avine-yard of Chardonnay grapes in Montrachet (1.7 acres).

As is well known, the wines of DRC are among the most expensive in the world, with Romanée-Conti itself at the very pinnacle. According to wine-searcher.com, currently the minimum retail price in the United States for a bottle of the 2016 vintage is $21,000. To place that in context, note that a bottle of 1945 Romanée-Conti sold at a Sotheby's auction in 2018 for $558,000.

Why do these wines command such staggering prices? An initial answer that is little more than tautological for readers of this journal is that the supply is miniscule (see the numbers noted earlier) and the demand is massive. So, why is the demand so great? Part of the answer is associated with the quality of the wines, due to superb *terroir*, high-density plantings, old vines, low yields, and only minimal intervention in the winery. Of course, much the same can be said of many other great, but considerably less costly wines. Surely, a larger share of the answer has to do with pedigree, prestige, and the existence of extreme wealth in many parts of the world.

The book takes two chapters to cover DRC's long history, a chapter to describe the *terroir*, a chapter for a close examination of Pinot Noir and Chardonnay, and two more chapters to describe the procedures used in the vineyards and the wineries. One long chapter takes us through each of the eight Cru of DRC, and another features an interview with Aubert de Villaine, which is among the most interesting and satisfying parts of the entire book. A final chapter provides Michael Broadbent's complete tasting notes going from the 1940 vintage through the 2013 vintage. From the first page to the last page, the beautiful photography of Jan Bartelsman illustrates the text; indeed, in many cases, the text is no more than extended captions for the photos.

At the end of this review, Burgundy aficionados may be offended by my bringing into the discussion the existence of new world Pinot Noir, and even more so by my referencing one of my favorite wine films, *Sideways*, which I reviewed in this journal about 13 years ago (Stavins, 2006). A high-point of the film is when Maya (played by Virginia Madsen) asks Miles (Paul Giamatti) why he is so into Pinot Noir. His response, which is both moving and revealing, is this:

> I don't know. It's a hard grape to grow. As you know. It's thin-skinned, temperamental, ripens early. It's not a survivor like Cabernet that can grow anywhere and thrive even when neglected. Pinot needs constant care and attention and in fact can only grow in specific little tucked-away corners of the world. And only the most patient and nurturing growers can do it really, can tap into Pinot's most fragile, delicate qualities. Only when someone has taken the time to truly understand its potential can Pinot be coaxed into its fullest expression. And when that happens, its flavors are the most haunting and brilliant and subtle and thrilling and ancient on the planet.

That is what makes Pinot Noir wines so distinctive, with the best coming from Burgundy — the highest expression of special *terroir*. And, of course, no wines of Burgundy are more celebrated that those of Domaine de la Romanée-Conti.

Having gotten through this massive volume about the history and the wines of DRC without ever having tasted even a drop of any of these legendary wines, I should mark the occasion by opening a bottle. But, alas, I cannot afford even the "humblest" of DRC wines, or, for that matter, nearly any other Grand Cru Classé Burgundy. Much to my surprise, however, just now I found listed in my cellar database three bottles of 2007 Domaine Chandon de Briailles from the Les Bressandes vineyard in the Grand Cru appellation of Corton. If you will excuse me, I will close this review, and make my way downstairs to my cellar, with corkscrew and glass in hand.

References

Ashenfelter, O. and R. Quandt. (1999). "Analyzing a wine tasting statistically." *Chance*. **12**(3): 16–20.

Stavins, R. N. (2006). "Film review: Alexander Payne, sideways." *Journal of Wine Economics*. **1**(1): 91–93.

Stavins, R. N. (2014). "Film review: David Leonard, a year in Burgundy." *Journal of Wine Economics*. **9**(1): 100–103.

https://doi.org/10.1142/9789811292415_0033

Chapter 33

Film Review: Jason Wise, *Somm 3**

Robert N. Stavins

John F. Kennedy School of Government, Harvard University, Cambridge, MA, USA

Resources for the Future, Washington, DC, USA

National Bureau of Economic Research, Cambridge, MA, USA

robert_stavins@harvard.edu

JASON WISE (Director): *SOMM 3*. Written by Christina Wise and Jason Wise, Produced by Forgotten Man Films, Distributed by Samuel Goldwyn Films, 2018; 1 h 18 min.

This is the third in a trilogy of documentaries about the wine world from Jason Wise. The first — *Somm*, a marvelous film which I reviewed for this *Journal* in 2013 (Stavins, 2013)–followed a group of four thirty-something sommeliers as they prepared for the exam that would permit them to join the Court of Master Sommeliers, the pinnacle of the profession, a level achieved by only 200 people globally over half a century. The second in the series — *Somm: Into the Bottle* — provided an exploration of the many elements that go into producing a bottle of wine. And the third — *Somm 3* — unites its predecessors by combining information and evocative scenes with a genuine dramatic arc, which may not have you on

*This chapter was originally published in *Journal of Wine Economics*, **15**(2020):423–426. doi:10.1017/jwe.2020.44.

pins and needles as the first film did, but nevertheless provides what is needed to create a film that should not be missed by oenophiles, and many others for that matter.

Before going further, I must take note of some unfortunate, even tragic events that have recently involved the segment of the wine industry — sommeliers — featured in this and the previous films in the series. Five years after the original *Somm* was released, a cheating scandal rocked the Court of Master Sommeliers, when the results of the tasting portion of the 2018 exam were invalidated because a proctor had disclosed confidential test information the day of the exam. And, if that were not enough, a *New York Times* investigation revealed in October 2020 a pattern of sexual harassment of female candidates by older male Master Sommeliers (Moskin, 2020).

That may be only part of the problem since a quick look at relevant data suggests that gender discrimination may also be at work. Of course, careful analysis would be needed to validate or reject such a charge (perhaps in a future article in this *Journal*?), but the numbers raise questions, with women comprising less than 17 percent of new U.S. Master Sommeliers over the past 20 years, falling below nearly all job categories in a recent assessment, except for truck drivers, where women are about 8 percent of the labor force (U.S. Bureau of Labor Statistics, 2020). This stands in contrast to the casual empiricism of many of us when we have noted that women we know seem to have, on average, substantially more discerning palates than our male friends (including ourselves), an observation that is pointed out in Wise's latest film.

The lynchpin of *Somm 3* is the 1976 Judgment of Paris blind tasting, which pitted a set of upstart California wines against renowned French versions of the same varietals, and resulted in a psychological win for the new world wines when they stood up to and in some cases beat their old world competitors when judged by a panel of French experts. That tasting — and issues surrounding the statistical analysis of the results — have been documented in this *Journal* (Cicchetti, 2006), and the story has previously been told with considerable humor and affection, if not great accuracy, in the feature film *Bottle Shock* (2008).

The 1976 tasting, which many believe launched the modern era of California premium wine production, provides a theme and a set of dramatic devices which bring together three legends of the wine world and a panel of young New York City sommeliers who engage in a blind tasting which in some regards is a natural sequel to the 1976 Paris tasting.

One of the legends is Fred Dame, who was celebrated in the original *Somm* as the first American to become a Master Sommelier in 1984. Another of the legends is Jancis Robinson, the highly respected wine critic and *Financial Times* columnist, whose autobiography I reviewed in this *Journal* (Stavins, 2007). Robinson talks about the historically small number of women in the wine industry but also emphasizes that women are playing increasingly important roles throughout the wine world, although she also notes that "competitive (blind) wine tasting is a very male thing." The last of the three legends in *Somm 3* functions as the hub of the film's narrative because this legendary character provides a real connection between the other elements of the movie — Steven Spurrier, the famed Paris-based proprietor of a wine shop and school, who organized and hosted the 1976 Judgment of Paris tasting.

There are virtually no simple "talking heads" in this documentary. Even people being interviewed are nearly always in action. More than this, the film provides brilliant cinematography of equally beautiful scenes (and inspiring music), which provide a most pleasant escape from social distancing during a global pandemic!

Blind tasting of wine is demonstrated in a session with Fred Dame, hosted by Jay Fletcher, which takes place for some unknown reason at a hotel in Big Sky, Montana. The session also demonstrates the film maker's creativity as Dame's commentary on the mystery wine is illustrated — sentence by sentence, and sometimes word by word — with a series of rapidly changing, beautiful, and appropriate images. Before the tasting begins, we are made aware by Fletcher that the wine Dame will blind taste is a 1995 E. Guigal Chateau d'Ampuis Côte-Rôtie.

Dame observes the wine in his glass, swirls it, tastes it, and as he speaks, the following scenes appear: "This is a classic wine from the Rhone Valley (aerial film of the Rhone River), it's Syrah (close-up of Syrah grapes ripening on the vine) with a little bit of Viognier (extreme close-up of white grapes on the vine). It's got new oak (oak barrels stained by red wine in a large cellar). The wine is a 1995 vintage (image of vineyard). So, we've got a 22 year old wine (glasses on the table). It's 1995 Côte-Rôtie." He nails it! Of course, if they continued to burrow down for the specific producer and vineyard, presumably he failed because the scene in the film stops there. Still, this was reminiscent of some of the captivating scenes from the original *Somm*, and hence fun to watch — but painful to write about now, after the recent disclosures of Mr. Dame's own involvement in the sexual harassment scandal documented in the *New York Times*.

In Paris, Spurrier mentions that if his 1976 blind tasting (which featured wines based on Chardonnay and Cabernet Sauvignon) were to be redone today, he would want it to compare new world and old world wines based on Pinot Noir. That provides the premise for the present-day New York City blind comparison of new world bottles of Pinot Noir with several prominent wines from Burgundy. This tasting is organized by and held in the Manhattan wine shop, Verve Wine, owned by Dustin Wilson, one of the four young men preparing in *Somm* for the Master Sommelier exam. (The three others make relatively brief appearances in *Somm 3*: Brian McClintic, DLynn Proctor, and Ian Cauble.)

As Wilson prepares his tasting event, he notes that Jancis Robinson's *Oxford Companion to Wine* (1994 to 2015) "has been part of my library from day one;" and some readers may recall that Miles characterized the same book in the movie *Sideways* as the "brilliant and exhaustive tome on everything you ever wanted to know about the universe of wine" (Stavins, 2006). Wilson invites several young New York male and female sommeliers to his tasting, before which he explains that they should not guess where the wines are from but simply rank them in order of their judgments of quality. Included are two premier cru from Burgundy, plus one wine each from the Willamette Valley in Oregon, Santa Barbara County in California, Patagonia in Argentina, and Geelong in Australia. I will not divulge the results, but I will say that the discussion among this group is as interesting as the outcome.

The various elements of the film are beautifully intertwined as we move from one part of the world to another: from elements of the New York City tasting to a get-together of the three legends — Dame, Robinson, and Spurrier — in a Paris restaurant, to historical vignettes about the three, the tasting with Dame, a visit to Spurrier's own Bride Valley Vineyard in Dorset, England, and much more.

The three legends of the industry proceed to describe and taste bottles each has brought to Paris of their respective "Aha! wines" — the bottle that had constituted a transformative and unforgettable experience which made them a lover of fine wine. For Robinson, it was during her student days at Oxford in the early 1970s. Out for dinner with her generous boyfriend of the time, she shared a bottle of 1959 Chambolle-Musigny, Les Amoureuses (Stavins, 2007). For Dame, it was a bottle of 1968 Ridge Cabernet Sauvignon; and for Spurrier, 1908 Cockburn's Vintage Port.

The film has a dramatic arc that progressively emerges, as much of the film appears to have been unscripted. While it cannot match the suspense and tension that characterized the first *Somm*, the various elements of *Somm 3* are brought together nicely at the conclusion, when Dustin Wilson takes the top three bottles selected at the blind tasting of New York sommeliers to Paris, to be tasted blind by Fred Dame, Jancis Robinson, and Steven Spurrier.

On re-watching the film, sitting with those three famous elders of the wine world in the private dining room of a Parisian bistro, there is much on which I found myself reflecting: the wines, the sommeliers, these three legends, and the recent successes of women in some aspects of the wine world, despite the awesome challenges and apparently terrible treatment so many have faced. Perhaps there is a story there for Jason Wise's next passionate and sensitive film about the world of wine and the remarkable people who seem to inhabit it.

References

Cicchetti, D. V. (2006). "The Paris 1976 wine tastings revisited once more: Comparing ratings of consistent and inconsistent tasters." *Journal of Wine Economics*. **1**(2): 125–140.

Moskin, J. (2020). "The wine world's most elite circle has a sexual harassment problem." *New York Times*. Retrieved from https://www.nytimes.com.

Robinson, J. (1994–2015). *The Oxford Companion to Wine*, 1st–4th ed. Oxford, UK: Oxford University Press.

Stavins, R. N. (2006). "Film review: Alexander Payne, Sideways." *Journal of Wine Economics*. **1**(1): 91–93.

Stavins, R. N. (2007). "Book review: Jancis Robinson, Tasting Pleasures — Confessions of a Wine Lover." *Journal of Wine Economics*. **2**(1): 106–108.

Stavins, R. N. (2013). "Film review: Jason Wise, Somm." *Journal of Wine Economics*. **8**(2): 238–241.

U.S. Bureau of Labor Statistics. (2020). "Labor force statistics from the current population survey: Employed persons by detailed occupation, sex, race, and Hispanic or Latino ethnicity." Retrieved from https://www.bls.gov/cps/cpsaat11.htm.

https://doi.org/10.1142/9789811292415_0034

Chapter 34

Book Review: James M. Gabler: Passions: The Wines and Travels of Thomas Jefferson*

Robert N. Stavins

John F. Kennedy School of Government, Harvard University, Cambridge, MA, USA

Resources for the Future, Washington, DC, USA

National Bureau of Economic Research, Cambridge, MA, USA

robert_stavins@harvard.edu

JAMES M. GABLER: *Passions: The Wines and Travels of Thomas Jefferson*. Bacchus Press, Palm Beach, 2016, 348 pp., ISBN 978-1533034700 (paperback), $25.00.

Having only recently read Ron Chernow's excellent biographies of Alexander Hamilton (Chernow, 2004), George Washington (Chernow, 2010), and Ulysses S. Grant (Chernow, 2017), I was eager to read a biography of Hamilton's great political opponent, George Washington's talented Secretary of State, and — of course — the third President of the United States, Thomas Jefferson. Instead, I "changed it up," as my son

*This chapter was originally published in *Journal of Wine Economics*, **16**(1), 102–114, 2021. doi:10.1017/jwe.2021.2.

would say, by reading this work by James Gabler that promised from its title to combine my armchair fascination with American history and my abiding interest and love of fine wine.

The book lives up to its title, as it provides what may be a nearly exhaustive (but sometimes exhausting) encyclopedic compilation of Jefferson's travels and wines. Apparently, seven years were required for Gabler's research and the writing, and it shows. The book draws on what I assume to be abundant original research and offers what must be the most complete and authoritative cataloguing of the wines Jefferson enjoyed (or not) from before the Revolutionary War, through Jefferson's time in Paris as ambassador, including extended travels to vineyards in France, Italy, and Germany, in the White House as President, and — of course — at his beloved Monticello.

Thus, the book can function as an excellent reference — presumably for someone who wants to check on Jefferson's travels in this year or that, the wines he was trying at the time, and the details of his transport, accommodations, conversations, and meals. Hmm, I wonder, in April of 1787, where did Jefferson visit, how long did he stay there, where did he sleep, and what wine did he drink? OK, on page 97 — we learn that Jefferson spent two days in Turin at the Hotel d'Angleterre, and drank for the first time Nebiule, made from the precursor of today's Nebbiolo grape.

So, this is a remarkable reference, and the book's reasonable cost may be justified by just two (of the five) appendices: one being a compilation of Jefferson's favorite wines that are "available today," that is, in their modern incarnations; and the other an inventory of Jefferson's White House wine cellar with detailed annotations. But even a great reference work is not necessarily a book I can recommend trying to read from start to finish (unless you have committed to write a review, of course). In too many of the book's 16 chapters, I felt like I was reading notes prepared for me by a very careful research assistant — from which I would then have to prepare a first draft of a chapter or article. Indeed, what I would love to read would be a long *New Yorker* article by Mr. Gabler summarizing some highlights of these 300+ pages.

For me, such highlights would include descriptions of dinners, dinner companions, cuisine, wine, and conversations at Jefferson's Paris residence on the Champs- Elysées, at the White House, and at Monticello. Likewise, it was fun to read excerpts from letters in which Jefferson gave advice about which wines to buy to three Presidents: Washington, Madison, and Monroe.

Yes, Jefferson's favorites from Bordeaux included Château Margaux, Haut-Brion, Lafite, and Latour, which I was surprised to learn were called "First Growths" even in 1784, fully 70 years before Napoleon III's 1855 classification. But Jefferson was not the ultimate wine snob, and purchased and drank a range of slightly lesser Bordeaux, including Gruard-Larose, Leoville-Las-Cases, Leoville-Poyferre, Leoville-Barton, Calon-Segur, Pontet-Canet, and — of course — from Sauternes, Château Yquem, which I learned was a very different wine in Jefferson's day, 60 years before infection with *botrytis cinerea* made d'Yquem the remarkable Sauternes it is today. Beyond Bordeaux, wines of roughly similar pedigree were Jefferson's favorites in Burgundy, the northern and southern Rhone, and elsewhere on the Continent.

Jefferson enjoyed a long retirement from the Presidency at his beloved Monticello from age 66 until his passing at 83 years of age. Those years included some marginal involvement in the political world, but mainly via letters to his successors pressing for some favored policy. Just two years into his retirement, in 1811, Jefferson abandoned his previous view of international trade policy, which was essentially based on the theory of absolute advantage of Smith (1776), and came to favor instead a somewhat isolationist policy, even more distant from Ricardo's theory of comparative advan- tage (Ricardo, 1817), which had not yet appeared, let alone diffused. At a time of European wars, this meant — remarkably — that for a time, Jefferson favored wines from Maryland, which he claimed to be "of the quality of the best Burgundy" (p. 215).

Not long after Jefferson sent a long letter to President Monroe, shortly after his inauguration, advising the new President of the wines he should add to the White House wine cellar, Jefferson became an advocate for public policies that would be favorable to wine drinkers like himself. Interestingly, he did so in ways that would be perfectly familiar to today's lobbyists. He argued in a letter to the new Secretary of the Treasury against a luxury tax on wine then being considered by Congress: "I think it is a great error to consider a heavy tax on wines as a tax on luxury. On the contrary, it is a tax on the health of our citizens" because it would reduce wine consumption and would be "in effect a condemnation of all the middling and lower conditions of society to the poison of whiskey. …" (p. 224).

To the end, Thomas Jefferson was a remarkable man — statesman, diplomat, architect, inventor, farmer, viticulturalist, and passionate oenophile. In regard to Jefferson's reputation as a "Renaissance man," my favorite quote in the book is not from Jefferson's many letters but rather is a quote from another President some 150 years after Jefferson left office. At a White House dinner on April 29, 1962, honoring Nobel laureates, President John F. Kennedy told the group, "I think this is the most extraordinary collection of talent, of human knowledge, that has ever been gathered together at the White House, with the possible exception of when Thomas Jefferson dined alone" (Kennedy, 1962).

References

Chernow, R. (2004). *Alexander Hamilton*. New York, NY: Penguin Group.

Chernow, R. (2010). *Washington: A Life*. New York, NY: Penguin Group.

Chernow, R. (2017). *Grant*. New York, NY: Penguin Group.

Kennedy, J. F. (1962). "Remarks at a dinner honoring Nobel Prize winners of the Western Hemisphere." In G. Peters and J. T. Woolley (eds.), *The American Presidency Project*. Santa Barbara, CA: University of California Press.

Ricardo, D. (1817). *On the Principles of Political Economy and Taxation*. London, UK: John Murray.

Smith, A. (1776). *An Inquiry into the Nature and Causes of the Wealth of Nations*. London, UK: W. Strahan and T. Cadell.

https://doi.org/10.1142/9789811292415_bmatter

Index

A
abatement costs, 309, 370
accounting treatment of ITMO transfers and use, 666–669
acid rain, 270
Acid Rain Program, 167–171, 186
Administrative Procedure Act of 1946, 269
adverse selection, 64–65
Affordable Clean Energy Rule, 289–290
Air Pollution Control Act of 1955, 267
Air Quality Policy Instruments, 276–284
Air Resources Board, 537
A.J. Meyer Professor of Energy and Economic Development, 8
Alberta, 139
Alberta's tradable carbon performance standard, 143, 152–153
Albert Pratt Professor of Business and Government, 8
Aldy, Joseph E., 10, 119
Alexander Valley Sub-AVA, 721
Allison, Graham, 8
allowance allocation, 185–188, 383–384
allowance prices, 145, 184
allowances, 144, 212
American Agricultural Economics Association, 5
American Clean Energy and Security Act of 2009, 221, 271, 285, 540
American Viticultural Areas, 690, 706
Andrew Dickson White Professor-at-Large (visiting) at Cornell University, 9
Annex I countries, 485, 523, 527
Annual Review of Resource Economics, 12
Appellation d'Origine Contrôlée (AOC), 690, 706
aquatic ecosystems, 279
Architectures for Agreement: Addressing Global Climate Change in the Post-Kyoto World, 10
Armco, 277
Article 17 of the Kyoto Protocol, 523–524
Article 6 of the Paris Agreement, 617
Assembly Bill 32, 236, 498

Assigned Amount Units (AAUs), 523
Assistant Professor, 8
Associate Professor, 8
asymmetric information, 64–65, 80–82
auction, 136
Australia, 516, 525
Australia's Clean Energy Act of 2011, 536

B

banking, 276, 282
banking of permits, 291
benefit-cost analyses, 37–38
Berkeley, California, 13
Berlin Mandate, 510–511, 541–542, 553
biodiversity, 23
Bodansky, Daniel M., 581
book and film reviews, 12
Borenstein, Severin, 407
Boston, 14
bottom-up architecture, 572–575
Brazil, 121, 149, 166, 526
British Columbia's carbon tax, 143, 151–152, 346–348, 386
Broekhoff, Derik, 677
bubbles, 276
Bulgaria, 145
Burgundy, 741, 747
Bush, George H. W., 166, 195, 200, 210–211, 220, 271
Bushnell, James, 407
Byrd, Robert, 197

C

Cabernet Franc, 715
Cabernet Sauvignon, 715–716, 721
CAFE standards, 61
California, 516, 543, 705
California's Cap-and-Trade System, 247–250
California's electricity crisis, 283
California's Global Warming Solutions Act of 2006, 537–538
Cambridge, Massachusetts, 6, 13
Cancun Agreements, 553
cap-and-tax, 227
cap-and-trade systems, 38, 123, 130–131, 135–138, 166, 170–171, 176, 227–228, 237–242, 272, 275, 291, 381, 494, 515
carbon dioxide, 271
carbon price volatility, 320, 377
carbon pricing, 130–131
carbon tax, 38, 130–135, 137, 150–151, 384–385
carbon taxes versus carbon cap-and-trade, 11
Caribbean, 149
Carnesale, Albert, 8
Carraro, Carlo, 423
certified emission reduction (CER) credits, 148
Chan, Gabriel, 165, 423, 443
Chapman, Jason, 8
Chardonnay, 715
Chernow, Ron, 763
Chicago Journal of International Law, 12
China, 121, 139, 166
China's emissions trading system pilots, 539
Clean Air Act, 11, 37, 195, 224, 268, 270, 272, 275–276, 278–279, 284–285, 288, 290–291
Clean Air Act Amendments of 1990, 167, 210, 226, 236, 283
Clean Air Act of 1963, 267
Clean Air Interstate Rule, 223–225, 227, 284
Clean Development Mechanism, 138, 158, 516, 521

clean energy standard, 130–131, 138–140
Clean Power Plan, 40, 285–286, 288–290, 412
Clear Skies Act, 222
Clear Skies Act of 2002, 184
Climate Change Economics, 11–12, 436–440
Climate Change Response Act of 2002, 148
climate club, 44
climate pledges, 682–684
climate policy, 12
climate sensitivity parameter, 25
clubs of countries, 41
CO_2, 149
coal, 133
coal-fired power plants, 219, 279
Coase, Ronald, 199
co-benefits, 280, 288
CO_2 emissions, 133, 290
cognitive limitations, 89–90
command-and-control, 177–178, 273
command-and-control mechanisms, 132
command-and-control policies, 280
command-and-control regulations, 131–132
Committee on Energy and Commerce, 198
common but differentiated responsibilities and respective capabilities, 124
competitiveness effects, 315
competitiveness impacts, 384
complementary policies, 384
complexity and administrative requirements, 379–380
Conference of the Parties, 120, 453, 581
conflict of interest rules, 431–433
Connecticut, 145, 534
consumer beliefs, 72–73
consumer heterogeneity, 78–79
Consumer Price Index, 710
continuous emissions monitoring, 281
convention, 453
Copenhagen, 512
Copenhagen Accord, 553
Cornell Department of Economics, 5
Cornell University, 4
Corporate Auto Fuel Economy standards, 288
Corporate Average Fuel Economy (CAFE) program, 285
corruption and market manipulation, 322
cost-effective, 170, 274, 291
cost-effective abatement, 136
cost-effective equilibrium, 275
cost-effective GHG emissions mitigation, 41, 43–44
cost-effectiveness, 286, 520–521, 564
cost savings, 214
costs to regulated firms, 312–313
cost uncertainty, 136, 147, 174–176
CO_2 tax credits, 134
Council of Economic Advisers, 32–34, 46
criteria air pollutants, 272
Crocker, Thomas, 199
Cross, Robin, 705
Cross-State Air Pollution Rule, 185, 226, 284

D

Dales, John, 199
Davis, Lucas, 407
D-Colorado, 201
decentralized approaches, 448–449
decentralized, bottom-up architectures, 157–158
Delaware, 145, 534

Democrats, 271
Denmark, 151
Department of Agricultural and Resource Economics at the University of California, Berkeley, 5
Department of Economics at Harvard, 6
Department of Transportation, 38–39
deregulation, 218–220
deregulation of railroads, 281
DICE model, 38–39, 41–42, 47
Dingell, John, 199
direct climate benefits, 286
direct linkage, 518–519
discounted net present value, 43
discounting, 23–24
Dismal Theorem, 45
distortionary taxes, 280, 291
distributional impacts, 313–314, 372–373, 564–565
Doctoral Program in Political Economy and Government, 9
Doctoral Program in Public Policy, 9
Domaine de la Romané-Conti, 753
domestic (national) policy, 11
double counting, 679–681
down-stream, 147
Duan, Maosheng, 677
Duke University, 53
DuPont, 277
Durban, 512–513, 516
Durban Climate Talks, 509
Durban Platform for Enhanced Action, 516, 542, 553, 558, 581
dynamically Efficient Time Path, 43
dynamic incentives, 132
Dynamic Integrated Climate-Economy (DICE) model, 33

E

earmarking revenues from taxes, 291
Earth Day, 267
Econometric Society, 21
Economic Report of the President, 34
Economics of Climate Change and Environmental Policy: Selected Papers of Robert N. Stavins, 2000–2011, 10
Economics of the Environment, 10
Edenhofer, Ottmar, 423
electricity generation, 273
electricity production, 412
Electric Power Research Institute, 172
eliminating fossil fuel subsidies, 140–143
elimination of SO_2 allowance market, 281
Ellwood, David, 8
Elmendorf, Douglas, 8
emission leakage, 135
emissions-reduction credit systems, 130–131, 138, 272
emissions trading, 500–501
emissions trading in the 1970s, 276–277
Emissions Trading Program, 277–278
emissions trading system, 272, 274
endangerment finding, 285
energy efficiency, 58–62
energy-efficiency gap, 54
energy-efficient products, 65–67
EnergyGuide, 66
Energy Information Administration, 280
energy price volatility, 144
energy star, 61, 66
Environmental and Energy Policy and the Economy, 11
Environmental Defense Fund, 5, 200, 210
environmental economics, 3, 20

Environmental Economics Advisory Committee of the U.S. Environmental Protection Agency Science Advisory Board, 10
Environmental Economics and Public Policy: Selected Papers of Robert N. Stavins, 1988–1999, 10
environmental effectiveness, 178–179
Environmental Law, 12
Environmental Protection Agency, 224–225, 269–270, 276–277, 279, 284, 286–289
Environmental Protection and the Social Responsibility of Firms: Perspectives from Law, Economics, and Business, 10
EU Emissions Trading System, 250–252, 526
Europe, 159
European Commission, 144
European Union, 139, 145, 516, 525
European Union Emission Trading Scheme, 130, 143, 167, 187, 497, 528–530
Evanston, Illinois, 13
Executive Order 12044, 35
Executive Order 12291, 35
Executive Order 13868, 40
Executive Order 112866, 35
experience with cap-and-trade policies, 331–339
experience with carbon taxes, 339
experience with hybrid policy instruments, 342–343
experimental research, 67

F

fairness purposes, 291
fat tails, 24–25
Fellow of the Association of Environmental and Resource Economists, 9
finance in international agreements, 469–470
Finland, 151
fisheries, 24
flexibility mechanisms, 382–383
Fondazione Eni Enrico Mattei, 9, 22
Forker, Olan, 5
formulaic approach to allocating responsibility, 491–492
fossil fuel subsidy reduction, 130–131
fossil fuel use, 40
Fowlie, Meredith, 407
France, 706
free allocation, 140
free allocation of allowances, 136, 212
Frontiers in Environmental Economics and Policy: A Symposium in Honor of Martin L. Weitzman, 20
fuel-switching, 219
FUND model, 39

G

G20, 141, 143, 483
Gabler, James M., 763
Gas Guzzler Tax, 61
gasoline prices, 71–72
geological sequestration, 134
Gerarden, Todd D., 53
Germany, 706
GHG coverage, 651–652
global climate benefits, 286
global commons, 42
global commons problem, 286
global costs, 286
global damages, 286
global warming potential values, 652–653
Goldman, Rudi, 747
Goulder, Lawrence, 7, 407
Grady, Robert, 200

Graff, Thomas, 5
Graff, Tom, 6
Grant, Ulysses S., 763
Grape production, 710
Gray, C. Boyden, 200–201
greenhouse gas, 123, 284
Greenland ice sheet, 45
Green National Accounting, 22–23
Greenstone, Michael, 407
Griliches, Zvi, 6–7
ground-level ozone, 283

H

Hamilton, Alexander, 763
harmonized domestic taxes, 154–155
harmonized national policies, 448
Harvard Business School-Harvard Kennedy School Joint Degree Programs, 9
Harvard College, 21
Harvard Department of Economics, 7
Harvard Environmental Economics Program, 8, 167, 203
Harvard Kennedy School, 8–9, 14, 53
Harvard Project on Climate Agreements, 8
Harvard's Department of Economics, 4
Harvard Seminar in Environmental Economics and Policy, 21
Harvard University, 4, 20–21, 53
hazardous air pollutants, 272
health benefits, 218
Heckman's two-step estimation procedure, 718
hedonic analyses, 67, 707
hedonic analyses of vineyard sales, 12
hedonic estimation, 689, 693, 705, 710–718
hedonic price equation, 724–725
Heinz, John, 10, 201
heterogeneity of jurisdictions, 637–638
heterogeneity of NDCs, 653–654
heterogeneity of policy instruments, 622–623
heterogeneity of targets, 644–645
HFC-23, 149, 526
high-sulfur Eastern coal, 270
Hoedl, Seth A., 581
Hood, Christina, 677
hot spots, 281
House of Representatives, 267, 270–271
Howard, Andrew, 677
human health impacts, 286
Hungary, 532
hybrid policy architecture, 614
hybrid policy instruments, 325–326, 380

I

Iceland, 24, 145
inadequate information, 65–67
independence property, 275
India, 121, 149, 166
indirect linkage, 158, 520
Indonesia, 121, 142
initial allocation of allowances, 275
initial allowance distribution, 135
integrated assessment models, 38
interactions with complementary policies, 321–322, 378
Interagency Working Group on Social Cost of Carbon, 33, 133
Intergovernmental Panel on Climate Change (IPCC), 10–12, 24, 417–422, 445
international climate change policy, 25
international climate policy architecture, 483–502
international competitiveness, 371
international cooperation, 44
international cooperation on climate change, 41

international coordination of carbon pricing policies, 153–154
international dimensions of climate change policy, 11
international emissions trading, 495–497
international energy agency, 142
Internationally Transferred Mitigation Outcome (ITMOs), 617
international monetary fund, 40
international policy, 415
international political strategy, 566–567
international taxes, 154–155
international tradable permit scheme, 155
intertemporal allocation of abatement cost, 215
Italy, 706
Ithaca, New York, 13

J

Jaffe, Adam, 6–7
Jefferson, Thomas, 763
Ji, Zou, 443
John F. Kennedy School of Government, 4
joint implementation, 158, 527
Jotzo, Frank, 677
Journal of Economic Literature, 11
Journal of Economic Perspectives, 11
Journal of Environmental Economics and Management, 268
Journal of Environment and Development, 11
Journal of the Association of Environmental and Resource Economists, 11
Journal of Wine Economics, 9, 12, 737, 741–742, 747, 753, 757, 763

K

Kaldor-Hicks criterion, 43
Kalt, Joseph, 6
Kennard, David, 741
Kennedy, John F., 766
Kizzier, Kelley, 677
Knights Valley, Rutherford, 725
Knittel, Christopher, 407
Kolstad, Charles, 407, 423
Korea, 166
Kotchen, Matthew J., 407
Krupp, Fred, 200
Kyoto Protocol, 44, 121, 138, 149, 453–457, 485, 498, 511–512, 524, 527, 541, 554
Kyoto Protocol's Clean Development Mechanism, 143, 148

L

Landry, Meredith, 8
Latin America, 149
Lazarus, Michael, 677
leaded gasoline, 237, 278
leaded gasoline phasedown, 277–278
Leadership in Energy and Environmental Design (LEED) certification, 66
leakage, 147
learning-by-doing spillovers, 58–59
learning-by-using spillovers, 82–84
Leonard, Dutch, 32
Leone, Sierra, 6, 13
Leontief Prize, 22
LeVeen, Phillip, 5
Liechtenstein, 145
linkage, 157, 376–377, 460–461, 499, 515, 559–572
linkage agreements, 620
linkage in international climate policy, 12

linkage in the Paris Agreement, 607–609
linkage of cap-and-trade systems, 12
linkage of climate policy instruments, 629–635
linkage of national policy instruments, 13
linkage with policies in other jurisdictions, 323
linking, 617–621
linking heterogeneous climate policies, 613
links between cap-and-trade systems, 623–625
links between heterogeneous policy instruments, 625–629
liquefied natural gas, 133
Los Angeles, 282
low-sulfur Western coal, 270

M

3M, 277
macroeconomics of global climate change, 46
Maine, 145, 534
Major Economies Forum for Energy and Climate, 483
marginal abatement cost, 274
market-based environmental policy instruments, 11
market failures, 57–67
market liquidity, 565
market structure, 61
Maryland, 145, 534
Massachusetts, 145, 534
Massachusetts *et al.* v. Environmental Protection Agency *et al.*, 284–285
Massachusetts Institute of Technology (MIT), 21
Mehling, Michael A., 605, 613
Merlot, 715
Metcalf, Gilbert E., 581, 605, 613
methane, 149
methane emissions, 132
Mexico, 166, 516
Mexico's cap-and-trade system, 539–540
Mitchell, George, 198
mobile sources, 273
monitoring and enforcement, 140
Montgomery, David, 199
Monticello, 765
Montreal Protocol, 270–271, 278, 462–463
myopia/short-sightedness, 87–89

N

Napa and Sonoma Counties, 717, 721, 728
Napa and Sonoma Sub-AVAs, 707
Napa County, 715
National Academy of Sciences, 33, 36–38, 46
National Acid Precipitation Assessment Program, 169
National Ambient Air Quality Standards, 269–270
National Bureau of Economic Research, 9, 53, 268, 299
National Emission Standards for Hazardous Air Pollutants, 269
National Highway Traffic Safety Administration, 288
National Income and Product Accounts, 36
Nationally Determined Contributions, 44, 301
National Research Council, 36
National Tax Journal, 11
natural gas, 133
natural gas prices, 68–70, 147
Nature's Numbers, 37
NDC Targets Under the Paris Agreement, 646–647

netting, 276
Newell, Richard G., 53
New Hampshire, 145, 534
New Jersey, 146
New Source Performance Standards, 178, 216, 269, 285
New Source Review, 216
New York, 146, 534
New Zealand, 516, 525, 532, 536–537, 543
New Zealand Emissions Trading Scheme, 147, 531–533
New Zealand's cap-and-trade system, 143
nitrogen oxides (NO_x), 168, 282, 287
nitrous oxide, 149
Nobel Prize, 31
nonuniform performance standards, 274
Nordhaus, William, 11, 31, 33–34, 45–47
Normative Theory of Policy Instrument Choice, 306–326
Northern European carbon taxes, 385
Northwestern University, 6
Norway, 145, 150
Norwegian Emissions Trading Scheme, 530–531
NOx Budget Program, 283–284
NOx Budget Trading Program, 284
NOx cap-and-trade system, 283
NOx emissions, 284
NOx prices, 283
NOx trading among eastern states, 282
NOx trading in eastern United States, 283
Nye, Joseph, 8

O

Obama administration, 39, 225, 272, 285, 288, 408
Obama Administration Climate Policies, 284–288
Obama, President Barack, 287
Office of Management and Budget, 269, 286
offset provision, 136
offsets, 276
Oregon's Willamette Valley, 707
Organization for Economic Development and Cooperation, 36
Organization of Economic Cooperation and Development, 142
Organization of Petroleum Exporting Countries, 142
ozone-depleting chemicals, 279
ozone depletion, 279

P

PAGE model, 39
Paris Agreement, 12, 44, 458–459, 614, 677
Paris Agreement Article 6, 673–674
Paris Agreement's Article 6.2, 12
Paris Climate Agreement, 301
particulate matter, 287
Peace Corps, 6
performance-based standards, 131
performance standards, 132, 272
petroleum, 133
Pigouvian taxes, 274
Pinot Noir, 708, 715
Plantinga, Andrew J., 705
polarization, 271
policy architectures for climate change, 446
policy instrument choice, 23
policy instruments, 272
policy instrument targets, 645–646
political demand, 328–329
political demand for policy instruments, 327
political equilibrium, 328
political obstacles, 681–682
political polarization, 159

political resistance, 324–325
political supply, 329–330
political supply of policy instruments, 327
politics, 291
positive theory of policy instrument choice, 326–330
Post-Kyoto International Climate Policy: Implementing Architectures for Agreement, 10
Post-Kyoto International Climate Policy: Summary for Policymakers, 10
Powder River Basin, 172, 218–219, 226
premium wine, 13
Prevention of Significant Deterioration, 270
price colla, 137
price stabilization, 565
prices vs. quantities, 23
price volatility, 284
probability distribution, 45
Professor of Public Policy, 8
program feature that prevents banking, 144
Project 88, 10
Public Policies for Environmental Protection, 10
Putnam, Robert, 8

Q

Québec, 543
Quebec's cap-and-trade system, 538–539

R

railroad deregulation, 220
raising revenue, 311
R&D Spillovers, 58
Reagan administration, 46
Reagan, President Ronald, 196, 211
rebates, 291
reference and target years, 650–651
Regional Clean Air Incentives Market, 236, 240–241, 282
Regional Greenhouse Gas Initiative, 138, 145, 236, 245–247, 275, 498, 534–536
Regional Integrated Climate-Economy (RICE) model, 42
Regional Programs under Clean Air Act Authority, 282–284
Regulatory Analysis Review Group, 34
Regulatory Impact Analysis, 36, 39, 46, 286–287, 289–290
renewable electricity standards, 139
Republicans, 271
resource economics, 3
resources for the future, 4, 9, 53, 172
Review of Environmental Economics and Policy, 9, 11–12
Review of Environment, Energy, and Economics, 12
Rhode Island, 146, 534
Rio de Janeiro, Brazil, 44
Rio Earth Summit, 510
Roach, David, 737
Robert, Matthew J. Kotchen, 397
Robinson, Kenneth, 4–5
Romania, 145
Ross, Warwick, 737
R-Pennsylvania, 201

S

safety valve, 137, 147
Salata Institute, 9
Sauvignon Blanc, 715
Schelling, Thomas, 32
Schmalensee, Richard, 209, 235
Schneider, Lambert, 677
Schrag, Daniel, 8

Schultze, Charles, 35
Schumpeter, Joseph, 47, 55
scrubber, 193, 270
scrubber installations, 194
Searle, S. R., 5
second-best designs of carbon-pricing regimes, 291
sectoral and geographic coverage, 651
Senate, 270–271
Senate Committee on Environment and Public Works, 197
Senator Timothy Wirth, 10
sideways, 755
size distribution of farms, 5
Smith, Kerry, 4
smog, 283
SO_2 allowance-trading program, 181
SO_2 allowance trading system, 226
social cost of carbon, 11, 38, 45, 47, 289–290, 398
social costs, 372
SO_2 emissions reductions, 220
soil characteristics, 718
Solow, Robert, 21
Somm, 731
Sommelier, Master, 732
Sonoma County, 715
SO_2 program costs and benefits, 188–191
SO_2 trading program, 215
South Africa, 166, 516
South Coast Air Quality Management District, 240, 282
South Korea, 516
South Korea's cap-and-trade system, 539
Spain, 706
Staller, George, 5
Stanford Law School, 6
Stanford University, 21
Stanton, Bud, 5
State Implementation Plans, 269, 284
state regulations, 215
stationary sources, 273
status under the Paris Agreement, 641–644
Stavins, Robert N., 677
Stern Review, 45
Stewart, Richard, 201
Stock, James H., 9, 397
Stowe, Robert, 8, 165
stratospheric ozone protection, 278–279
sub-AVAs, 715
sulfur dioxide (SO_2), 166, 270, 282, 287
sulfur dioxide allowance trading, 238–240, 279–282
sulfur dioxide cap-and-trade program, 270
Supreme Court, 285
Sweden, 150
Sweeney, Richard, 165
Swiss CO_2 Act, 531
Switzerland, 516, 525
Syrah, 715

T

target-consistent price, 399–401
target type, 647–650
tax on pollutant emissions, 274
Tea Party movement, 272
technological change, 47, 470
technological innovation, 192–195
technology-based standards, 131–132
technology-neutral performance standard, 139
technology spillovers, 58
technology standards, 272, 274
The Political Economy of Environmental Regulation, 10
terroir, 689, 705–706, 708

Tol, Richard, 39
transaction costs, 183, 322–323, 373–374
Trump administration, 289
Trump Administration Climate Policies, 288–290

U

uncertainty, 316–320, 374–376
UN Framework Convention on Climate Change, 271
United Kingdom, 45, 525
United Nations Framework Climate Change, 12
United Nations Framework Convention on Climate Change (UNFCCC), 36, 44, 119, 483, 509, 516
United States, 159
U.S. carbon-pricing policy, 11
US Clean Air Act, 267–268
U.S. Clean Power Plan, 11
US climate policy, 287
U.S. Congress, 166
U.S. energy and climate policy, 38
U.S. Environmental Protection Agency, 172, 216, 236, 267
U.S. lead phase-down of gasoline, 130
U.S. Senate, 159
U.S. sulfur dioxide (SO_2) cap-and-trade program, 130
USX, 277

V

Vermont, 146, 534
Vineyard attributes, 693–697, 728
Vineyard prices, 720
Vineyard sale prices, 705
Vineyard value, 710
volatility, 144

W

Wagner, Gernot, 19
Wara, Michael, 407
Washington, George, 763
Waxman–Markey Bill, 221, 271, 285, 498, 540
Weinstein, Jeremy, 8
Weitzman, Martin, 4, 8, 11, 19, 26, 45
Western Climate Initiative, 152, 543
Willamette Valley, 708
Willey, W. R. Zach, 5
Williamson, Jeffrey, 7
Wilson, Dustin, 735
wine production, 12, 687
Winkler, Harald, 677
Wirth, Timothy, 201
Wise, Jason, 731, 757
Wolak, Frank, 407
Wolfram, Catherine, 407
Working Group on the Social Cost of Carbon, 39
World Bank, 301
World Trade Organization, 549

Y

Yale University, 21

Z

Zeckhauser, Richard, 8
Zinfandel, 715
Zoellick, Robert, 200

www.ingramcontent.com/pod-product-compliance
Lightning Source LLC
Chambersburg PA
CBHW050448020625
27513CB00004B/192